PLOTS

PLOTS

By

Jay Dubya

www.bookstandpublishing.com

Published by
Bookstand Publishing
Pasadena, CA 91101
4524_8

Copyright © 2023 by Jay Dubya
All rights reserved. No part of this publication may be reproduced or transmitted in any form or by any means, electronic or mechanical, including photocopy, recording, or any information storage and retrieval system, without permission in writing from the copyright owner.

ISBN 978-1-63498-519-2

For Ginger

Other Books by Jay Dubya

Adult Fiction

Black Leather and Blue Denim, A '50s Novel
The Great Teen Fruit War, A 1960' Novel
Frat' Brats, A '60s Novel
Ron Coyote, Man of La Mangia
Pieces of Eight
Pieces of Eight, Part II
Pieces of Eight, Part III
Pieces of Eight, Part IV
The Wholly Book of Genesis
The Wholly Book of Exodus
The Wholly Book of Doo-Doo-Rot-on-Me
Thirteen Sick Tasteless Classics
Thirteen Sick Tasteless Classics, Part II
Thirteen Sick Tasteless Classics, Part III
Thirteen Sick Tasteless Classics, Part IV
Thirteen Sick Tasteless Classics, Part V
So Ya' Wanna' Be A Teacher
RAM: Random Articles and Manuscripts
Mauled Maimed Mangled Mutilated Mythology
Fractured Frazzled Folk Fables and Fairy Farces
FFFF&FF, Part II
Nine New Novellas
Nine New Novellas, Part II
Nine New Novellas, Part III
Nine New Novellas, Part IV
One Baker's Dozen
Two Baker's Dozen
Shakespeare: Slammed, Smeared, Savaged & Slaughtered
Shakespeare: Slammed, Smeared, Savaged & Slaughtered, Part II
Suite 16
Time Travel Tales
Snake Eyes and Boxcars
Snake Eyes and Boxcars, Part II
UFO: Utterly Fantastic Occurrences
The Psychic Dimension
The Psychic Dimension, Part II
Modern Mythology

First Person Stories
O. Henry: Obscenely and Outrageously Obliterated
Twain: Tattered Trounced Tortured and Traumatized
Poe: Pelted Pounded Pummeled and Pulverized
London: Lashed Lacerated Lampooned and Lambasted
Hawthorne: Hazed Hooked Hammered and Hijacked
Hawthorne Hacked, Shakespeare Sacked & Thurber Thwacked
THEMES
The FBI Inspector
Prime-Time Crime Time
The Arcane Arcade
Thirteen Tantalizing Tales
PLOTS, Part II
Homer's Odd Sea Odyssey
HOMER'S ILL ILIAD
The Timeless Time Machine
War of the Worlds
The Invisible Man

Young Adult Fantasy Novels

Pot of Gold
Enchanta
Space Bugs, Earth Invasion
The Eighteen Story Gingerbread House

Contents:

Edgar Allan Poe — 1

Edgar Allan Poe (1809-1849) — 2
"The Black Cat" — 3
"The Cask of Amontillado" — 19
"The Fall of the House of Usher" — 33
"The Pit and the Pendulum" — 43
"The Murders in the Rue Morgue" — 55

Jack London — 67

Jack London (1876-1916) — 68
"The Story of Jees Uck" — 69
"The Law of Life" — 83
"To Build a Fire" — 89
"The Story of Keesh" — 101
"Love of Life" — 115

O. Henry — 135

O. Henry (1862-1910) — 136
"The Gift of the Magi" — 137
"The Last Leaf" — 145
"The Higher Pragmatism" — 153
"The Cop and the Anthem" — 163
"A Retrieved Reformation" — 175

Mark Twain — 189

Mark Twain (1835-1910) — 190
"Boyhood Reminiscences" — 191
"Club Pilot on the Mississippi" — 201
"The Cat and the Painkiller" — 217
"Lost in a Snowstorm" — 225
"The Jumping Frog" — 241

William Shakespeare   **253**

William Shakespeare (1564-1616)	254
"A Midsummer Night's Dream"	255
"King Lear"	291
"The Merry Wives of Windsor"	373
"The Taming of the Shrew"	435
"Romeo and Juliet"	491

Description

Plots is a Jay Dubya acronym that represents a compilation of certain famous works by authors Poe, London, O. Henry, Twain and Shakespeare. Every good story, indeed, has a plot, or an essential problem (or problems) that must be solved. The problem could either be a direct physical threat, or an imagined mental-emotional crisis existing within the main character's mind; or perhaps various combinations of *those* separate elements. In any case, the main problem must be addressed and/or especially solved.

The particular stories selected by the author have been uniquely corrupted, and then creatively rewritten into satirical style where Jay Dubya effectively uses adult language and situations, thus adroitly modifying the general integrity of the original works.

Edgar Allan Poe

Edgar Allan Poe (1809-1849)

When author Jay Dubya was a New Jersey public school English teacher, the English mentor often enjoyed teaching and reading E.A. Poe's "influential literature" to his sometimes-enlightened middle and high school students.

Even though Poe (1809-1849) had died at a very young age, the literary contributor still managed to remarkably write over nine hundred pages of imaginative short stories and poems.

In addition to being a superb writer, Poe was also an excellent editor and literary critic, and is widely regarded as one of the most important authors in American literature. The now-esteemed writer is often referred to as "the father of the American short story", and as "the inventor of the detective story".

Edgar Allan Poe was born the son of traveling professional actors, and was orphaned at age three to the wealthy Allan family of Richmond, Virginia; and that is how Edgar acquired his middle name. Mr. Allan never adopted Edgar, because the wealthy man disapproved of Poe's literary ambitions, with the two often quarreling about authors seldom being able to make a decent and respectable living.

Poe was expelled from the University of Virginia on suspicion of gambling and other misdemeanor behavior. Edgar enrolled as a cadet at West Point, but was dismissed from that military academy as a result of poor grades. Realizing that reconciliation with Mr. Allan was impossible as long as he wished to become an author, Poe became disenchanted and depressed, and intentionally dropped-out of the prestigious school on the Hudson. But today, there is a commemorative statue at the academy dedicated to Poe, claiming that the famous writer had once attended college there.

Edgar married his thirteen-year-old cousin, Virginia Clemm, and made a very modest living as a writer and as a newspaper journalist. Poe had a nasty temper, took drugs as painkillers, and because of his volatile disposition, couldn't keep a job for any length of time. In 1847, Virginia died of tuberculosis, and Poe, underfed, pale and gaunt-looking, passed away two years later.

Poe's detective stories "The Murders in the Rue Morgue" and "The Purloined Letter" made him famous, in addition to his classic horror tales "The Pit and the Pendulum", and the genius's eerie, epic work, "The Tell-tale Heart".

"The Black Cat"

I don't expect anyone to believe the insane story I'm about to relate, because the world is fucked-up, the story is fucked-up, and I'm fucked-up, too. Even I can't believe the abnormal occurrences that had happened, and I'm now an avowed atheist, and currently believe in absolutely nothing except that everyone and everything on this planet and in the Universe, is fucked-up. Yet I maintain that I'm not *mad!* I'm just thoroughly pissed-off and simply am "angry-mad", but not "crazy-mad".

I know I'm not dreaming because presently I have a goddamned excruciating toothache that won't quit, and my hemorrhoids are three times their normal size and make my asshole feel like there's a saguaro cactus stuck inside it. But tomorrow, I'm scheduled to die, and today I must confess the true circumstances that have led-up to my impending execution by lynching.

My main objective in producing this writing is to inform the insensitive world about my dilemma, but the world is not a person having ears, so why the fuck should I even endeavor to do such an absurd thing? And besides all that self-destructive, life-curtailing bullshit, I have already established that the world is fucked-up, even without the planet having any ears to listen to and sympathize with my distasteful plight. But I'll describe my tale plainly and briefly, hoping that in the future, some reader will vindicate my conviction about the significance of life, and about my accompanying legal conviction by the fucked-up American judicial system.

I'll not try to explain the series of events, but instead, will simply and diligently describe them in detail in a sequential manner. Recently, I've experienced nothing but terror; terror of my environment; terror of other people, and terror of myself, and the attendant demons associated with virtually every fuckin' thing in this whole goddamned world, ranging from pets to cellars. I am literally a tortured, maligned, and defeated asshole, and I can't wait to die and escape this despicable, son-of-a-bitchin', horror-laden existence, so inappropriately mis-labeled as "life on Earth".

Some cynics may consider my account more strange than terrifying. I say to those asshole skeptics, "Fuck you!", because I'm the one that has to carry the extreme burden and bear the horrid reality every single minute, of every single hour, of every single day. A rational, calm person thinks that he or she is normal and will interpret my demeanor as being too excitable, and as too impetuous, but those cavalier, objective idiots are more fucked-up than I'll ever be, because the dumb shits will never admit that they're fucked-up in the first place. If someone reading this tale sees my descriptive tragedy as a mere sequence of causes and effects, then I say to that warped asshole, "Suck my dead dick!"

From the time after I had been protectively rocked in the cradle, I was always known and regarded as a cooperative, pleasant and subordinate person, possessing an affable temperament. My few teenage hooligan friends made fun of my wimpy personality, and often exploited my soft heart, and took advantage of my propensity for compassion. The antagonistic jerk-offs all thought that I was a naïve and gullible pecker-head, since I always attempted to please my peers instead of beating the fucking shit out of them like I should have done to achieve the lofty supreme position in their bully-oriented pecking order.

My heart had always been very fond of animals, and I quickly learned to like them better than I valued people. I enjoyed owning a great variety of dogs and cats throughout my late childhood and adolescence, and I found that my pets showed more honesty and truth in their emotions than my so-called arrogant, scumbag, facetious, untrustworthy friends did. Unlike my mercenary fucked-up peers, my pets were loyal and wise, and in many instances, more human than those uncouth imbeciles I had associated with at bars, dances, and taverns ever were. The animals in my house provided me with unselfish love and faithfulness; traits that my shit-head human acquaintances never acquired or developed.

I married young, and my pretty wife had a cheerful and benign disposition that generally corresponded to my own. She loved animals too, and we always had birds, dogs, goldfish, rabbits, gerbils, and even a small monkey inside the house. But the one pet that stood-out amongst the rest was a very large black cat with beautiful soft fur. The exotic creature exuded a docile wisdom that seemed to transcend all human knowledge, and I intensely felt its sagacity and serenity every single day, even without the perceptive animal ever saying a discernible word.

My wife was very superstitious in addition to being a cold, frigid piece of ass. "Black cats are really witches masquerading in disguise!" Beatrice often commented.

"Well, what about your black pussy?" I would occasionally jest. "Is there also a treacherous witch hiding inside that wet, pink, frigid mama, too?"

"Please take my great apprehension seriously," my wife sternly admonished. "There is something demonic about that black cat of ours. I can't put my finger on it, but our furtive pet always seems to be walking in a perverted *cat*atonic state!"

The black cat's name was Pluto, coincidentally named after the Roman ruler of the dark afterworld. At first, Pluto was my favorite pet in the whole house (which as I've already stated was sort of a menagerie), and the creature followed me all over, sniffing and smelling every damned silent or loud fart I would blast out of my asshole. My wife was absolutely afraid to feed the black cat, so I assumed performing that particular twice-daily responsibility. As I've already mentioned, the curious black prowler would follow me everywhere, even along busy thoroughfares and avenues, and also up and down narrow side streets and alleyways.

My friendship with Pluto remained intact for several years, but then one by one, the goldfish, the birds, the dogs, the rabbits, the gerbils, and even the small monkey, were viciously attacked and killed. Claw marks appeared all over their limp bodies. My wife and I never observed or heard Pluto kill any of the other pets, but one by one, the creatures all met their deaths by "inexplicable mutilation". My wife could not endure her emotional duress.

"I'm scared out of my wits," my spouse told me one afternoon when she had discovered the monkey's face, throat, head, and chest brutally clawed, almost beyond recognition. "I believe that Pluto has killed and abused all our other pets. That temperamental cat has turned into a horrible monster!"

"Don't be ridiculous!" I strongly replied. "Any cat probably would've eventually eaten the goldfish and the birds!" I insisted. "Their bodies were found clawed and mangled, but quite obviously, the other pets had not been devoured. And besides," I said; "an adult monkey ought to be able to aggressively defend itself and beat the living shit out of any ordinary black housecat!"

"I think you should call the police!" Beatrice ranted. "Something has killed our pets one by one over the last year, and it certainly wasn't you or I! I'm deathly afraid to stay in this house! It's more like an insane asylum!"

"Look," I replied, in an attempt to sound plausible. "The police aren't going to waste their time and energy investigating the death of house pets, especially with the abundance of murders and robberies occurring out there on the city streets! The cops have better things to do like delving into homicides, suicides and grand larcenies, not to mention eating doughnuts and getting laid," I stubbornly maintained.

"Pets aren't *murdered,* even if it appears that another animal had *killed* the goldfish, birds, dogs, rabbits, gerbils and monkey! Only humans are murdered, and only humans are murderers! Our pets were fuckin' killed, and not murdered!"

It was during that bizarre pet-killing rampage inside my house that I felt compelled to increase my consumption of alcohol. I loved rye, whiskey, gin, scotch, beer, and bourbon, and became quite addicted to all six Demons. As time passed, I became more cantankerous and more intolerant of criticism. I didn't give a flying shit about anyone else's feelings any-more, and began behaving exactly as my old hedonistic friends had acted ten years before. I swore at my wife, beat her violently on several occasions, and would deliberately piss on the floor to demonstrate my general animosity towards her and towards the cold, cruel, insensitive world.

Pluto sensed this radical fundamental change in my personality, and avoided contact with me; but still, I favored the wise creature and petted it whenever I found it hiding from me. My drinking problem became more acute, and the black cat was now growing old and aggressive, once fiercely scratching me on my right wrist. 'My wife was right about Pluto being evil!' I thought as I cleaned my wound and then wrapped a bandage around it. 'That fucked-up black cat has somehow transferred its satanic wickedness from its own heart, and now that ugly evil shit is savagely inhabiting mine!'

One summer night, I arrived home late, intoxicated from imbibing a quantity of liquor at a neighborhood tavern. I literally stumbled over the sleeping black cat in the hallway located between the living room and the bathroom. I angrily lifted-up the diabolical creature and squeezed its neck, but before I could strangle the despicable, furry, mongrel tomcat, the animal clawed my hands, and blood was dripping all over the wood-planked floor.

Maybe it was my inebriation, or perhaps my great fury, or both that motivated me, but a primeval hatred instantly consumed my spirit. I cornered Pluto in the parlor and then surreptitiously removed a penknife from my pants' pocket with my bleeding left hand. Next, I callously grabbed the savage black cat's neck with my right hand, lifted the hissing, evil creature up from the floor, and with a surgeon's precision, I frantically cut its left eye right the hell out of its fuckin' socket.

Presently, as I recollect and accurately document that gross damnable atrocity, I feel intense shame and guilt. But nevertheless, I cannot deny that the brutality had truly occurred, and that I had deliberately performed the abominable deed, and at the time, had delighted in doing so.

The following morning, I had sobered-up, and my random meditations were more lucid and less nebulous. I felt a degree of sorrow for my stupid-shit, animal-abuse crime, and an element of pity for the partially blinded black cat. But my regret was only superficial in magnitude, and I began heavily drinking my whiskey again in order to erase the memory of my uncivilized, horrid deportment. And when the bourbon, rye and gin bottles became empty, I switched my harmless addiction to chugging-down cheap wine.

Pluto had slowly recovered from his eye operation, and the black cat's hollowed-out left eye socket looked rather grotesque and frightening in appearance. The tomcat seemed to not carry any grudge towards me, and walked about the house as if he were a prince strutting around *his* opulent palace. But every time I approached the creature, its fur would then rise; it would violently hiss, and next the disturbed animal would scurry away to evade my further scrutiny. It was evident that Pluto plainly loathed and simultaneously dreaded me, and despised my antagonism towards him; towards my abused wife, and the brute also sensed my negative attitude towards the fucked-up world. The black cat's very obvious resentment of me ascended to the insane level of perverseness.

'Perverseness is a baneful, suppressed characteristic of the human emotional spectrum!' I objectively and academically thought like an asshole Harvard professor. 'The abstraction is understood as being both primitive and atavistic. Perverseness is indeed a baser emotion shared by everyone, even by horny whores and kinky prostitutes; and the negative quality is also a taboo frowned-upon by civilized society; but nevertheless, it dwells in the deepest pit of every human being's heart!'

I intensely and compulsively felt like leading the life of a contrarian, not only in thought, but also in deed. Every friggin' shit-head deep-down in his or her inner *core* wishes to be a rebellious Law Violator and a defiant Ten Commandment Maverick. But the superego, along with one's fear of public condemnation, discourages those primal feelings from surfacing-up to one's more docile learned-behavior world, rising from the goddamned dark and mysterious subconscious. And I so desperately wished to spite the holy morals and the legal principles that bond fucked-up society and law and order together, preventing most of us from becoming the sinful, hard*core,* decadent criminals that our dark side would like us to be. I firmly believe that laws and rules both prohibit and inhibit us from being our honest, happy, selfish selves.

This inner turmoil my erratic mind was experiencing gradually triumphed over my common sensibilities. I felt an overwhelming obsession to self-destruct (to emotionally implode), and I did not have the necessary fuckin' mental wherewithal to adequately combat that tendency. I felt a terrible, satanic need to become violent and to traduce and attack anyone I could. I feared I would *kill* my wife as if Beatrice were to transform into an animal, rather than merely *murder* her as a human being. 'I gotta' get the fuck out of this accursed house before I enact *that* dreadful, perverted fantasy, which my convoluted mind is fabricating!' I seriously thought.

I left the row house and ambled to the all-too-familiar neighborhood tavern. I drank four double shots of sweet bourbon, and my mind was swimming in silly numbness that excellently transcended the fuckin' mundane world that keeps us all civil and polite, with all (or most) of us stupid-shits being imprisoned inside our socially acceptable behavioral cages.

Then, the most beautiful well-built blonde woman I had ever seen entered the crowded bar and ambled over next to my stool. "Could I buy you a drink?" I courteously and artificially asked.

"Yes; a scotch on the rocks would do just fine," the knock-out doll coyly answered." Make that a double size, if you don't mind!"

The blonde broad and I conversed and drank for over an hour, and when I was thoroughly wasted, the now-standing, vivacious lady took my left hand and shoved it deep down into her skirt. I immediately knew that she was not wearing any undergarments. My palm touched her wonderful, hairy pussy, and the exotic female gently rubbed my super-sensitive fingers against her magnificent, thick bush. The thrilling, tantalizing sensation made me instantly think of Pluto's soft fur. I could not control my fury and my sense of survival that had buoyantly surfaced-up to my consciousness. I suddenly wrenched my hand out of her very magnificent pubic zone.

"Leave me the fuck alone; you fuckin' whore!" I screamed, getting the attention of every envious, sex-starved male jerk-off inside the crowded bar. "Fuckin' leave me alone to my own misery, you promiscuous, filthy pig slut!" I boisterously raved like a possessed, stark-raving-mad maniac.

I stormed out of the popular bar, leaving a generous tip on the counter, and also leaving a distinct hush in my wake. I was dominated by a *perverted* urge to enter my corner row-house and perform a most heinous act.

Precisely at midnight, I had cornered and captured Pluto, carried the black beast outside, and despite the animal's writhing and squealing resistance, and its incessant clawing and biting, I held its neck tightly, and before I had strangled the squirming creature to death, I took a rope and wrapped it around the screaming, frenetic animal's neck. I creatively hung the black cat from the lowest limb of a nearly-dead birch tree in my small backyard. I both laughed and cried in response to my perverse, perverted, maniacal sin.

'I've lynched Pluto because it loved me, and because I had loved its noble spirit!' I thought as I then sobbed and whimpered. 'I've destroyed the tremendous evil lurking in its heart! I know I've *killed* the wicked evil also lurking deep in his animal soul, just as *he* had honored a similar instinct, and had viciously killed my other cherished pets!' I sentimentally cried and sobbed with the bitterest sense of remorse.

My heart didn't give a shit at that moment if I had jeopardized my goddamned immortal soul and had condemned my spirit to the eternal fires of hell. 'Even the most Clement and Just God might not be able to salvage my wretched soul, following such inhumane and atrocious mal-conduct,' I suspected.

After I had eliminated what my mind considered the source of my evil by cruelly suspending and strangling the black cat from the birch tree, I slept in the spare bedroom, fearing that I might also be inclined *to kill* my already-abused wife. I was awakened from my slumber with hysterical shouts of "Fire!" originating from voices outside my dilapidated ghetto dwelling. The curtains around my bed, along with the sidewall, were already in flames. Soon, the entire house was engulfed in a raging inferno.

My frigid wife and I had separately escaped the dangerous blaze. I remember staggering out of the front door and falling down the white marble steps, clumsily landing on the pavement. 'Everything I've diligently worked for all my life will soon be reduced to ashes and cinders!' I despairingly thought. 'My life has been cursed, and my soul has been doomed! This fuckin' devastating fire is symbolic of the eternal flames of hell that my immortal soul will surely experience!'

Now, I'm logically and objectively presenting a series of irrefutable facts in the form of an intelligent sequence of events, but I'm not such a fucking fool to suggest that there exists any scientific cause and effect relationship between me dramatically hanging and killing Pluto and the terrible conflagration that had ensued shortly thereafter. But there are other very troubling, goddamned links to this bizarre chain of events that undeniably challenge my acumen and accentuate my fears.

On the day following the devastating fire, after a night of sobering-up and pacing the lonely Baltimore streets, I felt an untense need to visit the ruins of my demolished former home. Only one wall remained vertical, and it was the one situated in the center of the house. The head of the bed in which I had been sleeping had rubbed against that accursed wall. Remarkably, the plaster had withstood the fire's incredible rage, and I speculated that the standing wall's survival had been because the construction material had been recently applied, and the plaster was still fresh enough to fend-off the intense heat the blaze had generated.

A dense crowd had gathered around the only standing wall, and dumb-shit neighbors were gossiping and marveling about a certain phenomenon the crowd had been witnessing. I heard the adjectives "Strange!" and "Odd!" being babbled among the goddamned, disgusting horde of curiosity-seekers. I instinctively approached the lone standing wall to examine it more specifically. An impression of a rope wrapped around a huge cat's neck had been mystically embedded into the plaster.

My wonder quickly ascended and evolved into terror as I further-scrutinized the fucking hellish configuration. 'It's Pluto's ghost returned to further haunt my ass right into fuckin' insanity! I was plastered last night, and so was Pluto!' I naturally concluded. 'Try to settle-down and get a solid grip of your fleeting emotions!' I recall thinking. 'The special advantage that you have over these weak-minded, garrulous curiosity-seekers is that you have the capacity to be stoic and objective, and they're just a bunch of weak-minded, gossiping curiosity-seekers!"

My disheveled mind attempted to evaluate all of the evidence, and my disoriented brain reviewed all of the extraordinary circumstances. Pluto had been hung in the backyard from the birch tree. My keen eyes then looked at my hands with their many lacerations and scratches as observable, residual proof of that indisputable event happening. 'Someone in the neighborhood must've cut-down the cat from the birch tree immediately after he or she had trespassed upon my property, and after he or she had been allured and attracted by the house fire inferno!' I theorized. 'Then, the contemptible do-gooder must've hurled the dead cat through an open window (for it was then summertime) into my infernal bedroom, and I had been awakened by the thump, and soon heard the loud screaming originating outside.

'When the other walls collapsed, Pluto's body must've been pressed into the freshly-applied and heated wall plaster, making a permanent impression. And then, the plaster's lime had been chemically converted into ammonia, arising from the cat's sizzling carcass and asshole!' I methodically and deductively realized. 'This infallible hypothesis scientifically proves how the repugnant black cat had disintegrated, skeleton and all, and how its outlined form still eerily remains embedded into the wall's plaster.'

My delusional brain rationalized *that* rather fantastic theory and believed that I had made the correct and reasonable conclusion. My impeccable, flawless analysis represented fabulous confirmation of my intelligent assumptions explaining what had actually transpired.

There was nothing mysterious or supernatural about the fucking reprehensible, comprehensible event, whatsoever. The fucked-up incident just had the appearance of being incredible, but was entirely explainable if one rationally applied the science of chemistry to account for what had evidently occurred.

But still, my suspicions and my fears agitated my already-maligned sense of judgment. My discretion had been tinkered with, no fucking doubt about it. For the next half-year, I could not discard the image of "Pluto's fossil" being embedded in plaster from my psyche. 'I must vanquish these irritating manifestations completely, so that my mind can again enjoy tranquility!' I kept repeating to myself. 'Pluto's terrifying image in that standing wall can be explained by elementary science, and that's all that really fuckin' matters!'

The next year, my wife and I lived with separate relatives. In the meantime, I managed to borrow some money from reliable friends and vagrants, from several well-to-do unemployed cousins, and I had my former row-house reconstructed to the exact same dimensions to the ones that had been obliterated in the unfortunate conflagration. But still, each night I had crazy fuckin' nightmares haunting my psyche about Pluto, with his heinous animal soul crying-out to haunt me from the deepest, fiery pit of Hell.

My consciousness was dominated by the notion that I had to replace Pluto with a substitute cat, simply to redeem my killing of him. I wandered around that part of the city in search of a comparable black cat. I relentlessly paced all neighboring streets in the vicinity, but had the fucking bad luck of a born loser. Undaunted by failure, I resumed my exploration until I reached absolute fatigue.

I dejectedly entered an area tavern notorious for its debauchery and decided to get *plastered,* or at least as plastered as Pluto had been before being disintegrated by the intense heat of the house fire, and the subsequent chemical reaction that had mercilessly incinerated the dead creature somewhere into oblivion. After becoming groggy from an excess of liquor, I espied through a doorway a sinister black cat lying peacefully upon a large rum barrel inside the tavern's warehouse. 'That goddamned mammoth animal is indeed Pluto reincarnated!' I observantly thought. 'This is my opportunity for redemption. I shall possess the stray and give it the loving home that Pluto had been maliciously denied!'

I carefully approached the sedate creature and gently caressed it with my hands. The huge tomcat was virtually identical to Pluto, except for one outstanding feature. The fucking thing had a white blotch on its breast, which I naturally presumed symbolized an island of goodness amidst a vast sea of sin and depravity. 'This son-of-a-bitchin' black cat is begging me to be its master!' I shrewdly conjectured. 'It's definitely a docile, mature, friendly creature worthy of my deepest compassion and affection!'

The appreciative cat was purring loudly, apparently enthused about the good vibrations its sixth-sense ESP had been genuinely perceiving and interpreting as human kindness. The future pet rubbed his soft fur against my sweaty hands, and I was fully aware of our terrific compatibility.

"How much for your black cat?" I asked the suddenly surprised tavern proprietor. "He's sure a beauty!"

"It's not mine, and I've never seen the grotesque-looking critter before," the owner tersely answered. "You may claim it for your own, for I'm certain it's only but a stray tomcat looking for a warm meal and a comfortable litter-box."

I thanked the pleasant landlord for his cordial indulgence, and hurriedly returned to my recently constructed row-home, proudly carrying my new acquisition. The novel addition quickly found favor with my reconciled wife, who treated *him* with more respect and dignity than the frigid cold bitch had ever treated me. I soon became jealous of the new cat receiving more goddamned attention and approval in the house than I had been getting.

My interest in the new black cat gradually turned to jealous resentment. After several months, I abhorred and then despised the odious, totally detestable animal. Being somewhat paranoid, I avoided the creature, knowing full-well that I could be inspired to kill it on instinct for simply breathing anywhere near my face and sensitive eyes. 'I must not violate and abuse this cat as I regrettably had done with Pluto,' my mind guiltily pondered. 'I shall regard it as if it's diseased, and totally ignore its presence in my newly constructed abode.'

My conscience knew I was thinking and behaving like a derelict scumbag, but what could I fucking do? I never placed much credence in coincidences, until the following morning. I shuddered when I observed that the second black cat had its unlucky left eye missing, and now looked more than ever like Pluto (except for the singular patch of white fur on its chest). Beatrice then loved *him* even more because of his visual handicap, and I selfishly envied the second cat for meriting her devotion and tenderness, which I had been neglected throughout our marriage. I was livid, and my suppressed emotions were ready to volcanically explode into a tirade.

The more I hated the fucking second cat, the more it seemed to like me. Hades faithfully followed my footsteps as if it were a determined animal kingdom private detective stalking me down. It crouched at my feet whenever I sat my ass upon a chair. Sometimes, the son-of-a-bitch would hop onto my lap, begging to be cuddled. And whenever I clumsily sauntered down the hallway, the annoying animal would pass between my feet, and almost trip me into a tumble. Sometimes, Hades would insert its long, sharp claws into my pants, and playfully climb up to my chest. I was both puzzled and alarmed at those excessive liberties that the furry Pluto incarnate was exhibiting.

I soon desired to savagely kill this second offensive cat, and was contemplating appropriate methods of eliminating it from my daily experiences. 'This is absolutely fuckin' preposterous and silly,' I thought. 'Why should I feel unwarranted terror and dread from such a dumb, dependent stray cat? Even if it attacked me in my sleep, I would wake-up from the surprise assault, grab the mother-fuckin' piece of shit and wring its neck until it ceased breathing!' I graphically imagined. 'Sometimes I think that I'm almost as fucked-up as the mother-fuckin' world is!'

My wife kept reminding me how beautiful the new cat's white patch was, and that preposterous declaration instantly reinforced my certainty that the new pet had its own identity and its own agenda, and that the black creature was *not* Pluto's spirit reborn into another kindred mammal. And besides, when I had found the second fucked-up cat in the tavern storage room, it was at least three years old, and Pluto had been dead for less than a year, so any possibility of that new black cat being Pluto reincarnated was both chronologically and realistically infeasible.

I pensively thought about and seriously considered the white blotch on and below Hades' neck. At first, it appeared shapeless, without any particular definition; but now, the vivid image I observed upon its breast was the outline of *a gallows!* I recollected hanging Pluto from a limb on the backyard birch tree, and suddenly, the remarkable symbolism of the white gallows' formation on the second black cat's upper chest made me skeptical of the existence of such things as accurate science and a normal life on this goddamned, grace-forsaken planet. And soon, I felt an irresistible inclination to kill that second brutish beast, for it was not its physical appearance that I detested; but instead, its evil soul that, in my chaotic mind, was undoubtedly that fucking vicious stalker Pluto reincarnated.

I never thereafter had a decent night's sleep. I tossed and turned, anticipating with great trepidation that the bitchin' monster would go berserk, leap-up onto my bed, and slash my jugular with its sharp claws and fangs. I tried sleeping with my hands over my neck to prevent that feared incursion from occurring, but to no avail. I was restless, weary, incensed, frightened, and on the brink of becoming a fucking raving psychopath.

One October night, I arose from a light sleep and discovered that Hades had been breathing on my face. I hopped out of bed in a wild frenzy, chased the alarmed creature out of the spare room, and frenetically pursued it down the hall into my wife's chamber. When I flung open the door in a rage, my estranged, frigid spouse became startled and sat-up straight in her bed. My eyes glared crimson red when I witnessed the second black cat peacefully resting besides her right arm.

The following afternoon, my wife and I were stepping-down to the cellar to obtain some vegetables preserved in glass jars. We were poor folks, and my spouse began unjustly criticizing why she and I had reached an almost destitute existence.

"You can never hold a decent job, and we have little money to pay our many bills," Beatrice persisted. "And you're nothing more than a drunken failure and a pathetic loser!" my spouse wickedly instigated our quarrel while descending the cellar steps.

I wanted to take my hostility out on my shrew of a wife, but then I noticed that the black cat was also slowly descending the steps down to the dismal, dank cellar. When the frightful animal nearly tripped me on the fourth plank from the basement's floor, my total being went into an uncontrollable hysteria. I decided to transfer the intense animosity I had felt towards my wife to the very vexing black cat.

"What the fuck did you say?" I shrieked while lunging toward an axe that had been leaning against the cellar wall. But instead of taking my rancor out on my frigid spouse, I aimed a blow at the ubiquitous black cat. But my interfering "better-half" jumped into the way to protect the uncouth tomcat from my enraged wrath, and instead of killing the despicable Pluto incarnate, I had accidentally murdered Beatrice by mistake.

The axe's blade had penetrated her skull and was then buried deep inside her cranium. Beatrice fell to the cold cement basement floor, and ample blood spouted all over the goddamned place. It was a gruesome scene, and as I stood there crying at my malicious crime, I saw the hungry, hideous black cat eerily licking-up the puddles of crimson. I was afraid to savagely kill the demonic beast, since I was so distraught from recently butchering my innocent wife.

'I can't afford the expense of a funeral and a decent coffin, and the police are sure to conduct an intensive investigation! I must act with dispatch!' I quickly and anxiously decided. My brain thought of dismembering her body into small fragments, and then efficiently burning the various parts in a fire. 'I could fling her limp corpse into the backyard well!' I imagined. 'Or, I could do some concrete thinking. I could dispose of her remains by burying them under the cellar floor, and then resurfacing the section with fresh cement.'

Finally, my mind recollected an ancient practice that had been utilized by crafty European monks during the *Middle Ages*. 'I can seal her body up in the recently *plastered* wall, over there. The cellar has been damp, and the plaster has not hardened,' I reckoned. 'Any new plaster would easily blend in with the original composition and almost magically conceal my cunning camouflage!' I determined. "Fuck your damned remains, you no good frigid bitch!" I screamed at my spouse's lifeless corpse. "You would still be frigid, even if you lived in an Eskimo igloo!"

Then, I considered enacting other viable alternatives. I creatively re-evaluated my dilemma. 'If I remove the loose bricks from that decrepit chimney construction over there,' I theorized, 'I could stealthily stuff Beatrice's cadaver inside the wall, and then cover it up with fresh plaster; and then in the process, deftly conceal my heinous misdeed. No one will ever suspect that I had been capable of such a marvelous, expedient strategy! The fucked-up world is full of stupid fucks, most of the distracted assholes not half as clever as I am!'

I adroitly used a crowbar to further loosen and remove the aforementioned basement chimney bricks. When sufficient space had been made inside the still-wet wall to accommodate a standing corpse, I almost mechanically lifted my wife's limp body, and squeezed, and finally successfully manipulated her corpse inside the designated cellar wall. Next, I meticulously reset the bricks, and then blended mortar, sand, and some of *her* cut hair into a splendid plaster that when applied, looked identical to that which appeared throughout the rest of the tampered-with wall. It was indeed a most fantastic mixture which I had imaginatively concocted, and my propitious scheme would be far above and beyond any regular human detection.

I was perfectly convinced and satisfied that everything had been properly planned and deviously implemented. 'You're a fuckin' genius!' I proudly commended myself. 'I've picked-up all clues of debris from the grimy floor, and it appears almost immaculate after I had slyly eliminated all bloodstain traces with a powerful solvent that had been kept under the kitchen sink. Only the supernatural is aware of my dastardly deeds, that is to think if an omniscient Supreme Being actually exists!' I deliriously laughed. 'Now I must capture and execute that troublesome fucked-up black cat, which has caused all of the unnecessary pain and suffering that my heavily-laden heart must grievously live with for the remainder of my goddamned fuckin' life!'

After deciding that I must put the miserable, fiendish animal to *his* required death, the perceptive creature sensed my nasty mood and evaded my ongoing scrutiny. I searched and searched the house, but to no satisfaction. Finally, I took a much-needed nap, being exhausted from burying and sealing my wife inside the cellar wall, and from futilely ransacking the upstairs rooms, madly scrambling all over looking for the goddamned, Hell-sent replacement black cat.

I had slept fairly soundly as I hadn't done in many months, before and since the house fire. Then, three seemingly eternal days elapsed, and still no sign of Hades was evident anywhere. My elation was virtually exultant. 'The fuckin' black bastard has fled the house to escape my prescribed death sentence!' I gleefully thought. 'Its persistent evil will vex me no more!'

On the fourth day after I had conveniently executed and disposed of my wife, the police arrived at my residence to conduct a preliminary inquiry as to her whereabouts. Several neighbors had complained about hearing a minor disturbance, and after her relatives had conveyed to the authorities that Beatrice had not been in contact with them, the idiotic cops were compelled to make an official report. The police carefully searched all rooms in the modest premises, and then I confidently (without guilt or embarrassment) led the men-in-blue down to the interior of the cobweb-infested basement. The resolute investigators left no corner of the property unexplored. Four times the investigators made a rotation of the total cellar, and the frustrated officers found nothing suspicious or irregular.

I remained calm throughout the extensive inquiry, and did not tremble or show any indication of regret or emotion. I folded my arms in front of my chest and freely conversed with the dumb-assed detective and his incompetent, asinine crew of notepad scribblers, joking about the weather, and jesting about why my wife had mysteriously disappeared and had possibly fled to either Antarctica or the North Pole. 'I fear she's unfaithfully abandoned me for a richer man,' I hypothesized and stated. 'My wife was lazy, kept a poor, dirty house, and hated washing clothes and cooking meals,' I confidently stated. 'Beatrice had always sought a better life with a wealthy man, and did not hesitate to repeatedly emphasize those selfish desires to me!' I persuasively testified.

The concerns of the police had been satisfactorily addressed, and their superficial doubts about my integrity had been thoroughly alleviated. I felt victorious and exuberant as I began leading the investigative team up the cellar steps.

"Gentlemen," I announced. "If you need to come again, feel free to do so, and also be aware that you'll enjoy receiving my full cooperation. May you return in good health, and I anticipate again greeting you with my utmost courtesy."

Then, I felt an alien compulsion to say something completely casual in nature, and totally irrelevant to *their* purpose in being there; but the particular words that I uttered also happened to be very material to the truths that were dwelling deep within my soul. "Gentlemen," I continued my illustrious, concluding remarks. "You must admit that this new house is superbly constructed. The walls are dense and solidly built."

And during the culmination of my rather frivolous bravado, I deliberately and heavily rapped my black cane against the solid wall. But to my absolute horror, I had inadvertently initiated a most bizarre and diabolical reaction.

'May the mercy of God protect and isolate me from Satan's poisonous fangs!' I desperately thought. No sooner had my cane's blow echoed throughout the dank, dark cellar, that the five of us spectators discerned a pitiful cry originating from within the formerly nondescript wall where I had furtively deposited and concealed my wife's corpse.

At first, the horrible moan was that of anguish and agony, and as it increased in volume, the goddamned fucking noise swelled to a continuous, morbid and surreal scream that sounded like it had ascended from the very bowels of Hell. The cryptic siren was a most disconcerting combination of howling, wailing, shrieking, sobbing, screaming and fright. The spine-chilling tone was half-victory and half-horror; part-joy and part-damnation.

I felt thoroughly faint, and then my accursed body staggered around the dank cellar in a giddy dizziness. Random thoughts, ideas and weird emotions whirled-around inside my head, and together, became jumbled-up into one confusing, unbearable tornado of destructive mental excruciation. The four horrified police officials stood frozen upon the cellar steps, their perceptive eyes closely assessing my peculiar and unsettling behavior.

And then, the next thing I remember were eight strong arms actively hacking-away with *my* own various clubs and tools, their energy aimed at the recently-plastered wall. The policemen's strenuous efforts were virtually on target, hammering and banging away next to the artificial chimney from where the sensational howling and groaning utterances were still emanating. As a large section of plaster fell onto the floor, my wife's pallid-faced corpse suddenly stood before *our* horrified eyes. Then, I too panicked and quickly shared *their* extreme terror. Beatrice's horrid facial features appeared to be decayed and gory, and her cheeks, forehead and mouth were macabre in appearance, gruesomely covered with soot and wall dust.

On my dead wife's head sat a one-eyed, black cat with an opened-red-mouth. The beast's remaining eye blazed with a scarlet fire inside. The black demon's initial screams had alerted the police to study the recently plastered wall, and the sounds had simultaneously condemned me to the gallows. And then, in the midst of my cruel mania, at that moment, I recalled one insular fact. I then shamefully recollected that I had also walled-up the still-alive black cat with my wife during her most unorthodox burial.

"The Cask of Amontillado"

That bastard Fortunato is ironically going to encounter and experience a very 'unfortunate' tragedy of *his* own doing. The repugnant rogue has irresponsibly insulted me for the last time. Fortunato has poisoned my dog, has drowned my cat, has porked my daughter, has screwed my wife, but most importantly, the heinous nobleman-scoundrel has been having an ongoing affair with my gorgeous mistress. Now, I'm so extremely pissed-off that I could kill and mutilate the no-good shit-head, just at the mention of *his* despicable, abhorrent name.

'I intend to be so clandestine and so secretive about my need for satisfactory revenge that the arrogant asshole will never in his wildest imagination suspect my malicious scheme,' I shrewdly reasoned. 'I shall minimize risk of failure, and my retribution shall be swift and decisive. My vengeful heart shall efficiently execute my subterfuge with total impunity from justice,' I decided. 'Fortunato will be sufficiently punished, and will recognize my callous wrath only when his knowledge of it will no longer matter. *He* has wronged me and will die an animal's death; a death fit for a man that has lived as an indecent human being. My feigned *smile* of friendship shall be that dirty, mangy mother-fucker's guide that will ultimately escort his fat ass into the afterlife,' I vowed to my conscience. 'The obnoxious creep deserves to be my targeted victim!'

Fortunato never had any cause or reason to doubt my good will, or my benign motivations. I didn't mind when the son of a bitch killed my dog, and mutilated my cat, for the sake of diversion. I paid little heed when the fuck-head continuously fornicated my daughter, and had had intercourse with my attractive wife, but when *he* began hitting on and pumping the poop out of my lovely mistress, then that was what had converted my normally tranquil nature into a raging desire to savagely punish the horny, perverted philanderer. I intended to first humiliate the devilish villain, and then effectively eliminate the city's biggest ball-buster from mortal existence.

Every man has an obscure weakness, a concealed bad habit, or a fragile, predictable behavior that can be scrupulously converted into *his* Achilles heel. I deemed that Fortunato was vulnerable, and was no exception to *that* marvelous, unquestionable axiom of human interaction. Although respected, honored, and feared by his more gullible acquaintances, I happened to know that above anything else in life, the devious creep has always loved screwing women's love tunnels, including my daughter, my wife, and my treasured mistress. I was always aware that *that* scoundrel Fortunato was a connoisseur of excellent wines, especially Amontillado. In many subjects such as oil paintings, politics, investments, religion, philosophy and education, Fortunato was a quack, a veritable charlatan; but the repulsive aristocrat was no impostor when it came down to outstanding vintage wines. There the asshole was; an unrivaled authority, and I planned to use that impeccable wine knowledge of his to adroitly lure the scummy cock-sucker to *his* unexpected doom.

I also prided myself on being an epicure of extravagant gourmet foods and premium wines, and although I was always a mere dabbler, I was never in Fortunato's supreme league of discriminating tastes. I had adequate general acumen in the matter of distinguished vino to be used to connive, and then lure the reprehensible scumbag into a brutal inescapable trap. I myself have always been the possessor of an enviable collection of old wines, and my many sub-cellar casks I plotted to make into my modus operandi to imaginatively entice the loathed Fortunato to his final resting place.

One evening at dusk, during the culmination of merriment and lunacy of the late winter carnival season, I encountered my fiendish friend in front of the city's cathedral. Fortunato externally demonstrated a fake, warm reception, and I immediately discerned that the disgusting braggart was intoxicated both with wine and with his own egomania. The motley real-life jester was appropriately wearing a tight-fitting pin-striped gown, pretending to be a deranged gay cross-dresser, and exhibiting outrageous sin just before the end of carnival along with the advent of the sacred Lent 'fasting time'. On his big, fat, oval head was a cap cluttered with an array of imbecilic bells that jangled my nerves when I heard the annoying objects merrily ringing and jingling.

The two of us shook hands in a long-extended wringing manner as we stared into each other's cunning eyes. I was the first to initiate conversation with my most bitter adversary, who was certainly aware that I knew of his many transgressions against me. But because of social reasons, and the matter of our mutual community reputations, it was expected of us to extend insincere camaraderie to each other in public, especially during the winter carnival season. "My dear Fortunato," I falsely and pretentiously began my phony greeting. "You're looking quite well today, and seem to be in a most jovial frame of mind. But I must tell you that I've received from a distant Tuscany merchant friend a cask of delicious Amontillado, or at least I believe it's genuine vintage Amontillado. But not being a prestigious connoisseur such as yourself, I do indeed have my doubts about the wine's authenticity."

"Amontillado!" Fortunato euphorically exclaimed in his drunken state. "Ha, ha, ha! What a complete farce this is! Ha, ha, ha. You, my fine-feathered friend, must be a glutton for travesty!"

"Yes; and as I've already told you," I slowly emphasized so that the diabolical ingrate could perceive my every enunciated syllable. "I have my doubts."

"A pipe of Amontillado you say?" the verbose hand-job inquired. "In the middle of carnival season? Impossible!" my most hated secret enemy laughed and evaluated.

"Well," I keenly interrupted. "I was foolish enough to pay my reputable merchant friend from Florence the full Amontillado price. I realize I should've consulted you, the foremost authority on the subject, for verification of the wine, and also, to obtain a comparison price; but I could not locate you anywhere in the city on that particular afternoon, and I didn't desire to lose what appeared to be a most outstanding bargain. I trust you understand my predicament."

"Amontillado!" the wine profiteer bellowed once again. "You dare buy expensive wine from someone other than myself! Who was the rascal that sold you the cask? What exorbitant price did you pay?"

"I shall tell you those pertinent details later," I adroitly lied. "I'm sorry that you're enraged at my story. Right now, I'm on my way to see Luchesi to ask *him* to come over to my cellars and sample my acquisition, for that knucklehead will surely know how to determine whether or not the wine cask is indeed genuine Amontillado," I informed the drunken and now quite-infuriated Fortunato. "Luchesi will gladly tell me if…"

"That simpleton Luchesi cannot tell Amontillado from pedestrian merlot, or from crude port for that matter," Fortunato sarcastically ridiculed his chief competitor. "And the frivolous jerk-off doesn't know his dick from his own asshole, and always attempts defecating his solid wastes out of the former instead of out of the latter!"

"And I must confidentially confess that many famous aristocrats and clergy in this city actually believe that Luchesi's tastes are parallel to yours," I cleverly said and exaggerated. "But in all honesty, Fortunato, I deem that your impeccable taste in wines is definitely superior to his!"

"Come, let me accompany you to your residence," Fortunato suggested. "You have a refreshing air of truth about you that transcends all pretense. I volunteer to taste-test whether your Amontillado is legitimate, or a crude imitation sherry."

"To Luchesi's place?" I shrewdly asked. "You want to accompany me to Luchesi's mansion?"

"No, dunderhead. To *your* vaults so that I can confirm the validity of your suspect claim of owning a pipe of Amontillado."

"My dear friend," I replied to the advanced super-jerk off. "I shall not impose upon you to deviate from your marvelous carnival merriment. You undoubtedly have an appointment with a powerful government official, or maybe a scheduled engagement with distinguished members of the nobility later this evening."

"I have no appointments or engagements with anyone, rich or poor; fertile or impotent; straight or gay; or powerful or weak," Fortunato laughed as the costumed moron awkwardly staggered before me, shifting his obese weight from left to right to disguise his own wretched drunken condition. "I insist on accompanying you to your pole vaults; er, I mean your vaults."

"No, my friend," I dramatically dissuaded. "You seem to be afflicted with a severe cold tonight. My cellars are extremely dank and damp this winter's evening. The walls and floors are encrusted with dense moss and thick algae, and they're certain to trigger severe allergic reactions. You'll be sneezing your lungs out along with your mucus pneumonia all over the fuckin' place!"

"Enough of this meaningless debate, and let's proceed with dispatch, anyway," Fortunato confidently insisted. "The cold is really nothing that concerns me, for I once survived a severe winter in Siberia with minimal clothing, ha, ha, ha! On the contrary, I *am imposing* on you, and not you on me. And as far as that idiotic dick-licker Luchesi is concerned," my nemesis vehemently ranted, "Luchesi cannot differentiate the taste of Amontillado from the sweet flavor of virgin pussy, because that gay alchemist has never gotten laid, or ever even tasted the abundant delicacy commonly known as hair pie! Ha, ha, ha!"

Fortunato possessed himself of my arm, pretending to be the gay pervert Luchesi, whom he had been mockingly describing. The conceited ignoramus handed me a black silk mask to camouflage my familiar face in the raucous crowd of festival celebrators, and holding my hand like a bona fide homosexual, the pantomiming faggot/jester escorted me incognito to my own mansion to boastfully show me how much he knew about rare vintage wines.

None of my juvenile delinquent servants were wandering about at my palace. The crazy bastards and bitches were all getting drunk, getting laid, pissing urine into the harbor, or having porno' sketches of themselves being drawn by sex-addict artists renting booths and stalls at the sinful pre-Lent carnival. I had given each of my domestics a small amount of money as a bonus, so that the imbeciles would stay away from my *sanctuary* until the next morning. In that sagacious way, I would have sufficient time to creatively dispose of my deceitful, flamboyant, lustful arch-rival.

I took from wall sconces two torches, wishing that I could then and there shove *my* flambeaux through his gown and straight up Fortunato's enormous rectum, welding his sickening, lesbian, carnival dress right to his smelly colon. I bowed to my rare guest, showing him standard courtesy, but all the time, contemplating castrating the son of a bitch, and then solidifying and using his testicles in a neighborhood marbles or ping-pong tournament.

I escorted my dupe to an archway, an ancient portal leading to stone steps that descended-down to my sinister, dark and dreary vaults. I advised my still-droll visitor to be cautious as we meandered down a cold, stone spiral stairway, en-route to my glorious subterranean wine cellars. At the base of the dangerous curving steps was the burial ground of the Montresors, who were my venerable, deceased ancestors. A rectangular-shaped fifty-by-seventy-foot catacomb had been excavated twenty feet below the mansion's foundation, and the tunnel wove its way in labyrinth-fashion two hundred and forty-feet down to *our* desired vantage point.

"What's in these eerie crypts? *Dungeness* crabs?" my irreverent, half-inebriated enemy cackled. Fortunato's gait was wobbly; almost as if the despised bastard was walking with a limp. The nonsensical juvenile bells upon the moronic jester's cap jingled as we then proceeded to descend to an even deeper level.

"The pipe!" my unwary enemy snorted and chuckled almost simultaneously, as the ignoramus wiped saliva foam from his mouth with the back of his filthy wrist. "Where the fuck's the cask of Amontillado you promised to show me, Montresor?"

"It's farther down, perhaps two more winding flights of steps," I indicated as I rubbed my left hand along the wall and stopped my feeling near a web of niter gleaming upon the solid masonry. I glanced at *his* ugly, corpulent face, and noticed mucus running out of both nostrils of his mammoth nose. "Fortunato, you're sick," I melodramatically implored the obnoxious shit-head. "And you cannot languish down here too long, because the egregious combination of nitrogen and potassium could have a most detrimental effect upon your vulnerable health. You're not totally well-enough to make this underground expedition at this time," I humbly related with a well-concealed undercurrent of derision. "Perhaps it's best if you sample the sumptuous Amontillado another time!"

"Niter," the impetuous fool irrationally mumbled. "Niter! Fuck niter, I say!" the nut-job nastily exclaimed. "Yes; fuck niter day. Ha, ha, ha. I assure you Montressor, that no friggin' niter is gonna' keep me away from imbibing a well-earned quantity of your alleged vintage wine!"

"How long have you had that terrible cough and that waterfall of a running nose?" I innocently asked, seeing that Fortunato was gagging and about to choke from the distinct concentration of niter in the limited breathing air and space that was available.

"Ugh, Ugh! Ugh!" my rival replied like an Iroquois Indian with a severe speech impediment. "Ugh! Ugh! Ugh!" Fortunato choked-out of his throat like someone being strangled a third time. My encumbered foe found it impossible to clearly speak for several minutes. "It's nothing," the wine expert weakly uttered at last, while trying his best to transmit audacity in his raspy tone of voice. Then, the lunatic spit a huge green lump of mucus onto the stone floor. I quickly pointed my flaming torch toward the disgusting discharge. "It's nothing!" my inebriated guest repeated while still attempting to reflect strength and pride.

"Come Fortunato," I melodramatically begged, my torch temporarily igniting the hem of his ludicrous costume. "We'll go back upstairs where the air is fresh and clean. Your health is in jeopardy," I facetiously warned, "and you are a man cherished and revered by most everyone in our great city. If I die down here," I continued, "no one would notice or care a week after my funeral. But if *you* perish, it would be disastrous for both the economy and the politics of our fair metropolis. *Catastrophic* would be a much more accurate adjective to use than *disastrous*. I don't want to be responsible for any injury or affliction imposed by nature on you; this all-too-arduous trek might cause severe harm to Your Eminence."

"Enough of your mealy-mouthed, bullshit flattery!" Fortunato aggressively reprimanded. "The cough is only a cough; a temporary hindrance, and nothing more. Your flimsy monologue and your flagrant-fragrant niter certainly will not kill me, as you're so naively suggesting. I shall not die of a lousy fuckin' cough," the vain, wealthy merchant maintained. "Maybe I'll keel over from fuckin' syphilis, or perhaps from loss of sperm after a month-long orgy, but definitely not from excessive coughing. Ha, ha, ha; ugh, ugh, ugh!"

"Look Fortunato," I cunningly answered, noticing my adversary faltering. "Your competitor Luchesi is in excellent health. I'll simply ask him to come over and sample..."

"Nonsense!" my fully aggravated guest loudly bellowed as I took great pleasure in busting his microscopic balls. "That ninny, gay fuck-head thinks that a woman's vagina is a sink soap dispenser to get gook out of in order to wash his hands. Ugh, ugh, ugh, ugh!" my dupe demonstrably coughed like a tuberculosis victim searching for *his* last breath on *his* deathbed.

"Okay, I suppose you win," I cordially agreed. I removed a large flask dangling from a cord wrapped around my right shoulder. "Perhaps a few snorts of this dry sherry will clear your blocked trachea, and also your clogged throat of all that horrible phlegm. Then you wouldn't be so sluggish and so damned *phlegm*atic*!*"

"Ya know," Fortunato giggled in a weak, effeminate tone of voice. "You do have a sort of humor about you that rather amuses me. Remind me to invite you to my next bisexual orgy, ugh, ugh, ugh, ugh!" After clearing his throat and blowing his nose on his dress's long, silk sleeve, the chauvinistic, uninhibited swine muttered, "I have drunk most of the Medoc in honor of your deceased ancestors in repose all around us! Long live Montresor, I declare!"

"Drink more of it! Finish it off!" I cunningly recommended. I had never been so odious in my entire life. "In fact, I think you oughta' chug the whole damned flask down! It's guaranteed to clear the contaminated snot out of your snout, and the painful congestion right out of your acne-covered chest!"

My ornery visitor directly stared me in the eyes, searching for an iota of deceit; next the idiot slowly raised the flask to his pallid lips and awkwardly drank-down its remaining two-liters of content. His headdress's jester bells jingled and jangled, echoing their haunting melody all throughout my macabre, musky, subterranean cellars, and then resonating into my sacred family burial grounds.

My famous companion again grabbed my arm in imitation of the notorious faggot Luchesi, and we gradually descended another flight of narrow stone steps. "These vaults are rather extensive," the jerk observed and marveled. "I had no idea that your family was so wealthy!" the ninny deliberately manipulated in a statement designed to simultaneously berate and belittle me. "Do you have any poles in these vaults?" the bothersome ballbreaker reiterated. "Ha, ha, ha!"

"The Montresors have for centuries been a great and noble family all over the continent," I gleefully boasted to the incontinent, odor-assed fuck. "My ancestors were first warriors; secondly military officers, and finally, prominent merchants in numerous European cities. I'm most proud of their numerous accomplishments."

"I forgot your coat of arms," Fortunato replied while attempting to again indirectly insult my honorable kin and me by minimizing *our* valuable contributions to Italian society and to Renaissance culture. "What is on it?" the lousy, sick, drunken, pompous pig requested.

"The family coat of arms is a huge human foot in a field of azure, shown crushing a poisonous serpent with vicious fangs embedded in the man's heel," I explained. "Our family has always abhorred and vanquished evil, and the lethal viper symbolizes the general treachery I've just alluded to."

"And what is your family crest's motto?" the curious excuse for a human being inquired. "Is it the crest of a wave, ha, ha, ha!"

"Nemo me impune lacessit!" I sternly proclaimed.

"Speak goddamned Italian or dignified French!" the wine connoisseur demanded. "I loathe both English and Latin. Latin's such a terribly dead and forgotten friggin' language!"

I glanced to my right and searched his sparkling eyes and knew that the wine had had a heavy impact on diminishing his general stamina level. We descended to an even lower stratification and passed by piles of bones with casks, pipes, and barrels intermingled with the skeletal remains of past gallant Montresors. Each level down signified a descent further into my family's illustrious past, which was a rich, historic legacy, paying tribute to the dignified and knightly Montresors of yore.

I grabbed Fortunato's left arm above the elbow, and hesitated for a moment, before delivering my next salient remark. "The niter is now hanging like moss upon the walls," I dutifully noted, "which indicates to me that we're now below the river's bed. The moisture is trickling down these rocks, and when we finally get to our destination, it'll be almost cascading," I deceptively embellished. "Come, Sir. We shall ascend before…"

"Look here! You pathetic, asinine dip-shit!" Fortunato lividly rebuked. "It's nothing I haven't experienced before. Ya' know," my intended victim continued lecturing in a cocky, drunken tone of voice. "I got a pretty damn deep cellar of my own! Ugh, ugh, ugh, ugh!" the stubborn, suffocating fool repetitiously coughed.

I reached to a side recess where I had deliberately stationed a flagon of De Grave to capitalize on the imminent, opportune moment. I handed the powerful substance to Fortunato, who then greedily consumed all sixteen ounces in ten consecutive ravenous swallows. The dumb-fuck's eyes flashed with both envy and malice. The avaricious maniac didn't articulate any threatening words, but I could *feel* his enmity and his jealousy vibrating out towards me. The arrogant jerk-off laughed rambunctiously, and then nonchalantly tossed the empty bottle into the air. The object fell to the stone steps and shattered upon impact. I could not fathom the basis for his strange deportment. I stared at the evil man with a surprised expression upon my face. He repeated the gesticulation without employing any glass bottle to throw.

"You do not comprehend my antics or my semantics?" the famous fuck-head laughingly and mockingly asked.

"No, I honestly don't," I candidly replied. "What did that alien, fucked-up gesture mean?"

"Then you're not of the brotherhood," the diarrhea-mouthed bullshitter vociferated and oddly laughed. "You ain't nowhere in the 'hood, bro'! Ha, ha, ha; ugh, ugh, ugh!"

"What in the world are you insinuating or implying?" I defensively responded. "Your vague words are indeed incomprehensible!"

"You're not a mason," the intoxicated ingrate chuckled. "Any dolt in the organization would instantly recognize my mystic procedure with the designated wine bottle! Ha, ha, ha, ugh, ugh, ugh, ugh!"

"Oh yes, a fuckin', fucked-up mason," I instantly understood and remarked. "The clandestine guild of master craftsmen! The secrets of the building trade, I presume. Don't tell me that you're one of those mother-fucking, jerk-off wackos?"

"You do know the mason's sign?" Fortunato further verbally pursued. "There is a distinct sign that when conveyed, it symbolizes the brotherhood."

I alertly reached into a small alcove and produced a familiar tool of the mortar and stone trade. I deliberately showed the commonplace trowel to the half-cognizant wine authority.

"Yes, you're certainly jesting while you're gesticulating," my unassuming guest bantered and accused. "You're making a fiasco out of my sacred Masonic membership, aren't you, Asshole! But let's proceed to the Amontillado before I decide to make you pay for your most recent insensitive indiscretion when we return to the surface. Ugh, ugh, ugh, ugh!" the dunce choked-out while desperately struggling to catch his breath.

I deftly placed the trowel in a belt beneath my cloak, grabbed the tipsy aristocrat-womanizer by the right arm, and led the stupid bastard deeper into *my* private catacombs. Fortunato latched onto my elbow tightly as we passed through a series of narrow arches and then descended to an even lower level where the air was most thin, but where the foreboding smell of niter was very heavy. We eventually arrived at a crypt that appeared quite eerie in the ghostly light produced from our dual flames, and the vaporous air glowed, and the torches surreally illuminated from the faint trace of oxygen and from the surplus of niter that enveloped us.

We slowly entered another dark crypt adjacent to the first pitiful one on that lower level. My weakened weekend associate was breathing-in rare oxygen in a very labored manner, so I boldly held-up my torch to show "my mark" the piles of ancient bones heaped-up to a height of four feet, formed in a similar fashion to burial practices that had recently been discovered in the famous Paris catacombs. Three sides of this present vault were ornamented in that way, with the fourth a solid rock wall covered with dense niter deposits. When we were well into the interior of the second formation, a more remote, cold, dank chamber, I had some good news for my suffering trekker "friend".

"Proceed with joy, Fortunato," I audaciously informed my scheduled prey. "For here's where the splendid supply of Amontillado has been stored; and as for Luchesi, he will…"

"Luchesi is a pusillanimous pussy that squats down to piss! That retarded bastard has never stood-up like a man to take a damned leak in his entire life!" Fortunato exhaled, aggressively gasping for air. "Where the hell is the goddamned Amontillado, Montresor? Ugh, ugh, ugh!" the piss-head coughed, then discharging another quantity of green-colored mucus from his flu-infected lungs, and then spitting the semi-solid lump onto the cold-stone floor.

My grand scheme had been ingeniously designed and efficiently employed. Fortunato feebly leaned against the solid rock wall, his eyes rolling. And when I held my blazing torch-up to his pupils, his wrinkled face looked both grotesque and bewildered. I securely placed my torch in a wall sconce situated near where I had recently installed dependable shackles, and then I proceeded to fetter the dazed philanderer to suspended manacles that had cleverly been embedded into the granite wall. The secure iron fixtures were horizontally three feet distant from each other, and I soon quickly and deftly tethered Fortunato to my secret compartment's slimy, filthy rock wall. Next, I wrapped the links of a chain around my victim's wriggling waist, and in ten seconds, secured the chain with a third lock to an iron hook I had spent days pounding into the wall with a sledgehammer, just the week before.

I held the *skeleton* key to the three locks (up to the wall sconce's torch) to show Fortunato the vital object. "Try passing your hand over the wall," I brazenly challenged my almost-unconscious, drunken prisoner. "Feel the damp niter if you can; you mangy, aristocratic, no-good mistress-fucker!"

Apparently, my dazed and groggy captive did not yet realize that his erudite, vengeful host had competently shackled him to *his* area of well-deserved slow, methodical execution. "The Amontillado! Where's the goddamned Amontillado?" my intoxicated victim boomed almost out of breath without ever comprehending his immediate peril. "Ugh, ugh, ugh!"

Beneath a heap of bones, I had stored a cache of building stones and ready-to-use mortar. I quickly disassembled the pile and happily uncovered my masonry treasure. I soon detected that Fortunato's inebriation had been gradually wearing-off. His words sounded more rational, more sober; their essence revealing a detectable trace of anxiety dwelling within his present emotional condition. As I gathered my essential materials to fully enact my enterprise, I heard a low moaning, a sort of cry, emanating from *his* place of entrapment. I chuckled to myself at *his* utter futility; at *his* desperation; at *his* fateful justice, and at his ultimate destiny.

Soon, I listened to the loud vibrations of *his* chains as the dastardly Fortunato maneuvered around, endeavoring to liberate himself from his devious confinement. My prisoner was in anguish, terror-stricken, and momentarily evaluating the magnitude and the severity of his current dilemma. The chains vibrated even more furiously, and I thought to myself, 'He'll not be a prisoner much longer. Soon, this disgrace to humanity that has insulted my integrity for the last time will be dead! This scourge named Fortunato has finally met his implacable foe, and soon, the contemptible tyrant's heinous spirit will be forever conquered!'

Being fatigued myself, I sat-down upon another pile of bones to momentarily rest from my toil. Already, I had built a wall thigh-high between Fortunato's chamber of incarceration and my route to the four flights of stone steps leading-up to my cozy residence. When the annoying clanking of the chains against the granite wall finally subsided, I resumed my *constructive* enterprise. Soon, I had mortared the sixth and seventh tiers of available bricks, and my new masonry wall was now nearly up to my chest. I paused to honor an impulse I was feeling. I held the second flambeaux up over my masonry masterpiece so that the suffocating Fortunato's squinting eyes could perceive its flickering light.

A succession of violent screams and frightening shrieks burst forth from his mucus-infested lungs, and I was keenly aware of the terror originating from the pit of my hostage's heart. I hesitated for a brief moment to garner the right words to demean and castigate him, for I hated the educated scum-wagon with a passion for what he had done to my dog, to my cat, and to my mistress. 'To hell with my harlot wife and my whoring daughter!' I determined with great enmity in my heart. 'The two bitches are morally corrupt swine, just like this condescending dick-head Fortunato is! He's not even worthy of the four-sided grave I'm personally finishing for *his* final resting-place!'

I touched the thick niter encrusted upon the crypt's walls, and my heart felt both satisfied and inspired to thoroughly complete my most gratifying task. It was almost midnight, and soon the boisterous reveling above ground would cease, marking the end of the carnival and the beginning of sacred Lent. 'I must finish my skullduggery before the raucous revelry terminates, and the Holy Time of fasting and abstaining commences,' I seriously considered.

Working in haste, like a desperate man whose eternal soul was being gambled away, I very diligently assembled the eighth, ninth and tenth layers of my extremely magnificent, well-conceived brick architecture. Finally, a portion of the last layer of stones had been mortared, and only one more had to be inserted and plastered to form my very splendid partition. As I strained to lift the object up to its designated resting place, a low laugh echoed from the niche's inner recess. The hairs on my head bristled erect like those on a vicious cat when it has been threatened. A shrill, melancholy, repentant voice addressed me, and I had difficulty recognizing that the solicitation belonged to the eminent nobleman, Fortunato.

"Ha, ha, ha, ha!" the vile instigator then laughed with his last amount of dexterity being virtually exhausted. "That was a very fabulous joke indeed, you've just performed. A fantastic jest worthy of my true envious admiration," the nutcase cumbersomely and insincerely commended. "We shall enjoy many future hardy laughs at the palazzo when the two of us are reminiscing your brilliant ruse. Ha, ha, ha! All this trouble, and that new tedious wall you've constructed, all over stupid wine! Ha, ha, ha; ugh, ugh, ugh, ugh!"

"The Amontillado!" I audaciously yelled with new-found authority. "You are indeed a gullible stupid shit, if I've ever seen one!"

"Yes; the Amontillado, ha, ha, ha, ha; ugh, ugh!" the hostage freak-of-nature sputtered and coughed. "Will not our lovely wives be awaiting us at the palazzo! Release me from this incredible joke you've masterfully demonstrated. Ugh, ugh, ugh!"

"Yes," I snidely replied and concurred. "Let's depart to enjoy the end of the celebrating. Our festive wives are waiting, but both waiting for *me* to have a threesome!"

"Montresor, for the love of God!" my fated-victim hoarsely yelled with his last bit of strength. "Tear down that terrible wall and unchain me from this most imaginative prank! Ugh, ugh, ugh, ugh!"

"Fuck you, you belligerent asshole!" I yelled like a raving madman. "You've porked my mistress once too often; you pathetic, miserable piece of rubbish! Now *you* must pay the price for infidelity and for fuckin' with the wrong jealous man!"

"But Montresor, what are you saying?" my victim incredulously pleaded. "Surely, I'll compensate you for any reparations that need addressing! Forgive me Montresor; please forgive me for any harm I might've unintentionally committed! I'll gladly pay a king's fortune to ransom myself! Ugh, ugh, ugh, ugh!"

"Up yours you filthy piece of vermin shit! Up yours, garbage mouth!" I bellowed as my loud voice rumbled throughout my subterranean graveyard without any other ears than *his* to interpret their meaning.

I listened for a suitable reply to my bold accusations, and also to my admonitions, but none was forthcoming. All I could hear was disconsolate whimpering, delirious, and then, desperate weeping. "Fortunato!" I brazenly called three times.

Hearing no answer from the doomed rogue, I squeezed the torch through the remaining small aperture, and then assiduously sealed-up the cavity with the last necessary large stone. The only discernible sound my sensitive ears could detect was a gentle jingling of bells. I felt exhausted and nauseous, but not because of enduring a guilty conscience. I felt sick because of the catacomb's noxious dampness, and I had endured extreme exhaustion from my great labor. After stubbornly forcing the last stone into place with all the energy I could muster, I very meticulously plastered-up the final shred of evidence to my brilliant, nefarious deed.

Finally, I rearranged the bones that had been scattered on the stone floor back into a similar, tidy, neat pile. Presently, I am now an old man and can attest that I had perfectly restacked those sacred bones fifty years ago, and I am privileged to report that no one has viewed or disturbed them in the interim. In pace requiescat! May the souls of my valiant Montresor ancestors be vindicated and rest in peace, but may Fortunato's black soul burn for all eternity in hell!

"The Fall of the House of Usher"

In the early autumn of 1842, I had received a letter from an old college friend (or should I say acquaintance) Roderick Usher, whom I hadn't seen or heard from in over twenty years ever since we had worked together escorting people to their seats in a big city opera house. "Reticent Roderick" was a stand-offish loner, and basically, to tell the truth, so was I. But in contrast to Usher, I did belong to a heterosexually-oriented drinking fraternity, attended university parties (several of them wild orgies), and even got laid six times with different, inebriated, promiscuous girls. But Roderick just vegetated and degenerated inside the confines of his apartment, dropped-out of the University of Virginia in 1820, and according to my sage suspicion, never could amount to anything because he was a total asshole who even had trouble finding his infected anus.

I had known that Roderick had a twin sister, Madeline Usher, who back in 1820, said she would never marry either a man or a woman, but instead, wanted to always live with her eccentric brother and watch him masturbate eight times a day. 'They can't be identical twins,' I thought after considerable pondering, 'because then either Roderick would have to have tits, ovaries, and a vagina; or Madeline would have to have a dick and balls. The siblings must therefore be fraternal twins,' I deductively reasoned. 'But who the hell would want to fraternize with either of those two oddballs when they probably don't even fraternize with each other? What a fucked-up pair of psychos Roderick and Madeline Usher are!'

After re-reading the content of Usher's letter, my naughty mind did fancy certain other things too about Roderick and Madeline. 'Could they be having an incestuous-type of relationship and not be sleeping in *twin* beds?' I wondered. 'I've read that even Socrates was more than platonic with his protégé, Plato!' I recollected.

But then, a more serious conjecture dominated my contemplation after reading for the third time Roderick's invitation (or I should say solicitation) to visit the annoying, paranoid, reckless recluse, and his stranger-than-fiction twin sister.

'I've read in medical journals where twins are believed to have some magical telepathic power of consciously communicating with each other through a weird type of mental signaling, even over great distances,' I recalled. 'The two assholes could've had a stage or circus act with them performing as mentalists,' I mused, 'because if I remember correctly, the two dumb-fucks were classic mental cases to begin with! I'll journey up north and visit Roderick and Madeline just out of curiosity. I'm unemployed, have little money or savings, and who the hell knows?' I guessed. 'Maybe Roderick has become rich and can lend me a couple of thousand bucks so that I can open a bordello for horny gays and kinky lesbians just like I've always desired doing, but never had the initiative or the required capital to get the sex-boat cruise project to float!'

It was a long and difficult, week-long ride on horseback from my remote humble shack outside Richmond, Virginia all the way to Roderick's abode up in Massachusetts, twenty-five miles northwest of Boston. I slept in the woods, begged from farmers and strangers along the route for oats to feed me and my old horse Nads, who I would encourage and had the balls to coax my infirmed equine to go faster than a foxtrot by relentlessly imploring, "Go Nads, Go Nads, Go Nads!" And yes, my tender ass really hurt, and was badly chafed when Nads and I finally and gratefully crossed the Connecticut state line and entered the land of Samuel Adams, John Hancock and Paul Revere; good old Massachusetts.

'I suppose I'm riding way up here in response to Roderick's letter, mostly out of sheer curiosity, if nothing else,' I remember thinking as I politely solicited donations for Nads (and mine) next meal outside a country inn near Plymouth, for Nads had made a wrong turn after leaving Connecticut and wound-up in the vicinity of Cape Cod instead of heading north towards Boston. 'Maybe that wallflower Lady Madeline has developed into a decent-looking hussy, and I can get laid and blown while Roderick's out chopping wood or jerking-off in the outhouse,' I nefariously thought as some generous, churchgoing asshole dropped two pence into my stove-pipe hat that had a big hole in the bottom, and the head-gear was also rather torn and quite shabby in appearance. 'And according to my daily diary records, I haven't gotten laid or blown since college graduation, so when the next opportunity *rises*, I hope I remember what the hell to do with my dick besides taking hour-long pisses.'

As Nads slowly trotted along a lonely dirt trail through a dismal tract of forestland, and with shades of evening drawing near, in the far distance as *we* rounded a bend the House of Usher (as Roderick called his residence in his melancholy-sounding letter) came into view. My comical instinct stupidly thought at that moment, 'I'm glad it's not a country theater with only two ushers in it!' and then I further evaluated, 'Well Poe,' I thought; equating myself with the famous author; 'it's fuckin' time for you to usher in a new day in your life!' I further assessed. 'And 'I'm extremely fatigued, and my fuckin' ass really hurts from riding all the way up here just to see this bullshit decaying brick and mortar mansion, when as a standard shopping habit, I ordinarily boycott brick and mortar stores and buildings back in Virginia!'

The walls of the three-story House of Usher dump were rather bleak-looking, covered with soot and ivy, and looking like they hadn't been properly maintained in over fifty years. 'I've seen plantation slave shanties in better condition than this dilapidated eyesore,' I fancied, as Nads plodded ahead and approached the residence, which truthfully looked like it should have been condemned by some blind building inspector decades before.

'Even the goddamned oak and maple trees around this ramshackle estate are in a sad state of decay,' I observed and concluded. 'There's algae and fungus everywhere on this wreck's exterior, and I think I'm going to contract some sort of venereal disease just looking at the fucked-up place from over three-hundred feet away. If Lady Madeline's tits and cunt look anything like the house she lives in,' I seriously imagined, 'I'd be much better off sodomizing Roderick right up the old yazoo!'

A scruffy-looking, midget-sized servant, who looked as if he hadn't taken a bath since infancy, guided Nads to the barn, which would have been better off if it had collapsed into rubble a week before my arrival. The dwarfish jerk-off then returned to my company and escorted me into the dank and dreary House of Usher without ever uttering a damned word, which led me to believe that the miniature weirdo was indeed a potentially dangerous deaf mute with certain evil psychological issues.

The inside of the sinister and ominous-looking house was analogous to that of a funeral parlor, with every shadowy room lifeless, macabre, and morbid-like in atmosphere. And my first inclination was that I had to relieve my bowels because the place in general was literally scaring the shit out of me.

A doctor carrying his signature black bag (without his autograph engraved on it) descended the rickety wooden steps with a grim expression upon his aged face, and the medical asshole walked right by me without even acknowledging my presence; in fact, the in-a-rush sawbones almost knocked me over in his hasty departure down the unkempt, dark corridor, and then the restive visitor swiftly exited out of the building.

'I don't blame him!' I thought. 'I'd like to run out of this fucked-up house too! Oh crap! My diarrhea's acting up! I hope Roderick isn't taking a lengthy shit in the outhouse, or 'the Necessary', as my college chum used to call such an outbuilding back in 1820! There're two main things I have to remember when entering into a new unfamiliar environment. Where's the crapola, and where's the kitchen located, in that particular order.'

I cautiously stepped into what I believed to be the home's living room and sat down on a couch, when at least five pounds of accumulated dust billowed-up into the air, nearly choking me to death; for I have very bad allergies, and am prone to having long extended sneezing and sinus attacks.

The dreary room's wooden floor was planked and warped; the long, thin rectangular windows looked like filthy mirrors, and I also noticed feeble glimmers of crimson light somehow managing to filter through the transparent panes, and then refracting inside. The house's furniture all looked antique, giving me the distinct impression of an abandoned museum with cobwebs hanging from the ceiling; from the rotting cornice; from the fireplace mantel, and from the ugly, moldy walls. The descriptive adjective "gloomy" would have been entirely too complimentary to accurately describe the very hideous-looking and reprehensible-in-appearance House of Usher.

Then, in the dark, I became startled when I saw the outline of a man who was just lying there on a side couch, and upon recognizing my presence, Roderick sat-up like an Egyptian mummy rising from its coffin, and then rose-off of the side sofa and craziky stared at me. The ogre I witnessed was still six-foot eight inches tall, and apparently the cretin still weighed about ninety-three pounds, just as I had remembered him back inside his secluded dormitory room at the University of Virginia.

Roderick, who at best was always laconic and introverted, stared at me for a full mysterious minute, without even gesturing to shake my hand, or give me a lethargic high-five. Then, the gaunt-looking gentleman (I use the term loosely) commenced speaking.

"Is that you Edgar?" Roderick asked in an almost trance-like state. "I see that you've ridden all the way up here from Virginia. Your buttocks and rectum must be really sore from your ordeal."

Roderick's high and mighty demeanor, along with his eloquent, formal tone of voice, really pissed me off. "You still can't say common ordinary words like ass, asshole, jerk-off, shit, bitch, cock-sucker, mother-fucker, balls, cunt, bastard, and fuck, can you Roderick?" I angrily quipped. "Once an asshole, always an asshole! That's what I've always said over and over again since grammar school about your demeanor. How the hell have you been Roderick? From the looks of your lousy dump, er, I meant to say 'your exotic mansion', not too well! This house isn't even good enough to be in Philly's worst ghetto!"

"My twin sister Madeline is very ill and listless," Roderick said. "She's sicker than sick!"

"Why the hell does she need to keep a goddamned list in the first place?" I foolishly jested, as was my wont. "If she never kept a list, she would never be listless!"

"You don't understand *our* terrible plight, my dear Edgar," Roderick enigmatically answered. "Madeline is suffering from an incurable disease that the doctors cannot accurately diagnose. She's losing weight every day, and is now quite emaciated as if my twin sister is egregiously dying from starvation, although frankly, she eats incessantly all day long; in fact, eight pounds of food each and every day. If you were to see Madeline right this minute, Edgar, she'd have to be directly facing you. If my twin sister were to turn sideways," Roderick explained, emphasized and exaggerated, "then she's so thin and skinny that you'd have trouble seeing her."

'Well, it looks like I'm not going to get laid in this house,' I preposterously thought. 'The truth is I don't even feel like jerking-off anywhere inside this hellish disaster.' Then, I figured I had better mention something else, especially if Roderick really could practice mental telepathy, and really could read the dastardly and disparaging thought transmissions of my dirty, greedy mind.

"Perhaps if you were to take Madeline out of the house and visit Cape Cod, Coney Island, Atlantic City, Bunker Hill, Lexington and Concord, well just about any damned place in the Universe except here," I suggested. "And maybe, just maybe, such excursions would prove beneficial for both you and your twin sister's health."

"I don't think that either Madeline or myself is physically capable of making any long trip away from this marvelous House of Usher," Roderick eerily replied. "As you know from your college education, Edgar, the interesting word 'travel' is fundamentally derived from the nomenclature 'travail', which means 'hard and arduous labor'. Now tell me, Edgar. Who in Hades or on Olympus needs that kind of 'travel' bull feces?"

"Can't you ever say the simple word 'bullshit' without feeling embarrassed?" I admonished, raising my voice. "Listen to me, Roderick. Ever since I've known you that first day at college, you always said 'fellatio' instead of 'cock-sucking'; you always said 'cunnilingus' instead of 'cunt-licking'; you always said 'urinating' instead of 'pissing'; you always said 'intercourse' instead of 'fuck'; you always said 'testicles' instead of 'balls'; you always said 'Hades' instead of 'hell'; and instead of uttering 'farting', you always said 'passing intestinal gas'; and besides *that*, you always said 'vulva' and 'vagina' instead of 'cunt'; you always said 'toro feces' instead of 'bullshit'; you always said 'penis' instead of 'dick' or 'cock'; you always said 'male dog' instead of 'bastard; you always said 'sexual relief' or 'masturbating' instead of 'jerking-off'; you always said 'mother-copulater' instead of 'mother fucker'; and right up to today Roderick, you'd rather say 'female canine' than the word 'bitch'', and you'd rather say 'rectum' or 'buttocks' instead of 'asshole'," I loudly chided and vehemently criticized. "And now you have the unmitigated audacity to tell me that you're sick! Well Roddy, baby, I'm pretty goddamned sick and tired of this fuckin' sanctimonious, holier-than-thou bullshit you've been laying on me ever since we were freshmen in college. What the hell's the matter with you anyway, you dumb-ass prude! I'd rather curse than be accursed like you are, living in this garbage heap of rubble, any goddamned day of the week!"

Roderick ignored my perpetual protestations, and soon the nincompoop continued to methodically deliver his polite, defensive boring, and monotonous justification, confirming his typical lackadaisical prudishness. Out of the corner of my eye, I caught a glimpse of Lady Madeline flitting-by inside the adjacent corridor, looking like a moving, vertical cadaver; the pallid-faced, frail woman seeming like a panic-stricken whitish ghoul; her clandestine passage giving me the creeps, and making my foul-smelling colitis act-up. I then began farting incessantly as Roderick Usher completely ignored (or was oblivious to) the noises emanating from my hyperactive asshole, as the stupid shit redundantly continued spieling his lackluster monologue.

* * * * * * * * * * *

Over the span of the next week, I actually began relishing my stay at the very eerie House of Usher, because its ramshackle appearance made me feel good about my humble shack back in Virginia, and its pathetic residents also made me feel encouraged about my own mediocre existence. When someone witnesses the problems and the struggles of others that are far worse than he or she has to deal with, then conversely, that person's perception almost always makes the evaluator feel much better about his or her own life.

Roderick and I seldom spoke during that entire seven-day period, but I felt that we understood each other perfectly, with *that* rather peculiar observation lending credence to my secret "Usher telepathy theory". My friend Usher and I sat quietly at nights in either his mildewed-smelling library, or in his cobweb-infested living room, reading books, painting landscapes on canvas, crocheting socks, knitting bed quilts, and practicing elementary basket weaving.

At midnight each evening, my illustrious friend would quietly leave my mediocre company to check the condition of Lady Madeline, whom I had only seen once (during my entire stay) as a spectral-type figure zooming like a zephyr by the dusky living room. Everything seemed tranquil and copasetic until five minutes past midnight on Halloween Eve.

"Edgar, you must come with me immediately," Roderick imperatively ordered. "I believe we're having a dire emergency."

"Are we going to celebrate All Saints and All Souls Day?" I all-too-ignorantly asked. "I could use a nice glass of cold champagne right now to soothe my nerves!"

"No Edgar, you narrow minded Dolt! Madeline has passed-away, and the angels are escorting her to Heaven as I speak," Roderick ironically related, much to my consternation. "I need you to help me carry her body from her bed down to the cellar vault room. There, under candlelight, we'll place my beloved sister's mortal remains on a granite slab where I shall, in the privacy of my grief, apply lipstick and make-up to her face and hands to simulate her appearance as it might look at a public viewing; and then in two days Edgar, we'll slide her corpse into her crypt and seal it up!"

Normally, having a facetious and frivolous nature in terms of personality, I remained reticent while standing in the center of the House of Usher living room, merely nodding my head in tacit agreement, for I didn't wish to say anything alarming or blatantly hypocritical during Roderick's time of mourning. Even my own heart, which usually rejoiced in revelry, and ordinarily scorned any facet of suffering, disease, and illness, felt a genuine compassion for the terrible burden my friend Roderick was enduring.

My companion could have been a funeral director as verified by the meticulous way he was *undertaking* Lady Madeline's corpse in its preparation for burial. Lipstick, mascara, rouge, and nail polish, together made the dead woman seem almost like a contemporary Sleeping Beauty, but I was so petrified from the overall ordeal that I shuddered upon thinking that Roderick might appoint and assign me as Prince Charming to awaken Lady Madeline with a kiss.

"I'm afflicted with the same degenerative malady that has led to my twin sister's demise," Roderick verbally explained to me rather cold and matter-of-factly. "I shall die soon Edgar, and hopefully, you'll be here to attend to my corpse and bury me, too!"

"I'm generally not a superstitious person, but your fucked-up House of Usher, along with the scary passing of Lady Madeline, gives me the absolute creeps," I divulged to my almost-incoherent, genetically inferior host. "Let's leave this cellar vault room, stroll into the parlor, open a bottle of red wine, and drink to settle our frazzled nerves," I suggested. "That's why liquors and wines are called and labeled spirits. They'll change *our* deficient 'spirits', Roderick, from experiencing absolute melancholy and despair into positive tolerance and hope."

"And what shall we talk about while we're sipping our wine?" my disconsolate friend asked. "Truly Edgar, I can count on your comfort and support during my hour of need without us imbibing any alcoholic beverages."

"Well, if we get juiced-up enough," I remarked rather insensitively, "we could discuss all about our bygone college years and conscientiously review the fascinating topics of urinating, fecal depositing, intercourse, vaginas, vulvas and ovaries, testicles and penises, fellatio, cunnilingus, Hades, male canines, female canines, masturbating, buttocks and rectums, and also passing large quantities of intestinal gas; you know Roderick, all of the idiotic toro feces that immature college kids normally talk about."

My friend and I were soon downing our second bottle of foul-tasting port wine, and I had the feeling that Roderick was finally shedding his heavy depression and coming-out of his deep stupor. Suddenly, there was a disturbing clanging sound, as if a great chain was being rattled, and *that* startling interruption was followed by a frightening loud gong. Before I could swallow another ounce of putrid port, Lady Madeline shockingly appeared, standing erect in the doorway, her pallid face and her total image being gruesomely cadaverous. Roderick rose from his seat to grab onto his faltering twin, but the pale woman collapsed into his arms and instantaneously died a second time.

Momentarily, I was completely petrified and incredibly freaked-out, but then gaining some semblance of rational cognition, I was so disoriented that I failed to say even a perfunctory 'goodbye' to my old college friend, as my chum knelt-down on the cold wooden floor and affectionately caressed the body and cheeks of his again-deceased sister.

I scampered like an obsessed demon down the dark, drafty corridor, not even bothering to enter my assigned bedroom and retrieve my overcoat. Rushing out the front door in a full panic, I accidentally collided with Roderick's deaf-mute servant, knocking the surprised dumb-dick on his ass in the haste of my exit. I scurried as fast as my legs could carry me to the ramshackle stone barn, saddled-up Nads, rose-up from the stirrup, hastily clambered upon my shabby steed's mangy back, grabbed the shoddy reins, and then my faithful horse trotted-out of the shadowy enclosure and into the lane leading to the accursed House of Usher.

'I gotta' get the fuck away from this House of Usher, this diabolical House of Horrors as quick as a meteor,' I thought. 'Who the hell needs a goddamned, fucked-up, horrendous nightmare like this one while they're fuckin' sober and awake? I feel sorry for Roderick, but I must first look out for #1 while I can still do #2, whether I'm sitting on my horse's back, or whether I'm shitting a flurry of wet farts inside the nearest Necessary!'

My mind was so disheveled at that moment that I was virtually oblivious to the overhead thunder and lightning and the hard pelting raindrops that externally constituted my physical environment. Suddenly, my ears heard a great crumbling that sounded something akin to a violent explosion, or volcanic eruption.

At first, I thought that a catastrophic earthquake was in progress, but then my logical, college-educated mind reasoned that such a geological phenomenon would certainly be an anomaly in an eastern state like Massachusetts. Being both awed and curious in *that* particular order, I abruptly tugged the reins and stopped Nads on the summit of a hill. Next, I turned around to inspect the source of the tremendous ground-shaking reverberation that my auditory senses had heard.

Beneath a blood-red full moon, and amidst the relentless torrential rain, my disbelieving eyes witnessed a calamity like I hope to never again see. My disarrayed cerebrum was reeling from the great tragedy that my pupils were beholding. 'This is worse than Joshua blowing his horn outside the walls of Jericho!' I marveled.

My eyes perceived a cloud of luminous dust glowing in the distance, signifying to me that Roderick had finally joined his cherished twin, Lady Madeline, in the *hereafter.* 'What the hell am I here-after!' I considered. The House of Usher and its twin occupants were no longer in existence on the face of this all-too-fragile Earth. God rest your immortal soul, good friend Roderick.

"The Pit and the Pendulum"

Undoubtedly, my total being was in both emotional anguish and in physical agony. The dual pains were extremely excruciating, and every fiber that constituted *me* was aching from my head down to my testicles, right on down to my toes. When the anonymous guards finally untied me, I realized two things: I didn't know who the hell I was (apparently suffering from some memory disorder or amnesia), and besides that, I didn't know who the hell the black-robed judges were that had been heartlessly pronouncing my sentencing. Yes, those despicable bastards were in the process of unanimously rendering a verdict of "Death", yet at that bizarre moment in time, I was suffering from a distinct loss of identity, and my conscience was unaware of what egregious crime I had committed, or even in what goddamned country I was being convicted.

I recollect deducting that I was at that inglorious moment thinking in English, but conversely and illogically, the chief judge was communicating my doomed fate in Spanish. Thus, I reasoned and theorized that I was an Englishman being condemned to die for no apparent rationale or explanation somewhere in Spain.

Yes, those hideous macabre lips that the three black-robed judges flaunted were thin, grotesque, and white, as if the cheerless objects belonged on the mouths of goddamned, ghostly albinos. 'Those three inflexible and repugnant sons-of-bitches deserve to be butchered and mutilated,' yes, that's what my disoriented brain had reckoned as I stood there before the trio of reprehensible but all-powerful assholes! Indeed, those fucked-up, nightmarish lips were whiter than the paper on which I'm presently writing this incredible chronicle.

My recollection does not betray past reality. My eyes keenly perceived seven gloomy candles flickering on the judges' mahogany table, and I remember black drapes hanging above where the three ruthless dumb-fucks solemnly and reticently sat in a windowless 'Inquisition Chamber'. At the time, I imagined the seven tall candles as being white slender angels, especially assembled to escort me either to Heaven or to Hell, once my final breath had been inhaled, or perhaps exhaled. But in retrospect contemplation, how could my fucked-up mind be so vivid and observant when I had been experiencing so much agony and so much anguish?

Then, my creative brain thought of how serene, tranquil, and sweet a cemetery grave (or even a catacomb) would be compared to the horrendous suffering 'this nameless, helpless victim is suffering'.

Then I thought, 'Death will be my cherished reward; my salvation; my escape from this perpetual torture I've endured.'

And then the arrogant judges, like a triumvirate of omnipotent-evil-magicians, suddenly disappeared, a subtle clue that had momentarily deceived my senses; for as I author these words, the vanishing of the three ruthless pricks was really a blunt signal that I had gone unconscious from lack of strength, and from a basic deficiency in nutrition. I believed that the asshole judges would force me to drink something akin to cats' piss to continue living.

My spirit was falling into oblivion, but perhaps either into Hades or into the infernos of Hell itself. Yes, at *that* queer, surreal moment, the seven candle flames upon the mahogany table had inexplicably become extinguished as my cognizance of my surroundings simultaneously went totally blank. Then, quite mysteriously and ominously, my only fleeting sensation was a lone stark recognition that a bleak darkness had enveloped me.

I didn't recall any objects or furniture swirling around or floating in air. I believe that my immortal soul, or perhaps my subconscious post-mortal psyche, was passing through a supernatural void, or maybe an empty vacant medium of space and time; or perhaps my spirit was swiftly traveling through an obscure alien dimension.

Somehow, my present memory suggests that I had been descending, not by my own volition, or by employing the use of my legs down stone or wooden steps; but instead, being carried by invisible men to some black and dreary place of punishment. Was I imprisoned in some sort of fucked-up time portal? My fuzzy mind recalls that most everything I perceived as being a weird, fucked-up, nebulous combination of flatness, dampness, and most of all, total madness. But then again, my principal comprehension was that I was being conveyed to a designated area of atonement; and ultimately, my mortal demise.

Yes; my eyes were open, and I must admit that it required plenty of courage to do *that,* for I was still contemplating whether I was dead or alive. I finally realized that I was breathing, and that I had a pulse, and I could feel my heart beating in my chest; so, Descartes' classic maxim, "I think; therefore, I am" axiom had physical verification. According to the philosopher's sage logic, I was still a living human being. But indeed, I was frightened beyond reason or understanding, for having no memory as to my name, and being in a cold, dank, damp, dark environment with foul-smelling air, gave me an instant urge to vomit.

I was soon aware of lying on my back upon a hard surface that I presumed was solid stone or granite. My bravery increased as I stretched-out, and my damned lacerated fingers and left hand touched a slimy hard wall, which I ascertained was either metal or stone. I was still quite apprehensive about engaging in further exploration and discovery, because there was still absolutely *nothing* (no thing) to see or to identify through sight. The intolerable dark air seemed to be strangling me, as my lungs labored to perform their simple biological function. Sweat was profusely rolling-down my forehead and neck, and was virtually cascading down my condemned back.

Two essential questions dominated my befuddled thinking: 'Will I have to suffer more torture before being executed?' and 'How much sacrifice and pain can I possibly endure before either dying or attempting suicide?'

I decided that I should rise to my feet to determine exactly how large the dark dungeon (in which I believed I was being detained) happened to be. I suspected that I was not in a prison cell, for indeed, no ordinary prison could ever have such deplorable conditions as my present area of confinement.

But still, I dreaded advancing even a goddamned mini-step forward, for rationally, fear of the unknown could oftentimes paralyze a man's motivation to experiment doing anything. 'Am I in a tomb, my own personalized tomb?' I frightfully speculated. The mounting suspense was unbearable.

My eyeballs were straining (from their sockets) to observe even one scintilla of light; a wonderful phenomenon that would give my soul just one iota of hope. Finally, with my right hand sliding against the wet, mildewed wall, I gingerly took several counterclockwise steps along the macabre chamber's perimeter, which I fathomed to be circular in form by virtue of the roundness of the wall. And after twenty or so very slow and deliberate steps, no corner or meeting of walls had occurred. 'Have I been left abandoned in this dreadful, fucked-up incarceration to desperately meander around in circles only to eventually starve to death?' I wondered. But gradually, my mind's curiosity became the equivalent of my heart's tremendous fear. 'What fate could be worse than death? What futility should ever overshadow my desire to live?' I intrepidly conjectured, just like any other thinking asshole would naturally speculate under similar, mysterious circumstances.

Then, I instinctively felt my body to see what type of garments I had been wearing, and from my cursory, tactile inspection, I soon learned that I had no shirt, pants or uniform on my torso; but instead, had been clad in a thin robe of very cheap and tawdry cotton material. An inspiration filtered into my disheveled mind, and I quickly honored the suggestion by ripping a flimsy seam at the thin robe's hem, and then tearing a sizeable length of fabric that I immediately placed on the slimy, slippery floor directly against the wall. 'This way,' my sense of self-preservation dictated to my challenged will, 'I'll know when I've made a full revolution of the dungeon, and I'll then be able to estimate its circumference, area and diameter from my basic knowledge of simple Euclidian geometry.' But then my overall, hellish fatigue was all-powerful; and so, I collapsed upon the feces-laden floor and fell fast asleep.

When I abruptly awoke from my nightmarish slumber, my outstretched hand felt a loaf of stale bread and a pitcher of warm water. 'Is the goddamned water fresh? Is it stagnant? Are both the putrid-smelling water and the odorless bread fuckin' poisoned?'

I wasted no further valuable time assessing and debating the issue in the dark. I ate voraciously and drank indulgently, thinking all the friggin' while, 'Who' in either their right or wrong mind gives a flying shit about food poisoning? I'm fuckin' famished, and if I die from attempting to alleviate my hunger, then what the fuck do I care!'

Shortly after consuming my strange feast in complete darkness, I arose and began my exploratory circuit of the foreboding black chamber. A hundred-and-ninety-three paces around the unfamiliar room's circumference brought me back to the discarded piece of hem situated on the cold dank floor. 'Let's see now,' I logically guessed. 'There're two steps in a yard, so my foggy mind estimates that the circumference must be roughly around ninety-yards in length, or approximately three-hundred-feet. But am I standing in a room, in a dungeon, in a prison cell, or in my own personal sepulcher? I'm definitely not in a bordello!'

And so, wanting to investigate my arcane, dark environment some more, I bravely decided to move my feet and proceed in a straight line; my essential purpose being to traverse the chamber's diameter to establish if any useable objects could be found that I could cleverly improvise into tools; and in the meantime, my weak heart so deeply desired and hoped that such imaginary implements miraculously occupied the place's stench-laden interior.

My nostrils were keenly aware of a distinct, clammy, moldy vapor; My nose detected the peculiar smell of rotting fungus, when unexpectedly, my feet slid on the slippery floor, and my already abused body, honoring gravity, fell and made contact with solid stone. Despite the pain resulting from the hard impact, my face felt a chilling draft that wafted across my forehead and then my chin, and I was suddenly aware that I had nearly plummeted-down into the throat of a circular pit, probably intentionally designed to have a prisoner like myself drop into its horrid, total darkness.

Through the great exercise of diligent effort and excessive concentration, I managed to eventually dislodge a small fragment of stone from a narrow mortar groove that had been located inside the pit's rim; and then with a hysterical scream, I flipped the pebble into the well, only to hear a low splash occur several seconds later. 'Are dangerous and ferocious animals down there, perhaps a venomous snake or two, or maybe a very undernourished, carnivorous crocodile?' my rampant imagination vividly considered.

And at that alien moment, I heard a trap door in the ceiling opening, and then closing very quickly. 'I'm being fuckin' watched and scrutinized!' I pessimistically thought with my knees trembling and my sinuses leaking secretion. 'Yes, my pupils caught a faint glimmer of light,' I anxiously interpreted and considered. 'The brief ray soon faded, and everything was once again awesome, gloomy, black and intimidating! That timely and ironic accident of me falling near the pit has temporarily averted my shrewdly schemed death by design! But quite frankly, I'd rather die than suffer any more of that extreme mental duress! Danger must be ubiquitous in this horrifying black, fucked-up place!'

Shaking and quivering, I carefully sobbed and crawled my way back to the safety of the stench-infested round wall. 'How many other terrible wells are cunningly hidden in this fucked-up chamber's interior?' I contemplated while shuddering. 'Perhaps I should go back and plunge myself into that disgusting abyss, and swiftly end it all! But since when have I become a spineless coward? And who the hell am I, anyway?'

I fell asleep out of sheer exhaustion, suspiciously believing that the pitcher of water and the loaf of rancid-tasting bread must have been drugged with some ingredient that engendered hallucinating. But upon awakening, I soon perceived that my chest, hips and legs had been strapped-down upon a horizontal table. I comprehended that my left hand was able to come into contact with another pitcher of water, and a second loaf of crusty, stale, rancid bread. Again, I ate and drank ravenously, not caring one precious second whether I crapped myself excessively upon the table, or whether I fuckin' pissed myself through my gown. And according to my exaggerated comprehension of things, I soon felt my own urine arching directly into my expressionless, who-gives-a-shit face.

I dozed-off for an interminable period of time, and when my eyes again opened, I immediately noticed that 'the dungeon' was no longer black, but had been illuminated by a wild yellowish glow; its source or origin not at first traceable. Now, I was finally able to decipher the appearance and the size of the loathsome chamber, and I evaluated that it had been constructed of stone masonry walls. and 'the torture dungeon' definitely had a granite floor. The strange, sinister, amber light revealed to my grateful eyes that the circular chamber was around ninety-feet in diameter, and second and third observations confirmed and proved my keen analysis to be accurate.

Certain mentally demented drawings of hellish-looking demons, gargoyles, monsters, skulls, and skeletons adorned both the ceiling and walls, immediately suggesting that perverted lunatic monastery monks with a fascination for and an obsession with death had satanically drawn the weird and repulsive artwork.

I did gain some low comfort in visually realizing that there was only one pit in the entire area of confinement. And yes, the second pitcher and loaf of bread had been strategically placed upon the top panel of a wooden framed table to my left. 'But why?' I questioned my general ignorance. Although my hands and arms were still free, I was unable to maneuver or manipulate my aching body a trifle from the three tight ropes that tethered me horizontally upon the table.

Looking upward, my eyes and mind studied the chamber's ceiling, which in its center had a faded painting of "Father Time" looking exactly like the formidable and invincible Grim Reaper, carrying a gruesome scythe to obviously harvest his next unfortunate soul, which I perceptively gathered and intelligently understood must be *me*. But from out of the traditional curved scythe blade came the gradual sweep of an awesome pendulum; not a standard clock pendulum, mind you, but a pendulum in the shape of a warrior's battle-axe, possessing an excessively sharp blade.

And as my astonished eyes viewed the object's hundred-and-eighty-degree movement, back and forth and perpendicular to my body's prone position, I then fully fathomed that the goddamned thing was descending by degree an inch or so at a time with each successive oscillation. The visual horror made my heart palpitate, and I feared I was going into cardiac arrest before ever achieving another pleasurable erection.

* * * * * * * * * * *

A slight rustling noise distracted my strict attention from the almost-mesmerizing, slowly descending medieval pendulum. 'Oh rats!' I boisterously and coincidentally shrieked. My circumstance would have been humorous if it wasn't (in grim reality) such a drastic terrifying emergency. 'I'm not even circumcised, but now I might just be!' I feared and then moaned.

Several enormous, squealing, furry rodents had skillfully emerged from the now very conspicuous well situated in the center of the morbid-looking, dim chamber, apparently attracted by the amber light from above that had seemingly, supernaturally permeated my dreadful environment. The disease-carrying vermin seemed to methodically advance in troops, but without exhibiting any particular marching cadence. I knew right away that I should not procrastinate, but instead, should endeavor to scare the terrible, squeaking pests away, so I redundantly shouted 'Fuck the World!' a dozen times.

My initial exhortations were successful, and the result of my hollering afforded me a minute of welcomed relief. The sickening rodents had retreated and scattered, but soon they garnered the desire to eat the remainder of breadcrumbs that remained on the little side table. However, then I noticed several of the voracious rodents had overlooked globs of raw meat that evidently had been provided to me by my unscrupulous captors, probably as a farewell meal for me to devour. 'I must grab the meat before the goddamned rats do!' I surely reasoned. 'Those obscene and nauseating, disease-laden mother-fuckers will first aggressively eat the raw meat as an appetizer, and then start nibbling as a frenzied pack, like there's no fuckin' tomorrow, upon me. God save my penis!'

And yes, my attention again focused on the descending axe-pendulum, which instantaneously reminded me that I had dual problems to contend with, since the deadly weapon had lowered a full yard since I had originally recognized its imminent danger. Its foot-long, razor-sharp blade, from tip to tip, was gleaming in the artificial yellow light's glow.

'That sucker is both huge and heavy, and will easily plow right through my vulnerable chest like a sharp knife cutting through soft butter! And it's wickedly attached to a brass rod that hisses like a snake with each passing vacillation. Oh well, at least I won't be fuckin' decapitated or dismembered!'

And then, other disturbing thoughts haunted my psyche. 'Those craven, sons-of-bitchin' black-robed judges! I would love to violently bludgeon each of their asses with a heavy sword, if only I had the fuckin' opportunity! Yes, they're too fuckin' gutless to pick-up three sabers and kill me themselves. Or, if they had any decent-sized balls,' I angrily concluded, 'the Spanish deciders would egregiously and hatefully hurl my ass directly into the rat-infested pit! The weak-spined, feckless assholes want to see me accidentally kill myself!'

And then, my beleaguered mind had still another consideration. 'Yes; plausible reasoning must acknowledge that the pernicious pendulum constitutes a much milder death than a screaming plunge down into the dark abyss, where I would probably be fuckin' eaten alive by carnivorous rats or reptiles before I'll ever have a chance to drown! Yet inch by inch, that lethal pendulum continues its evil descent downwards, heading towards my helpless limp body.'

Throughout my colossal despair, all along I sensed that I had not been in the past (nor was I in the present) a devoutly religious man; but nevertheless, I began praying incessantly for either my fortuitous rescue, or in the worst-case scenario, for redemption and eternal salvation. If my moral conversion to a particular creed had been the principal objective of the vindictive robed judges, then the asshole jerk-offs could, with jubilation, regard their cruel Inquisition, and subsequent sentencing, as being a veritable success.

But soon, my idiotic fantasy/reverie vanished like an illusion from my fatigued and overburdened mind, and I once again dedicated my profound survival thoughts to denying the on-the-prowl rats of their precious raw meat; raw meat that ultimately would lead the abhorrent scavengers to feast on my exposed, cut skin.

And yes, the terror I was experiencing was indeed quite real, and in its twin lowest-common-denominators, very callous and brutal. To use the nomenclature "sadistic" to describe my diabolical tragedy would be entirely too polite; too courteous; too bland; too benign! But for several hours, the pendulum redundantly progressed back and forth above my chest, and simultaneously, those revolting squealing rats scurried about the base of the decayed, termite-infested, framed table, avariciously sniffing at the spoiled raw meat that rested upon the ledge above.

But my craving for sustenance suddenly afforded my mind a stellar inspiration. At first, I believed that the spectacular thought which had entered my cerebrum was merely a trite triviality, but then I set my mind to executing the crazy idea as a last resort before I myself would be savagely executed by the devastating, slowly descending blade's thrust and slice.

'The relentless sweeping of the pendulum's axe is now traveling only three inches above my chest,' I assessed. 'I must act with dispatch, or else I'll most certainly perish!' I very practically surmised. 'But who gives a shit or a flying fuck about my picayune, earthly plight? I'm just one doomed, pathetic, insignificant soul about to be systematically eliminated from existence on a tiny insignificant planet in the vast, mind-boggling-galaxy, in the infinite-sized, unending, eternal Universe!'

I furiously extended my left arm, and finally, my hand's stiff bleeding fingers were able to desperately grab the three balls of raw meat, which I then managed to smear against the main rope that fastened me to the execution platform. The distance between the dirty food plate to my mouth was the length of my grasp. 'There's only one fuckin' chance to evade this maniacal death ordeal, but it is not me trying to grab the pendulum and stopping it, unless I want my hands horribly severed from my wrists. It would be a lot easier to halt a massive avalanche rumbling-down an icy mountainside than to accomplish *that* foolish feat!'

I contracted my chest in with each time I inhaled, so that my breathing corresponded with the appalling pendulum's predictable sweeping intersection with my pounding heart. 'There's no more time for delay! I must act in a hurry, or most certainly, I shall be severed in two by this sharp weapon of those cowardly, black-robed, white-lipped, fanatical, religious hypocrites!'

But hope's voice whispered from another dimension into my yearning ear, so without hesitation, I boldly initiated my intrepid plan. Indeed, with the next several passes, the axe would be indiscriminately scraping away my thin black gown's fabric. But astonishingly, my resilient spirit was no-longer petrified beyond rationality! My arthritic hands began working feverishly with an obsessed nervous energy generated solely by my own despair and horror. I instinctively knew that I had to emerge as master of my environment. The numerous squealing rats were wild, brazen, and ravenous, yet I calmly resolved to make them my assistants and allies. Here is what ingenious machination I had set into motion.

I frantically smeared the rotting raw meat onto the rope that kept my chest and upper torso stationary upon the table, and then as if on cue, the hungry rats climbed up the frame's legs and began to bite away at the food that their sniffing noses smelled. Their greediness to eat was the phenomenal miracle for which I had been praying.

By the dozens, the on-a-mission army of disgusting vermin swarmed upon my horizontal torso, and soon their cold, animalistic lips met mine. With their long probing whiskers, the nauseous creatures meticulously squirmed and maneuvered around upon my throat, face and neck. Nevertheless, I lay still in a virtual panic-attack state of mind. My face was being smothered with stench-laden fur, and I honestly felt like regurgitating; but fortunately, I lacked sufficient food in my stomach to accomplish performing *that* rather revolting urge.

Out of the rodents' queer biological necessity, soon the teeth of the sickening, stinking vermin nibbled and bit away, until finally, the uppermost greasy strap encumbering my torso snapped from their jaws' activity. And I amazingly had the wherewithal to turn my body, and with the shifting of my weight, the sturdy table overturned and in an instant. Both it and I flipped over onto the cold granite floor; just as the sharp blade passed above exactly where my exposed chest would have been pierced. 'Oh, how precious air is; basic oxygen that I would ordinarily take for granted!' I momentarily rejoiced.

From my fallen position on the stone floor, I heard a sound and my pupils reflexively glanced-up. My eyes observed the near-fatal pendulum being hoisted back up to the ceiling by what seemed (to my erratic judgment) a mystical invisible force. My hands somehow garnered the strength to free the remainder of the ropes that had harnessed my body to the reprehensible execution bench. But no sooner had *that* arduous task been successfully consummated that the fickle rats began fleeing back to the safety of their resident well. I gradually got to my knees, and then rose to my feet. Standing there like an automaton, I was then cognizant of a harshly terrifying sensation that immediately diminished my will to live.

The aforementioned yellow light had been originating from a one-inch crack occupying the space between the stone-cold walls and the granite-cold floor; the physical dimensions that comprised the two major components of the torture chamber. 'The walls are separated from the goddamned floor!' I realized and marveled. 'Oh no! Oh my God! Holy fuck! What the hell is this?'

The final horrifying mystery of the demonic death chamber became quite abundantly clear and threatening. Then, the vague amber light gradually became more intense and brilliant. My senses were dazzled and enraptured, until the distinct smell of sulfur numbed my mind. 'The air's being contaminated! My already fucked-up lungs are now being poisoned with hot gas that will soon surely choke me to death. Enough of this abominable torture that you' anonymous assholes have so craftily designed! I want to fuckin' die! Do you hear me, Lucifer; you demented shit-head! How much more pain can I possibly take? Do you hear me Satan? I said that I want to fuckin' die!'

And then another unbelievable, ghastly danger plagued and terrorized my all-too-pathetic existence. The dungeon's walls were slowly-but-surely gravitating, and (by design), moving in speed and distance at what I estimated to be a foot a minute toward the pit, situated in the death chamber's center. I coughed, and spit, and gasped, and sneezed. 'My immortal soul's beginning to burn in the infernos of Hell!' my confused and blurred mind acknowledged. 'Hurry! Transform my body into embers before the pain of burning to death becomes entirely too unbearable!'

My grimy, bloodstained hands were cupped upon my face in total submission and dire resignation to my fate. I reluctantly accepted my destiny without any serious mental defense being rendered. My consciousness was positively and steadfastly resigned to the prospect of dying. My only human reaction was to bitterly weep and anticipate my inevitable demise.

The Inquisition had triumphed, and my conquered soul was about to surrender. Yes; the sulfuric walls were approaching me on all four sides, and within thirty seconds, I would have an accursed choice to make: either die by asphyxiation with my body being cremated, or voluntarily leap into the deep dark pit, and meet my predictable end upon impact with the watery bottom. All the while, the red, steaming walls moved steadily and morosely toward me in all four directions.

"The fuckin' pit!" I concluded and futilely yelled to the apathetic ears of Satan. "It'll definitely be the goddamned pit! My lungs are being stifled and feel like they're being incinerated! This atrocious sulfur is far worse a fate than being strangled to death!"

At the height of my dread, there was a discernible cessation of activity. My tired eyes stared between the fingers of my raised, cupped hands, and my pupils perceived a stoppage in the sulfuric fumes that had been filling the room. And then miraculously, the mechanical walls began to slowly recede back into their original positions. What on Earth (or in Hell) was happening?

My vocal cords screamed as loudly as they could, with me sounding much like an insane asylum maniac during an atrocious seizure. I tottered over to the right-side wall, and astutely listened to human voices conversing in French. Soon, the sound of military-trumpets was heard, and my hazy mind then envisioned God's obedient angels arriving on the scene to escort and accompany my soul to some distant afterlife destination. Then, a grating noise equal to a thousand thunders frightened the remaining daylights out of me.

I was quickly surrounded by a group of garrulous French soldiers, led by the very audacious General LaSalle. Then, it all occurred to me in a truly marvelous flash. The sadistic, black-robed, white-lipped, persecuting violators were now safely in the custody of the benevolent enemy. The cobwebs instantly disintegrated inside my foggy mind. I joyfully remembered that I had been a captured British mercenary fighting for the French against the wicked and reprehensible Spanish Inquisition.

"The Murders in the Rue Morgue"

The best private detectives are those persistent sleuths that perceive reality in a slightly different vein than the standard police inspectors do. Sometimes, what originally appears to be a vast, incomprehensible crime mystery can be easily solved with the examiner scrutinizing the very minute details that the average investigator tends to overlook.

Essentially, the most successful private investigators are shrewd-minded, distrustful crackerjacks, who are highly-skilled at analyzing, experimenting, hypothesizing, assuming, verifying and concluding. A dumb-ass critic might superficially say, "Well, those are the steps represented in the scientific method!" And *that* is a perfectly accurate definition on his or her part. But the most accomplished detectives are those serious-minded gumshoes that perform and execute to perfection the five characteristics evident in the "Scientific Method", and those coy investigators approach crime-fighting with much more guile and sagacity than do their police department counterparts.

In July of 1839, I had arrived with a purpose in Paris, France to conduct some valuable research on obscure materials to use in an upcoming novel I had planned on authoring. I was standing in a narrow aisle in an obscure, small, rinky-dink library in the Rue Montmartre, searching for specific information relative to the Normandy and Brittany peninsulas in Western France. And I also wanted to learn about the prominent families that populated those two sectors when I accidentally met a certain Mr. Cedrick Auguste Dupin, who incidentally was much more fluent in colloquial English than I was in French.

"Do you have a place to stay in the city?" Dupin asked me. "You look a little like a diseased mendicant to me!"

"No, not a permanent one," I chuckled and guiltily replied. "But Mr. Dupin; I do plan on staying at a downtown hotel until I can find adequate and inexpensive accommodations on the outskirts of the city. I'm an aspiring writer, you see, and I'm trying to amass a reputation and so unfortunately, I don't have a large revenue stream. Therefore, I must seriously limit my budgetary spending, because I'm basically a stupid, destitute, indigent bastard."

"I see," Dupin answered as the chief librarian in the far corner of the room cautioned him to keep his bass voice low, which it already was. "Mr. Poe, you can stay at my residence at 33 Rue Donut Faxbourg, St. Germain if you'd like," Monsieur Cedrick Auguste

Dupin invited. "It's not a deluxe hotel by any means, but the rent will be cheap, the wine will be good. and last but not least, I promise to be exquisite company, despite my habitual loud farting."

"You aren't a faggot, are you?" I discourteously and impertinently asked. "I fuckin' despise homosexuals who don't practice abstinence and celibacy. That's why I positively detest most Popes, Cardinals, Archbishops, Bishops, Monsignors, Priests, Brothers and Protestant Ministers, along with a few Hebrew Rabbis and Muslim Imams thrown in to boot," I emphatically qualified. "Those gay faggots either love to pork each other up the ass, suck each other's miniature dingles, or get their rocks off by molesting and sexually abusing vulnerable choir and altar boys. You might say that I have a phobia about those fairy fuck-heads that practice unnatural sex, but truly Mr. Dupin," I proceeded with my lackluster dissertation, "I find *their* perverted kind of lust to be unacceptably abominable when the gay fucks think that each other's assholes are wet, pink, juicy vaginas. An asshole is never a good substitute for a delicious, hairy, wet, pink pussy, wouldn't you tend to agree?"

"Absolutely, Mr. Poe! Absolutely!" Dupin promptly confirmed. "In fact, there's a terrific bordello only a block away from my dumpy residence, and I'll take you for a most gratifying visit there sometime later this week. But just remember," the keen-minded detective strangely pontificated. "I like to get the sloppy seconds. Please excuse me Mr. Poe, but that's an eccentric fetish of mine to which I happen to be addicted. I just love sloppy seconds!"

A week after my incidental meeting with the inimitable Cedrick Auguste Dupin, the nutcase and I were casually looking-over an evening edition of the Paris newspaper *Gazette des Tribunaux* when a certain front-page article attracted Dupin's interest involving a totally bizarre murder scenario. Two women were found dead, one was deceased inside, and the other near the same apartment, and there were no major clues as to the culprit's identity, or any hints about any particular motive.

"Were these women related to one another?" I phlegmatically asked Dupin. "Or were they lesbian lovers? Or perhaps they were bad-luck prostitutes?"

"The older woman was a certain Madame L'Espanaya, and the younger one was her daughter, Mademoiselle Camille L'Espanaya," Dupin read from the evening newspaper. "The two ladies lived in an apartment on the fourth-floor of a tenement building in the Rue Morgue. Eight neighbors and two gendarmes heard their loud, frantic screams, broke-down the locked doors, climbed-up three flights of stairs, knocked down the entrance door to their apartment, and the amateur rescuers were shocked at what they discovered."

"Well, what was in there?" I implored my new Parisian chum, who was then passing a quantity of intestinal gas. "Were these two ladies a mother-daughter prostitution team, and were the broads handling a lot of tax-free, illicit cash money? Aren't they the two sex-starved nymphomaniac bitches we screwed Monday night over at your favorite brothel? Ha, ha, ha, Dupin. That night you got your sloppy seconds twice! Ha, ha, ha!"

"You blundering Fool!" Dupin hollered with a lisp as the dumb shit inadvertently spit directly into my face. "You never mix business with pleasure. That's rule number one in professional detective work, so that the investigator can easily separate objectivity from subjectivity. Now then," my sagacious mentor continued his bullshit monologue. "The entire apartment was in total disarray, with items, objects, drawers, bras, tampons, unsanitary napkins, and assorted articles randomly-strewn all over the damned place."

"I see," I said with little thought or speculation. "So, the robbers were breaking and entering to steal personal property, and the women caught them in the act, and during their wild struggles, the ladies were killed by the criminal villains, who wound-up pilfering nothing. Those asshole murderers must've been rank amateurs because talented burglars never make the stupid mistake of killing anybody during a heist gone bust."

"Not exactly," Dupin answered with a puzzled expression displayed upon his hideous countenance. "Money, jewels, diamonds, necklaces and the like were left lying all over the friggin' apartment, so whoever committed the gruesome homicides didn't have robbery as a motive. The culprits had to be cold-blooded killers."

"Then, Dupin; it just doesn't make a whole lot of sense to wantonly kill two people just for the sake of killing them," I acknowledged. "Whoever enacted these brutal attacks must be a barbaric descendent of Attila the Hun, who incidentally was not gay!"

"Well Mr. Poe, according to the newspaper article, furniture had been broken, including legs of chairs, lamps, a bookcase, a prophylactic dispenser, etcetera."

"Monsieur Dupin, what about a jaded lover; a jilted boyfriend; a jaundiced husband, or perhaps a fiance with liver disease doing the killing?" I ridiculously asked. "Love and hate could also represent crucial motivations to extinguish human lives, especially during a crime of passion."

"Here's what is so baffling and mysterious about the entire scenario," Cedrick Auguste Dupin elaborated. "The mother, Madame L'Espanaya's hair, was pulled-out at the roots, and two long gray tresses belonging to her were found near the hearth, all dabbed with blood and dandruff. And also, a blood-stained, sharp razor was discovered on the Oriental rug, not far from the fireplace."

"So, the razor must obviously be the murder weapon," I concluded and verbally theorized. "The killer must either be a disgruntled or demented barber, or tailor! Who else could it have been? A jealous lesbian hairdresser from the local beauty salon?"

Dupin was not ruffled by my general lunacy. "A small metal safe was found in the main bedroom with the key still in the lock, but the contents inside were all still intact," Cedrick Auguste slowly read from the front-page account. "And situated next to the ripped-out gray hair tresses were found two cloth bags containing four thousand francs each, and nearby were four gold Napoleons, and three silver spoons," my friend monotonously read from the gazette.

"Well, Monsieur. I've heard of someone being born with a silver spoon in their mouth, but this is the first instance of someone dying with one almost stuck down their friggin' throat," I stupidly remarked. "I mean Cedrick; silverware might've been much more involved than either you or I can ever conjecture. Maybe the two unfortunate ladies were stabbed with a sharp knife when they refused to fork over the silver spoons."

"Stop speaking like you have diarrhea of the mouth and constipation of the brain," the normally unflappable Dupin cautioned and criticized my retarded cerebral functioning evident in my inane verbal commentaries. "Edgar, now please listen to me. Bona fide detective work requires total concentration, and no fuckin' fooling around, as is your demeanor, the meaner you get."

"Okay, Monsieur Dupin. I'll get serious for a moment, and for one moment only," I fraudulently pledged with my left hand being held over my testicles. "Tell me; what had happened to the rest of Madame L'Espanaya in that her pulled-out hair had been tossed all over the whole damned living room?"

"The gendarmes responding to the emergency soon discovered plenty of soot below the fireplace, so one of them stuck his head up the chimney, and to his utter horror, the corpse of the daughter Mademoiselle Camille L'Espanaya had been shoved up there with her head upside-down, and the girl's mutilated body came tumbling onto the hearth after being only slightly yanked by the astonished policeman."

"Holy shit in Turdsville, Cedrick!" I exclaimed. "It's bad enough when a person's nose gets stuffed-up with excessive snot, but when your chimney gets stuffed-up with your dead daughter, and you yourself are dead too, that's enough to make the average newspaper reader blow his or her stack. It's far worse than getting the damned flu (flue), that's for fuckin' sure!" I answered in a totally ludicrous, dumb-ass response. "But truthfully, my only Friend. no man would be strong enough to stuff Mademoiselle Camille L'Espanaya that far up a chimney! It's physically impossible to do, I would think!"

"Indications are from circumstantial evidence gathered that Mademoiselle Camille had been shoved up the chimney while she was still alive," Dupin reported from his newspaper column comprehension. "The young woman had bruises, abrasions, and lacerations on her face, chest, neck, right tit, asshole, and head; all coming from abominable friction happening between her formerly gorgeous body and the chimney stack."

"Was the mother Madame L'Espanaya ever found?" I asked. "Where was her hide if her hair had been discovered because usually, the city police can't find neither hide nor hair of anybody!"

"Well, Edgar, you clownish Buffoon; the neighbors and the police then heard shrieks coming from the back courtyard, and the snoops immediately ran to the apartment's back window. Below them was the body of Madame L'Espanaya, lying prone in the weeds. The alarmed searchers then dashed-down the building's three flights of stairs, and quickly entered the rear courtyard through a side wrought iron gate. The authorities found the mother's throat cut and her neck nearly severed. Upon raising-up her punctured body off the ground, the mother's head fell right off of her neck. Madame L'Espanaya is now fully decapitated!"

"Who could've done such despicable, gruesome, heinous crimes?" I rhetorically asked. "Remind me to lock the goddamned door to my room tonight. We have enough *cutthroats* already living in this neighborhood ghetto as it is, Monsieur Dupin, without me having to fuckin' worry about being literally decapitated, too!"

* * * * * * * * * * *

Two nights later at the supper table, Cedrick Auguste Dupin and I were seriously discussing a subsequent, follow-up, front-page article concerning the sensational Murders in the Rue Morgue that had just appeared in that evening's edition of the *Gazette des Tribunaux*. My friend, the singular and autonomous, no-client, unemployed private investigator, was reviewing for my information the reported depositions given to the Paris Police concerning the two strange killings. Dupin was in an extraordinarily contemplative mood as his analytical mind was methodically piecing-together relevant and irrelevant data that the regular charlatan police inspectors could not successfully connect, or had overlooked.

"Listen to this rather preposterous bullshit, Edgar," introspective Cedrick Auguste entreated. "Mrs. Pauline Dubourg, the whoring laundress for Madame L'Espanaya, claims that she's been washing clothes for the old woman and her naïve daughter Camille for three years. Pauline states in her deposition that the mother and the daughter were on good terms, and that the lesbians were affectionate towards each other, but seldom in public. And besides that," Dupin continued reading excerpts from the newspaper. "According to Mrs. Dubourg's testimony, Madame L'Espanaya always paid her cleaning bills on time, and was never late for a payment."

"Well, Monsieur Dupin," I said after a brief bit of contemplation. "Can we really trust Mrs. Dubourg's integrity? How do we know that she wasn't laundering money for Madame L'Espanaya and her daughter Mademoiselle Camille?" I frivolously jested. "Isn't there anything better to read on the Sports Page, or perhaps in the daily horoscopes section? What about all the ultra-liberal political bullshit printed on the editorial page?"

Ignoring my abundant facetiousness, my loyal companion (who incidentally was neither gay nor straight) described a second lengthy deposition given by Monsieur Pierre Moreau, an area tobacconist who sold the toothless Madame L'Espanaya several pounds of tobacco and a pound of snuff every week. "Monsieur Moreau testifies that the Madame was an independently wealthy woman, who often did fortune-telling as a hobby for area residents living in and around the vicinity of the Rue Morgue. What do you think about *that* new-found information, Edgar?"

"Well," I said before clearing my throat and sneezing into one of the dead women's recently obtained red-stained, unsanitary napkins. "If the dead old bitch had any advanced skill in fortune-telling, she would've known that she was going to be killed and would've strategically jumped-out of the goddamned fourth-floor window of her apartment, and the broad would've gotten the hell out of there before the tragedy ever happened to her. I mean, Cedrick Auguste," I editorialized while examining the newspaper's half-blank editorial page. "A person can't tell the future if she herself has no goddamned future. But what intrigues me the most about this remarkable case is that all of the doors and windows of the flea-bag apartment were shut and locked, and the only possible means of entry was through the fourth-story window that Madame L'Espanaya had been thrown out of. But the window is a full four-to-five-feet below the roof eaves, and I maintain that not even a triple-jointed acrobat could've gained access from the outside. And also, Monsieur Dupin; the chimney was way too narrow for anyone of any size to either clamber-down or up, and enter the premises."

Dupin remained in deep meditation, and heard not a word of my fantastic narrative. "And look here, Edgar; Isidore Muset, who was one of the gendarmes arriving on the scene, claims that he had heard some shrill sounds and a voice speaking in another language loudly emanating from the apartment. The language he had heard, of course, was other than French; possibly Spanish or Swahili."

"That makes some sense out of nonsense," I lyrically answered. "Madame L'Espanaya has a Spanish-sounding name, and perhaps she has a secret hot Latin lover; or maybe her daughter Camille was pregnant out of wedlock, and the enraged mother had been engaged in an argument with the prospective biological father."

"You think just like the regular, dumb-shit police do, and you're always fallaciously looking to the obvious in attempting to excavate important clues," Dupin offensively chided. "And the deposition of this policeman Isidore Muset can't be trusted either; simply because the deadbeat recently quit the force and is now recovering from insanity in a downtown mental institution. When the dedicated gendarme pulled Mademoiselle Camille out of the chimney, Isidore was so horrified that his mind and emotions automatically regressed back into his early childhood, a day later."

"Well Monsieur, what do you make of this anonymous male person in the apartment speaking Spanish?" I asked Dupin. "Who the hell was he? Miguel Cervantes, or Don Quixote reincarnated?"

"You're a complete horse's ass!" Cedrick Auguste vociferously indicted my true character. "In the paper's piss-poor account, it's specifically stated that a nosy neighbor named Henri Duval claims that he had heard someone in Madame L'Espanaya's apartment speaking in Italian just before the merciless murders had occurred, although this clown Duval doesn't understand a damned word of Italian. And some other area people giving lengthy, meaningless depositions reported that they had heard words uttered in Russian, German, and Hungarian, even though all of those other French assholes have indicated in their wacky signed testimonies that they don't know any fucked-up foreign words in Russian, in German, or in obsolete Hungarian."

But what really pissed-off Dupin more than anything else was a remote fact that had been barely mentioned in a related article on page three of the Paris newspaper, where it was casually reported that the police had arrested a petty thief named Adolphe Le Bon in conjunction with the atrocious Murders in the Rue Morgue.

"I know this lowlife vagabond Le Bon. True, the novice thief is a smalltime burglar and a petty crook, too. But the petty robber is definitely not a brutal murderer. Now Edgar," Cedrick Auguste emphatically expounded. "I fully intend to prove this ordinary jerk-off Adolphe Le Bon's innocence."

"How do you intend to accomplish that impossible task?" I challenged and then snickered. "The police must know what the hell they're doing! You're waging a losing battle against everyday reality, my delusional Friend. After all, Bon Ami; the police *are* the ultimate authorities, and they're going to resist and belittle anything of merit that either you or I have to say about this prime suspect, Adolphe Le Bon's innocence."

"The police are assholes, just like you're an opinionated rectum cavity for thinking exactly like they do," Dupin cryptically declared. "This morning, I received an urgent visit from Monsieur Gustav Ghent, the Prefect of the Paris Police Department. Ghent is quite baffled by these almost-indecipherable dual murders that had occurred in the Rue Morgue barrio sector, and the head honcho asked me to render my services in the ongoing investigation."

"And are you going to aid the police by them utilizing your great acumen?" I foolishly asked. "That could give you an excellent chance to clear the name of this petty local thug, Adolphe Le Bon."

Dupin then spoke as if he was describing the disunited pieces of a complex jigsaw puzzle, and I had to listen very intently in order to grasp the full gravity of his nonsensical lexicon. My pragmatic friend mentioned that he had met with Gustav Ghent earlier in the day, and that he had later accompanied the Prefect to the murder scene apartment, and that Monsieur Ghent had eventually agreed to allow Cedrick Auguste to keep the straight razor murder weapon in his possession for forty-eight hours in exchange for Dupin developing a definite solution to the baffling dual homicides.

"Did you uncover any new evidence besides the old evidence of the straight razor weapon?" I inquired. "After all, that *is* the murder weapon, isn't it?"

"It most certainly is," Dupin quickly concurred. "But sometimes the smallest, insignificant discovery could wind-up being the key factor in cracking-open a difficult case."

"Like what?" I interrogated my most ingenious colleague in crime fighting. "Like what?" I reiterated.

"Like this orange hair I discovered this afternoon in back of the apartment's living room sofa," Dupin answered, as the detective genius proudly showed me a long thick orange hair.

"Is it a pubic hair?" I idiotically laughed and then smirked. "I've never seen pussy hair quite that long; and come to think of it, I've never seen orange pussy hair, either. Some eccentric broad must've either dyed her head, or dyed her bush!"

"Don't be such a dumb fuck Ninny!" Dupin angrily reprimanded me. "I've examined this vital orange hair under a powerful microscope, and now I know exactly how the gory murders were committed. I've already arranged to place an ad in tomorrow morning's newspaper, and I hope to have this crime wrapped-up within the next forty-eight hours."

"You're fuckin' nuts; do you know that, Dupin! You're fuckin' nuts! In fact, your nuts are fuckin' nuts", I repeated. "You put more weight in a goddamned orange pubic hair, or possibly in a goddamned dyed-orange head hair than you do in the actual razor blade murder weapon! Forget your stupid-assed microscope analysis. I recommend that you stick your freakin' noggin under a telescope because you oughta' have your dumb-shit head examined!"

"Be here in my dining room two mornings from now at nine o'clock sharp if you want to learn exactly how the murders to Madame L'Espanaya and to Mademoiselle Camille had been strangely committed."

* * * * * * * * * * * *

Two mornings later, at a quarter to nine, I was in the prescribed place seated at the dining room table, and informally conferring with the brilliant and inimitable private detective, Monsieur Cedrick Auguste Dupin. At first, I felt a trifle fidgety, seriously thinking that I was being exploited as an accomplice to an elaborate hoax involving an orange pubic hair being the principal clue that would unlock the mystery of the intriguing Murders in the Rue Morgue. But then again, I generally trusted the eminent Dupin's judgment and his suspect professionalism, and I believed that the reputable fellow wouldn't be playing any grandiose trick on either me or the irresponsible Paris Police Department.

"Have you invited Prefect Ghent in on this frivolous session?" I anxiously asked Dupin while I twiddled my thumbs in a reverse motion, as was my bad habit ever since I was a toddler. "I mean to say, Cedrick; you do have to return the borrowed straight razor murder weapon to him this morning, don't you?"

"It is always easier to borrow than to invent," Dupin weirdly answered, using some arcane symbolism to establish a relationship that at that time I couldn't fathom. "But as I've told you a dozen times Edgar, the Prefect and his horde of nincompoops don't know bullshit from cat piss, or from the foul smell of boxwood, either."

"Well, Monsieur; you're doing all of this sidebar stupidity to exonerate a minor thug named Adolphe Le Bon," I continued our impromptu, unsensational conversation. "Why are you so concerned about the fate of a petty thief?"

"Because Edgar; Monsieur Le Bon, if convicted, will be a part of a travesty of justice entirely generated by police incompetence," Dupin replied. "That type of destiny shouldn't happen to anyone: to you, to me, or to vulnerable Adolphe Le Bon. The police are looking for an available dupe to blame; I believe being done just to cover their own lily-white, French asses."

I was totally miffed and stymied by Dupin's astonishing lexicon, and I needed several concrete explanations to preserve my rapidly diminishing confidence, along with my totally dwindled sanity. "Cedrick, what was the content of the ad that you had placed in the Lost and Found section of the morning paper?"

"Well, Edgar. I had advertised that I had in my possession a lost on-the-prowl orangutan, and that whoever had misplaced the itinerant ape, that person should come to my residence no later than nine o'clock this morning to claim their lucrative prize. Is that peculiar description perfectly clear to you, Mr. Poe?"

"Why Monsieur; now I really do think that this entire fiasco is a lot of insane jabberwocky and poppycock," I volleyed back, a bit flabbergasted. "You're now telling me that the orange hair you had analyzed under your defective microscope belongs to a goddamned orangutan that had committed the dual murders! I think I'm going to take you to London to be admitted to St. Mary's of Bethlehem. Yes, indeed, Dupin. Bedlam is where you need to be to fully recuperate from your massive, detri*mental* delusions!"

Just at that pivotal point in our important dialogue, there was a heavy rapping on the front door, and Dupin rose from his chair and answered the knocking. My illustrious friend returned into the dining room with a tall, brawny-looking, muscular fellow that Auguste introduced to me as Monsieur Jacques Trappe, who then was requested to have a comfortable seat in any of Auguste Dupin's uncomfortable chairs. After the three of us humans were fairly comfortably and uncomfortably situated, the private investigator initiated our three-way consultation.

"I see Monsieur Trappe that you're a veteran sailor?" Dupin cordially began. "Am I correct in making that assumption?"

"How in the world did you know that?" our guest incredulously asked. "I am indeed a sailor for fifteen years now."

"It's all not a very complicated matter," Dupin amazingly declared. "You have an anchor tattoo inked above your right wrist, confirming your nautical occupation."

"I see," Monsieur Jacques Trappe acknowledged with a sigh of relief. "I now understand that there was nothing mysterious about how you had figured-out *that* minor detail, after all! Now Sir; I've come to reclaim my orangutan. Do you have it here?"

"No Monsieur," Dupin indicated with a short smile flashing across his florid face. "It's too dangerous to keep inside a regular dwelling. It's being held in a cage at another location, and you'll be able to retrieve the creature in a few hours."

"What about the razor blade?" I awkwardly asked, nearly blowing Dupin's investigative technique.

Cedrick Auguste Dupin quickly produced the aforementioned murder weapon, and the agitated sailor attempted standing-up, but then the stellar private investigator held a previously concealed pistol in his hand, and threatened to use it against mariner Monsieur Trappe should the sailor attempt to flee the premises. Then, my wise friend demanded that Monsieur Trappe disclose everything that the ocean voyager knew about the caged orangutan, and about the very bewildering and gruesome Murders in the Rue Morgue.

As it turned out, Monsieur Trappe had acquired the orangutan on a recent ocean voyage to Borneo, and the lonely pet collector had trained the ape to accomplish certain tricks, labors and tasks. Upon arriving at the Paris docks, Monsieur Trappe was shaving inside his cramped cabin quarters, and the orangutan began imitating the behavior it had just witnessed by applying shaving cream to its hairy face, and then dangerously gaining possession of the straight razor.

The concerned sailor reached for his training whip to punish the impersonating ape, but fearing being punitively reprimanded, the Simian creature bounded out the door and fled the ship, carrying with it the long, sharp blade. Jacques Trappe chased after the powerful animal right to the vicinity of the Rue Morgue, where the frightened orangutan then skillfully climbed-up the side of the building, latched onto a flagpole, and next swung its hairy frame inside the back fourth-floor open window; launching himself directly into Madame L'Espanaya's apartment.

"And naturally," Dupin interrupted the sailor's woeful narrative, "neither elderly Madame L'Espanaya, nor her ill-fated hundred-pound-daughter Mademoiselle Camille L'Espanaya possessed the wherewithal, or the physical ability, to either discipline or fend-off the excited orangutan, who was wielding the sharp razor. So, the impressionable beast felt a compulsion to imitate *you* as its ideal model of impersonation, Monsieur Trappe; of course, you had been shaving your neck, and the ape...."

"The orangutan killed the lady in question by slitting her throat with the razor blade," the guilt-laden sailor finished. "When I heard the screams and shrieks coming out of the fourth-floor back window, that's exactly what had happened. The ape had gone absolutely ape!"

"And since you were exceptionally scared about what had just transpired," I contributed to the discussion, "you ran away from the crime scene like ape-shit on steroids. And I suppose that your orangutan barber is still on the loose somewhere in Paris."

"Not really," Dupin confidently clarified. "Prefect Ghent has advised me just an hour ago that the dangerous Simian had been captured while trying to gain admission, without any francs, to the Paris Zoo. The alert zookeepers had cleverly lured the animal into an empty cage by leaving peeled, rotten bananas inside the enclosure, and then shutting the door after the orangutan leaped inside."

"Will I be arrested?" the visiting sailor nervously asked. "I wish to avoid having a criminal record. I must re-board my ship that's scheduled to leave port by early Tuesday morning of next week."

"Well, Monsieur Trappe; that particular matter is for the Paris Police to decide," Dupin suavely replied. "But since the powerful ape had committed the two brutal murders, and not you, I imagine that your charge will be reduced from a major felony to a meager misdemeanor; that is, your leaving the scene of a crime, and then *you* not reporting it to the authorities. But since you're a fairly decent young fellow, Monsieur Trappe," Cedrick Auguste nonchalantly added, "I'll speak to Prefect Ghent personally, and I'm willing to predict that you'll be leaving port on your' assigned ship sometime next Tuesday morning; either with or without your treasured orangutan."

Jack London

Jack London (1876-1916)

Jack London died at the early age of forty, but the author left behind a rich collection of literature still read and admired today. London was a master at the literary writing technique known as *Realism,* where the literary genius skillfully describes struggles and life-or-death situations, pitting man against man, man against hostile environments, and often man against himself.

Jack London was born in San Francisco and helped to support his family at age fourteen, dropping-out of school to do so. Spending plenty of time in city libraries, London was a voracious reader who studied hard, and eventually passed the entrance examination into the University of California. The aspiring writer stayed as a college student for one semester, but then went to work as a sailor and a laborer. During the Gold Rush of 1897, London spent a year in the Klondike and Yukon territories, where the unlucky prospector gathered material and information about interesting characters that later would appear in his graphic novels and short stories.

Very fascinated by the Darwinian theory of "survival of the fittest", many of Jack London's works focused on the endurance of strong men driven by atavistic instincts and primitive emotions. His two most famous novels are actually direct reversals of each other. In the *Call of the Wild,* Buck, a very large dog, is stolen from a wealthy family's Santa Clara, California home, and is transported to the Alaska/Canadian Yukon to eventually become the lead canine in a dogsled team. In the classic novel *White Fang,* a wolf dog is taken from the tundra wilderness and then becomes domesticated.

The settings of most Jack London stories are in California, the Klondike/Yukon regions of the U.S. and Canada, and the South Sea Pacific islands in and around Tahiti.

"The Story of Jees Uck"

This is the story of Jees Uck, a swarthy-skinned, mixed-blooded, beautiful Indian/Eskimo woman, who was a native resident of the Yukon Territory of Northwestern Canadian. But it is also the story of a man named Neil Bonner, whose path Jees Uck had crossed (and possibly had double-crossed), and whose life the lady had significantly touched and influenced. Although Jees Uck had never learned how to read or write, her abundant wisdom is quite famous, and her tale is told around myriad nightly forest and mountain campfires, even to this day.

Neil Bonner was the only son of a wealthy trading tycoon, but the father-son duo constantly bickered and argued over even the slightest of trivialities. In order to discipline his son and indoctrinate him into the real business world at a low entry level, the inflexible and sanctimonious Mr. Neil Bonner Sr. had a close friend hire Neil Bonner Jr. as an agent for the P.C. Company, which operated by adhering to very strict, austere politically correct rules.

The large international trading corporation owned fleets of sailing ships that exchanged goods for furs, gold, and meat in the primitive Alaskan Klondike and in the Canadian Yukon territories. "Five years up there in the frigid north country will teach my son a good lesson in self-control, and compel him to implement sound business practices," the power-hungry San Francisco mogul told his P.C. Company associate. "It's so damned cold up there that only male polar bears get hard-ons!"

"If your son works-out well the first year in our junior management program," the father's friend explained, "then we'll really test young Neil's perseverance and mettle by assigning him to manage a small trading post up in the Yukon. I think that the one in Tanana Station will be manned next year this time, or else Young Neil will be in charge of the company's new Twenty Mile General Store. The damned trading post will be called Twenty Mile because it's twenty friggin' miles from nowhere; the nearest town being Dawson, which is nearly thirty miles away from *that* desolate area."

"That sounds like the perfect prescription to cure my obstinate, know-it-all son of his lackadaisical business disposition," Mr. Bonner replied with a smile. "Young Neil has two college degrees; one in pharmacy and another in basic chemistry, but the ornery fool doesn't want to enter either of those two professions. Neil wants to start at the goddamned top, but just like you and me George," the avid commerce broker stated to his company executive friend, "the little prick has to start at the bottom, learn the operation from the ground level, and then through hard work and achievement, pay his dues and earn the right to ascend into corporate administration. But first, Neil has to kneel!"

The newly-constructed post at Twenty Mile was a modest-looking log cabin the size of a corner grocery store. The place had two rooms to rent upstairs, and a kitchen and bedroom conveniently situated behind the main commercial area. The post was but one tentacle of the enormous P.C. Company empire; a sort of ice-bound Devil's Island where the neophyte Neil Bonner had been dispatched so that he could impress his superiors and simultaneously placate the lad's very strong-minded and highly regimented Puritanical father's uncompromising and indomitable iron will.

Young Neil Bonner's assistant at Twenty Mile was Amos Pentley, whose brother Andy had been fired by "the Company" just three months before down in Seattle. Amos was a short, hollow-chested, bossy fellow who frequently coughed, making Neil suspect that the jealous man was suffering from an advanced case of consumption. The new post manager felt sorry for Pentley's deteriorating health condition, but conversely, Neil Bonner just did not like or trust the whiny little man.

'Shit!' Neil thought. 'I love to party and flirt with beautiful women. But there's none of that neat city stuff going on up here. The only person I have to commiserate with is this wimpy, sneaky, fuck-head Amos Pentley, who hates to talk to anyone, including me! All the annoying bastard does is talk to himself in his sleep. But now that the outside temperature is seventy degrees below zero, I might just wind-up conversing with a goddamned igloo, a totem pole, a baby seal, or a glacier, simply to keep my general sanity intact.'

In January of that winter, Jees Uck entered the remote trading post to barter furs for food and supplies. Neil instantly observed the beautiful girl, and despite the freezing temperature, immediately Bonner got a boner.

'Oh my God!' Neil promptly imagined. 'This pretty Eskimo girl wants beads, flour, beans, and bacon for her furs. I wouldn't mind putting my bacon inside her fur pelt; yes, that's what the hell my warped mind thinks. My sensitive pecker throbs and bobs like a son-of-a-bitch every time that gorgeous doll looks me in the eyes.'

Amos Pentley noticed the flirtations going on between Neil Bonner and Jees Uck, and *that* scrutiny made him became even more envious of his newly arrived boss. During the Indian/Eskimo girl's third visit to the Twenty Mile trading post, Neil Bonner courteously carried a fifty-pound-sack of flour out to the young woman's dogsled when suddenly, his neck became exceedingly stiff, even stiffer than his erect penis. A quick spasm soon had the prodigal son rolling on top of ice and snow. Bonner became tense, and his body quivered, his back arched, and his general anatomy appeared distorted and twisted as his oddball convulsions continued.

Neil's forehead began to sweat profusely, despite the fifty below zero temperature, and his mouth started to foam. The love-afflicted man attempted crawling back inside the store on his hands and knees, but as soon as he got to the door, it opened and benevolent Jees Uck immediately intercepted the aching fellow's progress, and gingerly raised-up his head to promote his ability to breathe. Using all her remaining strength and dexterity, the benign girl dragged Neil back inside the log cabin, and then adroitly kicked the door shut.

"Oh Amos!" Jees Uck cried-out to apathetic Pentley. "Him die, you think? Him really paleface now!"

Pentley stood there in a nonchalant, reticent manner, shrugged his shoulders, and then uttered, "I believe he thinks he's Julius Caesar having one of his many epileptic seizures! Now I know how fuckin' Brutus must've felt!" Of course, Jees Uck was totally unaware of the historic symbolism of *those* fucked-up, malignantly-spoken words.

A minute further into the dire emergency, the tension in Neil Bonner's body eased, and during that auspicious moment of slackening, the trading post manager gritted his teeth before the onslaught of the next terrible spasm and sternly commanded, "Jees Uck; get medicine from wall cabinet. Never mind! Drag my ass over there, and I'll tell you what medicine to reach-up and get!"

Obeying the ill man's strict dragging order, even though the Eskimo doll was not a drag queen, Jees Uck tugged and pulled the incapacitated victim over toward the medicine cabinet that was hanging on the wall next to the store's wood-burning stove. Despite his hazy and cluttered mind, Bonner recalled that three of his sled dogs had exhibited similar muscular contractions, and the agonizing agent determined that he would utilize his academic knowledge of chemistry and pharmacy to alleviate his suffering. Neil pointed to a vial of chloral hydrate, and signaled for the native girl to pour an ounce of the formula down his throat, which she compliantly did.

"Listen to me, please, Jees Uck!" Bonner further instructed. "Stay by my side and guard me from Amos, but whatever you do, do not touch me!" And upon hearing what the sick man had directed, Amos Pentley retreated to the back bedroom, not wanting any confrontation with Jees Uck, who was an expert at hitting distant targets with the sharp knife she possessively kept inside her sheath. The girl also kept a sharp harpoon wedged inside her trusty dogsled. 'Neil is having regular contractions,' the Eskimo beauty considered, 'but I don't think he's pregnant. I'll check his eyes for dilation.'

A full day passed before Neil Bonner again opened his eyelids to marvel and gaze upon the pulchritude of Jees Uck, who was still loyally kneeling by his side without once having to use the bathroom. "Go into the kitchen and bring some food: biscuits, beans, and bacon," the recuperating trading post representative directed. "Take a lit candle in there because it's dark, and you might trip over some obscure object in the way. And get some coffee and the pint of whiskey on the table also, and then gees, Jees, come back in here and place those items on the trading post counter. I know you've never heard of a thing called science, but you're about to witness what we Americans call a *counter*-revolution!"

"Why all of yesterday's food? Are you going to eat like a snow vulture, Neil?" Jees Uck asked.

"Geez Jees; why the hell would I want to eat myself?" Bonner jested, finally exhibiting signs of snapping out of his lethargy. "But no; I'm not going to eat any of yesterday's food. I'm going to perform what the people in my country call 'a laboratory experiment'. I'm going to test it to determine if any of it has been poisoned!"

"What is a laboratory experiment?" the girl curiously inquired.

"A laboratory is a place where a white man often *labors* and mixes liquids together in what is called 'an experiment'," Bonner tried elaborating. "Try to pay attention Jees Uck. You will soon see what the hell I mean. All of that a scientist performs in a lab!"

'How the hell does anyone perform anything in a friggin' retriever dog!' Jees Uck wondered.

After the requested food items had been carefully arranged upon the trading post counter, the store's manager assessed his remedy theory. 'I believe that I had been suffering from a condition of tetanus,' Bonner suspiciously surmised as the science major began conducting his meticulous food analyses.

His initial research definitely demonstrated that the coffee had not been tampered with after the chemistry/pharmacy graduate had methodically mixed liquids of certain vials with yesterday's java taken from the pot. Then, after mixing other chemicals into different tumblers containing food, Bonner systematically determined that the baked beans had not been contaminated or tainted. All the while, Amos Pentley, who knew nothing of the sciences of chemistry and pharmacy, stuck his bald-head out from the kitchen from time to time, and at minute intervals, the craven asshole looked-on with abundant curiosity, and then again, retreated into the back room like a timid mouse scurrying into a wall opening.

"Is this white man's medicine a form of black magic?" Jees Uck asked. "It looks very strange and complicated. I did not know that you were a white shaman, Neil."

"I cannot speak wise words while I concentrate and mix," Bonner answered as the ailing chemist carefully studied the biscuit particles suspended in a salt solution, and then watched them change color. 'This next step is the most important part. I hope that this bullshit experiment works!"

Amos Pentley slowly and surreptitiously entered the main room, and the distrustful little man silently pretended to be concerned about Bonner's physical welfare.

"Are you feeling better Neil?" Pentley queried, feigning sincerity as best as he could. "I was worried that you'd be dead by now."

"Listen to me, you, dirty, puny, Lilliputian cock-sucker!" Bonner screamed at his new-found adversary. "You have to pack-up an outfit and hit the fuckin' trail before I fuckin' kill your ass right here and now! You can use the six company dogs out in the back shed."

"You don't mean to say that you're sendin' me out into fifty below temperatures at night to freeze to death?" the appalled assistant manager incredulously asked. "That type of irresponsible action could be construed as voluntary manslaughter, even in an Australian wallaby court of law! You might hang for it, if I die out there!"

"You fucked-up jealous bastard! Don't try threatening me with your perverted bullshit! You tried to kill me, and you failed!" Bonner accused, as the dumbfounded and confused Jees Uck listened to the dramatic exchange and attempted to comprehend what the exact nature of the white man controversy entailed.

"The company believes that Bob Birdsall had killed himself, but now I know better," Bonner vociferated to his pretentious enemy. "You, Amos Pentley, had evilly eliminated Birdsall by poisoning his ass right off the planet, you fucked-up, demented, dirt bag! In my case, my chemical analysis showed that you used strychnine in my biscuits to try to permanently send me to the Grim Reaper's happy hunting domain. Now listen carefully, Amos; if you don't want me to violently kill you right here and now. Twenty Mile is too small for the both of us to inhabit, and it's only two-hundred-miles on the trail to Holy Cross, the next company trading post," Bonner informed Pentley of *his* imminent journey. "Now I warn you, Asshole; mush the hell out of here with the six canines before I change my erratic mind and perform a fuckin' autopsy on you while you're still fuckin' alive! I attended-but-failed undertaking school before I ever studied chemistry and pharmacy!"

* * * * * * * * * * *

"You must go to bed, and I will take care of you until you're feeling better!" Jees Uck suggested after Amos Pentley got out of Twenty Miles like a fart zipping out of a challenged coward's asshole. "You, sick man, Neil; and need good squaw to nurse you."

Bonner licked his lips while peering at Jees Uck's magnificent breasts. "No Jees Uck; you go back to your camp and stay with your people for one full week," Bonner insisted. "Then come back here and by that time, you can *nurse* me into better health," the recovering fellow thought as his selfish brain contemplated sucking on the native girl's firm breasts and gorgeous nipples. 'I'll just pretend that I'm an infant again; yes, a cute little sucker with my anxious tongue greedily licking away!'

"You don't like me, Neil?" the attractive brown-eyed girl sadly asked as she slowly put on her warm parka.

"Only too well, Jees Uck! Only too well!" Bonner replied. "I promise you that by next week, I'll be strong enough for you to nurse me as you have suggested!"

Seven days later, Jees Uck showed-up at the Twenty Miles trading center with ten furs to barter for beads, food, scarlet cloths, moose-hide moccasins, Eskimo panties, and leather straps. After conversing in small talk for two full hours, Neil Bonner decided it was time for him to make his romantic move.

"I go now, Neil!" the pretty swarthy-skinned girl lowly and politely said with her eyes pointed-down. "Good night, Neil!"

"No, Jees Uck; you aren't going anywhere without my expressed permission," Bonner nebulously declared. And then the horny fellow kissed her on the forehead, and then again upon her lips, which seemed like a strange and eccentric behavior to the apprehensive native girl, who was unaware of Western Civilization male behavior.

"What do you call that caribou shit act?" Jees Uck asked her admirer about *her* peculiar experience. "Is that what white men do to white women?"

"Let me tell you all about a white man named Charles," Bonner affectionately said before kissing her again.

"Charles? Charles who?"

"A six-inch-tall fellow named Charles Dick-ins, who insists on being sucked and inserted at least three times a day!" the amorous and aroused white man stated as Bonner wrapped his muscular arms around the stunned native doll, and then planted a huge smooch upon her receptive mouth.

A month later, after Neil Bonner and Jees Uck shared a minimum of three fantastic intimacies a day, a P.C. Company employee named Sandy MacPherson showed-up at Twenty Miles with some bad news to convey to the trading post manager, which an hour later, was joyfully evaluated as 'a blessing in disguise' in Neil Bonner's self-oriented mind.

"This letter in my hands, Jees Uck, says that my father has died and that I must return to a far-off big village called San Francisco to manage his affairs and settle his will," Bonner endeavored to explain to the native girl who was ignorant of such complicated matters. "But do not worry. I will take good care of you during my absence from Twenty Miles, and one day, return and take you away to live with me in my country inside my big igloo. In the meantime," the goal-minded man announced, "I'll build a nice cabin for you to live in. and you can have a fine job being employed here at the trading post, yes, working with Sandy."

"Is your mother still living?" the compassionate girl wanted to know. "You've never spoken to me about your mother."

"Yes, and I must return home and help take care of her because she's very upset that my father has passed-on to stay forever with the Great Spirit," Bonner tried to express in words that Jees Uck could fathom. "Stay here and work with Sandy, and I shall come back and get you when everything back home in a place called California has been straightened-out!"

A week later, after the spring thaw had descended on the Northland, and the annual thick river ice had finally melted, Neil Bonner sincerely kissed Jees Uck "Goodbye" and then sauntered up the dock platform and onto the *Yukon Belle*, an antiquated steamer on its way out to the Bering Sea. "I'll be back before the first winter snow flies!" Neil Bonner yelled to his love from the ship's deck as the departure whistle blasted from the steamer's main stack.

'Shit!' Bonner thought as the ship's passenger again waved to his one and only girl. 'With dad's massive fortune sitting there for me to inherit, I can come back here and become the Cecil Rhodes of Alaska and of all the Yukon! Yes, you-con Neil,' Bonner's mind whimsically played and toyed with silly words. 'Yes you-con!'

* * * * * * * * * * *

Jees Uck was absolutely thrilled with her new log cabin, with enacting her "important job" at the isolated Twenty Miles trading post, and with her meteoric ascension into prominence among the white fur merchants and Indian pelt hunters that bartered in that part of the Yukon. The last fall steamboat left the local river dock, and the fierce winter snows arrived (including two savage blizzards), but yet, Neil Bonner had not returned to the Northland despite the native girl's admirable vigilance.

A full month later, John Thompson, who had replaced Sandy MacPhearson as the chief operator of the P.C. Company general store, tried to put the make on Jees Uck, and the impulsive Casanova almost had the blade of the angry female's dependable knife penetrate his jugular vein and nearby voice-box.

"Neil Bonner will return to me and to *our* new cabin in the woods," the faithful and vigilant girl communicated as the enraged female held her weapon to the quivering man's neck. "He is a good man, and will keep his sacred promise to me after his unknown business in his far away land has been completed."

"Look Princess Summer-Fall-Winter-Spring, I just read an article from a San Francisco newspaper that stated that your wonderful Neil Bonner has just married a very rich woman named Kitty Sherman, and that the pair intends to spend their honeymoon in a beautiful warm place called Hawaii," Thompson maintained, after the now-disconsolate native girl had placed the lethal knife back into her leather waist-belt holder.

"Neil will come back to me. And you lie to me, Mr. John Thompson. Do you think I am dumb Indian/Eskimo girl? Moon is not made of honey!"

"You have a hard head, Young Lady, and will never understand the white man's truth or the white man's reality," the new store manager maintained before gulping and then clearing his throat. "Neil Bonner will never return to this God-forsaken place, now that he's a very important businessman back in his big country. You'll never see him here again, and the only damned way you'll ever see him in the future is if you somehow travel down to San Francisco, California and witness the real truth I've just described, all for yourself; you naïve, gullible, beautiful, mixed-up mixed-breed!"

"I am, as you' white people call 'pregnant' with Neil Boner's, er, I mean Neil Bonner's child, and if you dare attack me again Mr. Mink-less," Jees Uck predicted, "I'll first slice your sex organs off your scummy body, and while you're bent over and bleeding to death, then I will get great pleasure from cutting a big second asshole in your fat, ugly neck! And now John Thompson, *you* can stack the maple syrup bottles used for the white man's pancakes on the log cabin shelf wall!"

Five months after the intense argument between John Thompson and Jees Uck, the girl gave birth to a son whom she named "Neil" in honor of the child's biological father. Four long years passed by, and with each successive month, Jees Uck's hope that her lover would journey back to the Yukon to resume their amicable relationship dwindled-down to almost nil.

But Jees Uck steadfastly kept her fidelity and refused to look into the face of the jilted John Thompson whenever the two had conversations inside the Twenty Mile General Store. And then three separate native hunters gladly offered to marry Jees Uck, despite the existence of her totally "mongrel son Neil", but the dedicated girl shunned the awkward verbal overtures of 'Oche Ish, Hah Yo', and 'Why Not Babe', because Jees still believed that the father of her child would still honor his pledge to come back to the Yukon; regardless of the false language about Neil Bonner's marriage, which had been printed in the newspaper announcement. All the while, the perplexed woman insisted for all literate white man customers to impatiently and orally read to her disbelieving ears before ever leaving the secluded Twenty Mile Trading Post.

* * * * * * * * * * * *

The sixth disappointing spring after Neil Bonner had left her stranded at the Twenty Miles trading post, Jees Uck took her life's savings and walked her son Neil down to the river dock to board the decrepit, old steamer *Yukon Belle*. Her journey took her and young Neil on an odyssey to St. Michael's; to Unalaska; to Metlakahtla, and next to St. Mary's at the terminal point of the Panhandle. Finally, she and her wide-eyed lad traveled south by ship through the strait of Juan de Fuca (which does *not* mean John the Fucker), and eventually arrived in the thriving metropolis of Seattle, where Jees Uck met-up with reassigned Sandy McPhearson, who painfully read the faded newspaper article about Neil Bonner and Kitty Sherman's wedding ceremony, about their elegant hotel reception, and about their elaborate Hawaii honeymoon. But still, despite the mounting evidence, Jees Uck refused to accept the printed truth about her former lover's new life in the all-too-modern and bewildering United States of America.

And adamant and determined Jees Uck was not intimidated by the great "iron horse" that transported her and her son along the jagged western coast from Seattle to San Francisco, nor was the Eskimo beauty overwhelmed by the masterful, industrial civilization and its attendant factories and immense warehouses that her amazed eyes were viewing outside the train window. This big train is nice, but I wonder if my good friend Neil has any loco-motives!' Jees inadvertently imagined and wondered.

With specific address information that the stubborn lady had obtained from Sandy MacPhearson in Seattle, the courageous woman and her awed son hopped-out of a hired buggy cab, and the weary travelers climbed up the white marble steps to Neil Bonner's opulent big city mansion.

A Japanese servant answered the mammoth-sized mahogany front door, and the valet escorted the woman and her child to a tile-walled waiting area. Five minutes later, a snobbish butler guided the pair through three elegant chambers (with crystal chandeliers suspended from ornate ceilings) until Jees and the wide-eyed toddler arrived inside an ostentatiously furnished parlor.

A vivacious, well-dressed, blonde-haired woman gracefully entered the room through French doors, and quickly initiated a polite conversation with the poorly-dressed but very unique Indian/Eskimo girl. "I understand that you wish to see my husband," the queen-like aristocratic lady prefaced. "Do you know my husband?"

"No," Jees Uck slowly answered, her disarrayed mind now boggled and disheveled. "I come here to see Neil Bonner."

"Neil Bonner *is* my husband!" the suddenly-amused, sophisticated woman laughed. "Neil will be arriving home for supper in about ten minutes. I presume you had known my husband when he had been stationed up in Canada. Please sit down. You've probably trekked a long way, and are quite exhausted from your long trip."

Jees Uck nodded her head in consternation, her stunned mind still swimming in a state of culture shock. A series of disturbing thoughts rushed through her addled mind, with the ideas ranging from salvaging Neil Bonner from certain death, to John Thompson's repelled romantic advances. And then, also, there was Sandy MacPhearson's most recent awful verification of Neil Bonner's marital activities and of course, finally, the fantastic excursion south on the "iron horse" from Washington State to Northern California. The culturally shocked, visiting woman and her amazed child sat back on the ridiculously comfortable sofa, as Mrs. Kitty Bonner resumed the rather awkward dialogue.

"You had known my husband up in Canada?" she graciously interrogated her unexpected, grimy-faced guest.

"Sure. I wash his clothes, and work in his trading post," the befuddled visitor honestly answered, obviously withholding certain essential facts from her sketchy account.

"And I presume that this sturdy lad is your boy? I have a little girl almost the same age," Kitty noted, never realizing that the two children might be kindred.

The alluded-to daughter entered the magnificent room accompanied by a manservant carrying a silver tray with a pot of steaming tea, along with two empty china cups. Soon, the youngsters had gotten over their initial shyness and began playing on the opposite side of the lavish room, while the disparate women sipped tea and continued their stilted conversation.

All the while, Jees Uck realized that she was out of her league competing with the charms and manners of the sophisticated former Kitty Sherman. A moment of silence was interrupted with a familiar male voice that featured surprise blended with an element of anxiety detectable in its intonation.

"Why mercy me! It's Jees Uck!" Neil Bonner exclaimed, not knowing exactly how to emotionally express his genuine feelings. "Kitty," the nervous man said to his unsuspecting wife. "This marvelous young woman had worked for me up in the Yukon."

The fidgety husband was still wondering precisely what Kitty had learned about the native girl and him in *their* past relationship, and so Bonner was reluctant to pursue any additional discourse with *her*.

"Hello Neil. I am fine, yes; very fine," Jees Uck clumsily replied. "You look much good!"

"Well, I must say how glad I am to see you," Bonner declared with a degree of alarm evident in his tone of voice. "What's happened? Did you strike a gold mine? When did you arrive here in San Francisco? I love this city! I'll never leave my heart here!"

"No Neil; I did not find any gold," Jees Uck emphatically answered her former bedmate. "I saved all my money and came all the way down here just to visit you."

"To think that you knew my husband all the way up there in the primitive Yukon Territory," Kitty chimed-in. "I understand that *that* part of the world is almost prehistoric!"

Jees Uck stared-over at her handsome son harmlessly playing with his half-sister, and noticed both children enjoying themselves tremendously; and suddenly, Jees' heart sank lower in her chest from the total weight of emotional pity, despair, and melancholy.

The man of both women tried filling a void in the cumbersome, three-way discussion. "Honey," Neil said to Kitty. "I've never told you this, but Jees Uck once saved my life after I had been poisoned by a diabolical fellow named Amos Pentley at the Yukon trading post. I truly owe my life to this fantastic young lady, and will be eternally grateful to this special woman as long as I live!"

"Why that is absolutely incredible to hear, Neil!" Kitty genuinely exclaimed. "I think that you should reward Jees Uck for her splendid loyalty. She should not have to live in abject poverty up there in *that* hostile wilderness. When she leaves San Francisco, I expect you to make her life more comfortable in every way possible."

Neil Bonner felt extremely guilty about his questionable past, and felt obligated (for his own good) to change the subject. "Is that your boy?" the father asked his displaced visitor. "He's a handsome young lad, and I'll see to it that he receives a good quality education when he grows-up."

"That would only be wise and prudent," Kitty confirmed and agreed. "What is your name Young Man?"

"Neil," the boy all-too-honestly replied.

"That's dumb Injun talk," Jees Uck interposed, realizing the futility of her present situation. "Him do Injun talk. Him name is Nee-al, meaning 'cracker' in white man's talk."

"And the boy's father?" the impressed wife wondered and inquired. "His father must be a fine man!"

"Oh yes, Nee-al's father is very good man," Jees Uck answered, squirming upon the sofa and awkwardly verified.

"Did you know Nee-al's father?" Kitty questioned her husband without showing any trace of suspicion.

"Know him! I knew him personally!" Neil Bonner attested. "He's as fine a man as ever lived in the Yukon, yes he is! I knew him almost as well as I know myself!"

* * * * * * * * * * *

But the story of Jees Uck is not one of total disappointment and misery. Human dignity has a way of rising above catastrophe, and ultimately triumphing over all contingencies. And so, the principal characters in this saga all found satisfaction in their individual endeavors, exploits, and enterprises.

The remarkably resilient Jees Uck returned to the Northland and led a straight, decent, moral life, and the modest lady never again slept with a man, or ever again considered marrying one. The Eskimo/Indian beauty stayed for a while with the dedicated Sisters of the Holy Cross Order, who patiently taught her how to read, study, pray, and write.

Out of her lucid fond memory of unreliable, materialistic and goal-oriented Neil Bonner, Jees Uck conscientiously learned the rudiments of nursing, medicine and surgery, and the "quick read" later in life had attended to the critical needs of many prospectors and trail-weary journeymen requiring first aid treatment.

And for the next two and a half decades, San Francisco socialite Kitty Bonner had made sure that her wealthy husband generously supported Jees Uck's humanitarian activities in the Yukon, where the native woman received a handsome annual stipend (and later a pension) of five thousand dollars. And finally, Mrs. Bonner encouraged her sometimes-forgetful spouse to make philanthropic financial contributions to the betterment of the education of children in the Yukon and Klondike territories.

And as for the child affectionately named "Neil," Father Champreau took the boy under his personal supervision and guidance. With great pride, Jees Uck received weekly letters sent from the Jesuit College in Baltimore, Maryland, and later from Paris, France, and then from Vatican City in Rome, Italy. The warm correspondence was from her loving son Father Neil, who eventually rose to a very eminent station in his religious order, and who steadfastly exhibited (with noteworthy distinction) all of the worthy qualities, characteristics and virtues that *his* self-indulgent father failed to master.

"The Law of Life"

Old Koskoosh was near death, and the elderly codger was well-aware of the consequences defined by tribal tradition as interpreted among the Eskimos. The needs of those that contributed to the community, and to the clan's welfare, preceded the needs of the individual, particularly those of the faltering aged and infirmed. Over the years, Koskoosh's eyesight had diminished, his hearing was no longer acute, his kidneys were weak and dysfunctional, his skin wrinkled, his pecker shriveled-up, and his loins shrunken and dry. The ancient former chief's vibrant granddaughter Sit-cum-to-ha was harnessing the dogs to the funeral sled, and her thoughts were not on her withered and broken grandfather sitting alone in the snow, forlorn and defenseless. Her troubled mind was focused on other more important concerns. Camp had to be broken, and the long trail awaited their passage, since the short period of energy-giving sunlight would certainly be abbreviated. The 'law of life' governed Sit-cum-to-ha's immediate duties and responsibilities, but death was the only prospect that was predictably imminent to old dependent Koskoosh.

The aged man's mind fondly reviewed his long history as a proud and honored hunter and revered village leader, but now, as his senses had declined, Koskoosh's terrible fate was predetermined. The elderly geezer gingerly felt the pile of wood next to his side, and realized that its existence would probably outlast his. His ears could faintly hear the women in the distance disassembling the hides that had constituted the temporary shelters of the nomadic tribe, and Koskoosh's decrepit mind vaguely visualized that it was time for the clan to follow the migration of the caribou, and move-on to a new temporary destination.

The shaman's voice could be heard barking guttural commands, and the cries of the recently born Koo-tee could also be discerned, the screaming child requiring food and nutrition, but in reality, an infant whose fate would in the future actually parallel old Koskoosh's. Koo-tee was besieged with bug bites, and the irritated bambino had a bad case of very large welts at that. In the bitter end, death stalked anyone and everyone, but its specter being especially imminent at present; the old man and the infant, both now thoroughly incapable of providing for their own personal needs, and thus, being dual burdens, affording little value to the traveling clan.

The whining dogs despised the work and the trail, at least that was Koskoosh's recollection of the past along with his present perception of reality. The hoary patriarch's ears heard the sleds departing one by one, as the 'sentenced by nature' grandfather sat motionless in the freezing snow. But much to the old fellow's comfort, his lone son loyally stayed behind to offer *his* last allegiance.

"Is all well with you?"

"As well as it fuckin' could be as death approaches and encroaches," Koskoosh, resigned to his fate, answered. "I was once in your role, ready to abandon my father, and I did so according to the fucked-up law of the wilderness clan. Now, I know exactly how the fuck my pappy must've felt at that moment, and my restless soul feels the same solitude and the same desolation. Why the fuck couldn't I have been born a rich white man?"

"I'll start your final fire, and I hope your wood lasts long," the compassionate son indicated. "The warmth of the fire will, for a short time, protect you from the cold as long as it lasts. The fire will remind you of your wife; my mother, who was your old flame!"

"Aye, it is snowing, and it is no wonder that my mind is flakey, if you fuckin' get my drift!" the old man attempted jesting to his son. "I remember my father saying those same fucked-up words before I left him behind to die; many meteors, asteroids, hemorrhoids, and also, many suns and moons ago!"

"I now hear the other men are summoning me to follow them," the son apologetically explained. "The hungry hunters have not feasted in a long time; the trail journey is long as *we* must travel fast without you holding back our progress. Such was true in your time, and I'm sure you understand the custom of clan necessity, no matter how fucked-up it all seems and sounds. But still, better you fuckin' perishing than me!"

"I fuckin' understand it, but don't fuckin' like it, when I know it's fuckin' happening to me," melancholy Koskoosh sadly replied. "Don't you get the idea, my son? I'm a degenerate leaf desperately clinging to its vine. Soon, I will fall, and nobody except me gives a shit. My voice is like a weak old woman's words, and my feet are heavy, and I'm more tired than a sex-starved whore after a night of intense humping and pumping. You'd better be on your damned way, to live and hunt another day, so that I can meet my scripted tragic end, with as much dignity as nature will fuckin' allow me."

The old, former tribal chief fathomed that his limited time would decrease in proportion to the duration of the fire's flames. Such was the overriding principal of *that* final inevitable phase of the law of life. Soon, the apathetic frost would take its toll with his feet yielding first, and then the cold and the numbness would dominate his other extremities; the old man's hands followed by his penis, his testicles, and then his head. 'It is easy. All men and women must die and maybe go to the great spirit in the sky, if that myth is not a lot of smelly moose shit; but the missionary people claim it is true, although I have my fuckin' strong doubts,' Koskoosh reasoned. 'But this death shit really hits home when it fuckin' has to happen to *you*, all alone in the frigid ice and freezing snow, and hoping that you die before the next Arctic blizzard fuckin' kills you! If this is the fuckin' meaning of life,' Koskoosh semi-rationally reckoned, 'then life has no fuckin' meaning or purpose at all!'

Koskoosh fully comprehended that nature had no sympathy for the individual, and that its laws in regard to man's existence were strict and unalterable. The laws of instinct and endurance valued the species and the clan over the person next in line who was distinctly designated to die. The strong survive, and the weak perish. The yellow leaf falls, but the green one thrives, but only during its ephemeral time.

The old men that Koskoosh had known as a boy had been acquainted with the old men before them. 'I'm now experiencing what generations of my dumb-shit people have known, honored and stupidly practiced for countless centuries,' the former tribal chief evaluated. 'I have produced a good son, and my name shall carry on through *his* deeds and exploits. I had been a skilled hunter in my youth, but am now being stalked and hunted by Death, and I now know how the prey feels before succumbing to a savage predator,' the dying man contemplated. 'And I had screwed several well-endowed women in my lifetime, but now can't even piss a yellow stream into a wide rock crevice. And those squawking squaws had been left behind with their wood and fires after famine hit the clan, and after their formerly luscious wet, pink cunts had dried-out. I, just like those lousy bitches from years ago, shall pass away like a summer cloud, with my descendants only to be replaced by the next moving cloud. Shit! Why's my memory so fuckin' cloudy?' the weary veteran questioned his mental alertness. 'Why is my fuckin' name Koskoosh and not fuckin' White Cloud?' the old man regretfully considered, as he placed another stick onto the fire and then resumed his lonely, futile meditating.

'Ah yes; the mosquitoes vanish each fall with the first frost, but what kind of brain could a tiny mosquito have? Does it even fuckin' know it's dying? The squirrel and the rabbit realize that they are old and slow, and can no longer outrace their famished enemies, but do those failing creatures have any concept of either death or dying?' And then the old man's thoughts became more morose and macabre. 'I remember leaving my father to die in a similar manner as my present predicament, yes, up in the Klondike Territory. But he passed on to that great hunting ground in the sky before camp was broken without ever fully digesting his last Eskimo Pie; and I had time to bury his body, but then, the hungry wolves dug him up, and consumed everything; flesh, blood, undigested Eskimo Pie, along with his bones! Shit, Great Spirit! Why the fuck was I ever born into this fucked-up world?'

And then the disconsolate, fatigued man thought about past famines, and the loss of his mother, and about how the salmon had not run the river that summer; and how the caribou never migrated through the territory that particular winter; and how only one in ten of the clan survived to hunt, to screw, to reproduce, and then to die. For what end? 'Ah yes,' Koskoosh logically concluded. 'The true meaning of life is to eat, sleep, screw and reproduce. Now I fuckin' get it! Ah yes!' the aged philosopher seriously reflected as if trapped in his own dream. 'There were good times too when the meat was plentiful. I'm fuckin' glad I've not been a dumb-ass vegetarian all these years, or else, I would've died decades ago from either fuckin' starvation or malnutrition! And the dogs were fat and healthy *that* warm July, and the horny women had nice firm breasts and delicious juicy pussies that were very accessible during the entire summertime mating season!'

Other fleeting random memories raced through the apprehensive old man's mind. 'When the men of my clan were fat-stomached and healthy, we then waged war with other neighboring clans, and out of sheer greed, we killed each other for each-others women to screw,' Koskoosh recalled. 'And then there was the amazing time when my friend Zing-ha and I witnessed a pack of hungry, ferocious wolves bring-down a colossal-sized moose, and then Zing-ha got so excited and disoriented that he fell into a deep hole, and when we finally dug him out six months later, my friend was frozen stiff; so, we had to thaw him out and eat him just so that we could survive the hostile winter! The zany son-of-a-bitch tasted pretty good though, I must admit. And I think I had acquired some of his hunting skills after munching on Zing-ha's delectable arms and shoulders! But that fucked-up story about Zing-ha's strange death doesn't seem quite so hilarious right now as it used to sound.'

Koskoosh's erratic psyche then reflected some more about his deceased comrade and trusty companion. 'Ah Yes,' the frail old man remembered as his fuzzy mind forgot all about all aspects of chronological order. 'Zing-ha and I had seen that old bull-moose that could no longer keep-up with the thundering herd, and the herd's patriarch was thus abandoned just like my worthless ass has been presently rejected and discarded. The wolves methodically separated the exhausted moose from his brothers and family, and then had him consumed for their dinner. Holy shit!' Koskoosh hypothesized and imagined. 'The same fuckin' thing might soon happen to me! I might be fuckin' wolfed-down by fierce snarling wolves! I hope I'm not greedily eaten alive just like Zing-ha was! And most of all, Great Spirit; I fear that my limp dick might be the first thing to be bitten-off and chewed right before my very eyes!'

The bloodstained moose had fought valiantly, going-down twice, and regaining its feet in the midst of the snarling and hissing wolves, two of which had been crushed to death by the weight of the falling animal, and subsequently, immediately consumed by their voracious peers. The entire episode had been carefully watched and followed by both Koshkoosh and Zing-ha. "The trail was red with the moose's blood," the two had told the dubious shaman, who in return succinctly declared, "I think both of you' juvenile assholes are hallucinating, because you've together eaten too much of the white man's stale 'chocolate moose' that we had luckily found in a village garbage dumpster, ha, ha, ha!"

'And now, after all of the great things I've done and accomplished for my ungrateful clan, the tribe leaves me out here to die like a sick animal!' Koshkoosh sorrowfully summarized. 'Such is the fucked-up Law of Life that I've helped to perpetuate!'

Then, the former proud chief pondered his adventurous youth and assessed his many contributions to the selfish clan. Koskoosh replenished his dwindling fire with fresh kindling and thought, 'If lazy Sit-cum-to-ha had only been more industrious and had gathered more firewood, I could survive out here on the frontier for another day and a half. But the arrogant, nymphomaniac whore is married to that relentless sex fanatic Beaver, the son of Zing-ha, who is an eager Beaver for my granddaughter's beaver, and every other goddamned hot beaver in the damned clan,' the faltering old man conjectured. 'But how could I envy, fault, or despise 'Eager Beaver', when he's only acting just like Zing-ha and I had done in *our* mutual 'hump and pump' every damned pussy' pasts.'

Momentarily, everything became still as the north winds seemed to cease. The old, shivering patriarch took a deep breath amidst the dreadful, all-encompassing silence. But hark! What was that very distressful rustle his still-perceptive ears were hearing? A great chill shot down his weakened spine. An all-too-familiar howl caught Koskoosh's attention, and the recognized distant noise further depressed his flagging spirit. 'Should I fight like a wild beast? Should I resist certainty as the bull-moose had ineffectively done? Or should I simply rationally accept my hideous fate and surrender to being torn apart and ravenously consumed?'

Soon, the inexorable circle of gray and white fur appeared, and the terrible sniffing and snuffling began, which was soon followed by the characteristic snarling, panting, and slathering dry mouths. Instinctively, the old Eskimo's hand shot towards the fire and grabbed a blazing stick; then desperately waving the contrived weapon in the face of the first suddenly-alarmed wolf, which promptly withdrew its nose from Koskoosh's throat. Several of the less brazen brutes retreated from the dwindling fire, but then soon again advanced, but this second time more audaciously. More fiery sticks were thrust forward and swirled about, but the determined, starving beasts refused to either scatter or disperse. The only inconclusive matter in dispute was which wolf would have the most flesh and muscle to rip apart and swallow.

The old man had now lost all of his desire to continue living. He dropped his burning stick and took one last sigh, voluntarily placing his head between his knees before being eagerly attacked. One last thought dominated Koskoosh's agony, and his anguish, before being devoured: 'I should not resist reality as the bull-moose had done.' Koskoosh accepted the principle of being conquered and defeated by the Law of Life; a covenant of nature that governed both man and beast in that remote Klondike Territory of northwestern Canada.

"To Build a Fire"

Dawn had broken under a cloudy sky, and the self-confident man deviated from the Yukon trail, and climbed up the steep, rocky bank to a higher, but less used pathway that led eastward through the spruce timberland. After ascending the incline and walking along for several hours with his wolf-dog trailing behind, the man inspected his watch and observed that it was already nine o'clock. The absence of the sun made the entire physical environment seem drab and gloomy. But still, the man was determined to persevere.

'In a few more days, the sun will be visible on the southern horizon,' the cocky trekker believed from past experience witnessing similar atmospheric phenomena. 'My fuckin' retarded wolf dog has no concept of the sun, of its function, or of its necessity! The stupid beast is probably much better-off being ignorant of nature and its laws! Basically, it's really all the old reason-versus-instinct bullshit college propaganda, and conversely, I possess the goddamned academic knowledge, and my dunce-dog does not!'

Looking beyond from his lofty vantage point, the observant man saw the mile-wide Yukon River frozen solid with three-foot-thick ice, and several-foot of snow had drifted upon the hard surface. The river's course wound its way around several spruce-laden islands in the same direction as to where the man would meet up with friends later that afternoon, and together, then continue their journey southward. The newcomer to the North stubbornly believed that the icy fifty-degree below-zero temperature was fairly tolerable, and not potentially dangerous to anyone with any element of courage in his character, and any spark of self-reliant determination in his spirit.

'Mittens, ear muffs, warm moccasins, fur hat and coat, flannel shirts, thick socks, and woolen underwear will insulate me from these abnormal elements,' the obstinate man rationally thought. 'But how the freakin' Eskimos ever have wintertime sex up here is far beyond my limited comprehension!'

The man spit some green mucus from his mouth, and was amazed that a sharp explosive crackle occurred when the liquid solidified in the freezing air before ever hitting the snow. 'The boys will be meeting me at Henderson Creek at six o'clock as has been planned,' the tundra ambler recollected. 'In an hour or two, I'll take out a biscuit and have it for lunch. But I'll have to eat that son-of-a-bitch in a hurry before it hardens, just like the spit did in the air. I don't want the hard bite to break my teeth. There aren't too many fuckin' dentists up here on the desolate trail, so I'd better be careful how I use my damned choppers!' the adamant man concluded.

And each biscuit was rich in fatty grease and wrapped in a nourishing slice of *bacon*. 'Not exactly a meal fit for a king, but up here in Northern Canada, it sure beats fuckin' starvation! Although I'd rather eat pussy, the bacon-covered biscuits are definitely more nutritious! I'll just pretend I'm eating Sir Francis, and then the delicious bacon will taste all that much better! Too bad I couldn't be devouring the Earl of Sandwich, too!'

He and his wolf dog maneuvered along the deep snow trail as the man occasionally rubbed his masked nose and cheekbones with his right hand's mitten. 'It's a little uncomfortable out here, but I'll endure,' the determined traveler haughtily convinced himself.

But the wolf dog knew that it had been too cold to be traveling anywhere, even though the animal lacked the arithmetical knowledge that the temperature was actually approaching seventy-five degrees below zero, and not fifty-degrees below as his master had erroneously believed. A hundred and seven degrees below the "frost-point" is an unbearable condition that is hostile to the survival and sustenance of human life. The trailing animal instinctively knew from past experiences with humans that its master should either seek shelter or enter a camp to get warm, and the canine's pea-brain mind wondered why the supposedly more intelligent human the animal was following persisted in struggling his meandering journey through the fierce harsh winds.

Every time the man attempted to expel juice from his chewing tobacco, the fluid would freeze and attach itself to his dangling red beard, because the brown liquid would not shoot-out over his chin onto the ground. In fact, an amber-colored icicle was forming between the man's mouth and chin from the extremely cold Arctic weather. 'This is not the time to give my boots a spit shine, or even a fuckin' brown spit shine!' the audacious fellow thought in an effort to amuse himself. 'Christ! If I was born in Belgium, I'd be even more fuckin' 'phlegm- ish' than I am right now! And this phlegm I'm discharging from my mouth can't possibly remind me of my old kinky girlfriend back in Fairbanks because she was a real spitfire!'

Several miles ahead, the trekker stumbled down a slippery snow embankment and reached the foot of Henderson Creek, a mere ten miles from 'the forks', his next intended rendezvous point. 'Let's see now,' the anxious fellow considered. 'If I average four-miles an hour, I'll arrive at the forks by around two in the afternoon. I'll hold off my stomach pangs until then, and enjoy swallowing-down my bacon-flavored biscuits. Then between six and seven o'clock, I'll meet-up with the boys at the camp and can finally examine some of their wonderful porno' magazines. Shit, I hope they've gotten some new nude centerfolds! Oh well. I'll just keep my current pace and extend the length of my amber icicle beard. Shit, the thing's already twice as long as my dick! But I can't wait to lick it and see if it's root beer flavored.'

But then, the encumbered adventurer noticed that his nose and his cheeks were numb, and that his facial skin no longer felt the sensations of warmth, touch, or pain. 'I'll put-up with these frosty, numb cheeks and numb nose for six more hours. A little discomfort never killed anyone! Shit!' the sufferer realized. 'How will I ever know if I piss myself if my dick becomes numb, too! Oh well; I'll just think about those porno' periodicals over at the camp. They'll keep me movin' on. It's amazing how the power of pussy can motivate a guy to ignore terrible things like fifty-to-sixty degree below zero temperatures out here in the bitter wilderness. If worse comes to worst, I'll just start singing the lyrics to 'Frosty the Snowman' to myself!'

* * * * * * * * * * *

The man's locomotion was not seriously impeded, despite the frigid cold and the high snow accumulation in his path. His awareness knew that although no deep-water creek could avert being frozen over, still, pockets of springs bubbled-out from the warmer hillsides, and the reality existed where the trekker could accidentally fall into a pool of water and drown. Such a horrifying misfortune would mean immediately building a fire to dry-out, and also changing his thick woolen socks to prevent getting frostbitten toes. The covered pools might be three-inches-deep, or perhaps three-feet-deep; the latter representing a life-threatening situation to certainly be avoided.

'I must be careful, because if I fall into a pool of water,' the man thoughtfully evaluated, 'I might as well be authoring my own self-destruction. And I don't need the delay of building a fire, if I could instead use my intelligence and my savvy to avert having to do it. And besides, I strongly desire to continue living, so that I could go back to Fairbanks down in Alaska and hump and pump my old spitfire girlfriend. Now that I've evaded the soft-snow water pool traps, I can resume my four-mile gait. I'm not going to allow nature's obstacles to fuckin' stymie my progress, so sir!'

Two hours later, the advancing man encountered another patch of soft snow that he recognized might be hiding unexposed water pools, so honoring an inspiration, the on-a-mission wanderer decided to make his wolf dog go first, but the beast refused to take an unaccustomed leadership role in the expedition. The man forcefully pushed the dog forward, and its weight suddenly broke through the thin ice, instantly wetting its front paws.

Immediately, the canine licked its paws and instinctively bit-out the ice between its pads; a natural reaction to its need for self-preservation. Fearing a loss of time, the man ripped-off his mitten and quickly helped the animal scrape-off and remove the remaining embedded ice chunks. Realizing that his right hand had become numb in less than a minute of exposure, the man quickly put his mitten back onto his fingers, and then pounded his chest thirty consecutive times to get vital circulation flowing again back into his wrists and knuckles.

At one-thirty in the afternoon, the fatigued trekker arrived at the designated forks to stop and consume his bacon-flavored biscuits, which had been strapped inside a pouch that was concealed underneath his warm fur coat. Again, his exposed fingers became numb at locating and removing his precious food. He then struck his hand two-dozen times against his knee to get the circulation and his feeling sensation going again. Now, the beleaguered traveler realized that his feet were wet, his nose, cheeks and fingers numb, and that perhaps starting a fire would be not only advantageous, but also fully necessary.

'That son-of-a-bitch old geezer back at the lodge at Sulfur Creek knew what the hell he was bullshittin' about when he said that it gets unbearably cold out here in the open country,' Jim Monahan recollected as the trekker continuously stomped his feet and thrashed his arms about as if performing improvised gym class calisthenics.

Using twigs and small branches from nearby spruce trees, the man built a fire to sit beside and then swallow-down his three biscuits while the obedient wolf dog sprawled-out just far enough from the roaring flames to not get its fur singed. After warming his hands and briefly smoking his pipe, the pathfinder speedily pulled on his sealskin mittens, adjusted the flaps of his fur cap over his tender ears, and then proceeded up the left fork trail that paralleled Henderson Creek. But as the middle-aged gent and his dog advanced onward, the canine knew that it was far better to dig a hole in the snow and curl its body into a semicircle to keep warm rather than to be walking along a creek in such hostile weather conditions.

'Ah, no signs of underwater springs on this left fork!' Monahan gratefully assessed. 'I should be able to maintain my schedule and meet the guys before seven. I hope the fuck those zany assholes don't wanna' play strip poker! Oh shit! I've just broken through down to my goddamned knees! That's what the fuck I get for losing my concentration for a second and letting my fucked-up imagination run amok! It's imperative that I lose another damned hour to build another fire or else risk freezing my fingers, toes and dick off!'

At the top of a rocky hill, the frustrated man industriously gathered grasses, twigs, sticks and branches, for time was of the essence. Monahan removed a piece of treasured birch bark from an inner pocket, scraped a match, and fortunately managed to ignite a fire. The Prometheus imitator very methodically fed the flames with dry twigs and grass, and much to his utter elation, the sparks and flames became greater, and soon began to roar.

'When it's more than fifty-degrees-below-zero, there's no room for error,' Jim plausibly concluded. 'If my feet are dry, I can run in the snow for a half a mile and get my blood flowing in my extremities again. But if my feet are wet, I gotta' build a fire and expose them to heat; otherwise, I'll be even worse-off than that famous Venus de Milo statue, having no legs in addition to no fuckin' arms! I must complete my scheduled route without any further complications! I can't get cold feet! Ha, ha, ha,' the man mentally laughed at his moronic cliché. 'No way Joseph; er, I mean, 'No way, Jose'!'

* * * * * * * * * * *

The encumbered man was not used to such severe adversity and realized that he should have adhered more diligently to the old-timer's advice back in Sulfur Creek. 'I gotta' act fast and not fuck-up again!' Jim frantically conjectured. 'It's early March, and I can't be as slow as molasses in January, because damn it, it's even colder now than it fuckin' was two months ago!'

To build his second fire to an appropriate level of heat and power, the pathetic struggler had to remove his mittens, and utilizing his overtaxed brain, Monahan promptly comprehended that his hands, in addition to his fingers, were completely numb; and also, his feet were now objects simply attached to his body. The full force of the swirling wind added more harsh reality to his treacherous dilemma.

'It's so fuckin' cold that I won't know if or when I shit my pants or freeze my balls off!' the perplexed man comprehended while persistently shivering. 'My blood is staying in the center of my body and my arms, legs, and head are feeling the hellish consequences. My skin can feel the loss of blood and all sensation had diminished, but let's hope this fire flourishes, because I don't know if I have the wherewithal to fuckin' start a third one!' Monahan lamented and regretted. 'Now I know. The next time the temperature drops under fifty below, I should stay the fuck under the covers in my bunk bed. Hell, my uncooperative gloved hands can't even feel the twigs that I'm feeding into the fire. Forget screwing my kinky girl down in Fairbanks! Oh, if I could only be alone in my bunk and be jerking-off one final time!'

The man attempted untying his ice-coated boots; however, the strings seemed like rods of straight steel, but upon acknowledging the folly of his actions, the desperate victim of nature drew his sheath knife to sever the strings. But then, an unanticipated fate occurred that would send shock waves from his brain down his spine. Jim had made the crucial mistake of building his fire under a large spruce tree, thinking that twigs and wood would be readily available.

The tree had a tremendous weight of snow upon its boughs. While yanking the fifth twig from the tree, that minor agitation precipitated disaster as a load of heavy snow descended from the top branches, until virtually all of the accumulated debris had descended into a mini-avalanche, and had in five-seconds had extinguished the fire that the determined man had labored so assiduously to ignite. A foot-deep mantle of snow now occupied the space where the benevolent fire had existed, just thirty seconds before.

'The old fuck at Sulfur Creek was absolutely right. I should've been travelin' with another trekker. It's as if my death sentence has just been cruelly announced,' Jim Monahan hypothesized with disgust. 'I'm never gonna' read those porno' magazines at the camp or ever get laid again by my spitfire bitch back in Fairbanks, or by any other horny whore anywhere else! I gotta' try one more time to build this fuckin' fire, but even if I succeed, I'm certain to lose a few fingers and toes to frostbite!'

Monahan gathered some twigs using his two hands, behaving like a primitive machine, but that next endeavor was performed out in the open away from any snow-laden tree branches. Jim could not separate the trigs from the worthless green growth around them, because of the lack of available dexterity in his fingers. All the while, the confused dog sat in wonder at the incompetence of the desperate man, who was ordinarily the skilled fire provider. Monahan then fumbled in his pocket for his second and last piece of birch bark to start the flames, but the gold prospector lacked the motor skills to effectively clutch the hanging tree limb. Realizing that his feet were now also frozen, the man's mind entered a panic-state frenzy.

'I gotta' beat my hands against my sides to get some feeling back into my fingers,' Jim worriedly thought. 'Just look at that dog peacefully lying there, all fuckin' curled-up in a ball; still warm and vibrant! Believe it or not, I would trade places with that dumb animal in a Seattle minute. I think that all-too-comfortable beast has more of a future than I fuckin' do! I can't believe it. I actually envy that furry, complacent son-of-a-bitch, who in reality, was basically really only a little son-of-a-bitch when he was born!'

"For an ephemeral minute, the overwhelmed man enjoyed with satisfaction an excruciating ache in his left hand, briefly indicating that a marvelous sensation again existed there. Jim was able to remove his pack of matches, which unfortunately then fell into the deep snow. Unable to pick the matches up with his numb fingers, Monahan devoted all of his energies on how he could ignite a fire.

Jim again used his two hands as an improvised machine/shovel to grab the elusive pack. Wearing his thick fur mittens, the poor fellow was able to again manipulate his hands like two shovels. Monahan managed to get the entire pack between his palms, and then he awkwardly raised his mittens up to his mouth, which had difficulty in opening because his lips had been ensconced in ice. Then, the overmatched man succeeded in lighting one flare, which then set the entire pack on fire, and burning brimstone soon ascended-up into his nostrils and down into his lungs, causing the man to excessively cough. The burning pack of matches plunged into the snow, and then its accompanying flames quickly faded-out.

* * * * * * * * * * * *

Jim stared avariciously at 'Czar', his curious-but-defensive minded wolf dog. 'You must think that I'm a total asshole if you have any fucked-up concept of what the hell a total asshole is!' Monahan thought during a moment of self-serving amusement. 'Once you realize that I'm dying and am no longer your personal fire provider,' the master visualized and considered, 'you'll sure as taxes and death abandon me as if I was a hard turd that had just dropped-out of your furry asshole.'

The battered man peered again at his bewildered dog, and the master's faltering mind successfully manufactured a fleeting idea. 'That's it!' Jim imagined as he again briefly glanced at Czar shifting his weight back and forth with anxious wistfulness, as the animal rested in the snow. 'The old-timer back at Sulfur Creek had once told me about a man caught in a blizzard who had miraculously killed a caribou, and then crawled inside its partially gutted-out carcass to stay alive until someone accidentally discovered him. That's exactly what I'll have to fuckin' do to survive! I'll try to kill Czar, and then stick my hands into its warm body to get the sensation of feeling back into them. It's my only chance of survival in this goddamned surreal, supernatural, life-or-death raffle that my accursed name has been entered in! I must fuckin' live at Czar's fuckin' expense!'

Monahan beckoned to Czar to come close to him, but the skeptical animal was used to listening to stern, distant commands, and the dog detected fear in Jim's weak voice. The canine's suspicious nature also sensed that ordinary things were out of kilter, and that his relationship with his master had somehow drastically transformed from dominant man and subordinate beast to something else more primitive.

Czar's ears flattened as the dubious animal ignored the man's feeble solicitations. Jim then got-down on his hands and knees, and very slowly crawled towards his furry companion, but again becoming wary and apprehensive, Czar slowly sidled away. The thwarted master then became cognizant of one important fact: he must rise to his feet and tower over the wolf dog if he expected Czar to obey his commands in any way, thus rendering his allegiance to his master. 'If I don't watch myself, I might somehow weirdly become a serf to Czar in a power-structure reversal of roles!'

After achieving the arduous act of standing erect, Jim had to wait a moment to verify that he was indeed in a vertical position, perpendicular to the ground; his energy reserve was rapidly sapping, and Monahan had no distinct feeling in his legs, feet or toes. The exhausted man attempted clutching the dog's neck, but instead, Jim collapsed upon the animal, endeavoring to either strangle or smother Czar beneath the weight of his body. All the while, the surprised dog snarled, whined, and struggled.

'If only I had the coordination and the strength to stab Czar with my sheath knife,' Jim thought during his mental and physical mania. With virtually all of his stamina expired, the physically spent man released the wolf dog from his greedy grasp. The creature wildly plunged away with its tail curved between its hind legs, panting heavily between snarls. Then Czar, with his ears pricked forward, halted a safe distance of forty feet away from Jim to then survey the man and his miserable plight. The dog's keen instincts detected weakness and craziness, and Czar did not value either strange entity.

Jim looked-down at his gloved hands in order to accurately locate them, and was surprised to see his wrists still attached to his dangling arms. 'I've never before had to use my fuckin' eyes to find out where my goddamned hands are,' the grieving man's mind fancifully thought. 'I'm just as doomed as the last asshole standing at the Alamo had been doomed!'

For five whole minutes, Monahan violently pounded his hands against his knees, and his heart was able to eventually pump enough blood to temporarily make his persistent shivering cease. But still, his extremities remained frozen and numb. 'Even my hard head is feeling no damned sensation. I'm truly the epitome of a human *numb*skull!' Jim mused. 'I'm no longer afraid of having my damned fingers and toes amputated! I'm now dreading the thought of losing my whole friggin' life! I swear there is no paradise, but I fuckin' pray there isn't any goddamned hell!'

Out of sheer desperation, Jim attempted to jog toward the logging camp, situated several miles distant, and the now-cautious Czar reluctantly and subserviently followed his trail. As the disoriented man floundered and staggered forward, his eyes perceived certain familiar objects that gave him renewed strength: the banks of the creek, the timber jams, the leafless aspens, the spruce trees and finally, the dull gray sky. 'Fuck. If I'm not careful, I might soon be stiff and dead, just like I want my useless pecker *not* to be!' Monahan poignantly assessed. 'I must make it to the camp before some carnivorous, nocturnal animal finds me. Even if I lose part of my face, hand, feet and ass,' the man decided, 'I don't honestly give a diarrhea shit! I gotta' somehow endure this awful mess and write a goddamned novel about it!'

Jim was both astonished and confused that his heavy legs could run at all on feet that were so terribly abused and so horribly frozen. The weight of his body was now indiscernible to his mind's perception. Monahan's feet had no relationship to the solid earth and thick ice, as his tottering body advanced, skimmed and slid ahead.

'I must not fall!' his stressed-out brain kept registering and reviewing. 'I wonder if that winged-helmeted Greek god Mercury could move as fuckin' swiftly as I'm moving now! And as for that fucked-up son-of-a-bitch bastard Prometheus, where the fuck is *he* when I really fuckin' need his services the most!' Jim illogically hallucinated. 'Why the fuck couldn't I be lost in the steaming hot Amazon jungle! At least I wouldn't be fuckin' freezing to death up here in nature's gigantic ice box! Shit!' Monahan realized during a moment of elevated frustration. 'I gotta' make sure I don't lose my balance tripping-over a goddamned crocodile or giant anaconda! Jesus Christ!' the hallucinating trekker imagined. 'I'd rather be nailed to a cross on Calvary than to mentally and physically suffer like this! I don't have the endurance to survive another mile!' the defeated man sobbed. 'My only fuckin' hope is to be found by the boys! But they're all egotistical, self-indulgent assholes! I'll bet they're all reading their fucked-up porno' magazines in their warm bunks, and looking at pictures of nude crocodile and anaconda centerfolds! Am I becoming fucked-up, or what?'

Then, the negative, pessimistic thought of his frozen arms and legs extending their numbness that was advancing to his chest and abdomen horrified Jim as the victim valiantly staggered onward. 'I'm more fuckin' afraid of panicking than of fuckin' dying!' the brave man concluded. 'I want to walk, but actually I need to run! Shit! When I used to play baseball in my youth back in Portland, Oregon, I used to walk all the fuckin' time!'

Jim abruptly fell to the ground with a thud, and Czar parked his gray and white furry body ten feet in front of the frenetic victim, as if deliberately taunting him and his futility. The warmth and security of the animal angered the jealous man, now wishing that Czar was a ferocious crocodile or a ravenous anaconda seeking to devour a near-frozen human being.

'I'm gradually losing my battle with the frost!' Jim academically reckoned. 'Why the fuck couldn't I have been a soldier at Gettysburg, or a frontiersman at the Alamo, and died battling other humans rather than being defeated by a goddamned, relentless, mean-spirited bitch named Mother Nature?'

Then, a certain peculiar simile entered the disenchanted man's distorted and disarrayed mind. 'I must sit-up and meet death with some degree of dignity. No sense in running around like a chicken without a head, because I'm not a goddamned chicken, even though I can't feel or even touch my goddamned head, or even the head of my limp and shriveled dick!'

Monahan stoically decided that he must encounter death decently and peacefully by going off to sleep, and then subconsciously surrendering his will to live. That imagined scenario appeared to be the best solution: to use sleep as an anesthetic, since the sensation of pain had been reduced to a mere conceptual fantasy, devoid of reality. Jim's last thought was his ghost accompanying his concerned friends, and together, the quartet discovering his frozen body lying motionless upon the uncaring tundra. The man's spirit had been persuaded by his diminishing will to abandon its imprisonment and exit his body in pursuit of its predestined place in the invisible Universe.

In his final thought, Jim's erratic mind conjured-up an image of the old-timer at Sulfur Creek being the immortal God-the-Father sitting upon his Olympian-like golden throne inside His marble palace in the center of Heaven. The dead man's initial words to his omnipotent Deity would be, 'You were right, Old Boss! I should've had a strong fellow along with me on the wilderness trail. You're always right and quite truthfully, omnipotent God; Your damned ubiquitous, eternal wisdom makes me want to puke!'

Gradually, Jim dozed-off into the most comfortable and satisfying sleep that is humanly possible, lying on even the softest and most desirable bed mattress. The puzzled dog sat restlessly, waiting for his master to awaken and to remember to ignite another warm fire. But the man's soul, half-Mercury and half-Prometheus, had peacefully journeyed into the afterlife. As the twilight drew closer, and dusk was imminent, Jim Monahan did not stir from his sitting position, having his head loosely bowed between his knees. The silence was quite extraordinary, and particularly alien to the confused animal's prior experiences.

A half-hour later, Czar wined loudly, and then aggressively yawned. The furry creature crept closer to its former master, and its superior nose smelled the scent of death. The baffled animal instantly bristled its fur, recoiled, and then backed-away in momentary confusion. A short interval of time elapsed, and then Czar howled under the canopy of night stars that had appeared overhead, coincidentally and inadvertently growling-up at Canis Major.

And finally, out of despair and disappointment, Czar turned and trotted-up the trail in the direction of the camp that his limited brain had memorized in a sort of biological map. From its knowledge of the local terrain, the wolf dog knew exactly where the other fire providers could be easily discovered.

"The Story of Keesh"

When I first heard the name Jack London (1876-1916) as an eighth-grade student attending a Levittown, Pennsylvania parochial school, I naively believed that the famous author was from England. London was born and raised in abject poverty in San Francisco. Although he resented formal education, Jack London was an avid reader and a frequent visitor to the local public library. As a roving teenager, Jack lived a rather unorthodox lifestyle where the adventurer was an oyster pirate, a sailor, a tramp, and the itinerant youth eventually wound-up in jail on vagrancy charges.

Jack London ought to be admired as a role model for young people, because he turned his life around full circle. He took night courses at the *University of California*, studied literature, and developed a respectable vocabulary. The reformed young man soon got caught-up in the Alaska gold rush fever. The avid reader didn't find gold nuggets up in the Klondike and in the Yukon, but he found something as good as gold if not better than the precious ore: Jack London discovered a wealth of material, settings, themes and characters to construct and support imaginative plots for wonderful novels and novellas.

The versatile author refined the writing technique known today as "Realism", and that very evident quality is reflected in his major novels like *The Call of the Wild* and *White Fang*. Most of Jack London's tales are about strong men, or animals, and their instinct to survive in very harsh environments. Realism is also definitely apparent in London's classic short fiction works such as "Love of Life," "To Build a Fire" and "The Story of Keesh".

Keesh was an Eskimo boy, who never in his life made or sold an Eskimo Pie or a Klondike Bar to anyone. Through courage and wisdom, the audacious youth ascended to the position of village chief, despite opposition from senile village elders, and jealous village rivals and hunters. By demonstrating steadfast virtue and an indomitable will, the proud lad was able to advance from the most-humble igloo in the village to becoming the most prosperous clansman. Here's how this incredible bullshit all happened.

Keesh was a bright boy, who sometimes glowed in the dark. At age thirteen, the healthy, strong lad had seen "thirteen suns", but not all at the same time during the same year. That's the terminology his Eskimo clan used in their native village to describe thirteen years, so naturally, the inhabitants probably also must have called the sun "a year", if they called a year "a sun".

Keesh's Eskimo elders were totally fucked-up. That's why he had to straighten all of the stupid assholes out, so that the proper things could be called the proper words and names; some of which might also have been proper nouns that were *commonly* used, and common nouns that were *improperly* used.

Keesh's father, Bok, had been a valiant fellow that had died during a *grave famine* when all the graves in the icy cemetery had starved to death. Bok sought to save the weaker members of the village by setting-out to hunt and kill a great polar bear, but unfortunately, the great dark beer drinker never came *bok*.

Keesh was Bok's only son, and over the years, the people forgot about Bok's bravery, so the proud boy and his poor indigent mother were demoted in rank to live in the village's smallest and most shabby, dirty-iced, small-assed, ghetto igloo. The igloo was made out of ice cubes from an ancient icebox, rather than constructed out of traditional large, carved, rectangular ice blocks as was the norm according to Eskimo construction codes. Keesh was pretty pissed-off about his relegation to the lowest social and economic echelon in the Eskimo community, which incidentally, also included the fucked-up Eskimo gay and lesbian community.

A council meeting in the big igloo of Chief Klosh-Kwan was rudely interrupted by a complaint from an angry upstart sitting in the rear. Keesh rose to his feet, showing the strong dignity of an elder, and demanded to be heard amidst the babble of a chorus of critical, condescending voices.

"Oh, great Klosh-Kwan," the acne-faced juvenile began his oratory. "The meat my mother and I have been apportioned has entirely too much fat, too much gristle, and too many bones. Hell, I demand better quality meat, and make 'no bones' about it. Know what the frig' I'm bitchin' about!"

The grizzled, elder, veteran hunters were appalled and aghast at Keesh's confident attitude, which the senile idiots interpreted as brash brazenness. The council lawmakers were perturbed that an audacious young punk pretending to be a man was attempting to arbitrarily break their balls in front of the entire Eskimo community, which included the fucked-up Eskimo gay and lesbian sub-community.

"Who is this impudent child that talks like a man?" one councilman asked. "He has absolutely no reputation as a skilled hunter, nor any track record as a proven scout. Sit-down Macho Boy, before we throw your ass out of the big igloo, and ostracize you from the entire Eskimo village, including banishment from the influential gay and lesbian village people, along with other less powerful heterosexual village idiots!"

Keesh was undaunted by the sudden outburst of criticism directed against him, so the lad stubbornly continued with his grievance. "I've heard from many of you demented charlatans that my father Bok was a fantastic hunter. It's said that Bok brought back to the village twice as much meat to share than any two other hunters combined. And it's also reputed that my father also knew how to beat his meat better than anyone else in this clan," Keesh reminded his disinterested listeners. "And Bok would then generously give his meat to the old toothless women of the village to suck on!"

"Nay, nay!" the old prune-faced men on the council *neighed* like discontented horses. "Put the disrespectful delinquent out of our company!" and "Send the infant wanna'-be back to his crib!" is what the incensed crowd boisterously yelled. "No man would ever insult the long graybeards as this lazy, juvenile punk delinquent is attempting to do!"

Keesh patiently waited for the assembly's clamor and the elders' protests to calm-down. Then, the determined lad incisively continued his critique, much to the chagrin of his already-peeved adult audience. "Ugh-Gluk," the Eskimo adolescent said to one of the humiliated hunters smugly sitting on the council. "Thou hast a wife, and for her do you speak."

"That's right!" The old man sitting in the assembly hollered-out. "Ugh-Gluk has some *ugly luck* with both married and unmarried squaws. Ha, ha, ha!"

"The old coot's insulted wife punched him squarely in the face as Klosh-Kwan banged his two hunting spears together to reestablish order above the hoots and jeers of the assembled crowd inside *his* huge igloo. Then, the wise old chief motioned for Keesh to continue his brazen oratory.

"And thou, Massuk; you have a mother, and for her do you speak. My mother has no one to speak on her behalf, except me, so that's why the hell I'm here," Keesh boldly declared. "Bok is dead because he hunted too fanatically for the benefit of others, who have now regrettably forgotten his glory," Keesh emphasized for everyone's consideration. "So based on my father's great contributions to this community, including the fucked-up gay and lesbian sub-community," the teenager cautiously proceeded, "I insist that my mom Ikeega and I be given better meat as long as this tribe has a plentiful supply. I, Keesh, the son of Bok and of Ikeega, have spoken. I say this just in case some of you deaf sons of bitches, seated on the other side of the igloo, and some of you deaf and dumb sons of bitches, whose smelly asses sit on the council, were wondering what the hell I was doing when I was moving my mouth and jaws!"

The brash kid sat-down in a huff with his ears perceiving the abundant dissension and commotion that his stinging words had generated. Keesh then alertly absorbed the intense, malignant harangue being channeled in his direction.

"That ungrateful boy talks disease out of his ass and shits out of his unwise mouth!" Ugh-Gluk mumbled to Massuk. "Let's face the music Massuk. Keesh is a sick, young, walrus pup trying to *seal* an easy life for his big fat cow mommy, and also for Keesh'! Ha, ha, ha!" Ugh-Gluk robustly laughed. "Massuk; tell that ambitious roughneck to fuck-off and quickly leave the council's igloo, so that we can conduct our important business!"

"Fellow Eskimos, shall the babes in arms tell us veteran, experienced men how we must distribute meat?" Massuk implored those parents still grumbling in the general attendance. "If Keesh was to have more meat, tell him to live in a 'porterhouse' instead of in the smallest igloo in Alaska! Ha, ha, ha!"

The entire assemblage. with the exception of saddened Ikeega, mocked and jeered Keesh's brashness. After order had again been restored, Klosh-Kwan commanded Keesh to bed to have 'white dreams' of delicious polar bear carcasses. "You shall have scheduled beatings administered to you by the council's administrators!" the livid Chief thundered at Keesh. "You're a most rambunctious, presumptuous, little tyrant, whose all-too-thin hide needs to be tanned! Have *you* no modesty or humility?"

Keesh's eyes flashed with heightened anger, and the blood in his veins, arteries and capillaries boiled. The defiant, very young prodigy/progeny jumped to his feet to challenge the council's supreme adult authority, all happening before the entire appalled village population. "Hear me speak, elderly retards and pedophiles!" the youth hostilely replied. "These are my last words to you. Bok was a great hunter. I, his son, shall prove to be a great hunter, also. I shall go and hunt the meat I shall eat without your goddamned, unjust welfare system, and I shall divide my meat and apportion it fairly," the agitated lad boldly stated. "First, I shall share my meat with widows whose husbands have been killed. Secondly, I shall share my meat with the mothers whose sons are dead; and thirdly, I shall give my meat to the impotent old men that sit on council and can go longer get erections or shoot an ounce of sperm juice. And I predict," Ikeega's son loudly communicated, "that in the days to come, the gluttonous, fat old men that arrogantly sit on this sham council shall know the meaning of the word 'shame' without the aid or use of a dictionary! I, Keesh, have spoken."

"You ain't gonna' screw me up the ass, you arrogant, piss-ant mother-fucker!" Massuk yelled at the audacious upstart, like a raving maniac. "Just come over here and suck my dick to see exactly how *impotent* I am in this damned village!"

Keesh did not answer Massuk's degrading insult, because the youth had told everyone at the meeting that he had spoken all he had wished to say. Jeers and abundant scorn filled his ears as the mocked lad abruptly left the meeting with his head raised high. Keesh's jaw was set tight, for the teen Eskimo looked neither left nor right as he silently battled his sudden lockjaw attack.

The next morning, the determined boy trekked along the coastline where the sea's ice met the hard frozen land. Several elders had witnessed him leaving the village with his bow, a handful of bone-barbed arrows, his father's enormous hunting spear, and a bulging hard-on sticking out from his thigh-length fur coat, which was made from the skin of Bok's last polar bear kill.

Never before had a thirteen-year-old fledgling gone-out to hunt, let alone gone out to hunt all by his lonesome. Many horny women stared with pity in their hearts at Ikeega, whose facial expression reflected both grimness and melancholy. "He'll be back before long, Ikeega," the considerate women encouraged their disconsolate, grieving friend. "He'll become tired, and return to the village, and eventually learn to curb his rash tongue. Your obstinate son is rebelling against a gross injustice, and blaming it all on adult authority."

"Let the junior jerk-off go; let him learn the meaning of 'disgrace' *without* the aid of an elementary school dictionary," the hunters laughed while mimicking Keesh's council meeting presentation. "And the callow wise-ass will come back soft of tongue and meek in speech, and he'll finally respect the wisdom of his sage elders; that young punk, double-fuck!"

And three days passed with strong gales and ten inches of snow, but there was no sign of Keesh. Ikeega pulled-out her hair, and smeared soot all over her face as tokens of sorrow, symbolically telling everyone it was better to do that than to smear soot onto her scalp, and to pull her face off. The village women all openly criticized their husbands for mistreating the haughty, naughty boy at the council meeting, and the clever wives cut-off their spouses' sex lives, and no longer sucked their partners' dicks, telling their husbands that those practices would only be resumed when the women could eat and enjoy Keesh's meat. The men of the village felt guilty, and were totally pissed-off by the stubborn women's statements, so the adult males reluctantly organized search parties to track-down and find the adamant, opinionated "lost boy".

On the fourth morning, Keesh entered the village, but the boy was wearing a cheerful, confident face. A bountiful supply of freshly killed meat was carried across his shoulders. Ikeega's son had triumphantly returned, and his success gave his militant personality a new-found cockiness.

"Go ye' men with your dog sledges, and travel my trail for a full day," the "Macho Boy" commanded the astonished residents, which included the gay and bisexual village people. "I've left much meat on the ice. A she-bear and two cubs."

Ikeega was filled with happiness at her son's apparent good fortune, and at his safe completion of his daring one-boy expedition. "Come Ikeega; let us eat meat inside our tiny, little igloo. After that, I shall sleep, for I'm quite exhausted from beating my meat out there on the cold ice!" Keesh suggested and confessed. "In the future, I'll have that ugly bastard Massuk pound my meat so that I can conserve my energy for future hunting expeditions!"

'Oh boy,' Ikeega proudly thought. 'Now Keesh will become rich and will give me enough money to open a village furniture store!'

Much discussion and debate abounded throughout the small tribal village concerning Keesh and his "lucky hunting foray". The killing of a she-bear attending to her cubs was very dangerous, considering *her* inbred maternal instinct to protect her young. The men could not believe that Keesh was a better hunter than *they* were, but the knuckleheads were glad that the youngster had come back, because now the jerk-offs could again receive decent sex and stimulating blowjobs from their sometimes-faithful wives, who actually preferred lesbian homosexuality to heterosexual activity with their marital partners. So, the grumbling men departed the village to retrieve the polar bear kills, remembering their wives' familiar refrains, "No sex or blowjobs until you retrieve and finally return with Keesh's fabulous meat!"

In northern Alaska, it was imperative that the polar bear carcasses be located as soon as possible. Wild animals in search of scarce food might discover the remains, or the exposed meat could freeze so solidly that it could break even the sharpest cutting knife. A three-hundred-pound polar bear is not easy to lift and deposit onto a sled when it is frozen-solid *dead weight*. But when the recovery team eventually reached the dead animals' location, the searchers observed that Keesh had already neatly and impressively quartered the prey in true hunter practice.

Keesh's mysterious hunting prowess became more and more evident with the passing weeks. On his second mission, the wonder boy killed a nearly adult-sized male bear, and on his third expedition into the Alaskan wilderness, a male and its female companion were slain. Both of those remarkable exploits had been condensed into rather short three-or-four-day journeys that Keesh had conducted into the snow-covered, frontier barrens.

"How does he do it?" the very concerned Massuk asked Ugh-Gluk. "He never takes dogs with him, and certainly, dogs can be of great assistance. I believe that Keesh is possessed."

"Daaa, I don't know!" the over-challenged Ugh-Gluk replied. "Daa, I don't know!" the old senile fool reiterated.

"Let's ask the lucky punk about this good-luck skein he's been on!" Klosh-Kwan chimed-in. "And let me do all the talking, you two old stupid jerk offs!"

The three decrepit council members ate humble pie (which is not as tasty as hair pie), and approached the valiant Keesh standing outside his humble igloo. "Why do you hunt only polar bear, Keesh?" Klosh-Kwan curiously asked. "Why not also go after Christmas and Easter Seals, and also sea lions?"

Keesh contemplated Klosh-Kwan's motivation for wanting to ask such a silly, damned, asinine question, and then the lad illustriously responded, "Are you three, ancient, cretin, stupid assholes, or what?" the teen scolded his elders. "Every Eskimo from here to the North Pole knows that there's more meat on a polar bear than on a seal, or on the kind of sea lions that frequent this God-forsaken part of the known world!"

"I think you practice witchcraft!" Massuk openly accused Keesh. "You hunt with evil spirits that gladly help you in exchange for selling your soul! You are an evil sorcerer!"

"Maybe the spirits that help me are good ones and not evil ones," Keesh alertly challenged. "Maybe my noble father's spirit is expertly guiding me, and allowing me to attain excellence and tribal reward through *his* fine example and wisdom."

"I think you beat and have pounded your meat too much!" Massuk criticized his young adversary. "That's exactly your fuckin' problem! You beat your meat too much! Ha, ha, ha!"

"At least I have meat that can be pounded!" Keesh smartly answered his narrow-minded opponent, whose last valid erection was on his eightieth birthday three decades before.

Keesh's accumulative kill production was quite prolific by Eskimo standards. The lesser skilled hunters were kept busy going-out and hauling in sleds full of polar bear carcasses. Just as Bok had done before him, Keesh's distribution of the meat was fair, and the village elders became extremely pissed-off when the popular boy became the first official Eskimo meat distributor getting advanced orders from neighboring villages.

The teenager was both just and democratic in his allocations, providing the least of the women and the weakest of the grandfathers (not on the council) with abundant portions. The lad was achieving great prestige and honor from his peers, along with recognition from the women, and many knowledgeable gossipers predicted that Keesh would replace ancient Klosh-Kwan as the village chief. But the obstinate boy remembered his promise, and never returned to the village council until Keesh would be invited by the bullshitting ruling elders to share *his* unique experiences, his expertise, and his precocious philosophy about village affairs. The sanctimonious, bureaucratic, senile elders were too proud and too ashamed to publicly compromise, relent, and invite the impetuous boy to address them in council.

One morning, in the center of the icy village, Keesh confronted Klosh-Kwan, Ugh-Gluk and Massuk, who were eagerly looking for a fourth member to sing bass to form a sort of un-harmonious Eskimo barbershop quartet.

"I'm considering constructing an igloo," Keesh began his oral statement. "And it shall be a very tremendous igloo to accommodate my mother Ikeega, and also my super-big ego. In fact, you wrinkled old farts; it'll definitely be the largest and most spectacular igloo in the whole damned village."

"Ay!" the three nodded in amazement. "Ay!" they hypnotically repeated and nodded.

"Ay! Ay! Ay!" Klosh-Kwan exclaimed. "Ay, Ay, *I* wish I was in *Dixie,* hooray, hooray, In Dixieland I'll take my stand, to live and die in *Dixie!*"

"Away, away, away down south in *Dixie!*" Massuk and Ugh-Gluk idiotically joined-in with Klosh-Kwan, to further aggravate their principal nemesis.

"Stop this crazy nonsense right now!" Keesh indignantly yelled. After silence reigned supreme, the boy continued his braggadocio-type monologue. "But I have no time to build my igloo because of my scheduled commitment set aside for hunting polar bear meat for the entire village," Keesh boastfully maintained. "I recommend that the old men and widows that eat my meat should construct my huge igloo during my absence."

And much to the council elders' humiliation, a week later the giant iced edifice was almost completed and being constructed to Keesh's strict specifications, and the huge structure was especially designed to be three times as massive as Klosh-Kwan's meeting hall. The spacious home was the first material comfort Ikeega would experience since the death of Bok, who according to village scuttlebutt, only came *bok* as a benign spirit, assisting Keesh in *his* celebrated hunting exploits.

Keesh's mother also earned admiration and recognition from the other village women, and Ikeega became the First Lady of the settlement, despite the fact that the place had no President, and that her husband was deceased. Many squaws asked the matriarch's sage advice on sensitive female matters like dealing with menstruation, and having multiple sex partners, and Ikeega competently showed the other women how to masturbate like crazy using both hands, and how to use a whalebone dildo to achieve multiple orgasms when not engaged in formerly forbidden lesbian sex.

One day, Klosh-Kwan, Massuk, and Ugh-Gluk accosted Keesh in front of the youngster's work-in-progress, almost completed igloo. The three elders appeared rather annoyed and in prosecutorial moods, despite the fact that the trio had recently found a talented bass singer to complement the correct rhythm for their inharmonious Eskimo barbershop quartet.

"What's this shit about a new culinary sensation being attributed to you?" Klosh-Kwan jealously asked the Eskimo boy prodigy. "Stop stealin' our fuckin' thunder!"

"My new eating delight is when a person puts seven slabs of polar bear meat on a skinny stick, and flame broils the flesh over a fire," the now-famous young hunter gloated. "Ikeega calls the new fabulous dish Eskimo *Keesh-ka-bob*!"

"It is charged," Ugh-Gluk yelled, deliberately changing the topic of conversation, "that thou Keesh dealest with an evil spirit; wherefore thou hunting expeditions are rewarded by dead demon shamans with plentiful polar bear meat."

"There is 'spirit' involved," Keesh readily acknowledged, "but it's not an evil spirit. When I see a polar bear about to attack me, I simply *spear-it!* Ha, ha, ha! Get it! Spear-it, ha, ha, ha!"

"Don't give us any of your polar bear comedy shit, or we'll excommunicate you from the village!" Massuk sternly warned his young formidable enemy. "Your new ice house is probably held together by E-glue, because types A, B, C and D glue were ineffective."

"Is not the meat good that I give you?" Keesh objected while getting back on subject. "Has anyone in our village taken sick from eating it? Is your accusation of witchcraft being involved in my skill a slick cover-up for the envy and jealousy that consumes your black, selfish souls?"

"That's enough out of you; you disrespectful, insolent, walrus pup!" Klosh-Kwan admonished the proud youth. "Keep your nasty fucked-up thoughts to yourself!"

"You three senile, deranged, stupid shits can *Keesh* my smooth, white Eskimo ass!" the boy-prodigy-genius quite vehemently and contemptuously answered his mortified superiors.

And the three elder councilmen fearfully withdrew from Keesh's illustrious company with their hands trembling, and the gossipy eavesdropping village women intensively snickered at the "three charlatans" failure to effectively intimidate the emboldened lad. At a council caucus meeting, the trio of embarrassed elders asked for "suggestions from the ice" on how to deal with Keesh's blatant defiance of their authority.

After much discussion, it was finally decided to send four scouts out on patrol to spy on Keesh, and to see if witchcraft was indeed associated with his sinister hunting activities, or if skill was the dominant factor responsible for the boy's uncanny success. Four crafty hunters, Bim, Brim, Baum and Bum were assigned to trail the boy wonder into the icy wilderness, and then report back to the pissed-off council elders precisely what they had witnessed.

Five days later, the four fatigued spies re-entered the shabby village and addressed a closed-session of the council. Their eyes were bulging out of their sockets, and the neurotic men's hands were shaking as if each spy had contracted Parkinson's disease during the five-day absence. Klosh-Kwan requested that one of the four hunters step forward to the front table, and then orally review exactly what the spy had personally observed.

Bim reluctantly approached the elders seated behind a rudely fabricated table made from timber imported to the northern tundra from the Alaskan taiga forests. "Aged Brothers; the four of us had done as commanded by the council. We cunningly trailed Keesh, and we did it so secretly that he never suspected our furtive presence, our eyes scrutinizing his every move," Bim prefaced.

"Get to the point, or we'll have Bum tell us what the fuck happened!" Klosh-Kwan characteristically chastised the all-too-vociferous, gossiping villager. "You have a shit-mouthed tendency to prevaricate and equivocate!"

"Well, midway in the first day, Keesh encountered a ferocious large bear with teeth longer than Bum's dick!" Bim cockily asserted.

"I've never seen such a gargantuan bear in my entire life!" Baum verified. "But the amazing thing was that although provoked by Keesh's spear, the monster refused to fight him. It all was quite fuckin' extraordinary to witness, to say the least."

"And what transpired next?" Massuk demanded to know. "Make it short and sweet, just like Bum's abbreviated dick. I gotta' leave the meeting soon, Bim. It's almost time for my ugly wife to give me my nightly enema."

"The strange-acting bear turned and moped slowly over the ice," Bim elaborated with mild excitement. "And Keesh chased after the beast, which became very much unafraid. And the obnoxious boy shouted insults at the great brute, which just ignored the dumb kid's nasty comments. Some jerks get all the friggin' luck!"

"And then," Brim enthusiastically interrupted Bim. "The bear became so antagonized that it stood-up on its hind legs and growled fiercely. But Keesh stepped right up to the giant polar bear as if it were a baby seal pup."

"Next," interrupted a very nervous and stuttering Baum, "Keesh ran-up to the enraged, ferocious bear, and prodded him with his father's magical spear. I thought that the asshole must be insane to be acting so aggressively!"

"Ah, witchcraft!" Ugh-Gluk surmised and exclaimed. "The little bastard was using witchcraft! The spear is bewitched! I knew all along that *he* was fuckin' communing with evil spirits!"

"Perhaps!" Baum continued and acknowledged. "Keesh then ran away, and the aggravated mammoth bear took-off in pursuit of his ass. But Keesh then dropped a little red round ball upon the slippery ice, and the mammoth bear amazingly stopped, smelled it, and finally chewed and swallowed the circular sphere!" Baum exclaimed. "And then Keesh dashed-away some more, and dropped his balls all over the ground, and the irate bear continued to devour them."

"What are you four fucked-up simpletons expecting us to believe?" Massuk incredulously asked. "Are you four assholes fuckin' delusional or what? I think the four of you neurotic, imbecilic cunt-lappers are infected with evil spirits, too!"

"We all saw it with our own eyes!" Bim confirmed.

"With our own eyes!" Bum corroborated.

"With our own eyes!" Brim affirmed.

"With our own eyes!" Baum verified.

"Fuck your own eyes!" Klosh-Kwan boisterously derided. "Your eyes can only behold evil witchcraft, and nothing else!"

"But eminent elders," Baum facetiously answered. "This red-ball activity continued until the immense polar bear stood erect, cried-out in agony, and then thrashed its forepaws wildly about as if it was going absolutely crazy. The lunatic bear paid no attention to Keesh as it growled and groaned in excruciating pain," Baum added. "The goddamned polar bear became very weak and exhausted, rolled over on its back, and then seemed to beg Keesh to kill it, which he soon accomplished with his father's bewitched, supernatural spear."

"The spear was a charm! It was an evil object not intended for Eskimo use in this accursed world!" Ugh-Gluk exclaimed. "The spear definitely belongs to an evil sorcerer! A fuckin' shaman of the forbidden black arts!"

"Exactly what happened after Keesh killed the bear with Bok's haunted spear?" Klosh-Kwan insisted on learning.

"When we left the incredible scene," Bim summarized almost out of breath, "Keesh was preoccupied skinning the bear, so we came sprinting back to the village in record time to accurately reveal the unearthly truths that we had witnessed."

"All four of you shit-head clowns, get the fuck outa' here right this instant!" incensed Klosh-Kwan nastily screamed. "Besides sucking Keesh's dick, you four assholes must also eat his little red balls, too!"

That afternoon, the humble women of the village all earnestly pounded Keesh's meat, while their aggravated husbands attended an emergency council session in Klosh-Kwan's igloo; now the second largest ice building in the whole damned village. A courier was dispatched to Keesh, ordering the vernal hunter to attend the important meeting, and of course, the young man considered and then declined to go, even though he believed "the order" was "an invitation" by the elders to formally address the council. "I'm too tired and hungry this time," the polar bear killer told the shocked and disappointed messenger. "But my new igloo is the largest in the village and can easily accommodate all of the councilmen, along with the gay and lesbian sub-community," the kid just entering puberty shrewdly answered, effectively breaking everybody else's testicles and tits.

Klosh-Kwan and the others were so curious about inspecting Keesh's new igloo that the ignoramuses all got their asses up and paced over to the recently-constructed "Ice Palace". Keesh was busy eating his one-man banquet, but the lad took the time to welcome the elders and the rest of the 'rank' and file clan, and next seated them according to their positions of importance. Ikeega was proud of her son's evident haughtiness, and the loyal mother became the hostess with the most flair, going around the tremendous-sized igloo and cordially serving everyone delicious Eskimo pies without any pubic hairs in them.

During the formal council meeting, Klosh-Kwan presented the testimonies of Bim, Brim, Baum and Bum. "So, young Keesh," the tribal chief concluded and articulated. "I believe that an explanation of your fantastic activities is indeed warranted. Describe to our village people, Macho Boy, your secret method of hunting polar bears. Is there any witchcraft or evil spirits involved?"

Everyone listened intently for Keesh's explicit accountability. "Nay, old Klosh-Kwan," the lad nonchalantly answered. "A boy, such as I, knows little about witches or about the forbidden black arts. I have but cleverly developed a means to successfully kill ice bears. I assure you, Mighty Assholes perched on the council, my genuine hunting methods involve good head-craft, and not evil witchcraft as you presume."

"And may any hunter perform the same method?" Massuk inquired. "Could I be able to kill a polar bear?"

"Yes, even you Massuk!" Keesh amusingly responded as the other men in the audience loudly heckled and jeered the village's old codger. "If you can still pop a load into a hairy pussy, you could kill a polar bear with my proven strategy."

"And will thou share with us this wonderful hunting secret?" the aged Ugh-Gluk pleaded. "I'd love to kill more polar bears if the process could be made easier, and if it didn't involve any fucked-up satanic witchcraft!"

"Yes, I'll tell thee now, since the council has had the courtesy to assemble in *my* igloo!" Keesh lectured and stated. After sucking on a rich marrowbone, the young hunter stood on a crate and again spoke to the astonished Eskimo community, including the influential gay and lesbian Eskimo sub-community. "It is all quite easy and simple to comprehend, you asinine simpletons!"

The lad picked-up a thick strip of whalebone cartilage and showed it to his captivated audience. The ends were honed like sharp needle- points. Keesh then meticulously coiled the cartilage strip until it released and sprang open in the palm of his hand. He next picked-up a piece of red blubber, and made the mass hollow on the inside.

"Then, I place the coiled whalebone cartilage inside the blubber, add another layer of red meat, and next form the mass into a rounded red ball," the young hunter orally described and demonstrated for all to see. "Next, I take the Eskimo 'meatballs' and allow them to freeze outside. The bear swallows the red ball, thinking that it is delicious food, which in a way it is," Keesh convincingly explained. "But it happens to also be deadly food. When the blubber melts, the whalebone cartilage either uncoils in the bear's throat, or in its stomach. The polar bear becomes ill, chokes incessantly, suffers from internal bleeding, and when it's too weak to fight, I kill it with my father's trusty spear that is not haunted, as *you* especially fucked-up idiots on the council falsely presume."

And Ugh-Gluk exclaimed "Oh!" and Klosh-Kwan yelled-out "Ay!" and old Massuk boomed-out, "You conniving smart-assed little bastard!"

Soon, Keesh became the eminent chief of the remote village located on the rim of the great polar sea. His loyal hunters practiced good head-craft instead of evil witchcraft, and the Eskimo village was soon the most prosperous on the entire Alaskan coast. Neither widow nor weak grandfather clamored for fresh food, even during the fiercest winter blizzards.

Keesh instituted a tradition in the village that is still practiced today. The new teen Chief declared the warm month of July "Polar Bear Month", and every resident was required by law to crawl around stark naked on all fours inside his or her igloo in imitation of the great white animals whose flesh and meat sustained the village's population. The horny men would sniff their wives' hairy asses and crotches all day long for that whole warm summer month, and every calendar period between March and April of the following year, the village was blessed with many new baby Eskimos.

The promulgation of surplus Eskimos trained in the art and skill of "head-craft" led to the tribe's great prosperity, and vastly expanded the clan's already-renowned reputation. Even some of the avowed village lesbians surprisingly became plumply pregnant, and reproduced their own healthy kind, thanks to wonderful Keesh's incomparable genius and indispensable wisdom.

"Love of Life"

The two very fatigued men hobbled-down a steep embankment. and staggered across rough jagged rocks. Each was heavily encumbered with blanket packs strapped to his shoulders, while having head-straps across the forehead, used for stabilizing and also supporting cumbersome camping paraphernalia. The very tired men both wished they were situated in a more pleasant and less hostile natural environment.

"I wish we had a couple of those cartridges in that cache of ours," the second man disgustedly stated to his traveling colleague. "Then, we could either shoot an animal and live, or pop a few slugs into our brains and get the fuck outa' this goddamned cruel world."

The man's disgruntled tone of voice was very mechanically spoken without evident emotion or motivation, and his utterance was completely ignored by the second man, who was thinking about getting laid on a tropical island, and not about trekking across the worst, desolate part of Alaska.

Soon, the two gold prospectors splashed and staggered through a stream of icy cold water, making their feet and ankles even more numb than they already were. The trailing man slipped on a smooth, underwater rock and uttered a sharp expletive.

"Fuck!" the follower exclaimed and objected. The trailing trekker reeled around and attempted to balance himself from falling over into the icy water. "Thank God the ice will make the goddamned swelling go down!" the staggering gent yelled as the man thought about his throbbing ankle, and not about his throbbing dick penetrating the lead man's gorgeous native princess on the ideal tropical island. But the lead man was still thinking about getting laid on the tropical island paradise, and ignored the following man's loud cry for assistance.

"I say, Bill; I've fuckin' double-sprained my right ankle!" the second injured trekker hollered.

But the man in front again ignored his companion's entreaty, as the leader awkwardly stumbled onward through the icy-cold, shallow river. The first fellow's eyes were like those of a dazed, wounded deer, as his distracted mind pleasurably imagined experiencing a wonderful sperm ejaculation. Then Bill ascended up the stream's embankment without ever looking back and acknowledging his faltering companion. 'I'll now think about my next fuckin' sexual fantasy!' the lead hiker selfishly considered. 'Yes, fantasy! That's really the only fuckin' thing that's keepin' me alive,' Bill concluded.

The man left stranded in the stream still had sufficient energy to give his abandoner a stiff middle finger. His lips were trembling from his pain and from his general exhaustion. A rough mustache and a thatch of brown hair encircled his quivering lips. The beleaguered man's tongue moistened his mouth, and the fellow was pretending that he was licking the imaginary native princess's hairy beaver on that wonderful, fanciful tropical island.

"Bill!" the man left behind frantically yelled with all of his strength. "Don't leave me out here all alone, you fuckin' degenerate!"

But Bill never turned his head to recognize his friend's desperate plea. William kept on lurching forward up the embankment toward the dull gray skyline, where his sex-starved mind now imagined that a dozen horny babes on another tropical island were wildly masturbating and waiting for him to arrive. 'I hear the bastard callin' me, but I don't give a shit about Jack!' Bill thought. 'I don't care Jack about Jack. I'm gonna' keep all my gold, and sail from Tahiti out to Samoa, so that I won't have to dream about *some moa'* goddamned pretend sex! I want the real fuckin' thing!'

The deserted man stared ahead in the direction of Bill, and Jack observed his friend's form passing through the mists and vapors as if he had entered an atmospheric portal into another weird dimension. While placing his weight on his good ankle, the abandoned man standing in the frigid stream still possessed the wherewithal to pull-out his watch, which faithfully indicated four o'clock.

'It's just about the First of August, and the damned sun is in the northeast,' Jack perceptively reckoned. 'The Great Bear Lake is to the south, and then after that lies the Canadian Barrens. I wanta' fuckin' stay away from that desolate place. And this stream I'm in feeds into the Coppermine River, which flows into Coronation Gulf near the Arctic Ocean. God, I'm sure glad I won that shitin' Geography Bee in elementary school!'

The man again surveyed his bleak environment of low-lying hills that were devoid of vegetation. 'No damned trees, shrubs, grass or ladies' bushes,' Jack regretted. 'And Bill still has two good legs, and the determined bastard is liable to eventually make it back to civilization and to the nearest whorehouse, way before I do. Fuck you Bill, even if ya' gotta' be sodomized! Fuck you I say!' Jack mentally repeated in what constituted an introspective rage.

The abandoned man stood shivering in the icy water, cowered-down, and then examined the empty gun in his hand. His shaking allowed the gun to fall from his grasp into the cold stream, and the almost-delirious fellow groped in the water until his searching hands finally located the weapon. Then, Jack weakly trudged-out of the stream onto the solid, hard, frozen land. 'Why the fuck did I ever leave San Diego?' the prospector wondered and regretted. 'Now I remember. I wanted to find gold up here in Alaska. I'd rather die of venereal disease recalling fond prostitute memories than drown is this lousy, scumbag creek, and wind-up being polar bear food,' the wincing man mused.

Next, the determined stream escapee struggled-up the rise and gradually reached the hill's crest. Jack noticed no trace of Bill limping forward, anywhere. Instead, the fellow's weary eyes perceived a shallow valley showing no signs of life, so Jack stubbornly lurched forward thinking about how Bill had left him in *his* moment of dire need, even though his fiendish friend was hallucinating and didn't know what the hell he was actually doing.

'Jack and Bill went up the hill, to fetch two sacks of gold,' the man from sunny California recollected and laughed. 'Jack fell down and sprained his leg, and Bill never heard his partner beg! Fine partner I've been fuckin' associated with!'

The valley's basin was extremely soggy, and moss-covered rocks were prevalent in that God-forsaken sector of the Alaskan Tundra. Each time the man struggled a step forward, the muddy water squirted out from under his boots, causing a sucking sound, which immediately made the survivor fantasize about getting the best Samoan blowjob of his life. Jack slowly meandered through the muskeg *marsh,* looking for delicious marshmallows to eat, and then sampled the disgusting mint-green moss, only to spit the foul-tasting slime out of his mouth. But Jack was as doomed as Biblical Abel.

'I'm not lost, even though I'm all alone,' Jack pensively and hopefully pondered. 'Pretty soon, I'll be south enough to reach the dead, stunted trees on the shores of the little lake the Eskimos call the *titchin-nichille*. That means 'little sticks', and logically, they're the only kind of erections the damned Eskimos could achieve in this fuckin' frigid temperature. I'll locate the stream and follow it to the Dease River, where *our* cache of supplies is hidden under the overturned canoe. I'll be able to find my gun bullets, fishhooks, lines, a small net, flour, bacon, beans, and my treasured porno' magazines,' Jack remembered, enjoying a brief moment of felicity. 'Yes; the memory of those fuckin' porno' magazines; *that* is really the only goddamned thing keepin' me alive. There aren't any boondocks out here to be out in the boondocks, and there are no sticks around here to be even out in the goddamned *titchin-nichille!*'

When I regain my full strength,' Jack reckoned, 'I'll locate the hidden canoe and paddle-down the Dease to the Mackenzie River, and successfully race south ahead of the encroaching winter. Next, I'll finally reach the Taiga, where the frontier Hudson Bay Company post had been constructed in the northernmost coniferous tree line. Food will be aplenty, and after being rejuvenated, I could then use my precious gold to hire the myriad services of several enterprising, itinerant Eskimo prostitutes.'

And meanwhile, Jack still possessed some semblance of distorted reality. 'Bill will probably be waiting at the cache with Tippycanoe and Tyler, too,' Jack's inventive mind fabricated. 'I haven't eaten for two days, and for the first time in my life, I actually desire chomping on food more than eating juicy, succulent pussy!'

So, the man stooped-down and picked-up a handful of bitter-tasting muskeg berries and carefully chucked them into his mouth. And as Jack chewed on the sour-flavored vegetation, he imagined that even dingle-berries would taste better than a handful of friggin' mushy muskeg berries.

The distracted trekker seriously stubbed his big right toe on a protruding rock at nine o'clock. Jack faltered and then toppled over in response to the pulsing excruciation inside his big right toe, which augmented the pulsating pain in his double sprained right ankle. He knelt-down on the permafrost and roughly slipped off his backpack straps, wishing that he could convert to being a Muslim, die, and then shack-up in heaven with a minimum of seven virgins eager to lose their virginity. As twilight settled in the eastern sky, the man built a fire out of dried moss, and then heated a tin pot of water to drink in the absence of good hard whiskey.

Jack next unwrapped his pack, and with his mind in a bewildered, fuzzy state, meticulously counted his remaining matches, and twelve consecutive times the counter reached the sum of sixty-seven, wishing he had two more so that he could contemplate 'sixty-nine'. Bill's paranoid, left-behind companion divided the matches into three nearly-equal piles, and then placed one pile into his empty tobacco pouch; the second handful in his pants' pocket, and the third batch inside his battered and tattered hat's headband.

'I can't remember how many matches I have,' Jack thought while doubting his own judgment. So, the perplexed survivor counted his three sums an additional time to verify the validity of his former mathematical determination.

Jack placed his wet boots next to the smoldering fire, and then he briefly removed his socks and examined his abused feet, which were pallid, lacerated, and bleeding. 'I'm glad my dick and my ass aren't in the same condition,' his twisted mind considered. 'Then, I would need four socks. Two socks would cover my tender feet, and another pair for my dick and my ass to wear. And my ankle's' now the size of my knee, and my knee looks like a baby watermelon. Christ! I must have *water*melon on the knee!' his warped, exhausted, deteriorating mind deducted. 'And this fuckin' swollen big toe is really aggravatin' my excruciating gout condition.'

The gold prospector tore the seam strips from one of his two blue blankets and recklessly bound them around his severely injured right ankle. The rest of the strips Jack ingeniously used to wrap around his feet to serve as suitable protection until his saturated socks would dry near the gentle fire. Next, Jack poured the hot water into a tin cup and greedily drank, pretending that the bland liquid was powerful rye whiskey. He next wound-up his watch, momentarily studied the heavens, crawled between his blue blankets, and finally dozed-off.

The Land of the Setting Sun had only brief darkness around midnight, and soon, the Earth's nearest star rose in the northeast, and the flickering object was discernible amidst ominous gray clouds. Jack woke-up hungry, and realized that he required nutrition to continue his arduous journey to the hidden cache stashed under the hidden, inverted canoe. He turned over and then shrieked to the barren wilderness, "Holy shit! I need a delicious fuckin' sizzlin' steak!"

A nearby bull caribou had been inspecting with curiosity Jack sleeping, tossing and turning on the cold ground. The nervous man heard snorting and then fully awoke. 'That bastard animal probably wishes he was a wolf rather than a weak grass eater,' the man suspected. 'I sorta' wish that he was a goddamned wolf, too!' "Eat me, you son-of-a-bitch!" Jack futilely screamed, scaring the bull caribou into thinking about flight and about sex with its mate, rather than wasting time studying a stupid, silly, sleeping human stranded many miles from civilization.

Jack instinctively reached for his gun, pulled the trigger, but no bullet was released from the chamber. The bull caribou soon had escaped the desperate man's range of vision. At that moment, the lonely human wished that he did have a bullet in his pistol's chamber to blow his own brains out, and escape to Muslim heaven and start pumping the poop out of those seven gorgeous, horny virgins.

In sheer contempt of his hostile environment, the miserable fellow groaned and finally managed to stand and assume an erect posture. The commonplace task of standing required a full minute to complete, because Jack's joints felt like rusty door hinges needing lubrication, and his tender ass felt like it weighed the equivalency of a ton of bricks. Next, the aggrieved prospector attempted taking a leak, but that simple process required a full half hour to perform, mostly because of faulty internal plumbing, along with a bad case of bladderwort infecting his aching bladder.

The weary survivor stumbled and crawled up a small knoll, and still had the presence of mind to survey the distant scenario. Everything appeared gray, including the prospect of *his* returning to the overturned canoe. The lakelets, sky, moss, rocks, streams and distant caribou all were gray, symbolizing stark uncertainty, old age, and the encroachment of death. 'I've lost my fuckin' sense of direction!' Jack eventually realized. 'But now, I remember! I'll just proceed in the opposite direction from which I came! I say, how many fuckin' matches do I have left! I'd better count the suckers again just to make sure I'm in control of my sanity!'

After carefully tabulating and double-checking his matches, Jack seriously considered having 'sixty-nine' instead of 67 with the bull caribou, but then immediately exited his peculiar delusion when the beast (in his mental manifestation) started kicking the man's face with its hooves as it started to orgasm. 'Christ! My mind is really fucked-up now!' Jack concluded. 'I gotta' use-up another match, burn and singe my numb finger, and get this friggin' sixty-nine bullshit fixation out of my goddamned head!'

Then, the delusional prospector assessed his moose-hide sack containing fifteen-pounds of gold nuggets. 'Should I discard this precious ore?' Jack wondered and evaluated. 'It's fuckin' weighin' me down, and it means nothin' at all to the goddamned caribou and wolves in this most secluded part of Alaska. Oh well, I'll take it with me in hopes that I can reach the Hudson Bay outpost and buy some sixty-nine with a decent hooker rather than dream a nightmare of doin' it with a fuckin' male caribou! Damn it! I gotta' use up one more of my freakin' matches, or else I'll fuckin' go insane!'

Hunger pangs gnawed-away inside Jack's stomach as he fancifully craved all sorts of food, and would even kill and cannibalize a weak vegetarian caribou if one were within choking range. He haphazardly descended into the ugly-empty valley, where rock ptarmigan rose with flapping wings, pecking away at the scattered muskeg berries. "Ker, ker, ker" the birds squawked as their beaks picked at the tart berries randomly growing between rocks and ledges. Jack pathetically stalked the bad-tempered birds on his knees, just as a hungry cat might hunt a family of yard birds (outside a prison). His abused legs left a blood trail as the hapless man squirmed and wriggled over wet moss and rocks, futilely attempting to clutch and strangle an unwary mother ptarmigan nesting its young.

"Ker, ker, ker," the disturbed birds mocked as they communicated danger to one another.

"Fuck! Fuck! Fuck!" Jack answered in frustration, repeating in his language what he had interpreted "Ker, ker, ker!" had meant to the apprehensive wary ptarmigans.

Almost in tears, the thwarted man crawled-upon what must have been a sleeping deaf bird. Jack impetuously grasped at the suddenly surprised creature, which quickly regained its consciousness, and frantically flew-off. Only three gray tail feathers were present in the man's dirt-smeared palm. "Come back and retrieve your ass-end steering feathers!" Jack yelled to the escaped ptarmigan flying overhead in a circle. "Come back you fuckin' birdbrain, and I'll surely kill your ass the second time around!"

The dazed man rose and clumsily tripped his way forward. In the afternoon, the disoriented fellow entered a valley of marshes where animal life was more abundant. Twenty caribou played peek-a-boo with him, and aimlessly ambled and grazed a hundred yards away. 'If only I had a loaded rifle,' Jack thought. 'I would easily take-down the biggest of the herd. And if I could sprint, I could surely catch the swiftest of the pack. Holy Christ! Are my totally angled thoughts fucked-up, or what?'

A black fox accidentally came ambling toward the incoherent man, and it was carrying a squealing ptarmigan in its mouth. "Drop that fuckin' bird!" Jack shouted at the sly fox, which quickly and skillfully leaped-away onto higher rock ledges, and then hastily disappeared over a hill's crest. 'Even sloppy seconds from a wily fox seems tantalizing,' the desperate man supposed in self-sympathy.

Jack then glanced-down at his dungaree zipper. 'The next thing I gotta' prevent from happenin'' is to keep that freakin' fox away from *my* damned bird, especially since *he* carries his cherished food away to eat and enjoy in secrecy!'

The overwhelmed man came upon a milky, lime-colored stream that flowed through multi-shaped patches of green grass. Jack pulled the grass rushes up from their roots, which to his jumbled mind, reminded him of onion sprouts, hardly the size of a pinky fingernail. The fibers were tough and stringy, and the small bulbs were hardly as palatable as the famished man had wished.

And next, the tenacious struggler got-down on his hands and knees and wildly foraged and munched the grass like a distraught bovine would, even though Jack hated everything about cows, including their sweet milk. 'I'd much rather have a nice juicy *Porterhouse* and chew the fat with a homosexual friend, rather than to suffer the indignity of lying here in this isolated marsh imitating a lowly cow chewing its cud!' the weary wanderer decided. Then, another basic consideration surfaced in the all-too-frustrated prospector's troubled cerebrum.

'Damn it; I wanna' find some nourishing food,' Jack lamented. 'I need meat! I'd even eat live frogs, or squiggly worms, if I could only find them!' the pathetic wanderer thought as he aggressively dug away into the muddy marsh grass with his fingernails. 'I'd even eat a horny toad! God, how I really love frog legs! Shit! No frogs, toads or worms live in this far north wasteland, but I'm gonna' keep on diggin' for reptiles and amphibians, anyway!'

Jack searched every shallow water pool hoping, to see a small fish. And then, almost miraculously, the fanatic spotted a tiny old *minnow* that, to his warped mind, looked like it was a carryover from the ancient Greek *Minoan* civilization. The starving fellow plunged his arm up to his shoulder into the cold pool, but the daylight had been refracted, going from the medium of air to the medium of water, and the slippery minnow eluded his frantic lunge. The incensed man then used both hands exploring the depths of the pool, trying to use tactile sensation to locate the tiny old fish, which nearly had died from fright during its most recent misadventure. The unfortunate human fell and splashed into the murky marsh, getting wet up to his chest.

'I have to wait until the sediments settle so that the water is clear again,' he concluded. 'I must stay on task and not lose sight of my *mission!*' the food searcher thought as his destitute mind conjured-up an image of the *Alamo*.

After the muddy water became somewhat clear again, Jack attempted capturing the evasive minnow, which again wildly avoided his frenetic effort. The encumbered man anxiously began bailing water out of the pool with his tin cup, while boisterously screaming, "Everybody out of the pool! Everybody out of the fuckin' pool!" the asshole shrieked as if he was a maniacal lifeguard. His freezing hands were shaking, and his heart was rhythmically pounding inside his chest cavity. In a half hour, the pool was nearly empty. The tiny fish had managed to squeeze itself though a tiny crevice between two stones, and had escaped to a larger adjoining pool that was big enough for a small whale to swim in.

'Damn it!' Jack mentally cursed. 'If I had known of that fuckin' crevice, I could've plugged it up.' Then, his attention was directed toward his rusty zipper. 'Shit!' the famished survivor realized. 'My limp pecker will never again plug-up any damned female crevice, diminutive or otherwise, unless I fuckin' find some food fast!'

The virtually-defeated, lost rambler slowly climbed out of the freezing-cold pool and rolled over upon the wet ground. Jack cried loudly to the apathetic and heartless marshes, mountains, hills, and dull gray sky. His soul felt as desolate as his insensitive surroundings seemed to be.

In a moment of sheer inspiration, the stubborn survivor managed to build a campfire and warmed several quarts of hot water, which he indulgently gulped-down to keep his fragile body warm. Jack next conscientiously checked his supply of matches, and ascertained that they were still dry. 'Now I only have sixty-five, I think, the counter sulked. 'How the hell do you do sixty-five with a naked woman?'

Jack's blue blankets were moist and clammy, and his right ankle, knee, and big toe ached with incredibly intense pain. He again wound his watch and eventually fell asleep, dreaming of Viking feasts, of huge wedding banquets; of exotic-magnificent Hawaiian luaus; of cheap Eskimo smorgasbords, and of fast-food brothels. The dozer awoke from his disturbing slumber feeling physically cold and emotionally irritated.

'What the fuck's goin' on?' the lost gent thought in disgust. 'Snow flurries are ornamentin' the hills, makin' them pure white; and a heavy wind is blowin'. The dampness from the larger flakes has put out my fire! Why the fuck was I ever born!'

The poor soul carelessly packed his wet gear, awkwardly strapped the blankets to his back, and proceeded onward. 'Fuck the land of the little sticks, and the cache under the canoe on the bank of the Dease. All I wanna' do is eat some grub. I can't believe I'd rather eat broccoli or celery than savory wet pink pussy! I must be turnin' into either a goddamned lame wimp, or a fuckin' gay son-of-a-bitch! One thing's for damned sure!' Jack irrationally decided. 'I'll never follow Bill into the goddamned wilderness again, gold or no goddamned gold nuggets!'

The pessimistic adventurer again stared at his heavy moose-hide sack of gold. 'This sucker's weighin' me down,' the trekker assessed. 'It's worth a fortune anywhere in the Klondike or the Yukon, but it ain't worth shit out here with the various hungry animals. No creature would accept a fuckin' ransom for me, that's for damned sure! But I'll try and preserve my strength to carry the sack to the damned Dease. Then, the gold will be worth something again!'

Jack re-cinched his ankle with his blanket strips, and blood oozed through the fabric. The hilltop snow had partially melted, and after identifying the position of the morning sun, the man valiantly set-out on his quest to reach the secret cache. 'I gotta' go about five degrees to the right,' the treader roughly estimated. 'I believe I've gone slightly off course. I don't want to wind-up somewhere in shitin' Siberia or fuckin' Antarctica.'

The man's tongue felt dry and enlarged as he trudged along. He frequently paused to rest, and his heart was irregularly palpitating, going "thump, thump thump" as if it was a big brass drum lodged deep in his thorax. 'My goddamned parched tongue feels like it's growin' hair!' Jack thought. 'Could it be that it's turnin' into a woman's fuzzy beaver?'

The woebegone trekker came upon a fairly large marsh pool with two minnows darting about in it. 'This damned basin is much too large to bail-out!' the observer accurately determined. Showing less excitement at finding a marsh pool than he had exhibited before, Jack slowly pushed his tin prospecting bucket through the water's surface and (through noteworthy perseverance) managed to isolate and catch several of the small creatures. And then after taking a deep breath, he thrust the wiggling fish into his mouth, and avariciously chewed them raw, all-the-while imagining that he was enjoying a wonderfully delectable baked flounder dinner.

That evening, Jack successfully caught three more minnows and saved them for breakfast. 'I gotta' cover at least ten miles a day,' the prospector reckoned. 'I gotta' stay strong. The goddamned wolves are huntin' the old and weak caribou. I can hear the carnivorous critters howlin' in the distance. Fuck breakfast! I better *wolf* down these three squiggly fish before those friggin' wolves wolf both me and my arrogance down.'

The perplexed man had a tough decision to make, and finally rationality triumphed over greed. He divided his gold nuggets into two piles. Jack stashed half into a crack in a prominent ledge inside some blanket material, and the remaining half he returned to his *moose-hide* sack, which entirely was too small for even a baby moose to hide inside of. 'I'll keep my gun for as long as I can,' the grim-faced struggler convinced himself. 'I can get ammo' when I finally reach the overturned canoe. I might even need bullets to kill Bill, that fuckin' dirty, faggot prick!'

Jack was overwhelmed from giddiness that had been caused by a lack of nutrition and plenty of weariness. His bewildered and befuddled brain was as befogged as the strange-looking atmosphere. He stumbled and fell five times, got-up, and continued his weird one-man procession. His bedraggled body stumbled a sixth time, falling squarely into a well-concealed ptarmigan nest. Jack's blurred vision detected four squealing, newly hatched chicks, little day-old specks of life. The man honored his impulse to act quickly.

The desperate human eagerly hi*jacked* the tiny birds, flung them into his mouth, and chewed them ravenously (ptarmiganly), his teeth crunching them as if they were shelled peanuts. 'These little critters taste much better than those tart minnows did,' the starving trekker reasoned and appreciated. 'I can't wait to find and catch a warty frog, or a couple of earthworms, and see if I like the taste of them better!'

The alarmed mother ptarmigan returned from scavenging food, tried protecting her nest, and chirped and squawked all about, just managing to elude Jack's wild lunges. The frustrated prospector endeavored using his gun as a suitable club, but the annoyed bird dodged his erratic thrusts. He then hurled stones at the protesting bird, one of which injured her right wing. The distressed mother ptarmigan forgot all about her maternal instinct, entered a survival mode, and subsequently always maneuvered to stay several steps away from Jack's incessant clutching and smashing.

'Those chicks have whetted my appetite,' Jack realized. 'A bird in the hand is worth two in the bush!' the crazed Californian concluded as he lustily rubbed his limp *Johnson* while pursuing the thoroughly agitated 'lady-bird'.

The chase brought Jack across several swampy swales in the bottom of the valley where his fertile mind conjured-up a half-dozen valley girls masturbating like crazy. Then, amazingly, the dazed pursuer discovered recently formed footprints. 'Those suckers look like Bill's,' Jack theorized. 'They must be Bill's. That snot-nosed bastard must not be far ahead. I know the six valley girls are safe from molestation, because my buddy Bill's a goddamned, impotent, one-balled, homosexual.'

The mother ptarmigan lay exhausted ten feet in front of Jack's grasp, but the exhausted predator lacked the stamina or the will to leap and land upon her. Both the man and the bird required rest, and each existing only a mere ten-feet apart from one another. 'No more delicious *smorgasbirds!*' Jack mused in despair. 'And when the guy mustered-up sufficient power to lurch forward, the petulant-but-frightened mother bird also had reserve energy to elude his exaggerated effort by nervously fluttering and hopping forward. Jack tripped and fell flush on his face, cutting his pallid cheeks and chin between two sharp-edged stones. The courageous man did not move a muscle for an hour. Then, he diligently wound his watch, shit his pants, and went to sleep.

The following foggy morning, a nasty wind and a light drizzle had completely obscured Bill's footprints. By midday, the weight of the backpack became too oppressive, so Jack discarded the balance of his gold nuggets, and blatantly cursed man's proclivity toward valuing avarice. Starvation was setting in, so the temporarily lost soul also threw-away several items of necessity, and carried only his blanket, the tin sifting bucket, his knife, and his gun.

'I'm so goddamned hungry I'd even eat a smelly Eskimo hair pie,' Jack whimsically reflected for a moment. 'I believe I have one bullet remaining in my gun.' He industriously checked the weapon and was dismayed that his hope turned-out to be a mere fantasy. Jack next plodded and tramped ahead in disappointment, trying to ascertain how reality and his imagination had merged into one entity.

During the next two hours, the plodder fancifully inspected his gun six times, searching for the indispensable bullet that his undependable mind had created. The serious hunger pangs were increasing in severity and in frequency. The man robotically advanced southward, acting like a strange automaton devoid of compassion, self-sympathy, or other common human feelings. Suddenly, a fierce sight caught the trekker's immediate attention.

'Holy horseshit!' Jack's mind thought. 'It's a giant bear lookin' for its next meal!'

The ferocious carnivore was studying the pathetic hiker with bellicose scrutiny. 'I must do something before the animal goes into an irreversible attack mode!' Jack decided. 'If I run, I'm dead meat; and if I fight; I'm dead meat! I'm about to get my ass kicked and my whole body eaten! This is all ironically fuckin' un*bear*able!'

Jack remembered that he had not thrown away his trusty hunting knife that was still fastened to a leather sheath strapped to his belt. He touched its pointed blade, making certain that it was sharp. The worried gold rush participant's strained heart again began beating irregularly, and he felt as if his knees were wobbling and about to buckle. 'I'm going to pass out!' he frightfully thought.

In a gesture of total desperation, the dumb-ass man rushed forward with his raised knife and screamed as loud as he could, 'I'm gonna' kill you, you fuckin' ugly brown bastard!' The bear reared-up in a defensive, combative posture, considered its circumstances, and then retreated back three steps. Jack's grisly eyes met those of the big grizzly, and the man menacingly growled as the shouter crazily gestured with the raised knife. His startling animation had effectively intimidated the fierce predator, which was momentarily stunned by the mysterious human's uncharacteristic antics. Jack stood still as a statue, and then commenced roaring in imitation of a vicious circus lion he once saw as a boy. The gigantic, brown bear scampered-away on all fours, figuring that it would judiciously select a less insane and more predictable prey for its next meal.

The man wept and sobbed for a full half-hour; his psyche had been completely overwhelmed by his latest bizarre ordeal. 'I don't give a flyin' shit about dying like a man!' despondent Jack contemplated and wept. 'I don't want to be violently ripped to shreds and then devoured by a fuckin' wild, ferocious Alaskan bear, or consumed by a pack of savage wolves. Oh, dear God; isn't my troubled soul deserving of a more favorable fate?'

Over the next several hours, full-bellied wolves crossed his path in packs of three and four, but the wily predators steered clear of the vertical creature weeping and screaming like a mental patient escaped from an insane asylum. The carnivores were hunting and feasting off of old, weak and young caribou, which did not stab, or scratch, or bite like the weird human standing and shouting crazy expletives in a threatening, erect, defensive stance.

An hour later, Jack discovered scattered caribou *calf* bones. The backpacker felt the rear of his knees and thought, 'I'm fuckin' lucky to still have my two *calves* attached to my legs. Look what the fuck those carnivorous wolves have done to this poor, innocent, grass-eating animal!'

And then, the unstable man did something grotesque and unthinkably primitive. He solemnly touched the bones and thought, 'Is this what the fuck I'm gonna' look like tomorrow? These remains can't be Bill's dismantled skeleton!' And then an additional thought brought some consolation to *his* chaotic mind. 'There is no pain or suffering in death! Only the desire to live brings about misery, hurt, and anguish! Heaven, please help me! I'm not ready to fuckin' die!'

Jack was soon squatting in the damp moss, and sucking on a pink bone, biting off every savory shred of flesh and available sustenance left behind by the already-satisfied wolves. The sweet meaty taste sent Jack's mind into a mild ecstasy. He chomped-down on the bone with his weak jaws. Sometimes the caribou's bone broke exposing its rich marrow. Sometimes the intense crush broke several of Jack's molars.

Then, the almost-vanquished man had an inspiration. He smashed the bones against the nearby rocks, pounding them into small fragments, and then Jack swallowed the almost-pulverized remains. His fingers were bleeding from the times his descending rock missed the bone, or when the white femur or clavicle broke, scraping the skin off of his exposed knuckles and wrists. 'I'm livin' like a freakin' caveman!' the man sobbed and anguished in languish. 'Neanderthals had more dignity than I have right now. At least those primitive assholes had the security of bein' with their moronic family upon leaving *this* life!'

The next two days featured a mixture of snow, sleet, and rain, and Jack behaved like a machine that was not synchronized with its environment. His sleeping patterns were irregular, with him traveling both during the day and at night. Sometimes, he gingerly walked, and other times, he irresponsibly crawled and groveled. Jack was unwilling to surrender his soul to death's beckoning. He repeatedly made and then quickly broke camp at whim, and did not honor any standard practice or regular habit.

The desperate man carried in his pack remnants of the caribou calf's bones, and he actively sucked and crunched them whenever he felt a need to react to his biological compulsions to eat and live. Jack now loyally followed a wide, fast-flowing stream, and his hazy mind was filled with exotic visions and mirages, none of which were entirely comprehensible.

The following morning, the tormented nomad awoke; his body lying on a rocky ledge. The fatigued wanderer felt the sun's rays shining upon his countenance, and heard the sounds of curious caribou calves to his left. 'I want to live and I also want to die!' he ambivalently thought as his disoriented mind grappled with fathoming the significance of the two extreme alternatives. 'But if pain, anguish, and suffering are all that fuckin' life has to offer,' the lost fellow regrettably pondered. Iin the final analysis, I would truly prefer dying.'

But the warm sun reflected off his bearded face, and provided the obstinate man with encouragement to continue his intrepid travail. He rolled onto his side and perceived the wide fast-flowing stream, the identity of which challenged and puzzled his memory. Jack observed the dismal, bare, distant hills devoid of vegetation. Only the river valley had grass and caribou feeding-off the vegetation supply, and eager wolves feasting-off the once-healthy, captured caribou. The worried man's emotional state was very melancholy, and quite apparently, now lacked interest, motivation and enthusiasm.

As the pitiful human being gawked into the distance, he believed his mind was playing cruel tricks on him. 'There's a ship out there on the shining sea,' Jack interpreted and comprehended. He closed his eyelids, opened them, and then rubbed his face to confirm his recognition of the familiar object outlined on the horizon. 'It is a ship anchored in a bay, and several small islands are surrounding it. I wonder if they're the friggin' *Illusion Islands* between Alaska and

Siberia! I just gotta' get my bearings straight!' his giddy mind mused. The hopeful vision persisted, and did not fade into oblivion, and *that* particular realization (mirage) energized Jack's spirit and afforded his weakened heart the far-fetched prospect of being rescued.

But then, the obstinate trekker's soul plunged into despair. 'There's no bullet in my friggin' gun,' he sadly remembered. 'And also, no ship on the shining sea. What a fuckin' living nightmare those goddamned lousy illusions are!'

The vanquished explorer soon heard a snuffle behind him, that was actually a combination cough and pant. He shifted his body weight and witnessed a most despicable companion. Jack noticed the gray head of a wolf, and its primitive-looking jade eyes were greedily peering at him through several jagged rocks, twenty or so feet away. The predator's green eyes were glassy and bloodshot, and its head was drooping, and almost crestfallen. The animal blinked as if it too was witnessing a terrible mirage.

'What the fuck's this shit?' Jack thought in total consternation. 'A fuckin' sick wolf! And the goddamned bastard is waitin' for me to expire so that it could enjoy its last meal. What a travesty of justice if a dumb abstraction such as justice exists in this lousy survival-of-the-fittest animal world!' the giddy man neurotically considered. 'If there's justice anywhere in this fucked-up misadventure of mine, it must indeed be a freakin' miscarriage of justice!'

Jack turned his bloodied head left toward the nebulous ship on the shining sea, and then rotated his face right toward the very real diseased wolf, and the befuddled observer attempted to plausibly distinguish between the 'dual mirages'. Then, the suffering man chuckled,' A weak dying wolf! What utter irony! What a fuckin' appropriate fateful conclusion to a goddamned, meaningless human life!'

The whimpering sufferer closed his eyes and reviewed the dramatic events of the past few days. His difficult journey had been heading south by southwest, moving away from the Dease Divide in the direction of the fabled Coppermine River. His unexpected destination was well-defined on the wall map at the Hudson Bay Company outpost. 'That damned shining sea is the majestic Arctic Ocean!' Jack hypothesized. 'And there's a damned whaling ship anchored in Coronation Gulf! God save both the Queen of England and my lily-white ass!'

The hope of deliverance gave the temporarily defeated man additional emotional energy. He carefully felt his aching feet, which were now deformed lumps of raw meat. 'My fuckin' gun and knife are now several miles behind me,' he reasoned. 'I still have matches in my pocket. It's eleven o'clock,' his brain realized, and his eyes stared blankly at his still-ticking watch. 'I've been through too much to simply give up and sacrifice my life and my body to a goddamned, sick, gangrened, lustful wolf!'

The exhausted American attempted remaining calm and prudent. All awareness of pain had now disappeared, and even his lips and fingertips had little sensation. Jack thought of swallowing food, but that ignorant idea made him feel nauseous, and his stomach felt like vomiting. The beleaguered gold prospector re-cinched his swollen ankle, causing blood to drip upon the surrounding rocks. 'I still have my tin cup and my matches,' he doggedly considered. 'I'll be able to drink boilin' water and kill off the bacteria. I wonder if I could set the wolf on fire? That's one fuckin' advantage I still have. The wonder of fire is my staunchest ally over that repulsive, sick animal.'

Jack's hands now shook as if he was afflicted with a palsy. He gathered dry moss into a heap to ignite into an improvised blaze. Man's mastery of fire could be used against the filthy offensive wolf. 'He's probably been abandoned by his pack, just like Bill had abandoned me,' Jack accurately concluded. 'How terribly merciless and inhumane could nature be?'

The brave man inched forward toward the diseased wolf and peered directly into the creature's glassy, bloodshot eyes. The animal was still fearful of Jack's unorthodox behavior, and the wolf reluctantly yielded territory to the crazed, strange-behaving human. The wolf greedily licked the sides of its mouth, contemplating food (once Jack would die), but the man noticed that the revolting beast had hardly the strength to curl its flaccid tongue.

'Jesus S. Christ!' the dejected man thought. 'The goddamned enlarged tongue isn't even red! It's yellowish-brown and coated with a layer of thick, germ-infested mucus! I'm not goin' to be this hideous, diseased animal's next son-of-a-bitchin' meal. No way!'

After Jack drank nearly a liter of hot water, the injured prospector found that he still possessed adequate strength to rise-up on his abused feet and stand almost erect. 'If I die, it'll be with a man's dignity, and not with a sheep's cowardice!' Jack proudly thought. 'I can walk at least four-miles toward the anchored ship on the bay, even in this debilitated condition. I hope the ship's not an illusion created by my horribly stressed-out psyche!'

All night long, Jack habitually blinked his eyelids and could not fall asleep. The sick wolf's coughing and wheezing, along with the squawking of distant ptarmigan and caribou, kept him awake. 'I am this sick wolf's only hope of living,' Jack pragmatically evaluated. 'If I live, it fuckin' dies! If I die, it fuckin' lives! Fuck philosophy! The basic formula is so amazingly simple, yet at the same time, so terribly brutal!'

The repulsive creature stood on its four legs, assessing Jack's every movement, including his most recent bowel movement. Its mangy tail was tucked between its legs in a subordinate, defensive position, and the sickly animal lacked the strength to even snarl or moan. It very deliberately and slowly skulked in a circle around the frightened human, who now regarded the dying beast as a mutual companion in suffering. The infected wolf even seemed to broadly grin at Jack's rueful face, when the shocked human orally addressed the disgusting, sick animal using sarcastic and obscene language.

That afternoon, the weak man's legs dragged his vulnerable frame three miles forward, but fatigue rapidly set-in, and soon Jack was slowly advancing on all fours, just like the sick wolf had been avariciously trailing him. 'Thank God it's an Indian summer day. If it were three weeks from now, my Caucasian butt couldn't be distinguished from an icicle's asshole in broad daylight!'

As Jack slowly progressed on all fours toward the glittering ship on the shining sea, his form came across a small pond where he triumphantly captured four minnows in his tin cup. "Here," he declared to the diseased wolf while tossing the smallest of the fish before the creature's maw. "Eat to your goddamned heart's content. You've been officially reduced to a lousy, goddamned scavenger, just like me, but I see that you don't give a shit!"

Jack crawled along for several-hundred-yards, following the trail of another man that had also crawled that doomed path. A heap of fresh-chewed bones was surrounded by wolf footpad marks that had been imprinted in the soggy moss. The recent arrival observed a moose-hide sack, similar to the one he had been carrying, and Jack automatically theorized that the skeletal remains were those of Bill. "These pinky, white bones are yours, Bill," Jack acknowledged and sobbed with tears forming in his eyes. "But don't worry, good buddy! I will not suck your bones. I'm not a fuckin' cannibal or a goddamned fuckin' civilized queer, either. I'll never suck another man's bone! Never I say!"

An hour later, the distraught, paranoid man arrived at a deep pond of water where the deflected sunlight reflected his wretched-looking face. He spotted three minnows swimming inside the pool, and thrust his arm inside the cold water in an unsuccessful attempt to acquire his next snack. 'I'm afraid that if I accidentally tumble into the pond, I'll certainly drown,' Jack regretted. 'And I know that I could easily friggin' drown in only six inches of water if I was lyin' on my face. Tell me, bitter destiny; explain to me, fate; how the hell did I get to be so totally fucked-up in this totally fucked-up world?'

The next morning and afternoon, Jack was able to stumble and crawl another three-additional-miles towards the tantalizing gleaming ship upon the shining sea, and the following day, his labor gained him two-more-miles. 'This is how Bill expired,' Jack remorsefully thought. 'He was crawling, and fainting, and sleeping, and inching his way, but his labor was all in vain. Who needs this raunchy crap? Who needs this fuckin' Alaska Tundra shit?' the man's addled and cluttered mind questioned.

And then, as Jack turned his head, his pupils observed the lugubrious-looking, infected wolf diligently licking *his* trail of crimson with its gruesome, enlarged, yellowish-brown tongue. But the defiant man was adamant about persevering and enduring, so he pulled and dragged his abused carcass across the desolate ground with the wolf scavenging and licking-up his recently shed blood.

'If the wolf were a healthy one, I would gladly surrender to death,' Jack contemplated. 'But since the ugly bastard is diseased, the thought of him eating my flesh is absolutely repugnant. I'd prefer sucking Bill's raunchy dick when *he* was alive rather than have this son-of-a-bitchin' loathsome disgrace of its breed biting my tender ass and sensitive balls off!'

Jack's intervals of lucid mental activity now alternately appeared into and then quickly faded from his disoriented mind in more rapid succession. Hallucinations perplexed his perception and cognizance, and doubt plagued his sensibilities, especially his misgivings about the 'artificial glistening ship on the shining sea.' Late that afternoon, the man was awakened from a deep slumber by a faint sniffle at his ear. When Jack reflexively moved his head, the rancid-furred wolf leaped back and stumbled, exhibiting an almost ludicrous, awkward demonstration of its current pathetic plight.

'I guess that the glowing ship's only about four-miles away now,' Jack estimated. 'That is to say, it's four-miles away if it's really a ship anchored in the bay.' The survivor rubbed his eyes so that his peepers could focus with more clarity. 'It has white sails; but fuck! I can't even crawl a half-mile, let alone four wicked miles! Why the fuck didn't I join the navy like my parents wanted me to do!' his stark madness sarcastically concluded. 'Then, I'd be a safe, contented sailor, standing at attention aboard that gleaming ship on the shining sea!'

The grief-stricken man closed his eyes and visualized his existence speeding toward a tunnel's entrance with a small intense bright light glowing at the other end. 'I'm dying!' he happily thought. 'Thank God I'm fuckin' finally dying!'

As Jack lay on his back gasping for his next breath, his left hand felt the sick wolf's putrid-smelling breath wheezing against his left cheek. Next, the petrified fellow felt the sick wolf's huge, discolored tongue pressing against his mud-smeared face. It's persistent lapping had the horrible feel of sandpaper grating against his almost-numb skin. 'I'll not move until the exact right moment!' Jack promised his in-flux conscience.

The wolf showed tremendous cunning and patience, but Jack's stubborn attitude was equal to his adversary's resolve. The man lay still for a whole half-day, allowing the wolf to gain confidence and to begin initiating its disrespectful feast. Jack dreamed of a spectacular beautiful blonde whispering in his ear, only to awaken to the despicable wolf's harsh, coarse tongue caressing his face and lips. 'This must be a gay fuckin' wolf that only wants to eventually lick my dick!' Jack conjectured during that very traumatic moment. 'I'm still vulnerable in the neck, and this scumbag scavenger is liable to accidentally puncture my throat and sever my goddamned jugular!'

Soon, the infected dying wolf's tongue began lapping at Jack's bleeding right hand. The animal's fangs pressed against the man's palm, and attempted to penetrate the already lacerated skin. Jack wrapped his left arm around the wolf's neck, and the prey's mouth was soon full of flea-ridden, stench-smelling, dark, gray fur. 'I can't choke him to death, but I think I can sever the gross creature's throat with my teeth!' he hoped. 'Maybe I can smother the damned carnivorous wolf. Take that; you mangy, ugly, foul mother-fucker!'

Five-minutes later, the pathetic man's entire weight had pinned-down his immobilized adversary, and thirty-minutes thereafter, Jack felt a very unpleasant warm trickle rolling down his throat. 'He's dead!' the man realized and concluded. 'The mother-fucker's dead! My will has prevailed!' Then, the victor slowly rolled over, closed his bleary eyes, and dozen.

A whaling ship, *The Bedford,* had brought a contingent of scientists to northern Alaska to expertly conduct pertinent experiments, and to assiduously record observations of polar flora and fauna. The alert sailors on the ship's main deck had binoculars and noticed a large, strange creature moving like a crippled crustacean along a riverbank. The mariners instantly climbed into a 'whaling harpoon boat', and set-out to discover exactly what they had seen. Jack was squirming forward like a mammoth worm. He then was writhing and twisting about, wrangling and wrestling with an imaginary sick wolf in his volatile, semi-conscious mania.

Three weeks later, Jack sat-up in his bunk bed on *The Bedford* to disclose to his fascinated audience the elements of his incredible tale, which the listeners regarded as mostly bunk being told from a *bunk* bed. Tears cascaded down the man's cheeks as he recalled and vividly described each episode of his extraordinary adventure. Intermixed with his revelations about caribou, a bear, the gold, the ptarmigans, the sick wolf, and Bill's morbid fate, were recollections about his mother, his family, and sunny California. Somehow, orange groves got blended in with muskeg berries, and semi-tropical flowers were intermingled with lichens upon hard Arctic rocks, which added a certain dimension of implausibility to Jack's disheveled mind.

The following morning, the still-confused man sat in the ship's galley, and he gobbled-down his hardy breakfast as if he had just survived a horrendous famine. 'They're goin' to aggressively steal my fuckin' food!' the distrustful eater imagined and believed. 'These fuckin' surreptitious sailors are no different than that black fox and that bastard dying wolf! The scumbag bastards think my story's a gaudy lie!'

After breakfast, the rescued man briefly toured the ship, and paid particular attention to where all of the food had been stored. And he voraciously ate like a hog in heat, stuffing every available morsel into his mouth, making each bite swiftly disappear into his esophagus before any crumb could be stolen by his 'jealous and envious ship mates'. In three weeks, Jack had added four inches to his waist, and began exhibiting a most prodigious girth.

All the way from Alaska to San Francisco, Jack hoarded hardtack biscuits, and ate with suspicious eyes. He clandestinely stuffed and hid biscuits inside his mattress and inside his bunk bed. Jack steadfastly guarded his 'highly-coveted food supply' from the *Bedford's* 'less intelligent crewmembers'.

'I must take precautions so that no one pilfers my goddamned food,' Jack greedily thought. 'All of these treacherous son-of-a-bitches are ruthless! I must survive for the sake of my love of life!'

O. Henry

O. Henry (1862-1910)

Even though O. Henry had died at a very young age, the author still managed to remarkably write over five hundred short stories and anecdotal sketches. William Sydney Porter's fiction often occurs in familiar environments and settings that he had known well during his short tenure upon this Earth.

O. Henry was very familiar with New York City, and so his famous stories "The Gift of the Magi", "The Last Leaf", "The Furnished Room", "After Twenty Years", "The Higher Pragmatism", "The Cop and the Anthem", "The Green Door", "The Caliph, Cupid and the Clock" and "Mammon and the Archer" all take place in Manhattan, at or around the turn of the twentieth century during the emergence of the exciting Golden Age of science and technology.

William Sydney Porter was born in the South in Greensboro, North Carolina, and so the prolific author was quite familiar with the culture of the post-Civil War Dixie states, and some of his popular stories are set there: "The Whirligig of Life" (Tennessee), "One Dollar's Worth", "A Call Loan", "The Pimienta Pancakes" (in Texas), and "The Emancipation of Billy", also take places in the American South.

Most interestingly, many of O. Henry's terrific short stories were authored while he was in jail. In 1892, Porter moved to Texas and soon became a teller at an Austin bank where the institution's officials accused him of illegally manipulating funds into his own private account. Porter fled to Central America, but upon returning to the States after his wife became very ill, the on-the-lam author was captured and then convicted. Thus, one of O. Henry's most famous stories "A Retrieved Reformation" involves safecracker Jimmy Valentine getting out of prison and also, the writer's humorous stories "Shoes" and "Shoes and Ships" take place in Coralio, an imaginary seacoast village in Central America.

It is widely believed that the rather unique writing name "O. Henry" had been conceived in honor of a certain security guard named Orrin Henry, who had been employed at the federal penitentiary where the literary genius William Sydney Porter had been serving his sentence.

"The Gift of the Magi"

A measly one-dollar-and-eighty-seven-cents had been scattered all over the small living room coffee table; a paltry pittance even in this inventive age-of-machinery, 1910. That was all the saved money that Jim and Della counted, and sixty cents of that minuscule sum was in copper pennies. And the accumulated chump-change had been obtained from Jim, who had been arguing monetary trivialities with the neighborhood grocer, with the corner vegetable huckster, and with the parsimonious German butcher who often threatened his more belligerent customers with razor-sharp cleavers raised and held high above his bald head.

Sadness prevailed in the couple's hearts. One dollar and eighty-seven-cents wasn't enough money to buy a soap pack for two, or even a carton of sanitary napkins, and the worst aspect of this entire sad story was that the next calendar day would be Christmas, and no presents had yet been bought or exchanged inside the James Dillingham Young household.

Della flopped-down upon the apartment's tiny shabby couch, which was more of a miniature ratty loveseat than a bona fide comfortable sofa. The sorrow-laden wife sobbed while the more pragmatic husband speculated, 'Just look at that fuckin' bug-infested sofa! My last fuckin' name should be Davenport instead of Young. Why the hell doesn't Della go out and get a goddamned sweat-shop job and earn a few extra bucks, instead of foolishly sitting there crying and sobbing all day long about our destitute situation? And we don't even have any wise-mouthed kids' stomachs to feed! What a wagon load of horse manure this whole, rotten, domestic scene is!'

The Youngs' piss-poor flat was crudely furnished and cost eight dollars a week to rent. Jim, a lazy door-to-door mascara and perfume salesman, often wished that he was talented enough to sell encyclopedias, or girly magazines, or durable pots and pans, but the jerk had been emphatically rejected during thirteen separate short job interviews after Young had become overly argumentative and confrontational with his prospective employers. And besides *that* bad social habit of being crude and rude, un-dynamic Jim had never learned how to read or write proficiently, flunking first-grade at Brooklyn P.S. #13 several years in a row.

The downstairs vestibule mailbox had a dysfunctional electric button that would surprisingly shock any finger that accidentally touched it, and the lettering beneath the flimsy container bore the accursed name "James Dillingham Young," but the "D" in Dillingham had been missing ever since Jim's weekly salary and commission had been diminished from thirty dollars a week to a mere twenty American bucks.

But on the positive side of the family ledger, whenever James Dillingham Young returned home at 6 p.m. with a defeated attitude and having his stubborn head crestfallen, Della instinctively hugged him dearly, yanked-off all her husband's sweaty and smelly clothes, kissed his ass and every other exposed part or organ, and then gave her chosen mate a really exotic and erotic blowjob, followed by some fantastic pussy penetration.

Then, after serving her love-mate a traditional supper of broth, bread and city tap water, Della would sit almost in a trance-like state and annoyingly weep on the small shabby couch, and with her avaricious fingers, physically recount the un-spectacular dollar eighty-seven cents over and over again. 'I've been saving-up this amount since the Fourth of July, but Jim had to curtail my weekly allowance because of the drastic decrease in his wages and in trying to survive in his present pauper status. Oh well; I can't afford to get him a decent Christmas present,' Della whimpered. 'Maybe by Easter, things will change. I suppose I'll ambush and attack him in the shower and give my adorable hubby another round of fellatio. Damn it! I knew I should've married my old high school beau Bill Lingus and changed my lousy first name to Connie!'

Della sadly gazed at her reflection in the living room's shoddy-looking and faded pier-glass mirror. The very self-conscious wife removed her barrettes, and next methodically pulled-down her long brown hair and simultaneously thought, 'I'm still pretty curvaceous and attractive, especially when I smile. I think I know what to do to get some additional cash to buy Jim a nice Christmas gift, and my solution doesn't even involve selling my gorgeous body to lowlife, dirt-bag men! Yes; I know exactly what I'm gonna' do!'

Now there were two personal possessions that the James Dillingham Youngs separately took great pride in having. One was Jim's highly coveted gold watch that he had (by sheer accident and serendipitous good fortune) found lying on a train station bench. The other prized item was Della's magnificent, long-brown, wavy hair that would have had the ancient jealous Queen of Sheba shear-off her nipples just to own. And had envious King Solomon lived in the dingy upstairs apartment across the hall, Della would have certainly teased and tempted his colossal libido by sending the greedy ruler photos' in the mail of her being stark naked and showing her long, wavy tresses draping-down and tantalizingly covering her more personal body areas.

'Holy crapola! My fabulous hair reaches way below my knees and must weigh at least ten pounds! No wonder I have a stiff neck! I guess I don't have to join the Hair Club for Women now after all!' Della mused as the wife assessed and admired her fantastic appearance in the tawdry pier-glass mirror.

The next morning, when Jim was wearing his retread shoe-leather out traipsing throughout dangerous Bronx ghettos, trying to sell perfume and mascara that both smelled somewhat like cow piss, Della donned her black wool jacket and meticulously arranged her old brown hat upon her head, and with a certain sparkle of determination in her big brown eyes, the goal-minded spouse walked six blocks west to a frequented Manhattan salon owned by entrepreneurial Madame Sofaronie, who also was the proprietor of a number of popular and well-patronized bordellos in the bustling city's five boroughs.

"My name is Della Young, better known as Mrs. James Dillingham Young. Oh, how I hate all of this aggravating male chauvinism bullshit, starting with women having to change their last names when getting hitched! Now tell me Madame, will you buy my hair?" Della asked as she dropped her extraordinary tresses down to her knees. "It hasn't been cut in over ten years!"

"We'll buy your pubic hair too if you'd like," Madame Sofaronie stated with a forced smile. "There's a big market in the pussy replacement business, you know. When teenage girls and regular housewives shave their crotches to pose nude, lots of times their domineering boyfriends and spouses become upset, so the dolls then glue my company's bushy crotch wigs that fit quite beautifully around their precious cunt cracks. I use the newly manufactured crotch wigs all the time in my network of prosperous brothels when certain discriminating male clients insist on having girls with nice pussies, even if the bushes being screwed are artificial! Even my most demanding lesbian and dyke patrons are showing more than a mild interest in my gorgeous pussy wigs! But I must tell you Mrs. Young, there isn't such a big black market for underarm hair!"

"No thank you about shaving and selling my pussy fur Madame," Della politely declined. "My husband James is an old-fashioned bush man, even though he was born in the United States and not in Southern Africa. And besides," Mrs. James Dillingham Young confidentially articulated, "my affectionate Jim usually likes to beat around the bush before he pumps me silly!"

139

"Well then, Lady, er, I mean Mrs. Young, I'll give you twenty dollars for your marvelous flowing tresses," Madame Sofaronie offered. "I figure I could make at least three-to-four fine wigs from your nice thick locks."

"Show me the money!" Della shrieked with great delight saturating her intense verbal reaction. "I'll return to your salon in ten years when my hair finally fully grows back. In a decade, I'll be able to feel decadent again!"

Two hours later, Della was euphorically parading up and down Manhattan's Fifth Avenue in quest of the ideal Christmas gift for her beloved Jim. Finally, the object that fit her special purchasing needs was observed through the sidewalk window of an exclusive men's shop. 'That's it!' Della imagined and realized. 'It'll make Jim have a premature ejaculation for damned sure! Maybe his sex rocket will even be able to blast-off twice!'

The totally thrilled wife paid twenty-one dollars cash for the handsome and expensive platinum fob chain that she believed would complement Jim's highly-treasured gold watch. 'I still have eighty-seven cents left in my pocket,' the ecstatic woman calculated. 'Hey, I still have enough change left over to purchase a high school jock sweater for Jim to wear on cold winter nights! Maybe I'll head over to Macy's right now!'

Prudence once again governed Della's delicate mind, after she had merrily reached and entered the dismal, all-too-familiar upstairs low-budget apartment. The wife found her curling irons stashed-away inside her bureau's right top drawer, and next, carefully began maneuvering the difficult short locks that remained growing from her scalp. 'Maybe I should trim my pubic area after all and paste some hair patches needed in the sparser regions of my head,' the wife whimsically considered. 'I now really look cheap and sleazy in the mirror, just like one of those Coney Island chorus girls that work their butts off on weekends at wealthy Madame Sofaronie's Brooklyn bordello, after the exploited chicks have done their exhaustive striptease dancing over at those disreputable Surf Avenue honky-tonk lounges. Oh well; at least Jim will have a tremendous orgasm when he sees his new platinum present!'

At six p.m. the coffee was perking on the hob, and the leftover pork chops were sizzling in the frying pan upon the corroded stove. Jim was a half-hour late, and Della began worrying. 'Maybe he's been mugged by some ruthless teenage hooligans, or maybe Jim's found another woman to pump the poop out of!' But then joy filled the woman's heart when her perceptive ears detected the sound of familiar footsteps ascending the antiquated, condemned building's fire-hazard stairs.

The husband slowly opened the apartment door, and his overall appearance seemed weak; his posture poor; his knees buckled, and his face pallid. 'My husband needs a new overcoat, gloves, pants and rubbers; yes, especially rubbers!' Della automatically thought. 'Yes, Jim indeed needs plenty of rubbers! What wife in her right mind wants a couple of bratty, snot-nosed, totally obnoxious kids further ruining her already-miserable life and crazily screaming their damned, infected tonsils out?'

A peculiar expression of alarm showed upon Jim's pale countenance as the man of the apartment gazed at and studied Della's new short hairdo. The guilt-afflicted wife approached the slightly-warped, wooden coffee table to expressly comfort and console her special man.

"Jim, darling," Della greeted, tenderly feeling and massaging his whiskered face with both hands. "Please don't stare at me that way. I've done some huge sacrificing for you; yes, I have! I couldn't have survived the holiday season without giving you a most appropriate gift that I'm sure will bring you much joy and happiness. And please don't fret, even though you never learned how to play a guitar," the wife jested, trying to get her mate out of his very obvious negative mood. "I just had to follow my conscience and do it. My hair grows pretty fast. Please now Jim', let's be happy and not be so glum! Wait until you see the nice thing that I've bought for you!"

"You've cut off your goddamned hair!" the husband squawked and protested, pounding and collapsing the frail, wooden coffee table with his clenched fist before it collapsed to the dusty floor. "Cut your hair off! That's just like me cutting off my dick!"

"But my hair will grow back and your magnificent penis wouldn't!" smartly argued the wife, thus gaining a definite advantage in their dispute. "Don't you like me for what the hell I am, either with or without my tresses? I had my sensational hair bravely cut, and I sold it for a good price just for you, Jim!"

"You'd better not have sold your pubic bush, too!" yelled the infuriated man of the apartment. "Della, you're saying to me that your majestic hair is gone? Where did you hide it? Where the fuck did you hide it? I hope not under the coffee table!"

"You needn't search for it," the wife soberly related. "It's sold for a handsome profit, I tell ya'! Sold for your benefit Jim! Maybe the hairs on my exposed scalp are numbered, but nobody could ever count or weigh my tremendous love for you! Are you now ready to eat your leftover *chops* and quite prepared to forget about busting mine?"

The disconsolate husband reached into his cavernous coat pocket and removed several objects that were guaranteed to be future family heirlooms of sentimental value. "Forget about the goddamned broken coffee table, and check-out these nifty items before you wrongly judge my character. This extremely bizarre coincidence has to be the ultimate irony imaginable! Not even that clairvoyant asshole Nostradamus could've predicted this incredible bullshit!"

Della stared incredulously at the two excellent and exquisite sterling silver combs being held in the center of Jim's right palm. "Holy dog shit!" the wife marveled and exclaimed. "I've worshipped these things in a certain ritzy Fifth Avenue jewelry store display window for over a year now! I never thought that *we* could ever afford to possess these beauties in a million years! Oh Jim; you shouldn't have done this for me! You're the finest husband a dumb-ass wife like me could ever desire!"

The appreciative spouse gladly threw her skinny arms around her man's thick neck and began smooching away incessantly. "Oh Jim! My hair grows pretty damned fast, including my fluffy pubic bush and the vexing bristles that are always-sprouting under my armpits! I think I'll be able to proudly wear these luxurious combs in six short months. Please forgive me Jim for acting so freakin' hysterical! I promise you! By the next Fourth of July, I'll be proudly wearing them in my new hair on the Coney Island Boardwalk!"

And then Della realized something very relevant and pertinent, and she quickly reached inside her bra and swiftly removed the fancy platinum fob chain she had especially purchased for Jim's cherished gold timepiece. The item's stunning precious linked-metal gleamed; the radiant reflection seemingly matching the wife's bright, ardent, upbeat spirit.

"Jim, take a look at this little article I've acquired for you this morning, my dear benevolent soul mate. I bought it on Fifth Avenue just for you to have and to own. Isn't this incredible specimen a real dandy?" the exuberant wife declared. "You'll have to admire your gold watch at least a hundred-times a day now. Give me your timepiece so that I can immediately attach this most splendid platinum fob chain!"

Instead of obeying Della's suggestion, Jim tumbled onto the less-than-mediocre couch and momentarily cupped his hands over his face. Then, possessing a broken heart, the melancholy fellow had a rather extraordinary announcement to make.

"Della, let's put both our real and our imagined Christmas presents away for a while," the husband strangely prefaced his remarks. "They're entirely too superb for us to use, or even think about right now. Are you ready for a real shocker?" Jim rhetorically asked. "You have to understand that I had sold my gold watch so that I could purchase the sterling combs for your long brown hair; that is, for your now non-existent long brown hair! Damn it! Why couldn't I have attended and graduated from *Auburn* or *Brown* and made something big out of my boring, lackluster life!"

"Don't despair Jim," the supportive Mrs. Young answered in a bittersweet tone of voice. "It's not the expense of the gift that matters. In the final analysis, it's the true love in a fine marital relationship that genuinely represents the honest motivation for giving a special gift that really counts."

* * * * * * * * * * * *

The Magi were three important ancient Kings of the Orient, namely Melchior, Balthasar, and Gaspar, who had brought gifts of gold, frankincense and myrrh to the Christ Child lying in the stable manger in Bethlehem, expecting nothing in return for their heartfelt acts of kindness. Hence, the Magi are often referred to in literature and in standard Christmas carols as "The Three Wise Men". And in this magical chronicle of human wisdom, Della and James Dillingham Young discovered and confirmed the greatest gift of all: eternal and non-pretentious love for each other.

"The Last Leaf"

In the southern district of cosmopolitan New York City known as Greenwich Village, the narrow streets are arranged in an irregular configuration, and those small strips situated west of Washington Square are called "Places". Many of the houses in that overcrowded section are apartment buildings; inferior tenements that are rented-out primarily to artists, actors, painters, sculptors, prostitutes, and musicians. The city canvas artists, along with the newspaper and magazine pornography sketchers, prefer the uppermost floors that feature eighteenth century gables, certain secluded Dutch attics that the avant-garde artists call "studios", and of course, the modest dwellings command low-rents to accommodate the highly populated colony's Picasso, Rembrandt, Norman Rockwell, and Thomas Nast aspiring wannabes'.

At the top garret of one of those antiquated old Dutch-style tenements, two young lesbians named Sue and Johnsy (that wanted fame and fortune as contemporary artists) resided in their cozy and modest "studio". One frigid mid-December night, the pair had been impatiently standing inside Delmonico's Restaurant, where the main dining room had been very jam-packed, and so the wishful artists (possessing similar interests and ambitions) had coincidentally met in the long reservations' waiting line, and then ultimately agreed to share a table.

In January, just after the New Year had been celebrated in Times Square, an insidious villain identified in the newspapers as "Mr. Pneumonia" had infiltrated into the shadowed ghettos of New York City, smiting victim after victim, and the result of *his* wicked, heartless pandemic had rapidly filled virtually every remaining gravesite in the city's cemeteries.

Sue was from New England, and had developed good resistance to rampant respiratory diseases, but Johnsy had lived most of her young life in Southern California, and was very susceptible to any bacteria or virus that the eastern winter atmosphere had to offer. The afflicted West Coast girl lay motionless in her single bed, and poor Johnsy steadfastly stared-out the studio apartment window, her body in a trance-like state; and her bloodshot, blue eyes being fixated directly on the rear red brick wall of the adjacent, crowded tenement house.

The second Monday morning of January, 1914. the overworked arts-community doctor climbed the humble tenement's rickety steps, entered the back studio room, carefully examined Johnsy's pathetic physical condition, and then summoned Sue out into the hallway for a brief consultation.

"No, your blonde-haired friend does not have any life-threatening venereal disease," Dr. Wynan communicated to alleviate Sue's initial concern. "Instead, she's contracted the dreaded pneumonia that's been contagious throughout the city, and Johnsy has maybe a one-in-ten chance at surviving the current epidemic that's on an evil crusade. The mercury in my thermometer registered an all-too-high one hundred and three temperature, and I'm sorry to report that the local hospital's beds are all filled to capacity, and that they're not admitting any more patients. In fact, Miss Sue," the medical man elaborated, "there are no more large enough areas left in the facility to effectively quarantine the great number of extremely sick pneumonia victims. Even the goddamned undertakers are dropping like flies and dying from the major epidemic menace. If I may jest a bit Miss Sue, I'm even considering taking equestrian lessons and becoming one of the Horsemen of the Apocalypse! I mean, ya' gotta' have a flexible sense of humor to endure and survive this horrendous urban holocaust in progress! Wouldn't you agree?"

"Is that your definitive prognosis?" Sue lethargically asked Dr. Wynan. "Johnsy and I were just getting to know each other intimately, and were even thinking about inventing something called 'same sex marriage' right here in New York. We first met in line at Delmonico's. Now everything's being tossed into the hopper!"

"Your little lady friend has made-up her mind that she wants to die," the traveling physician sadly revealed. "Tell me Miss Sue; did Johanna, or should I say Johnsy as you affectionately call your girlfriend; did Johnsy have any particular interests or goals she wished to pursue before becoming so horribly incapacitated?"

"Yes Dr. My roommate wanted to paint the Bay of Nipples, er, I meant to say the Italian Bay of Naples," the aggrieved artist sobbed, blowing and then vigorously wiping her nose mucus upon her long dress sleeve.

"How the hell could she ever paint the Bay of Naples?" Dr. Wynan marveled and exclaimed. "That absurd project would require at least a million-million-million gallons of dark blue paint, and that's just the damned primer coat! Doesn't your gay roommate Johnsy understand that paint doesn't adhere to water?"

"No Dr.; I had meant that Johnsy wanted to paint the Bay of Naples on a canvas placed upon her easel," Sue clarified. "And after doing that, while still vacationing and working in that beautiful part of Italy, Johnsy had plans of painting Mt. Vesuvius, too; that is to say, painting the inactive volcano on a separate canvas!"

"What I had meant to articulate to you, Miss Sue, was this," Dr. Wynan said before removing a tin flask of hard liquor from his suit jacket's secret compartment, and then chugging-down several very ample swigs. "Excuse me! That imbibing you just witnessed was for medicinal purposes only! Now then Miss Sue; I meant to ask you if Miss Johnsy had any special man in her life to think about. That kind of hope might give her the necessary inspiration and the emotional strength she needs to valiantly combat the potentially-lethal disease that's taken over her body."

"No Dr. Wynan. Johnsy and I have a sort of civil union going where we share everything including our bodies," the slightly embarrassed roommate confided. "The plus side of our relationship is that neither of us has to worry about becoming pregnant or having an abortion. But that's all changed now that Johnsy seems to have purchased a one-way ticket to Heaven!"

"Well, Miss Sue. I'll provide you with some medicine and some pain pills, and we'll just have to let Mother Nature randomly practice her will," the local tablet dispenser and drug dealer bluntly summarized. "But as you're well aware, science can only do so much, and no more. Try getting your frail companion to speak and talk about fashion, or gay marriage, or anything else that floats her boat. Otherwise," Dr. Wynan predicted, "get ready for the Grim Reaper's lethal stalk. That roaming son-of-a-bitchin' prowler doesn't miss eliminating his targeted victim too damned often!"

After the bad news doctor departed the premises by tripping and then violently tumbling down the stairs, Sue darted into the small side room and cried her eyeballs out; her tears causing a quickly saturated Japanese napkin to turn to pulp. Then the young red-hair woman grabbed her drawing board and stepped into the studio where Johnsy was lying prone in a comatose state of existence.

'I'll start that pen and ink freelance drawing I plan on sketching for that literary magazine where the editor is a male homosexual that wants to see me succeed,' Sue fondly recollected. 'I should go into the asphalt and macadam business so that my road to success would be more easily paved!' the aspiring artist mused.

As Sue diligently sketched an Idaho cowboy wearing a monocle while riding a fierce bucking bronco, her concentration was suddenly interrupted as Johnsy began uttering a bizarre numerical sequence in her unconscious state. Immediately, the alarmed listener ceased her intellectual art experimentation, wondering what evil influence had been the cause of the suffering girl's weird, oratorical aberration. 'What kind of satanic bullshit is this? Whatever happened to the goddamned alphabet? She's obsessively counting her memorized numbers backwards!' the roommate recognized.

"Twelve, eleven, ten," Johnsy distinctly uttered those designations at three-second intervals. "Nine, eight, seven, six," she continued her strange countdown-in-reverse.

'Holy shit!' Sue nervously thought. 'Johnsy either thinks she's firing off a rocket, or counting the number of bottles of beer on the wall! What the frig' is this fucked-up anomaly all about?'

Then, the petrified woman from New England looked solicitously out the studio's window and quickly fathomed the reason for Johnsy's weird verbalizations. The neighboring brick house's rear outside wall was a mere twenty-feet away, and what had over the years climbed the residence's exterior was a gnarled ivy vine. Autumn's chilling winds had claimed most of the vine's withered leaves, and had shaken them to the ground but still, *five* extremely vulnerable growths still remained.

"What is it that you're counting?" Sue gently whispered into her roommate's left ear. "I can count on you to tell me!"

"Five," Johnsy spoke in a scary, monotone voice. "Four," was her next utterance three seconds later. "When the last leaf falls, then I must go, too," the girl answered and prophesied, sounding as if she were speaking from another dimension or world. "There're only four leaves left," the sick girl stated from her unconscious condition. "When the last leaf falls off," the bedridden girl expressed, "that's when I'll fall and disappear, too!"

'Holy crap! I'd better not write all of this crazy shit down on *loose leaf* paper!' Sue's disheveled mind imagined. "Here Johnsy! Try to swallow-down some of this delicious broth! This tasty bouillon will make you feel like a billion. In fact, Johnsy, this tasty yellow bouillon is much better than gold bullion, as far as your deteriorating health is concerned!"

"Sue," the sick girl said from her horizontal, trance-like state. "When the last leaf falls, so do I. Four!" the infirmed roommate reiterated. "Four!" Johnsy frightfully repeated. "The fuckin' ivy vine seems to be stuck on four!"

"Keep your eyes closed and don't look out the damned window!" Sue imperatively commanded. "I need to sell a few drawings in a hurry, so that *we* can afford a friggin' window shade! Otherwise, if I don't, it'll certainly be curtains for you, my precious Johnsy!"

"I can't wait to die! I need to succumb! Come on, you stupid, goddamned leaves! Drop the hell off so that I can swiftly journey to paradise!" Johnsy scarily declared.

'I know what I'll do! I'll call old Mr. Behrman up here to pose as a miner sitting on a rock,' Sue decided. 'Behrman will be my model, and while he's up here, I'll tell the fossil-faced asshole all about poor Johnsy's dilemma. Maybe he'll be able to give me some sound advice, or be able to help my roommate recover from this shit respiratory disease called pneumonia! I've heard rumors that Behrman had once studied to be a voodoo witchdoctor before he ventured into painting murals, frescoes, and canvas portraits. Now the dumb-ass, drunken, old-coot, insane bastard has to settle for painting dilapidated rooms, shanties, and sleazy whorehouses!"

* * * * * * * * * * * *

Old Wilhelm Behrman lived on the ground floor, and the dumb fuck honestly believed that he had been Michelangelo, Marie Curie, Cleopatra, a ferocious mastiff, and Moses in his previous lives. For forty frustrating years, Wilhelm Behrman had wielded a brush, and never once was invited to have an art exhibit, and never once had he ever sold a canvas painting while canvassing all of Greenwich Village. But the ancient fool's major dream was to paint a masterpiece, but in order to pay for his next meal and his cheap apartment rent, Behrman often posed as a model, even though he wasn't a model citizen. And the old lush's severe drinking habit was indeed an abominable curse; drinking-down gin and tonic, often swallowing hair tonic stolen from another mentally confused and deranged apartment resident, who believed that *he* had been a Teutonic (two-tonic) knight during the fucked-up medieval period in European (Your-a-peon) history, a weird period when most the living, unwary, assholes frolicked amid-evil!

The inebriated Wilhelm Behrman gladly accepted the assignment of posing as a gold-panning miner sitting on top of a boulder, symbolizing to his degenerate mind that he was somewhere between a rock and a hard place and not getting any *bolder,* because of the very hard and uncomfortable huge stone.

Sue was encouraged to observe that Johnsy was sleeping soundly in her fleabag bed. She and Wilhelm then apprehensively paced to the studio window, and both were greatly relieved to witness that a single leaf still remained clinging to the ivy vine. Wilhelm then assisted the red-haired artist in hanging a bed-sheet over the window to serve as a makeshift curtain. After working-up a sweat from his most recent laborious ordeal, the exhausted old wheezer then further irritated his itchy hemorrhoids by faithfully sitting for four long hours, all the while pretending to be a determined Western gold prospector taking a five-minute break from his arduous toil. Unfortunately for Behrman's bothersome rectal discomfort, without *his* knowledge, Sue had left the apartment to go to the pharmacy, and then to the grocery store, to obtain medicine and nourishing food supplies to keep her soul-mate Johnsy alive.

* * * * * * * * * * * *

The following morning, after Sue awoke from a terrible nightmare, the loyal roommate brought Johnsy some cold orange juice to drink in order to lower the doleful girl's fever. "I'll give you a nice sponge bath to further cool you down, and I won't forget to thoroughly wash your personals. Don't worry, Johnsy! I'll take good care of you! What am I fuckin' saying? I can't even take care of myself!"

"Sue," the blonde young lady replied almost-miraculously, and then opening her swollen eyes. "Tear down that dirty bed sheet so that I can see if the last leaf has fallen."

Afraid of what might *not* be behind the opaque sheet, Sue reluctantly did as her dying friend had requested. And lo and behold; the fierce, gusty winds of the night before had not removed the last leaf, which still bravely clung to the ivy vine.

"I thought for sure that it would've dropped by now!" Johnsy said, almost with remorse. "I heard the strong gales blowing last evening, and without a doubt, tonight the leaf will plummet, and so will my soul; right into Hell for being a sinful, self-centered, practicing lesbian! If only I could've shown behavioral restraint. If only I could've been celibate, and chaste, and faithfully exercised good Christian abstinence."

"Johnsy, please get your mind off of dying and of going straight to Hell," Sue mildly reprimanded her dear friend. "If you won't worry about yourself, please think of me and my wretched circumstances! If you die like you want to, I'll have to masturbate at least four times a day until I finally find a suitable, cute, little blonde-haired replacement for you! It's not easy being a tough-chick dyke nowadays, let me tell ya'!"

But Johnsy was so weak that she again closed her heavy eyes without ever answering. The most lonesome thing in the world is a soul when it is making ready to take its journey into the unknown afterlife. The daylight hours slowly passed, and all night long, the extremely strong winds blew, and fierce torrents of rain pelted against the century-old Dutch eaves, but when sunrise gradually arrived, the amazing last leaf had not fallen.

Johnsy rested in her bed, and for several hours, her bloodshot eyes peered-out the garret window at the incomparable last leaf. After consuming her chicken broth and sipping-down a glass of cool refreshing water, the guilty-minded pneumonia victim confessed to her empathetic roommate, "I've been a naughty girl, Sue. That last leaf is still up there against the brick wall to show me how utterly wrong and selfish I had been; wanting to sinfully die and end it all! Bring me a little more broth, some milk and a glass of port wine," the indisposed young lady requested. "And also, please bring me two more pillows for me to prop-up my head. I'll sit-up in bed and watch you draw, and then later, I'll see you prepare lunch."

"If you get better, Johnsy, I promise to take you to Italy so that you can paint the Bay of Nipples, er, I mean Naples!"

Later in the day, Dr. Wynan paid the apartment's occupants an unscheduled visit, and the gentleman was astounded at noticing the vast improvement in health that petite "Johanna" was experiencing and exhibiting. "I'm not a gambling man, and I don't even play bingo at the local Catholic Church, but from what I can observe, I give her a fifty-fifty chance of beating it!" the M.D. told Sue. "With good nursing and tender loving care, she just might beat the despicable disease! Her spirit must be invincible after all the sickness crap that she's encountered! But now, I must go and visit another very sick patient downstairs."

"Who is it?" Sue curiously asked. "I know everybody that lives in this piss-poor tenement!"

"His name is Behrman; a kind of an oddball artist, so I hear," the beleaguered physician related. "He's somehow had the bad luck of contracting pneumonia, too! But I understand that he's an old weak fellow, and his attack has been both acute and severe. There's little hope for him, I'm afraid to say!" Dr. Wyman stated with mild regret. "I just hope that his Guardian Angel was alert and has already escorted him to the Pearly Gates."

The following morning, the on-the-go doctor again visited Johnsy and reported to Sue that her art partner was "wonderfully out of danger". Then, the family practitioner sagaciously advised, "But I warn you; no perverted lesbian sex for at least a goddamned week! I suggest that you now scamper over to the fish store and buy for yourself a dozen clams without beards to tide yourself over!"

Later that same day, Sue entered the secluded studio and had a brief-but-enlightening, meaningful-but-direct conversation with her recuperating companion. "I have some rather bad news to report Johnsy. Mr. Behrman had died at the hospital at dawn from the dreaded pneumonia. The cleaning lady had found him lying on the floor of his hideous, rodent-infested room. Wilhelm's shoes and clothes were soaking wet through-and-through, and icy cold, too."

"How did he ever get himself into such a horrible condition?" Johnsy wondered and asked. "He had often told me that he never wanted to visit either Siberia or Antarctica!"

"Well, there were some obvious tell-tale clues that hinted at what had actually happened," Sue joylessly informed her courageous girlfriend. "The cleaning lady had found a lantern, a ladder, and some scattered brushes, along with a palette with green and yellow colors mixed on it."

"Why is life such an ugly travesty Sue? You don't mean to say that..."

"Yes, Johnsy; I believe that your assumption is absolutely right! Just look out the window at that last stout ivy leaf! Didn't you wonder why it had never fluttered away?"

"Yes," Johnsy replied. "And it never swayed or moved when the wind blew!"

"That last leaf is Mr. Behrman's masterpiece that he always wanted to complete! He had painted it up there on our neighbor's rear brick and mortar wall; the same damned night that the last leaf fell!"

"The Higher Pragmatism"

This might be a marvelous story about Divine Intervention, or it might not be; the ultimate verdict would be depending on the interpreter's religious/moral/scientific orientation. Call it fate; call it destiny, or for the more cynical-minded, call it the result or the consequence of transcendent *chance*. Some critics will believe that an idea is only practical if it actually truly works. Regardless of the individual decider's unique perspective, positive thinking should always triumph over negativity, and then emerge victorious over skepticism and over doubt. And *that* particular sage conclusion is what is meant by the following appropriate nomenclature: The Higher Pragmatism.

I had found Richard (or "Big Dick" as the vagabond wanted to be known) lying prone on a park bench in Lower Manhattan's Washington Square Park. After Big Dick had routinely asked me for a meager quarter donation, and when I adamantly refused his panhandling solicitation, that perchance was the opportune moment when I half-heartedly initiated our rather remarkable conversation. For the sake of brevity, here's precisely how our minor chance encounter had actually occurred.

"Hi; my name's Mack, and I'm a struggling newspaper reporter searching for my next big scoop," I falsely began my salutation. "May I sit down and join your dignified company?"

"If ya' want a scoop, go sit your ass down inside an ice cream parlor and leave me the fuck alone," scruffy-looking Big Dick snottily answered. "If ya' ain't got a lousy quarter for me, then I ain't got the time of day for you."

I momentarily hesitated, but then reached into my pocket, removed fifty cents, and next reluctantly handed the loose change to the gregarious and pretentious mendicant. "Now Big Dick," I proceeded with my phony introduction. "My demanding editor has assigned me to document the experience of an unfortunate victim of fate such as yourself; a person that might be illegally loitering while occupying a park bench here near Greenwich Village this fine evening. Tell me Sir; what do you suppose might have heavily contributed to your downfall from our American culture's socio-economic graces?"

My rather corny-but-un-hilarious initial presentation was swiftly interrupted by a strong laugh, which soon morphed into a loud roaring guffaw. Then, the totally uncouth fellow identifying himself as Big Dick coughed-up a quantity of disgusting green phlegm, spit at and hit an unwary. slow-walking pigeon that was pecking-away at some discarded pretzel crumbs upon the ground, and then the itinerant philosopher addressed me in what my ears discerned as a facetious tone of voice.

"Okay, Asshole," Richard disrespectfully stated. "You ain't no goddamned newspaper reporter, that's for damned certain. A genuine story-seekin' gumshoe just pretends to be a city bum, and is usually disguised to look like one, too. You don't appear to be any hobo or tramp on the lam; or a freeloader that's just jumped-off of the last freight train from St. Louis," Richard shrewdly determined. "Over time, us park derelicts get to be fine judges of human nature, and we're much more aware of reality than your goddamned average psychologist or college professor happens to be. We develop our keen insights by sittin' on park benches all day looking and seriously studyin' people's antics and semantics, so I don't give a flyin' fuck about the abstract quality of certain things like most academic assholes do! As a matter of fact," the tramp rambled-on, "I can size-up most any man much better than your average asshole tailor can! Well now, Sir, that's the true advantage of bein' a regular, fucked-up neighborhood bum like myself."

"Well then, Big Dick," I articulated with a degree of chagrin evident in my stilted intonation. "How do you size me up? Do you have a customized tailor-made answer for that specific inquiry of mine, too? Did you graduate from Prophecy University, or from What's a Matter U.?" I mockingly challenged.

"Look Mack, my initial assessment was that you were in the contracting business, but then I surmised that maybe you worked your ass off in a department store, or perhaps now you're a damned unemployed sign painter," Richard haphazardly speculated and guessed. "But I presently conjecture that you've stopped here in the park to finish smokin' your expensive imported cigar, and thought you'd amuse yourself for a few minutes by pickin' away at my pea brain. But still, ya' might just be a parasite lawyer, or a mobile wall plasterer lookin' for his next gullible customer. It's getting pretty fuckin' dark out," Big Dick observed and vociferated. "And my most recent analysis is that I think you and your wife just had a violent argument, because the untamed shrew won't let you smoke your malodorous cigars anywhere inside the house."

"I think you're full of shit all the way from your asshole right up to your hyperactive larynx!" I angrily replied. "You don't know shit about shit; so ya' can't just simply be an idle asshole who's laid-off from the city's sanitation department!"

"But judging again on hindsight," Big Dick continued his analysis, while completely ignoring my general diatribe. "On second thought, I'd say that you don't have any bossy wife after all; even though your intolerable disposition amply suggests to me that you're absolutely henpecked. Are ya' married or divorced?"

"No, no, no!" I exclaimed, wildly motioning my hands in animation. "I'm proud to say that I'm pretty evasive and have skillfully avoided Cupid's speeding darts. If I may say so, that…"

"I detect that you have a fucked-up story to tell me from either guilt or need," the vagrant accurately hypothesized and declared. "Here are your crummy fifty cents back, and a goddamned five-dollar bill to boot. Now's your one and only chance to have an unbiased, philanthropic expert objectively help you along the road of life! I won't even charge you a penny for my professional services."

Somehow, Richard's exceptional attitude and extraordinary demeanor caught my vulnerable fancy, and so I immediately gained some curiosity about the extent of his intelligence, and therefore, had to attempt measuring it through dialogue. "Confidentially, I've never disclosed to any of my friends my personal dilemma, so why not share my innermost thoughts and fears with you, Big Dick?"

At least that was my mental inclination at that specific moment in time. After all, my new, almost-anonymous acquaintance seemed perfectly harmless and innocuous. So, like the proverbial sentimental fool often featured in popular song lyrics, I've always been governed and influenced by inferior-minded people, ever since my early adolescence. Consequently, on that city park bench in late October of 1910, I naively opened my heart and confided the essence of my sorrows to that obnoxious, foul-smelling 'imperfect stranger'.

I told 'Richard the Mouse-hearted' that I had spent many months adoring a voluptuous, big-breasted, sophisticated doll named Mildred Ingram. I shared with Big Dick my grievous days of uncertainty; my vacillating hopes; along with my crushed romantic dreams, and finally, I divulged my countless hours of overwhelming emotional stress and duress that I had suffered. The devil-may-care night prowler even heard plenty of confessions about my perpetual frustration in not being able to overcome the lofty position that her distinguished family had maintained in genteel New York City high society. "Mildred has grace and dignity, and her parents have big bucks going back at least a century," I sadly lamented to my new guidance counselor.

"Why don't ya' just ask the rich bitch to marry ya?" Big Dick impulsively advised with a prodigious smirk showing above his chin. "Take the hot-to-trot hussy out to Coney Island for some honky-tonk entertainment, and during the height of your recreation and revelry, ask the high society bitch if she wants to screw and do sixty-nine before the wedding day!"

Showing deep cowardice when it came to expressing myself about one gorgeous Mildred Ingram, I explained to Poor Richard (lacking his almanac) that I had (like a total ignoramus) lost my entire savings gambling in the stock market, and also had amassed major deficits out at the local race track, and that I lacked the courage to hock my most prized possessions at the neighborhood pawn shop and purchase a cheap diamond ring that would accompany my belated marriage proposal. "When I'm in Mildred's illustrious company," I complained to my new shabbily-dressed consultation guru, "the only overt behaviors I can exhibit are stammering, stuttering, drooling and blushing. Mildred probably thinks that I'm the biggest jerk if not the biggest jerk-off in all of Manhattan!"

"The rich bitch sounds like a real professional when it comes to bein' a goddamned tease," the erudite Big Dick sagely evaluated. "You're overwhelmed by her dignity, her beauty, her family name, and her firm ass and big tits, aren't ya' Mack?"

"She's all of those things and much more," I remarked. "She's Venus reincarnated! She's Aphrodite's twin sister!"

My casual comment instantly inspired my lowest-income-level friend to again begin lecturing. "Tell me the truth; Mack; does this high society dame have any sisters?" my new-found psychologist asked. "Sometimes, ya' can cleverly use sibling rivalry to your own advantage in order to achieve the upper edge you're fuckin' lookin' for. Do ya' know any other girls that might make this Mildred jealous if she sees you grabbin' and feelin' their tits, or pinchin' and goosin' their tight, desirable asses?"

"I know dozens of beautiful girls, but none of them would ever permit me to do those vulgar things to them; either in pubic, er, I mean in public, or exclusively in front of Mildred," I revealed a little too honestly. "But I wouldn't be afraid to hold any of their hands in the dark over at the nickelodeon; that is, any of 'em but the most attractive Mildred Ingram."

"It seems that you're just basically afraid of this rich bitch, and no other woman seems to faze you," Big Dick perceptively theorized and concluded. "Now let me tell ya' *my* real-life case as a model example for you to study, and perhaps imitate. Just feel my muscle!" the almost-penniless bum said, flexing his right upper arm.

I consented and followed his strange command, and mechanically and obediently felt his upper right appendage. Then, I was flabbergasted at what Richard told me, because his profound wisdom amazingly pertained to my own personal, actual long-term problem with Mildred Ingram, but the comparative relationship existed in a rather ironic-but-convoluted way. Here's the exact, rather-incredible language that went down between him and me.

"Four years ago," Big Dick commenced his relevant narrative, "I could beat the shit out of any man in the city; and I often did just that," the unshaven and unkempt vagrant seriously boasted. "Now listen carefully, Mack, because your situation and mine are even more parallel than railroad tracks, and believe me; I know a fuckin' lot about railroad tracks, empty freight cars, cabooses and the like. I was in a pissed-off mood that particular night and feelin' pretty goddamned pugnacious, as opposed to you, usually bein' altogether recessive and pusillanimous. Anyway, Mack," the on-a-roll fellow resumed his bizarre braggadocio, "I was a formidable street brawler when I was only ten-years-old, and when I was twenty, I was the best amateur middle-weight fighter in the whole shit-eatin' metropolis, and nobody could go beyond four rounds with me. I had a devastatin' right cross and a hammer-of-Thor left hook, not to mention my Herculean uppercut to the victim's jaw! I went undefeated boxing all over the West Side at charity benefits, at private parties, and at backyard barbecues, but never fightin' for money; just for the sake of sport."

"Did you ever consider fighting professionally, since you were so good as an amateur?" I sincerely asked. "Both you and my love Mildred Ingram do have something in common after all. You're both knockouts!" I idiotically commented.

Big Dick pretended that I didn't say anything, either smart or stupid. "Listen Mack; every time I got into the ring with a professional pugilist for money, my confidence dwindled; my knees buckled, and then I egregiously got the shit beaten out of me; really pummeled ya' might say! My face saw more fuckin' canvas than that crazy asshole Picasso ever did!" the derelict grossly exaggerated. "The minute I saw the large crowd in the arena that had paid big bucks to see me perform, I became terribly intimidated, and the minute that my opponent stepped through the ropes, I shit my pants, er, I mean crapped my trunks!"

"Well then, Rich, if I may call you that, you' poor slob," I bravely editorialized. "How the hell did you ever solve your perplexing confidence problem? You must've been in a friggin' panic mode with the advent of each successive professional bout crisis!"

"Well, after I quit jabbin' and parryin' as a failed professional boxer, I was so fuckin' pissed-off that I went around the city after dark and then wildly beat the shit out of anybody that looked at me the wrong way," Richard astoundingly communicated his general woe. "I even knocked the snot out of the nostrils of a couple of belligerent cab drivers; several hostile milkmen and mailmen; a handful of knife-wieldin' pimps, and a few loud-mouthed cops, too."

"Wow, you beat the crap out of so many people that no one in the entire city was full of shit anymore," I foolishly jested. "You should've focused your energies on all the bullshitting politicians, and done the rest of us an enormous public service!"

"Anyway," Richard proceeded with his illuminating commentary. "One fine evening, I was walkin' down near the Bowery lookin' for some self-satisfyin' fighting adventure. Seven drunken assholes came paradin' in my direction, all dressed in tuxedos, tails and carryin' canes; the group lookin' like a gaggle of fuckin' penguins. One of the brazen punks pushes me to one side of the pavement, and I didn't take kindly to his discourteous gesture. The jerk-off in question put-up a decent fight, just like the ones ya' see in those new-fangled silent motion pictures. In fact," Richard elaborated. "The other guy had some science and artistry, but then I creamed his ass with a savage right cross that could've been a five-hundred-pound crucifix as far as my doomed foe was concerned."

"Wow! What a tremendous story! Did ya' ever discover the unfortunate victim's name?" I inquired. "Did the dumb drunken shit require hospitalization? Was there any significant brain damage that you had so mercilessly inflicted?"

"Well, Mack, here's the goddamned irony that I had been tellin' ya' about," my ingenious new buddy proudly disclosed. "One of the unconscious jerk-off's friends, his manager, a clown named Easy Ed Elliott, then tells me right there on the Bowery Park scene, overlookin' the in-cherry-condition Statue of Liberty, that I had just brutally knocked out Reddy Burns, the reigning middleweight champion of the whole goddamned world. I learned that Burns had arrived in town just the day before, because the famous boxer was tryin' to get a promotional match with the invincible Jim Jeffries," Richard convincingly related. "But truthfully, if I had known I was fightin' Reddy Burns, I would've thrown in the towel and folded right away when the lousy arrogant bully had deliberately and roughly shoved me into the nearby shrubbery, because the fuck-head had thought I was a wimpy weakling *pushover* standin' in his goddamned way."

"I'm not a boxer, or any other breed of dog," I quipped, showing-off my fucked-up personality's comedy side. "What does prize-fighting have to do with *my* bewildering predicament involving Mildred Ingram? I'm not a fighter, and apparently, I'm not a very good lover either," I told Big Dick. "Perhaps I need some dynamic sex hormone pills, or maybe an effective aphrodisiac to get my sticky sperm juices flowing in the right freakin' direction, so that I could pop the mess right-out of my enlarged. erect love tube and directly into Mildred's warm and loving crotchola!"

"You're destined to fall even deeper in love with this enticin' Mildred bitch, just like I had been destined to get my ass kicked a multitude of times in the professional ring," Big Dick pessimistically predicted as the park-bench philosopher sat there next to me, his left hand vigorously scratching his testicles. "In boxing parlance, you're afraid to enter the ring and pursue the biggest conquest of your unenviable, piss-poor life! When it comes to this rich dame that you're so mesmerized with, you're a rank amateur, Mack. And I strongly recommend that you not stick your head through the three vertical ropes, because you're fuckin' afraid of entering the ring."

I was so impressed with Big Dick's oratory that I gave him a ten-dollar tip, which the contemporary "Bowery" Socrates eagerly and enthusiastically accepted as well-deserved compensation. At that 'epiphany moment', my mind was in a perpetual frenzy after hobnobbing with the modern-day genius for a full hour.

But then, my suspicious and imaginative brain construed Big Dick as my personal enemy. 'I'll show this know-it-all two-bit tramp that I can fight the high society equivalent of Reddy Burns, and emerge as the victor. Within the last hour, I've miraculously turned into the foremost authority on the esoteric art of successfully proposing marriage. In fact,' I pledged to my growing ego, 'I'm gonna' demonstrate that I'm about to become totally invincible at love; just like champion Jim Jeffries is at boxing.'

I hurried to a nearby public telephone near Wall Street and Broadway, and excitedly rang-up the ultra-conservative, Uptown Ingram residence. I gulped as a female voice answered my dramatic rushed call. The moment of truth and courage had finally arrived.

"Is that you, Darling?" I asked, feeling quite omnipotent and virile in my presentation. "I need to talk with you, Honey, about a terribly urgent matter."

"Yes, this is, I!" came back angelic, beautiful language in a very grammatically correct and utterly sweet female voice. "Who is this please? Your voice sounds awful, er, I mean awfully familiar!"

"Why it's me, the inimitable and irresistible Mack Gordon!" I politely yelled, showing an excess of feigned anger at not having my masculine baritone immediately recognized by my favorite woman over the telephone. "And furthermore," I very confidently added in my most mellow tone of enunciation. "I have a few rather pertinent items I need to speak to you about, so I might as well promptly get right to the point and address them to you right now."

"Dear me!" exclaimed the suddenly thrilled Ingram girl. "Oh; yes; it's you Mr. Mack Gordon! You sound so energetic and so stimulated! What's on your mind?"

"I just gotta' get down to brass tacks," I neurotically insisted. "You know, of course, that I'm madly in love with you; yes; ecstatically in love with you, right to the brink of insanity. I gotta' confess that I've been incarcerated in this idiotic slave-like infatuation state for over a year now, so I guess it's truly more love that puppy infatuation, or something like that!" I awkwardly expressed in circumlocutory language. "Now mind you; I demand a definitive answer right now, so be prepared to respond. I wanna' truthfully know; will *you* marry me or not? Here's a bland suggestion. Let's be adults about this very crucial subject, and approach this matter with measured maturity!"

"Holy shit! Oh Mack; why certainly! I'll be more than thrilled-to-death to be your ever-lovin' wife! Oh Mack, please flag-down the next cab and come up to the mansion right this minute! I just can't wait for your wonderful embrace! I want you to kiss and caress me all over!" Click.

* * * * * * * * * * *

Well, I hastily arrived at the Ingram's Park Avenue palace as quickly as I could get there. I forcefully rang the harmony-toned doorbell and impatiently waited; twiddling my thumbs in the interim. A handsomely dressed butler, wearing a white, curly Revolutionary War era wig and matching impressive, red coat with an accompanying compatible white and blue uniform, greeted me, and then the benign servant formally announced my presence.

'Oh well,' thought I, with my big brown eyes turned upwards, closely examining the ornate, intricate cornice work, and also the delicate-looking crystal chandelier anchored into the foyer's ceiling. Then, my wandering mind made a powerful realization. 'I'm presently a big step up and above *that* obnoxious park bench scumbag Big Dick now!' I thought. 'His incidental knocking-out the notorious Reddy Burns has absolutely nothing over on me and my recently discovered love prowess! God; do I feel potent!'

Suddenly, my trembling knees began to knock as I heard footsteps descending the upper part of the Park Avenue castle's magnificent spiral staircase. Foolishly, I looked around for a convenient window or trap door from which I could escape my sudden anxiety attack. But then fortunately, my rationality took command of my fluctuating emotions, when I plausibly considered exactly how much I actually loved the stunning and dazzling debutante, Miss Mildred Hortense Ingram. 'The hard part is over!' I rationally reckoned. 'She's already consented to my proposal over the phone.'

But just then, the side dining room door swung open, and in stepped little Betsy Ingram, Mildred's charming younger sister, who at that confluence of space and time, looked like a radiant, glorified angel herself'.

"Hi Betsy," I greeted, unaware of any impending surprise. "You look just as beautiful as Mildred always does, and I just gotta' flatter you some more. Your impeccable blue eyes are a sight to behold, and also, your firm breasts, er, I mean your firm hands are indeed an alluring sight to be held."

"Why Mack Gordon," Betsy replied with a florid, blushing face. "All the while I thought it was my sister Mildred that you had the royal hots for. Oh my God! You don't know how positively euphoric I am that you've asked me to marry you over the telephone! How original and daring! You do have audacity and style, Mack; I just have to concede you that!"

Amazingly, in conclusion to my small fascinating tale with a twist involving a certain degree of 'Higher Pragmatism,' I suspect that *that* pathetic failure known only as Richard or "Big Dick", and me, Mack Gordon, will always be helpless amateurs no matter how long we each might live upon this majestic Earth. But in *my* singular matrimonial/marital bliss case, I'm mighty glad of my amateur status; and furthermore, I hope and plan to be married to my second marriage choice, vivacious Betsy Ingram, until "Death do us part"!

"The Cop and the Anthem"

As any above-average, acne-faced, eighth-grade student knows, O. Henry was William Sydney Porter's (1862-1910) penname. Porter's short stories are notorious for their "twist", or surprise endings, that usually involve the literary element of irony appearing in a parallel dual development situation.

Soapy sat uneasily upon a New York City park-bench, looking at the dying flowers that had been planted inside a circular Madison-Square-garden. A brisk, late autumn wind and overhead honking geese signaled the end of Indian summer, and the belated approach of nasty winter. The vagabond knew he needed a warm place to stay until the arrival of the next vernal equinox. A dead leaf fluttered-down from a tall oak tree and fell upon Soapy's lap, symbolically representing the dire coldness soon to envelop the city.

'It looks like the end of fall!' Soapy thought as he glanced-up at the now totally barren oak tree. 'Jack Frost is right around the corner, so I guess it's time for me to find a comfortable warm sanctuary to chill-out until spring before Mr. Winter pays the metropolis an unwelcome visit!'

The human indignity commonly known as the American "work ethic", along with the responsibility of maintaining a bank savings' account were both as alien to the whimsical tramp as much as tropical flowers and coconuts were to Eskimos. 'I gotta' commit some major misdemeanor, or some lesser felony, so that I can spend the winter as usual in a cozy *East River* jail cell on the Island!' Soapy thought. 'And now it's time to intrepidly collide head-on with the New York City justice system! I can only dream of exotic places like Mt. Vesuvius towering above the Bay of Naples, or a luxurious Mediterranean cruise ship to Greece that I've read about in vacation books over at the free library,' the idle tarrier mused. 'Those majestic places and things I'll proudly let my imagination visit, once I've guaranteed myself a bunk bed with a hard mattress on the Island! That's the splendid three-month vacation my heart truly desires!'

Some of Soapy's more fortunate old pals that had leeched off of rich old widows, or that had hit it big at the race tracks were now destined to Palm Springs and to the French Riviera that coming winter. But the disconsolate derelict had no alternative other than to connive an innovative way to facilitate his upcoming annual pilgrimage to 'the venerable Island'.

'Three discarded Sunday newspapers can't keep my chest, stomach and ass warm!' Soapy soberly realized. 'And I can't fall asleep at nights if my butt-hole is a degree under fifty on a standard rectal thermometer! A frozen ass is worse than a frigid woman; that's for damned sure!'

The happy-go-lucky drifter scorned the city's charity, especially crowded Bowery soup kitchens and raunchy fleabag hotel accommodations. The bum instinctively loathed dependence on institutionalized humanitarianism, thinking that some humiliation or obligation for the act of being socially reformed was attached to the taxpayers' benevolence. Soapy's plain and simple rationale was that the Law was more objective and logical about his future incarceration than any "Municipal Philanthropy" ever suggested or warranted.

'Those city shelters all make me shave, take a bath, and thoroughly wipe my ass after taking a shit!' Soapy considered in defense of his faltering ego. 'I'd rather have dirty brown-stained underwear on my own accord than a mandated clean lily-white ass any damned time,' the mendicant concluded as his eyes carefully scanned his immediate environment. 'Who needs a litany of questions and a dumb-dick inquisition for a lousy loaf of bread and a cup of coffee? It's my way or the highway; that's what the hell I believe!' the tramp rationalized. 'I friggin' hate when obnoxious do-gooders get their talons into my soul, and their snooty brown-colored noses stuck all-the-way up to my colon!'

Soapy rose from the hard, wooden, park-bench, stretched his arms out above his head, scratched his itchy balls, and then recollected exactly how he had managed to gain adequate residency during past harsh winters. 'I'll do something brash like dine at an exclusive restaurant,' the conniver whimsically imagined. 'And after I declare insolvency, the waiter will then dutifully notify a policeman; who will predictably notify an impartial city judge; who will quickly contact the sympathetic warden. Getting arrested and convicted is almost as easy as committin' the illegal act in the first place!'

Soapy departed the garden not far from Madison Square, and felt like a semi-*macho man* as the bum walked through throngs of apathetic Soho and Greenwich *Village people.* He kept strolling along concrete sidewalks and across asphalt streets until the vagrant came to the junction of Broadway and Fifth Avenue. The drifter turned-up Broadway, and soon halted in front of a glittering café, where local socialites, celebrities, and expensive horny prostitutes usually gathered to mingle, to conduct business, and to network their fame and fortune. The newly arrived dinner guest had confidence that his superior scheme would yield handsome dividends in earning a very pleasurable hiatus at "the Island", conveniently situated away from mainstream civilization in the center of the *East River*.

The vagrant was unusually clean-shaven that particular morning, sporting only a two-day-beard. His black overcoat looked fairly presentable, and the necktie the tramp was wearing had been given to him on *Thanksgiving Day* by a *Salvation Army* lady lieutenant, trying to reform his chronic waywardness. 'All I gotta' do is reach a table in this fancy restaurant, and success will ultimately be mine!' the old amateur swindler plotted. 'The tablecloth will conceal my shoddy trousers, which have indeed seen better days, months, years, and decades.'

'Ah, roasted duck and a glass of fine imported white wine will adequately fill my belly, and then I'll feel quite satisfied being ushered-off the premises by a man in blue to later appear before my favorite sympathetic judge,' the big city hobo imagined. 'If only I didn't always have to go through all of this disturbing preliminary bullshit just to get to the damned courtroom!'

When Soapy set foot into the gourmet restaurant, the beggar's disheveled appearance was immediately recognized by the alert headwaiter, who was a veteran identifier of mendicant intrusions.

"Get your frayed trousers and scruffy-looking shoes out of this reputable establishment immediately!" the headwaiter commanded to the ill-starred (and now-thwarted) famished diner. And with that hostile evaluation being articulated, two husky assistant waiters savagely grabbed Soapy by the shoulders and by the seat of his wrinkled pants, and proceeded to hurl the destitute fellow out onto the hard, cold Broadway sidewalk.

"Fine hospitality you extend toward decent prospective patrons!" Soapy complained to his assailants as he got up and methodically dusted himself off from grime that had been caked onto his pants, prior to his ejection from the famous restaurant. "Give my damned regards to Broadway!"

"And don't come back here again until you're President of the American Telephone and Telegraph Company, or Commander-in-Chief of the United States Armed Forces!" the wily headwaiter yelled-down at the recently evicted wily trespasser lying on the sidewalk. "Your slovenly, unkempt appearance couldn't even evade detection if you were standing stark naked inside an overcrowded nudist colony!"

Soapy soon turned from Broadway, and trekked north to find another location in which to reconnoiter and loiter. Before reaching

Times Square, the itinerant fellow was aimlessly pacing west on Fortieth Street. 'Only three-thousand or so more miles until I enter the outskirts of San Francisco!' the homeless wanderer mused. 'That inhospitable restaurant headwaiter can't tell an epicure from a cancer cure!' the bum decided. 'Ya' might think that by now that the dumb-shit could accurately distinguish quality from quantity! What a friggin' retard that oversized asshole was!'

At the corner of Fortieth and Sixth Avenue, Soapy had a sudden inspiration. Electric lights and a storefront plate-glass window elaborately displayed an intriguing array of dinnerware, silverware, and cutlery sets. The fine China plates and soup tureens made the frustrated observer remember being recently, mercilessly, and embarrassingly tossed-out of the posh Broadway restaurant. The ambling derelict spotted a loose cobblestone on the street corner, picked it up, and then heaved the heavy object at one of the delicate gold-gilded place settings that had been neatly arranged on the other side of the plate-glass window.

A host of pedestrians had heard the window-glass shatter, and a horde of spectators soon gathered around the suspected perpetrator until a New York City patrolman arrived at the crime scene to conduct a proper investigation. "Okay, okay folks! I'm here to restore law and order!" the policeman imperatively indicated. "Ya' all can go about your business while I professionally perform my personal interrogation!"

After the curious crowd scattered in all directions, the policeman conducted a rather brief inquiry into the vandalism. The cop inspected Soapy, who was casually standing there with his hands in his pockets, and broadly smiling like the legendary Cheshire Cat. "Okay Mister; where's the criminal that's broken the window?"

"You're talkin' about me!" the big-city-bum shamelessly confessed. "I'm the villain that exclusively did the damage! And I gotta' admit that this ain't the first damned store window I've ever broken with a loose cobblestone, either!"

"Who the hell do ya' think your shittin', old man!" the cop snarled back. "Destructive scoundrels that smash windows don't hang around to get their asses' arrested! Do' ya' think I'm some kind of damned rookie officer that's still wet behind the ears?" the policeman rhetorically asked. "Do ya' think I'm some kind of goddamned virgin eunuch, or some kind of a friggin' faggot left over from the naughty-naughty Gay Nineties?"

"Don't ya' figure I had somethin' to do with this particular case of vandalism?" Soapy inquired to the cop in a very disappointed tone of voice. "I want ya' to know that my whole damned family is nothin' more than a bunch of violent criminals and dangerous convicts. My grandmother was a notorious safecracker, and my Aunt Harriet was a mass murderer, and my father was..."

The policeman turned and astutely observed a man running to catch a horse-drawn cab a block down the avenue. The dedicated keeper-of-the-peace drew his club and instantly sprinted in that direction yelling, "Stop running away; you' vile rogue!" as the determined officer took-off in hot pursuit of whom *his* mind had evaluated as the principal suspect in the quite mysterious storefront window-breaking offense.

Soapy felt disgust and depression accumulating inside his weak heart, as the drifter sullenly watched the policeman dash after a completely innocent man, who just happened to be in 'a New York hurry'. The dejected wanderer next noticed an unpretentious-looking restaurant across Sixth Avenue that catered to the tastes of modest, casual clientele. 'That place has thick stone plates, thin soup, and watery coffee,' Soapy critically thought. 'But it's better than nothin'! I'll just have to eat a considerable amount of food, and then refuse to pay the bill; claimin' I got indigestion!'

The cunning, scheming, sly diner entered the busy eatery and remarkably made it to a comfortable seat unchallenged. The shabby-looking fellow parked his wide buttocks at a table-for-two, and successfully ordered and then consumed bacon, eggs, pancakes, toast, coffee, orange juice, more coffee, apple pie, a Danish, a chocolate doughnut, and finally, a huge slice of carrot cake. The busy waiter finally came around with the hefty bill, and presented it to his most satisfied, hefty, rapidly-farting non-customer.

"I ain't got no money to pay the tab," Soapy haughtily admitted, "so kindly call the police. I wanta' speak with a jerked-off law officer right now!"

"No goddamned cop is gonna' enter this establishment for street scum like you!" the aggravated, livid waiter hollered, drawing the instantaneous attention of fifty gossipy breakfast patrons. Two monstrous, muscular restaurant employees immediately emerged from the kitchen and came over to Soapy's table, latched onto the full-bellied leech, and then flung his ass out onto the Sixth Avenue sidewalk, which was equally as hard and cold as the Broadway pavement had been.

"I'd prefer *tossing* salad in the kitchen rather than having to slime-up my hands and have to toss scum like you outside!" the original waiter shouted-out the restaurant's front door at the slow-moving, bruised-up bum lying on the sidewalk.

"You're lucky we were very busy today," one of the huge muscular waiters yelled. "Anyone that's got the time to scrutinize ya' will quickly realize ya' ain't got two lousy nickels to rub together!"

"I've seen better scum on bathroom tile!" the third strong-looking waiter hollered-down at the sidewalk as the brute grabbed the handle to the restaurant's front door. "This is New York City and not Shanty Town!" the incensed waiter violently screamed.

Soapy slowly arose as pedestrians wove their way around his recently ejected shabby form. The notorious panhandler beat some dust from his black coat's threadbare sleeves, and then deftly noticed a policeman standing beside him.

"Ain't ya' goin' to arrest me?" the evicted diner asked the jovial-looking cop. "I just tried to scam that joint out of a decent meal."

"The restaurant has to register an official complaint for me to take that action!" the Irish-accented patrolman matter-of-factly informed. "They're too busy making money rather than havin' to spend time in court sendin' the likes of you to jail!" the experienced cop elaborated. "The business knows ya' ain't worth the time investment of a formal court appearance!"

"I gotta' do time at the Island for not payin' the bill!" the astonished tramp argued and insisted. "I deliberately committed a crime, and I wanna' be arrested!"

"I know your motives!" the shrewd cop verified. "And if I were you, I'd go out and get a freakin' job, earn some honest money, and then at least pay my simple restaurant bills!"

"I'd rather lose my fingers, my toes, and my mouth to frostbite!" Soapy nastily answered and protested. "I'd rather die of hunger than hold a despicable, sweaty, menial job anywhere in this shit-eatin' anti-beggar metropolis!"

"I think ya' was born on the wrong freakin' planet, not to mention the wrong side of the tracks!" the extremely-amused policeman bluntly replied. "The paradise ya' seek is supposed to be in the next damned world, and not in this stupid one! Ya' just happened to get off the *Eternal Express* train a stop too early! Ha, ha, ha!"

'It's easier for me to get laid with an expensive hooker than to get three months at the Island!' Soapy concluded as the failed vagrant observed the jolly policeman stroll north on Sixth Avenue, twirling his nightstick as if it was a band major's baton.

The disgruntled indigent despondently walked five blocks south in a woebegone frame of mind. A rare opportunity to be suddenly arrested soon confronted his still-determined mental state. A young woman was standing, and apparently window shopping, looking at a store's handsome display of inkstands, clothes' stands, and umbrella stands. Six feet away a horny policeman was admiring the petite woman's hourglass figure, which was still quite evident outlined underneath her late autumn overcoat.

'If worse comes to worse, I'll just pretend I'm a masher and grab and squeeze her two chest spuds, and then wildly mash her potatoes!' the tramp imagined. 'That bitch's firm cantaloupes are nicer than any melons I can find or steal anywhere."

Soapy straightened-out his ready-made tie, exposed his rusty cufflinks by extending his arms out of his sleeves, and tilted his top hat downwards. The self-appointed masher swiftly approached his designated well-built female target.

"Ah, good to see you, Matilda!" the impostor began his cruel and calculated solicitation. "Don't ya' want to come and play some ball in my yard!"

"Why certainly," the woman surprisingly agreed. "I'm a damned horny high society hooker, but since that cop over there is waiting for me to solicit you," the lady of the night stated, "then there's not anything illegal about taking you up on you trying to hit on me! It might be a tad immoral, but certainly not illegal, if it's just sex without money involved!"

The promiscuous prostitute then grabbed the astounded Soapy's arm and proceeded south on Sixth Avenue. "After ya' buy me a couple of beers and a delicious steak dinner," the female continued, "we'll see how well ya' can perform in the damned sack! I hope ya' have more damned stamina than you're showin' me right now!"

"I don't need to get laid or have a blow-job!" Soapy shouted to his new-found female companion. "I don't even need any good blowjob! I just was fantasizin' about playing with your beautiful knockers! That's all I was doin'!" the dirty old rascal voluntarily and very honestly admitted.

"Well, ya' can massage, caress, and lick both of them until ya' get tired, or until your' damned tongue falls off!" the bombshell blonde hooker promised. "But first, ya' gotta' buy me dinner and a few mugs of suds at Mickey's Bar over there!"

At the next corner, in front of Mickey's Bar, Soapy broke free from the hot woman's grasp, and hustled across the avenue, nearly getting run-over by a fast-moving milk wagon's team of brown horses. "Hey Bitch, I ain't had a decent hard-on in fifteen-years!" the tramp turned and arrogantly yelled back at the totally shocked, well-proportioned harlot. 'And I ain't got a damned dime to even buy her an average cup of coffee!' the tramp thought and regretted as he continued scurrying-away in the opposite direction from the aggressive blonde dame.

Four blocks later, the on-the-move vagrant abruptly stopped to catch his breath in the fifty-degree late morning temperature. Soapy was now situated in an upscale section of Manhattan, where the women wore warm fur coats, and the men were expensively clad in the finest haberdashery, being covered in rich wool great coats. 'I need to get arrested quick!' the visitor to that exquisite section of that glorious city thought. 'Maybe if I act like a complete imbecile and cause a major ruckus, then that dumb-lookin' gullible cop over there will put the cuffs on me for disturbin' the peace in a fine, upscale neighborhood!'

"Screw New York!" Soapy defiantly yelled. "This is the most ridiculous, fucked-up, shit-eating metropolis in the entire damned country! Fuck this rotten city!" the unkempt protester boisterously shouted as the charlatan whirled-around, raved, and howled like a confident maniac for the distinct purpose of being rudely apprehended by the vigilant law officer.

"Aren't you going to take that shrieking idiot down to the station?" a well-dressed pedestrian asked the equally-observant policeman. "His foul and vulgar language is offending my wife! Isn't that right Beatrice? That poorly dressed asshole is really fucked-up and deserves to be goddamned arrested!"

"Sir and Madam," the patrolmen said, doffing his hat out of courtesy to the fine citizens he was addressing. "I'm absolutely certain that the annoying fool is one of those obnoxious *Yale* students celebratin' the big victory in the football game against *Fordham University* last night!" the policeman incorrectly surmised and garrulously answered. "I'll wager he had drunk one-too-many brewskis, and is now not in control of his regular senses. Just ignore the zany idiot! He'll quiet-down once he realizes he doesn't have an audience, and can't bother or pester anyone!"

The sophisticated couple politely smiled and ambled into the nearest highbrow-oriented bistro. "Get along now!" the officer prodded Soapy with his nightstick. "You're a little old to be one of those insolent *Yale* students! I'll betcha' you're one of the university's deans that's downed one-too-many *boilermakers*! Been to *Purdue* lately? Ha, ha, ha!"

Soapy was rather disconsolate from again failing in accomplishing his noble objective. 'The Island today is as unattainable as my next damned erection!' the deeply saddened fellow imagined. 'The only functional things my dick can do is piss and stay limp, but not necessarily in that specific order; damn it!'

Soapy next glanced into a tobacco and cigar store entrance and observed a short, skinny man lighting-up a dollar "Cuban Special". 'The unassuming jerk has leaned his silk umbrella next to the entrance!' the tawdry-dressed observer perceptively noticed. 'I'll skillfully snatch that expensive baby and not run too fast or too far, before getting the long arm of the law's attention to interrupt my abbreviated escape!'

The conniving schemer keenly noticed a policeman stepping up the avenue, so Soapy reached inside the doorway and adroitly snagged the expensive black silk umbrella, and then fiercely banging the pilfered object against the tile floor, the demonstration designed so that its owner would turn-around and witness the theft-in-progress. At least, that was Soapy's clever strategy.

"My fuckin' umbrella!" the victim shouted at Soapy as the tramp stood on the sidewalk in front of the alarmed policeman, who was inspecting and assessing the characteristics of a crime in the making.

"Oh, it's not *your* umbrella; you lyin' bastard!" Soapy exclaimed in an indignant tone of voice. "Well, here's a policeman standing right here!" the brazen mendicant hollered at the appalled victim. "Protest to him what ya' claim to be true!"

The umbrella owner began stammering and stuttering. "I, I, er, I mean, er, I wanta' say that, er.."

"What the hell is goin' on here?" the patrolman questioned. "Who's the freakin' jackal here, and who's the friggin' coyote?" the cop asked as the patrolman curiously studied the behavior and the facial expressions of the two extraordinary men, who each claimed to own the black silk umbrella.

"Er Officer," the fancy-dressed gentleman guiltily responded. "Well, er, you know that occasionally, errors and mistakes happen sometimes when certain objects look similar," the pedestrian self-consciously continued. "But apparently this, er, this beautiful umbrella belongs to the other gentleman making the claim. I, er, had accidentally picked it up by mistake at a crowded restaurant over on Park Avenue this morning!"

"What the fuck' are ya' sayin'?" Soapy adamantly balked. "I just stole the goddamned. son-of-a-bitchin' thing from ya' out of the doorway! And now you're fuckin' claimin' to be a dirty crook, too?"

The formally dressed umbrella fella' retreated from the doorway as Soapy extended his wrists out, so that handcuffs could be suitably applied. At that moment, a woman's scream from down the block attracted the policeman's attention, so the cop devoted his dedication and energy to resolving what appeared to be a more dire emergency than an already settled mild dispute over the mere ownership of a black silk umbrella.

When Soapy walked away with the imported British umbrella, the poor bloke soon came to an area of recent building excavation and property renovation. The walker flung the closed silk umbrella into a heap of crumbled bricks and mortar, pretending that the rubble pile had been that last wifty New York City law enforcer he had most recently encountered. "If I didn't want to be apprehended," the tramp considered and lamented, "then I would've already been arrested at least a half-dozen times!"

The disillusioned stroller wandered east, and kept walking until he reached a certain Manhattan Avenue that, in the distance, paralleled the Brooklyn side of the East River. 'I'll just keep trekking until I finally make it safely back to Madison Square, just like the goddamned pigeons that inhabit that park always do,' the disappointed old mendicant thought. 'I've got more damned bad luck than Judas Iscariot and the Biblical Job put together!'

At an unusually quiet intersection, Soapy came to a standstill, and sized-up an old, historic church. The tramp ascended the granite-stone steps, entered the edifice, stepped to a rear pew, sat-down, and his bloodshot eyes admired the magnificent stained-glass windows. A low rumble of "Rock of Ages" filled the dim chamber, and the somber melody momentarily entertained the building's sole occupant, who was kneeling in a pew and praying to be arrested. The meditation of the audience of one was then rudely interrupted. A man's huge hand latched onto the tramp's weatherworn topcoat, and Soapy's concentration on the solemn church anthem had quickly become effectively fragmented.

"Why hello, officer!" the city's most luckless homeless man exclaimed. "I'm not preaching to the choir when I tell ya' that I was just prayin' for salvation while seekin' temporary sanctuary from the bitter elements!"

"I guess you aren't visiting here to redeem some grocery store coupons. If ya' can't resurrect a dollar from your pocket," the patrolman emphatically declared, "then I'm afraid I'll have to arrest your ass for vagrancy!"

"I was just in church prayin' for an exclusive job as a delivery clerk for a regional fur importer," the shabbily-dressed visitor disclosed and fibbed. "But now I see that my special wish has little chance of ever materializin'."

"Come along with me to the station!" the burly policeman commanded in a soft-but-persuasive voice. "I'm sure the Magistrate will confer on you three months of worthwhile rehabilitation on the ever-popular Island!"

"What a cruel and reprehensible world!" Soapy answered as the law offender rolled his eyes upward toward the church's resplendent cathedral ceiling. 'Thank God! My recent, solemn prayer has been heavenly answered!' the grateful drifter concluded and relished with a wide smile.

"A Retrieved Reformation"

On February 13th, a blue-uniformed guard entered the prison shoe-shop where notorious inmate Jimmy Valentine was diligently preoccupied stitching leather.

"This shoe is a lot like a policeman," Jimmy complained to a fellow prisoner. "It's a big heel with no friggin' *soul!*"

"Okay Valentine," the guard began his announcement. "I gotta' escort ya' over to the front office. The warden wants to see your wise-ass right now!"

"Is the Warden a certified proctologist?" Jimmy humorously yelled to the martinet guard. "I want him to check my prostate while he's probing away in *that* sensitive area."

Five minutes later, the Warden transferred to Jimmy Valentine *his* official pardon, which had been signed by the accommodating state governor that very morning.

"Ya' only served ten months on a four-year sentence," the Warden griped. "That's only just enough time for a woman to get pregnant and have a crying baby."

"Warden, ten-month-sentences take a long time to write, and the grammar also must have a lot of commas and colons," Jimmy joked. "Actually Warden; I had expected to be outta' here in only three months, or just about as much time as a woman takes to have a goddamned abortion."

"I guess your powerful high-society friends on the outside are dying-off and losing their influence with the state's corrupt politicians," the Warden sarcastically concluded and opined. "Look at it this way Valentine. Ya' got ten-good-haircuts that cost ya' absolutely nothing; not to fully mention a good bunk bed, along with three-square-meals to round-out your day. You're luckier than most damned lottery and sweepstakes' winners are after taxes!"

"Everybody on earth would be luckier if the dumb-shits were never born in the first place," Valentine weirdly objected. "And stop talkin' to me like I was born yesterday."

"Now Valentine; I have a word of sound advice," the all-too-conscientious Warden preached. "You'll be officially outa' the pen in the morning. Correct your errant ways, and lead an honest life. You're not an evil person at heart, and you've got a good personality goin' for yourself," the prison director commended and praised. "Stop cracking safes and start pumping safe cracks of the feminine variety, if ya' know what the hell I mean!"

"Me?" Jimmy Valentine questioned while feigning surprise. "Why Warden; I've never cracked a blessed safe in all my life!"

"Oh no!" the Warden laughed. "Let's establish a little time line now, Valentine. How was it that you happened to get convicted on that widely publicized Springfield heist? Was it because your alibi might have compromised an important Congressman, or an unethical Senator?" the warden candidly accused. "Or maybe it was because a mean old jury finally decided to render an honest verdict based on the damned evidence? It's always some lame-brain excuse with you innocent victims that have somehow been deprived, depraved, and exploited by our unparalleled American free enterprise society!"

"Not me!" Jimmy answered with a broad smirk exhibited upon his face. "Why Warden; I've never been inside Springfield in all my life? I'm not too proficient at geography. What damned state is Springfield in, anyway?" Valentine virtuously replied.

"Okay Cronin, I've listened to enough of *this* wise-ass prisoner's arrogant malarkey," the Warden indicated. "Take Mr. Valentine to the prison tailor-shop, and have him fitted with some decent street-worthy haberdashery. Then, unlock Jimmy Boy at seven sharp tomorrow morning, *Valentine's Day*. What a fuckin' holiday misnomer in addition to being a bizarre fuckin' coincidence!"

"What should I do after that?" Cronin asked. "Sacrifice him to Zeus or Neptune?"

"Then take Mr. Valentine to the bullpen to warm-up. Keep him in the bullpen until it's time for us to release him after the tenth inning," the Warden jested and specified. "The barred room will help Jimmy V. meditate about reforming to an honest future. You'd better carefully weigh my advice, Valentine!"

At seven-thirty, on February 14th Jimmy Valentine impatiently stood in the Warden's outer office, studying and admiring the prison official's secretary's solid rock-hard breasts. 'Maybe I should imitate my throbbing dick and go straight!' Jimmy thought as the sex-starved jailbird squirmed-around in his chair, attempting to diminish his huge erection. 'Going straight with the right woman sounds like a pretty sound suggestion. But straight women nowadays are as hard to find as men with Z-shaped erections!'

Jimmy was villainously wearing a black pinstriped suit; a felt hat, and a pair of rigid squeaky shoes that he himself had personally stitched for his recently announced prison departure. 'These are standard items of apparel that the state provides for all its compulsory detainees,' Valentine deducted. 'God; I gotta' get me an inflatable rubberized woman to sleep with; one who has got solid firm tits like the Warden's knockout personal secretary has!'

The prison clerk presented Jimmy with a complimentary railroad ticket and a crisp five-dollar-bill, which the naïve law establishment provided its former residents to hopefully rehabilitate into good prosperous, contributing American citizens.

"Here Valentine, take this cigar with my best wishes," the Warden requested. "I hope ya' don't choke on it before it explodes in your goddamned criminal face."

Jimmy thanked the prison operator for *his* exceptional wisdom and for his mediocre gifts, and soon "Inmate Valentine, 9763" was recorded on the books as being "Officially Pardoned by the Governor". At eight a.m., James Valentine stepped out of the front gates and into the dull February sunshine. The area winter songbirds chirping away in the barren deciduous trees seemed to be singing: "Go back to a life of crime, Jailbird! You have no fuckin' alternative! Go back to engage in crime!"

'I'll head for a restaurant and have a delectable meal,' Jimmy thought. 'I'll have some barbecued chicken, and a cheap bottle of white wine. Then I'll puff on a new fancy Cuban cigar!' Valentine decided, as the released former convict chucked the lousy nickel cigar that the Warden had given him into a convenient street corner waste receptacle.

Having enjoyed his tasty meal, Jimmy leisurely exited the ordinary restaurant and headed toward the local train depot. After casually tossing a coin into a blind beggar's hat, the notorious safecracker purchased his railway ticket, and casually boarded a westbound train. Three hours later, the liberated man stepped off the *Pullman* and into a little hamlet located near the Illinois/Iowa state line. The paroled gentleman entered a popular local watering-hole and shook hands with the proprietor, a certain old acquaintance named Mike Donaldson.

"I'm sorry Jimmy my boy that we couldn't arrange this little conference seven months sooner," Mike whispered and confided. "But the big boys had that legal complaint from Springfield to iron-out, and the wimpy politician Governor had to be negotiated with. Now tell me, Doctor V. How the hell are ya' feelin' after your unfortunate tenure in the pen?"

"Just as fine as could be under the circumstances," Jimmy admitted. "Some shit-faced inmates tried to sodomize me on two separate occasions in the middle of the night, but I punctured one of the prick's balls with an ice pick, and I flipped the second fucked-up asshole into the other homo's bunk, and listened all friggin' night to them getting it on. Say Mike; doesn't anybody just jerk-off any more? The whole fuckin' world is getting into this perverted and gay sex bullshit!"

Mike Donaldson smiled and handed Jimmy the key to *his* old upstairs room, which had remained unoccupied since *his* ten-month incarceration. Valentine climbed the rickety steps, and then soon found that everything in the modest quarters was exactly as it had been situated the previous April Fools' Day. The detective Ben Price's collar button (that had been torn in an intense scuffle) even still remained on the floor. 'That police raid was rather rough and disrespectful,' the gentleman criminal remembered. 'Why the hell don't they go after blue-collar criminals like pimps, prostitutes, and transvestite bank robbers! This white-collar professional, namely me, felt friggin' humiliated when the rambunctious cops had the unbridled audacity to put the goddamned cuffs on my wrists! And that totally fucked-up extended two-month criminal court trial was nerve-racking, too!'

Jimmy slowly pulled-out the folding bed from the wall, and behind a well-concealed sliding panel was stashed his dust-layered suitcase containing his indispensable safecracking tools. Valentine gingerly opened the piece of luggage and admired the finest set of vault neutralizers in the entire Central United States. 'I feel like popping two loads just lookin' at these magnificent babies!' Jimmy laughed as the owner respectfully touched the fabulous assortment of drills, augers, clamps, special screwdrivers, "Jimmy's jimmies," braces, and drill bits. 'I've even meticulously designed and manufactured several of these tools all by myself'.'

A half-hour later, Jimmy Valentine was standing downstairs inside the small café, reminiscing shared history with his old loyal colleague, Mike Donaldson. The suave white-collar criminal was now dressed in more dapper apparel, which was reflective of his high society lifestyle. Jimmy's recently-cleaned black suitcase remained on the café's floor at *his* side.

"Got any jobs goin'?" Mike personally asked. "I really like harboring a person of your high caliber upstairs, and I treasure our memorable gigs done in area banks. Jimmy, ya' really taught me plenty about the profession."

"Are you referring to me?" Jimmy answered in a feigned bewildered tone of voice. "Mike, I'm now a top salesman for the California Amalgamated Short Crispy Biscuit, Cracker and Scumbag Frazzled Wheat Company, Incorporated!" Valentine imaginatively replied. "We specialize in distributing hookers and madams, all having shaved beavers of course, all over the country. Next year, my fledgling company plans to go international."

The safecracker's witty comment delighted Mike Donaldson, who had gone through three separate divorces, and had envied Jimmy Valentine's class and style with the ladies; those dolls having either shaved crotches, or those horny whores having wonderfully hairy bushes of all pubic colors.

The following week in late February, the Midwest newspapers accurately reported a well-performed bank-safe burglary in a Richmond, Indiana institution, with "no apparent significant clues left behind'. Two weeks later, a highly touted burglar-proof safe in Logansport had been opened; its contents heisted, and a large sum of stock securities, currency, gold and silver had been purloined. Detective Ben Price and his acclaimed team of rogue-catchers took immediate notice, and the federal authorities catalogued the pattern that was developing.

"It sounds like Valentine's on the march again," Ben Price informed his incompetent investigative partners. 'I'm targeting Valentine for a cardiac arrest! Ha, ha, ha!"

"How the hell can Jimmy V. be on the *march* when it's still only friggin' February?" Price's fellow detective answered and chuckled.

"Stop talkin' like a stupid shit-head and get serious about the art and science of detective investigating," Inspector Price chastised his wisecracking novice colleague. "You would make more fuckin' sense to me if you had been born in the China hinterland, and never learned a damned word of English!"

"Okay, the recent job's gotta' be Dandy Jimmy Valentine's signature," Detective Price's numbskull associate deduced and offered. "The tumblers were punched-out clean, and there was only one hole that had been neatly and skillfully drilled. That reminds me, Ben. My wife also has one hole including her ass, and I drill it all the goddamned time! In fact, sometimes three times a day! Every once in a while, my deep drilling hits oil!"

"When I capture the evasive bastard this time," Ben Price predicted as the renowned federal inspector gritted his teeth, "he'll serve his full sentence. The next time, I'll get my hanging judge brother-in-law to show Valentine no clemency for his incessant insolence to my regional authority!"

Ben Price was an expert on the proclivities of the criminals whom the detective adroitly followed, and the investigator kept a keen eye on every reported Midwest bank robbery. "Valentine's established pattern is long distances established between larcenies; rapid getaways; no accomplices, and a definite flair for high society vogues and habits. Yes Harry, Jimmy's a quick dodger of law apprehension," Ben told his pathetic apathetic assistant. "And the slippery felon is as elusive as a frightened cheetah fartin' its ass off in the open field. If I were a vile criminal, I would indeed model myself after stealthy Jimmy Valentine."

One morning in June, the accomplished safecracker and his heavy suitcase climbed out of a horse-drawn carriage that incidentally was used to send mail from one rural Arkansas village to another. Jimmy had landed in Elmore, a town of three thousand hicks, located five miles off the nearest railroad in the Arkansas blackjack territory. Valentine looked like a handsome *Yale* senior in search of his first authentic piece of ass. The visitor ambled down the board sidewalk in the direction of the *Planter's Hotel,* where all guests mysteriously always wound-up with gigantic in-grown warts on their feet.

A comely young lady wearing a semi-formal floral-designed dress and carrying a matching colorful parasol above her sophisticated bonnet, entered the Elmore Bank. Jimmy took one glance at the attractive vixen and immediately fell in love. 'Women like that make instant male erections and premature ejaculations possible,' Valentine mused. 'Even when those kind of gorgeous, cock-teasing, vivacious women have all their goddamned clothes on, the dolls still heighten a male viewer's sex urge into overdrive. Who the hell needs pornography with lovely, sophisticated bitches like her struttin' all around?'

Jimmy accosted a young boy, who was loitering in front of the livery station across the gravel street from the Elmore Bank. Valentine asked the acne-faced kid a catalog of questions about the special sights of the town. Jimmy kept transferring dimes to the receptive lad with every positive answer provided, as if *he* was an accomplished animal trainer rewarding a seal or a tiger with food after the creature had successfully performed each successive circus trick. Then the beautiful well-endowed lady exited the bank and acted unaware of Jimmy's or anyone else's presence. The gorgeous female then nonchalantly sauntered down Elmore's Main Street.

"Isn't that knockout bitch, er, I mean that proud young lady Miss Jennifer Sampson, the horniest and kinkiest woman in the whole southeastern United States?" Valentine very deliberately asked the callow lad.

"Naw," the ornery adolescent honestly returned. "Her name's Annabel Abrams, and her rich pa' owns the darn bank. Hey Mister;

that particular information will cost ya' a quarter instead of a mere dime. Say, Mister. Why in tar-nation did ya' come to a freaky, country-bumpkin town like Elmore for? Did ya' fall off the stage coach or something?"

"No son," Jimmy laughed. "I'm lookin' for a decent little community in which to settle-down in. I'm tired of travelin' all over creation searchin' for my seven-year-niche, ha, ha, ha!"

"Say Mister, is that a gold watch chain ya' got there?" the all-too-curious kid asked. "I'm savin' up money to buy a pedigree bulldog to scare the crap outa' senior citizens in wheelchairs that live in my neighborhood. Say Mister, ya' got any more dimes or quarters?"

Jimmy left the youthful informant's fantastic company, and ambled over to the *Planter's Hotel* that originally accommodated only vegetable and cotton farmers who habitually did only a *sow-sow* job. The Elmore visitor imaginatively signed the register as *Mr. Ralph D. Spencer*, pretending to be a prominent national salesman of primitive, prototype vending machines.

"What brings you to Elmore Mr. Spencer?" the amiable (but nosy) hotel clerk inquired. "Are ya' a Yankee trying to flee the Civil War fifty years too late?

"I wanta' get out of the machine dispenser business and find something more profitable and lucrative," Jimmy Valentine, alias Ralph D. Spencer, fibbed. "I've noticed you hicks around here ain't got no exclusive shoe store in this primitive-lookin' village, so I'm plannin' to open a fine shoe business right here on Main Street."

"The General Store down the block sells shoes," the slightly offended clerk corrected in defense of Elmore. "But quite truthfully, its limited selection is rather shitty, er, I mean limited. Most Elmore folks go into Little Rock to buy their foot-gear."

"Yes, but those obsolete-lookin' shoes in the General Store's window look like they're used leftovers from the time of the Massachusetts Pilgrims and the early western pioneers," Ralph (Jimmy) humorously maintained. "And if I ever need a diamond wedding ring, I'll surely go into Little Rock to purchase one."

"Well, Mr. Spencer, I'm really quite impressed with your city slicker clothes and shoes," the envious desk clerk confessed. "Show me how you achieve that exquisite tie-knot, and I'll introduce you to every damned whore in town that frequents the *Planter's,* and the *hot* bitches expertly giving their customers fantastic venereal warts rather than common ordinary planter's warts."

181

"This remote burg looks like a very pleasant community, and the people seem to be obnoxiously sociable," Jimmy congenially responded. "Say, could I pay my bill in rare porno' magazines?"

"Sure can," the young hick clerk said with a smile. "I'll buy 'em from you, and then you can pay me back so that I could put the money in the cash register. But I warn ya'; I wanna' see lots of wet pink hairy beaver slits, or it's no damned deal!"

"Now then, I'll stay here for three nights and check-out all aspects of beautiful metropolitan downtown Elmore," Jimmy politely returned. "And you needn't call a bellboy to carry my suitcase. It's rather heavy and loaded with the latest porn' mags' from around the globe. Those Danish and French model bitches are really super-hot! I'd give ya' one of my mags' right now as a deposit, but then you'd be squirtin' sperm juice all over the damned lobby, and that obviously would be detrimental to conductin' civil business."

Ralph D. Spencer felt like the proverbial *Phoenix*. He had risen out of his own criminal ashes, and now the free man had designs on leading a moral, straight life, especially with his new hard-on for Miss Annabel Abrams. 'I'm gonna' remain here in Elmore, run a legitimate shoe business, marry and screw Annabel Abrams, and then get promoted to vice-president of the bank.'

True to his promise, a month later Ralph D. Spencer opened a modern shoe store with the latest available styles, and the handsome entrepreneur attracted a respectable trade, knocking the shoe department of the Elmore General Store into economic extinction. Socially, the new arrival instantly made many friends, and in a matter of three months, became Master Sergeant-at-Arms of the eminent "Elmore Perverted Sex and Dildo Society".

Ralph finally managed to meet Annabel Abrams, selling her a pair of black leather army combat boots, and then smelling and licking her rancid putrid bare feet. Spencer soon became fascinated with Miss Abrams's many appealing 'charms', and the reformed safecracker asked Annabel where she had purchased her glittering bracelet, along with all its dangling cheap, tawdry trinkets.

By the following April Fools Day, Ralph D. Spencer had been elected President of the Elmore Perverted Sex and Dildo Society, rising to that high privileged office in the shortest time of any newly sponsored member. His popular shoe store was prospering, and his kinky sex reputation was rapidly proliferating. Even Annabel's stringent father, a demented pedophile child molester, found favor with the new Elmore businessman. Mr. Abrams already liked Ralph better than his other daughter's irrelevant husband, Waldo, who was leading a unique double-life as an area Catholic priest in another backward Arkansas community. Martha and Waldo had two children, Agatha and *May*, who were both born in September of different years.

Jimmy Valentine was now happily reformed as the socially reincarnated Ralph D. Spencer. The satisfied gentleman sat-down at his apartment desk and authored a letter of regret and happiness. Then, the shoe entrepreneur mailed the informative missive to a former criminal confederate in St. Louis:

Dear Louie the Lip in St. Louie:

I want to meet you at Riley's place in Little Rock next Wednesday night at nine p.m. I intend to consummate some final details with you professionally representing me as my personal fence. My kit of precious tools is now available for instant black-market resale. You couldn't duplicate the special set for many thousands of bucks. Perhaps you can negotiate a sale to one of those new upstart male/female Little Rock amateur felony teams, either Bonnie and Clyde or Bill and Hillary.

Now, I shall regretfully review the personal sentimental crap. Louie, please don't give me any lousy lip about my expressed intention that I'm confidentially sharing with you. I've retired from the unpredictable safecracking banking business, and have purchased a fine shoe store down here in rural Arkansas. I'm making an honest living, and I'm going to wed the most gorgeous bombshell this side of the Hudson, or is it the Mississippi? Anyway, the straight life is the only life for me, Louie; and my throbbing dick also intends to go straight, along with my budding professional shoe store occupation.

After I get married, I plan to sell my upstart business, and take my new wife to California where Ben Price will probably never track me down, since his law enforcement office has a very scarce budget for traveling expenses.

I tell you Louie, my new girlfriend is an absolute angel, who believes in me as if I'm a true religion. I wouldn't perform another crooked thing in my life, especially with my erect straight pecker. Be sure to be at Riley's place in Little Rock to negotiate the final specifics of the anticipated transaction. From now on, I'll just be using the tool between my legs.

Your old buddy,

Jimmy V.

On the following Monday, after Jimmy had posted the letter, Ben Price unobtrusively arrived in Elmore, searching for the whereabouts of an infamous, itinerant safecracker. The nationally celebrated detective casually strolled around the town, telling every inquisitive native who asked that he was a tourist in quest of founding a "Pet Shop" business in a vacant storefront situated off of Main Street. The clever detective carefully scrutinized Ralph D. Spencer's shoe store from a rented room's window above the Elmore Drug and Marijuana Shoppe, centrally located directly across Main Street from Ralph's flourishing commercial enterprise.

'Well Jimmy, I understand you have designs of marrying the banker's unsuspecting daughter,' the eminent detective imagined. 'Now that's what I really call an inside job! What a fuckin' impractical dreamer and schemer you are, Mr. Ralph D. Spencer!'

The next morning, Jimmy was enjoying a country breakfast at the Abrams' spacious kitchen. The conversation was both genial and genteel. But Annabel's always-suspicious banking father was quite inquisitive with his interrogatives.

"Why are you going to Little Rock?" Mr. Abrams asked his ambitious, future, favorite son-in-law.

"I'm going to *Little Rock* to buy a *big rock* for your daughter's hand," the gleeful soon-to-be fiancé ludicrously replied. "And I gotta' purchase my fancy wedding togs, too. This will be the first time I'll be leaving Elmore in over a month, Mr. Abrams, so I sorta' have island temperature living isolated here in Elmore, or cabin fever, or some other crazy mental condition like that!"

Two hours after consuming the very spectacular breakfast meal, Mr. Abrams, Mrs. Abrams, Annabel, Martha, along with her two daughters, visited Jimmy at his apartment to say "farewell" and to wish him "Godspeed" on his prospective shopping expedition to Little Rock, Arkansas.

"What's in the suitcase?" Annabel Abrams innocently asked Ralph. Then, she tried lifting it. "The thing feels like it's got gold bricks inside. Are you a slippery, side-winding goldbricker!"

"Oh, it's just a few blacksmith anvils and plenty of nickel-plated shoehorns," the shoe store owner defensively laughed. "I'm gonna' sell them in Little Rock to cover the expense of your soon-to-be-coveted big rock, and also use the excess money to pay for my extravagant wedding costume."

"Okay," Mr. Abrams lustily laughed. "Carry your heavy luggage downstairs. I've hired Adolph Jensen to take you in his buckboard to the railroad station. But Ralph, first I want to show you a surprise. Let's all go over to the bank and inspect my most recent prized acquisition! It's a real dandy!"

Everyone else hopped into two carriages, while Ralph D. Spencer (alias Jimmy Valentine) almost got a double hernia lifting the heavy suitcase onto Adolph Jensen's classic taxi-buggy.

Five-minutes later, the merry entourage excitedly entered Mr. Abrams' landmark Elmore Bank. The town's financial kingpin (and the principal pillar of the community) had recently installed a new vault that had been especially obtained for holding safety deposit boxes and major cash storage. The new steel enclosure featured a modern-designed, patented door, configured with three solid bolts that latched simultaneously, and the massive safe also had an accurate clock timer, which constituted a novel, avant-garde technological addition. Naturally, the new vault represented an alluring temptation to one Jimmy Valentine.

"This vault is the most advanced one in this section of Arkansas," Mr. Abrams proudly articulated. "And not even Bonnie and Clyde or Bill and Hillary could break into it."

Martha's children, May and Agatha, took an instant interest in the new contraption, but Ralph D. Spencer prudently showed a courteous-but-remote fascination with the new-fangled enclosure. While the family was marveling at the bank's latest advancement, Ben Price strolled inside and observed the occupants chatting and complimenting Mr. Abrams on his impeccable judgment to safeguard his cherished customers' accounts.

"I don't want to make a deposit or withdrawal," the master detective informed the listless teller, who was preoccupied reading the latest gay and lesbian county LBTQAKRFP pamphlet. "I'm just waiting to speak with someone I know who's intendin' to open a sizable savings account here."

Suddenly, a loud, shrill, scream permeated the air, and the shriek immediately threatened to ruin the momentous occasion. The alarmed elders all turned their heads to learn the cause of the great commotion. Five-year-old May had been playing an impromptu game of "Hide and Seek" with nine-year-old Agatha, who had accidentally locked her younger sister in her grandfather's shiny, new steel bank vault. The emergency presented itself as a tremendous mental dilemma to Ralph D. Spencer.

The elderly bank executive hastened to the vault and vainly tugged at its immovable handle. "I can't budge the damned door!" Mr. Abrams bellowed and hollered. "The clock hasn't been synchronized, and the combination hasn't been set yet! Woe is me'! Woe is me'!"

Martha was screaming hysterically, as if a porcupine and a saguaro cactus had been shoved-up her sensitive love canal.

"Hush Martha!" Mr. Abrams admonished his older daughter as the rattled bank executive raised his right hand to fend the emotionally distraught mother off. "Your maternal instinct can only complicate matters right now! Shut the hell up, so that I can think rationally for a goddamned minute! Panic will not solve this friggin' crisis!"

"My precious May!" "My precious May!" Martha hysterically and repeatedly yelled. "She'll die of fright! Break open the damned door! Can't anyone here do something!" the distraught mother wailed.

"The closest expert that can open this door is a hundred-miles away in Little Rock!" Mr. Abrams answered in a defeated tone of voice. "Spencer, what the hell can we do? May is an epileptic, and will surely go into convulsions, and soon have a wicked seizure! She'll most certainly use-up all of the goddamned oxygen in that confounded airtight safe," the melancholy bank director informed. "And in a matter of minutes, when May wildly rolls around the vault's floor, swallowing her tongue, she'll eventually be dead!"

Martha was frantic and began having her own epileptic fit, deliriously rolling around on the bank's floor, and being awkwardly attended to by Annabel and by Mrs. Abrams.

"Ralph, can't you do anything?" Annabel cried and pleaded from her kneeling position. "Why are you looking so dazed and puzzled?"

"Dynamite is not a dynamite idea!" Mr. Abrams boomed. "It might blast poor May and my expensive, uninsured vault all the way to Kingdom Come!"

Ralph D. Spencer momentarily studied Annabel's large, bloodshot, blue eyes that profoundly reflected both anguish and fear. The former safecracker felt compelled to intervene in the dire situation to rescue May, knowing full well that his past clandestine activities, and his widespread disreputable safecracking identity, would be discovered.

'Oh well; my inglorious past is gonna' jeopardize my secure future,' Jimmy Valentine realistically thought. 'And I must do what is right and save May's life, even though I despise with a passion the raunchy, little spoiled bitch!' Then Ralph D. Spencer gazed again into his woman's despairing eyes. A smile from his lips brought hope to her soul.

"Annabel," Ralph said. "Please give me that rose that's pinned on your dress. It will give me emotional strength."

Annabel stared at Ralph incredulously as if he was mystically speaking to her from another dimension. The future Mrs. Ralph D. Spencer did exactly as the safecracker had strangely requested, and gently handed him the flower, which Spencer immediately stuffed into his exposed vest pocket. With the transfer of the symbolic red rose, shoe-man Ralph D. Spencer instantly transformed back into the notorious high society rogue, Jimmy Valentine.

"Get away from the door, all of you!" Jimmy commanded the still-shocked, helpless family members. Valentine then dashed outside, obtained his heavy suitcase from Adolph Jensen's buggy, carried the necessary tools into the Elmore Bank, and then assiduously went to work practicing his ignoble craft. Jimmy laid-out his wonderful equipment upon the bank's white marble floor, and strangely (to the consternation of the Abrams' family members), whistled a cheerful tune. Everyone watched spellbound as the former convict confidently demonstrated his very remarkable (formerly secret) skills.

A minute later, Jimmy's favorite drill was smoothly biting a small cavity into the vault's solid steel door. Breaking his fastest entry record, Valentine adroitly moved back the three bolts and then easily opened the sturdy portal.

May was gasping and panting, wildly rolling around on the vault's metal floor. Annabel gently dragged her niece out of the compartment, and used Jimmy's augers as convenient tongue depressors for both the almost-paralyzed girl, and next, *her* hysterical, epileptic mother, who was still rolling around on the white marble floor while frantically clutching *her* aching throat.

Jimmy Valentine put on his suit jacket, stepped outside the vault area, and paced toward the front doors as if in a mesmerized trance. The safecracker hesitated as he felt a hand on his shoulder, and a bass voice saying, "Hello Ralph!"

"Oh, hello Ben!" Jimmy greeted his old nemesis. "I figured you might catch-up with me sooner or later! Well, let's go and get my arraignment going over at the courthouse. Take me into custody, so that I can be spared the embarrassment of having to explain my arrest to my beautiful fiancée and her prudish, wealthy, WASP family!"

"What the hell' are you talkin' about Mr. Spencer?" Ben Price surprisingly answered. "I don't believe I've ever met anyone by the name of Ralph D. Spencer before today. But I gotta' admit; that rescue was a damned wonderful humanitarian thing I had just witnessed, perhaps the greatest act of self-sacrifice and courage my eyes have ever seen."

"Do you mean I'm not goin' back to the slammer?" Jimmy Valentine asked in amazement, as the reformed criminal realized his possible retrieved reformation. "I mean, I've feared all throughout today's Elmore bank caper that *that* was my ultimate fate!"

Ben Price simply winked at the new straight contributor to Elmore, Arkansas high society. The famed police investigator knew quite well when the exercise of moral justice should be warranted and justified, and now the acclaimed detective's keen eyes and mind had ultimately recognized it. A brief announcement ensued.

"Well, Ralph," Ben Price declared. "Strange and peculiar things often happen on April Fools' Day," the famous inspector coyly commented. The master detective courteously doffed his felt derby in respect to Ralph D. Spencer, and then slowly ambled out of the Elmore Bank onto gravel-topped Main Street. The flabbergasted, notorious safecracker now had permission to start a new life with a clean slate; thanks to the wise and sage discretion of the very judicious Detective Ben Price.

Mark Twain

Mark Twain (1835-1910)

Remarkably, Samuel Langhorne Clemens (1835-1910) was both born and died the same years that Halley's Comet had made its seventy-five-year revolution around the solar system. Clemens acquired his pen name "Mark Twain" from Mississippi River steamboat terminology of "twain" being a water depth of two fathoms (twelve feet), the allowable safe level for a riverboat to navigate over a reef or shoal, and the depth was measured by a leadsman who threw a heavy lead weight overboard, and then after lifting it out of the river, would *mark* the *twain*.

Sam Clemens became a successful riverboat pilot under the direction of a captain named Horace Bixby, but after the Civil War broke-out, the Mississippi River was closed to commercial traffic. Being unemployed, Clemens journeyed out west to try his hand at gold prospecting in Nevada, and then later at newspaper journalism in California. The writer gained international recognition with the publication of his classic, humorous short story "The Celebrated Jumping Frog of Calaveras County," first published in 1865.

Mark Twain is generally regarded as a humorist, but he is also understood by literary critics as being a serious philosopher and an astute analyzer of the antebellum and post-Civil War American societies of his time. Twain's most famous novels are *The Adventures of Tom Sawyer, The Adventures of Huckleberry Finn, The Prince and the Pauper,* and *A Connecticut Yankee in King Arthur's Court.* Other important Mark Twain works are the books: *Roughing It, Life on the Mississippi,* and *Innocents Abroad*, and also, some short literary sketches taken from the last-mentioned three books have been used in organizing *this* quite outrageous satire/parody collection.

In 1870, Mark Twain married Olivia Langdon of Elmira, New York, and the couple had two daughters, Susy and Jean. After becoming rich and famous, Clemens built a fabulous mansion in Hartford, Connecticut that had a porch and staircase which made the spectacular dwelling resemble a Mississippi riverboat.

"Boyhood Reminiscences"

When I finally became old and famous after a lifetime of hard work, and coincidentally developing arthritis in my hands from writing manuscripts on paper too damned much, my very demanding publisher insisted that I author an autobiography of my screwball life, because common folks throughout the country wanted to know more shit about me than I fuckin' knew about myself. In organizing *that* monumental assignment, I was smart enough to use some of those early life experiences in my book *The Adventures of Tom Sawyer*, which took place (just like my childhood did) in the mid-nineteenth century along the Mississippi River. And so. me and some of my dumb-dick boyhood friends (and *our* outlandish real-life adventures) actually became Tom Sawyer's and also Huckleberry Finn's unique exploits later on in literary fiction.

My school reminiscences began when I was about six years old, and my mere existence soon manifested itself as a real pain in the ass as far as the adults in the somnolent community of Hannibal, Missouri were concerned. In those primitive early days, long before Abraham Lincoln had ever ascended to the Presidency, Missouri had no public schools, but private schools were quite common and popular. Hannibal boasted of two private institutions of lower learning, and the standard tuition for attendance (even for an irascible asshole imp such as myself) was a meager twenty-five cents a week, although my two-bit teachers often told me that my "babysitting expense" should've been quadrupled, with *that* meager bargain-basement amount of money also being paid by the parents of the average "good behaved Hannibal student".

Mr. Sam Cross (who was reputed to be both mean and cross all the goddamned time) taught the older kids their irrelevant academics in a frame schoolhouse situated up on a hill just outside town. Mrs. Horr conducted her martinet-oriented grammar school/log cabin at the southern end of one-block-long Main Street. Although the nasty schoolmarm was married, the old hag (with thick-rimmed glasses hanging upon her lengthy snout) never screwed around with any men (besides her husband) like her weird-sounding last name might suggest when spoken orally.

And so, I figured and accurately assessed at a very early age that Mrs. Horr was not a regular harlot, or an everyday prostitute, as was the infamous rumor all around the morning playground. And after sixty-five years of what could only be characterized as growth and immaturity, I still can recollect some significant incidents involving curious, little, nefarious me that had occurred under Mrs. Horr's austere classroom jurisdiction.

A particular episode happened on my first day of formal education. Being my normal non-compliant self, I easily violated several basic and easy to understand school rules, and Mrs. Horr warned me that continued mischief and recalcitrance on my part would automatically warrant the well-deserved penalty of receiving a "royal whipping" to be administered swiftly and directly to my tender ass by the snotty, pompous-acting churchgoing Bible-toting, old lady pedagogue.

After my second minor misdemeanor (which involved scratching my itchy testicles in front of the girls in the legendary cloak room), Mrs. Horr told (*instructed*) me to go outside and fetch a functional birch switch, so that the ancient bitch could proceed to beat the living and dead shit out of my asshole. Well, I was appointed to complete that important responsibility, And I truly believed that I was the most qualified student, and that I could practice more judiciousness in doing so than the average stupid-shit classmate, who out of pure jealousy and spite, might've been harboring grave animosity towards me because of my extreme popularity with the more-kinky girls, all of whom wanted to closely examine and inspect my itchy balls, and also examine my corresponding, miniature pecker apparatus.

I diligently searched the swampy mud located behind the fire-hazard log cabin schoolhouse, and soon discovered a cooper's shaving; the remnant of an old decayed barrel that had been originally crafted out of solid oak wood. The piece of "punishment tool" was a quarter of an inch thick, and two-foot-long; and it rose to a shallow curve at one end. I really liked the new-found rod because it was rotten, and I reckoned that the improvised object would break into shreds after making hard contact with my skinny bony ass. Upon my hasty return inside the dimly-lit log cabin, Mrs. Horr didn't at all like my personal selection, so right then and there, I knew that the old witch bitch wanted to administer a rather cruel beating, and that she was basically a vindictive, bloodthirsty sadist left over from prehistoric Puritan times, where stocks and bonds in the town square (and not the Wall Street type) were the goddamned rage to punish suspected classroom violators.

Despite my contrived attitude of overtly exhibiting meekness and self-depredation, Mrs. Horr didn't buy into or fully appreciate my choice of an appropriate torture weapon-device, so the hostile-to-me villainess called me by my full name of Samuel Langhorne Clemens, which fuckin' meant that my ass was grass even before she would ever begin to wallop the hell out of it.

"I'm ashamed of you Young Man; so therefore, Samuel Langhorne Clemens, you should be adequately prepared to experience some pain in your bottom because you're definitely a royal pain in everybody else's ass in this humble classroom."

Well now, Mrs. Horr appointed this kid possessing a gigantic gut and accompanying massive abdomen named Jim Dunlap to go outside and find a more suitable "birch switch" for her to beat the digested and undigested feces out of my vulnerable asshole. I was excessively worried from that moment on, because that belligerent kid Jim Dunlap hated my entire being, ever since *that* morning out on the playground when I had told him that I thought he had a bad terminal health condition called "Dunlap's disease", where his inflated stomach "done laps over". Anyway, five minutes later, that junior jerk-off Dunlap returned inside the building with a pretty usable, sturdy switch rod; so, I immediately comprehended that the obese punk was an expert on the matter, a moron-dumb-fuck who wanted to see me suffer severely, and become penitent and submissive to the wicked teacher's basic hostility.

Now, it was known all throughout Hannibal that Mrs. Horr had originated from up north in Rhode Island, and everyone in Hannibal was aware that she was a treacherous New England bitch that loved to switch the rear-ends of devious little boys for personal gratification. The old abuser opened her little Inquisition hearing with a prayer read directly from the Good Book; yes, that weird fuckin' psalm that begins with some oddball passage like "Walking through the valley of death and fearing no Devil-generated evil". The conclusion to her brief requiem happened to be the screwed-up, pathetic, prophetic words, "Ask and you shall receive!" Then, the raunchy, bizarre, barbaric woman, without me ever asking for a damned thing, tanned my hide so hard that I thought I was being turned into the leather remains of a slaughtered cow, and that I would wind-up becoming a part of another freaky kid's jacket, hat, belt or shoe soles.

After I had gotten the shit knocked out of me by my new-found adult enemy, I soberly concluded that perhaps I should give the oddball "Ask and you shall receive!" philosophy an honest try. I solemnly prayed for some scrumptious gingerbread to eat as a reward for surviving my brutal Puritanical-style persecution, and coincidentally Margaret Kooneman, who just happened to be the town baker's daughter, had brought a slab of the delicious baked item to school on that propitious first day of kindergarten.

At age six, I was not only a penitent sinner, but also a junior culinary authority in addition to being remarkably sexually precocious and inquisitive for my tender age. When I finally finished my silent "gingerbread prayer" to Heaven, I glanced behind to Margaret's desk directly in back of me, and her gingerbread treat was sitting there on the top slate while she was leaning over and retrieving a scrap of paper that had floated onto the wooden floor. I immediately became a convert to being a devout, grateful Christian, because I had been fortuitously rewarded for my religious reverence and steadfast devotion twofold.

First of all, I had the delightful opportunity to snatch the freshly baked gingerbread slice, and then quickly devour the delectable snack in three wonderful bites and swallows. Secondly, I got a fantastic glimpse of Margaret Kooneman's snatcheroo because her legs were wide open when she was leaning over and grabbing her coveted scrap paper; but unfortunately, even though Margaret wasn't wearing any type of underwear beneath her dress, I perceptively noticed that she only had a weird-looking Z-shaped slit between her legs, and no damned pussy hair was yet growing down there in her future pleasure garden. 'No wonder why all the girls in the class want to see my balls and pecker!' I then realized and understood.

* * * * * * * * * * *

I prayed incessantly the entire next week, but never received any more scrumptious gingerbread samples, or any more sensational young girl hairless crotch glances, so I became disenchanted, evolved into an instant atheist, and soon gave up prayer; my skeptical mind regarding the mystery mental communication as a thing that only magically worked once for a young mischievous fella' like myself. And amazingly, the miracle happening only once on my first day of school.

My more-than-tolerant mother experienced a great deal of trouble raising my ass through puberty, but I think she rather enjoyed the impossible challenge. My brother Henry, who was two years younger than me, was the ideal "lily-white conscience" kid who never caused problems and who wasn't one himself. So, mom looked at *my* mischief as a counterbalance to Henry's obedient and angelic nature. My negative deportment tended to furnish her with adequate relief and variety from Henry's trite contriteness and his general hatred of mayhem. My junior brother was not a normal, vicious youngster, but Henry definitely was too damned righteous, wanting to grow up to be a schoolmaster, a minister, a pope, or some stupid-shit adult like that.

Henry often reported my radical and rebellious misdemeanors to mom because of my negligence to ever indict myself, and in the novel *The Adventures of Tom Sawyer*, the fictional character Sid (who always squealed on Tom) was actually benevolent Henry in disguise. When I was approaching thirteen, I had often planned to push Henry out of my second-floor bedroom window and impale his never-spanked ass upon the white picket fence below, but then I logically figured that the extensive cleanup (with all of the blood, piss and shit all over the damned backyard) would have been too laborious for a lazy jerk-off like myself to have to perform.

One sunny, summer afternoon, just before suppertime, Henry brought it to mom's wicked attention that the thread that she had meticulously sewn my collar together with (to prevent me from playing hooky from school and going swimming down at the secret pond) had strangely changed color from black to white. Well, mom became quite piqued at my outrageous audacity, and based on insignificant circumstantial evidence, and Henry's speculative testimony, the woman viciously cracked me a dozen times on the head with her metal thimble, nearly riveting me right through the goddamned wooden floor planks.

When I finally got Henry alone outside, I believed that I had to mercilessly whip his ass for ratting on me, which my strong-willed conscience considered *his* fundamental disloyalty, his squealing being a grievous mortal sin of the greatest magnitude. And I had to exhibit to Henry my physical dominance over him during *my* pre-pubescent adolescence. But right when I began administering my justified retribution, mom detected the clamorous backyard commotion, rushed outside, immediately sided with that no-good-prick Henry without even initiating a brief investigation, and then savagely used two metal thimbles (on both her left and right index fingers) to make my totally abused scalp feel like a large bag of marbles as more and more nasty big skull bumps materialized.

Henry was such a despicable saint that the juvenile nutcase never once pilfered any sweet objects inside the kitchen cookie jar without first obtaining permission from mother. But one morning, an itinerant demon must've possessed my younger brother, because I caught him with his paws inside the bear-shaped jar, and upon his realization that I had nabbed him performing the pilfering act, the little, conniving bastard dropped the revered container from his grasp, and then, the ceramic old English mamma bear (along with its precious sugary cargo) splattered all over the new linoleum.

"Now I'm gonna' tell on ya' just like you always do on me," I threatened the guilty culprit. "Not only did I catch you with your hands in the cookie jar, I've also witnessed you breaking the damned thing, you idiotic, clumsy oaf!" I warned. "I hear mom enterin' the house right now. You're in big-ass trouble Henry, and now I'm goin' to enjoy you receivin' your first terrible whippin'! Maybe ya' better scamper upstairs and put on three more sets of underpants for sufficient padding to endure all the brutal agony! But never mind your fat ass! Breaking the damned cookie jar probably means you're gonna' get the thimble-head-denting treatment!"

Mother entered the kitchen, keenly observed the recently caused debris, and then stood there with her arms folded under her huge, flopping breasts that extended down to her ankles when mom was not wearing a bra. I figured I would savor the wonderful, joyous moment of Henry's beating, so I procrastinated before acting like the county prosecutor engaged in convicting a heinous felon. But mom never interrogated her two offspring by asking, "Who did this shit?"

Well now, I had made a grave error in situational miscalculation by not speaking-up and making the allegation as direct evidence against Henry, because mom instinctively presumed that I had been the wicked villain, so the livid parent aggressively gave me an assortment of cracks upon my already throbbing skull with her metal thimble, which I felt when excruciating pain descended-down my spine clear to my quivering heels. My bad experience was all pretty damned close to being executed.

"But Mom, you've punished the wrong person!" I exclaimed and explained. "Henry broke the cookie jar, I swear it! I saw him do it despite the fact that it was an accident!"

"Don't be absurd, Sam!" mom yelled in staunch defense of her erroneous disciplinary actions. "Henry is incapable of doin' such a terrible thing as pilferin' from the cookie jar without first askin' my approval. But Sam, I'm glad I thwacked ya' a few times on the head to make-up for some sneaky violations that you've recently committed that had somehow escaped my scrutiny!"

Another misadventure implicating Henry occurred when I was twelve and he was ten. A stairway outside the Hannibal house led to the upstairs' hallway, similar to what is called a fire escape nowadays. One day, Henry was climbing up those rickety steps, so I wasted no time and sprinted upstairs and locked the door from the inside, isolating the subservient asshole on the top steps outside the modest home. Then seeking revenge for his myriad trespasses against me (especially his tattling), I felt obligated to make Henry atone for his past transgression, so I started hurling wet black mud clods at him as he began ducking-down left and right like a target in a modern-day shooting gallery.

"You can use that tin bucket in your hand as a deflector all ya' want," I boldly hollered-up. "But that ain't gonna' protect your ass for too long, because I got at least a hundred more mud clod balls to throw up at your puny, scumbag body!"

The wet, smelly clods were loudly smacking against the house's weatherboarding, and soon mom appeared on the back porch steps conducting her usual visual and olfactory investigation. She and Henry immediately formed an alliance, and the pair began sprinting after my frightened ass, so I frantically bounded over the side white picket fence, and almost castrated my tiny testicles on the same four-foot-high boundary that I had unscrupulously plotted to impale Henry's body upon.

Several hours later, I surreptitiously ventured back to the family property, and was happy to observe that no one (conspiring to annihilate my entire being) was in sight. But then Henry suddenly appeared from behind a magnolia tree, and tossed a stone in my direction. The hard object ricocheted off my noggin and left a sizeable welt above the center of my forehead, the damage to my forehead having the spectacular shape and appearance of that Matterhorn Mountain over there in Europe.

Mom came running out of the house to evaluate the source of the commotion. "That's what you get Sam for always pickin' on poor little Henry!" the woman accused and concluded. "That's what the hell you deserve after you were throwin' those dirty wet mud clods at your younger brother. Now Henry," mom commanded, "go inside and eat a piece of that warm apple pie I just baked, and as for you Sam, get a bucket of water, some soap suds, and a couple of washcloths, and start cleaning-up that horrendous mud mess you've made up there on the weatherboarding!"

* * * * * * * * * * *

Besides being engaged in mild sibling rivalry with the family's apostle-in-chief, Henry, in late autumn of 1849 (during the height of the exciting California Gold Rush), my older sister (who wishes to remain anonymous in my monastic-type monk writings) gave a huge party, and invited most of the horny teenage males and females of the village, virtually all of whom were obnoxious, future village idiots, of course. Although I was biologically driven by my newfound sex hormones, my basic bashfulness felt overwhelmed in the company of mature girls that had tits with half-dollar-sized nipples puffed out on their magnificent chests.

My irascible sister had arranged for me to be part of the "jolly entertainment segment", and dress-up in a bear costume during a "fairy-play" that was to be performed. "You'll just stand there for eight minutes and then foolishly cavort around in circles like a gay homosexual carnivore for the remaining two minutes," I was directed. "Don't worry Samuel! I'm sure you'll be the hit of the party! The girls and I will be doing a forest dance scene from William Shakespeare's *A Midsummer Night's Dream!*"

At half past ten, I was told to go to my room and put on the furry bear outfit, and patiently wait to be called to perform my indispensable role. Then, if I wanted to further rehearse my amateur baptism into show business, I should advance up to the attic in full disguise, and practice marching around in circles like a completely fucked-up asshole impersonating an inebriated bear.

After arriving up inside the dark attic, I heard some giggling originating from behind a translucent dressing screen, and instantly recognized the high-pitched voices of young members of the opposite gender mumbling and conversing next to a candle-lit table. 'Perhaps this theatrical thespian bullshit is not so damned gay after all!' I plausibly reasoned. 'Maybe unlike my little gingerbread caper with Margaret Kooneman back in Mrs. Horr's first grade, this time if I'm lucky, I'll get to sneak a big-time peek at some mature hairy teenage pussy cracks!"

I had not yet donned my bear disguise, and so I stripped-down bare-ass naked to be able to facilitate my tedious clambering inside the cumbersome ensemble. Boy, was I in for the shame and embarrassment of my formative years of development, when my limited cerebrum failed to keenly anticipate the 'unexpected'.

No sooner had I gotten all my clothes off my anatomy that the translucent dressing screen tilted over and tumultuously collapsed to the floor, revealing in the dull candlelight six masked naked girls with real nice tits and furry brown bushes being exposed in their various personal body areas. The naked snickering young ladies simultaneously rushed my nude form, tackled and knocked me down, and one by one rubbed their hairy brown snatches against my nose, tongue and face. It was a boy's absolute delight, a sort of perverted college sorority-type, sex initiation being enacted on a gullible-yet-defenseless, petrified fourteen-year-old, willfully-victimized boy. Five long minutes later, the thoroughly amused girls all darted with their (lesbian/dyke) fairy costumes under their arms down the attic steps to my anonymous sister's room, where they would ultimately get changed for their anti-climactic nightingale performance.

'Holy shit!' I remember thinking. 'One of those brazen, conspiring smelly cunts might've been my older masked sister! I mean,' I considered with a frown of disgust, 'licking your older sister's hairy brown anonymous crotch is far worse than just having to kiss the bitch on her other lips!'

* * * * * * * * * * * *

When I had left Hannibal several years later to seek my fame and fortune on the Mississippi River, I had all but forgotten about the peculiar attic female sex assault. At the time of my older sister's party, one of Hannibal, Missouri's dearest and prettiest teenage girls was the stunning and dazzling Mary Wilson, and every boy in the village (that could muster an impressive erection) wanted to get his noodle wet inside Mary's highly desired love tunnel. But I always stood in awe of the voluptuous, mature broad, and could only get an erection thinking about her luscious love tunnel when the adorable doll *wasn't* standing or sitting in my presence.

The scene now shifts to Calcutta, India forty-seven years after the long-forgotten attic incident. I had arrived in that distant country in 1896 as part of a formal lecturing tour I was conducting to promote my books and my authoring career.

As I entered my hotel lobby to check-in at the main registration desk, a heavenly angelic vision passed by me, and the young attractive girl my eyes had spotted looked identical to the radiant Mary Wilson I had known and admired back in Hannibal. 'That's impossible,' I decided. 'Mary's my age; even several years older, and she sure as hell would be subject to nature's cruel aging process, just the same as any other human being would be!'

Come to find out, the beautiful young damsel I had noticed in the lobby was the granddaughter of the Mary Wilson I had once known back in *our* hometown. Mary had learned that I would be staying at her Calcutta hotel, so she sent a messenger to deliver a handwritten invitation for me to join her at six for supper in the main dining room. I immediately sent a memo' back to Room 224 agreeing to meet my former dreamboat (whom I had greatly admired long before I had ever stepped foot on a steamboat). I had also known through reliable sources back in Hannibal, Missouri that Mary was now a widow and was possibly looking to renew some romantic ties with old acquaintances.

The now-wrinkled, wealthy, gray-haired woman met me at her table and we warmly shook hands. "Won't you sit down Samuel, er, I mean Mark?" she commendably requested. "It's been a mighty long time since we both left Hannibal!"

"Yes, it has been Mary," I merrily concurred. "Ya' know, when I was a youngster, I, like every other horny boy in the village, had a mad crush on you. I guess you've known that fact all along."

"Yes Mr. Twain, but before we reminisce old times and the glory of our memorable youth, there's something rather cute and relevant that I wish to tell you."

"Are you gonna' talk about that un-hilarious line that I had to deliver in the infamous Shakespeare' forest scene: 'What's so special about dried herring'?" I asked my former girl idol.

"Well, Mark, if you insist on knowing, I was one of the six masked girls that sexually molested you up in your house's attic," Mary confessed with a wide grin being evident on her countenance.

"Oh my God Mary! That splendid assault was the first time I ever tasted delicious pussy juice in my life, and I haven't stopped seeking more of it ever since!"

"Now Mark," Mary naughtily giggled. "I'm awfully afraid that my personal area is now a dried-up herring, just as your one and only play line suggests!"

"Who the hell gives a shit!" I exclaimed with a hardy laugh. "At my advanced age, you valiantly fight for every damned sniff of Heaven you can get!"

"Club Pilot on the Mississippi"

Samuel Langhorne Clemens (1835-1910) was undoubtedly one of the most influential early American authors, and was also a prolific contributor to United States literature. The literary genius was born the year Halley's Comet made an appearance, and died seventy-five years later, when the celestial object made another solar system pass past the earth and then around the sun.

Sam Clemens acquired the writing pseudonym "Mark Twain" from Mississippi River steamboat jargon. A worker on the riverboat would toss a lead weight attached to a rope overboard, and "mark the twain". If the water was two fathoms deep (twelve feet), then a riverboat could safely navigate past a shoal, or over a hidden underwater reef.

Growing-up in the quiet town of Hannibal Missouri, young Sam Clemens knew more about the Mississippi River's 'muddy waters' than the blues/jazz musician Muddy Waters ever conceived of. As an imaginative boy, Twain's prime ambition was to become a Mississippi riverboat pilot. His dream eventually did come true, and Clemens' classic, humorous, autobiographical story "Cub Pilot on the Mississippi" retells one of his first rich experiences on the *Pennsylvania,* a typical steamboat of the antebellum (pre-*Civil War*) era. Herein lies an unworthy, decadent corruption of one of Mark Twain's more popular tales with the ordinary word "Cub" being mischievously changed to "Club".

When I was a boy, and I do believe that happened some years before I became a man, my happy-go-lucky friends and I had one principal aspiration. We lived in somnolent Hannibal, Missouri on the west bank of the mighty Mississippi River, and each of the guys wanted to become a steamboat man, which in reality is sorta' fuckin' easier than actually becoming a steamboat.

I must confess, I had other fanciful notions circulating in my hyperactive cerebrum, but those hankerings were but transient, fleeting impressions, and mostly totally juvenile perceptions. When an occasional circus came to town, I wanted to be a clown. But then I realized that my grammar school teachers had always persisted in calling me "a clown", so why should I grow up to become what I happened to be already? So, when the damned circus pulled-up its tent and packed away its midway concession stands, I lost interest in becoming an acrobat, a lion tamer, a ringmaster, a midget, a bearded woman, and also a dumb-ass clown.

I recall a minstrel show coming to Hannibal, and my buddies and I were all enthused and psyched-up about the prospect of becoming traveling troubadours. But then that was during our 'minstrel period', and we all soon realized that only girls had that kind of stupid-assed bloody bullshit to deal with each and every month. And to tell you the truth, who the hell needs that kind of monthly bull crap? That's the only period during the entire month when pussy juice absolutely tastes worse than tomato juice!

My pals and I also wished that God would allow us to become formidable pirates, even though Missouri was plenty far away from Pittsburgh. Then, we figured we could ambush travelers taking the stagecoach into Hannibal and profit from selling them corn on the cob for a *buck-an-ear*. And if our captives refused our generous ransom terms, or didn't particularly savor the taste of corn kernels, then my creative young colleagues and I schemed-up an honorable penalty. The guys all reckoned we would rob the rambling bastards, and simultaneously rape the more-voluptuous stagecoach bitches passing through "our territory", all done in the noble tradition practiced by our notorious, villainous, high seas' heroes, Blackbeard and Captain Kidd.

Once, in my later youth, I wanted to be a riverboat cabin boy, so I could exit the steamship's kitchen area wearing a white apron and proudly shake all the crystal saltshakers and pepper-shakers, and then nonchalantly loosen the embedded breadcrumbs off the dining area's tablecloths. Finally, I fuckin' realized I could be a cabin boy just by staying at my pop's cabin in the woods, and in that stellar capacity, I really didn't have to wear any fancy white apron, or deal with the crummy passengers' crumbs.

Later, in my fairly-pleasurable youth, I thought I would prefer being a deckhand standing conspicuously at the end of the vessel with the lead weight in my hands to officially "mark the twain". That might've been tolerable for a year or two, but confidentially, who the hell wants to measure the depth of river water for the rest of his or her damned life? I needed to do something more adventurous and more dynamic in my future, like robbing trains, and amusing myself terrorizing the appalled passengers; or perhaps wrestling aggressive gorillas or ferocious grizzly bears at exciting summer carnivals.

Most of my childhood amigos eventually managed to find work on the local riverboats. The minister's son, who despised the four gospels with a passion, abhorred the total *Bible,* and hated *his* inflexible, straightlaced, holier-than-thou old man, and smartly became a riverboat engineer. The doctor's and the postmaster's sons became "mud clerks", and that seemed quite appropriate for them in that both a physician and a postal worker deal with prescriptions and writings of some sort all the damned time. At least working on a steamboat seemed much better than going the traditional doctor route or as they say, "going postal".

The local liquor merchant's son became a bartender on a riverboat called *The Delta Queen*. On that same boat, the county judge's son became a *pilot'*, whose first job each morning was to carefully move a barrel, a piece of equipment, or a cargo bundle from one side of the boat and then "pile it" on the other side of the spectacular vessel.

A real authentic riverboat pilot was the most wonderful elite position of all. The assignment commanded a sensational salary of perhaps two-hundred-dollars a month, even in those lean years of trivial wages prior to the catastrophic event known as the *Civil War*. Twenty-four-hundred fabulous dollars a year! That's six times as much as a preacher's annual salary was in those hard times, because as we all know, cheap words command cheap compensation for cheap services rendered.

But many of *our* overprotective parents and guardians were against us boys getting employment on riverboats. The dumb-shit Missouri adults pompously claimed that interesting stuff like gambling; itinerant people; drinking whiskey; fighting; enjoying immoral fellatio and cunnilingus; patronizing forbidden bordellos; participating in totally erotic, pleasurable prostitution, and fingering loose, flirtatious women's hairy love tunnels were bad influences on our characters. But that's exactly why the hell we all wanted to get hired and work on the riverboats! I mean, fuck morality! Who the hell wants to grow-up (I think it's impossible to grow-down) in any way, shape, or form to be a facsimile of their prudish mother or their sexually frustrated father? Even Hannibal's un-liberated parents envied *our* penchant for exploring freedom's limits, and also *our* noble desire to escape the listless mediocrity of the restricted lifestyle generally associated with middle-class WASP culture. I say, "Hooray for horny promiscuous women wanting to share their eager beavers!"

So, I ran away from home, escaping from responsibility; from rules of society, and from the dictatorial standards of Christian values, and sought sanctuary riding on Mississippi riverboats', which to me symbolized liberty and escape from parental influence and from social tyranny. I vowed to my conscience that I would not return home again to Hannibal until I achieved my childhood wish of becoming an eminent and esteemed pilot on the mighty Mississippi. The colorful, glamorous excitement that goes on inside a riverboat was also an incentive to want to leave the dull tranquility of rather rustic Hannibal, Missouri.

I proudly served under many honorable pilots during my three-year apprenticeship aboard the stately *Pennsylvania*. My education involved not only mastering the art of being a riverboat helmsman, but my fascinating function also entailed meeting people and learning about their occupations, interests, vices, and in the final analysis, all about the good and the bad of human nature. That was the kind of stuff good authors' greedily study, and by virtue of my stellar steamboat preparation, I had sufficient material to begin organizing a variety of short stories, and then later, tackling novels. And I readily admit, I owe it all to mingling with all kinds of whacko charlatans, slippery con-artists, cagey gamblers, attractive hookers, and sinister villains. Who the hell wants to read a novel with nothing but goody-goody-two-shoes praising each other all day and all night long as the key element in the fucked-up plot? That kind of lackluster, dull, lousy, high falutin' fiction might as well be cemetery fodder with a big family burial *plot!*

Now then, a pretentious jerk-off named Mr. Brown was my immediate superior on the good ship *Pennsylvania.* Brown was a middle-aged, tall, bony, and thin, smooth-shaven, donkey-faced, miserly, stupid, mealy-mouthed, faultfinding, snarling, despicable martinet that made that bastard Napoleon Bonaparte seem like an innocent altar or choir boy. I always dreaded going on watch with the loathsome imbecile. I knew *he* was a malicious asshole looking for someone like me to daily shit-on, just to make himself look like an important disciplinarian to the judicious captain. I could be flying high after winning a bet, or thrilled after seeing a gorgeous female take-off her costume in the ship's entertainment dressing room. But as soon as I approached the inevitable pilothouse, my heart sank into my bowels, knowing that I had to contend with Brown's bossy, cynical, sarcastic, idiotic, and authoritative happy horseshit.

The first time I had a negative encounter with the captain's chief "*Brown*-noser" was in St. Louis, when the steamboat had just backed out from the wharf. I sprinted as usual up the rickety wooden steps to the pilothouse. Brown was standing at the helm, wondering whether he should piss, shit his pants, or loudly fart; and so, being cautious, I deliberately paused in the center of the room. My intent was to make a very prolonged and exaggerated theater stage bow, out of respect for the ship's chain-of-command, which was traditionally extended to anyone in authority.

I suspected that rude and crude Mr. Brown, as usual, decided to feel self-satisfied; his hands gingerly maneuvering the *Pennsylvania* from its dock. I also cleverly reckoned that the haughty asshole was deliberately ignoring my miniscule presence. My astute brain sensed that the neurotic shit-head was furtively aware of my appearance inside the pilothouse, but I dared not interrupt his pretended concentration. If a collision with another boat occurred, *he* naturally would surely blame the event on my distracting him from the performance of his vital duties. I tip-toed very softly and cautiously to the stepped "cub pilot observation bench", where "students of the profession" ardently learned basic, essential knowledge of the unpredictable river, and mastered the very intricate and difficult mechanics of riverboat helmsmanship.

A pregnant ten-minute silence elapsed without a word being exchanged between that sarcastic pecker-head Brown and me. I don't think that I was sitting 'on the bench' like a bump on a log, or like a court judge acting ostentatious, or anything out of the ordinary like that. Then the friggin' dumb ass turned-around and examined my body from head to foot, for what seemed like a good half-hour. I suspected that the reputed faggot wanted me to perform some gay activity on him, so I was mentally *cog*nizant and emotionally prepared to grab his scrawny head and insert it between two of the pilot wheel's *spin*dles. Finally, the friggin' gay jerk-off broke the ice and initiated a rather peculiar, unsavory dialogue.

"Are you Horace Bixby's new cub pilot?" the illiterate asshole asked as if he was addressing a baby bruin through iron zoo bars.

"Yes sir, yes sir," I defensively and politely answered. "My name is Sam Clemens."

"I didn't ask for your goddamned name," Brown snarled back, demonstrating great rancor and a deficiency in civility. "Speak when you're fuckin' spoken to, you, you obnoxious little punk! All I asked you was if you were Horace Bixby's new cub pilot!"

'Fuck you shit-head!' I thought but refrained from uttering. "Yes sir!" I volleyed-back with intense fire raging in my heart. "Yes sir!" I firmly reiterated.

After that initial verbal sparring, there was another pregnant pause, and that fucked-up ignoramus Mr. Brown again feigned sincerity and gruffly asked me, "Now sonny boy. What's your goddamned name again? Ya' got me so pissed-off that I forgot it!"

I felt like administering the stupid fuck a swift knee-lift to the testicles, but then I seriously doubted if the creep had any bona fide nuggets dangling-down between his skinny bowlegs. "My full name is Samuel Langhorne Clemens," I replied as mannerly as I humanly could under the bizarre circumstances.

"Samuel Langhorne Clemens!" the miserable fuck-head repeated like he had amnesia, dementia, or schizophrenia, or some other common asshole mental disease. "Where was ya' born Langhorne?" the repugnant creep asked without the courtesy of saying either my first or last name.

I felt like offering him something smart-ass like "I was born in a bed"; or "in a hospital"; or "in a hospital bed"; or "on Planet Earth," but amazingly, I exhibited remarkable self-control. "In Florida, Missouri, but I grew-up in Hannibal on the banks of the Mississippi," I answered as nicely as I could.

"Well, which damned state was it!" the preoccupied asshole boisterously insisted. "Was you born in the state of Florida, or was you born in the state of Missouri, or was you born in Mississippi, or was you born at all?"

"Er, Missouri," I affirmatively *stated.*

"Ya' shoulda' stayed there, ya' little snot-nosed twerp," Mr. Brown admonished without mentioning any of my name. In fact, in retrospect, the stupid shit never ever called me by name; always addressing me with "Hey you sonny boy!" or "Cabin boy, I wanna' tell ya' something!"

Brown then extracted my family history from me by asking a series of irrelevant questions that had no pertinence to the art and science of riverboat piloting. Mr. Brown's interrogation was interrupted when the fanatic had to steer around several sharp bends, and that enormous responsibility (and test of ability) made the very high-strung knucklehead even more self-conscious and petulant. The insufferable imbecile's face suddenly became beet-red, and every muscle from his forehead to chin began twitching as if the moron was having a terrible bout with St. Vitus palsy. Then, Brown, in lunatic fashion, nastily shrieked without provocation, "See here, you wise-assed simpleton! You gonna' just sit there collectin' splinters in your little fat ass all day?"

"Sir, I have no particular orders to enact!" I diplomatically volleyed-back. "I'm simply here to learn, and you're simply here to teach me something!"

"Ya' say ya' have no orders!" my principal adversary stormed-back like a livid maniac. "My; what a prissy little pussy piss-head you are! How come ya' ain't wearin' a goddamned dress, bra or petticoat?" the belligerent fuck belittled. Then, Brown went on an illogical tirade that when the fool finally finished his diatribe, the nincompoop sounded more like an incoherent asylum patient. "You've had no *orders*, ya' say!" Mr. Brown vehemently ranted. "You think you're some kind of dizzy blonde waitress or somethin', workin' in a goddamned gourmet restaurant? Ya' have *no orders!* This ain't the military son, and I ain't your daddy either, even though I might actually be, since I called ya' son. *Orders* is what ya' want, huh? I'll learn ya' to swell yourself up like a blowfish, or a pregnant bullfrog, and march around this here ship thinkin' you're a freakin' spoiled prince, or a friggin' rich duke. Get away from the damned wheel!" the tyrant imperatively thundered. "Ya' ain't that kind of big wheel yet to take over the *Pennsylvania's* helm! In fact, you'll never amount to anything besides the young discourteous punk ya' already are! Sonny boy, ya' ain't worth your weight in horse manure or termite shit!" the pathetic despot maliciously ridiculed. "That's for damned sure!"

I was stupefied and flabbergasted by the unsolicited and unwarranted verbal assault I had been innocently receiving. I moved back a step, feeling like throwing the egotistical bastard headfirst overboard into the murky, muddy water.

"Ya' ain't fit to be a cabin boy, let alone an ambitious cub pilot on the Mississippi," Brown nastily criticized. "Now, take this ice pitcher down to the Texas Tender. Ya' can be the officer's waiter down in their quarters for the rest of the friggin' mornin'. Better yet," the accomplished ballbreaker continued his impertinent lecture while again changing his detestable, ever-vacillating mind, "deliver the pitcher and then come back here to do some minor chores for me!"

I knew that the Texas Tender was the largest room on the boat where the officers stayed, sort of like a combination office and pleasure lounge. But I was new to the *Pennsylvania,* and didn't know exactly where the damned tender quarters were located. Since the tender was the biggest room on the boat, it was naturally referred to as "Texas". 'Texas on the *Pennsylvania!'* I whimsically thought. 'That's as fuckin' bad as Florida located in Missouri!'

When I finally completed Brown's ball-bustin' errand, I sprinted back up the rickety steps to the pilothouse to avoid further verbal abuse from the "crazed psychopath". Instead, the fanatical fiend yelled, "Hey you, dumbwaiter! Where were ya' sonny boy all that time you've been gone!" the shit-mouth boomed, intentionally breaking my chops and bustin' my sensitive balls simultaneously.

"Sir, I couldn't find the Texas tender, so I had to go down to the pantry and get accurate directions," I indirectly apologized by providing a wonderfully feasible excuse. "I beg that you can fully appreciate my predicament."

"Darned likely phony story ya' just fabricated!" Mr. Brown instinctively chided. "Now fill up the damned stove with fresh firewood, and do somethin' useful for a goddamned change!"

Brown watched me load the stove like a red-tailed-hawk sizes-up its intended prey. Then, the junior dictator went into another nonsensical, inane outburst. "Put that damned shovel down!" the zany freak characteristically exploded. "You're the damnest numbskull I've ever seen in my life. Ya' ain't even got the wherewithal to load-up a goddamned, cotton-pickin' stove! Were ya' raised in a redneck barn by savage cannibals, or were ya' raised in a goddamned Neanderthal cave?" my volatile, incensed, immediate superior contemptuously rebuked.

That kind of haranguing from the egocentric Mr. Brown went on all throughout that morning watch. And for three whole months, I had to endure a multitude of *his* perpetual sarcasms. I dreaded coming on duty and daily being verbally maligned and butchered with his vitriolic remarks. Brown was like an insidious serpent, always in quest of a pretext to spit-out some hideous venom in my direction. The charlatan would start by commanding, "Here, take the wheel Rookie. I gotta' take a serious healthy crap!" Then, my testy mentor would change his unscrupulous mind and yell, "Where in tar-nation are ya' takin' us, sonny boy? Give me back the goddamned wheel! Give me back the goddamned wheel, I say!" the temperamental pervert fiercely clamored. That particular interaction would be repeated at least twice every day. I was never immune to either Brown's grouchy disposition, or to his continuous wrath.

George Ritchie was the other cub-pilot "learnin' the trade" on the majestic riverboat. The kid was from Pittsburgh, and seemed more at home on the *Pennsylvania* than I did, being from Missouri. Ritchie got along splendidly with his good-natured mentor, George Ealer; and truthfully, I envied the other cub because I had to contend with Mr. Brown's vile, cruddy shenanigans every single day. Ritchie had steered for Brown the previous year, and my friend and peer knew exactly what I had to tolerate and endure from that sorry excuse for a riverboat tutor, namely Mr. Brown.

Whenever I was lucky enough to take the wheel on Ealer's watch, George Ritchie would bust my sensitive testicles by successfully imitating Mr. Brown. "Snatch her! Snatch her!" my buddy would yell without either laughing or smiling. "Pull her down! Pull her down! Damnest greenhorn mud-cat I've ever seen on this here fucked-up planet! Sonny boy, ya' gonna' stay a rank amateur for the rest of your goddamned life!" George affectionately berated. "Don't cramp over that shoal! Watch-out for that damned reef! Give me the damned wheel you stupid whippersnappin', delinquent weasel!"

So, I always had to overcome abundant derogation and denigration, no matter whose watch I was assigned to, George's or Mr. Brown's. And sometimes, George Ritchie's good-natured badgering seemed almost as abusive and almost as abrasive as Mr. Brown's poisonous commentaries. I eventually realized that a cub had to take all the distasteful relegation that a pilot felt obligated shooting in *his* face.

I was expected to appreciate the time-honored riverboat tradition that "critiquing" (harassing) was a vital part of a cub's basic training, so that an apprentice such as myself would be able to keep his cool in any emergency.

George Ealer once confidentially told me that it was a federal crime to ever strike a riverboat pilot, regardless of *his* pessimistic disposition, and if I ever committed that type of heinous felony, I would be dispatched at once to a United States' penitentiary. And so, although I secretly wanted to make Brown into a genuine homicide victim, I reconsidered *that* specific option, and decided to stay the course and absorb all of the savage acrimony *he* could barrage me with. I was determined to survive anything that the arrogant asshole could throw in my direction.

Two trips later down to New Orleans, I got into some serious trouble involving the despicable Mr. Brown. The fucked-up dolt was steering the *Pennsylvania* south down the scenic river. Henry, my impish younger brother, appeared before my alert eyes walking on the hurricane deck. Young Henry knew of the dramatic conflict going on between Brown and me, so my perceptive sibling yelled-up to the very volatile pilot, "Stop at the next landing and leave me off!"

Brown pretended he didn't hear Henry's innocent request, and the bellicose ignoring asshole went about his routine business as usual. The condescending ingrate never compromised his arrogance to simply recognize the vocalizations of an under-clerk like Henry, or of a cub pilot like me. I knew that Mr. Brown was virtually deaf, even though I perceived that he was dumb. Anyway, Brown always vainly attempted to disguise *that* very obvious dumb and deaf fact. I remained discreet, waiting to see if Brown would honor or ignore my younger brother's request to dock. I didn't want to defiantly challenge my "straightlaced professor" by repeating my sibling's intent to disembark at the next landing, a mile or so down the river.

Well, sure enough, the *Pennsylvania* cruised right past Henry's appointed destination. When we sailed by the designated plantation platform, Captain Klinefelter suddenly appeared on the pilot deck and intensively interrogated the already-frazzled Mr. Brown about the apparent oversight.

"Didn't Henry request to get-off at that landing back there?" the captain authoritatively inquired.

"No sir!" Brown neurotically stammered. "I heard no such request from that irresponsible pipsqueak!"

"Mr. Brown," Captain Klinefelter imperatively said. "Do you realize I'm the one that sent Henry up to the hurricane deck to do it?"

"He did come up to the deck," Brown deviously maintained, "but the little squirt never said a damned word about anything, but just stood there lookin' at me stupid-like the way that *his* immature, older brother does, all the damned friggin' time!"

The *Pennsylvania* was far away from any ocean, or from the *Gulf of Mexico,* so I couldn't understand why Captain Klinefelter would want to *harbor* someone of Brown's low-character ilk on *his* prestigious riverboat. I was shocked when the captain asked me a poignant question.

"Well Clemens; didn't *you* hear Henry's request to get-off at the plantation?" the chief officer asked. "Certainly, if anyone would heed Henry speaking, it would be you."

I knew that if I spoke the truth, then I was indirectly declaring war on Mr. Brown, and that the mercurial son-of-a-bitch would then wrongly deduce that I was betraying him. "Yes sir; I heard Henry tell Mr. Brown to stop!" I courageously responded, spontaneously aggravating my normally volatile instructor, and daringly baiting *him to* now go ballistic in the captain's midst.

"Shut your goddamned mouth!" Brown furiously hollered in my direction while in the benign captain's presence. "You never heard anything of the kind, and if ya' ask me," the infuriated nutcase continued his wild dissertation, "ya' are an insolent young punk wise-ass seekin' to take over my job by deliberately lyin' to Honorable Captain Klinefelter!"

An hour later, Henry casually sauntered into the pilothouse, unaware of the confrontation that had recently transpired. I knew that Brown would show no mercy toward my younger brother and would generalize that Henry was fair game because *he* and I were genetically similar in the Clemens' family tree.

"Here, here, you fucked-up little squirt chimpanzee!" Brown began his standard didactic vituperation. "Why didn't ya' tell me

we'd got to land at the plantation instead of just standin' there like a dimwitted asshole scratchin' your ass like it was infected or somethin'!" the dip-shit irately condemned my sibling. 'Ya' could always swim back to the plantation, if 'ya so desire!"
"But Mr. Brown, I did tell you to stop the boat!" my usually calm and inoffensive brother sincerely answered. "But ya' either didn't listen, or ya' didn't hear!"
"That's a fuckin' boldfaced lie!" Brown cursed and accused. "You lie better than a whore on a wool rug! Both of you Clemens' boys are young, inexperienced hemorrhoids. And you, Henry. You're nothin' more than a dreamin' schemin', no good, smart-assed, sonny boy, punk, just like your nasty older square-assed brother is!"
"That's a bold-face lie!" I exclaimed in honorable defense of Henry and me. "You aren't even fit to be a respectable pilot teachin' anybody anything about this boat, or about this river!"
Brown glared at me and was momentarily speechless at my unanticipated audacity, and at my enviable rhetorical ability. Then, the livid dick-head anxiously shouted like a maniac, "Shut the fuck up! I'll attend to your situation in a minute!" the ninny yelled at me. And next, the insane nutcase vilely criticized Henry by saying, "And you get your silly ass out of this here pilothouse right this minute! You're trespassin' where ya' don't belong and instigatin' trouble, just like your older brother does all the goddamned time!"
The inflexible "pilot law" had to be obeyed, because according to George Ealer and George Ritchie, if it wasn't respected, then Henry would have to spend a month in the county jail for leveling Mr. Brown and sending him to either the hospital or the morgue. When Henry obediently trudged to the door with his head crestfallen, my principal adversary performed a rather deplorable act. The emotionally unstable pilot picked-up a lump of coal weighing a full pound, and with unbridled fury, ran toward my brother and was about to smash the black object into the back of Henry's head. There was absolutely no time for Henry and me to form a *coal*ition against lunatic Mr. Brown.
I first picked-up a small low chair, and hit the *stool* pigeon on top of his noggin', making his dandruff-infected scalp bleed. Then, I picked up a nearby 'club' and violently clobbered Brown on top of his already aching head, exactly like a good "club pilot" should. The uncouth, hostile villain fell to the floor, and was found to be temporarily unconscious from the dramatic impact he himself had perpetrated. I just had had enough of *his* relentless invectives, but

when Brown was about to injure my precious brother, I just could not harness my temper and felt compelled to retaliate.

Well, I fully understood I had committed the riverboat crime of crimes, and would more-than-likely bypass the county jail, and that a federal judge's verdict would no doubt sentence me to incarceration in a government penitentiary. 'At least I got *some* personal satisfaction out of this terrific altercation!' I remember thinking. So, I figured I would really get my money's worth of serving two years in prison. I angrily got-down on my knees and began brutally pounding and pummeling the living shit out of the uncivilized, dictatorial asshole, who was still lying prone and dazed upon the pilothouse floor. Fortunately, Henry heard and observed my rage, and my loving sibling interceded by wrapping his arms around my flailing fists. Then, my brother lifted me to my feet and proceeded to wildly tug me to the other side of the pilothouse.

A few seconds later, Brown regained consciousness, and instead of launching an attack on my physical presence, the jerk-off jumped to his feet, and the paranoid moron dashed over to the ship's wheel. In the heat of our out-of-control fight, I had forgotten that the riverboat was heading south with nobody at the helm for five full minutes; the ship was going about fifteen-miles an hour downstream. Thank goodness that Eagle Bend was two miles wide, and the water twenty-five feet deep. Thank God no collision with shifting shoals or with existing dangerous reefs was imminent. The magnificent riverboat was in no immediate jeopardy from *steering itself* down that particular stretch of the mighty Mississippi.

Recovering from the shock of receiving the well-deserved thrashing of *his* life, Mr. Brown required a full minute to comprehend that the *Pennsylvania* had miraculously escaped the attendant perils associated with self-steering river navigation. Brown picked-up the giant spyglass that had been set atop his cluttered desk, and raising the instrument as if it was a weapon, the lunatic boisterously ordered me out of the pilothouse. I figured I had sealed my doom and would be ostracized from all riverboats as a result of my blatant insubordination to an immediate, intolerable, egotistical, narcissistic superior. "Get the fuck out of here right now you piss-faced hooligan!" Mr. Brown blustered with his bulging eyes appearing in their sockets as red as rubies.

But I was not afraid of Brown now, because I had just beaten the shit out of him, and was resigned to the idea of being conducted to a federal penitentiary as subsequent punishment. I tarried in the pilothouse, and easily found fault with *his* propensity to use colloquial English when becoming enraged. I said, "Mr. Brown, you should've suavely indicated 'Leave my premises right this instant you, recalcitrant individual'!" I rather perceptively and intelligently corrected *his* poor grammar.

Apparently, Mr. Brown was not acclimated to this sort of controversy involving an underling, so not knowing exactly what the hell to do in that situation, *he* put-down his venerable spyglass on top of his cluttered desk and resumed command of the wheel, generally ignoring my physical presence. Sensing that I had achieved the upper hand in our rocky relationship, I leaped-up on the cub's observation bench and intensely studied *his* body language, which immediately suggested to me that Mr. Brown's despotic spirit had been effectively vanquished by my undaunted tenacity. All *he* did for the next full minute was deliberately stare at the river in sort of a hypnotic trance, while shaking his head back and forth to gesticulate his disgruntled attitude, along with his basic disapproval of recent events.

Our intense scuffle had caused a racket that was heard on the deck below, and soon a dozen very alarmed shipmates and the concerned captain were standing inside the pilothouse. I trembled when I saw Klinefelter's face incredulously staring at both Brown and me.

'Now, my goose is really cooked!' I fearfully thought. 'I've taken away the captain's options, and he has no alternative other than to dismiss me from the ship and report my ass to the local constable!' I anticipated the maximum penalty, since I had endangered the lives of the passengers (without them even knowing it), and I could've inadvertently sunk the *Pennsylvania* and destroyed all of its costly cargo it was carrying downriver to New Orleans.

"Sam Clemens; I'll talk to you in the privacy of my office!" Captain Klinefelter austerely commanded. "I insist that you follow me right this minute!"

I was led to the spacious Texas tender's parlor. The captain closed the after-door, and next closed the forward one; his stern actions giving us the privacy he had promised up on the pilothouse deck where I had recently and satisfactorily kicked the brown crap out of ignoble Mr. Brown. I stood erect like a loyal soldier at attention as Captain Klinefelter adroitly interviewed me.

"So, Mr. Clemens," the good man deliberately began his narrative. "I see you've stooped to fighting with Mr. Brown!"

"Yes, Sir," I politely and meekly replied. "I guess I got tired of his constant abuse. He was going to hit…"

"Do you realize that what you've committed is regarded as a very serious offense?" the riverboat's captain impatiently interrupted.

"Your impulsive action could result in your dismissal from the ship, and a minimum year's vacation in jail!" the chief officer informed.

"Yes, Sir; I'm fully aware of that!" I blandly responded. "I really should've shown more self-discipline! Sorry, Sir. I suppose I was acting too impetuous."

"Are you aware of the fact that the *Pennsylvania* was plowin' down the river at fifteen miles an hour with no one steering it?" my Captain professionally reminded me. "Automatically piloted boats haven't been invented yet!"

"Yes, Sir," I guiltily admitted. "I should've known better I suppose. I guess I'm the ideal asshole!"

"Did ya' strike Mr. Brown first?" my very intelligent boss appropriately and professionally interrogated.

"Yes, Sir, I must confess that I did," I replied without a trace of remorse for my most egregious deed.

"With what did you hit Brown with? Your fists? A hammer?" Captain Klinefelter asked with a grim expression on his face.

"With a stool, Sir," I answered, thinking that Brown himself was a piece of *stool* inside an outhouse's shit hole pit.

"Did ya' clobber him really hard with the stool?" the captain curiously inquired, exhibiting the vocal skill of a highly qualified court prosecutor.

"Fairly hard!" I somberly attested. "At least hard enough to knock him down!"

"Did ya' follow that up?" Captain Klinefelter systematically asked. "By that, I mean, did you continue to hit him without using the stool?"

"Yes Sir," I honestly testified. "I pounded him pretty well with both my fists, and bruised-up his face a trifle, and bloodied his nose, too!"

"Well, did you pound Brown more than much? By that I mean, did you fuckin' pound him relentlessly?" the captain further inquired.

"One might describe it like that," I verified.

"Well then," the captain paused. "Don't repeat this to anyone, but I'm really happy to learn that you, pardon my French," my superior hesitated to grasp the proper nomenclature, "that you kicked the fuckin' shit out of the no-good bastard. You did to Brown what I've always wanted to do to that dirty cock-sucker, but I was prevented from accomplishin' my goal by my high position on the ship, and by my good reputation on the river."

"Why thank you, Sir!" I exclaimed with great surprise as I glanced into a nearby wall mirror and detected a sparkle in each of my suddenly rejuvenated eyes.

"But Mr. Clemens, please don't let this incident go to your head!" the captain solemnly warned. "Remember that you've committed a great crime worthy of expulsion from this boat, and banishment from every other ship on the Mississippi," the commanding officer meritoriously proceeded to lecture. "And never be guilty of it again, do you hear? I rarely give any cub pilot a reprieve of any kind, let alone a major one of this nature."

"Yes, Sir. I'll always bear your words in mind," I promised my venerable mentor.

"Now, before the ship docks at the next port, I want you to do *me* a big favor," the captain suavely requested.

"Anything you say," I agreed to cooperate.

"I want you to go up to the pilothouse, and this time *really* beat the living brown feces out of Brown," the captain ordered with a very evident smile upon his countenance. "Do you hear me Clemens? Pulverize the lousy, obnoxious scumbag! A whelp like you is allowed one, and only one official crime on my ship, so go up-deck and finish the damned job you had started!"

I scampered upstairs and accosted Mr. Brown in the pilothouse. "Well, I hope the captain has laid down the riot act to you!" the asshole uttered while staring at the river below and not giving me the courtesy of looking me in the eyes. "Well, you impudent wimp; what do ya' want now, sonny boy!" the cunt-lapper chuckled without mentioning my name.

"I want to beat the livin' shit out of you again!" I boldly yelled as I clenched my fists and quickly administered to the dirty slime-ball a rather violent right cross that was soon followed by a vicious uppercut to the chin. "I'm gonna' hit you over and over for each of the hundred people that always wanted to smack ya' in the face, but didn't have a chance to finish the task!"

An hour later, Brown was all black and blue, and the paper-tiger bully hobbled over to the boiler deck where Captain Klinefelter was conversing with several sophisticated, well-dressed male and female passengers. Brown demanded that I should be put ashore at the next stop, and that the county sheriff should be summoned and notified of my "brutal assault and battery" that had been performed on him.

"That punk Clemens has a criminal mind," Brown asserted, "and I'm never gonna' turn a wheel steering this boat until that insolent ruffian is put in the slammer where he belongs."

"But that cub needn't come around the pilothouse when you're on watch, Mr. Brown," the captain casually replied. "I'll just re-assign young Clemens to George Ealer's watch instead of yours, that's all!"

Brown had too much pride to admit to Captain Klinefelter that I had twice beaten him up, fair and square. "Sir; I refuse to even stay on the same boat with that pugnacious, hooligan, delinquent thug!" Brown argued and complained. "One of *us* has gotta' go ashore and stay there permanently!"

"Very well then; have it your way," Captain Klinefelter cordially acceded. "Let Mr. Brown go and stay ashore, and let Samuel Clemens be a permanent part of my crew!" the ruling officer of the *Pennsylvania* justly decided.

During the remainder of the trip down to New Orleans, I knew exactly how an emancipated slave must feel after escaping the treacheries of the Deep South. For in a certain inexplicable way, I too had finally been emancipated by Captain Klinefelter's benign proclamation liberating me from arrogant Mr. Brown's perpetual tyranny.

"The Cat and the Pain Killer"

Tom Sawyer was extremely depressed. His favorite girl Becky Thatcher was not attending school, and the melancholy lad was mighty concerned that something drastic had happened to her. Perhaps she was going through puberty, and having her first period, or maybe she was pregnant by the sperm juices of another twelve-year-old boy popping his first load. Or maybe that distrustful son-of-a-bitch Huckleberry Finn was hitting on Becky, without ever sagely consulting Tom's unparalleled wisdom.

Young Tom Sawyer began finding himself (without the use of a mirror) surreptitiously hanging around in the vicinity of Judge Thatcher's mansion (well, a mansion by Missouri and Mississippi River standards), and the perplexed youth was feeling more than a tad sick and miserable because of Becky's prolonged absence from school, and possibly, her apparent absence from existence.

'Is she ill? What if she should die?' Tom thought and negatively considered. 'She's pretty rich, and she's rich and pretty; and Becky's quite popular, too. I hope the young doll didn't run away to join the circus as an acrobat, or as a fortuneteller, or I dreaded that she had been captured by dangerous pirates or bandits. Maybe she's finally getting some hair around her luscious cookie, and running a mild temperature. Gee, if Becky is becoming an eleven-year-old prostitute without my permission or approval, I'll be really pissed-off,' Tom Sawyer assessed. I'll become so pissed-off that I might commit suicide, or maybe even homicide, and go to jail for life without ever getting fuckin' laid!' Tom dejectedly contemplated. 'What a horrible thought, that's sure to weigh-down my heart like a heavy anchor! I'd rather go to war and have my balls and dick blasted-off than to have to put-up with all of this silly love bullshit!'

So, the charm associated with the pleasures of Tom Sawyer living; and breathing; and eating; and sleeping; and dreaming; and pissing; and shitting, was absolutely gone; totally vanished into oblivion. 'No more playing with my petrified dead bat, or throwing my ugly cat out of my second-floor bedroom window, because those sources of entertainment no longer amuse me,' Tom reckoned.

And Aunt Polly was alarmed that Tom was getting physically sick, and the on-a-mission lady tried a variety of new home remedies on him to determine what prospective cure was the most optimal and viable solution to correct his chronic misery. The domineering woman mercilessly unloaded a heap of her conventional verbal propaganda on poor Tom to accompany the creative snakebite medicines she was prone to buy, not at the town drug store, mind you, but from any on-the-run peddler jumping off the late afternoon steamboat and aggressively promoting the elixir's sale and distribution door-to-door on his way to the next town (and its gullible citizens), either up or down the enchanting river.

"Tom Sawyer, you have to first read a chapter from the Good Book, and then obediently swallow-down two tablespoons of the patent medicine I've just bought for you that's sitting on the kitchen table," Aunt Polly authoritatively insisted. "Now, I've read all sorts of literature about the need for resolving your major health problem in the monthly periodical I've subscribed to, and all the published experts say that you have to defeat a cold in its initial stages before you're bedridden and about to go unconscious after receiving an enema," the sagacious woman maintained. "And during your health crisis, don't forget to keep your room well-ventilated with your window half-open, even though it's almost the height of winter. And do some exercising, but not with your greedy little hands down inside your pajamas," Aunt Polly continued orating her relentless diatribe. "You might be going through a terrible growth process called 'puberty', and you're coming into what Reverend Thompson refers to as 'the Temptation Zone', with the diabolical Devil becoming more active and tantalizing in your mischievous life. Church services twice on Sunday will also aid and cure you in overcoming your current malady!"

"Aunt Polly, your family doctor must look like a duck with all of these quack medicines and cures that you believe in and try to practice," Tom nastily and defensively answered. "And as for the Devil and his subordinate demons, Huck Finn and me, and the rest of our gang will beat the crap out of those red-tailed varmints, either on Earth, or in Hell, or in Purgatory, after we all finally get there and organize our rebel army!"

"Tom, I do believe that you've already become susceptible to Satan's evil influence. I swear that I'm going to get the preacher to march over to this house and exercise an exorcism on you," Aunt Polly adamantly replied. "If he can't do it, I'm sure that the bishop can! You're probably the most defiant mouth in the South when it boils-down to being insolent. Now just pretend, Mr. Sawyer, that I'm the Angel of Healing, and agree to sample this new medicine that I've recently obtained. It's called Pain Killer; and it's guaranteed to remove all of those evil germs and wicked spirits out of your vulnerable, diseased system."

'If the Pain Killer would make me have my first ejaculation and wet orgasm,' Tom mentally reckoned, 'then I might consider drinking down the whole fuckin' bottle.'

But then young Sawyer became more rational and boldly challenged his guardian on *his* moral and logical battlefield. "Aunt Polly, you ain't gonna' get me behind the woodshed and pour buckets of cold water on my naked body, because you ain't gonna' be able to see my naked body anymore," Tom Sawyer courageously argued, attempting to establish his independence and his about-to-happen teenage puberty rebellion. "I'm startin' to get some important peach fuzz around my dingle, and pretty soon, I'll be squirtin' sticky sperm juice all over the damned place, especially on my bedroom walls, and maybe even up on the ceiling, should I produce a real gusher. And besides those potential acts," the thoroughly upset lad editorialized, "I'll no longer consent to bein' wrapped-up in a wet blanket; so, Aunt Polly, it's lookin' like you're goin' to be the only damned wet blanket and crepe hanger in this here house!"

"Tom Sawyer! You vulgar, obscene little Imp!" Aunt Polly yelled and scolded. "I'll make sure that the harmful yellow infection stains ooze right out of your pores, and that you profusely sweat your entire body clean under ten pounds of heavy towels. But I'll allow you to take your hot sitz baths in private, if you insist on not being scrutinized. And then, Young Man, there's going to be numerous mustard plaster applications I'll administer, and also a strict oatmeal diet, too!" the livid lady ranted. "But listen-up, Tom! You're going to have to drink-down these two tablespoons of Pain Killer, or else I'm going to make an appointment for Minister Thompson to come to the house, and through an hour of intense Bible prayers and chants, the beloved Reverend will skillfully remove all of those pesky evil demons that are greedily possessing your body and your juvenile mind. Now, here you are Tom Sawyer. Take and gulp-down this wonderful medicine so that I can begin retrieving your soul from Lucifer's covetous clutches!"

"Okay, Aunt Polly. But I think I'd rather pal around with Satan than buddy-up with either you or Preacher Thompson!" Tom vehemently protested. "Yuck! This junk tastes like liquid shit! It's gonna' rot my stomach and asshole away!"

"Tom, you watch your foul language and show more respect for your elderly Aunt Polly!" the aggravated woman commanded. "I'm thinking about making you join the church choir, or maybe go over to that Catholic Church across town and become an altar boy! That's it!

We'll have the town doctor cut-off your testicles, and you'll instantly become a Castrati choir boy!"

"Great ideas Aunt Polly!" Tom vehemently balked. "That's just what I need! I don't want to be molested by either that faggot Reverend Thompson or by that gay pedophile Catholic priest, either. All I want to do is screw Becky Thatcher, get her pregnant, and then go into politics just like all of the successful, immoral assholes in this messed-up town do!"

"Sakes alive Tom! Your rudeness is incredibly intolerable! You need to rinse your mouth out with detergent after you take another dose of this delicious Pain Killer!"

"Aunt Polly wants a cracker, so why don't you find a good white man to sleep with and get yourself pregnant!" Tom impertinently answered. "At least that's what all of the black folks around town have been sayin' about you!"

* * * * * * * * * * * *

Being excessively naughty and unscrupulous, Tom began asking his beleaguered relative for Pain Killer at every opportunity, and the fiasco eventually reached the point where the boy's constant utterances became a plain nuisance, and Aunt Polly was getting awfully suspicious of young Mr. Sawyer's all-too-furtive motives, and the old lady was often yelling into his face, "Quit bothering me with your asinine requests!" But the aged woman persistently distrusted her nefarious nephew, and closely watched the Pain Killer bottle clandestinely, endeavoring to catch Tom pouring its contents out the nearest window an ounce at a time; but Tom's guardian's vigilance and perseverance were to no avail. All that Aunt Polly could daily observe was the liquid level inside the brown medicine bottle upon the kitchen shelf gradually diminishing in volume, day after precious day.

But all the while, instead of mending his poor health with the magic Pain Killer formula, wily Tom was each and every afternoon assiduously mending a narrow crack in the wood-planked sitting room floor. One Wednesday afternoon, mischievous Sawyer was secretively filling the aforementioned crevice with some new Pain Killer, when Aunt Polly's near-death yellow cat Peter came purring into the vicinity, and then keenly eyeballed the cherry red liquid rather avariciously.

"Well, Peter; let's see if this powerful shit will make your peter erect!" Tom whispered out of fear of getting caught administering the all-potent drug to the rapidly deteriorating tomcat. "Let's see ya' lick this foul-tasting crap down your throat, and we'll see if it rejuvenates you back into your youth when ya' used to be the best damned fighting, sex-starved cat in the whole damned town. But don't blame me if this shit makes you jump-up to the ceiling, hit your head hard, and then die as a result of you bein' cured of distemper, or whatever the hell's wrong with you. I warn ya' Peter. This nasty mixture tastes a lot worse than cod liver oil, or even that horrible castor oil shit."

So, then, Tom gingerly pried-open Peter's mouth and poured-down an ounce or two of the omnipotent, putrid-tasting Pain Killer remedy. Well, that ornery tomcat sprang several yards up into the air, with its normally kinked, curly fur standing straight-up on its back and tail. And upon honoring the rules of gravity and hitting the floor on all fours, the suddenly-obsessed animal screamed incessantly, and wildly whirled around in circles at least two dozen times, violently knocking over flower pots, ramming against furniture legs, and pissing a long yellow streak while crazily and repeatedly scampering around the confined area in full velocity.

Next, Peter, being exhausted, ceased his frenetic frenzy, and then pranced around the room like one of those trained white Austrian stallions, flamboyantly showing-off his fantastic, new-found, energized disposition. But then the possessed cat accelerated again to full speed, tearing around the house like a creature possessed with demented demons, and in his self-created chaos, the furry marauder was plowing into any object or obstacle in his erratic path.

Aunt Polly immediately stepped into the normally tranquil sewing room, put her wet hands on her hips, and promptly (in an exasperated tone of voice) interrogated innocent-looking Tom about what all the commotion and racket was about.

"I don't know what the heck's gotten into Peter," Tom politely and uncharacteristically testified, showing very little remorse or humiliation for his naughty actions. "I think Peter's entered his second childhood and wants to be the kitty in a poker game over in the smokey back room down at the pool hall!"

"I don't know what ails that strange-behaving tomcat, but I'm glad to see that he's getting over his general lethargy, even at the expense of breaking a couple of flowerpots," Aunt Polly stated in a confused state of mind. But then, the old lady bent-down and discovered the telltale handle to the tablespoon sticking-out, and quite visible, under the sewing room's table. The irate woman immediately fathomed exactly what had occurred to Peter, so she swiftly raised Tom up by his right ear, and repeatedly clobbered his cranium with the heavy tablespoon until his scalp and skull fully ached. Then, the extremely livid woman placed her metal sewing thimble upon her index finger, and made several impressive rivets and dents directly upon Tom's already-throbbing forehead.

"Tom Sawyer, why did you have to treat poor Peter with such unbridled malice?" Aunt Polly very loudly chastised her principal nemesis. "You know that the creature is nearly blind, can't hear a lick, and can't even smell his own feces! Stop deliberately torturing and abusing that poor animal."

"I only gave him the same damned medicine you was givin' me," Tom effectively debated the issue. "I was only treatin' old Peter like he was a human being. I done it out of sheer pity, because Peter ain't got a wonderful caring aunt like I do; a lady who gives me delicious medicine to cure my illnesses!"

Aunt Polly suddenly felt a wave of charitable compassion envelop her, and she soon experienced a pang of remorse (penetrate her forgiving heart) for the excessive punishment of her saintly and considerate nephew. The old bag's eyes watered, and she put her hand on young Sawyer's shoulder saying, "I'm sorry for hurting you, Tom. I was meaning the best for you and Peter, so that's why I unfortunately pounded and pummeled you!"

"Well, Aunt Polly; the Pain Killer really did Peter some good because his peter became erect, and now the cat can journey about and screw all of the pussy in the neighborhood; even pumpin' the hairy ass of the gay faggot male cat moochin' a living next door. And that psyched-up Tom-cat of yours is feelin' young and virile once again, thanks to the wonderful wizardry of your most fabulous Pain Killer formula."

"Oh Tom; get to bed early so that you can arrive at school tomorrow morning well-rested," his protective guardian advised. "I just know that you're going to grow-up to be a famous scientist, inventor, mathematician, or comedian some day!"

* * * * * * * * * * *

Anticipating a punctual rendezvous with Becky Thatcher, Tom reached school early the following morning. The impulsive lad anxiously loitered around the playground gate, hoping to catch a glimpse of Becky's frock approaching from the distance, but the boy's intense surveillance was noticeably unproductive. Young Sawyer had felt both swindled and hoodwinked by the whims of fate, if not being egregiously exploited by human nature. The kid twice entered (and exited) the play area and half-heartedly chased some friends around the perimeter, pretending to be a twelve-year-old successful hooligan, but out of the corner of his eye, Tom was stealthily doing espionage and reconnaissance work looking-out for any sign of his imagined sweetheart. Jeff Thatcher then paraded through the open gate and into the dirt and gravel area, and Tom accosted the free spirit, and felt compelled to ask him a question or two about *his* absent sister.

"Hell Tom; I ain't got the time of day for Becky, no way," Jeff responded to Sawyer's dire inquiry. "My parents treat her like she's some sort of special royalty, so the conceited little bitch thinks she's a princess and a goddamned queen-in-waiting! See ya' around Tom! I got my eyes on that cute little Mary Lee Chapman doll standin' all by her lonesome over there!"

Tom heard the teacher's hand bell ring, and reluctantly entered the schoolhouse with his head crestfallen. All during morning roll call, the boy's head rubbernecked toward the side window, looking for any sign of his missing girl-Venus. 'Maybe she's eloped with some older punk, and they've run off to Ohio or the Amazon!' Tom imagined. 'No; Becky wouldn't do anything drastic like that! She's too spoiled-rotten at home by her overprotective parents to ever consider doin' anything like that kind of dumb stupid shit!'

Soon, one last frock came ambling into the schoolyard, and Tom's heart nearly leaped out of his chest. Against the alarmed teacher's wishes, the overzealous lad jumped-out of his desk and zoomed out of the schoolhouse, dashing full-throttle towards the petite girl of his dreams. Young Sawyer intentionally grabbed a tardy boy's hat off his head, as the youth was entering the ramshackle building, and then nonchalantly tossed the object onto the schoolhouse's roof.

"My goodness Tom!" Becky Thatcher exclaimed in indignant disappointment. "Some rebellious asshole I know thinks he's mighty important around these parts and always showing-off."

"Look Becky," acne-faced Tom replied. "I see a big zit on your forehead, so that pimple either means that you're getting over the chicken pox, or having your first monthly period and goin' through what the local, pious, adults call 'puberty'. If that's the case," Tom said with a sparkle in his eye, "let's go inside Aunt Polly's tool shed after school so that we can play a friendly game of doctor, and curiously examine each other's newly-formed pubic fuzz!"

"Lost in a Snowstorm"

Samuel Langhorne Clemens (1835-1910) was undoubtedly one of the most influential American authors ever, and was also a prolific contributor to United States literature. Sam Clemens was born the year Haley's Comet (Halley's Comet) made an appearance, and the literary master died seventy-five years later when the celestial object made another solar system revolution past the Earth, and then sped again around the sun.

Mark Twain was a trend-setter because Clemens was one of the first authors to present characters speaking dialogue using poor grammar, the way ordinary people would converse with regional accents, rather than the stilted, formal, academic style practiced by his literary predecessors, and also by his pompous New England literary contemporaries.

I never liked blizzards or volcano eruptions, but instead, always preferred hurricanes and massive earthquakes. But here is one zany snowstorm tale I'll never forget. One morning, it was snowing like a son-of-a-bitch when the three of us boarded the decrepit *Overland Stagecoach*, which could not float on the ocean, so naturally, the stagecoach usually always went over land. The snow was already several inches deep, and the dirt trail could not be seen by the horses, if ya' get *the drift* of what the fuck I'm tryin' to accurately describe here. Visibility was only about three-hundred-foot or so, and it really didn't matter if the three stagecoach passengers were blind or not during that particular wicked shit-eatin' trip that I'm lucky to have lived through and now write pertinent details about.

Ollendorff was an old, snotty, arrogant, senile Prussian asshole, and Ballou happened to be an elderly blacksmith that were travelin' with me to Carson City. Ollendorff thought he knew everything about anything, and bragged that he could tell when the stagecoach driver would deviate one inch off the goddamned center of the dirt road. All during our lengthy ordeal, I suspected that both Ollendorff and Ballou, prior to being born, neither of the two morons could find his way out of his mother's birth canal.

"How can ya' be so sure of your claim?" I asked the garrulous, old European fart. "Do ya' have some kind of compass implanted in your goddamned cerebrum, or maybe inside your epididymis?"

"Be careful!" the decrepit, inflexible Prussian cautioned. "I happen to be just as much an expert on fucked-up deviants as I am on fucked-up deviation!"

Then, the driver accidentally came-upon a fresh trail, and Ollendorff egotistically shouted, "Boys, I knew my senses are as good as that mental compass we were just talkin' about! The driver spotted someone else's recent tracks in the snow, and we ain't lost one iota out here, meandering around in the wilderness."

"I'd believe the driver sayin' those words before I'd ever believe an old fossil-faced-fool like you!" Ballou asserted and challenged the militant Prussian. "Ya' just ain't got no credibility here in America, and I think ya' ain't got none back in wherever the hell ya' came from, either."

"Ballou's right!" I insisted, just to further break Ollendorff's supersensitive balls and to continue the bullshit conversation. "Now if we were travelin' somewhere in Prussia instead of in the Nevada Territory on this lackluster North American continent, then I would be half-inclined to give ya' credit for makin' an intelligent observation. Speakin' of a continent Ollendorff," I continued with a wry smile featured on my countenance, "by your putrid body odor, Ballou and I both think you're incontinent!"

The driver put the horses into a trot, and although I knew we was lookin' at a mirage through the snowflakes, that flakey dude, fellow passenger Ollendorff, insisted that we were gainin' on our predecessors (ridin' in the imaginary speedy stagecoach ahead of us), because the discernible tracks embedded in the snow were apparently becoming more distinct.

"Why don't ya' just drink another pint of rye whiskey?" Ballou mentioned to the indignant Ollendorff. "You're as drunk as the Lord at the Last Supper already, and I've seen walls not half as friggin' plastered as *you* already are!"

"Ballou's right!" I keenly added, to further bust the Prussian's balls. "I believe we're followin' a phantom stagecoach, or possibly a mystery Conestoga wagon, or somethin' ridiculous like that."

"Look you two excessively dumb-shit Americans," Ollendorff criticized in some kind of distinct perverted German accent. "The damned tracks in the snow are looking fresher and newer all the fuckin' time. And now, instead of two sets of wheels, there appears to be four. We're not alone on this treacherous journey to Carson City, that's for goddamned sure!"

"I'll bet it's a company of stout-hearted soldiers from a nearby frontier fort," Ballou theorized and suggested about the new-found wheel tracks. "Those Army guys know this territory better than we traveling assholes do."

"Get a grip!" I ranted before taking another swig of blackberry brandy to finally end the main course of my impromptu and improvised dinner. "Soldiers ride on horseback, and those veteran eunuchs, who have lost their testicles from bouncing up-and down inside horses' saddles, well, those pony riders don't leave damned stagecoach or Conestoga wagon tracks in two-foot of snow durin' inclement weather. It's a good thing you're not an optometrist Ollendorff, because you'd make a spectacle out of yourself daily!"

In another hour, the visible wheel tracks advanced from four to six sets, and Ollendorff felt compelled to mercilessly chastise Ballou and me for being agnostics (or maybe even atheists) to his omniscient claims. "That platoon of soldiers is expanding as more troops are joinin' the regiment," the Prussian idiot confidently declared. "If worse comes to worse, the soldiers will feel obligated to rescue us from impending tragedy."

"Yeah; there's gotta' be at least a hundred soldiers out there ahead of us, deliberately getting lost in this goddamned snowstorm, too!" Ballou humorously maintained. "Got any more fucked-up claims to make Ollendorff?"

"You Americans are so damned cynical, it's absolutely sickening!" the irate Prussian admonished Ballou and me. "You two wouldn't believe Christ if he came-down from the cross and was sittin' here tellin' ya' exactly what I'm tellin' both you freakin' constipated, nutcase nitwits right now!"

"Right!" I sarcastically ridiculed the snotty, conceited European. "As if Jesus Christ has nothin' better to do than hop off His cross and miraculously appear inside this here stagecoach to tell us that you Ollendorff know what the fuck you're talkin' about. I think I need to take a healthy shit after poor Jesus hearin' all this fantastic poppycock, and then givin' us His supernatural advice!"

"The military has wagons attached to horses too, you know!" the regimented Prussian argued in his special brand of jabberwocky. "Why do you fucked-up Americans think you have a monopoly on logic, or on truth?"

"Right, and a thousand Indians in the vicinity feel like fightin' the soldiers from the fort right this minute in the center of this massive mother-fuckin' desert blizzard!" Ballou comically yelled and then laughed. "Grow a goddamned second brain, will ya', Ollendorff?"

The driver abruptly halted the *Overland Stagecoach,* and the cowboy sauntered to the cab and declared, "Boys; I can't see the damned trail any-more, and I suspect we might be goin' in circles followin' our last trail. What's your pleasure?"

"Alcohol!" Ollendorff defensively proclaimed.

"Gamblin'!" Ballou instinctively added.

"Loose women, good sex, big firm tits, hairy beaver, and perfect smoking tobacco!" I reflexively confessed.

"I knew I should've kept futilely ridin' into Death Valley instead of tryin' to be serious with you three degenerate jerk-offs!" the petulant driver chastised. "I was much happier bein' all content sittin' up there exposed in the freezin' cold, tryin' to get you three mental-case fools to Carson City."

Two-minutes-later, the stagecoach jerked forward, and then Ballou again felt it appropriate to bust Ollendorff's sensitive testicles and scrotum sac. "I ain't never seen nor ever heard of such a fucked-up, self-centered imbecile as you are," the old blacksmith ranted to the emotionless, stoical Prussian. "Ya' probably try to take a piss every time your dick gets hard!"

Ollendorff was indeed pissed-off, but without having any noticeable erection. And the fuck-head dared not belligerently defy and challenge the muscular old blacksmith to a fistfight inside the stagecoach, because we were caught in a monster snowstorm, and still over a hundred miles away from the nearest hospital or the closest mortuary.

"Look!" I indicated to my riding companions while pointing to the right. "There's the bank of that frozen stream that we've already passed three times in this mean-assed snowstorm. If my thinkin' is correct," I hypothesized and mentioned, "the next inn oughta' be only five hundred *kilometers* or so away," I estimated, deliberately using a European distance measurement instead of the standard American word "miles" to further aggravate the traveling Prussian seated diagonally across from me.

The *Overland Stagecoach* smashed right over and through that frozen stream, and headed-out into the middle of nowhere. Everyone temporarily professed confidence in the clueless driver's good instincts, and in his sense of direction and overall experience, considering this was only his first trip to Carson City. To our utter astonishment, the three of us momentarily spotted a second swift-moving stagecoach directly in front of us, and the object was speeding along as if the vehicle was on a sleigh, rather than moving along on mundane wagon wheels.

"I still say that's a mystery illusion we're followin' up ahead," I mentioned to initiate another meaningless conversation with my extraordinary, opinionated companions. "I know a fuckin' phantom when I see one!"

"You have the faith of a condemned cynic and are a certain candidate for the infernos of Hell!" Ollendorff accused. "You were probably baptized in a contaminated swamp by some uncertified infidel, or by an unqualified, defrocked priest or pagan rabbi!"

"I think you two imbeciles would get along better if ya' just jerked each other off!" Ballou obnoxiously stated. "I've seen better rectum wipers in the *National Historic Asshole Museum* that's conveniently situated in downtown Boston!"

Our driver's horses were no match for the other "phantom stage's team", and the fleet object soon disappeared into the vast relentless snowstorm. Ollendorff insisted that the current "matters really didn't matter", and that our driver could still follow the freshly-made tracks that were being laid down by "the disillusioned stagecoach pilot, and by the reckless delusional ghost driver".

"Despite the blizzard those recently made ruts in the road are deep enough for our driver to easily recognize and follow," the Prussian idiot insisted. "It doesn't matter if the fuckin' artificial tracks are a goddamned mirage!" the drunken bastard conjectured and firmly stated.

"I think your freakin' mind is in a pathetic, damned rut," Ballou answered and admonished Ollendorff. "I'd believe you more if ya' was a tad more drunk than ya' are right now!" the argumentative old blacksmith further reprimanded the austere Prussian.

"Pretty soon it'll be night, and our driver ain't got no lantern to follow the imaginary trail left by the phantom horses and by the specter driver!" I concluded and emphatically stated. "We're fuckin' lost in a snowstorm!"

Night did descend on that remote part of the Nevada Territory, but the snowfall was still thick, as the severe winds cycloned around in the lingering twilight. Visibility had been reduced to fifteen human paces, and the glistening snowflakes had virtually covered the desert sagebrush, making each of the objects look like sugar or salt-covered edible mounds. The first stagecoach's grooves had been reduced to mere traces in the deep snow, and for the very first-time, concern filled the three passengers' hearts, instead of levity or rancor.

Now the snow-laden sagebrush was mostly around three-to-four-foot-high, and some of them formed a lane of a sort of surreal avenue out there in the desolate desert; so, I told my traveling companions that we might be headed out to obscurity, or to infinity, or to oblivion, or some obscure place like that down one of those imaginary sagebrush avenues leading to the end of our lives.

"You Americans are all doomsayers, skeptics, and obnoxious pessimists," Ollendorff denounced and generalized, before loudly belching and simultaneously farting six times. "But a true-blue European aristocrat is more rational, and certainly much more logical about accurate probability, and other exceptional scientific bullshit like that."

"What do ya' groom your hair with?" I questioned the Prussian. "I'll bet ya' use a *sage*brush because you're so damned smart. Your goddamned ancestors must've been two-tonic knights!"

"Ollendorff ain't got no damned hair for neither a comb nor a brush to groom with," the equally-baldheaded Ballou cackled while slapping his knees. "And I understand that these friggin' Prussian dudes are so low-browed that they'll even comb or brush their bald heads to try and impress us all-too-savvy Americans."

I thanked the Lord that we were still alive while anxiously riding in that forsaken stagecoach; we being nature's cold victims freezing our asses' off in the middle of an unmapped and uncharted desert wonderland (wasteland). I suppose imagining having a sheet of ice shoved-down one's back could graphically make the reader understand the intense chill that penetrated my fragile heart, my immortal soul, and also, my frozen dick and my frosted buttocks. We yelled for the driver to stop the damned stagecoach so that the passengers could get out; stretch our legs; take pisses in the snow; walk around and test the ground, and then attempt to build a roaring sagebrush fire to melt any icicles that might have begun forming inside our already-frozen assholes.

"Let's build a fire!" Ballou authoritatively bellowed. "I gotta' warm-up my ass and pecker before I can move and climb my genitals back into the damned stagecoach."

"That's an exceptionally good idea," the amiable driver agreed. "I need to thaw-out this nice bottle of frozen blackberry brandy over a roaring campfire."

"I had no idea I was traveling with a gang of accomplished alcoholics!" the half-drunken Ollendorff bitched while facetiously condemning his alleged immoral traveling associates. "Give me a scenic beer garden in Munich any goddamned time over rank drunks like you three whiskey-randos lost out here in an ugly American desert during the fucked-up blizzard of the century."

"Okay, you three ingrates. Let's get the fire started," I constructively suggested. "First we gotta' assemble some sorta' dry sagebrush, and stack it into an orderly pile."

"What are we gonna' do after we gather the sagebrush fragments?" the driver curiously inquired. "How's the pile gonna' ignite? The damned sagebrush is all wet and saturated from the fuckin' snow!"

"Indians used to scrape sticks together to create a spark," I academically stated. "Ollendorff here seems to be an authority on working his stick."

"We'll rub our dicks together and the friction might generate a lucky spark to ignite a fire!" Ballou inspirationally replied and laughed. "If that esoteric strategy doesn't work, we'll then try and piss fire out of our shriveled-up fadorkinbenders!"

"You're full of shit!" Ollendorff criticized Ballou.

"We'd all have to have hard-ons, and with this freezing frigid temperature," Ballou laughed and coughed, "that phenomenon would be virtually impossible. Not even the fuckin' Abdominal Snowman could get and maintain a regular erection in frigid weather like this freakin' blizzard!"

"For your information," the very disciplined Prussian clarified, "it's the *Abominable Snowman* and not the Abdominal Snowman. And besides Mr. Ballou, I'll just shoot my pistol into the sagebrush and lots of sparks will be created, and then a magnificent flame will automatically result," Ollendorff nonchalantly volunteered. "There is indeed a rational solution to our dilemma, you know!"

"Have ya' ever done such a thing and started a fire that way?" I reasonably asked the know-it-all European visitor. "Ya' seem like a damned tenderfoot to me that's shot his damned ankle at least several times by accident."

"No; but once I read in a book about it being done," the serious-faced, intoxicated Prussian confidently answered. "In fact, I read about it several times in a couple of different books."

"What was the name of the first damned book?" Ballou nastily queried. "Was it *Shooting Off My Mouth*?"

"I believe the book's title was *Flames in Paradise*," Ollendorff grimly replied. "And the setting was on a beautiful, picturesque, tropical Pacific Island."

So, then we all crouched-down and huddled together on our knees in the two-foot-deep-snow, while swirling snowflakes eddied and spiraled all around our heads in an oddball atmosphere that seemed to transcend all of our previous boring and dull experiences on planet Earth. I perceptively scanned my immediate surroundings, and observed that Ballou, Ollendorff and the bewildered stagecoach driver all looked like paralyzed, white, stooping statues, taking royal shits out in the middle of an unknown, hostile, barren, frigid frontier.

After five minutes of assiduously arranging the assorted sagebrush twigs into a handsome heap, we all retreated fifteen paces as the genius Ollendorff applied his pistol to the mound, pulled the trigger, and next an array of sparks flew all over the damned place, except inside the friggin' sagebrush twig pile. The crazy Prussian (in maniacal frustration) then emptied the remaining five bullets into the center of the mound, blowing the entire pile clear out of the Nevada Territory as if he had been using extremely potent dynamite sticks.

The four of us heard a wild neighing, and then quickly realized that the gunfire had frightened the resting team of horses. The alarmed animals panicked and took-off, leaving the driverless unhitched stagecoach behind them, and also abandoning the four of us humans to our miserable, pitiful, lonesome fate; all lost in the biggest blizzard of that entire cold and frigid winter.

"Got any other clever brainstorms?" Ballou defiantly asked General Ollendorff. "How many malignant tumors did ya' say ya' got inside your fucked-up, infected brain?"

The beleaguered Prussian attempted to transfer blame for the failed incident to the now dumbfounded and innocent stagecoach driver. "Why the hell did *you* dismount the stagecoach before I fired the gunshots into the sagebrush mound?" Ollendorff boisterously yelled at the accused defendant.

"That was not half as stupid as *you* blastin' the shit out of the mound and destroyin' what was supposed to make the goddamned fire!" I countered in defense of the poor, persecuted stage driver. "When brains were distributed by the Almighty, ya' must've stupidly gotten in the asshole line *a second* time!"

"Those cocksuckin' unhitched horses are off to the races, and we'll probably never see those frightened bastards again," Ballou lamented and noted. "We gotta' be at least two hundred miles from the nearest populated whorehouse!"

"Those lying library books," Ollendorff disgustedly complained. "They all stated that horses always remain close to their masters for companionship and for support during times of crisis," the Prussian regretted and commented. "I apologize to you, Mr. Driver, for lambasting your character about not staying up there perched in the stagecoach's driver's seat."

The four stranded travelers, with our faces turning purple from the frigid cold, were now transformed into four marooned nomads. We endeavored building a second fire, and after a mound of sagebrush had finally been gleaned and gathered into a classic heap, Ollendorff again obliterated the semi-wood pile by depositing six errant bullets into its center. "Let's try rubbing some sturdy sticks together," the shit-for-brains Prussian recommended. "I gotta' feeling that the widely acclaimed pistol method I had read about in library books is ineffective in subzero weather at precisely midnight in the midst of a terrible desert snowstorm."

"No fuckin' shit!" Ballou nastily replied to the loony, drunken European dude. "You're about as useful as a dried-out turd on a paper plate that's baking in an oven! What pecker-headed library did ya' go to over in Munich, *The Duncecap Academy's!"*

Mr. Ballou methodically dug deep into his pants and produced four healthy matches from a fifth pocket, which the retard never knew he had. In the meantime, the other three of us reviled all native American Indians; frontier hunters; *pioneers;* cake-in-ears; island cannibal; uncivilized savages; friendly barbarians; happy Eskimos; books, and anyone or anything else that inanely maintained that fire could be made by systematically rubbing sticks together.

"Four matches are better than four bars of gold bullion at this particular place and time," I stated to break the stone-cold silence that prevailed at that very moment. "Any kind of money right now is useless, with us being stranded here outside of civilization!"

"That's right," the stage-less stagecoach driver concurred. "Money, silver, platinum, and gold are completely useless right about now. Survival is the only damned thing that really matters."

"If we ever survive this cursed ordeal," Ballou promised with his hand over his heart, "I'll buy everyone a big steak dinner, a horny prostitute, and a bottle of your favorite whiskey when we finally return to civilization."

Mr. Ballou lit the first match, but it burned-out in ten short seconds. The second match was extinguished by a sudden gust of howling wind that sent a series of chills up and down my vulnerable spine and shrunken pecker. The third match was on the imminent brink of being a wonderful success, when suddenly, it too faded and then eventually expired.

The group all huddled closer together, hoping that we could block the effect of the overwhelming wind for the fourth and final match. Mr. Ballou scratched the igniter tip on his rough, jagged, belt, and the baby flame burning blue and true, and then astoundingly, flared into a robust little inferno. Gentle tongues of fire formed on the edge of the sagebrush mound, and the four of us were all instantly optimistic that our improvised campfire would wondrously ignite-up into a nice glowing blaze.

Ballou was so absorbed in watching the sagebrush that the absurd dingleberry had forgotten that the match was still burning in his right hand's fingers. "Ouch!" the senile cretin loudly shouted as his curled fingers and knuckles became scorched. The excessive breath from the old blacksmith's exclamation traveled out of his mouth and onto the sagebrush, causing the tiny fire to immediately lose its original robust vitality.

"Nice goin', you totally incompetent fuck-head!" the normally dispassionate Ollendorff uncharacteristically cursed at Mr. Ballou. "Who's good at diggin' graves without a goddamned shovel! And I don't mean any goddamned snow shovel either!"

Then, no one else dared to say a word for a full five minutes as the strong northern wind howled, and the chaotic snowflakes swirled around our heads, and slammed into our exposed faces. We all peered into each other's saddened eyes, and as midnight encroached under an ominous full moon, all of us realized that the horribly unbearable darkest hour might be our last one staying alive upon the apathetic Earth. In my heart, I knew that each of us shared the same fearful conviction, and that our ultimate demise was probably inevitable, if not imminent.

Ollendorff began all of the stupid solemn bullshit that followed, by him sanctimoniously stating like a bizarre, fucked-up church minister: "Brethren; let us perish together in this frozen wasteland, and let our hearts discard any animosity or discord, so that we may forgive all of those that have sinned against us," the Prussian fool began an unwelcome dissertation.

"Shut the fuck up!" Ballou yelled at the inebriated Prussian.

"I fully realize that some of my charming companions might still hold a grudge against me for bragging about the truth; for me being more academically gifted; and for me exploring the circumference of circles with a mile-long-diameter here in the brutal desert blizzard," the delusional Prussian preached. "But as you all are aware, I meant well and never intended to bring harm or insult to any of you. I confess that I did have some hard feelings toward Mr. Ballou for calling me 'a carnival stooge', which, of course, has no significant worthwhile meaning on the entire European continent," Ollendorff pontificated and elaborated. "Let it be known right here and now that I forgive our simpleton companion, the illustrious Mr. Ballou, with all of my heart, and with all of my soul."

"I said shut the fuck up!" Ballou reiterated as the infuriated blacksmith clenched his fists. "If only I had my anvil available to tie around and hang from your big fat neck!"

Ollendorff then became emotionally disheveled, broke-down, and began sobbing like a weak wimp: Prussian, American or otherwise. Ballou's eyes were creating crocodile tears, too; and then the weeping, muscular blacksmith apologetically told Ollendorff, "I forgive you, too; even though you were, are, and always will be a fucked-up asshole!"

The pathetic Prussian then ceremonially removed a full pint of powerful whiskey from his interior coat pocket, and instead of twisting-off the cap and quickly swallowing-down a major chug, the haughty fool pledged, "I'll never again take another gulp of this poison if my life is super-mundanely spared from this impending calamity. I shall be totally reformed, and shall dedicate all of my energies to assisting the poor; to nursing the infirmed, and to lecturing various civic service clubs about the need to practice temperance," Ollendorff wholeheartedly promised in a weird type of perverted prayer. "I will first and foremost be an exemplary fine example for today's misguided youth; for them to model their easily tempted lives after."

Then, the penitent Prussian threw-away the bottle of sinful liquor, which Ballou, the driver, and I desperately needed to drink in order to stay alive. Next, it was Mr. Ballou's turn to describe his vices and to forgive all his myriad enemies of their particular trespasses, transgressions, offenses, crimes, and excessive sins, along with innumerable violations against him.

Ballou reached inside his external coat and removed a new deck of playing cards. "I never made a habit of gamblin'," the old bald-headed blacksmith began his repentance. "But I admit I've played a game or two of poker with righteous bankers, preachers and undertakers from time to time. No man is without sin or vice, and I am consistent with that particular axiom of life. Therefore," Ballou proceeded, "I pledge and vow to discard these virtue-less gamblin' cards, and hereby abandon all immorality for the remainder of my tenure on this sometimes cruel and unusual planet. I am *obsoletely* (absolutely) certain that the Almighty's benevolent mercy will fairly and impartially judge my soul on the scales of truth and wisdom."

The blacksmith's sorrowful nomenclature affected him as if the ideas he had presented had actually been very intelligible and erudite remarks. Ballou openly cried, shook like a Quaker, and then quivered as if possessed by a plethora of diabolical, evil demons; and then the distressed gambling fanatic strenuously hurled his new deck of cards out into the desert wilderness, in the same direction that Ollendorff had thrown his full pint of whiskey.

The aggrieved stagecoach driver then professed to sacrifice his future existence (should he successfully live through our present hardship) by giving up sex with men, with children, with space aliens, and with horny women, and then having some kind of perverted sex operation performed, and finally entering a secluded convent as a novitiate hermit nun, or some highly peculiar religious function like that.

My own remarks were laden with remorse for practicing a thoroughly unfilled and unrewarding life. "I, like you three honest gentlemen, am also in the presence of death," I prefaced. "And with all honorable and sincere motivations, I hereby proclaim to separate myself from my former dependence on tobacco." I then threw-away my corncob pipe in the same direction as Ollendorff had tossed his whiskey bottle, and that Ballou had heaved his new deck of poker playing cards. "If only I could be spared a few additional years on this majestic Earth," I pleaded; "then the new reformed me could engage in charitable and civic service enterprises of all kinds." Next, without any indication of faltering, my fake fortitude suddenly collapsed, and I lost my sense of manliness, crying like a hysterical widow at her damned bankrupt husband's funeral.

The four of us put our weary arms together in a tight circle as if we were faggots or lesbians, or bona-fide fucked-up people like that; and then each of us bade the other a final farewell. "Take us dear Death!" I implored to the distant and merciless heavens. "Let us struggle and suffer no more!"

I shuddered, and was aware of other certain, non-spectacular neurological sensations, and then a queer numbness spread inside all of my appendages including my shriveled-up, limp penis. A gentle anguish gathered-in and dominated my spirit, and my intense shivering quickly ascended into violent trembling. 'This is the envelopment of my soul, ready to be transported into the afterworld,' I sadly surmised. 'It's the macabre encroachment of Death! We'll all soon be tasty meals for starving coyotes!'

Soon, my hallucination was brought back to reality by an emphatic statement from Mr. Ballou's lips. "Will one of you fine gentlemen have the decency to kick me really hard in my stupid ass?" the aged blacksmith astonishingly uttered like a fallen disgraced angel.

I rose-up from my position lying on the snow-clad desert ground, and to my right, outlined inside the gray dawn, my eyes perceived a stagecoach station, and inside stood the team of four horses (that had abandoned us) and our weatherworn *Overland Stagecoach*. At first, I doubted my eyes' veracity; thinking that I had been observing a desert-snow mirage, or some sort of tricky optical illusion.

An arched igloo fractured before my amazed eyes, and out of the white shell popped the unmistakable figure of Ollendorff, and to his right hatched the equally white form of the convivial stagecoach handler. The whole situation was so abnormal and so unreal in appearance that the four of us simply stayed there staring at each other with our mouths agape.

"Where the fuck are we?" Ballou shouted.

"This scene has got to be a fantastic supernatural apparition!" Ollendorff shrieked. "It's gotta' be akin to a mass hallucination!"

"We've all been fuckin' fools confessin' our sins and vices to each other like church children, while we were only standin' and shiverin' a mere fifty-feet away from the next stage station!" the thoroughly embarrassed novice stagecoach driver uttered.

"We really *were* goin' around in monotonous circles after all," I concluded and indicated. "We should've known the horses knew where they were goin' all the damned time, and we shoulda' trusted *their* natural instincts."

I have hardly exaggerated in this descriptive narrative any pertinent details of the three travelers' most absurd stagecoach misadventure. It all occurred in precisely the exact chronological order as I have personally recalled, and have professionally authored. We had actually held a midnight holy prayer vigil in the snow-covered desert, and nearly had died twenty paces away from a warm stage depot with lots of wood and matches (inside the building) situated near a hot, black, potbelly stove.

The four new arrivals entered the fairly warm stage station, sat apart in four creaky wooden chairs, and contemplated the entire fiasco in disgust, soon silently experiencing two full hours of suffering personal humiliation. Then, Ballou had the courage to finally initiate a conversation.

"Well men," the elderly anvil-slammer said before clearing his abominable throat. "It's now evident why our horses deserted us. The animals were seeking shelter from the fierce snowstorm and galloped under that shed outside in fifteen- seconds-flat," the blacksmith lectured. "Those horses must've been neighing their asses' off anticipatin' us grown men makin' silly public confessions like we had become reformed alcoholics at a woman's temperance meeting!"

Ballou discovered some coffee and eggs inside a cupboard, and the new arrivals shared a rather delicious breakfast that ordinarily would be quite a utilitarian-type morning meal. Zest again saturated our spirits, and we all discussed how we had been complete, contrite assholes, just several hours before.

As Ballou rather adroitly and expertly persisted in busting Ollendorff's balls, I ruminated about how I had been enamored with the sensation of again smoking my corncob pipe, and how I had missed the attendant pleasure more than I had craved delicious lobster-tail, or having non-stop-sex with the best piece of ass in the universe. 'The spirit is as weak as the flesh!' I thought. 'I want to smoke my corncob pipe right now. I need the vice of tobacco at this moment more than I need to listen to either Ollendorff or Ballou's illogical bullshit. And that ain't no goddamned *pipe*dream, either!'

I sneaked out of the rickety old stage depot and wandered around the building's barn pretending to be inspecting the condition of the four horses should one of my colleagues happen to accidentally discover my wayward solitude. Satisfied that no one had espied my escape from the insular stage station, thirty minutes later, I embarked on an important mission to locate the singular corncob pipe to which I had become addicted.

I shortly found my legs honoring my compulsion to meander about the nearby snow-laden sagebrush growths in a noble attempt to zero-in on my wonderful missing corncob pipe, already filled with tobacco. I amazingly fell upon my objective and avariciously repossessed it, first caressing the common item, and then stashing it securely inside my tan cowhide overcoat. 'Why are all of these footprints around the exact area where I've found my pipe?' I wondered. 'There must be phantom ghosts haunting around these parts, besides phantom stagecoaches and phantom horses!'

I guiltily hid behind the dilapidated red barn that housed the fatigued horses and the weatherworn stagecoach for a while, fearing that I might be spotted by my ruthless companions, who would then proceed to tease and verbally crucify me to no end because I had been caught red-handed abandoning my promise never to smoke again, a mere three-hours or so after I had made it. 'Oh, what the hell?' I conjectured. 'Who gives a flyin' shit if Ballou, Ollendorff or the driver catches me in the damned act of smoking!'

I frantically lit the pipe (with some matches I had taken from the depot), and felt the resplendent joy of pure evil surging throughout my entire being. 'Selfishness is a virtue,' I imagined as I diligently puffed-away. 'There's definitely more pleasure in sin than there is in abstinence!' I rationalized. All that artificial, pious justification because I was ashamed of being trapped inside my own self-centered, pitiful, subordinated ego. I dreaded the notion of Ballou or Ollendorff peering-out the stage station's side window and seeing me violating my heavenly pledge, so I advanced to the edge of the old red barn and turned the corner. Straight ahead I detected old Ollendorff turning the opposite corner simultaneously, and I was immediately cognizant that we had coincidentally caught each other's furtive acts.

Between our positions was naughty Mr. Ballou sitting in deep concentration on the snow-covered ground, playing what he considered an exciting game of solitaire. 'I reckon the old gent's simply enjoying the fine sensation of just feeling those very special poker cards in his hands!' I instinctively imagined.

I glanced over at Ollendorff. He stared me straight in the pupils and then winked. The militant Prussian was first to articulate rhetoric.

"I'm not goin' to tell anybody about this un-fortuitous encounter, and about all of that reform bullshit we had initiated; and about being a good model of behavior for the upcoming generation to imitate," the traveling European baron dishonestly stated.

"And I know *you* enjoy your whiskey as much as Ballou down there likes his cards, and just as much as I savor my indispensable corncob pipe," I all-too-honestly returned.

"We're all fucked-up in our own separate ways," Ballou injected as the brawny, retired blacksmith temporarily escaped his stupor while still gazing at the cards in front of him, that remarkably and ironically represented both chance and uncertainty. "My lips are sealed except for imbibing sassparilla (sarsaparilla), eating the finest pussy, and swallowing-down the best of foods that this goddamned planet has to offer," the elderly blacksmith solemnly promised.

"The Jumping Frog"

When Samuel Langhorne Clemens (a.k.a. Mark Twain) was a barefoot lad growing-up in Hannibal, Missouri, the boy worked as a typesetter for his older brother Orion's newspaper, the *Journal*. Later, the master storyteller ventured-out onto the muddy *Mississippi River* and learned the challenging trade of riverboat pilot under the expert tutelage of Horace Bixby.

Then, the tragedy of the *American Civil War* broke-out, so the mighty *Mississippi* was closed-down to commercial navigation in 1861. Out of his piloting job, Mark Twain packed his bags and headed west, seeking a new career as possibly a gold prospector, or an aspiring newspaper journalist. In May of 1864, Twain left the Nevada Territory and journeyed to San Francisco, where the industrious journalist penned his first (and most famous) classic tall tale, "The Celebrated Jumping Frog of Calaveras County". The innovative, satirical work appeared in the New York *Saturday Press* on November 18, 1865, and the cynical humorist Mark Twain became an overnight sensation. Herein, lies a vain retelling of the literary giant's inimitable landmark story.

A stranger rode his horse into Angel's Camp, an old dilapidated mining village situated in Calaveras County, California. The visitor was seeking information about a friend of a friend of his, and the former Angel's resident was reputed to be one Leonidas W. Smiley.

The traveler tied-up his horse at a hitching post and entered the nearly deserted Angel's Saloon, where the visitor came across an old geezer sleeping and snoring in a rickety, antique, wooden chair that looked as if it indeed had rickets. Upon waking up, the fat, elderly bald-headed, gentleman introduced himself to the itinerant eastern guest as the Honorable Simon Wheeler.

"Where can I find Leonidas W. Smiley?" the visitor to the camp inquired. "He was a boyhood friend of a close friend of mine, and supposedly, later became a devout minister of the Gospel; and that's the Gospel truth, and not random bullshit. Last reports indicate that this Smiley character was prospectin' for gold right here in Angel's Camp, Calaveras County."

"Well, howdy there, stranger," old garrulous Simon Wheeler casually greeted his unexpected visitor. "We don't get too many easterners visitin' us out here in fool's gold country. That gold rush everyone's in heat about is nothin' but a big bust. Yessiree stranger; that's exactly what the hell it is. A big bust!" Simon Wheeler emphasized as his dilated pupils turned to a wall calendar and intensely scrutinized a big-breasted nude woman massaging her impressive, huge tits, featuring big brown succulent nipples.

"Well, Sir, what about Leonidas W. Smiley?" the eastern dude with a distinctive New England accent asked Mr. Wheeler. "That is to say, the Reverend Leonidas W. Smiley."

"You must mean old Jim Smiley!" the bald-headed, slightly addled old codger exclaimed. "I've known cucumbers and eggplants that are smarter than him. Well anyway, Stranger," Simon Wheeler disclosed. "Jim Smiley's the only Smiley I've ever had the pleasure of knowing here in Angel's Mining Camp, so just sit back and relax while I tell ya' all I can think of about that stupid asshole."

The friendly stranger pulled-up a chair and sat-down between a cracker-barrel and a hot potbelly stove, politely listening to the exaggerated tale manufactured and presented by the pot-bellied old whiskerando, Simon Wheeler. The old feller' leaned forward in his creaky chair, corralling and blockading the visiting dude in one trapped corner of the cobweb-infested saloon.

Old Wheeler never smiled or frowned, nor did his voice vacillate or waver one iota. The camp orator began his contrived narrative without any noticeable enthusiasm or animation, as if his utterances were of some worldwide significance or academic profundity. The stranger dared not interrupt the loquacious speaker by stating any declarative or interrogative sentence, preferring to absorb the total impact of the preposterous story that *he* suspected was being facetiously fabricated and related.

"Reverend Leonidas W., well now, yes; Reverend Leonidas. Well Sir," Simon Wheeler began with a forced smile, "in the winter of '49, or maybe in the spring of '50, I ain't no goddamn historian ya' know; so, I don't recollect the time and date exactly. But I remember the giant mother-humpin' water flume that existed back then wasn't finished being built yet, when Smiley took his first half-hour piss in Angel's Swamp, and nearly killed all of the brave pike and the shiners swimmin' around in there. Smiley was the most curious jerk-off ya' ever wanted to see or meet, but above everything else, the asshole loved to bet and gamble on anything and everything."

"Bet and gamble?" the visitor challenged. "But I had deliberately said that Reverend Leonidas W. Smiley was a minister of the…"

"That's right, Stranger," Simon Wheeler asserted and stubbornly maintained. "This pud-puller Smiley was only happy when he was gamblin', playin' poker, or rollin' the friggin' dice. But the young bastard was lucky, uncommonly lucky," the old storyteller continued.

"And that freakin' ball-buster would bet on anything from whose wife had the biggest knockers, to whose dick was the longest, either when soft or hard. Smiley would take any side he pleased, and when he wasn't bettin', he was always scratchin' his pimply ass or rubbin' his hairy balls; whichever happened to be closest to his overanxious right hand."

"Sir, in all due respect," the all-too-polite visitor earnestly insisted, "your description doesn't seem to match the Reverend Leonidas W. Smiley I was asked to...."

"Never mind that nonsensical, stupid bullshit!" Simon Wheeler exclaimed as if the chatty storyteller was a renegade mental patient exclusively hanging out at Angel's Saloon. "Now if there was a horse race, the lucky shit would either be flush, or be a big fuckin' loser at the end. Smiley even bet on which mare would have the most colts or fillies, claiming to be a sort of a *stud'* meister himself. But let me tell ya' Stranger," the old, whiskered fellow indiscreetly added, "I ain't never seen him stickin' his tiny dick inside of the old gray mare that ain't what the hell she used to be; now that she's authentically dead. And if there was a ..."

"Now, just wait a minute," the sophisticated eastern Yankee passenger passing through Angel's Camp objected. "I come from a genteel Atlantic Coast town where all the folks are mannerly and docile, and I'm not used to hearing this sort of slang language being..."

"That's fuckin' perfectly all right!" reasserted old Wheeler as the accomplished speaker shoved his astonished guest back into *his* squeaky wooden chair. "Now, as I was stipulatin', this shit-head Smiley would bet on dog fights, catfights, chicken fights, female mud wrestlin', and on jerkin-off and female masturbation contests to see who would come to an orgasm first, or who would pop the biggest load the farthest. That son-of-a-bitch was the luckiest son-of-a-bitch I've ever..."

"I think I've heard enough!" the appalled visitor decided, and as the insulted guest attempted to rise and to vacate the premises, old Simon Wheeler roughly pushed him back into *his* chair to continue his remarkable dissertation.

"Now, Sonny," the bawdy, risque narrator proceeded, "once there were two birds sittin' their asses on a fence, and instead of bettin' which one would fly away first, old Smiley bets the mayor which bird would take the first crap. Then, this fella' Jim again bets the mayor which bird would shit the most turds in the first half-hour. And once a straddle-bug was skitterin' all over the shit-eatin' wood-planked floor, right here in this armpit saloon, and old Smiley bet the visitin' governor of Vermont where the bug would eventually skitter to. Well," Wheeler elaborated. "The bug skittered its way right up the governor's wife's stockings, and tickled her crotch and aroused clit really good, until the cultured bitch wiggled and wriggled her fat fanny all over this here crowded saloon lookin' like a drunken hooker. The damned governor laughed so fuckin' hard that he gladly paid old Smiley the fifty dollars *he* had bet just to…"

"Now, Sir, I believe I've heard enough of this barroom vulgar conversation coming from your filthy mouth," the embarrassed stranger balked. "So, if you don't mind, I'll be on my…"

Old Simon Wheeler forcefully knocked the red-faced guest back into *his* rickety chair, that actually looked like it had a worse case of rickets than the storyteller's flimsy rickety chair had. "Now Sir, like I was pertinently sayin', this bitchin' bastard guy named Jim Smiley would bet on anything. Once he bet Parson Walker when the preacher's wife took sick that she would die of malaria, and when she did pass away, the grievin' Parson had to pay Smiley a hundred dollars, and Smiley insisted that the bet be mentioned in the woman's obituary in the local *Gazette*. Smiley was a lot smarter than your average everyday ass-wiper, that's for damned sure. And also, when he…"

"Please, Sir," the new arrival angrily-and-bitterly protested. "I have an important appointment in San Francisco and I must be on my…"

"Never mind about trivialities!" Simon Wheeler yelled in a very contrary tone as the saloon proprietor manhandled the thin, weak dignified visitor back into *his* creaky, rickety chair. "Ya' ain't leavin' until I get to finish the whole damned friggin' story. Now, this here Smiley had a mare he called the fifteen-minute nag, that reminded Smiley of *his* dead wife that he had shot in the head six times with a revolver because the nasty bitch always *nagged* the hell out of him. Anyways," Wheeler editorialized, "this female horse always would lose the goddamn race because she was pregnant and had distemper and asthma, and everything' else; so, Smiley had it all figured-out. The genius at betting used to give the old gray mare that wasn't what she used to be a hundred-yard head start, and the goddamn bitch would win the race every time by a lousy cunt hair; yes, she would. And the curious folks around these parts…"

"Sir, please excuse me, but I must take my horse to the livery station because he needs a new…"

"Now just a cotton-pickin' minute," chastised old Simon Wheeler as the aged control freak twisted the stranger's arm and thrust him back into *his* unstable wooden chair. "I thought you eastern guys was notorious for courtesy and for manners. You is actin' mighty uncivil and rude by wantin' to leave this here cozy room before I'm done with my intriguing tale. Now then," Wheeler commented and transitioned, "this asshole Smiley has this here bull hound dog pup he owned, and to look at the freak, ya' wouldn't want to give two red cents for his leash and collar, let alone for him. But Smiley had the vicious pecker-headed pup trained, ya' understand. As soon as money was placed down on the table in the form of a bet," the long-winded speaker elucidated, "the mutt's under-jaw, nose, and impressive dick all stuck-out straight ahead, and then the energized canine was a totally different *animule* altogether."

"What did Smiley call this weird-looking dog?" the stranger asked, exhibiting s degree of mild curiosity.

"I'm getting to that important detail," Wheeler mildly scolded. "Smiley named em' Andrew Jackson as a joke, because *he* knew his dog would do something *unpresidented (unprecedented).* When Andrew Jackson would get into a mean dogfight that was bet on, the old rascal would win every time by latchin' on with his choppers to the other dog's hind legs, and then bullyraggin' the other mongrel all over the damned place, until the other dog was whimpered into fuckin' submission," Simon Wheeler explained. "Andrew Jackson really knew how to kick ass really swell, and if his sharp teeth missed the other dog's hind legs, then the mutt would viciously bite the other cur's dick off, and swallow the tasty morsel just like it was a little hot dog wiener."

"Did Andrew Jackson ever lose a dogfight?" the stranger wanted to know. "I hope that this is the end of the Leonidas W. Smiley story!"

"Now I was getting to that prominent detail when *you* so rudely interrupted me," old Simon Wheeler gruffly reprimanded. "One day, Andrew Jackson got shucked-out bad, because the shaggy mutt that the critter had to fight was as ferocious as a grisly grizzly bear. And besides that-rather-fairly-pertinent fact, the new dog everyone was bettin' on against Smiley had no friggin' hind legs; and when old Andrew Jackson went to bite the bitchin' freak, he didn't know what the fuck to do!" Simon Wheeler described in detail. "So, the other damned dog took the initiative, and bit and beat the shit out of old Andrew, and then bit *his* tender loins off and chewed them up good. Then, Smiley's dog just curled-up and died, and it always makes me feel remorse for old Andrew Jackson; yes, it does; the way it all ended for him, and the way his fightin' career was radically terminated."

"Well, then," the totally dismayed stranger interrupted. "Did Smiley change his evil gambling ways after what had happened to his precious dog, Andrew Jackson?"

"No indeed!" Simon Wheeler testified. "Smiley became even more intent on bettin' and riskin' the damned odds. This here Smiley had rat terriers, and chicken cocks, and tomcats, and all them kinds of dip-shit varmints, and the addicted gambler would throw all of the nasty cantankerous *animules* into this here cock fightin' pit, which was really like a fuckin' *animule* sports' arena. The seven or eight species would have a big brawl," the storyteller expounded, "and everyone would put their dollars-down and bet which one would be the last creature standin'. That's how fucked-up Smiley was, and how fucked-up he had made everyone else stayin' here at Angel's Camp, preposterously prospectin' for fools' gold."

"Look, Mr. Wheeler, I appreciate your fine hospitality," the uneasy visitor mentioned and exaggerated, "but I think I've heard enough equivocation about your Jim Smiley when I really need some tangible biographical data on the Reverend Leonidas W. Smiley."

When the visitor attempted to rise and escape *his* captivity inside Angel's Saloon, Simon Wheeler kicked the newcomer in the testicles, and then punched the stranger in the gut, knocking the air out of *his* lungs. Then, the eastern traveler had to sit there in excruciating pain and listen to the remainder of corpulent, bald-headed Simon Wheeler's stellar description of Jim Smiley's immoral and illicit betting exploits in Angel's Camp.

"Well, Stranger," the old talkative fellow proceeded. "This here Smiley catched a frog down at the swamp one day, which was easy to do, because the swamp was swamped with frogs. The obsessed gambler then took the creature home and teached him how to jump great distances, even though it wasn't fuckin' leap year anywhere in Calaveras County. Old Smiley educated that frog in all the basics of jumpin', settin-up a pole, and next increasin' the pole's height each time. That fantastic frog even whirled in the air like a dizzy doughnut, doing somersaults, and tumble-saults, and table salts, and the like, and the critter always came-down flat-footed like a smilin' Cheshire cat that intentionally falls outa' a tree."

Although the exasperated stranger was still in agony from the flurry of blows that had been administered to his solar plexus, which the decent gentleman had received from the incomparable Simon Wheeler, *he* still had the wherewithal to ask a rather relevant question. "Did Smiley's frog have a name?"

"I was just getting to that pertinent point, so don't fuckin' *jump* to conclusions!" the senile storyteller bristled and acknowledged. "Old Smiley would train this friggin' frog by makin' the thing leap-up and catch flies the master would dangle above the jumpin' poles. The two practiced the art and the science of jumpin' every single mornin', noon, and night until the fuckin' frog was the most skillful *hopper* in the whole damned area, even though he didn't look anything like a goddamned toilet!" Wheeler amusingly ascertained.

"But did the frog have a damned fuckin' name?" the frustrated fit-to-be-tied visitor, also a dedicated minister of the Gospel cursed.

"Well, Sir; I saw Smiley place old Daniel Webster down on the planked floor of this here dusty saloon: incidentally, Daniel Webster was the fuckin' flyin' frog's name, and then Smiley would yell out, 'Flies, Daniel, flies!' Well Sir," Simon Wheeler euphorically pointed out, "there weren't any damned flies around anymore to reward the damned hungry frog, but old Daniel Webster would jump-up a storm anyway, and break all existin' records, and win lots of cash for everyone interested in bettin' on *his* phenomenal leapin' ability!"

"Look, Shit-head!" the virtuous, self-righteous minister turned ordinary person in and around Angel's Camp yelled. "How did the son-of-a-bitchin', mother-fuckin, cunt lappin' frog ever lose a turd-eatin' bet for Smiley?"

"Well, Stranger; now you're finally talkin' my language!" Simon Wheeler answered and commended without even using a single curse word. "Ya' never did see a frog so modest, so humble, so gifted, and so straightforward as this fucked-up Daniel Webster was. Yes siree; when it came-down to fair and square jumpin' on a dead level plane," Wheeler boasted, "Daniel could cover more ground in one leap and hurtle over any obstacle better than any other non-royalty frog of his mediocre breed. Smiley would ante-up two twenty-dollar bills, and everyone else in attendance would cough-up and bet the incredible sum of forty dollars against Daniel, just to attempt bankrupting Smiley, so that *he* would quit gamblin' and bustin' everyone's friggin' stones all the goddamn time."

"Well, you crazy old, demented mother-fucker; what the fuck happened next?" the irate and now belligerent traveling minister demanded in a totally out-of-character rant.

"I'm getting to that particular highlight," Simon Wheeler promised. "But Stranger, ya' gotta' oblige me with some old-fashioned western patience. Old Smiley was monstrous proud of his special frog, and he kept it in a latticed box', I guess more of a cage than a goddamned box. One day, a feller,' a real wise-ass in the camp came across Jim Smiley carrying his box containin' Daniel. The braggart asked Smiley rather matter-of-factly, 'Say; what the fuck does ya' got in that peculiar box'?"

"Look Mr. Wheeler, I really have to..."

"Just sit-down and fuckin' relax your testicles before ya' make me have conniptions!" Simon Wheeler insisted, as the saloon owner smashed the visiting minister back into *his* rickety wooden chair.

"And Smiley answered the feller' sorta' indifferent like saying, "It might be a parakeet; it might be a mongoose, or it might be a castrated canary, but it's not. It's a goddamn fuckin' ordinary, non-fancy frog sittin' quietly inside this silly box!' And then the camp newcomer looked at the frog careful-like, slowly turning the latticed box all around this way and that, and the jerk-off starkly says to Smiley, 'Say, Buddy; so it is a goddamn fuckin' ordinary, non-fancy frog. What's he good for'?"

"And what the fuck did that stupid asshole Jim Smiley say in response?" the almost-livid visitor to Angel's Camp asked from his imprisonment in the rickety wooden chair.

"Oh well," Wheeler genially replied. "Smiley says rather easy and carefree. "He's good for one thing, I should ascertain; and that is he can out-jump any other goddamned frog in Calaveras County'."

"This story is absolute bullshit!" the visitor-minister vociferously objected. "I'm getting' the hell outa' here right now!"

Old Simon Wheeler administered a frenetic flurry of expert karate and judo' chops to the parson's neck, diaphragm, groin, penis, and ass, and soon the stranger was once again seated, slouched-down in his all-too-familiar squeaky, creaky, rickety, wooden chair.

"Now then," the tale's principal narrator proceeded speaking to his now unconscious audience of one, "the rookie passin' through Angel's Camp peered-inside the latticed box and cleverly says to Smiley, 'I don't see any points about your asshole frog that's any better than any other asshole frog I've ever seen'!"

"Maybe ya' do, and maybe ya' don't know didley-squat about frogs and am-fib-ians," Smiley said to the limp and listless injured stranger. "Maybe ya' don't understand the science of frogs, or maybe you're still a rank amateur just like most local assholes are. I'll risk ya' forty dollars sayin' that old Daniel Webster here can out-jump any other frog in Calaveras County. Well Stranger, the new fellow studied the latticed cage and its sole occupant for a full minute, and then aptly answered Smiley, 'Sir, I'm only a dumb greenhorn here in Angel's Camp, but if I had a healthy frog, I would surely bet ya'!"

After a brief pause, old Simon Wheeler continued his expository narrative. "Then Jim Smiley felt compelled to favorably respond to the suave man's blatant challenge. 'That's okay, that's all right!' the native resident said. 'If you'll hold this lattice box for a minute, I'll hustle-down to the swamp and catch ya' a comparable frog that will jump against old Daniel'!"

The listless stranger that had been brutally assaulted, mugged and molested by Simon Wheeler was now regaining full semi-consciousness. The parson shook his head and reacquired some semblance of sensibility. "What the fuck happened?" the groggy minister asked in reference to *his* recently administered pain and suffering, and not requesting more details about Simon Wheeler's hyperbole involving Jim Smiley and Daniel Webster.

"Well Sir," Wheeler characteristically blustered, "the feller' put-up his forty dollars next to Smiley's bet, and then he sat-down to wait for Jim to return from the pond with a capable specimen to jump against Daniel Webster. Then the wily jerk-off got a most brilliant idea," Simon Wheeler indicated with great admiration. "He took a teaspoon out of his coat pocket, filled it up with quail shot, and meticulously poured the special ingredient down Daniel's throat. The guileful asshole repeated this deceitful act with the spoon at least twenty shit-eatin' times, until Daniel finally weighed at least five more pounds than usual!"

"Look Asshole!" the stranger-minister defiantly blurted-out. "I don't give a shit about Jim Smiley or his mother-fuckin' frog. I only came here to fuckin' find-out some information about the Reverend Leonidas W. Smiley."

"I'm getting' to that essential idea, so just mind your p's and q's, and I'll tell ya'. My God, Mr.! I ain't never met somebody as rambunctious and as spoiled rotten as you are, and with such a goddamned short attention span! Anyway," Wheeler snorted after spitting a large green lunger into a floor spittoon. "Smiley stepped out to the swamp and slopped-around in the mud like a happy pig in shit. Jim catched a nice-lookin' frog, and brought it back to this here saloon where the thrillin' jumpin' contest was goin' to be held."

"If you don't tell me about Leonidas W. Smiley soon," the perturbed Reverend threatened, "I'm gonna' tear this fuckin' saloon apart and crush your goddamn balls into mince-meat!"

"I'm tellin' ya' about Leonidas in a minute, so stop threatenin' my ass," Simon Wheeler pledged and demanded. "Smiley hands the new frog to the stranger and commands, 'Now when you're ready, set your critter alongside Daniel, and I'll give the startin' numbers.'

Well, the greenhorn did exactly as Jim had dictated, and then Smiley yelled out 'One, two, three-jump!' The new frog from the pond hopped off lively-like, but old Daniel had indigestion and couldn't budge an inch; just like he was anchored into the floor planks. Smiley was surprised and disgusted, but Jim didn't have no clue as to what the fuck was wrong with old Daniel!"

"I wanta' know what the fuck ever happened to that evasive bastard Reverend Leonidas W. Smiley!" the visitor-Preacher screamed like an incensed maniac.

"Just hold your damned horses, and I'll tell ya'!" wildly exclaimed Simon Wheeler. "The scamming feller' took Smiley's forty-dollars and paced to the swingin' doors over yonder, and turned and bellowed, 'I don't see any points about your asshole frog that's any different or better than any other asshole frog I've ever seen before'!"

"Damn it! What about fuckin' Leonidas W. Smiley, or I'll rip your balls right out of your scrotum and then fanatically choke you to death with my bare hands!" the normally passive Minister deliriously boomed at Wheeler.

"Now then," the master storyteller calmly proceeded, "Smiley just stood there scratchin' the damned dandruff out of his scalp; lookin' at Daniel Webster for the longest time and sayin' over and over again, 'What the hell's wrong with this fuckin' frog!' at least five hundred times. Jim catched and lifted the fat frog by the neck and saw that the critter weighed at minimum five pounds, and understood that Daniel couldn't leap worth a damn if *his* hopping-mad life depended on it. And then," Simon Wheeler paused as the old codger inhaled a large quantity of air. "Jim Smiley turns the frog upside-down, and the *animule* belched-out two handfuls of heavy quail shot. And then Jim became madder than all hell that's being full of aggravated hornets. Smiley threw the frog onto the planked floor, and sprinted-out through the swingin' doors, runnin' hard after the abominable, clever feller' that sneakily tricked him; but Smiley never catched-up with him and..."

"But what about that stupid jerk-off asshole, fuckin' Reverend Leonidas W. Smiley?" the traveling Preacher insisted.

"Well, Stranger," Wheeler tersely added. "The greenhorn with the victorious frog happened to be your Reverend Leonidas W. Smiley. He's the one that broke Jim Smiley's balls but good with the quail shot trick, and also in the process, broke Smiley of his terrible gamblin' habit, too!"

Just then, wrinkled-face Simon Wheeler heard a saloon patron calling his inglorious name from the other end of the bar. "Just stay where ya' are, Stranger. I'll only be gone for a second once I serve that drunken lush a double-shot bourbon. I just gotta' tell ya' about this here mother-jumpin', one-eyed, quill-less porcupine that didn't have no tail or testicles, but only a short, stumpy projection, and a nose that was a weird cross between a very green banana and a very ripe watermelon."

At that junction, the traveling-Minister became so fed-up with, and so pissed-off at old Simon Wheeler, that the itinerant Preacher reached his right hand down to the old timer's huge testicles, and squeezed with all his might. The Reverend effectively and literally crushed the storyteller's balls, as those tender nuggets had never been crushed before. "There Fuck-head!" the traveling Parson triumphantly hollered. "Just like Jim Smiley had been cured of gamblin', I hope that you're balls bein' busted will ultimately cure you of your idiotic exaggerated storytellin', you obnoxious, arrogant, egotistical asshole!"

And with those magnificent words, the self-satisfied Preacher limped-out of the almost-empty western saloon, unhitched his black stallion, and climbed atop *his* faithful horse, leaving old Simon Wheeler bent over in sheer agony inside Angel's Saloon.

The recipient of the traveling Minister's vengeful wrath was wishing that he had the balls to tell the old drunk seated at the bar the fascinating story about the quill-less porcupine without a tail, and having a nose that was a weird cross between a green banana and a ripe watermelon. Fortunately, discretion prevailed, and old, agonizing Simon Wheeler remained perfectly silent as the bullshitting Western bard poured the old drunk a delicious double bourbon.

William Shakespeare

William Shakespeare (1564-1616)

William Shakespeare was born (just like the rest of us fragile mortals) in Stratford-on-Avon, England, situated about eighty miles northwest of London. The registers at the Holy Trinity Church indicate that Shakespeare was baptized (and nearly drowned) on April 26, 1564, probably three days after the future playwright popped out of his mother Mary's snatcheroo. William was the third of eight children born to John and Mary Shakespeare (maiden name was Arden), and *his* merchant father was once mayor of the somnolent community, who would knock on residents' doors and humorously and ridiculously announce, "Stratford-on-Avon calling!"

William courted and dated an attractive girl named Anne Hathaway, who lived in Shottery, a village around a half-mile (half-a-way) from Stratford-on-Avon. Anne was actually robbing the cradle since she was twenty-six and William was a mere eighteen when the pair wed in 1582, and even though Shakespeare never took drugs and seldom got drunk, as a horny youth he was often seen entering the "half-a-way house" in Shottery with a huge bulge in his pants. The couple had three children, Susana in 1583, and twins Hamnet and Judith in 1585. All three raunchy kids had to sleep in twin beds, even though only Hamnet and Judith were bona fide twins.

After moving from the countryside to London, Shakespeare soon became an actor, playwright, poet and businessman, becoming a partner in the ownership of the now-famous *Globe Theater*. His acting company The King's Men often performed at the *Globe,* and it is frequently and accurately said, "All the King's horses and all The King's Men, couldn't put Humpty-Dumpty together again!"

William Shakespeare is reputed to have written thirty-seven plays, and since he died at age fifty-two, it is believed that he regularly wrote at "super-sonnet speed." Shakespeare often had trouble holding his sword or spear steady while standing on stage, and hence, his physical appearance and trembling mannerisms often matched the structure of his last name. In his work, the playwright demonstrates a tremendous knowledge of a variety of subjects such as music, history, politics, the *Bible,* along with other remarkable assorted bullshit. In 1611 William became pissed-off and bored with the *Globe Theater,* so he lived the last five years of his life as a country gentleman in Stratford-on-Avon. W.S. was buried in Trinity Church where he had been violently baptized fifty-two years earlier.

"A Midsummer Night's Dream"

Act I

On any warm and fuzzy magical, midsummer night, anything (including Cupid's amorous love spells) is possible. On such a mystical late summer evening in ancient Athens, a man could be changed into a donkey, and mortal women and Mt. Olympus goddesses could passionately fall in love with *the* ugly-looking beast. Could this exotic, erotic tale all have been an illusion? A joke? A wondrous dream you may think? Or perhaps the entire allegory was pure asinine bullshit? Who the hell knows?

A long-long time ago in mythological antiquity, before drunken historians began recording human events in a fairly rational and logical manner, Theseus, the renowned King of Athens, was all set to marry the all-too-hip Hippolyta, the former notorious Amazon and Amazon.com Queen. The much-anticipated and joyous mythology marriage ceremony was all set to occur four days later under the full harvest moon.

"Well Hippolyta," Theseus said to his former warlike fiancée in his ornate throne room. "In four short days, we're going to get hitched. And to think we were once former enemies belligerently fighting a raging war. Fortunately, my very competent Athenian army defeated your tribe of Amazons, and there's now tranquil peace in the valley; and soon, a much-deserved piece each and every evening we'll share in our warm, cozy bed, ha, ha, ha."

"The four days until the full moon will pass quickly, dear Theseus, as if it was one night," Hippolyta shrewdly replied and predicted. "And then, my prospective Husband, I can't wait to give you a full moon each and every evening with my firm, plump ass."

"Ah yes," Theseus acknowledged. "That splendid, erotic thought haunts my psyche daily. I'm fuckin' hornier now than that goddamned bullshitting Minotaur I had killed in the shadowy labyrinth underneath King Minos's palace on the island of Crete. I kicked the gargantuan monster's ass really good, but I intend to lick yours Hippolyta; instead of punting it around the palace, assuming that you'll wash your rear-end clean before I instinctively go-down sixty-nine-style on you."

The perverted King then summoned his official "Director of Revels", Philostrate, to the opulent-looking throne room and commanded, "Go-out into the hinterlands and into the boondocks and announce to the lowlife citizens of metropolitan Athens and vicinity that they're all welcome to attend the sensational wedding and subsequent, spectacular dinner feast afterward, scheduled for four evenings from now at precisely midnight under the full harvest moon. And Philostrate," Theseus seriously added. "Tell your big-penis, gay brother Dickostraight that he's formally invited to the gala shindig, too!"

No sooner had the gregarious Philostrate departed the throne room (where the King's royal toilet was situated) that Egeus, an old, wrinkled geezer with dysfunctional bowels and myriad urinary tract disorders, entered the royal chamber. The wealthy old fart was followed by his daughter, Hermia, and two young men; a blond-haired Adonis named Lysander, and a stocky brown-haired stud named Demetrius.

"Welcome elder coot Egeus," Theseus greeted his old (and I mean really old) friend. "Are you in quest of some wondrous aphrodisiac formula; or perhaps a mild and gentle laxative to move your fucked-up erratic bowels?"

"No, my courageous King," Egeus answered and then gulped from heightened nervousness and anger. "But here, before you stand my gorgeous, well-stacked brunette daughter Hermia, and I wish for her to marry the brown-haired suitor Demetrius, because I fuckin' don't like blond-haired, male assholes, and have a deep and definite prejudice against each and every one of them."

"So; what in Hades is your damned problem?" Theseus asked Egeus. "Your daughter Hermia desires to marry this brown-haired fellow Demetrius, and I presume that this blond-haired muscular Lysander dude standing next to him is going to be the Best Man; that is, figuratively speaking, ha, ha, ha!"

"That fuckin' *is* the exact damned problem!" old Egeus grieved and complained. "Demetrius wants to marry and hop into the sack with my Hermia, but my witchy bitch of a daughter wishes to marry and shack-up with this blond-haired son-of-a-bitch Lysander, with poor young Demetrius being relegated to being the goddamned Best Man, literally speaking!"

"What do you have to say for yourself Hermia?" King Theseus asked the beautiful brown-haired maiden. "From the way things look, you've really immensely fucked-up your senile father's plans. And Athenian law specifically states and enforces certain family and marital traditions, but please don't ask me where the fuck it's recorded and documented," the King solemnly qualified. "Anyway, Hermia; the legal precedent states that a daughter always must obey the commands of her father, regardless of what the bitch might prefer doing. In other words, you must sacrifice and surrender your selfish will to your father's strict commands. Do you now understand the fuckin' dilemma you're causing here? If every broad decided to break our time-honored traditions, then mass chaos and social disorganization would dominate my peaceful kingdom, and hostility would reign supreme in every damned household."

"Lysander is a fine man whom I love and cherish," Hermia dejectedly bitched, "so shouldn't that be the prime consideration here? I mean, don't I have any damned choice in this apparently cut-and-dry matter? If you care to hear my personal opinion, King Theseus, I believe *that* that particular Athenian male chauvinism law that you're citing really sucks."

"Are there any missing pieces to this rather-intriguing puzzle you're now describing?" the sagacious King Theseus requested knowing. "In other words, Hermia; what the fuck else is going on in your love life besides what's been revealed here today? For example, young lady; is there some kind of secret immoral love triangle in progress? What about a goddamned love quadrangle, or how about a friggin' love pentagon?"

"Well, King Theseus," Hermia respectfully answered. "In the beginning, Demetrius loved my best friend, a blonde-hair chick named Helena, and I'm not referring to Helen-a-Troy either. This brown-haired bastard, Demetrius, won Helena's heart, but then he dumped her, and now wants to marry me in a new relationship, against my will. And your good cunning and conniving pal Egeus, my lunatic Old Man, is actively conspiring with this brown-haired son-of-a-bitch Demetrius."

"Watch your foul mouth young woman!" King Theseus imperatively warned. "I, too, have ordinary brown hair, and now indirectly, you're calling me a deceitful bastard and a son-of-a-bitch by association when you capriciously condemn this brown-haired suitor that your hard-working father prefers; what's his fucked-up name; oh yes, Demetrius."

"But your obsolete law is skewed to favor male domination and female discrimination!" Hermia staunchly objected. "I feel like a piece of shit; a worthless piece of property being arbitrarily bartered and being cruelly traded in matrimony. And I feel like during the whole screwed-up process that I'm being given the royal shaft, even though I'm not having sex with any snobbish king or monarch."

"Look, you upstart Bitch!" King Theseus chided and reproached. "I must enforce and support our chauvinistic law that states a daughter must always obey her father until after she marries, and then she must be subordinate to her husband first; to her father second; and to her father-in-law third, in that fuckin' order. Now Hermia, you have four days to think over your limited options, which in reality constitutes actually only one choice. Then, I demand that you obediently return to this palace and inform me of your sage decision. Following that subservient appearance, I mandate that on *my* nuptial day, when I intend to marry the vivacious, voluptuous Hippolyta, who incidentally doesn't in any way, shape or form resemble a hippo', I hereby decree that *you* Hermia must tell me which man you intend to marry; and it better fuckin' be brown-haired Demetrius, or I'll really get pissed-off on my special day and go absolutely berserk. To tell you the honest-to-Zeus truth, Hermia, I don't want any mongrel-looking sandy-hair next generation asshole kids' running around the streets, alleys and ghettoes of Athens."

"Aren't there any last-ditch alternatives?" Hermia desperately begged the monarch. "Surely, My King; some other viable solution or salvation is possible."

"Yes, there is," King Theseus chuckled and then snickered. "If you stubbornly refuse to marry your father's choice, Demetrius, then you must enter a convent that's recently been constructed for the virgin priestesses of Athena. Now, do you know what in Hades *that* idiotic bullshit means?" Theseus rhetorically asked. "My dear Hermia, in translation, it means being one of Athena's devoted priestesses and obedient temple sweeps, and that's explicitly defined as nun in the morning; nun in the afternoon; and none in the evening! Ha, ha, ha!"

"Well, my King," Hermia strongly objected. "At first Demetrius loved my best companion Helena, but then the ball-breaker, or in this case the tit-deflater, changed his whimsical mind, and now desires to marry me, just to curry my father's favor and to spite my desire."

"Male prerogative!" Theseus claimed. "Too bad you Hermia, and your blonde-haired friend, lovely Helena, were born of the wrong and powerless sex! Now stop boring me with your monotonous, redundant female feces!"

After the crazy, bizarre audience with King Theseus concluded, Egeus consented to Hermia having a few minutes to privately say her final goodbyes to Lysander in the palace's adjoining parlor room.

"Oh Lysander, if only I could run away and elope with you," Hermia cried as she melodramatically began her silly sob story. "I've saved my virginity just for you, but now that obnoxious shit-head Demetrius is going to violently pluck and de-stem my cherry. And my beloved Lysander, if I don't marry someone soon, I might unfortunately wind-up in the local hospital's infamous cherry-at-tricks ward."

"Holy Zeus Hermia! Your cheeks have turned as pale as the ones on Hades' pallid ass! And presently, your disheveled life is just as melancholy as the god of death's morbid existence is! But don't despair my love!" the blond-haired Lysander told and encouraged the brown-haired Hermia. "I have a tremendous plan that'll knock your girdle right off your portly ass. A wealthy aunt of mine, a benevolent rich-bitch dowager who favors me because I'm the only blond-haired male in the whole damned family, lives south of here in Sparta where the freakin' harsh marital laws of Athens don't apply. We'll elope and go south, and be married in the other Greek city-state if you don't mind living a lousy Spartan existence for the next several years, or maybe centuries."

"Holy crapola!" Hermia marveled and exclaimed. "I can escape my father's loveless house tomorrow night while he's preoccupied making wine and getting drunker than either Dionysus or Pan. Where shall we meet?"

"What about in the forest picnic area where you, Helena, and I first met, and both of you dynamic bitches gave me terrific, simultaneous blow-jobs!" Lysander (who was merely a simple stone smoother and adroit apple polisher) suggested to Hermia. "Speaking of Aphrodite personified!" the blond-haired young man gasped and exclaimed. "Here comes Helena walking-up the palace marble steps now! Man, I still remember munching on her magnificent blonde beaver when the three of us got naked that first night we met in the forest and formed a really neat, nude daisy ring! Hermia, if you go south to Sparta with me, I promise to go south on you!"

Brown-haired Hermia expected that blonde-haired Helena would be cordial, civil, and happy towards her best girlfriend (and the corresponding good eloping news). But much to her chagrin, the opposite kind of reception was true.

"Hermia. you whoring harlot Bitch!" Helena yelled at her former best friend and confidante. "What the hell's this dumb-ass bullshit all about that you've stolen my Demetrius from me'! Where's your goddamned screw-ples!"

"Oh, dear Helena! You must be having wicked PMS mood swings!" Hermia diplomatically responded. "Demetrius loves me, but in truth, I totally despise him," Hermia attempted to explain. "Instead, I love Lysander, but my fucked-up father wants me to marry your precious Demetrius, instead; and *he's* effectively solicited the King's discretion, and now chauvinistic Lord Theseus has explicitly sided with my asshole Old Man. Now Helena, could anything in the domain of romance get any more fucked-up than this retarded, ass-backwards dilemma?"

"Holy Zeus atop majestic Mt. Olympus!" Helena exclaimed in astonishment. "And you think that *you* have a nasty bitchin' problem. The more I love my Demetrius, the more the fickle prick fuckin' hates me. I'm salt, and he's pepper; and regrettably, salt loves pepper, but pepper loves mustard, and in the final analysis, mustard loves spicy paprika. What a lot of emotionally disturbing, asshole bullshit our mixed-up relationships are!"

"And the more I frown upon and curse Demetrius, the more that thick-headed moronic jerk-off loves and pursues my ass with my father's complete blessing and approval!" Hermia lamented and anguished.

"You lucky Bitch!" Helena dejectedly remarked. "I wish the Hades that I was you! I'm even thinking about dying my hair and my damned bush brown! And perhaps, Hermia; you should consider dying your hair and your bush blonde to adequately please your lover-boy Lysander. That way, you can continue to successfully woo him when he comes around to dote on you, and suck-cessfully get into your hairy pink crotchola."

"Don't worry Helena," Hermia comforted her distraught blonde-haired friend, loud enough for Lysander to hear. "I swear by Cupid's best golden arrow that I'll let you in on a nifty secret, and please confidentially, guard it with your precious life. Lysander and I are running away soon to get married, so therefore," Hermia paused to catch her rapidly-fading breath; "so therefore you'll have muscular Demetrius all to yourself. Soon, he'll forget all about me and concentrate completely on trapping your hairy, blonde beaver."

"Yes, that's quite wonderful, Helena," the eavesdropping Lysander yelled and *confirmed,* even though Christianity hadn't begun yet. "Hermia and I are having a love rendezvous tomorrow night in the forest at the familiar picnic area where the three of us first snacked and munched on each other's sexual equipment."

"That's really great news!" Helena commended and congratulated the two thrilled lovers. "I promise to only tell Demetrius about your elopement agenda, and he and I will follow you from the dense forest to the *outskirts* of Athens; and if Demetrius is lucky, he'll get under my out-skirts and get to work on my sweet, delicious, eager, blonde beaver pelt."

Hermia and Lysander gleefully left Helena's company, and exited the palace via a side door. The lovebirds were chatting and clandestinely finalizing their scheme to escape both the adamant old fart Egeus, and the by-the-book King Theseus's male-by-preference autocratic jurisdiction.

* * * * * * * * * * * *

A group of frivolous, gay artisans (with aspirations of becoming famous lesbians and thespians) assembled in an Athenian back-alley workshop to rehearse a selected play designed to commemorate the upcoming nuptial of King Theseus to the totally voluptuous Queen Hippolyta. The corny, preposterous craftsmen (all suffering from delusions of grandeur) were Peter Quince the Carpenter; Snug the Wood Joiner; Rocco Bottom (also known in and around Athens as Rock Bottom) the Weaver; Flute the Bellows-Mender; Snout the Tinker, and Starveling the Tailor. A jolly conversation soon ensued in Quince's carpentry workshop.

"Is everybody here?" Peter Quince inquired above the din of inequity (sic, den of iniquity). "Let's get this ridiculous show off the road and into my cluttered workshop immediately. I'm in a rush because I don't want to miss tonight's male couch dancers' routine that's scheduled to be performed two hours from now over at the faggot Sappho Lesbos Inn and Gay Bordello. Now, the sooner we get this preliminary bullshit over with," Quince said to his merry friends, "the sooner I'll be able to attend to more important duties."

"All present and accounted for!" Snug the Wood Joiner amiably reported. "All's perfectly fine as long as that brown-noser Snout doesn't start tinkering inside our grimy assholes with his flea-infected nose. That curious, dumb bastard always has his nose into other people's business!"

"Okay, you disgusting vermin jerk-offs; listen-up to what I gotta' say!" Quince the Carpenter imperatively insisted. "We've already agreed that we're gonna' perform a special play for the King's amusement, and that Snug and I will build the sets and props. Are there any oddball, preposterous questions pertaining to that easy-to-understand relevant bullshit?"

"Well then, my gracious host; what play have you decided on performing Quince baby?" Rocco Bottom, the rock bottom Weaver, boldly asked. "How about something upbeat by Homer like the *Iliad* and the *Odd Sea?*"

"No, you fucked-up moron!" Peter Quince sternly admonished his inane companion Rocco Bottom. "Snug and I have been assiduously studying the art form known as drama, and we've mutually decided that *we* should do *our* creative rendition of a most lamentable, little-known Babylonian comedy/tragedy entitled 'Pyramus and Thisby'. It's actually a very serious one-act play about a lover named Pyramus that unfortunately kills himself after he loses his fortune in a crazy Pyramus scam. Rock, er, I mean Rocco Bottom," Quince lectured, "my good buddy, Snug, and I hereby assign *you* Bottom to play the part of Pyramus, and you don't even have to dress-up like a corny Egyptian Pharaoh; or like the *Nile River* to satisfactorily perform your very important part, ha, ha, ha."

"I accept the stupid-assed part!" Rocco Bottom the Weaver reluctantly consented. "I'll make everybody cry, especially the soap opera-oriented, fatuous, fat-laden ladies. Then, I'll pick-out which gentlemen guests attending the King's wedding reception to sodomize, and ball the hell out of them during the last scene; that is to say, while the fucked-up bitches are bawling their ugly tonsils and larynxes out. I predict that this crazy, absurd play for King Theseus and Queen Hippolyta isn't going to be that terrible after all!"

"Great rhetoric Bottom! Really terrific and admirable speech!" Quince, the burly carpenter, praised. "Now then, Flute; you totally dumb fuck; you're assigned the very important part of Thisby. That's spelled T-h-i-s-b-y and is pronounced Thisby, not fuckin' 'this by'."

"What the hell does that nutcase jerk-off have to do in the play?" Flute the Bellows-Mender anxiously asked. "Does he kick or kiss ass? Is he a gay or straight jerk-off?"

"For your information, you notorious dimwit, Thisby is a fair maiden that's in love with the self-destructive Pyramus," Quince aptly clarified. "And you won't even have to shave your thick beard off Flute, because you're going to be wearing a mask with a grotesque-looking female face drawn on it. I know you're going to be disappointed Flute, because Thisby is a straight heterosexual young lady, and Pyramus is a straight guy, even when he isn't sporting a huge erection. But that's the fuckin' breaks that often happen with stage productions in the standard, all-too-moral, traditional Greek theater."

"What about me?" Snug the Wood Joiner asked, even though he already-knew what his theatrical part would be. "Am I to be a prop; a tree, or a *stump* that asks riddle-like questions, and who stumps Pyramus and Thisby? Will I get to wear a vizard?"

"No, you annoying hyena's ass, but that's not such a bad idea that I think we could somehow incorporate into the script later on; perhaps a century from now," Quince the Carpenter lauded the frivolous imbecile. "You, Snug, will play a fierce lion, and your only line as a lion will be repetitiously growling 'Raaaa! Raaaa'!" Peter Quince informed the mentally-challenged fellow possessing the notoriously short memory. "Now don't become too smug, Snug! I think you could handle that simple-assed detail. Just take *pride* in your fuckin' acting stint as a savage lion, that's all the hell I ask. Do you require any further explanation?"

"Holy shit!" Snug joyfully exclaimed. "This is all quite amazing, and I can't wait to participate! If I fuckin' growl backwards, then I could get my gaseous bowels in an *uproar!* Won't that phenomenon be just dandy?"

"I want to play the lion with the irritable bowels!" Rocco Bottom objected. "My stomach growls so heavily and loudly that I won't even have to fake my boisterous grumbling using my voice box. I'm sure I'd make a really fine *dandy lion*, ha, ha, ha. And I hope that the lucky lion gets to swallow fuckin' Pyramus whole, and gets to marry Thisby in the end."

"Now Robin Starveling, you attention-deficit pinhead," Quince addressed the inattentive Tailor. "You'll have the distinct honor of playing Thisby's stressed-out mother, and then *you* Snout," the Carpenter announced to the almost-asleep Tinker. "You're assigned the extraordinary part of Pyramus's fucked-up father, without even having to try out for the role. What the fuck more could you irresponsible idiots possibly want? And Snout, you can even tinker with Robin Starveling's bush, since *he's* been assigned to be a *crotchety* old, disgusting woman holding a hideous-looking azalea as a prop', ha, ha, ha, ha."

After the rogue Peter Quince assigned the remainder of the lesser parts to the bizarre play 'Pyramus and Thisby', the demanding scoundrel had one last salient announcement to convey. "I'm really in a *jam"*, Quince facetiously remarked to his tradesmen colleagues. "I'm afraid, Rocco Bottom, that your thunderous farting and your raucous growling will un*fart*unately scare the tits and the beavers off of all the sophisticated, impressionable ladies that'll be in attendance!" Quince criticized his associate with a contrived frown expressed upon his face. "Now, I want all of you excessively gay asshole thespians, including myself, to learn our difficult lines by tomorrow night, so that we can rehearse this screwed-up drama and see how badly we can fuck-up and crucify this supposedly serious tragedy that's gonna' be shrewdly misrepresented as a comedy." Quince then paused to gauge the impact of his speech. "Does everybody hearing my dumb-ass words fully understand my impeccable bullshit?"

"To be perfectly candid, Sir Director, I'd feel much more comfortable performing as a clown in a variety act than being involved in a ridiculous, fucked-up play such as this one," the always vacillating Robin Starveling told Peter Quince. "It's bad enough that I'm a detestable asshole in real life that I gotta' also be one on the damned stage standing in front of the King and Queen. I'm afraid that we'll all be hung for insulting all those regal aristocrats and distinguished guests at the wedding reception. Can't we uneducated tradesmen just do a simple acrobat or juggling routine, instead? My acting ability leaves much to be desired."

"According to your libido-dissatisfied wife, your goddamned sexual ability *also* leaves much to be desired," Quince answered Starveling, much to the delight of his fellow thespians. "In fact, all of us gay thespians suck when it comes to performing gratifying heterosexual, marital sex!"

Act II

The following night, brown-haired Hermia and blond-haired Lysander met at the designated picnic area inside the dark forest, and the muscular Demetrius secretly trailed their ramble deep into the woods with blonde-haired Helena keeping a distant eye on the jealous pursuing brown-haired fellow (that the gorgeous doll wholeheartedly loved).

But Quince, Rocco Bottom, and the other nutcase actors were also congregating inside the forest to rehearse their highly-anticipated presentation of the one-act play "Pyramus and Thisby". None of the mortal trespassers ever realized that the forest was uniquely enchanted and occupied by hundreds of fairies, governed over by Oberon, King of the Fairies, and by Titania, Queen of the Pixies (including *their* meddling obnoxious Fairy Godmothers).

Puck, a naughty, zany sprite (wearing a stupid-looking jester's cap) who was especially loyal to King Oberon, encountered a dazzling female fairy disciple of Queen Titania. The pair of gay pests instantly engaged in a curious conversation.

"Say; you look like one of the Pixie chicks! Where are you heading, oh most beautiful Pixie?" Puck asked the girl fairy, who was working for his boss's rival, Titania. "Oh, I wish I was in Pixie, who's she, who's she? In Pixie's crotch I'll take my watch, to live and die in Pixie! Go down, go down, go way down south on Pixie!" the waggish chick/sprite sang and laughed.

"What's your problem?" Puck asked the Pixie. "Are you drunk?"

"Don't bug my flying ass, because I'm on an important, special assignment for Queen Titania," the attractive Pixie explicitly explained. "But don't ask me what the hell the job is, Puck, because I can't fuckin' remember anything ever since you scared the damned wits out of me during our most recent, almost head-on flying collision over yonder mountain."

"Maybe your job should be giving me a hand-job, Pixie. Well then, anyway, fair Fairy. I have some excellent news for you that might refresh your muddled memory," Puck confidentially declared. "My boss Oberon, the fucked-up Fairy King, will be here inside the forest tonight causing huge trouble for mortals who are foolishly meandering around. He and your employer Queen Titania, who has tiny breasts, have had...."

"Have had an enormous argument that was capped-off with a mammoth power struggle," the cute, adorable Pixie remembered and finished Puck's sentence. "And there's bound to be all kinds of unprecedented trouble and raucous chaos later tonight around this neck of the woods."

"It's my good sound advice Pixie to keep Queen Titania away from King Oberon this evening, until his pissed-off mood passes!" the impish, pesky Puck suggested. "He's liable to change all the human interlopers this evening into avid gay practitioners. Say Pixie; please tell me why are all of the zany forest fairies gay? And seemingly, why are all of the human buffoons that enter this ass-backwards forest weird-behaving straights?"

"It's a fundamental rule of nature," the informative Pixie stated, "that 'the Sexual Preference Separation Law' will in the near future remain between the mortal and the fairy domains, but soon," the flying female faggot qualified, "as humans gradually become gay, there'll be less and less faggot fairies like you and me around to pester and torment the homos; er, I mean homo sapiens. And when the human population becomes entirely gay," the intelligent little fairy continued, "then according to Mother Nature's queer seesaw, things will reverse, and the fairy population will become entirely straight. Does that odd truthful bullshit profoundly register and settle inside your minuscule brain?"

"Well yes, sort of, Pixie. But don't sprinkle any of your crazy fairy dust down my pants, because your action might start into motion the simultaneous transitions among mortals, and also among us fairies that you've just crazily alluded to. I'm perfectly content being a fucked-up, flying faggot midget jester," Puck honestly confided.

"Now tell me, Puck. What's the basis for the ongoing conflict between my Queen and your King all about?" the Pixie curiously inquired. "That's all *we* need around this strange, enchanted forest is an all-out gay sex war in this already fucked-up environment!"

"Well Pixie," Puck matter-of-factly replied. "Your distinguished superior, the incomparably alluring Queen Titania, has stolen a lovely Indian boy servant from Bombay, whose father owned a *new deli* there. Now my boss, King Oberon, is jealous and wants the Indian boy all to his own, but Titania will not surrender the lad in question under any circumcisions, er, I meant to say circumstances."

"I believe, naughty Puck, that King Oberon wants to convert the Indian boy into the first official gay human, which will begin the process of making all of the Greek humans, male or female, authentic faggots; and then all of the forest fairies will become straight; just for the sake of pursuing *his* own sport and diversion," the Pixie pointed-out to her attentive, all-too-goofy listener. "And if you ever thought that being gay sucked, just fuckin' wait until you experience what it's like being straight! Look-out, Puck! Here comes your boss King Oberon approaching from the left woods. You'd better pucker-up Puck, and get prepared to kiss your boss's fat smelly ass."

"And here comes your Queen Titania approaching from the right-hand-side woods with a contingent of obese attendants!" Puck observed and exclaimed. "Get ready, my friendly Pixie, for a fuckin' roaring forest fire to ignite! If we fly high enough, I won't get my tiny dick scorched, and you won't get your luscious, lesbian bush seriously incinerated!"

King Oberon and Queen Titania coincidentally met in the center of a meadow, which was not far from the mortals' favorite picnic site. Soon, a not-too-pleasant dialogue transpired.

"This indeed is not a happy confrontation," Oberon said to the equally pissed-off Fairy Queen. "I'm angry with you for not giving the little Indian boy to me, so that I could perform a radical sex experiment on him that would start a new sexual revolution occurring among the dumb-shit mortals and their presently mundane, monopolistic, heterosexual community. Someday, Titania," Oberon boldly predicted, "there's going to be an extensive gay and lesbian community among the humans that'll gradually fuck-up their inferior race; it'll become even worse than it is right now. How long do you plan on staying in the forest?"

"I'm staying until King Theseus of Athens weds the Amazon Queen Hippolyta during the height of the full harvest moon," Titania candidly answered her male counterpart. "Next, I'm off to recruit and steal more vulnerable innocent Indian servant boys, just to be a bitch; and then, I'll focus my efforts on successfully breaking your gay balls some more. Now Oberon; as a temporary overture of truce, you're entirely welcome to accompany my pixie entourage to the gala wedding if you'd like."

"No, Titania. I refuse to accept your invitation unless you surrender that straight little Indian boy you had *kid*napped while he was innocently sleeping," the obstinate Oberon demanded. "Give the pathetic ignoramus to me, and I promise I'll gladly accompany you."

"Go sodomize yourself at least a dozen times a second, you arrogant faggot!" Titania admonished her principal adversary. "Come on, my prized pixie followers. Let's go and have our wet pussies eaten by the forest's abundant gay munchkins."

"You'll be sorry, Fairy Queen, for your brazen insolence to my omnipotent authority!" Oberon yelled, raising his clenched right fist high into the air. "I'll get even with you, because as you're well-aware; *odd* fairies like me always try to get *even!"*

After Titania, Pixie and the corpulent, lesbian female sprites abandoned the popular, centrally-located picnic zone, Oberon and Puck had a frank conversation, even though neither of them had ever been named Francis or Frances.

"Listen carefully Puck, you totally dumb fuck!" King Oberon emphatically threatened his chief accomplice. "If you don't heed my royal words, you're going to spend the rest of your life as an abused, miserable object being mercilessly battered around an ice hockey rink. Now then," Oberon continued. "Do you remember the time I saw a big-breasted mermaid riding on a dolphin's back?"

"Yeah; she was riding the porpoise on purpose I suppose," Puck recalled and mentioned. "A *siren* must've gone-off in your mind when your eyes first perceived that beautiful mermaid, ha, ha, ha!" the flying jester remarked and indulgently laughed. "It's hard to pull a fast one *over on* Oberon, ha, ha, ha! Sometimes I just make me piss myself silly, ha, ha, ha! Oberon must live ober-on Smart Street!"

"Shut the fuck up, you uncouth asshole, and hear the rest of my stellar oration!" Oberon shouted at Puck. "Now then, Fool; that flying little bastard-archer Cupid came flitting-by, and soon shot his golden love arrow at the siren-in-transit, but the dart fell short of its mark and landed in a bed of white flowers situated on a cliff overlooking the sea. The flower that was de-flowered, pardon the terrible pun Puck," Oberon proceeded narrating his intriguing tale; "well, that first arrow had penetrated a white flower that instantly turned purple. Puck; I hereby command that you retrieve that indispensable magical purple flower and immediately bring it to me, so that you and I can inventively perform some queer mischief on the defiant and insubordinate Queen Titania."

"I'll get the purple flower and be back in a flash; that is, if lightning accidentally strikes my lily-white ass on my return trip!" Puck promised and giggled. "I'm sure that your mysterious scheme is gonna' teach that bitch Titania not to fuck with Puck and Oberon."

After Puck flew away to execute his unusual floral assignment, Oberon imagined and mentally reviewed his marvelous plan for the implementation of the magic purple love flower. 'I'll squeeze the love sperm out of that purple flower directly onto Titania's eyelids the next time she goes to sleep in the forest,' the Fairy King creatively thought. 'And I won't remove the crazy love spell until my female rival gives me that straight little Indian boy jerk-off, so that I can surreptitiously conduct my revolutionary queer sex experiment on him. I intend to eradicate the whole human race by making all of those miserable, mortal assholes gay. Then, the dipshits won't be able to reproduce, and eventually the whole retarded civilization of straight-turned-homo' bastards and bitches will, within a century, become extinct, ha, ha, ha!' Oberon gleefully considered. 'It's really great being a scheming, omnipotent ball-breaker and tit buster! Ha, ha, ha! Oh my; what's that I hear behind those bushes? It's human voices. I'll fuckin' eavesdrop on their ludicrous conversation, even though there are no buildings having eaves anywhere around here.'

Oberon and the other gay and lesbian fairies and pixies were invisible to human eyes, so there was no logical reason for the Fairy King to be stupidly crouched-down, listening to the humans' ever-unfolding melodrama. Blonde-haired Helena had finally encountered brown-haired Demetrius, who had been stealthily following his love, the gorgeous brown-haired Hermia, who was eloping with blithe blond-haired Lysander. Demetrius was not-too-thrilled learning that gorgeous Helena had discovered him ambling in the vicinity on *his* furtive forest ramble.

"You had said yesterday outside the King's palace that I would find Lysander and Hermia here," Demetrius screamed at the love sick Helena. "You fuckin' bitch liar! If I do see that dirty, wimpy blond-haired prick Lysander, I swear with all my heart that I'll kill the filthy, rotten bastard for stealing away my charming Hermia!"

"Oh Demetrius, I love you!" Helena cried and pleaded. "Why must it be that almost every eligible bachelor in Athens loves me, and the one thick-headed asshole I do love despises my guts! What kind of fucked-up poetic justice is that? Once upon a time, everything was in black and white. Now today, everything is in brown and blonde."

"Well Bitch, I happen to hate your guts; your cunt; your tits, and your stench-laden asshole, too!" brown-haired Demetrius rebuked the blonde-beavered Helena. "My stomach turns sick just at the sight of you! In fact, Helena, I feel like vomiting my breakfast, lunch, and putrid dinner all over the fuckin' forest ground right now!"

'It makes me sick, too, just to look at you!' the disconsolate Helena lamented and thought. 'Why do I have to be in love with such a repulsive and *bellicose* son-of-a-bitch! Oh handsome, belligerent Demetrius,' Helena pondered and sadly mused. 'Please don't hit me in the *belly, 'cause* it already aches!'

"Now Helena, since you have nothing further of relevance to say," Demetrius angrily stated as mighty Oberon listened-in on the heated human argument, "I'll rapidly run away and leave you far behind; and hopefully, you'll then be attacked and eaten by a horde of hungry, wild beasts. You can only be fuckin' wolfed-down and digested one time, you know!"

"The carnivorous wolves, the ferocious lions, and the bears from mythical Chicago can't be half as cruel and vicious as you are!" the distraught Helena sobbed and wept. "You're an emotionally lost asshole! Demetrius, sometimes you can't see the damned forest for the trees!"

Chauvinistic Demetrius was so insulted from being savagely reprimanded by a mere female, whom he now thoroughly despised, that the muscle-bound bully rambunctiously sprinted-off, leaving poor, sensitive blonde-haired Helena behind to drown in her sorrow. The eavesdropping Oberon then got an inspiration (besides an earful), and mulled the strategy over in his immortal, roguish mind.

'I feel sorry for the blonde young lady being maliciously dissed and jilted by that petulant brown-haired jerk-off!' Oberon decided. 'I'll use the effects of my fantastic magic to soon have that brown-haired bastard crave that lovely blonde-haired girl's luscious bush.'

Moments later, the impish Puck returned with the aforementioned purple love flower that Fairy King Oberon had assigned the zany jester to obtain. "Here's the flower you had specifically stipulated,"

Puck said to his master. "This beautiful sucker looks like a damned rendezvous point for the birds and the bees, ha, ha, ha."

"I'll squeeze the sweet sperm juice out of this love flower onto the sleeping Titania's eyelids," Oberon proudly informed Puck. "Now carefully take a portion of the potion and place it upon a nearby angry Athenian man's eyes, also. Then perhaps I have tricked the gay Pixie Queen Titania to fall in love with the temperamental sleeping Athenian straight asshole. The Fairy Queen will then beg me to lift my enchantment, and next she'll surrender that little straight Indian boy to me, so that I can corrupt his morals and make *him* the first gay, perverted, kindergarten kid in either mythology or history. What do you think of my naughty plan, dear Puck?"

"This super-mischievous, erotic bullshit really excites my psyche," Puck commented. "It's a definite departure from everyday boredom. Maybe, My King Oberon; I'll squirt any remaining purple flower drops onto *your* eyes, and then you and I can have a *budding* affair going! Ha, ha, ha!" the flying jester chuckled. "Just kidding Lord Oberon! Ha, ha, ha. Just kidding!"

"Get the fuck out of here, you little squirt-blooming idiot!" Oberon inadvertently double-punned. "Now the first lady that the jilted Athenian jerk-off will see after opening his bleary eyes will be the babe he instinctively falls in love with; possibly against his own asinine free will. I must voluntarily get involved with this human heterosexual crap before I can get the handsome Indian boy into my greedy custody, and then I'll further interfere by transforming the entire mortal straight population into a global community of gay bastards and lesbian bitches."

"I'll do precisely as you say Master!" Puck cooperatively complied. "And if there's any drops left over after I administer them to the sleeping Athenian asshole, then I'll squirt them onto my diminutive dick, just to see what the fuck happens!"

"Get that shit done before the cock crows at dawn!" Oberon commanded silly Puck.

"I've been watching my dick for many centuries now King Oberon, and I've never seen my cock crow once; be it morning; afternoon or evening, when I'm always intensively examining my tiny pecker!" the silly Puck laughed and cackled. "Oh well, Boss. I can attest that there's certainly more significance to being a frivolous flying fairy than being a common, ordinary, peon pecker-checker!"

After Puck flew away to conduct his clandestine mission, Oberon discovered Titania sleeping in the forest, and the mischief-maker proceeded to squeeze several love-drops from the magic purple flower onto the forest queen's eyelids. 'I hope that the first creature she sees is a grotesque-looking, vile-tempered beast, so that this stubborn Bitch is adequately punished for her imprudent impudence. These enchanted love drops will make this impertinent Pixie Queen Bitch come to her senses in a hurry. Then, my rival Titania will surely comply with my expressed wishes!'

* * * * * * * * * * * *

Not far away inside the dense forest, blond-haired Lysander and brown-haired Hermia were having second thoughts about defying King Theseus's mandate. The pair of lost lovebirds were feeling quite queasy in their stomachs.

"We'll rest and relax here until dawn," Lysander said to the beautiful Hermia. "Then, we might get lucky and see the light when the sun rises. But I caution you that we're not out of the woods, yet."

"Okay, my dear Lysander. I'll sleep under this bush and you can sleep over there under that tall oak tree," Hermia suggested. "I know you'd prefer sleeping under my bush, but that kind of kinky sex-play won't happen until after we're officially married in Sparta."

"Or we could move to a far-off land called Australia where I could become a boner-fide, transplanted, African bushman down-under," Lysander joked. "Let's get some much-needed shuteye so that we're well-rested to continue our arduous trek to Sparta. I hope my rich aunt doesn't fuckin' drop dead before we get there."

When Hermia and Lysander dozed-off into pleasant dreamland, the frolicsome imp Puck showed-up, mistook Athenian Lysander for his rival Demetrius, and then the flying instigator squirted the powerful love potion/aphrodisiac onto the blond-haired youth's eyelids; all the while thinking that he had been fulfilling Oberon's imperial decree. 'These juices will efficaciously activate the sex juices in your defective mortal testicles!' Puck evaluated and giggled after effectively squirting the dozing Lysander. 'Now then, you lucky heterosexual recipient; you're guaranteed to wake-up with a massive hard-on! Oh, how envious I'll be!'

After the sportive Puck abandoned the scene, brown-haired Demetrius came into the vicinity, pursued by the bad luck blonde-haired Helena. The brown-haired strongman then sprinted even faster, and soon easily outdistanced and lost his blonde-haired female chaser. Completely out of breath, Helena stumbled and accidentally came across blond-haired Lysander, sleeping with his enormous head resting against the base of the tall oak tree.

'Holy Zeus! It's Hermia's prospective husband, Lysander!' Helena shockingly thought. 'I must wake him up. He could help me find Demetrius, and be a good arbitrator to help soothe *our* all-too-rocky relationship. On second thought, screw that brunette shrew Hermia! I desperately need Lysander to help me solve my lovers' quarrel.'

Helena violently shook Lysander's shoulders, and woke him up; not realizing that the love potion from the purple flower would instantly make the blond-haired fellow fall deeply in love with the voluptuous blonde-haired Athenian chick.

"Oh Helena! I never realized how fantastic you look and how much I love you!" Lysander strangely wooed the extremely beautiful girl. "I would run through the flames of Hades just for you, because my great balls are on fire right now! Holy shit! What in blazes am I actually saying?"

"What the hell's wrong with you?" Helena challenged Lysander. "You're acting like you've just contracted that brutal Angry Steer/Mad Cow Disease!"

"Please tell me, kind Helena. Where is that dirty bastard Demetrius who has been incessantly shunning and abusing you?" Lysander insisted on knowing. "Even though I'm a feckless wimp, I'll beat the living shit out of him for arrogantly offending your virtuous integrity!"

"You're mocking me Lysander, because you know that Demetrius resents and abhors me as if I were a bitchy whore," Helena mildly reprimanded her new suitor. "But now, you feel you must persist in making fun of my already overwhelming emotional suffering. Don't you know the meaning of the words 'compassion and empathy'? The least you could do is be a sentimental slob! I was totally mistaken when I had erroneously thought that you were more considerate than you actually are; you pathetic, male chauvinist pig!" blonde-haired Helena chastised blond-haired Lysander. "Now go find and grovel to brown-crotched Hermia, and pump the poop out of her; you contemptible, creepy crawler! You'll never get to see and lick my golden beaver again; that I solemnly promise you!"

Helena was so distressed and out-of-kilter from her resisting Lysander's peculiar, unexpected advances that the knockout babe instantly scurried away with her new-found suitor in hot pursuit.

Meanwhile, brown-haired Hermia awoke from her extended forest sleep and wondered what had happened to her handsome but now missing blonde-haired Lysander. The horny beauty impulsively dashed into the woods, searching after the dashing young man, who was preoccupied (by his all-too-forceful love spell) dashing with a full erection after the completely bewildered and totally frightened blonde-haired Helena.

Act III

Meanwhile, in another part of the dark, dense forest, the dumb-ass aspiring actors Quince the Carpenter, Snug the Wood Joiner, Flute the Bellows-Mender, Rocco Bottom the Weaver, Snout the Tinker, and Starveling the Tailor had congregated in a clearing to begin rehearsing the preposterous comedy/tragedy play "Pyramus and Thisby". Queen Titania was still sleeping nearby (simultaneously) under the enchantment of the purple love flower's juice (that had been administered by Oberon).

"Let's get started on learning the lines of this nonsensical play," Quince insisted. "As we all know, Snug and I still have to build the sets and nail together the cheap props."

"I smell trouble both developing and enveloping us here," Snout detected with his keen long nose. "Maybe we should rehearse this dumb bullshit in your workshop, Quince?"

"Nonsense, you preposterous, gutless wimp!" Quince yelled at the gay fellow whom he sometimes deliberately called "Tinker Bell," who incidentally needed his bell rung.

"Well, wait a daisy-picking minute!" Rocco "Rock" Bottom the Weaver joined-in. "Snout, as argumentative as he is, has a very good point besides the one situated on top of his pinhead. I think that several necessary, significant changes have to be made in this totally fucked-up play."

"I agree, and I'm a true *believer* who now categorically concurs with the *Weaver,*" Starveling the Tailor rhymed and contributed to the oddball discussion. "Several much-needed *alterations* have to be made, ha, ha, ha!"

"Like what?" Quince lividly retorted. "Like you two Assholes want to be bigger stage assholes than you are in real life? Like you two assholes ought to master how to play billiards so that you can better learn your cues."

"This mixed-up lover Pyramus that I'm playing must kill himself, and I don't know if I'm ready to commit suicide, either in real life or on the stage!" Rocco Bottom argued as his mind hit rock bottom. "In my humble opinion, I'd rather commit homicide than suicide! And besides," Bottom futilely debated with the all-too-inflexible Quince.

"All of the dignified ladies in attendance won't savor seeing violence and the like, especially the ones whose husbands come home drunk every night, and beat the living shit out of them."

"I agree with Rocco Bottom a hundred percent," Flute, the long-winded Bellows-Mender, piped-up. "We have to leave sins like killing, manslaughter, lady slaughter, and cow slaughter out of the plot, or else the wimpy women will be boisterously screaming 'Bloody murder'! Perhaps if a prologue is written into the script explaining what'll be happening next, then the maudlin broads won't be so maudlin when Bottom, according to his fucked-up lines, commits suicide."

"Okay, you three inane retards in leotards!" Quince was finally convinced. "I'll make that minor adjustment just to tailor to your concerns Starveling, and also for *you* Bottom. Now, I suppose I'll have to become a playwright to get this play right. Instead of cabinet smithing, I'll have to learn the fucked-up art of word-smithing, too!"

"And what about the ferocious lion scene?" the inquisitive animal hater Rocco Bottom asked the already-flustered Peter Quince. "The beast will certainly scare the ladies out of their underwear during the *mane* event, and they'll all probably start wildly masturbating out of nervousness during the play's climax!"

"Well then, exactly what should I do about that exciting lion scene bullshit, Mr. Bottom?" Quince worried and appropriately asked his principal, real-life antagonist. "I never really felt a need to consider *that* unnecessary possibility!"

"In the beginning, during your drab, boring prologue, also tell the audience that the lion is also make-believe; just like Rock Bottom's, er, I mean Pyramus's suicide is a staged pretend activity," Rocco Bottom suggested, because only Starveling the Tailor could skillfully tailor a recom*mend*ation along with Flute the Bellows-*Mend*er.

"You two frivolous jerk-offs should've been alchemists, since you both have strange solutions for everything," Quince commended his garrulous, gay comrades. "Now then, let's begin rehearsing this serious production because before you know it, it'll be the crack of dawn, and you're all fully aware of how we all hate pussy, even Dawn's pink, dew-laden slit; even though unfortunately, each of us had plopped-out of a mother's wet, smelly, bloody crotch when we were hatched, er, I mean born."

While the fussy actors were having their own real-time dialogue about the upcoming play, Puck nonchalantly flew into the area in his "invisible mode" and discovered the exotic Queen Titania sleeping nearby. The spritely fellow then heard the arguing actors' voices, and had an amazing inspiration, even though Puck was breathing (inhaling here) and really didn't require any inspiration at all. 'Just for my own amusement, I'll change the guy in the purple robe by giving him a donkey's head!' Puck thought and giggled. 'Ha, ha, ha! That guy looks like a dumb-fuck jackass even without a goddamned donkey's head!'

When Bottom had departed the imaginary stage, Puck converted the idiot's head into a huge three-dimensional, real-looking donkey's face, and when Rocco the Weaver, playing the role of Pyramus, again entered from stage left, the donkey-headed Bottom scared the living shit out of his three thespian companions, who all instantaneously shrieked, and then imitating frightened jack-rabbits and antelopes, hightailed it the hell out of the rumored-to-be enchanted forest.

"What the hell's wrong with those crazy faggot assholes!" the surprised Bottom said to himself as the naughty, invisible Puck listened and chuckled. "This must be some childish prank or trick they're playing on me, and I don't relish their nursery school shenanigans one iota!" the donkey-headed queer gent (who was unaware of his new queer physical appearance) sulked and bellowed. "Those trouble-making jokers can't make either a horse's ass or a damned donkey out of me!" Then, to dramatize his absurd point, Bottom began hee-hawing and braying like a psychotic, neurotic, stubborn donkey. His frenetic disturbance woke-up the sleeping Titania, who instantly became aroused, both from her slumber, and sexually as well.

"Oh, magnificent, handsome beast; your sweet melodic voice has thrilled me, and I feel quivers and tingles traveling all over my horny body!" Titania solicited and propositioned the peculiar man with the donkey's head. "I love you fair creature, but if you also have a donkey-dick to match your donkey head, then quite possibly, the idea of sex is out of the question!"

"What the fuck's going on here?" the beguiled Rocco Bottom hollered. "You're not in the fuckin' play, Lady! And I fuckin' despise women, especially beautiful dazzling ones like you!" Then Bottom reconsidered. 'On second thought, getting propositioned and getting laid don't seem like such repugnant and alien ideas after all. I'll just stay here and see if I can dicker my dick with this attractive bitch! Great Zeus on Olympus! I feel my dick rising already! Maybe I should change my name to Richard. Wow! What an experience! I suppose I'm ready to dicker right now!'

"Don't you dare leave my company you strong, dark, and handsome fellow," Titania begged the partially-transformed beast-of-burden, Rocco "Donkey" Bottom. "You've successfully aroused my primal animal instincts. I'm a rank pixie of high rank, and I feel I love you madly, and desire getting vigorously pumped for the first time up my furry snatcheroo, even if you possess an incomparable, tremendous-sized, two-yard-long donkey-dick. In my love-struck mind," Titania qualified to the bewildered Bottom, "I don't give a shit about that donkey-dick phobia notion anymore, or even about abandoning boring gay sex either!"

"What the fuck's wrong with *your head* lovely woman!" Bottom the Donkey Head inquisitively asked. Then, the Weaver thought deeply for a moment. 'Shit, I've never gotten good head from a lesbian fairy queen before. Just wait until I tell Quince, Starveling and the others about this incredible bullshit. Those greedy faggots might become jealous when they learn that a lesbian pixie sucked me off free of charge! They'll never believe my fantastic story in a million years, but on second thought, *this* scenario is the fuckin' imaginative and stimulating play-in-progress *we* ought to be giving for King Theseus's and Queen Hippolyta's entertainment, instead of that fucked-up melodrama 'Pyramus and Thisby'.'

Titania then summoned all of her tiny pixie subordinates to attend to Bottom, by putting flower garlands around his ears, and then petting, caressing and stroking his body and hideous-looking head, while Titania riveted her wet tongue in and out of the very gratified Donkey's left ear. "Sleep, oh magnificent creature, so that I may admire and covet your body!" Titania encouraged the totally gratified and delighted Rock Bottom, who ordinarily was as stubborn as a mule. "I'm certainly glad that you're being cooperative and not stubbornly bull-headed like my former bisexual boyfriend, the cretin Cretan Minotaur was!" the Pixie Queen romantically and dramatically praised.

* * * * * * * * * * * *

While Titania was wasting her valuable time admiring the sleeping Donkey-headed Rocco Bottom, the flying sprite Puck, alias Robin Goodfellow, reported back to his vindictive master Oberon, King of the Gay Faggot Fairies. At first, the casual conversation was cordial and pleasant.

"Guess what happened to Titania?" Puck rhetorically asked. "She awoke from her one-chick slumber party and has miraculously fallen in love with a grotesque-looking animal; a hideous donkey-headed human freak of nature, I do believe. Some wannabe' moonlighting actors were in the forest rehearsing a really bad play the assholes plan to perform at King Theseus's wedding reception, and Titania was fast asleep nearby all during the fiasco. I then magically changed one of the fool actor's odd-shaped head into a donkey's moniker," the impish, irascible Puck communicated to Oberon. "And when the shithead returned to the makeshift stage, the victimized asshole scared the Hades out of his astounded buddies, who all ran the hell out of the forest. I'll tell you, Boss; it was a gas without me even farting! Then," Puck proceeded to comically relate, "Titania awoke and instantly fell in love with the half-man, half-animal; and I mean this literally, Lord Oberon, instantly fell in love with the stupid *ass!"*

"Well done, Puck; you fabulous simpleton fuck!" Oberon congratulated his mischievous, chief errand boy. "Now then; did you come across the Athenian young fellow that I told you to put the magic drops into his sleeping eyes?" Oberon sternly inquired. "If you did as I had commanded, I'll promote you from Lieutenant Jerk-off Jester to full-fledged Senior Captain Jerk-off Jester."

But before the ecstatic Puck could answer his austere Master, blonde-haired Helena casually stepped into that particular forest area, followed by the brown-haired Demetrius (and not by the blond-haired Lysander). Immediately, Oberon recognized that Puck had been incompetent, and had completely fucked-up his important assignment by casting the spell on the wrong Athenian male target. Oberon and Puck (invisible to the humans) listened to the mortals' heated quarrel, almost vicariously wishing that *they* themselves were human. But then, Demetrius speedily dashed away, and Helena soon stumbled upon the sleeping Lysander. The brown-haired chick immediately awoke the blonde-haired stud.

"I love you, Helena," Lysander claimed. "I've forgotten all about brown-bushed Hermia, and presently think only of you. Now give me a kiss or two, right here on my kisser! I can't wait to marry you and fuck the Hades out of your luscious pink, hairy love tunnel."

"I absolutely loathe you Lysander!" the totally-addled and confused Helena retorted. "I love Demetrius, but I feared that you had already killed him while I was sleeping. If my apprehension is correct, Asshole," Hermia admonished the young man, "then I insist that you murder me, too, so that *our* hapless souls (Demetrius and mine) could be reunited in the daffodil-laden Elysium fields of Hades."

"What does Demetrius have that I happen to lack?" Lysander asked. "Surely, not greater strength, bigger biceps, and a longer, thicker dick! Even though I'm a feckless wimp, I just can't fathom your illogical reasoning during this crucial time of our relationship."

"Demetrius is sincere;' 'sina cera', meaning 'without wax' in another language," Helena definitively replied. "You're too fickle and moody, and you're much like a poorly-carved statue with patches of wax covering-up your all-too-numerous flaws. In other words, Lysander, despite your alluring blond hair, you're a detestable bully and a deplorable brute, and I despise every ounce of flesh on your stocky body, including the meat inside your goddamned pulsating penis."

"Well Helena, I want you to know that I've not either hurt or injured that puny, punk jerk-off Demetrius, although I've been tempted to beat him to a pulp on many occasions, and that's no pulp fiction either!" Lysander honestly replied. "But if that interfering asshole ever again pisses me off," the blond-haired Adonis falsely bragged and threatened, "I'll punch him in the jaw with a solid stiff uppercut, and consequently, send that brown-haired, handsome, bastard soaring all the way to the goddamned moon!"

"I hate you more than I loathe sin itself'!" Helena screamed at Lysander. Then, the upset and puzzled blonde-haired Helena sprinted away to escape the relentless advances of the desperate, love-struck blonde-haired suitor. Soon, the emotionally exhausted and physically drained Lysander sat-down, and (then after becoming somewhat comfortable) the young man rested in a horizontal position, lying near a pond, and soon gradually fell asleep.

Meanwhile, Demetrius (without being accompanied by any gladiators) became exhausted, and slept in the deep dark forest. Oberon and Puck quickly discovered the fatigued brown-haired Athenian snoozing and loudly snoring.

"Puck, I have another rather vital assignment for you!" Oberon commanded while the goofball jester was singing gay melodies.

"Puck the magic Fairy, lived by the sea. And frolicked in a land the natives called, tiny Athen-ee. Oh, Puck the magic...."

"Shut the fuck up Puck and hear my command!" Oberon's thunderous voice boomed. "Go and fetch the blonde-haired woman, and I'll make this insane asshole Demetrius fall in love. And don't fuck-up this time, or you'll be busted down to Fairy First Class!"

"I'll zoom faster than a meteor, and promise not to *comet* suicide before I safely return with the gorgeous blonde-haired doll!" Puck promised Oberon, and then hardily laughed before energetically zipping across the moonlit sky.

Oberon meticulously crushed another petal from the purple love flower that had been *arrow*neously anointed by Cupid's errant dart, and then let the drops gently fall onto the sleeping Demetrius's eyelids. 'This ought to cure this volatile dolt's need for a complete attitude adjustment, and if it doesn't work,' Oberon thought and chuckled, 'then I'll cure this petulant wise-ass mortal's temper by supernaturally kicking his ass, even if I'm generally reputed to be a non-violent, peace-loving, immortal faggot,' the majestic Oberon pledged his conscience.

Soon, Puck returned, followed by the knockout blonde-beauty Helena, who was being tailed by blond-haired Lysander, and according to *his* dastardly habit, was always in pursuit of some additional tail in which to insert his dick, in order to enjoy a satisfying and refreshing '*cocktail'!* The King Fairy, and his irascible Jester, who both never had tasted the flavor of beer, suddenly felt immense trouble brewing.

'These mentally-deficient mortals are truly super-assholes of the greatest magnitude!' Oberon concluded. 'Now I sense that there's going to be another heated altercation developing, and I can just feel the emotional energy gathering; and quite frankly, it's actually turning me on! Being immortal, and being gay, well, the situation happens to be so damned boring after so many millennia!'

Demetrius awoke with a rare clear mind, and his bloodshot eyes perceived Helena, whom he had always malevolently shunned and ridiculed. "Oh, sweet, delicious Helena, you look more stunning than the divine Aphrodite attending to her flourishing African diaper service," Demetrius flattered and exaggerated. "I feel compelled to reveal that I love you, and wish to hump and pump your goddess-like pussy right into the next century!"

A dilemma was quickly evolving because now both Demetrius and Lysander both loved the blonde-haired Helena, since she was the first woman that the two men had seen upon waking-up. Soon, the two virile Athenians confronted each other, and got into a heated argument over Helena, who now thought that the young colts were both making fun of her. An ancient soap opera was in progress.

"Cut the fancy, sugarcoated bullshit, Demetrius! You've always ignored and dissed me in the past!" Helena loudly protested. "And Lysander; I think that you're conspiring with Demetrius to further insult my sensitivity. You're both dirty rotten bastards as far as my judgment is concerned!"

And then, to complicate matters even further, brown-haired Hermia (wandering through the forest) found the three others in the clearing, and demanded to know why her lover Lysander had thoughtlessly abandoned her. When the blond-haired fellow announced to Hermia that he now loved blonde-bushed Helena, that's when the shit really hit the spinning oxcart wheel.

"What the fuck's going on here, Lysander?" Hermia yelled like a hyperactive maniac. "Just an hour ago, we were happily in love and joyously eloping to Sparta to live with and mooch off of your rich dowager aunt!" Hermia reminded her strange-behaving lover. "And now you're hot-to-trot over blonde beaver, and I don't savor your fickle nature one bit! You're like two dysfunctional sun dials Lysander; you lousy fucked-up two-timer!"

Helena still thought that she was being mocked and was being the brunt of what constituted a very sadistic, three-sided joke. "I understand it all perfectly clear now, Hermia!" the blonde-haired girl screamed at her former best friend. "You're in on this ugly joke along with Lysander and Demetrius, who I'll wager is responsible for causing me this gross humiliation. You've forgotten all about our wonderful friendship, Hermia, and you've conspired with your two male friends to make merry sport of me. Life is cruel enough, but you three assholes are even much crueler; in fact; much crueler than even a goddamned French cruller."

"You've stolen my lover Lysander from me, you whoring Bitch!" Hermia screamed at Helena in defense of *her* ego as she menacingly raised her fists in an offensive attack posture. "Why don't you just go indiscriminately screw every available erect pecker in Athens; you filthy harlot Bitch?"

"Protect me from this ferocious out-of-control she dog!" Helena implored Lysander and Demetrius. "She's even more vicious than you two abominable creeps put together!"

"Don't be afraid, Helena!" Lysander valiantly exclaimed. "I'll protect you from this crazy out-of-control hussy! She'll not harm a hair on your magnificent golden bush!"

"Never mind Lysander!" Demetrius asserted in defense of his abundant pride and manhood. "The beautiful Helena's all mine, and I'll kick your plump, puny ass all across this forest, and then mercilessly hang you from a tall tree, just to prove my manhood!"

"Lead on Demetrius!" Lysander yelled, accepting the pugnacious bully's reckless challenge. "I've been pushed around by you for far-too-long, and now it's time for me to defend my honor, as well as my relentless love for blonde-haired Helena! Let's find the nearest clearing and have a brutal sword-fight to the death! You've verbally cut me up all these years, Demetrius; and now's my remarkable chance to literally cut you up!"

Act IV

While Lysander and Demetrius departed from the astonished girls to find a wide-enough area in which to conduct their dumb-ass man-to-man combat, Helena anxiously ran away and left Hermia, refusing to get involved in a female altercation with the thoroughly pissed-off, jealous wench. Oberon and Puck watched in alarm at viewing the evolving dual crises.

"Puck, you've really royally fucked-up things this time!" Oberon criticized his now-worried, normally irresponsible errand fairy. "It looks like we'll have to intervene in this prospective fracas, otherwise we're going to have at least three dead humans on our consciences. Of course, Puck," Oberon rationalized and declared. "We could always transfer the blame on wifty Cupid's bad aim, missing the big-titted mermaid riding on the porpoise's back in our comprehensive and biased final report to Almighty Zeus."

"What should we do, King Oberon?" Puck apprehensively asked. "Should we move to Egypt and become river nihilists there? Working for Zeus and the Olympians is bad enough, if you want my personal, prejudiced opinion! In all honesty, I'm not really ready for all that Ra-Ra shit!"

"Here's my ingenious plan of action!" Oberon instructed his zany helper. "Go and patrol that section of the forest where the two dense-headed humans are going to sword-fight. Then, cover the ground with *our* special magically-induced heavy fog. After an hour or two of swinging their heavy swords at nothing but air, the two assholes will become weary and eventually fall asleep; hopefully not one on top of the other, or else the impact of their bodies might wake them up, and the idiots will again proceed to kill each other. Shit Puck," Oberon said with some optimism evident in his tone of voice. "If we can pull this one off, Zeus might elevate me from being the Forest Fairy King to the prestigious title of Chief Gay Faggot god, and we'll then be able to evacuate this fucked-up, low-budget woods, and live our existence in luxury on opulent, marble-templed Mt. Olympus."

"After I create the thick fog, and the puny Athenian men fall fast asleep from exhaustion, what should I do next?" Puck wondered and asked. "Piss on them both to wake them up? Boss; I truthfully don't think my kidneys are big enough to do that particular job!"

"No Asshole!" Oberon scoffed at his childish-minded underling. "Put some of this remaining love juice from the purple flower into the blond-fellow's eyes. In that way, he'll go back to loving the brown-haired girl once he sees her, and everything ought to fuckin' work-out according to my grand design. I'll make sure that the blonde-haired jerk-off sees her first."

"Where will you be while I'm performing this essential service?" Puck asked his very evasive mentor.

"I'm going to check-out what the hell's happening with Titania and her hee-hawing donkey-headed companion," Oberon answered with a broad smile. "I got to get her back to fantasy (here, Fairy and Pixie reality), convince her to give me the little Indian kid, and get her away from that half-human, half-donkey smelly creature before we'll accidentally have created a whole colony of new fucked-up beasts like the Centaurs are. If that happens, I'm sure that Zeus will automatically condemn us to work for his brother Hades in the Kingdom of the Dead, and I fear we'll then never be elevated up to Mt. Olympus. And besides all that terrible horse manure, Puck," Oberon admitted. "I don't want to lose Titania to any donkey-dicked, half-human, since I feel I'm actually falling in love with her, and am ready to have an honest-to-goodness heterosexual love affair. We'll only have one real-time opportunity to solve our evolving dilemma, so let's get our asses moving!"

"Oh shit, Master! Look to the east. It's almost dawn!" Puck observed and articulated, pointing to the horizon. "We gotta' work fast while our midsummer night magic is still potent and effective!"

Puck flew over the section of the forest where Lysander and Demetrius were about to commence sword fighting, and the frivolous imp skillfully covered the woods with a mystifying thick mist. 'I'll complete this insane detail, and then hang-around to see what the *fog* happens next!' the sprite reviewed in his fanciful little mind. 'I'll be creative and speak to the idiots one at a time, while deftly simulating the other's voice. That neat ruse will entirely confuse the already fucked-up combative assholes!'

"Demetrius you extremely craven Retard; now where the hell are you?" Lysander arrogantly called.

"I'm over here! Catch my ass if you can!" Puck whimsically beckoned. And then the little aggravator yelled to Demetrius in Lysander's disguised voice, "Come on; you tough guy! I'm over here! Find me and I'll cut the shit right out of your raunchy bowels!"

Naturally, Lysander and Demetrius started hacking-away with their heavy swords, moving and swinging their weapons in opposite directions in the thick-as-soup fog. And when the frustrated young men had inadvertently gotten within fifty-feet of one another, the rascal Puck called to each combatant in the other's voice, and the pair separated again, each in quest of his virtually invisible, avowed foe. This incredible bullshit went on for over an hour until Demetrius and Lysander finally collapsed to the ground in sheer fatigue, lying only ten-feet away from one another.

Then, as luck and coincidence would have it, lost blonde-haired Helena entered that section of the woods, and she too became weary and fatigued. The gorgeous girl dropped to her knees in a fellatio position, and realizing that there was no erect dick to toot, she too rolled-over onto the ground and quickly fell asleep, only three feet from her original beau Demetrius. And if that unbelievable horse crap wasn't enough, brown-haired Hermia staggered through the thick fog, and becoming tired, keeled over and rolled her body onto the ground, winding-up lying right next to her former lover and intended husband, Lysander.

Next, Puck magically lifted the mist-ifying fog and remembered to squeeze the love juice onto Lysander's eyes, so that (upon waking-up) he would again love the brown-haired Hermia. 'Now finally, my backfired mischief episodes ought to be effectively reversed!' Puck imagined. 'It's all dawned on me now!' the clownish imp realized as his head turned and his eyes scrutinized the eastern horizon. 'I still have time to visit Oberon at the place where Titania's sleeping, and see what the hell happened with the knockout Pixie Queen and with the donkey-headed human actor asshole!'

In her sleep and under Oberon's powerful hypnosis (and with Puck as his unreliable witness), the Fairy King persuaded Titania to surrender the little Indian boy, who had been designated by Oberon to become the first authentic gay human. Soon, the awakened Pixie Queen had been entirely liberated from her deep love spell that had compelled her to become infatuated with Rocco Bottom, the donkey-headed Weaver/aspiring actor.

"Now, fully awake, my beautiful Queen, and become your old bitchy self once more!" Oberon entreated his new heart-throb. "This antidote I'm rubbing on your breasts will be a great anecdote for me to gossip about to drunken tavern patrons in the future."

"Oh, Oberon, what queer un-queer dreams I had experienced!" Titania revealed to her new-found champion. "I dreamed that I was in love with a very interesting donkey that was eager to share his filthy stable stall with me, so that we could then roll around in the shit-covered hay together! Holy Crap, Boss Man!" Titania exclaimed while recognizing Oberon's rank over her. "I'm sure as Hades glad that you showed-up and rescued my firm ass from who knows what!"

"Your former love stud is lying asleep over yonder!" Oberon exclaimed as he pointed-out to Titania a certain freak-of-nature having a man's body with a donkey's head. "Someday, when we're both happily intoxicated and feeling uninhibited, or after sharing a sweet sexual afterglow, we'll chat and I'll explain the whole fuckin' complicated mess to you. But first, my Fairy Queen, your mind must be free of all anxiety and angst."

"Hurry Master! Dawn is coming fast! It is almost morning!" Puck (alias Robin Goodfellow) reminded the very forgetful Oberon. "You must command me to change the sleeping fellow wearing the purple robe back into a full-fledged human, while your colossal night-power is still functioning."

After Puck received permission to transform Rocco Bottom back into a complete male human again, Titania and Oberon danced in the new day's twilight, as the cute imp/jester loyally practiced his very special magic touch on the sleeping Weaver.

* * * * * * * * * * *

At sunrise, King Theseus, Queen Hippolyta, and their blithe entourage led a merry hunting expedition into the dark forest as the first part of celebrating the couple's much-anticipated, upcoming marriage. Soon, the enthusiastic revelers encroached upon Hermia, Lysander, Demetrius and Helena, all sleeping on the forest ground, right next to each other, in a row.

"You obviously have the most wonderful hunting dogs in all of Greece and perhaps all the world?" Hippolyta said, flattering her royal husband-to-be. "Some of them are black, but I especially like your gray hounds!"

"What the hell do we have here?" Theseus bellowed with mild astonishment as the King noticed the four Athenian young adults sleeping in the forest. "Can't these acne-faced teeny-boppers find a decent inn or lodge to shack-up in? What's this moral-less, younger generation coming to, anyway?"

"You're absolutely right in your astute. analytical criticism, my Theseus!" Hippolyta agreed. "These four misguided youths seem to be lacking in both decency and common sense!"

Then, Hermia's elderly father spotted his daughter lying on the ground next to Lysander, Demetrius and Helena. "I've heard of twosomes and threesomes, but a fucked-up foursome sleeping together is quite extraordinary and bizarre!" the astounded old Egeus gasped. "I had always suspected that my daughter Hermia was an addicted nymphomaniac, and this embarrassing discovery evidently confirms my worst-case-scenario concern. Daughter; why must you mortify me in front of my royal aristocratic friends?" Egeus shouted. King Theseus, she's not waking-up!"

"Perhaps you're being a little too presumptuous, Egeus!" Theseus objectively questioned the old man's apprehension and accusation. "Maybe these four young adults weren't committing groupy sex at all. Perhaps they had no ulterior motives, and we've caught them in the innocent act of getting here a little too early to participate in the widely-publicized, scheduled hunting festivities. The well is always half-full as opposed to being half-empty, at least that's been my lifelong philosophy, Old Man. And after all, Egeus. You've got to give Hermia the benefit of the doubt. She was not caught in the act of having sex with her three callow friends! But honestly, revered and elderly Egeus," Theseus recollected and then commented. "Isn't this the day that your daughter Hermia will decide exactly what to do in regard to marrying Demetrius?"

"Er, yes, King Theseus," the demented old fart remembered and verified. "Today's the Zeus-damned day all right!"

The King then directed his musicians to sound their horns to suddenly startle the four, horny, young adults, who soon heard the blasts and were embarrassed and quite shocked to see their illustrious-but-amused King standing above them.

"Lysander and Demetrius," King Theseus noted and stated. "Rise to your feet. You seem to be passive friends now, when several days ago, I've heard that both of you were seething with venomous hate for one another. What the hell's happened to you two fickle devils?"

"Oh, just and mighty King Theseus. I really can't explain my radical change of heart towards Demetrius," Lysander stammered. "But Hermia and I ran away to the forest to use the enchanted woods as a staging area for us to elope and get married, and then live in Sparta with a rich aunt of mine."

"What!" aged Egeus loudly protested, almost having a massive cardiac arrest. "King Theseus, you must punish this arrogant upstart Lysander for defying *our* adult authority, and for violating our chauvinistic Athenian laws! My rich widow cousin has promised to leave her fabulous fortune to me! That's why the hell I intend to outlive the old Spartan witch!"

"And what's your incredible story?" the wise King asked the muscular weightlifter, Demetrius. "How come you're here too, and with Helena, the beautiful blonde girl that you've occasionally professed to despise ever since she amazingly kicked your ass really good sixteen-years-ago in nursery school!"

Much to everyone's astonishment (including the old coot Egeus), Demetrius uttered, "My temporary love for brown-haired Hermia is no more. Now I get warm and fuzzy vibrations every time my eyes gaze upon fair, blonde-haired Helena, and I get so excited, and then imagine licking her magnificent golden bush! What a sensational drug-free high that wonderful ongoing feeling is!"

"This entire event is indeed excellent, unprecedented bullshit!" King Theseus acknowledged for all to hear. "I hereby rescind and nullify the ancient, archaic, Athenian law, and hereby propose that three blissful couples are to be wed on the temple steps: Lysander and Hermia; Demetrius and Helena, and Hippolyta and me."

And then, the whole assemblage of revelers conducted their successful hunt, and returned to Athens with the exception of old, mentally-challenged Egeus, who stayed behind searching for a tall tree to jump from and commit suicide. Fortunately, for the old geezer, he was too feeble to climb to any first limb, and a competent "quest party" was dispatched to find him. The searchers retrieved the old loon (suffering from dementia), and truly saved the old fart from himself.

* * * * * * * * * * * *

In another part of the enchanted forest, Rocco Bottom finally woke-up from his donkey-head enchantment. 'Where the hell am I? Did I get drunk last night? Where the hell are Quince, Starveling and the other fuck-heads?' Bottom angrily thought. 'Those insane-shits must've run away like cowards and left me to be devoured by legendary gay faggots, and by very real, vicious beasts! What a crazy fuckin' dream I had!' Bottom thought, pensively rubbing his eyes. 'I'll get Quince to write a play about my incredible, fucked-up dreamland experience, and we'll make a fortune!'

Meanwhile, Snout, Flute, and Starveling arrived at Peter Quince's carpentry workshop to begin seriously rehearsing the scheduled play. The guild tradesmen were upset that Rocco Bottom had never returned home the previous night, and that a half-donkey/half-human monster had probably killed and eaten the beloved Weaver.

"We're in big trouble!" Quince sadly told his melancholy comrades. "Bottom is the only one capable of playing the main part of Pyramus. Now that stupid fuck-head just *has* to be maimed and devoured by some grotesque-looking, donkey-headed, mutated creature eerily residing in the forest. I hope that King Theseus never makes that fucked-up forest into a goddamned national park!"

Just then, Rocco Bottom nonchalantly entered the workshop, all ready for his dramatics' rehearsal. Bottom strongly expressed his desire to have Peter Quince change the play to *his* phenomenal forest experience, which he had shared with a regal Pixie Queen.

"Tell me all about it later, Rocco!" Quince gleefully replied. "Right now, we gotta' prepare for 'Pyramus and Thisby'. But after our performance," Quince promised his former missing-in-action pal, "I'll gladly listen with both my ears to your fucked-up story."

Act V

The three joyful couples were married (by a certified Justice of the Piece of Ass) on the temple's white marble steps, and then the principals and their invited families and guests walked inside King Theseus and Queen Hippolyta's majestic palace to celebrate the fantastic royal reception for the triple nuptials. The euphoric King graciously proposed a toast to the pair of young couples, Hermia and Lysander, and Helena and Demetrius. Then, there was a brief interlude where everyone socialized while the Athenian King and Queen anxiously approached and sat on their purple velvet thrones.

"Those fantastic stories that the newlyweds, that is to say my dear Hippolyta, the newlyweds besides *ourselves*," Theseus declared and clarified to his bride, "well, those fabulous tales were really rather incredible. I have a hunch that the four of them must've drunk several gallons of cheap wine the night before the idiots had innocently entered the legendary enchanted forest. What the hell do you think about their seemingly fictitious accounts? How could four days possibly be magically condensed into one night?"

"My Husband and King," the elegant Hippolyta politely and eloquently replied. "Who really gives a flying shit? But upon second thought, I must admit it does seem especially strange that all four adolescents had remarkably shared the same rather incomprehensible midsummer night's dream."

Philostrate, the renowned Master of Revels, and Prostrate, the Grand Master of Ceremonies, and his deranged triplet-brother Prostate, the Grand Gland Master of Ceremonies, were presently pissed-off because King Theseus had overruled them, and had chosen to hear and see the amateur play "Pyramus and Thisby" performed in *his* honor, rather than watching and listening to a more sophisticated drama produced by the officially unionized Professional Athenian Amphitheater Thespian Players Association Guild. Disgusted and aggravated, Philostrate reluctantly introduced the inimitable Peter Quince, who then orated a lengthy, boring prologue to the audience, explaining that there would be a lion attack scene, along with a possible suicide or homicide scene, also being performed by the improvising actors. Quince's expressed purpose in making the speech was to eliminate the possibility of weak-hearted women sitting in attendance from later screaming, fainting, and crapping inside their expensive formal gowns.

"That ignoramus carpenter narrator made absolutely no sense at all," Theseus whispered to Hippolyta. "Perhaps we had indeed made a terrible mistake in judgment, and should've had the professional company perform the formal play that those envious triplets Philostrate, Prostrate and Prostate selfishly wanted me to accept. Confidentially, I've never heard of this unfamiliar backwoods' play that features a lion and a speaking wall having major roles," the King told the new Queen. "This better not be an exhibition of simpleton plebeian bullshit, or else, I might lose my reputed temper if I feel that my invited guests have been either deliberately or inadvertently embarrassed. Do I make myself perfectly clear?"

"Nonsense," Hippolyta objected and disagreed. "Contrary to your biased opinion, I find this harmless company of simple tradesmen rather refreshing and amusing. Now, my devoted Spouse; let's see what the heck transpires next. Sit back Husband, and learn to relax. It's our special wedding day, remember?"

"I am a Wall," the Wall (an awkwardly-disguised Snout the Tinker) explained to the somewhat-worried and apprehensive audience. "Essentially, I separate the lovers Pyramus (Bottom the Weaver) and Thisby (Flute the Bellows-Mender). Up until now, that's been my only damned function and claim-to-fame in my whole lackluster life. The two lovers sometimes speak through a missing brick in my faulty construction, but despite the fact that neither Pyramus nor Thisby has had any formal education, all in all, each character is but another brick in the wall, that structure symbolically being the wall of life," the omniscient Wall philosophically clarified and disclosed to the suddenly-captivated audience.

"I hope that Thisby, even though she's a man, both in real life and on stage, doesn't forget to meet me here," Rocco Bottom, acting as Pyramus, articulated for the amused attendees' information and viewing pleasure. "Please assist me in communicating to my lover!"

"Oh, Wall; why do you have to be such an obstacle and keep me separated from my true love," Thisby rhetorically asked, exhibiting a very obvious speech impediment, which was sort of an obstacle all of its own. "Oh, talking Wall, stop being such a difficult fucked-up sound barrier!"

"I see a soft voice, and I hear Thisby's enchanting face!" dumb-shit Pyramus (Rocco Bottom) accidentally uttered in reverse grammatical logic from the other side of the wall, as the alert audience began boisterously laughing.

"All's wall that ends wall!" the sagacious talking Wall perceptively remarked.

"Will you meet me tonight in the enchanted forest, so that we can watch the ecstatic fairies and the sexually-active pixies in motion," Pyramus smartly suggested. "Oh crap; I just remembered dear Thisby. We can only hear the fairies and the pixies romping around, because we can never see them."

"I'll be there with tinker bells on!" Thisby answered, as the audience cracked-up, not knowing exactly what or whom *she* had been referring to. "Where the hell did you get this obtrusive division; this ugly barrier to our properties Pyramus; at a local Wall Mart?"

"I've executed my job without delay, but now I, the Wall, even though I have no legs or feet, must go away," the male-sounding Wall (who wished he was a fence) loudly yelled and rhymed to the delight of the howling audience (without any aroused wolves seated or laughing in it).

In the following scene, a Lion (Snug the Wood Joiner) came-out with a sword and violently attacked Pyramus, who then loudly growled, scaring both the crap and the urine out of the supposedly ferocious predator, which then cravenly sprinted-off the stage in fright. Being quite scared, too, Pyramus also quickly dashed-off the stage in the opposite direction. But then, Thisby aggressively tugged the intimidated Lion back onto the rudely constructed wooden platform, and (much to the audience's satisfaction), proceeded to beat the hard and soft shit out of the reputed king of beasts.

Thisby next single-handedly dragged the defeated, dead Lion off the stage, and then Pyramus re-entered, saw the Lion's blood splattered all over, and logically concluded and thought that the crimson stains belonged to his true love Thisby. Pyramus (in utter despair) lifted his sword from its sheath, and was about to ironically commit suicide, when Thisby came-back on stage to intervene in her (his) boyfriend's impending suicide. The two lovers embraced, but then the Wall, (who was thoroughly pissed-off from hearing the lovemates melodramatic conversations all the damned time), became extremely hostile, grabbed Pyramus's sword and wildly killed both lovers during a most turbulent fit of rage. The audience (including King Theseus and Queen Hippolyta) felt obligated to give the amateur performers an enthusiastic, standing ovation.

"Splendid! Most excellent!" the King commended Peter Quince, Bottom and the other tradesmen turned amateur thespians. "Okay everyone, it's almost midnight, and if we're lucky, it's time for the forest fairies and pixies to exuberantly dance, sing, gambol, and frolic. As you all know," King Theseus elaborated, "this being twilight, on the approach of midnight, is the only marvelous time of day when both the straight and the gay and lesbian communities can mutually come together and blend-in as one compatible entity."

Oberon, Titania, along with their sometimes invisible, gay minions, gracefully flew into the palace from all directions, singing and dancing in the air as the jubilant, celebrating humans were doing likewise on the palace's white-marble floor. The non-stop party went on all evening until dawn began showing its red hues upon the eastern horizon.

Then, the irascible Puck flitted-around and screamed in a shrill faggot voice, so that all in attendance could hear his noteworthy proclamation. "The mistakes in this mix have all been completely fixed. And if you all don't believe this evening's theme, think of it as just a midsummer night's dream!" the naughty rascal adroitly rhymed. "And furthermore, all that are present right here and now should take a close gander, at Demetrius and Helena, and at Hermia and Lysander!"

Silence reigned supreme throughout the white-marble dance floor as King Theseus and Queen Hippolyta, and everyone else, stood still as statues pondering the exact meaning of the shrill queer voice's haunting comments. And then, seconds later, everyone standing on the palace dance floor again began singing, cavorting, frolicking, and laughing, until the stellar sun finally rose in the east.

"King Lear"

Act I

The setting for the tragic Shakespearean play "King Lear" is medieval Britain after B.C., which was also long *before* the invention or popularity of B.A.'s, BB's, BeeGees, BJs, B.M.'s. BO, BP, BS and BLT. The Earl of Kent and the Earl of Gloucester were discussing King Lear's recent, unorthodox behavior, and the pair suspected that the Ruler had gone daft, particularly in relation to the division of his kingdom, as the merciless onslaught of dementia was interfering with the Monarch's better judgment.

"I tell you Earl," Kent said to Gloucester. "I used to believe that King Lear favored the Duke of Albany over the Duke of Cornball, er, I mean Albany over Cornwall, but now I'm not so sure."

"Well, Earl," Gloucester said to Kent. "I've thought the same fucked-up bullshit, too! I'll level with you Cunt, er, I mean Kent; nobody knows what the hell's going on in terms of the distribution of property, castles, White Castles, estates, palaces, and manors after Lear's imminent death, which can happen any decade now! The only thing that we both really know is that Lear is totally fucked-up," Gloucester told Kent. "And our King's disintegrating mind vacillates somewhere between insanity and senility."

"Is that not your mentally disturbed son, my Lord, scratching his balls standing directly behind us in the throne room?" Kent asked Gloucester. "I'd wish the hell he'd scratch my balls! My scrotum is really itching something fierce!"

"Yes, Kent," Gloucester guiltily and embarrassingly verified. "But I must say your interrogative was all-too-polite! Often, I'm ashamed to acknowledge him in public because Edmund is my bastard son, who I keep around simply for the pleasure of child abuse. Actually, my plow horses have better breeding than Edmund does," the Earl of Gloucester confided. "The idiot's now nineteen years old, and still wipes his ass with tablecloths, tapestries, handkerchiefs, washcloths, and drapes. But Kent, Edmund's mother was a wonderful whore who could do it all, both in and out of bed, and the slut really knew how to please a man. It's too bad that ten-minutes of sexual pleasure with a horny strumpet has led to a lifetime of humiliation and aggravation for me. Thus, Edmund is the penalty I've received for thinking with my dick and not with my brain for a lousy ten-minute interval of intense carnal gratification. And I sorrowfully regret that the end-result of my sexual exploits as a young man is fucked-up Edmund."

"If I had a defiant son that looked and behaved like Edmund, I'd certainly keep him locked-up in a gorilla cage!" the Earl of Kent told the Earl of Gloucester, who was a distant cousin of the famous Duke of Earl, and the mild-mannered dog Duke of Marma.

"I do have a legitimate older son named Edgar," Gloucester reminded Kent, "and for some remote, inexplicable reason, I do favor Edmund over Edgar, just like Lear favors that asshole Albany over that low-down prick Cornwall. The psychology behind these parallel cases is too difficult for my limited intelligence to fathom, yet it makes for a damned good story. All I know, Kent, is that the whole world's fucked-up, and that my family and King are, too!"

"How could you love a freak of nature like this dunce Edmund standing and loudly farting behind us?" the Earl of Kent inquired. "He looks and behaves like some kind of fucked-up gargoyle!"

"It's not fuckin' easy being me, that's for damned certain," Gloucester readily admitted to Kent. "Of course, I was a delinquent asshole too when I was an acne-faced teenager, but I never had grotesque features like this monstrosity Edmund does! I think that his whoring mother had to have Medusa, the Sphinx, the Minotaur, and the Chimera for ancestors or relatives."

"Father," Edmund alerted Gloucester as the retard approached the conferring men, and then pinched the Earl's portly ass. "The King is coming, but even with my perfect vision, I still don't see any trace of sticky semen either flying or dripping-around anywhere!"

Elderly King Lear entered the palace chamber, and the Duke of Cornwall, the Duke of Albany, and the Ruler's three daughters Goneril, Regan, and Cordelia were following close behind in what appeared to the observing Earls and to the dunce Edmund as an unmajestic, clumsy-looking, chimpanzee procession. King Lear next awkwardly sat-upon his ebony throne and leered left, right, and then left again, as was his bad habit when the Monarch felt a little leery of his covetous Dukes, and of his unpredictable daughters.

"Earl of Gloucester, go into the adjacent room and shoot-the-shit with the Duke of Burgundy, while I have an informal chit-chat with my three daughters," King Lear directed. "If I'm lucky, I'll remember what the hell I want to talk to them about. I mean dear Earl, sometimes I even forget to wipe my big fat ass after I take a prolonged healthy piss."

"I shall talk to Burgundy about his wine vineyards and about his profitable vino bootlegging operations," the usually early Earl of

Gloucester remarked. "Then I'll interrogate the bastard and find-out if Burgundy personally knows the Duke of Merlot, the Duke of Chablis, the Duke of Champagne, the Duke of Chardonnay, and the Duke of Cabernet-Sauvignon."

After the comical Earl of Gloucester had left the dreary throne room, King Lear leered and stared at his three daughters, and then it was time to get-down to business. "I was never good at fuckin' geography," the aged Monarch admitted. "Hand me a map of Britain so that I can map-out my strategy. I plan on dividing my realm, which is ordinarily outside the realm of reasoning, into three distinct separations, and apportioning each territory into the possession of each of my three daughters," Lear prefaced his mediocre dissertation. "If only I had possessed enough sperm to produce a valiant son, I wouldn't have this fuckin' lousy problem that I intend to address and solve right now! My daughter Gonorrhea, er, I mean Goneril. What noteworthy platitudes and accolades do you have for your all-too-generous Old Man?"

"Oh Father; I love you and Britain more than you can ever imagine, because to tell the truth, you have a very minuscule imagination," Goneril illogically began. "In fact, I love you Daddy, more than I love my own cherished tits and pussy!"

"That evaluation has been very well-enunciated and is most commendable," King Lear' praised Goneril. "Would you shave your pussy for me, my Dear?"

"Yes, Father, with full knowledge that my cherished pubic garden would grow even bushier and even darker once again!" Goneril smartly answered.

"Well then, my dear Gonorrhea, I mean Goneril, wife of Albany," the demented King replied. "How the hell could you be married to an entire city? I often wonder in my sleep about that mighty strange arrangement! Do you have any other wonderful words to cordially deliver for my personal satisfaction?"

"Yes, Father; I love you more than I love your power, your admirable wisdom; your fantastic property; and your fabulous wealth!" the eldest daughter Goneril falsely answered.

"And how about you Regan, wife of Cornball, er I mean Cornhole, er I mean the Duke of Cornwall!" King Lear stuttered and asked. "Do you have any meritorious opinions about your munificent King and Father?" Lear solemnly asked.

"I'm made of that same rare metal as my sister Goneril, so obviously, I also have a heart of gold," Regan aptly lied. "The major distinction, Father, is that my love for you is at least three times that of Goneril's, which I must admit is very excessive and extraordinary! I love you more than I love my tits, my pussy, my ass, my clit', my vulva, my vagina, and my goddamned ovaries! That's how much I fuckin' love you, My Liege and Father!"

And then being completely flattered, elderly King Lear inquired about his third daughter's devotion; the normally blunt and all-too-honest Cordelia. "Do you love me more than your body, the air you breath, and the good food that you eat?" Lear asked his youngest daughter. "Tell me all about your commitment to me, Cordelia."

"I'm not pretentious like my two older whoring sisters are," Cordelia critically stated. "So, I'll tell it like it is, Pop. I do possess a little allegiance to My Liege! But my love for you is in my heart, and not in my forked tongue, so I can't express to you false words that are based on disguised greed and evil avarice! I refuse to speak untrue praise and worship to you from a ponderous mouth as my siblings Gonorrhea, er I mean Goneril, and Regan have so fraudulently and so maliciously done!"

"Do you realize what you're presently jeopardizing?" Lear yelled at his youngest, sweetest, and most independently honest daughter. "If you shower me with an abundance of sweet nothings as your bitchy sisters have done, you'll most certainly inherit much! Bearing that obviously propitious result in mind, youngest Daughter, what laudatory phrases do you have for me?"

"None!" Cordelia sharply answered. "I have nothing to say in the line of false bullshit!"

"Holy Fuck!" King Lear boomed. "Nothing really means two words: no-thing! What the hell's wrong with your sense of discretion? Out of the kindness of my own heart, I'll give you another chance to redeem your reprehensibly poor judgment. Cordelia, speak to me and kindly make your remarks pleasant."

"Look, Big Daddy; I'm not an eloquent orator, so I can't stick my heart into my mouth and utter the exact words that express how I truly feel!" Cordelia all-too-realistically explained. "I somewhat love you, and have nothing else to articulate, except maybe a few graphic unsavory expletives!"

"How dare you, Cordelia!" King Lear yelled as the monarch fell off his throne, and then the nearby Earl of Kent helped the senile Ruler up from his knees and back onto his proper, elevated, purple-cushioned seat. "Cordelia, even though you can't mend an irregular hem or a common cotton dress, please mend your disrespectful speech, or else I shall be inclined to disinherit you! I advise you to keenly weigh the consequence of your spoken language!"

"Father, you have begot me, and now you've got me," Cordelia smartly commented. "I obey and honor you almost as much as I do the amorous and handsome French Duke of Burgundy. I would love being *marooned* with Burgundy on a lavender and oxblood-colored island. And that isn't any Bristol bullshit, either."

"Daughter, you've blatantly disgraced and insulted my dignity before all of these gathered distinguished and covetous assholes," Lear bellowed in front of his formal audience, with only the Earl of Gloucester and the Duke of Burgundy missing. King Lear then further admonished his youngest daughter, Cordelia. "I warn you by citing an ancient quote: 'Don't come between the dragon and his temper.' Now Kent, I have an academic question to ask. Are there really such dangerous animals as fire-breathing dragons?"

"If you say so, My Liege," the very diplomatic and amenable Earl of Kent sagaciously responded. "Then certainly, there must be such dangerous creatures as sure as God made dicks and pussies, and little green apples! If venerable St. George was alive today, he'd most definitely testify to the existence of dragons!"

"Fuck you Cunt, er, I mean Kent!" King Lear shouted. "I'm now so damned pissed-off at Cordelia that I'm going to disinherit her. Her prized third of my kingdom, upon my death, will now go to Goneril and Regan, and also to their worthless, lazy, spouses: Albany and Cornball, er, I meant to say Cornwall!" Lear raged and ranted. "And because of Cordelia's unnecessary arrogance and lack of cooperation, her future husband, that scumbag, always-whining French Duke of Burgundy will receive nothing, either! I might be a trifle dour from citing all of this troubling death and last will and testament bullshit, but I guarantee to everyone present in this dusty chamber that insolent Cordelia will be both powerless and dower-less!"

"But My Liege," the Duke of Kent politely protested on Cordelia's behalf. "Your decision is quite retaliatory, and grossly heartless! You're punishing Cordelia for being honest!"

"Look Cunt, er I mean Kent," King Lear hollered as his ebony throne began wobbling on its tiny wooden platform. "Stop acting like a freshman and a junior jerk-off with your sophomoric senior citizen commentaries, while I myself am having a challenging and annoying senior moment!"

"Kind King; power should not bow to flattery, but it should align with truth, justice, and tradition!" the Earl of Kent candidly spoke in defense of Cordelia. "Your Majesty should not fall to folly, even though you've already clumsily tottered and plummeted off your regal throne several minutes ago. I swear to you Lear that your youngest child does *not* love you the least, but in reality, Cordelia actually admires and honors you the most! What the fuck's wrong with you, anyway? Don't you know anything about basic character evaluation? Your two older daughters know how to kiss ass, but are totally ignorant of how to kick it!"

"Shut the fuck up Kent, or else, you'll be decapitated and dismembered before you die!" King Lear boomed and threatened. "Now get the fuck out of my sight, even though according to the modern laws of science, you can't fit inside my goddamned eyes!"

"I've always been loyal to you, My Liege, against all kinds of awesome enemies and foes, and now you treat me like a fuckin' pawn on your tilted chess board, after you had just rooked Cordelia!" Kent challenged and defied his obstinate, senile King. "Your safety and survival have always been my paramount considerations! Now you pretend that I'm a mere vassal, or some kind of meager serf. You're suffering from dementia, Old Man!" Kent accused Lear. "Look at Cleopatra's River because you see-Nile in the morning, and then you carelessly leap into Paris's River, for you're definitely in-Seine at night, especially during the daunting full and new moons! Lear, learn to value tradition more than to pursue extradition!"

"Kent, you have but ten-days to get your butt the fuck out of my kingdom!" King Lear screamed at his new adversary and only true friend. "Now vanish and be banished! You're hereby relieved of your geriatric babysittin' responsibilities. Now Kent, I reiterate. I want you the fuck out of Britain! I repeat! You have ten short days to hit the channel, and navigate the European bays!"

The berated and demoted Earl of Kent gave the virtually blind Lear the middle finger (which the poor-sighted King did not see), and then promptly exited the throne room. Next the Earl of Gloucester re-entered the royal chamber, accompanied by two Frenchies, the King of France and the Duke of Burgundy.

"Here's France and Burgundy," the Earl of Gloucester informed King Lear as the eminent men gracefully entered the chamber. "And how we've managed to squeeze an entire country and also a part of that fucked-up kingdom into your diminutive throne room is far beyond my mortal comprehension."

"Duke of Burgundy," King Lear stated while staring blankly at the ceiling. "You and the ambitious King of France here, both desire to screw and marry my youngest daughter, Cordelia. Let me determine how strong your rivalry happens to be. My daughter has just been disinherited and will receive nada, *not a* single thing from my estate, which happens to be the whole fuckin' country. Cordelia might just as well be a destitute peasant, and pregnant with quintuplets. She comes with substantial heavy-baggage debts and liabilities. But there she is Burgundy, ripe for the fucking, er, I mean plucking!"

"Holy Shit!" Burgundy pessimistically exclaimed. "Who needs a dowerless princess as a wife; a disowned and disinherited insolent wench at that! Now that I see the total picture, I believe I'd rather screw a rag doll than hop into the sack with petulant Cordelia. With your permission, King Lear, I'd like to abandon this futile courtship quest and return to Burgundy and get drunk with some lowlife assholes inside a fleabag whorehouse. Your abrupt announcement has definitely turned me off!"

"Then Burgundy, your wish is granted, so get the fuck out of here and never return!" King Lear hollered. "And don't let the rusty gate above the alligator moat hit your ass on the way out! And what about you King of France?" the Monarch sternly asked. "Do you desire to get laid so badly that you risk going bankrupt with a dowerless woman as your queen? You'd be better off being the Earl of Bristol because the Earls of Bristol are dumb as a pistil (flower part). when they do the Bristol pomp!"

"Cordelia is definitely most beautiful!" the pompous King of France acknowledged. "It's too bad she ain't worth a tit-less turd. Are you sure Lear that you won't restore her dowry for Burgundy or for myself to confiscate? Then, I'm sure he'd reluctantly marry your youngest daughter if I couldn't."

"I've already sworn that Cordelia will get nothing from my estate, and I'm rather adamant about enforcing that decree!" King Lear lectured as the aged imperial ruler stared at a sconce's blazing torch on the wall, thinking that it was the sun's radiance. "Cordelia will be poorer than the poorest scrub-woman in Burgundy, and far worse-off than the lowliest, begging bag lady in all of France."

"I would never be Burgundy's wife now that I know what's lurking in his jealous, covetous heart," Cordelia yelled-out for all present to hear. "Fortune and power are his great loves, and the libido-driven, greedy French bastard can try screwing his gold coins and his golden throne instead of me."

"What about me, Cordelia?" the now-insulted King of France interrupted. "Even though I have a tiny dick. most of my constituents regard me as a really big prick. And furthermore, oh unjust Lear, on second thought, just for spite. I'll take Cordelia to France, marry her, honeymoon in Sweden. and then make her my dancing queen. Now in conclusion, I say screw you Lear, and screw you too, Burgundy!

Despite my embarrassingly small genitalia, I know a good piece of ass when I see it."

"Take her then to France for all the hell I care!" King Lear bellowed as his beady eyes stared at the marble floor and thought it was a ship's wooden deck. "Be gone with my daughter, and never disgrace me with your uncouth presence again! Forget all of this compatibility bullshit between our two countries! And disobedient Cordelia; you're permanently devoid of my blessing, of my love, of my grace, and of a third of my enormous wealth! Now get the hell out of Britain, for I'm certain that there is substantial hell awaiting you in France!"

"Cordelia, I urge you to say goodbye to your two phony sugar-tongued sisters," the French King suggested and gestured with his middle finger. "They're both accomplished liars, betrayers, schemers, and prevaricators! You'll have a much better future in France as my dower-less, penniless, exploited wife!"

"You two whoring bitches ought to disintegrate into dust," Cordelia screamed at Goneril and Regan. "I hope you tramps enjoy licking pig shit out of each other's crotches the next time you two strumpets do sixty-nine!"

"Go to Paris and see what's under the King's underpants!" the smiling Goneril hollered at Cordelia. "I see London, I see France, I see the King's, oh, foolish Sister, must I finish the all-too-familiar childish nursery rhyme?"

"Go to France and screw your King in all the Paris-sights, you whoring destitute queen bee!" Regan exclaimed, loudly condemning her innocent and truthful-to-a-fault sister. "France, both the country and your prospective husband, suck, and so do you, Cordelia. So, in that sense, you two human disasters fuckin' deserve each other!"

"That's right Cordelia!" Goneril haughtily boasted and concurred. "Regan and I have been generously rewarded by our feeble-minded father, who has forgotten where his pecker and his asshole are, and exactly what their easy-to-use functions happen to be. Our Liege is an aged fool pursuing delusional folly, and Regan and I have expeditiously profited from his ever-increasing lunacy. Both *you* sister Cordelia, along with your future French husband, have made wrong decisions."

"Come my fair Cordelia, before I come right here and now and get my silk tights all messy and sticky!" the King of France urged. "Vive le France. Vive le bon sex, too!"

"Ah, yes!" Goneril whispered to her equally selfish sister Regan. "It's no damned secret that father loved Cordelia most of all three of his beautiful daughters! But what good has it gotten my youngest sister, who has lost a third of the estate of an old foolish man suffering from senility and dementia. Our father's judgment is worse than his terrible eyesight, and he can't see shit in a manure storm!" Goneril maintained to Regan. "Our Liege can't think straight; can't speak right, and can't act normally. He's entirely fucked-up!"

"That's a hundred percent correct," Regan softly added and concurred. "He's banished the Earl of Kent, his most loyal supporter! The stupid weak-minded imbecile! He's liable to inadvertently start an unnecessary war between Britain and France based on his own suspect mental disability and horrible indiscretion."

"Where's my chessboard!" screamed Lear like a bratty toddler in a highchair. "I want to beat France right now! I don't give a pauper's shit how many knights, bishops, and rooks the stupid prick has! I'm gonna' kick his butt and teach that conniving son-of-a-bitch a lesson for eloping with my disinherited, betraying, biological daughter, Cordelia!" the King yelled. "Where's my fuckin' cheeseboard, er, I mean chessboard, anyway! I wanna' be white!"

* * * * * * * * * * *

The following morning Edmund, the mentally-challenged, ogre-looking bastard giant entered his father's castle drawing room where the Earl of Gloucester was preoccupied sketching a nude woman. The semi-retard was carrying a forged letter, which Edmund had obtained (and had paid handsomely for) from illegal Viking aliens who were unscrupulously counterfeiting and falsifying official-looking government documents. All the while, the distrustful creep was mentally reviewing what the bastard son intended to say to his father, the eminent Earl of Gloucester, who never gave an aristocrat's shit about what anyone else (except maybe King Lear) ever thought, did or said.

'You know Father that I'm more loyal to you than my prick half-brother Edgar, who ordinarily has a reputation for doing everything legitimately!' the illegitimate Edmund thought-out his greatly rehearsed discourse as the schemer furtively approached his patriarch still sketching in the drawing room. 'Although I'm not a chronic alcoholic and have no illegal whiskey-still sitting in the barn, Edgar happens to be some twelve or fourteen moonshines ahead of me. I'm your son, too, even though I'm definitely a bastard, both biologically and socially, literally and figuratively,' Edmund pondered as the out-of-kilter dolt tripped over a vertical armored knight stand, which then crashed to the floor along with himself. The deformed, awkward fool swiftly arose without even fixing the fallen armored knight back into its rightful, upright position. Next, the bastard son stealthily paced to his oblivious, unperturbed father (who was still engrossed in *his* artwork while thinking about the Earl of Kent being banished from Britain, and that the same thing might happen to him). Then Edmund interrupted Gloucester's contemplation by handing his father the falsified letter.

"What does this envelope envelop, Edmund?" Gloucester grumpily grumbled. "What do you have here? Have you flunked-out of military training school again?"

Feeling uneasy and somewhat deficient in confidence, Edmund snatched the letter back, and then ineffectively attempted concealing the already-sealed envelope.

"What's in that damned letter?" Gloucester demanded as his attention was again momentarily distracted from his nude drawing and Kent's terrible fate. "What are its contents? Are you dying from a plague? Do you need your hemorrhoids removed by the incompetent, partially-blind castle surgeon? Did you get a pig or a cow pregnant, and now want me to pay for the abortion? Speak-up Edmund! Put your tongue to good use!"

"Nothing weird like *that,* My Lord," Edmund quietly answered, shrewdly feigning embarrassment. "I'm afraid that the letter contains information that might infuriate your ass, and make you have conniptions, and go into a damned panic-attack-rage. That's why I feel I shouldn't show you its sentences and paragraphs."

"Now that you've disturbed my sage meditation, I insist that you show me the goddamned letter, or I'll show you the nearest prison, after I show you the door!" the Earl of Gloucester insisted and warned. "Get with the fuckin' program, Edmund!"

"Forgive me Father, but it's a letter from Edgar that I've intercepted and have partially read," Edmund insincerely revealed. "I became so nervous that I sealed it back up, and was struggling with my conscience, whether or not I should share it with you. You might get so pissed-off after reading the missive that you could commit suicide, and then go completely nuts, and then possibly kill me!" Edmund illogically uttered. "Since I have limited reading skill, I figured I should bring this vital note to you for your examination!"

"Stop the stupid bullshit!" Gloucester admonished his bastard son. "Give me the fuckin' letter, Edmund, and then I'll decide who is at fault, and who might be fuckin' to blame. You certainly know, my bastard son, how I like having the guards tie you to the rack, which then converts to a very utilitarian rotisserie, rotating your exposed ass over roaring flames. Confidentially, I can think of no better way, Edmund, to keep my castle warm in the wintertime."

"I only hope for my brother Edgar's sake that this letter is just an experiment in creative writing gone amok," Edmund lied as the scammer handed his father the contrived document. "Evidently, Edgar thinks you're going senile just like King Lear, and that you're too old and feeble to enjoy power and authority. My half-brother wishes that you were dead, so that *he* could take over as the new Earl of Gloucester, which might not be such a bad fuckin' idea after all."

After reading the falsified letter, Gloucester picked-up a plumed pen and hastily colored in the bush on the drawn nude's body to symbolically demonstrate his new-found animosity for Edgar conspiring against him, and diabolically wishing to surreptitiously (or violently) supplant the elderly Earl.

"How did you obtain this indicting autobiographical piece of distasteful literature?" Gloucester asked Edmund. "Who brought it to you? Was it delivered by messenger or by oxcart?"

"No, my benevolent Lord and Father," Edmund deftly lied. "I found it in the castle's rubbish heap just before I was to burn the disposable trash. Edgar probably thought that his little exercise in fiction writing would not be discovered or exposed. I mean Pop," the power-hungry bastard son maintained, "who the hell else besides illiterate me and a couple of area homeless peasants ever comb through smelly garbage and stinking trash?"

"This weird scribbling does seem to be Edgar's ugly chicken-scratch writing," Gloucester plausibly determined. "In fact, his lousy handwriting, devoid of standard penmanship, looks almost identical to yours Edmund; and incidentally, both of your sloppy, illegible, un-cursive renditions, in my humble scholarly estimation, are equally abominable and atrocious in appearance!"

"I never write-down anything on paper from my own head. All I ever do is copy sentences out of books word-for-word to try and learn how to read," Edmund idiotically clarified.

"Has Edgar ever discussed with you about supplanting me in power?" Gloucester asked his sly but dunce-headed Edmund. "I know that your brother has never sought my counsel on the matter, and that we've never actually discussed it. If he has those kinds of rebellious intentions, then I do believe that fucked-up Edgar is even more of a dirty bastard than *you* are!"

"Never Father, but I've heard through the local grapevine that Edgar often says that he's now at the proper age to take over your lands, and that you're an adamant Old Fart that's too old to fart," Edmund deliberately lied. "Edgar has often stated to me that your health and mind are declining, almost as quickly as your failing realm, and that only *he* could bring your fucked-up estate back to good reputation and prosperity. As part of Edgar's diabolical plot, I suspect and believe that his first bold act will be to take over your internal revenue. At least that's what the hell I hear around town."

"My flesh and blood son Edgar has become a manipulative, devious villain!" Gloucester yelled as the patriarch grabbed the nude drawing and demonstrably ripped it to shreds. "Edmund; I demand that you seek-out your half-brother. Then, I'll have the dirty bastard apprehended and incarcerated, even if he is my legitimate son and heir. I know exactly how to quell a family insurrection. But tell me my bastard Son; where the fuck is Edgar right now?"

"Don't aggressively pursue and punish Edgar until you have more sufficient evidence against him," the brazen Edmund dishonestly recommended. "I mean to say, Father; even though I've never been in a hotel or lodge, I do have reservations about discussing the evil essence of that letter to you. I know how pissed-off you get when you read anything, let alone a horrible message such as this crazy one I had discovered while innocently rummaging for discarded gold inside the conveniently located rubbish heap. What do you now think of your legitimate older Son?"

"I can't believe that Edgar could be such a vile, inconsiderate, conniving monster," Gloucester confided to Edmund. "I never suspected that Edgar could be a mutinous asshole just like you are! Perish the goddamned thought! Perish the goddamned reality! I insist Edmund, that you go and find Edgar and then bring the purported traitor into my custody."

"I'll track him down as if he was a wild animal," Edmund promised the Earl of Gloucester. "And then, I'll feign courtesy and tell the slippery dick-licker that you desire to surrender your land to him. I'll use that savvy ploy as bait to get him to accompany me back to your ruinous, in-need-of-repair, damp, cold, drab castle. My appropriate actions will prove my pledge of allegiance to your authority and to you, also. It's quite ironic, Father, that I can talk a good game, but can't read or write worth a shit!"

"Then go with dispatch Edmund, even though I know you'll be traveling to Edgar's anonymous residence all by yourself," Gloucester commanded. "An unscrupulous son plotting against a just father; father against child; and a repugnant, ambitious half-brother thrown into the goddamned mix! The Earl of Kent has been banished by Lear, and if the fucked-up King learns about this developing scandal going on in my house, the unpredictable asshole might banish me next!" Gloucester screamed like one possessed. "There is tremendous insanity all over fuckin' Britain, and we're in the muddle, er, I mean, *we're* in the 'middle' of the maelstrom, Edmund; whatever the fuck *that* terribly erratic, bullshit, useless expression means!"

As Edmund exited the Earl's castle, *he* contemplated that liars, adulterers, drunkards, knaves, thieves, thugs and fools, just like himself, were abounding all over Britain, with their sinister intent to exploit and extort honest, sincere, chaste, sober, law-abiding nobility. 'Ravenous New Age politicians like myself need to outsmart honest, unassuming victims like my gullible half-brother Edgar. I was born under the constellation Ursa Major,' Edmund reckoned, 'so there's a distinct possibility that my mother who bore me was a ferocious bear. Father is reputed to have screwed sheep and mares in his younger days, when he couldn't get his dick inserted into a virgin filly,' the bastard son mused. 'And so, by my fraudulent birthright, I'm both a rough and lecherous bastard; and besides that, also a stupid, academically-ignorant bastard to boot!'

Edgar was looking out of his small, isolated, only castle window (with nothing better to do) when the ingrate observed his half-brother approaching and encroaching on horseback. 'Oh shit! It's that expert at causing bedlam, Edmund! I can expect a trick or two of tomfoolery, with some wickedness thrown into the stew, too! I wonder what brings him here? Of course! It's his fuckin' horse! What else would bring the ruthless son-of-a-bitch here?'

After Edgar dismounted his ignoble steed, the brother slowly entered the small white castle and was coldly met by Edmund, who was not grilling any hamburgers. "Why are you here Edgar? Are you here to cause more strife and friction in the family? Don't you know anything else besides abundant corruption?"

"No Edgar; I was watching the moon and the sun recently, and I gotta' say that nothing can eclipse the importance of your visit," the lying son-of-a-bitch stated. "Astrology has warranted that the stars predict that Father will soon die, and that you'll inherit all of his property. Furthermore, the stars oracle that you must visit father during his critical time of decision-making, to help and allow for the smooth transition of power from him to you."

"Since when have you become an expert on the difficult subject of astrology; let alone an authority on the art of fortune telling?"

Edgar incredulously asked. "You still haven't mastered jerking-off and getting laid yet."

"You recently had spoken with Father, and the Earl has expressed to me that he was happy and satisfied with your relatively calm disposition," Edmund lied to Edgar. "But he seems to be in a rage about your more outstanding negative personality traits, and today you must make amends, pacify the old fool, and settle-down his uneasy mind, so that you might profit from your grand inheritance. Father is becoming just as rash and irrational as our fucked-up King."

"Are you suggesting that someone in the Castle Gloucester is feeding bad propaganda about me to Father, and now Pop is actually believing the outrageous lies?" Edgar rhetorically asked. "What dickhead or contriving bitch would be doing such a dastardly thing? Who could possibly be so downright deceitful?"

"I'm just a dumb bastard, and not smart enough to speculate about who the contemptible, treacherous villain might be," Edmund equivocated and answered. "Share your loyalty and your confidence with Father until the fool gradually stabilizes his emotions back to rationality. When I left Castle Gloucester, which is just right over there to our left, Father was mentally returning to his youth, and had expressed to me that he wanted to go-out and start screwing sheep, mares, fillies, and imported polar bears again. Edgar, I strongly suggest that you go see him, with you being armed with weapons, for Father's mind is presently in an unstable state."

"I go everywhere armed," Edgar replied. "My fuckin' arms are always attached to my goddamned shoulders. Haven't you ever noticed my splendid anatomy?"

"Take your weapons with you, for you might need them to protect yourself from Father's wild mood swings, and perhaps from his anonymous evil adviser, too," Edmund told Edgar. "Who really knows what kind of raunchy shit is going on in Castle Gloucester; aside from all of the fucked-up crap going on at King Lear's court? Parallel developments evolving in separate locations! It's all like a fuckin' double-insanity paradigm in progress!"

"You're right Edmund!" Edgar agreed. "There are dirty bastards all over this land, starting with you and me!"

"On the other hand, perhaps it would be wiser for you to just temporarily run away from the area rather than hang around and face our father's lunacy," Edmund wickedly suggested. "Our Father, who isn't in Heaven, is in the process of having an emotional meltdown! In his fucked-up delirium, the senile Earl might accidentally have you tarred, feathered, and then executed! Be prepared to defend yourself against his unpredictable fits of rage!"

"For the first time in your fucked-up life, you might remarkably be right," Edgar commended Edmund.

* * * * * * * * * * * *

Meanwhile, King Lear's eldest daughter Goneril was at her husband the Duke of Albany's palace having a personal discussion with Oswald, her private steward and sex-on-demand servant.

"Harvey Lee (which was Goneril's unique nickname for Oswald), King Lear has gone-off the deep end, and thinks he's a robust, young stud again. His renegade knights are out of control, riding crazily all over Britain while terrorizing and raiding convents, taverns, drug dealers, and whorehouses, everywhere that those places exist," Goneril told Oswald. "And the King upbraids us every time the spirits move him, the alcoholic fool! And I don't need my goddamned braids upbraided any more, thank you very much! My predictably unpredictable Father is becoming just as contemptuous and petulant as Lear is! What the hell am I saying? My rapidly deteriorating Father *is* Lear!"

"Perhaps a little sex will get your mind off of your family problems and onto sharing a common ecstasy," the always turned-on Oswald advised the disenchanted woman. "It sounds like you need my hard stiff cock plunging and riveting-away inside your ravenous, cavernous love canal."

"No time for that type of physical pleasure right now, Harvey Lee," Goneril politely replied to Oswald. "I think I hear my ungainly husband stepping-down the corridor as we speak. Unfortunately, my wonderful lover, we don't even have time for a delightful quicky! Maybe tomorrow morning, we'll have a delightful chance to secretly rendezvous, Harvey Lee."

"What should I do?" Oswald asked. "Assassinate Lear? All because his asshole undisciplined knights are running amok all over fucked-up Britain?"

"No, you inane, insane, idiotic Ninny!" Goneril exclaimed. "Go and prepare supper as is outlined on page seven of your job description. Don't get too hungry for power, Harvey Lee; even though I allow you to wildly screw me three times a day. Now I highly recommend that you closely follow my orders, or else you'll wind-up at the local unemployment office again; standing in line with all the other area, lowlife degenerates!"

* * * * * * * * * * *

The Earl of Kent did not evacuate Britain as King Lear had commanded, but instead, disguised himself as Baron Folly, and soon arrived at Duke Albany's palace (wearing a jester's uniform) where it was rumored Lear had been tarrying. Kent was determined to bring Lear back to sanity by making the King aware of his horrendous plight, and by convincing the addled monarch that his two older daughters were dirty-rotten, thieving, bitches that were bent on betraying Lear's love and trust. The King (adorned in his lion-skin cape) entered the dinner chamber, accompanied by various knights, *men-in-knights'* clothing, and basically, other fucked-up, degenerate, subordinate attendants.

"Who are you that is blocking my view of the dinner table?" the nearly-blind Lear demanded. "Are you a wayward beggar? Are you a visiting vagabond? Are you a talking asshole? How about a traveling lesbian thespian?"

"I am but a man," the stranger (the insane Earl of Kent pretending to be Baron Folly) answered in a raspy voice. "I merely wish to serve you King Lear, but for your information, I do not serve food or tennis balls. I only serve My Liege. But to my honorable credit, I eat no spoiled fish because it smells too much like unclean pussy."

"Do you know me? What services can you perform? I'm too old for adolescent-type blow-jobs and for second-party hand jobs!" Lear sarcastically commented.

"I can do it all, Your Majesty," the Earl of Kent disguised as the fake jester Baron Folly answered. "I can ride horses and women; I can deliver messages to enemies, and also, I can deliver blows to the midsection if necessary; I can change diapers for infants and royalty alike; I can kiss and kick ass, but most importantly, I can keep a secret. You must admit that I'm a very versatile and valuable son-of-a-bitch to have around the castle and keep you company, and keeping you well-amused, too."

"How old are you?" Lear asked. "My vision is very poor, especially when I wear a battle helmet with a very tiny visor. But your phantom voice doesn't seem a day over sixty-nine, which used to be my favorite number in my more virile days."

"I'm sixty-eight, My Liege, and I can still have sex just like my meals, three times a day," Kent, really thinking about sixty-nine, exaggerated. "At any rate, I'm a better-than-average adviser, too, when it comes to helping mentally deficient, incompetent, and incontinent rulers make important decisions. I go by the royal title Baron Folly."

"I like your style, Baron Folly; so you can be my guest at my table for this evening as I conscientiously pursue conducting a little social experiment," Lear communicated. "And if I like your personality and find you witty, and if you have an interesting fuckin' story line that's filled with asshole intriguing and humorous anecdotes, and then successfully share them over the next several dinner hours," Lear added, "then I'll invite you to stay, and I'll gladly listen to your astonishing bullshit every goddamned night."

"Thank you, My Liege!" Baron Folly happily replied. "According to my mathematics, I've got more bullshit than a dozen cow pastures squared. Doesn't that arithmetical comment sound rather gross?"

"Where is that scoundrel servant Oswald?" King Lear blustered. "I need that grouchy, pathetic, big-dick bastard to clown-around and entertain us at supper."

"Harvey Lee, er I mean Oswald, is attending to your daughter Goneril, who says she's experiencing a severe migraine in her pelvic area," an undependable knight informed the table, even though the table was inanimate without any ears or brain. "I think that your daughter just had some violent sex with Duke Albany, and now she needs Oswald to comfort her, and gently attend to her feminine emotional needs. And besides that, King," the double-agent knight continued his tattletale speech. "Everyone in the palace, including the Duke, Goneril, and even Harvey Lee, or I meant to say Oswald, thinks that you've lost your sanity and will never again retrieve it."

"You arrogantly say that I am insane! Well, it was insane for me to divvy-up my kingdom to Goneril and Regan, and now be subject to a variety of sinister plots and schemes being greedily organized against me behind my hairy back," Lear concluded and opined to his sitting counselors and dinner guests. "Listen-up, assholes. I'm now second-guessing my inheritance decision, and wish chronic constipation on everyone younger than me in the whole of Britain. Now go from my presence, informative, gossipy Knight. You've temporarily been relegated to courier until you return and report back to me," Lear sneered. "Now here's your important assignment. Go and tell Goneril and Albany to fuckin' get their asses to dinner, or else face my mounting wrath, even though I'm now an honored guest in Albany's modern castle, and have no soldiers loyal to me in this whole fuckin' place."

The assigned Knight eventually gathered-up sufficient audacity, and boldly rapped and then entered Goneril's chamber, finding her engaged in a passionate embrace with Harvey Lee Oswald. "Lady Goneril; your father the King demands your presence at dinner immediately, and His Majesty also wishes to be entertained by Harvey Lee."

A half-hour later, Goneril, Oswald and the messenger Knight made it into the freezing-cold banquet room. King Lear was not-too-enthralled with the late arrivals' appearance.

"You whoring Dog!" Lear barked at Goneril while he was thinking about Oswald, and actually in *his* mind, directing his verbal venom at Harvey Lee. "You Knave, you Slave, you Gigolo, you mangy Mongrel! You dare try to stare your King down with beady eyes, you culpable lowlife Bastard!" Lear vehemently screamed at Goneril while attempting to reprimand Oswald. "Take that, you scumbag Asshole!" Lear boisterously shouted as the King aggressively tripped Goneril onto the floor while thinking that his victim had been Oswald. "I can still kick your wimpy ass, despite the fact that I'm nearly on my goddamned deathbed."

The Earl of Kent (disguised as Baron Folly) leaned-over and advised the thuggish Oswald in a whisper, "Arise and get the fuck out of this room while your dick is still attached. Lear collects balls and has them uniquely attached all over his castle's game room walls! Now leave this chamber immediately, if you ever wish screwing Goneril again!"

Wanting to distract Lear from Oswald's stealthy departure, Kent suggested that the demented King remove the Fool's jingle-bell hat, because only a Monarch with a jester's mentality would leave his kingdom to his two conniving, illegitimate daughters, and disinherit the one biological child that was 'a true blessing and a Providence'. "I'll teach you proper logic and ethics, and I'll be your personal psychiatrist, and also instruct you on how to control your bowels and your kidneys when in public," Baron Folly (the Earl of Kent) related to the oblivious Lear.

"You offend me, Baron Folly; and you deserve to be manacled and whipped; you lousy, knavish masochist," King Lear wildly shouted to the total amusement of his fascinated dining audience. "You're quite like a wild dog that must be periodically whipped into submission, and then into obedience."

"Before you whip my ass and the rest of my frail body, too," Baron Folly answered in a slightly-intimidated tone of voice, "please allow me King to teach you an eloquent speech."

"This better be good, or I'll have you ground right into the ground, get it, ha, ha! I'll have you, Baron Folly, ground into the ground," King Lear laughed as his entire assemblage of diners loudly guffawed too, out of fear of being also ground into the ground upon the maniac King's arbitrary order.

"Leave thy drink and thy whore, although King Lear, we all know that you haven't gotten laid in decades," Baron Folly preached while imitating a loquacious, self-righteous bishop friend. "Lend less than you owe; speak less than you know, and have more than you show. Everyone is a fool in *his* (chauvinistic masculine by preference) own way, be he a baker, a barber, a carpenter, a butcher, a candlestick maker, or a fucked-up illiterate King. We're all fools at our own levels Lear, and the less we do and say, the more we capably conceal our foolishness!"

"Do you blatantly and brusquely call me a fucked-up fool, Baron Folly?" Lear challenged as everyone else in the chamber gasped and then became hushed. "Your foul words sound like treason!"

"You've haphazardly given-away all your other titles and grants to your two older daughters and their deceptive husbands," Kent valiantly stated. "You've recklessly traded your power and kingdom for two scheming daughters and their power-hungry spouses. You've given your gold to two daughters possessing wooden hearts, and have ignored and shunned your biological daughter with the true golden one. An ape has more damned wisdom than you've thus far exhibited, Lear."

"You'll be brutally and viciously whipped by my youngest but very competent whippersnapper!" King Lear screamed at the not-too-cleverly disguised Earl of Kent. "Keep jabbering and you'll pay the ultimate price for your insolence!"

"Your two older daughters would have me whipped for telling you the gospel truth, and conversely, you would have me whipped for lying," Baron Folly argued and maintained, while everyone present listening to the peculiar dialogue again gasped with their mouths agape and their hands upon their lips. "And sometimes, those greedy surrogates acting in authority would indiscriminately whip me without me ever saying a single or married word to deserve the flagrant flogging. What a cruel bullshit world I've been born into!"

Just as King Lear was about to order Baron Folly beaten and scourged, Goneril re-entered the dining chamber (she had unobtrusively left the hall for several minutes to wash the blood off of her lacerated knees and to take an emergency crap). Her second appearance further confused the already-perturbed Lear, and had coincidentally and miraculously salvaged Folly from certain torture.

"How now Goneril," Lear said as the warped-minded King amazingly recognized his eldest daughter's loud, consistently irregular gait. "Why have you a frown on your face? Do you have gas pains? Have you gotten a large foreign object stuck up your crotch? It's too bad you've missed most of my eloquent speech!"

"People used to listen to your silly drivel when you still were deciding whether or not to divide up your kingdom," Baron Folly whispered to Lear. "You're now an enormous zero without a whole number in front of it, and if there was another number, you'd then be a double zero, you old frivolous, delusional Fuck!"

"You're more of an utter fool than my father is or ever was," eavesdropping Goneril admonished the straight-talking Baron Folly. "And my pathetic father allows his knights' horses to gallop with impunity all over his kingdom in an undisciplined fashion, the crazed knaves randomly raping both heterosexual women and defenseless lesbians in every city, town, village hamlet and macbeth. Why can't those unruly dumb bastards ride their horses here to Albany and start riding me? You're a total and complete asshole, Father, without having either the decency or the honesty to either overtly acknowledge or admit it."

"A good King is not an obedient father," Baron Folly counseled and lectured Lear. "Why do you take this backtalk bullshit from your belligerent daughter? I'll tell you why! Because you've already committed to the Bitch half of your formerly illustrious kingdom upon your death, which the treacherous whore is probably planning to enact right this minute."

"You, Father have allowed castles around your kingdom to become riotous inns and also chaotic, immoral whorehouses; all the castles except Albany's, Cornwall's, and yours," Goneril accused and asserted. "Shame on all those asshole earls and barons that permit such debauchery to occur in their manor residences, in their estates, and in their castles. Your kingdom is in total disarray, Old Man! Get the fuckin' territories in order before I inherit half of them as my fucked-up dowry!"

"Saddle my horse!" King Lear yelled to no one in particular as the astonished assemblage again gasped, with each person holding his or her breath and crotch. "I must stop all of this sinful and banal misbehavior in my kingdom before I die, or I must die doing so! I must straighten-out all these fucked-up, crooked crooks at once, before I'm prepared to meet my Maker! Why should I want to meet and be reunited with my fucked-up father, that dead skeletal prick!" the extremely perplexed Lear questioned his previous illogical statement. "Anyway, I must learn if Regan and Cornwall's lands are in similar tumult. Why must my pitiful life be such a disorganized tragedy? A fucked-up disorganized travesty?"

The Duke of Albany finally entered the banquet room *to re-join* his wife Goneril, who in Lear's confused mind, somehow had become dismembered. The tardy Duke was greeted with venomous remarks from the emotionally unstable and mentally imbalanced, King Lear.

"You've arrived just in time to prepare my horse for a serious gallop," Lear unexpectedly screamed at Albany. "You ungrateful, marble-hearted Fiend; you're more hideous than a sea monster, which of course just like a flying dragon, exists only in preposterous myths and legends. So why do I persist in giving such bullshit examples and ludicrous metaphors?"

"What the fuck are you talking about, old man father-in-law?" the Duke of Albany answered with a snarl. "Has my henchman Oswald adroitly twisted your nuts into a knot? Why have you all-of-a-sudden turned into a delirious Old Fart?"

"My knights are the most valiant in the entire world, and your crooked-tongued wife has seriously denigrated them in my presence!" the King asserted. "Yes, I'm referring to your goddamned ungrateful wife, whom I have pledged half my kingdom! She has less discretion than a Dover whore, yes, she has! In fact, she performs head on every dick around, just like a sweat-laden, stinking Dover whore does! You and your unfounded derogatory remarks give me a *fuckin' headache,* Goneril!" Lear shouted as the disoriented King demonstratively stuck his two middle fingers up to his forehead as the monarch's disheveled mind pictured Goneril giving both Albany and Oswald simultaneously blowjobs.

"Lord, I'm guiltless of any of this crazy bullshit to which you allude, and I'm unaware of exactly what psychological condition is afflicting you! Perhaps I should assign Oswald to perform a little light skit for this schizo," Goneril stated in her defense.

"I implore Almighty God to make Goneril's womb sterile and fruitless, and to dry-up all her infected pussy juice. Better yet," the crazed Lear continued his heightened tantrum, "I pray that a monster be born to *you* and Goneril, so terrifying a creature that both you, Albany, and my daughter, your perfidious betraying wife, will someday regret ever tricking me into promising you two ingrates half of my disintegrating kingdom, making this ingenious *King dumb* to all of his rebellious subjects and predicates."

"What's caused Lear to go mad?" Albany asked the astounded, gasping, gossiping diners gathered at the banquet table. "The ancient goofball has lost his senses, and also his assumed power, and is virtually a lame duck with clipped wings; and in addition, our ruler has a troublesome, plugged-up asshole inhibiting him from correctly shitting. Level with me. What the fuck's wrong with you Lear? Do you need a new cork up your ass?"

"I'm ashamed to my core that I've surrendered half of my realm to plotting cowards like you and my daughter," Lear sneered at Albany. "If only my eyes could form daggers to directly shoot right into your brass balls! I have another derelict, renegade daughter, Regan, who with her husband, I can't remember his goddamned name right now, will welcome me and make me feel comfortable in their acceptance and hospitality. I shall go and tarry with Regan and Cornball, er, I mean Cornwall, who will, unlike you, Albany, treat me with honor and with reverence."

"I'd like to tarry with you, My Lord," Kent, disguised as Baron Folly, offered his illustrious services. "My jester cap, if it were magical and stolen from Merlin, the hat then ought to fetch two hangman's nooses utilized to lynch two arrogant, bragging, nuisances in our midst."

"You two stooges are lucky we're allowing you to venture-out with your lives," Albany threatened Lear and Kent. "Let him, this laughable senile fool who pretends to be our King, let him futilely attempt to assemble a hundred knights in his traitorous defense while war with our persistent enemy France is imminent. This King and his vigilante knights should be confined to the perimeter of a chess-board game room! Ha, ha, ha!"

"Before you get laid tonight," Kent softly stated to Albany, "*check* your *mate*. She might already have contracted eight types of venereal disease from Harvey Lee, er, I mean from Oswald."

Just then, by sheer coincidence, Oswald entered the banquet room from which he had earlier exited. The reprehensible servant wished to converse with Goneril, while additional barbs and insults were still being exchanged between Lear and Kent versus the predator Albany.

"Oswald, have you finished writing that letter to my sister that I had dictated to you while we were having foreplay before sex?" Goneril softly asked her lowlife paramour.

"Yes Madam; and I even sealed it with some sperm juice since there was no available glue around," Oswald replied.

"Take three of my husband's fucked-up servants with you, and ride to Cornwall and Regan's castle and deliver the important letter," Goneril commanded.

"How can four of us ride one damned horse?" the dim-witted Oswald asked. "My balls get pulverized with me alone on top of a rambunctious steed."

"No Asshole; take four horses, one for each rider," Goneril clarified. "Get your shit together to negate the diarrhea coming out of your filthy mouth, along with the immense volume of constipation flowing out of your limited brain. And Harvey Lee, embellish the letter's contents with hyperbole to make my sister Regan's attitude towards and treatment of our Father parallel mine. We must drive the incompetent bastard completely insane, so that we can prematurely take-over his lands while the nutcase still breathes; just like you and me. And Harvey Lee; please don't prematurely ejaculate while you're still breathing heavily."

"Yes Madam!" Oswald exclaimed and bowed. "But you've gotten me so excited and aroused that I just popped a load simply thinking about penetrating you and that cheating Regan, both at the same time, which as you know Lady Goneril, is physically impossible."

Act II

King Lear and Baron Folly (Earl of Kent) rode their horses from the Duke of Albany and Goneril's castle to Cornwall and Regan's domain, and their tender sore asses were becoming chaffed from all of the repetitious bouncing up and down. All the while Lear was giving Folly (whom he thinks is a new trusted acquaintance) some last minute-minute instructions.

"We'll ride separately for the last part of our journey," Lear told advisor Kent. "I want to see if I can get into a few brawls with yeomen, or be attacked by wild animals to determine if I still possess my heavy mettle. First Baron Folly," Lear instructed. "Deliver these letters to the Earl of Gloucester, and then continue on to Regan and Cornwall's castle where I shall meet you. And don't worry about my folly, Folly! I can still kick ass including your skinny butt if I have to get physical! And if Regan and Cornball, er, I mean Cornwall, are visiting the Earl of Gloucester over in Gloucester, then I'll meet you at *his* castle."

"I'll not sleep until I deliver your important letters to Gloucester," Baron Folly promised his mentally-failing King. "I might be fucked-up, but I'm fucked-up on my own terms. Your two older daughters are like identical, crabby crab apples, both equally poisonous and lethal. Remind me, Lear, not to eat any goddamned crab apples when we meet again in Cornwall, or in Gloucester, because I already have a bad case of crabs, ever since I was eight-years-old," Baron Folly (the Earl of Kent) related. "But in the final analysis, Lear, we must always be more devious than our devious enemies in order to decisively defeat and trounce them!"

"We're both ignorant fools; you more than I, and we deserve each other's company!" Lear realized and expressed. "I think I'm regaining my mental health after only brief exposure to one of your asinine seminars. By the way, you make an excellent fool, Folly."

"Thank you, Kingy!" Kent responded like a gay retard. "You're never too old to be an accomplished fool, or to become one, that's my motto! The wisest men alive today are fools, for only a fool recognizes that he *is* one, when everyone else in the world is one, also. The pompous assholes that think only other people are fools are the biggest fuckin' fools of all."

"Make me sane and wise again, sage Baron Folly," King Lear sincerely entreated, "so that then I can teach all of those bigger fucked-up fools in my dysfunctional family a valuable moral lesson that they'll never forget."

* * * * * * * * * * *

Inside the Earl of Gloucester's dank, musty, castle, *his* bastard son Edmund was having a conversation with Curan, a court courtier, and also just a plain, old, nasty. country bastard like Edmund. The pair was discussing the anticipated arrival of the Duke and Duchess of Cornwall. Regan, Lear's second daughter. who like Goneril, had also falsely flattered the King so that Lear would by mistake give her half his estate and lands, while Cordelia, the third and most-deserving daughter, would receive nothing, because of her' honesty.

"Save thee, Curan," Edmund began his rhetoric. "And I'll save thee in a bank because Heaven doesn't want anything the hell to do with you and your perpetual skulduggery."

"And your salvation will also never occur since you have a heart blacker than pitch, and that's precisely why we get along perfectly," Curan cut-up and identified with Edmund. "Now, I just want to remind you that the Duke and Duchess of Cornwall will be coming soon to Gloucester Castle, and I don't mean sexually, ha, ha, ha!"

"How do you know that particular information you, blundering Knucklehead?" Edmund asked. "Are you a soothsayer? Are you an augur without an auger that delves into prognostication? Ha, ha, ha!"

"Go fuck yourself, Edmund!" Curan nastily snapped back. "I place more trust around here in gossip than I do in truth. The whispers among the peasants are usually more accurate than official notices in the public square that no one can read, because virtually all of Britain's subjects and commoners are fuckin' illiterate."

"Are you aware of any other rumors circulating around primitive, metropolitan, downtown, deserted, fucked-up Gloucester?" Edmund questioned his sneaky nobleman pal. "Is there an epidemic of smallpox that I'm not aware of? Are the Duke of Cornwall's knights running amok just like Lear's sworn protectors are? Has the King learned how to read?"

"There are no likely wars on the horizon between the Duke of Cornwall and the Duke of Albany, just as sure as there are probably likely no whores on both men's horizons," Curan cleverly answered.

"In time, you might hear of such exciting bullshit. and much more strange stuff besides!" Edmund replied. "Now Asshole; return to your duties once you figure-out what the hell they are. And if I knew what the hell they were, I'd fuckin' tell you to do all of them."

After Curan left to do nothing but pretending to be doing something, the wily Edmund thought about recent developments. 'My father is all set to apprehend my brother Edgar, and punish the good-hearted prick for wanting to possess *his* lands prematurely,' the Earl of Gloucester's bastard son rehashed in his mind. 'And the Duke of Cornwall is equally pissed-off at Edgar, just like Pop is, for it's gotten-out that my legitimate brother has also furtively plotted against *him*. According to damaging gossip initiated by me, Edgar has spread ugly rumors about the Duke of Albany desiring to kick Cornwall's ass and obliterate his highly touted knights; and it's all to my clever doing. Now, Almighty Fate; ain't I the fully-successful, truly-veritable, fucked-up, evil genius? Ha, ha, ha!'

Edgar ambled onto the castle property to chit-chat with Edmund, who had more malicious things on his sinister mind to cause further conflict between his benign legitimate sibling rival and his father. Soon the conversation took a bizarre twist.

"Edgar, let's together draw our swords and fake a duel," Edmund suggested as the dastardly bastard observed their father, the Earl of Gloucester, approaching in the distance behind Edgar. "I'll kick your ass good just for the sake of kicking your ass!"

"Fuck-off, Bro'!" Edgar exclaimed. "Look you bumbling, inept delinquent Fool! You just cut your arm drawing your sword! I'm getting the hell out of here before you blame your lack of coordination, and its bloody consequence on me."

Edgar fled the scene and Edmund complained to the Earl that his "hostile brother" had injured him in a brutal, savage sword fight that Gloucester had inadvertently broken-up by intruding on the supposed wild and ferocious fracas.

"What were you two goofballs quarreling over?" Gloucester asked. "Who has the longer dick or the bigger balls?"

"No, Father!" Edmund answered with a false grimace upon his countenance. "My villainous brother surprised me, insulted your integrity and dignity, and then I challenged him to an altercation explicitly to defend your honor. I was about to kill the obnoxious bully when the feckless shit-head became extremely frightened of my fierce resistance, and rapidly fled to escape your notorious temper and your proud justice."

"Where did Edgar go?" Gloucester insisted on learning. "Did he vanish into thick fog?"

"Father, look at my arm. I'm profusely bleeding because of that bastard Edgar, who isn't even an authentic bona fide bastard like I am. The rotten knave is lucky I didn't intrepidly swipe his reproductive apparatus off!" Edmund bragged while brandishing his blood-stained sword to impress his almost-blind dad.

"Well, young Edmund, what the fuck are you standing there for? Verbally submitting me to all your exaggerated braggadocio?" Gloucester yelled. "Pursue the dirty bastard; you clean bastard! Even though Edgar is legitimate, he's still a dirty bastard in my book after authoring that traitorous letter you had showed me!"

"Not only did Edgar write that terrible letter about prematurely wanting your property, but now the fucker has mercilessly wounded me; and also, the lunatic cock-sucker's been spreading nasty, scurrilous stories about the Duke of Cornwall and the Duke of Albany and their sex-hungry wives, along with their craven bloodthirsty knights," Edmund lied. "What should I do Father against such a belligerent and horribly offensive sibling foe?"

"Edgar will not remain uncaught for long inside my territory," Gloucester predicted to his bastard son, whom the Earl now exclusively favored by believing a series of deliberately fabricated lies. "The scurrilous Duke and his wife Regan are coming to my castle tonight, and I'll convince Cornwall that Edgar is *his* enemy too, and a bounty will be put on my legitimate bastard son's head;

and anyone who protects or hides him will be hanged, and *his* body mutilated, and butchered, and presented for dinner at the nearest orphanage," Gloucester said, exhibiting a degree of hyperbole. "The coward, my own flesh and blood, will burn and be barbecued at the stake, especially since the stakes are now high here at normally tranquil Gloucester Castle."

"Edgar told me he desired killing me because I was a disowned bastard and because he was always favored by you," Edmund lied to Gloucester. "How can you have possibly trusted someone like Edgar, who is totally deficient in virtue, in honor, and religious faith, in that he had cursed your name; and therefore Father, I had no viable alternative other than to defend your noble prestige and honor?"

"I thank you Edmund for being only half as fucked-up as your half-brother Edgar is. Therefore, I think that you're more deserving of my property than he is, when I'm finally called by Gabriel's trumpet to visit St. Peter at the Pearly Gates," Gloucester commended his bastard son. "Holy shit, Edmund! I now hear the rebellious Duke's out-of-tune, dissonant trumpets blaring in the distance. I'll persuade Cornwall to block all the ports to prevent Edgar from fleeing Britain. All the ports will be blocked as well as all the starboards; yes, you'll see my impeccable wisdom, my illegitimate-turned-favorite son!"

Cornwall and Regan entered the Earl's castle, and were formally greeted by Gloucester. Immediately, the Duke revealed to the Earl that he had heard "strange news", and wanted to hear Gloucester's opinion about rumored developments.

"My heart is cracked just like my legitimate son Edgar's brain and corresponding morals," Gloucester confessed and lamented to Cornwall. "Everything in my turmoil-oriented life is going askew!"

"We've heard via the royal grapevine that your eldest son, Edgar, who is my father's god-son too, desires to have you rubbed-out," King Lear's second daughter Regan declared to Gloucester. "And it's also wild hearsay that Edgar is a companion of the boisterous drunken knights that are partying all night long, terrorizing and raiding every profitable royal brothel and inn in the land! Their repulsive antics are causing widespread instability and insecurity throughout our realm. That damaging activity is eating into my husband's cut of the royal treasury!"

"More hideous shame being associated with Edgar," Gloucester regretted and sobbed. "I didn't know about his hanging-out with the riotous, radical, renegade knights' bullshit, though. You'd think that Edgar would be smart enough and horny enough to be consorting with kinky whores and hookers instead of with bellicose playboy knights, many of them muscular gay pinheads."

"I've learned of Edgar and the knights' destructive activities from my trustworthy sister Goneril," the always-conniving Regan informed the increasingly bewildered Earl.

"So, with Edgar being a dangerous fugitive from justice, then that leaves Edmund here the next in line," Cornwall added, just to further break the Earl of Gloucester's already-fragile testicles. "I trust that you're dispatching a few reliable, non-renegade knights to apprehend your treasonous son?"

"That conclusion is correct, Duke Cornwall," the distressed Earl of Gloucester sadly concurred. "Edgar has egregiously violated my will at his own selfish volition. And my previously neglected and disfavored Edmund has pledged his loyalty both to you and to me. He's triumphantly ascended above cowardice and disfavor, when all along in the wrongful past, I had erroneously believed my bastard son to be a fucked-up moron! I state from my heart that Edmund is now my one and only future heir."

"That's marvelous rhetoric! Simply marvelous bullshit rhetoric!" Regan commented and commended Gloucester as Lear's second daughter sneaked a peek and admired the bulge in the center of Edmund's tights. "You, Earl of Gloucester, are to be congratulated on your wonderful discretion. I'm sure that noble Edmund possesses some superior tools to aid both you and me, er, I mean *you;* and also, give comfort to my pedophile husband, as well as to me."

"Such weird language you have employed," the concerned Duke said to his always-cheating whore wife. "Now kind Earl," Cornwall continued speaking. "Do you know why we really came to visit you? If you thought it was to talk about trivial matters like your disobedient and treacherous son Edgar, then you're most certainly mistaken. We have much more important shit on our minds."

"Why no; I thought you came to ally with me in apprehending my fugitive son Edgar, and to tell me all about King Lear's clamorous and riotous knights," Gloucester attested.

"Well, dear Earl; we really came to Gloucester Castle to solicit your advice on certain pertinent situations that have recently arisen," Regan declared to her subordinate royal, as the horny bitch again glanced at the large bulge in Edmund's tight pants. "We've learned from my sister Goneril certain incredible facts concerning King Lear's disjointed kingdom, and we must share them with you in the utmost confidence!"

* * * * * * * * * * * *

    Harvey Lee Oswald (Goneril's steward and paramour) confronted the Earl of Kent outside the gates of Gloucester Castle. Being a visitor arriving from Albany Castle, Oswald curiously inquired about Kent's identity.
    "Good morning, Sir," Oswald said and snottily greeted. "Are you connected in any way to the inhabitants of this fair-but-mediocre country castle?"
    "Yes; I happen to know all of the devious shit-heads that live within," Kent acknowledged. "And in fact, I knew all of the poop-heads before they became genuine shit-heads."
    "Where may I set my horse?" Oswald asked. "He's as tired as I am after our long ramble from afar."
    "Over in the marsh would be just fine," Kent negatively responded. "Yes, your horse should be mired in the mire; that's exactly what the hell I think."
    "If you love me, Old Man, you should give me a polite, honest answer instead of acting like a complete jerk-off!" Oswald bristled.
    "I don't love you because I completely abhor homosexuality," Kent indignantly replied. "Even if you are bisexual or tri-sexual, I would still say 'Up your fat, ugly ass!' That was a figurative reference and not a literal one!"
    "Why are you abusing me, Man?" Oswald loudly challenged, looking to instigate a fight where Harvey Lee would be dominant. "I know you not, old fool, and regret ever encountering you; you ornery, scruffy-skinned, aged Wolf."
    "I know a knave and a rascal when my keen eyes perceive him," Kent further insulted Oswald. "I strongly suspect that you're a lily-livered, whore's son, wannabe' noble. Now then, you uncouth, risqué Asshole. My keen intuition detects that you're a combination beggar and coward, and a son of a mongrel bitch; and if you further annoy me with your asinine drivel, I'll beat and whip you to your already-wobbly and buckling knees!"
    "What a barbaric, monstrous, old-coot fellow you are, railing me as if I were an ordinary banister!" Oswald countered. "Ha, ha, ha!"
    "You ignorant, Varlet," Kent volleyed. "You pretend that you don't know me, when several days ago, you were in my presence at Albany's castle. Draw your sword you reprehensible, delinquent rogue! Draw your sword, you lowlife whore's son!"

"Get the fuck away from me, decrepit Old Man!" Oswald yelled. "I'll have nothing to do with your macho bravado! That's all I need is a senior citizen murder on my hands!"

"I suspect that you've come to Cornwall carrying letters that malign our good King Lear," Kent indicted his new-found adversary. "You impugn Lear's regal legacy, and smear what His Liege intends to be his glorious posterity. Draw your sword, you ruffian Coward, and fight like a man, you pestering Wimp!"

"Help me, someone!" Oswald shrieked and screamed. "Save me from this Old Fuck madman assassin wannabe'!"

Edmund was out for his early morning constitution around the castle grounds. His auditory perception heard the altercation-in-progress, and the bastard came sprinting to that destination to investigate the nature of the *mayhem,* although it was fall, and nobody was sewing.

"What's the fuckin' matter here?" Edmund inquired. "Is somebody having a cardiac arrest? How about a prisoner arrest?"

"I'll stab and slice you to ribbons, and have your parts displayed on the winning prize table at the county fair!" Kent irrationally yelled at both Edmund and Oswald. "You, Edmund along with *this* punk impostor whore's son, will both experience your bloody demise!"

Then coincidentally, the Earl of Gloucester, the Duke of Cornwall and Regan had all heard the developing ruckus, and the three swiftly meandered from the castle and out into the fracas setting. The newcomers were appalled at what their pupils (here, eyes and not students) were witnessing.

"What the hell is going on here?" Gloucester demanded knowing from Kent and Oswald. "If you can't tell me what's going on, then tell me what's coming off!"

"The dirtbag that initiates the next blow will die," the Duke of Cornwall sternly predicted. "Now, somebody please explain what the fuck is the matter here?"

"These two newcomer clods must be the messengers sent from my sister Goneril and from my father, King Lear," Regan theorized and stated. "I'll wager that both of these arguing jerk-offs arrived here simultaneously, and then got involved in a fucked-up imbroglio as to whose message was more important. What are you two pathetic dumb shits fighting about?"

"I'm so out of breath from this queer ordeal that I can scarcely breathe," Oswald testified as his lungs sucked in air. "I'm so nervous and anxious that I don't know what I'll do first, vomit or shit!"

"You craven Knave are the son of a tawdry tailor and mother whore," Kent, dressed in tawdry peasant clothes, vilified Oswald. "Your father was either the village tailor, the village blacksmith, the village painter, the village stone-cutter, the village drunk, or the village idiot, for your whoring mother had sex with each of those scumbag assholes, each and every lousy night, even during her bloody periods!"

"Enough sarcastic bullshit from your lips!" Cornwall interrupted Kent. "Now what's this minor donnybrook all about, or you'll both hang from the gallows!"

"This sword-toting, caveman, impostor, your Dukedom," Oswald panted, "whose life I had generously spared at the Albany banquet room, now has the unmitigated audacity to...."

"Thou whore's son!" Kent vehemently interrupted Harvey Lee. "You carry a letter full of malicious lies! I'll tear you Villain to shreds with my sword, and then decorate the mortar and bricks of the Earl of Gloucester's newly-constructed, state-of-the-fart, outhouse with your unworthy flesh and entrails."

"Peace, you beastly Knave!" Cornwall rebuked Kent. "Have you no reverence for arbitrary royal authority; er, I mean respect for royalty in your midst; arbitrating wild disputes among commoners?"

"Yes Sir; I've been bred a gentleman, but sometimes I transform into an unpleasant peasant criminal mindset," Kent egotistically explained. "And that rare phenomenon occurs especially when I'm confronted by a trouble-making, ambitious rogue servant on a simple mission where the dumb punk thinks he's some kind of vital entity."

"Why are you so bent out of shape Old Man?" Cornwall asked. "Do you need a laxative or an enema, for you certainly are too old and gray for an aphrodisiac!"

"This uncouth lowlife servant standing across from me wears a sword and pretends to be a royal personage," Kent angrily attested. "A filthy rat has more honesty and integrity than this lowly knave whore's son possesses. This vulgar joker has a dog's mentality, and a ferocious, untrained canine's personality and character, to boot. Beware of him, oh royal ones, or else you'll find your assumed safety in fucked-up jeopardy."

"Are you daft Old Man?" Cornwall answered and chuckled. "You appear to be quite mad and mentally incompetent, just like feeble King Lear, who now I understand desires to move to Italy and be called King Lira, ha, ha, ha! But why now do you call your chosen opponent a knave? Aren't you both fucked-up messengers originating from the same source?"

"I hate *his* countenance, for it forebodes conflict and chaos for all of King Lear's Britain," Kent obtusely and vaguely uttered like a self-ordained soothsayer. "He's a pox and a pestilence that must be thoroughly eradicated," Kent yelled while pointing a shaking hand at the craven swine Oswald.

"What the fuck are you attempting to express, Old Man?" Cornwall bellowed. "My patience is growing as thin as *your* body, and I'm about to blow my top and go on a rampage, delightfully executing both of you dueling Assholes!"

"Listen to me; speak and then listen to that lowlife, disingenuous rogue enunciate grotesque lies," Kent entreated impatient Cornwall. "And then, Honorable Duke, you'll understand that I'm noble bred, and that my dipshit adversary is a scumbag derelict of low ancestry, whose inferior genetics can't be trusted one iota in either royal circles or in public squares."

"What verbal or physical offense have you rendered to this old demented Windbag?" Cornwall intelligently asked Oswald. "Did you blatantly pilfer his enema bag or his surplus diapers?"

"Sir Duke; I was just arriving at Gloucester Castle when this dirty Old Prick accosted me, derided me, railed me, ridiculed me; all after the same jerk clumsily had tripped me several days ago at Albany Castle," Oswald claimed and exaggerated. "This old buzzard is favored by fucked-up King Lear, and therefore he's a very dangerous committed enemy of the Duke of Cornwall and *his* fair wife Regan."

"Fetch the stocks in which to imprison this loud-mouthed, gregarious Old Fart," Cornwall imperatively ordered several subordinates that were spectators to the crazy insult-swapping frenzy. "You, Old Fart Braggart, will be amply humiliated in public and scorned by all of those who despise fucked-up, country soapbox orator-rebels, such as yourself'."

"I serve the King!" Kent strenuously protested to no avail. "I am not a militant insurrectionist! I deserve respect and royal treatment because I represent Lear when in your royal presence."

"Nonsense!" Cornwall exclaimed in exasperation at Kent's cocky attitude and language. "Fetch the stocks for this old geezer to sit and meditate in until noon. The sun might boil and melt this aged prick's brain, and then perhaps he'll be able to think more rationally."

"To hell with *until noon* today!" Regan objected. "Until noon tomorrow would be a more valid applied punishment. The stocks will enable this old, destitute, vulgar coot to take better stock of his all-too-fluent words; don't you think so Husband?"

"If I were your father's dog you would not use and abuse me so," Kent staunchly defended his own intelligence and sanity.

"For your information, Old Geezer; I used to kick the shit out of my father's hunting dog every single day," Regan clarified. "So, you ought to be glad that you just have to suffer and endure your merciful and very fair stocks' situation."

"King Lear might not like what you're doing to his appointed dopey messenger," Gloucester butted-in. "After all, the irrational fellow is still our Monarch."

"Fuck that old senile Asshole!" the Duke of Cornwall exclaimed. "I'll take full responsibility for this punishment order, and if Lear doesn't fuckin' like it, the dumb-fuck could find the nearest forest and start chopping-down trees with his bare fists! Now insert the old fool's legs into the holes and secure the lids!" the pissed-off Duke commanded. "I really like stocks, but not nearly as much as I love bondage, and being regally whipped and belittled by Lady Regan!"

Everyone left the "area of squabble" except the Earl of Gloucester and the Earl of Kent, who didn't at first recognize each other, although the pair had been close, intimate friends since childhood.

"You've been a victim of the power-hungry Duke's pleasure," Gloucester sympathetically stated to the shackled Kent. "Cornwall is a sadist at heart, except when he's being bound and whipped by Lady Regan. Then, in his convoluted hypocrisy, Cornwall does a deviation from reality and becomes a practicing masochist! I'll ask the obstinate Duke for mercy once he simmers-down a bit, gets laid, and then gets bound and whipped," the Earl of Gloucester promised Kent. "That abuse should make him forget his animosity towards you, and after being reformed and rehabilitated, behave more suavely and royally once again."

"Don't worry about me!" the manacled Kent maintained. "I'll stay out here in the stocks until noon tomorrow, and feeling sorry for myself. Sacrifice and suffering have always appealed to me because they're analogous to diminishing my punishment in the afterlife. More pain now, less pain later on. That's how the fuck I see it."

"I still blame the dimwit Duke for overreacting to your annoying, talkative nature," Gloucester consoled his old boyhood (and recent) friend that he still didn't fully recognize. "But once the sex-driven Duke shoots some of his excess sperm from his peter, I assure you that he'll become more tranquil and passive. He might then extend to you more clemency than he has thus far exhibited."

'I still have the precious letter in my possession,' Kent recollected with a smile. 'The stupid money-hungry Assholes, in their rush to have me placed into stocks and bonds, had overlooked the letter I was to deliver, and the royal imbeciles are totally ignorant of its contents.'

* * * * * * * * * * * *

Edgar, meanwhile, appeared in a nearby woods, and pretended being a madman. The idiot passionately spoke to the barren trees and to the scrawny bushes, and shared his plight and his feelings.

"I've miraculously thus far escaped the hunt and the pursuit," Edgar orated to no one except the pristine physical environment. "All ports, sherries, and muscatels have been alerted of my accursed fugitive status situation. I'll be vigilant and still attempt to escape my father's unwarranted wrath. I'll disguise myself as a pauper by griming-up my face with dirt and animal manure," the distressed fugitive announced to the apathetic trees and rocks. "I might even join a band of beggars if the commoners can play musical instruments. I'll bypass mills, hamlets, macbeths, and random villages in my path until I finally reach safety; wherever the hell that remote refuge is! I've been reduced to nothing by vicious human treachery, and I must accept my dire situation as a non-entity, or else be run-down by trained hounds, and torn apart by their sharp fangs before their owners ever arrive with intentions of formally executing me for the mere benefit of public scrutiny and personal amusement."

Dauntless King Lear had ridden his miniature horse "Hercules" to Regan's castle in Cornwall, only to learn (for lack of basic telecommunications) that his middle daughter and the hormone-driven Duke were away, visiting the Earl of Gloucester. The King then journeyed onward, and upon arriving at his detoured second destination, had the cerebral wherewithal to realize that Kent has been maliciously put into stocks. The royal rider dismounted his panting steed, and became excessively pissed-off at his amazing discovery.

'It's strange that the Duke and Regan have left Cornwall and not sent my messenger back to inform me of their journey,' Lear suspiciously wondered and thought. 'And now I have a really sore buttocks from all that fuckin' rough riding from Albany, to Cornwall, and now over here to Gloucester. I don't know what hurts worse; my pride or my swollen ass.'

"Hail to thee, Master!" Kent yelled up (from his encumbered position in the stocks) to his frail, weak King. "It's me; your annoying, humble advisor. Horses' heads are tied by their bridles; dogs and bears are leashed by the neck; monkeys are tethered and controlled by their loins, and punished men are tied and taught punitive lessons by their legs," Kent cryptically uttered. "And my toes and knees are really cold out here, being exposed to the raw elements, most of which are understood and categorized by dumb-fuck university alchemists. My Liege; I still have a fuckin' sense of humor despite by present handicap! Ha, ha, ha!"

"Lord Advisor; who the hell has put you into this embarrassing predicament?" the confused Lear asked as he tripped over a low tree stump, winding-up upon the ground, and then eventually and slowly turning-over and awkwardly rising to his feet.

"Your son-in-law, the Duke of Cornwall, along with your abusive daughter Regan, ordered my punishment," Kent orally conveyed. "Yes Master, the two cretins felt threatened by my sagacity, so the pair of freaks subjected me to this ludicrous, goddamned, ridicule as imperial retribution for my esoteric verbalisms."

"By Jupiter; I can't believe that Regan would do such an unsavory thing to you," Lear incredulously sighed and sobbed.

"By Juno; the vengeful Bitch certainly has!" Kent asserted from his difficult and encumbering stocks' situation. "Your mendacious daughter has defied your sense of justice, My Lord. I attempted to deliver your letters to her, but then this saucy knave, Oswald, I believe, showed-up after being simultaneously dispatched by Goneril and Duke Albany. We got into a boisterous argument, and the next thing I know, I'm confined to stocks and bonds without the aid of a goddamned financial adviser," Kent strenuously protested. "Your daughter and her husband read Goneril's message, and then felt obligated to treat me quite harshly. My Liege; I don't know what hurts me more, my ass or my vain pride? I was perceived and interpreted as being a vile trespasser, and now you're observing the consequence of *their* collective anger."

"I know precisely what the fuck you mean!" Lear ascertained, identifying with Kent's agony while rubbing his own ass. "I could really use a gratifying rub massage from a escort dating service." Then, the fatigued King reflected for a moment and pondered, 'I wonder where the nearest, inexpensive whorehouse is?' "Tell me; Lord Adviser; where is my daughter Regan? She needs a good spanking, although contrary to chauvinistic male dominance, I've heard peculiar illogical reports that Regan viciously spanks and whips Cornwall!"

"Listen to this my Royal Fool!" Kent implored Lear. "The person that serves and seeks gain, and who follows another just for the sake of form instead of for the sake of principle, that person will pack-up when it starts to heavily rain, and then leave you alone to suffer in the storm! If you don't fathom my queer analogy," Kent clarified, "I'm fuckin' speaking about your daughters Regan and Goneril, and their power-hungry, self-indulging husbands, those hazardous Dukes Cornwall and Albany, who are out to pilfer your wealth and power!"

"Where did you learn this pedestrian poetic verse, from the Dead Poet's Club?" Lear sardonically quipped. "But Noble Advisor; there *is* a certain reason in your rhyme that is like a clarion bell ringing true! I trust your lucid judgment, Old Fellow, even if it's contrary to my family genetics and my basic better instincts!"

Lear then entered the Earl of Gloucester's castle, forgetting to hitch Hercules to a post. The petite animal wandered-off into a deep marsh, got bogged-down in the quagmire, and then slowly drowned.

"You want to deny me from speaking to Regan and Cornwall!" the King yelled at the Earl of Gloucester. "And you're now protecting them by lying that the conspirators are sick and weary after their lengthy journey here! Well Earl, I'm sick and tired, too, but I'm fuckin' sick and tired of what the hell's been going on!"

"Well, my Lord, I've personally informed the pernicious Duke and your Daughter Regan, the Duchess, that you've arrived and that you wish to speak with them, and apparently, they don't give a shit, and have elected to remain and dawdle alone in their quarters," Gloucester reluctantly and hesitantly explained.

"I don't care if both the Bitch and the Bastard have fevers of a hundred and twenty degrees; I want to speak with them now!" the lame duck King Lear screamed at Gloucester. "My kingdom is dying, and you tell me that my daughter and her greedy, delinquent, derelict husband are predisposed in their quarters, resting from a grueling ride, after I've ridden my horse several hundred grueling miles to get here? Where the fuck do you think I arrived from, the nearest hinterland village! Tell the two plotting deserters I want to address them now, before I have a massive heart attack, or suffer a colossal stroke!"

"As you like it, Sire!" Gloucester mockingly prattled. "I'll endeavor to fetch your exhausted and fevered daughter and your fatigued and dunce-brained son-in-law from their daily, afternoon, monotonous, amorous, foreplay routine."

Five minutes later, Gloucester escorted Cornwall and Regan into the castle's foyer. Regan addressed her father in a phony voice.

"I'm happy to see Your High Ass, er, I mean Your Highness has safely arrived!" Regan impudently stated. "What's up Pop?"

"Cut the sanctimonious crap!" Lear crazily yelled. "Your sister Goneril has betrayed me, and now I fear that you're mimicking her high-stakes treachery. Regan; give me your full understanding of this unbelievable bullshit that's currently transpiring over in Albany."

"Father Dearest; my well-intentioned sister in her letter I just received has referred to the great chaos being generated throughout the countryside by your impulsive, renegade, whoring knights," Duchess Regan related. "Goneril has not abandoned her obligations, and my sister and her husband will bring discipline and order to their half of your often-bellicose-and-tumultuous kingdom. Your oldest daughter and Albany are not to blame for all of the disorder that prevails throughout the kingdom, but indeed, your recalcitrant, maverick, iconoclastic knights are truly responsible for the disturbing fucked-up crisis flourishing throughout Britain!"

"I curse her a thousand times for her infidelity to my authority," King Lear cynically replied to his second illegitimate daughter. "That eldest Bitch is insolent and defiant to my jurisdiction, and Goneril deserves to be stripped-down naked and mercilessly spanked, and then severely flogged."

"Look, Big Daddy," Regan disrespectfully replied. "You're now quite old and of feeble discretion. I think you owe Goneril an apology. She's straightening-out all of the insurrection in her share of your kingdom, and you, like a complete fool, ride your miniature horse hundreds of miles from Albany to Cornwall to Gloucester, just to further sully her fine name. You big decrepit, senile, despicable Bully! I believe that you should immediately return to Albany and ask, er, I mean beg Goneril for forgiveness."

"I'd rather ask the Devil for a dozen fire-torches and vats of hot sizzling volcanic ash to shove up my ass!" Lear shouted like a zealous maniac. "Now, I realize that I'm old and quite feeble, so I beg you Daughter, to offer me food, lodging, a comfortable bed, and an affectionate harlot to arouse my latent libido, which has been conspicuously missing for several decades now!"

"Return right now to Goneril over at Albany Castle and ask your eldest daughter for food, lodging, a comfortable bed, and an accomplished strumpet hussy!" Regan irreverently hollered and berated her father. "I'm now treating you, Big Daddy, exactly as you had always treated Goneril and me; with absolute disdain and contempt!"

"Your sister has spoken to me with a serpent's tongue, and her words were quite viperous," the perplexed Lear recalled and stated. "Now, I wish such similar revenge and justice on you, daughter

Regan! Both you and Goneril are, without a doubt, dual scheming sisters, vile gorgons, ignorantly conspiring bitches against my rightful power!"

"You have no power, Old Man!" Cornwall yelled. "Your power is as impotent as your dried-up testicles and flaccid dick are!"

"You and Goneril had both viciously lied in your false praise, and also in your fraudulent devotion and loyalty to me," Lear finally realized and accused. "I had bestowed you two hussies with equal portions of my kingdom, and now you show your true colors as my contemptuous, avowed enemies. I had erroneously divided my kingdom between my two unnatural daughters, and have stubbornly ignored my sole legitimate offspring, Cordelia," Lear concluded and anguished. "There really is a lot of truth about fucked-up family genetics, and about the merits of inferior royal traits being biologically transmitted from generation to generation."

Then, unexpectedly, Harvey Lee Oswald swiftly entered the white castle's foyer, and the un-sage herald attempted addressing Regan about Goneril.

"You slithering Varlet; you London barrio Dirt-ball!" Lear screamed at the shocked and surprised Oswald. "This slave tried to assassinate my dear Lord Advisor, who is now confined to stocks and bonds outside this formerly splendid castle. This dolt is a traitor; a dangerous spy!"

"What the fuck are you' ranting about Lear?" Cornwall insisted on comprehending. "A bumbling imbecile makes more sense than you do! You're unfit to be a mentally challenged human being, let alone the supreme King of all Britain!"

"Lady Goneril has just arrived at Castle Gloucester," Oswald announced. "She graces us with her presence."

Leary Lear, momentarily confused by all of the ongoing commotion and pageantry, of outside cornets flourishing, and various attendants quickly gathering, ignored Goneril's appearance in the castle foyer and asked Duke Cornwall why *his* Lord Adviser had been put into stocks and bonds when "knowledgeable Baron Folly" was just a plain ordinary political Adviser, and not even a criminal financial advisor.

"I set him there, my dear Lear, because the Asshole Sophist was making no sense at all arguing with everybody, including poor Oswald from Albany here," Cornwall calmly related. "Your so-called Lord Advisor seemed to be the instigator, and also the cause of all the turmoil occurring outside our kind host Earl of Gloucester's polluted castle, so I took charge of the situation, and brilliantly commanded that the punishment be instantly meted out."

"It was conceited idiots like you that had convicted Christ and then had Him nailed to the cross!" Lear bellowed at Cornwall. "Just because you screw my daughter's beaver like she is a mink, *that* doesn't mean that the two of you have to screw me out of my authority and my cherished throne."

"You're miserably weak and deranged, old, feeble, Father, and nobody listens to your inane bullshit anymore," Regan sternly stated. "Learn to accept those facts and adjust to the new reality."

"You want me to be slave and vassal to these fucked-up men you consort with and perpetually screw," Lear hollered at Regan while inaccurately pointing at Oswald and Gloucester. "I'll not condone being submissive to the illicit decisions of unqualified underlings that have overrun their decision-making boundaries. I don't want to see any more of you two illegitimate, whoring daughters again! I don't know which is worse: bastards like Edmund and Oswald, or bitches like you two defiant, insolent broads! I should've never disowned my precious Cordelia!"

"You have always been too tolerant, too moderate, and too liberal with your knights and servants," Goneril lectured disconsolate King Lear. "And turmoil has flourished like a pestilence throughout your lands, because of your careless lackadaisical attitude. You can't friggin' control Regan and me any longer, because you never controlled your own internal affairs, you unassuming, all-too-trusting, incapable Fool! Father Fuck, that's who you are. You lack benign motivation to improve your nation, but Regan and I, and our covetous husbands. do not lack motives."

"I gave you, my two bitch daughters, everything, and now I have nothing of value left; and no one in my family respects or honors me anymore," the woebegone Lear lamented and complained. "I now know nothing but despair, and I greatly despise *that* terrible, all-too-real abstraction. I should've kept reticent about my estate and given everything to Cordelia, my only candid, and truly loving daughter."

"You're a superfluous, old idiot, who has gone absolutely major cuckoo, you miserable screwball," Regan again belittled her grieving father. "You now aren't worth a copper coin, since you're in *our* custody, and we can dispose of your fat ass however we wish; you sniveling Weasel!"

"I'm full of grief, and wretched in body and spirit, while my wicked, cruel daughters are full of crap, and evil in mind and heart," Lear sobbed, shaking his head in despondency and remorse. "Someday, you two recalcitrant Bitches will be wrinkled old hags with sons or daughters usurping your thrones, and causing massive strife and insurrection within your damned families, and within your damned realms. It'll only be then that you Goneril, and you Regan, will know exactly what anguish and suffering I presently feel."

"Let's withdraw to the castle's interior for a severe storm is approaching, as my reliable, weary, arthritic bones are forecasting," the Duke of Cornwall encouraged all of the guests at the Earl of Gloucester's less-than mediocre castle. "Maybe Lear will get lucky, and a tragic tsunami, or a massive tidal wave will sweep across the plain and wash his carcass right up to Heaven, where ever-vigilant St. Peter will introduce the outrageous fool to Noah! Ha, ha, ha!"

"I want a pedigree horse, and I want to ride out of this dump right now," Lear insisted. "I'll ride and ride until there's finally no violent storm. I'll borrow one of your finest horses Gloucester, and disappear into the night winds, and race the raindrops into oblivion, if necessary. I'm not afraid of a turbulent storm, and some swirling gales! I'm dauntless Lear, King of Britain, and don't any of you dumb bastards and stupid bitches forget that salient fact!"

And with those astounding words, the King opened the castle's front door, and ambled-out into the thunder, lightning, and the very heavy downpour. The soaking-wet pedestrian found an old plow-horse in a nearby barn, amazingly mounted it and then rode-off into the raging bluster.

Drenched by pelting rain, and having severe bronchitis developing into pneumonia, Kent (at noon the following day) was finally released from his stocks and bonds, and then the completely groggy counselor wandered into the mushy heath, accidentally tumbling down a muddy slope, and then plopping into a mire, where the Earl finally almost-drowned in the mucky, six-foot-deep mud.

After trudging out of the nasty swamp a half-hour later, the courageous Earl of Kent (Baron Folly) stubbornly roamed over hill and dale, and across wet meadows, and through crap-laden sheep and cow pastures, until the weary trekker eventually stumbled across a gentleman (too tired to seek shelter), sitting next to a tree on the fringe of a tangled forest, getting saturated also. Soon, a benign conversation ensued.

"Who the hell goes there besides a foul hurricane-type storm?" Kent hoarsely shouted. "Are you animal, vegetable, or human?"

"I'm a follower of King Lear," the gentleman answered as Kent wrapped his arms around his shoulders, and then a quantity of water squirted-out of his garments, as if they were sponges. "I've followed

the King all the way from Gloucester Castle to here, which was a difficult task because Lear was on horseback, not knowing where the fuck he was going, and I was running for many hours on barefoot. I seem to know your voice?"
Lear seemingly recognized a somewhat-familiar voice. "Are you a sit-down comedian? Are you an unemployed sit-down entertainer? How about an unemployed, handicapped, sit-down ventriloquist?"
"I told you that I'm a loyal follower of King Lear and have followed him this far, and because I can't follow him any further, and because of the mean-assed storm, I'll have to wait until tomorrow to find him. Even the wildest of beasts including the wildebeests are huddled together in families this evening, keeping their fur as dry as possible. Just like you, I'm thoroughly drenched, and could right now use a hot bath, a clean shave, and a warm, nsked whore inside a dry hayloft."
"Sir, I do know your voice from somewhere, so I shall share with you some important tidings," Kent intimated to the shivering gentleman, who at that moment didn't give a shit about any news, or pertinent or impertinent details about anyone or anything. "Now Sir; a distinct conflict is forming between the House of Albany and the House of Cornwall, and because of it, I had been put under house arrest in stocks and bonds in the storm for over twenty-four hours," Kent informed the sitting stranger, whom he believed to know by virtue of hearing the man's voice.
"Please tell me more crucial developments," the drenched stranger (Edgar) urged.
"The King of France, because of his connection to King Lear's daughter Cordelia, is sending knights and soldiers to rescue Lear, who might actually be dead by now from either starvation or from sickness. I don't know you from Adam, and I never had the pleasure or displeasure of meeting Adam," Kent stupidly elucidated. "But I'm going to entrust you to travel to the White Cliffs of Dover to convey vital messages and instructions to Cordelia. I'm a man of high breeding and I own seven pedigree dogs, five thoroughbred horses, and one pedigree girlfriend back in Albany, and my natural instincts, which are correct fifty-percent of the time, tell me that you too are a distinguished, eminent man of good breeding," Kent evaluated and declared to the renegade Edgar. "So, whatever you do, Stranger with the familiar voice, don't breed any more chaos throughout King Lear's Britain."
"I need to know more essential information about this fucked-up assignment you're sending me on!" the sitting-in-the-rain stranger

with the familiar voice requested. "Who' the fuck are you? How do I know that this isn't some ornate ruse you've concocted, to have me walk over two-hundred-miles all the way to Dover for nothing! I've never ever been to Dover in my entire goddamned life!"

"It's all quite extraneous for me to explain!" Kent told the stranger with the all-too-familiar voice. "Now, take this leather pouch with the aforementioned documents to Cordelia in Dover, immediately. Show her this ring of nobility that I'm inserting into the pouch, and then Cordelia will know in an instant exactly who has confidentially dispatched you to Dover. Say now, you aren't a petty thief hanging around in this forest in a typhoon, just waiting for your next easy mark to show-up, are you?"

"Give me your fuckin' hand Man," the gay-sounding, sitting-in-the-rain stranger implored. "Your plan is so fucked-up that I just have to participate in it. Have you anything else of interest or of consequence to relate?"

"No!" Kent shouted to Edgar through the heavy cold raindrops. "Now get the hell out of here before I change my mind and perform the sidebar errand to Dover myself. But presently, it's my great task to locate King Lear and see if the senile, inflexible-minded fool is still alive."

Act III

Meanwhile, in another part of the waterlogged, windswept heath, King Lear was physically exhausted, camping-out in the rain without a fire going. Lear was shivering and having a queer conversation with Baron Folly's voice (in his head) that he imagined was not only a real person, but also his trusted Lord Advisor.

"Blow you fierce winds until you've drowned the cocks on top of the steeples, the bats in the belfries, and the cocks of the men screwing their whores and old bat wives in the church belfries," Lear hollered at the howling, dispassionate, apathetic elements. "Singe my whitehead and my blackheads, too! Erode the round Earth, and make it flat, or erode the flat Earth, and make it round; whichever premise is fuckin' happening at the time. I say bust and rupture every man's fertile, hanging balls, and deflate every woman's balloon-sized tits, for all the hell I care!"

"This night has no sympathy or mercy for either wise men or fools, or wise men that are fools, or wise fools that are men," Baron Folly's voice articulated, eerily mesmerizing Lear's concentration.

"Ask for your daughter's blessing, but I'll leave it up to you whether I mean Goneril, Regan, or Cordelia. Oh, valiant and intrepid Lear, on the verge of having a complete mental breakdown, if this inclement downpour were holy water, we'd be the most blessed, lucky, fortuitous assholes in all of Britain."

"If I could, I would tax *you* bitter-cold elements, and also *you,* nasty storm, right into submission, and compel you to pay tribute," Lear lamented and stated to the imaginary Baron Folly (Kent's alter ego). "Pound and beat the shit out of me, for all I fuckin' care! Just give me a break every six-hours or so, in order for me to pull my pants down and take a long shit, or a relieving piss. Oh; what should I do with my two pernicious daughters and their fucked-up Duke husbands?" Lear cried-out to the inhospitable rain. "They'll either tear each other apart on the battlefield like vicious, feuding cats, or will form an alliance to combat the King of France and his minions; and then if victorious, the thieves will start a civil war between their armies. Look at what a mess my old age benevolence has caused."

"You've really fucked-up your kingdom in an admirable way!" Baron Folly's voice registered in Lear's mixed-up cerebrum. "Have you considered suicide as a feasible alternative to what may aptly be described as ultimate failure and rejection?"

"Fuck you, Baron Folly! Fuck you Baron Folly!" Lear deliriously shouted and repeated. "Your warped ass ought to be sodomized all the way from legendary Mt. Everest's summit down to the lowest levels of Hell! A goddamned cunt hair has more intelligence than you do, Folly! Do you hear me Baron! A goddamned cunt hair!"

Kent miraculously stumbled in the torrential rain to the vicinity where Lear was then sitting stationary in the muddy mess, arguing with the imaginary Baron Folly. The nobleman bent-down to examine his pitiful Liege. "Who is there sitting on the soggy ground and leaning against the barren oak tree, having conniptions and delusions during this most severe storm?"

"Oh, it's you again, Baron Folly," and not the barren tree speaking to me, Lear almost listlessly responded, even though he was not reading from any list. "I thought I'd taken you captive in my mind. How the fuck did you escape your incarceration?"

"I'm here to help your suffering ass, even though you strangely perceive me as your adversary," Kent informed his anguishing King. "Neither rain, nor snow, nor sleet, nor hail could keep me from my appointed duty, which at the moment evades my feeble and disintegrating memory. Anyway, King Lear; do you welcome my honorable assistance, or will you shun me as Goneril and Regan have likewise ostracized you?"

"Get me out of this blasted mud puddle, Man," Lear commanded Kent. "How am I to know whether or not I've pissed my pants if my clothes are all fuckin' wet? There's more mud on my grimy ass than on all the goddamned ground around me!"

Kent struggled and lifted Lear up off the saturated turf, and stared his weak Master directly in the eyes. "Kind King; a very unique Kind King; please listen to my entreaty that there is no treaty between Britain and France. In the meantime, your entire kingdom is in disarray with an intense power struggle going on between Albany and Cornwall and their wives; who happen to be your two older daughters, not to mention that your party animal knights that are running amok all over the fuckin' land. All of this fucked-up mania and frenzy is *your* responsibility to resolve."

"I'm too cold and old to even think, piss or shit," Lear confided to his devoted aide, "and my renegade two older daughters have defied my will, and have banished me, but I can't do shit about it. I'm now a senile Old Fuck, once a smart young buck!"

"Your wit is just a little temporarily dampened," Kent encouraged his discouraged King. "But I shall rehabilitate you without initiating any elaborate, physical therapy. I shall reconstruct your spirit and give you a dynamic outlook on life that you haven't experienced in many moons, or in many exposed male or female assholes."

"Are you sure you're not some sort of misguided heretic, or pagan agnostic?" Lear asked his loyal, royal Lord Advisor. "There are enough hedonistic barbarian pagans over in Germany, let alone those invading cowardly gay voyeurs from France. Who the hell did Cordelia link-up with anyway?"

"Politics and circumstances make strange bedfellows, indeed!" Kent affably agreed. "And strange bed ladies too, if I may add!"

* * * * * * * * * * *

Meanwhile, the Earl of Gloucester and Edmund were conversing in a secret room (designed for sharing secrets) inside the Earl's in-need-of-repair castle. Gloucester was bitching about recent shenanigans going on in his revered-but-mediocre domicile.

"I'll tell you Edmund what's really pissing me off," the disgusted Earl began his litany/tirade. "The Dukes of Cornwall and Albany, and their spoiled-rotten wives, won't allow me to speak anything of King Lear in *my* own castle, let alone utter polite words about the monarch's extraordinary character. Lear is a good fellow who allowed too much chicanery and hanky-panky to go on during his faltering regime," the Earl of Gloucester related to his bastard son, who didn't give a shit about what the old fart was saying. "And then no one budged a finger to prevent Lear from wandering-out into the relentless storm. That's gratitude for you Edmund. I know you'd never plot anything so despicably treacherous against me, as Lear's seditious daughters have done against him!"

"No Sir; I don't have a dishonest finger on my feet!" Edmund jested and lied. "Honesty is the best policy, even when you don't have any goddamned life insurance!"

"Now here's a secret that you mustn't share with anyone," Gloucester whispered to Edmund in a low voice, although no one else was within two-hundred-feet of their private conversation in the locked-room. "Not only are Albany and Cornwall about to start a damaging civil war right here in Gloucester Castle. The greedy knuckleheads are quarreling over Lear's kingdom, but also, I've received a letter outlining how Cordelia, with the help of the French King and his faggot army and navy, are about to invade Britain and kick all of our asses all the way up to Scotland," Gloucester told Edmund. "Then, Lear will, by a stroke of amazing fortune, take back his kingdom by default, so that he could then surrender Britain to Cordelia, his only legitimate daughter. You must remember, Edmund; bastards always lose in the end because they're basically dumb-ass buffoons; fucked-up sons-of-bitches to begin with!"

"Yes Father, I'll always perish, er, I mean cherish that thought," Edmund flattered Gloucester in a similar manner that Goneril and Regan had falsely praised King Lear. "When the old stalwarts fall and/or die, the young rise to the occasion, but in that regard, they automatically rise to power. Thanks Pop, for informing me of what's going on in Britain, since I'm too narrow-minded, and too stupid, and too lazy to observe and interpret it all by myself. Your fucked-up secrets are safe with your low-intelligence bastard son. I guarantee it! Is it true that Cornwall wants to start a university for pedophiles and have it named after himself?"

* * * * * * * * * * * *

Back in the blustery mini-hurricane, Kent led Lear to a man-made hovel and requested that the King enter the improvised shelter to be afforded a degree of protection from the pelting rain. Rather than quickly going inside, the king preferred to engage in trite dialogue.

"Here's the hovel I was telling you about, Sire," Kent pointed-out to the half-dazed and fully crazed Lear. "It'll offer a bit of soothing insulation from this tyrant of a storm."

"Baron Folly," Lear stated, incidentally mistaking the Earl of Kent for the advisor's impersonated self. "This unprecedented, ferocious land-tempest is a worse tyrant than that ancient despot Nebuchadnezzar ever was. And besides, this very soggy entrance isn't exactly the portal to my imperial palace, now, is it?"

"Beggars can't be choosy, even when they are kings, earls or barons, my dear Lear," Kent emphasized. "Now get the hell in there before we both turn into fish or crustaceans, or some other kinds of all wet, fucked-up, aquatic animals!"

"The tempests in my mind and those raging in my heart are more tremendous than this natural phenomenon that's enveloping our abused asses," Lear figuratively expressed in a magnificent metaphor. "And I shall weep no more because no one including you, kind Baron, will be able to see my tears with ten-million rain drops ricocheting against my face, beading upon and presently cascading-down my forehead and cheeks. Goneril and Regan deserve to be out here in this abandoned hovel, and not sitting comfortably in Gloucester's inferior, poorly-constructed castle. Where is the fuckin' justice in this convoluted world?"

"Lear, please just duck-down into this improvised nest that seems like a duck blind, and then slide your huge anatomy inside," Kent impatiently advised, since that was his primary function. "And My Liege, don't tell me I'm still wet behind the ears because I'm fuckin' wet all over!"

"Go in first, Baron Folly, for I have the stamina and the tenacity to outlast this old persistent windbag we call Mother Nature," Lear exhorted. "I'll stay out here and pray for heavenly justice for my plight, and then I'll sleep standing-up, if I have to."

"I wish you lots of luck while implementing that silly method, My Liege!" the realist Kent remarked. "You can catch the flu out here despite the unavailability of any chimneys flying around. I'm going to crawl inside this hovel, and if *you'* Sire wish to become drenched through-and-through, then that's your moronic bad decision to stay outside with the inclement elements."

"This relentless storm is being sent by Heaven as a sign of what will soon transpire in my kingdom through either civil war, or by French invasion," Lear yelled to Kent inside the hovel during a rare moment of mental clarity. "That's why the storm is so savage and incessant! It's a supernatural omen communicating to me what's going to happen with my kingdom."

"Get your corpulent, farting, fanny fully inside the makeshift shelter, you garrulous, stubborn Asshole!" Kent screamed. "Must you grovel near my hovel'. Say now Lear, there's somebody else inside this fucked-up primitive skunk's hut with me! Don't come completely inside Lear, until I determine if this anonymous clown is dead or alive; is friend or foe."

"Who the hell is it?" the King yelled. "Is it a man or a woman; a gay or a straight? I think you're just imagining that the damp smelly straw is talking to you Folly."

"He says his name is Tom, but don't worry Lear," Kent hollered through the torrential downpour. "He has no last name, so you don't have to worry about it being Foolery."

"Get away from me, you stinking itinerant mendicants!" Tom (Edgar on the lam) acerbically yelled at Kent and Lear. "You foul, reeking Fiends! If you nothing-to-offer Piss-Heads weren't so goddamned destitute, you could confer upon me some charity."

"This indigent man has a blanket Lear, so stop being an obstinate wet blanket yourself and come over here," Kent loudly and jubilantly articulated.

"May faults and curses descend on his two eldest daughters," the thoroughly-puzzled Lear preached while substituting Tom (Edgar) for himself. "There's treachery and evil in every goddamned family, rich or poor."

"Tom says he's not married and has no daughters, Sire," Kent answered from inside the poorly-fabricated shelter. "So, this Tom chap doesn't give a shit about your mammoth family dilemma. He ingeniously claims that a female for a wife or girlfriend is enough of a curse, without any next generation offspring of the lady gender permanently ruining and dooming his life."

"Your elderly companion standing in the heavy rain outside this mansion is an absolute loon," Tom (Edgar) mentioned to Kent (Baron Folly). "The unkempt man looks, pardon the expression, a little under the weather! He also looks like a veritable madman; a fucked-up madman becoming madder and madder by the second. But he's right about one thing. There is little or no justice in this world, and pray tell, the next life might be even more fucked-up than this one is!"

"Who speaks this wisdom that my ears perceive?" Lear asked. "Are you Socrates or Plato reincarnated? Say Baron Folly; did the Earl of Gloucester build this fucked-up hovel all by himself?"

"I've led a decent life, loved my father, was always obedient; ate my spinach and broccoli; said my prayers; went to bed early; avoided brothels and inns, and look where the fuck it's gotten me," Tom (Edgar) bitched and moaned. "I've been banished from my title, and must stay out here in the boondocks as a crabby hermit; eating mice, rats, and for a feast, an occasional groundhog. All of this because I've been disowned in favor of my dastardly bastardly, brother!"

"It's a sad day indeed when illegitimacy ascends to power, and it manages to trump legitimacy," Kent acknowledged and agreed. "I do sincerely believe, young Tom, that first of all, you're not a Peeping Tom, and secondly, that fate has brought my Master and me to this about-to-collapse hovel to make your fine acquaintance, and to lay the groundwork for *our* future collaboration. Does that far-fetched theory make any fucked-up sense to you?"

"Baron Folly; don't make friends with this callow, churlish upstart philosopher until I quiz the dopey fool on some fundamental scientific matters," Lear ordered his Lord Advisor. "Tell me young Aristotle; what causes thunder to happen?" Lear asked as a bolt of lightning and then a loud boom shattered a nearby tree, scaring the hell out of the three stranded individuals.

"That's a rather easy question," Tom (Edgar) eagerly replied. "It's Jupiter farting loudly after releasing a colossal-sized lightning bolt from his gigantic erect dick."

"That's quite an impressive answer," Lear marveled and uttered as he tottered and leered near the wobbly hovel's crude entrance. "Now what particular fields of study do you specialize in?"

"The methods of identifying the fiend and how to trap and kill vermin in order to survive out here in the lonely wilderness," Tom (Edgar) ecstatically answered. "I'm sort of like a contemporary John the Baptist, who specialized in eating locusts!"

"I have one more pertinent inquiry to make of you," Lear informed Tom (Edgar). "Are you a virgin?"

"Yes, I am!" Tom (Edgar) exclaimed with pride. "I am a virgin, even though I've never had my period, and don't rightly know if I have a cherry to be busted, or a vagina to be penetrated."

"Great!" Lear stated in full accord with Tom's response. "Fie, fi, fo, fum, I smell the blood of a British man! As soon as this blasted tempest subsides, you, young Tom, can assist my associate Baron Folly and me on a very crucial mission. If you like getting your ass kicked, then you'll be in rare totally excellent company! I've always professed that fucked-up people mutually deserve each other's fucked-up company!"

* * * * * * * * * * * *

When the violent storm finally diminished the following morning, the contemptuous Edmund visited the Duke of Cornwall and gave the Royal One false information concerning *his* father, the kind-hearted Earl of Gloucester. Cornwall was receptive to the nefarious power-hungry traitor after the pair had clandestinely met in a chamber inside the Earl of Gloucester's very ordinary-but-deteriorating castle.

"Give me some news that'll allow me to have revenge on someone; on anyone," Cornwall strangely instructed his power-hungry subordinate. "Edmund, give me some useful information that I could use to destroy my enemies, whoever they may be."

"My brother Edgar, as you know, possesses an evil disposition and covets my father's estate and territories," Edmund lied to the Duke of Cornwall, who happened to already govern over all of the Earl of Gloucester's estate and territories, but who also coincidentally yearns for Lear's entire kingdom. "Now in this letter I'm holding, Edgar expresses that he's a staunch ally of France, and that my evil brother plans to commit a treasonous act against *you* Cornwall, and also against Britain. If my asshole, iniquitous, half-brother was any more good-hearted, Edgar would be a felon! This letter intercepted from *his* possession officially makes Edgar not a phantom enemy of ours, but a villainous traitor!"

"Come with me to the Duchess so that we could discuss this important matter in detail," Cornwall suggested to Edmund. "If all this bullshit is true, my forces would have to be allied with Albany's soldiers and knights to wage war against the French aggressors trespassing onto Britain's sacred soil. Get ready, Edmund, for a turf war on our own turf. And if Britain will be lucky enough to win the war," Cornwall told the bastard; "then quite obviously, my prick brother-in-law, Duke Albany, and I can duke it out over who controls all the mediocre bullshit happening on this side of the *English Channel*. That's one reason why France cannot win, for then the body of water would be called the French Channel, and we can't let that crap happen. And furthermore Edmund," the Duke of Cornwall elaborated. "If I could emerge triumphant in these impending struggles, then I could alternate between screwing Goneril and Regan while Albany is sitting tied in a chair panting with his damned two-foot-long tongue hanging-out."

"Then you're the new Earl of Gloucester by default, once your father is apprehended and conveniently disposed of," Cornwall finished his now-delighted protégé's statement.

"I pledge my loyalty to you, Duke Cornwall, and to the glorious future of Britain," Edmund falsely vowed with his left hand held over his appendix. "Furthermore, I'll even generously contribute to the construction of your new pedophile university!"

"I trust you Edmund, and would like to be your substitute father once we defeat the French, vanquish Albany, and imprison your old man Gloucester," the Duke of Cornwall lied. Next, I'll adopt you as my heir, because you and I Edmund, share plenty of similarities, both in our characters and in our personalities."

* * * * * * * * * * * *

Kent, Lear and Tom (Edgar) exited the hovel two days later, when the weather finally cleared, and then the fatigued nobles hobbled their way to one of Gloucester's remote outbuildings that stunk like feces. Kent found the Earl of Gloucester leaving the crap-shack, and asked permission for Lear and him to stay and hang-out for a while. Benign Gloucester gave the men *his* consent, and promptly returned inside his in-need-of-repair castle to try and figure-out why he had ever left it in the first place.

"What kind of stench-odor dump is this? This disaster looks familiar to me!" Tom (Edgar) asked his companions in a dissatisfied tone of voice. "Fiends and murderers should have such a fate as this, and not reputable assholes like us."

"Lear, do you suppose that a madman can be a gentleman or a yeoman?" Kent asked his King while ignoring Tom's (Edgar's) vehement protest.

"A King! A King!" Lear answered. "All Kings are fucked-up, despite the fact that most don't start out that way. And all yeomen are fucked-up too, but not so much as monarchs and their inbred families are. And our whole planet is entirely fucked-up also because all of its human inhabitants are self-centered dolts and practicing assholes. Wasn't *that* conclusion a clever redundancy, Lord Folly and Tom Foolery, ha, ha, ha."

"You're a pathetic Madman!" Tom (Edgar) exclaimed to Lear. "A pathetic Madman, I say! Several rungs higher on the psychology ladder, and you'd be labeled insane!"

"I invite you two colleagues to sit-down in my court as I judiciously mete-out justice," Lear commanded Kent and Edgar. "We'll just pretend that these smelly, shit-covered straw mounds are soft velvet cushions. You two Nincompoops can be my panel of auxiliary judges. I shall arraign Goneril first. The Bitch is charged with kicking her father, the King of Britain, off his property. Say Guys; this meaningless prosecution bullshit is fun!"

"Goneril is guilty as charged and convicted of treason!" Kent and Edgar enthusiastically and simultaneously shouted.

"And here may I present Regan," Lear proceeded with his weird theatrical prosecution. "And her heart is full of corruption and lust for material gain. Her surface emotions are false and contrived, and her garbage statements of love and devotion to her father are all counterfeit and hollow. Regan is a vile, vicious snake whose husband desires to be king; yes, King Cobra is his name; that lunatic cornball scoundrel from Cornwall."

"Regan only loves mammon, and the witch is guilty as charged and hereby convicted of treason!" Kent and Edgar boisterously declared in unmelodic unison.

"Now that your official business has been commendably conducted," Edgar said to the disillusioned Lear, "allow Baron Folly the privilege of drawing the curtain (shut the barn's door) so that you may get some much-needed sleep."

When Kent stepped to the door to shut it, the Earl was confronted by Gloucester, who anxiously inquired about his tarnished King's safety. "He's over here, Earl," Kent indicated by pointing. "But I would not initiate conversation with poor Lear because I believe him to be somewhere between daffy and daft. Our Liege is comfortably resting, and it's a major miracle that the fellow ever survived the hostile storm out in the bitter open while staying in a decaying hovel," Kent related to Gloucester. "Yesterday, the King was barking and meowing all over the place because Our Liege actually believed it was raining cats and dogs."

"Perhaps Lear is pursuing a career to become a ventriloquist. But it's too bad for the fragile royal liberal," Gloucester mildly empathized. "There're all kinds of plots evolving in this castle that not only threaten the King, but *his* entire beloved Britain as well. Wake Lear up at once, and take the raunchy dozer to Dover where you'll be welcomed and given protection by Cordelia and the foreign king's army of French kissers, er, I mean French soldiers. I'll show you the way. but that's all the hell you can expect out of me at the present," Gloucester related to Kent. "I don't like fighting because I think it's basically cowardly, immature, and juvenile behavior, and that's why every bully in my youth beat the living shit out of me. Now then, Kent," Gloucester continued without ever recognizing his own son Edgar standing next to *his* old friend. "Cornwall must not learn of the three of you hiding-out in this dirty, stinking, malodorous, barn, so I recommend that you evacuate right this instant. And besides, I don't want to get my ass kicked by a big bully, who incidentally kicked the feces out of my ass on the royal playground when nasty Cornwall was a little six-year-old potential bully."

"King Lear! My King Lear!" Kent screamed as the Earl shook his superior's shoulders and aroused him from his deep snoring. "Sorry to wake you after only ten-minutes of rest, but we have to get the hell out of here right now!"

After Lear, Kent and Edgar fled Gloucester Castle's primitive-looking barn (all of the guards in the palace's ramparts were drunk, sleeping, or getting laid), Cornwall, Regan, Goneril, and Edmund got together inside the dilapidated fort for an impromptu strategy session.

"My dear sister-in-law," Cornwall said to Goneril. "Return to Albany at once, and show your fuzzy-minded husband this letter of paramount importance. The French army has landed, and part of their mission is to steal and fry all of our potatoes. Find that traitor, the Earl of Gloucester, who is accused of aiding and abetting our prime enemies, King Lear and Burgandy, the potential French monarch. Gloucester must hang! I don't mean the city, but I do mean Edmund's betraying old man."

"Pluck the shit-head's eyes right out of their sockets and hang Gloucester from the highest oak tree," Regan chanted three times until everyone finally understood her thoughts. "The Earl deserves the worst of early painful deaths! Too bad Gloucester can only die once, the lucky, old wimpy son-of-a-bitch!"

"Edmund, keep Goneril company while Regan and I seek immediate revenge on that no-good prick Gloucester," Cornwall imperatively ordered, as Goneril glimpsed-down at the center of Edmund's tights and noticed his sausage-like apparatus coiled around three times like a long snake resting. "Farewell Goneril and Edmund, and don't do anything that Regan and I wouldn't do!"

Before Cornwall and Regan could exit the throne chamber, Oswald, Goneril's servant and paramour, entered the room all out-of-breath to make an official announcement. "Thirty-six of Albany's knights had met the determined Duke at *his* castle's gate, and then the posse's horses quickly galloped-off in the direction of Dover. Of course, there are several hundred villages and towns between Albany and Dover, but I presume that's where the fuck they're heading." Then, Oswald noticed the tremendous bulge in Edmund's tights and began rubbing his own genitals.

"Oswald; instruct my handlers to get horses prepared for journey; have the steeds ready for Duchess Regan and myself," Cornwall austerely directed. "What are you doing staring that way at Edmund?" the agitated Duke chastised Oswald. "Are you a gay faggot son-of-a-bitch, or what?"

Goneril, Edmund, and Oswald departed the Gloucester Castle throne conference room to have a three-way interlude, while Cornwall and Regan discussed their anticipated vengeance against the now-targeted Earl of Gloucester, along with their upcoming expedition to Dover. The Duke and the Duchess were extremely peeved and vindictive as the pair reviewed current events and contemporary foes.

"I'm going to have Gloucester's nuts ground into sawdust," Cornwall told his wife. "Regan, you never saw dust like the saw-dust I'm going to manufacture from that two-faced, double-crossing, dirty bastard's shriveled-up testicles."

Just then the Earl of Gloucester, who had stupidly stayed at his castle rather than fleeing to Dover with Edgar, Kent and King Lear, entered the dimly lit, Lilliputian-sized throne conference chamber.

"It's the goddamned Traitor in the flesh!" the Duke of Cornwall bellowed when Regan's husband recognized his doomed host. "Grab this old Fuck-head's left arm Regan, and we'll wrestle this feeble old derelict to the floor without a prolonged tussle."

"You craven, ungrateful, Slime-ball!" Regan yelled at the aged Earl of Gloucester as the ambitious woman strenuously twisted his left arm and shoulder, bringing the abused old fart to the stone floor.

"You're my guests, so stop administering all of this pain attacking your benign host like two out-of-control Viking barbarians," Gloucester protested from the hard cold floor. "Why all of this foul play? Is this some new kind of sado-masochism? If so, I don't relish it one damned bit! It's too goddamned rough on my torso!"

"Bind him!" the Duke of Cornwall yelled to two guards that had just entered the conference room. "Bind his bowels, too, so the scheming bastard can't shit anymore! Bind him while I blind him!"

"You filthy, Old Fart Traitor!" Regan screamed and repeated while the Duchess repeatedly kicked Gloucester in the scrotum two dozen times. "This double hernia is exclusively for you! And it doesn't matter if I kick you from your blind side, because both of your disloyal eyes have just been gouged-out by my tyrannical husband, the Duke of Cornwall."

"Bind the blind imbecile and his raunchy ass to this poorly constructed chair!" Cornwall boomed to his guards, who were primarily Gloucester's mercenary guards to begin with. "And then you can look for his miniature balls rolling-around somewhere on the slate floor."

"I don't mind you kicking me in the testicles, but keep your slimy, grimy hands off my beard," Gloucester screamed at his attackers, as the sadists eagerly tethered the now-blinded hostage to a flimsy chair. "You can ruffle all my feathers, but leave my motherfuckin' chin hairs alone!"

"Come now, Gloucester; the game part of our little intriguing interview is over," Cornwall summarized. "If you value your life, you'll tell Duchess Regan and me the exact contents of the secret letters Lear had recently received from Cordelia in France."

"Be succinct and answer candidly and bluntly," Regan added. "For Earl Gloucester, we already know the damned truth, and are only in quest of verification. Answer us our inquiries now, or suffer more excruciating torture!"

"I had a letter in my possession from one that had a neutral heart, and not from one that regards himself or herself as your enemy," Gloucester diplomatically replied without disclosing any particulars.

"Okay Gloucester; that was cute, cunning and evasive," Cornwall evaluated and expressed. "The letter was from Cordelia, telling of the French landing on our shores, somewhere near Dover. This we already know from local scuttlebutt. Where have you sent the King? To Hell I hope!"

"To Dover!" Gloucester screamed as the Duke of Cornwall unmercifully squeezed what remained of the Earl's sensitive gonads. "To Dover!" the blinded victim loudly and tearfully reiterated.

"Tell me why 'to Dover', you blind Bastard, or I'll flip the chair over, step on your face, and then have Duchess Regan lift her dress, kneel-down, and suffocate you with her smelly, lice-infected cunt!"

"Help me my servants and guards!" Gloucester futilely shouted. "I don't want to suffocate! Help me I say! I don't mind being blinded, but I absolutely detest being smothered to death by raunchy-smelling pussy that I can't even see!"

"Fuck you, Old Man!" a formerly loyal guard exclaimed at the extremely bruised and frustrated Gloucester. "Your ass will turn into your brain, before I'll ever come to your fuckin' aid!"

But another foolish guard (enraged that Gloucester had been blinded) charged Cornwall, and a brief sword fracas ensued. The protesting guard was run through-and-through and killed, and during the brief combat, Cornwall had sustained a severe wound.

"Edmund will help me!" Gloucester pleaded. "Where is he?"

"You futilely call for the one that hates you even more than we despise do," Regan reproached the Earl. "Edmund doesn't give a flying fuck about you, now that he's allied and in-tight with Duke Cornwall and me."

"Guards, carry this blinded jerk-off outside, untie him from his bondage, throw him upon the dung pile, and then let the Old Fart either suffocate in pig and horse shit, or smell his way to Dover," Cornwall ordered.

Act IV

Edgar, his mind in a dismal quandary, was out on the heath searching for an imaginary heathen named Heather, while blind Gloucester was also out on the heath where he soon met an old heathen named Heathro. By coincidence, the blind Earl of Gloucester (Heathro) (somehow accompanied by the implacable Earl of Kent) encountered *his* disowned son in a thick mist without the foggiest idea of what was actually happening.

"Who comes here out in no man's land?" Edgar wondered and yelled. Then, Edgar considered, 'The taller, gaunt, old asshole looks like my curmudgeon Father, who had disowned me in favor of that no-good bastard Edmund!'

"Oh, Good Man," Heathro (Kent's new identity) greeted as Edgar was shouting curses and expletives in the distance. "I've been your tenant and your father's tenant living in one of your tenement houses for many years; fourscore and seven I believe. Am I being presumptuous in thinking that you don't recognize me?"

"Get away, Heathro," Gloucester moaned to the tenement tenant heathen heaving heavy air on the heath. "Fine material comforts can do me no good any longer, and when I decipher what the hell I just said, I'll be able to explain my perception of reality better. What the fuck's going-on that my mind cannot fathom?"

"You're blind my Lord, and can't see a blessed thing," Heathro (Kent) observed and volleyed. "And because it's so fuckin' foggy out here, I might as well be blind, too, because I can't see a damned fuckin' thing either! All I see is a vague figure in the distance with a very familiar haunting voice."

"I'm lost in life dear Heathro, so what the hell do I need eyes for?" the blind Earl of Gloucester uttered to Kent, while being swamped in despair, even though they were conversing on the heath. "I sense by that beckoning I hear that we're approaching another suffering, lost human being. Oh my God! The horrific distant odor smells like my son Edgar! It's almost as if my nostrils have eyes!"

'Oh shit!' Edgar reckoned. 'I definitely know that old coot! Of all the miserable people in Britain to run into in this God forsaken place! If I were in my right mind, I'd kill the no-good bastard,' Edgar angrily thought. 'He must be a no-good bastard just like Edmund is, since *he* disowned me and favored my crazy, genetically inferior bastard half-brother. This chance meeting is the absolute pits, and I'm not thinking about my damned underarms either.'

"Are you a lost beggar or pilgrim?" Heathro (Kent) asked as the itinerant Earl squinted his eyes while holding his left hand to his brow in the thick mist and fog. Then, Heathro addressed blind Gloucester. "Probably this person is a crazy man and a tramp, too, if he's like everyone else in this remote hick sector of Britain. If anyone possessing a cerebrum had any common sense, that idiot would've stayed home after such a howling, mother-humping, three-day-long rainstorm. But unfortunately, in the whole of England, common sense is not too common."

"Ah, Heathro; I tell you this man might be a beggar now, but yesterday his name was indeed a particular Tom Foolery, and his voice *is* certainly a match for my disloyal son Edgar," the totally bewildered, disenfranchised blind Earl of Gloucester maintained. "I believe my exhausted brain is turning into wiggling, wriggling worms! This might sound like some alien mumbo-jumbo, Heathro, but everything swimming around inside my head is one big, jumbo jumble! Edgar is up to his old tomfoolery, as either himself, or as that all-too-tricky rascal Tom Foolery."

'This incredible scenario I'm witnessing looks like the blind leading the blind. But I've finally come to realize that anger and revenge don't contribute to solving anything,' Edgar benignly surmised and concluded. 'Perhaps I should try thinking morally and logically for a change, just like the fucked-up priests and ministers preach. An ordinary son would murder the old son-of-a-bitch on the spot, but I pity the senile old geezer, and feel sorrow for him, even though a more rational, vengeful son, in this particular circumstance, would contemplate more gruesome consequences. In a similar situation, I'm quite certain that Edmund would draw his dagger and start daggering, of *that* assault I'm very sure!'

"Are you heading to Dover?" Gloucester asked his disowned, legitimate son. "I understand that the peasants and the yeomen have beautiful White Cliffs there."

"Did you say Rover?" Edgar intentionally asked to further confuse his father. "I see that you still remember my old mongrel dog."

"No Son, or Tom Foolery, or whoever else you may be," Gloucester rankled, "I had asked you, my fellow heath trekker; are you heading for Dover, for that is *our* destination."

"Perhaps I can merry myself by traveling several-hundredmiles out of the way to Dover, just to have something different to do," Edgar cheerlessly stated. "Yes, I'll gladly accompany you on your fanciful ramble. I've read some fictional stories about that strange place on the *English Channel,* and those queer tales were real cliffhangers!"

"Good! Excellent!" Heathro (Kent) exclaimed. "Right now, my blind companion is dreaming of how he could go from rags to riches. I'll go and fetch, or maybe steal, my friend here some decent apparel so that he doesn't look like such a penniless mendicant who doesn't have two bronze coins to rub together."

After Heathro (Kent) scurried off to either find Gloucester some presentable clothes, or disappear into oblivion altogether, the discouraged Earl and his estranged son engaged in a meaningful conversation.

"Do you know the way to the White Cliffs of Dover?" the father inquired of the estranged stranger. "I don't know if I have the strength and the vitality to finish my arduous trip there, but I'm driven by two psychological needs: First I'd like to see King Lear again, even though I'm fuckin' blind; and secondly, I'd like to end my life by jumping off a high cliff, and to tell you the goddamned truth, I don't even give a shit if it's white or not!"

"I've already specifically told you, Old Man, that I intend to journey to Dover with you and your insane associate, and maybe kick some ass or get my own ass kicked upon arriving there," Edgar frankly responded. "Isn't that what life's about, Father? Self-preservation and advancement at the expense of others?"

"Good!" Gloucester exclaimed, without exactly realizing what his rejected son had just articulated. "Very good then! Being young and strong, you'll probably be able to get to our mutual destination before me. Now Young Man; take this purse to Dover; meet-up with King Lear and Lady Cordelia, and present it to them. And please enjoy being my disinherited messenger, in addition to being my disowned Son; er, I mean disenfranchised brother; or whatever the hell you are to me, that I had meant to say."

"Thank you very much, my ball-breaking Father!" Edgar ungratefully acknowledged while accepting the important purse. "I'll certainly present the contents to either King Lear, or to his daughter Cordelia, once I get there ahead of you, if I ever get there."

"Upon my arrival to the coast, bring me to the highest and whitest cliff in Dover," Gloucester begged and instructed his legitimate son. "I'll jump off that high mother, despite the fact that it isn't leap year! I don't want my inglorious, suicidal end to be any ordinary goddamned melodramatic cliffhanger!"

* * * * * * * * * * *

Goneril and Edmund the Bastard soon arrived on horseback (actually two horsebacks) at the Duke of Albany's magnificent castle/palace. The new arrivals were welcomed by Harvey Lee Oswald, the Steward, who was really stewing over the newly-found friendship of Edmund with the Duke's flirtatious (and then some) promiscuous wife.

"Where's my husband?" Goneril asked Oswald. "I don't see him swimming in the moat with his pet crocodiles, or are those reptiles imported alligators?"

"I had told your spouse of the French army landing, and Albany said that flying ships haven't been invented yet, or some stupid shit like that," the jealous Harvey Lee answered. "And then, I told him that you were coming, and Albany revealed that you were a sexual pervert, and that you're always coming, either when awake or in your sleep," the horny Steward recounted to Goneril. "And when I related to your husband the Duke about the Earl of Gloucester's disloyalty, and about Edmund's faithful service, your husband called me 'a bungling blockhead', even though, as you can plainly see, my head is perfectly shaped; round and not cubed. I really suspect that your spouse's stated fucked-up, reverse logic description is actually intentional reverse psychology, custom-designed and enunciated to piss me off."

"That's the way my spiteful husband behaves when he's jealous and envious of someone hitting on me," promiscuous Goneril informed Oswald. "Now Edmund; I want you to go back to Cornwall to see if he's been mortally wounded by another mortal. Right this moment, I must pacify my husband, and pretend I love him to get him out of his deep melancholy," Goneril instructed and explained. "As you ride back to Cornwall, staying over at Gloucester Castle, remember the sweetness of my juicy pussy, and for the time being, forget all about Cornwall being a dumpy town elsewhere in Britain."

"Madam, I'd better get the fuck out of here because here comes your mercurial-tempered husband now with a heavy frown encumbering his face," Edmund observed and stated. "I'd better take-off despite the fact that flying ships have not yet been invented as your husband has often objectively testified. That guy's even smarter than either of us had ever given him credit for being."

Edmund sallied forth in a heartbeat, and his steed quickly galloped off over the nearest knoll. Goneril then dismounted her mare, and approached Albany with the intent of stealing the thunder from his stormy disposition by endeavoring to confuse her bed-mate.

"When we were first married, you would run out to greet me," Goneril bitched. "But now I must kowtow to you at every moment. Are you screwing another woman, or are you pumping and sodomizing a whole bevy of other whoring hussies? Tell me, my unfaithful Husband!"

"Goneril, how long have you been practicing this preposterous speech?" Albany questioned his wife. "I have a feeling that what you're accusing me of, in reality, is what you've been guilty of. I comprehend all about reverse psychology too, you know! I've heard from reliable sources that over the years, there've been more dicks inside you than there are Richards in all of Britain!"

"You're an uncouth, milk-livered, grotesque monster with juice-less testicles!" Goneril snapped-back, intentionally belittling Albany's manhood. "France is invading our beloved homeland, and you're feeling insecure about me getting laid outside of wedlock, and about you not being able to satisfy any eager beaver in my absence. Petty Husband; I want you to understand that you have no monopoly on my sweet pussy, whether we're married or not!"

"You're a whoring, fiendish Bitch!" Albany hoarsely yelled. "A whoring, treacherous, fiendish Calypso, who incidentally gives tremendous deep throat blow-jobs, but unfortunately. to any and all sex-starved men! That's why I'm both envious and jealous of all of your myriad amorous, extra-curricular activities! You're the Devil's Advocate masquerading in a goddamned curvaceous woman's body; a goddamned, very sexy, curvaceous woman's body at that!"

A gay servant entered the castle's foyer, and with a lisp-voice, announced some additional negative news to the already-infuriated Duke. The oral communication described the Duke of Cornwall's death from wounds received from a sword fight with a common knave, and also, there was (on the other hand) secondary news confirming that the Earl of Gloucester had been blinded.

"These felony crimes must be avenged!" Albany bellowed. "At least Cornwall's premature birth, er, I mean death, ought to be!" the infuriated Duke corrected himself while gleefully hypothesizing that, with Cornwall out of the picture, the Duke of Albany could now easily become the next King of England. "I insist that justice for Cornwall must be rendered!"

"Are you fuckin' crazy?" Goneril skeptically criticized. "Your country is being invaded; you stand to lose your royal title, along with your regal lands, and you say you want revenge on a scumbag lowlife that killed Cornwall? What am I saying? I'm actually calling poor dead Cornwall, my former brother-in-law, a lowlife scoundrel, too! And I thought that only you, Husband, were fucked-up and drunk with ambition!"

"This letter from your sister Regan might provide additional crazy information," the messenger told Goneril as the courier handed the Duchess a confidential report.

"I'll read this letter in private," Goneril said to her mentally (emotionally) unstable husband. "I'm certain that my sister Regan is quite sorrowful about being an instant widow, and the widow may be a bit sad that Gloucester's eyes have been plucked-out, and now the Old Coot can't practice his notorious voyeurism on her anymore. Such tart news is making my pussy turn sour, and I can feel my love cave shriveling-up! I must seek requiem, Husband, and share my sister's grief in spite of the fact that the country is being invaded by the horny, affectionate, long-dicked, bisexual Frenchmen! I emphatically say now; hurry-up with the goddamned conquest!"

Before leaving the castle's foyer to scamper to a private room, Goneril thought about her present state of affairs for a moment. 'To hell with that lowly knave Oswald, and my roguish, aristocratic husband Albany! Oh shit!' the distraught Duchess considered. 'That scoundrel Edmund has gone back to Cornwall, and after the degenerate Duke is buried, *he'll* be pumping Regan's well dryer than a desert! I'm jealous! I'll soon have to find an Edmund substitute in a hurry if I need a jiffy lube during a sexual emergency! Oh well, good old Harvey Lee will just have to do!'

Meanwhile, the Duke was conducting a brief interrogation. "Where was Gloucester's bastard son Edmund when Gloucester's eyes were plucked, or should I say gouged-out?" Albany asked the neurotic messenger, who feared being killed on the spot.

"He had already headed toward your castle on horseback along with Lady Goneril!" the servant recollected and told the perplexed Duke. "No, that statement is not correct! They came to your castle on two horsebacks! No, that is still not completely accurate! Edmund was on one horse, and your wife was on another!" the under-duress servant irrelevantly recalled and shared. "Those two irresponsible lovers are always horsing around, Duke!"

"Tell me all that you know!" Albany demanded of the messenger as he held a gold coin incentive in the palm of his right hand. "On second thought, you degenerate Piss-head, tell me all that you know about Goneril, Regan, Edmund, Gloucester, King Lear and Edgar. Contrary to popular belief, I'm now beginning to think that Lear is the most sane, intelligent person in all of fucked-up Britain!"

* * * * * * * * * * * *

Several days later, at the bustling French encampment near Dover, parallel events were occurring when the Earl of Kent and King Lear surprised themselves by amazingly arriving at their destination, just as military conflict was about to ensue. The duo stopped their forward progress, and bilingual Kent then spoke with a cooperative French cavalier.

"Where's the King of France?" Kent asked the knight, who incidentally spoke fairly good Anglo-Saxon English. "I don't see his tent occupied at the moment. Is he still back in Paris trying to perfect his nebulous formula for making plaster?"

"It was necessary for Burgundy to return to France to conduct urgent business, the nature of which no one knows or really cares about," the cavalier suavely answered Kent. "We care as much about our King as you do about your great-great-great-great grandfather's embalmed asshole!"

"Who is commanding his feces, er, pardon my poor English, I meant to say his forces?" Kent asked. "An accomplished general I presume. Are there any accomplished French generals at all?"

"So far, it's been Monsieur La Far, our myopic, nearsighted Marshal of France, who has marshaled this huge assault contingent, while the King is away on contingencies that are contingent on unknown factors," the officer accurately and cavalierly explained. "And I don't know what was in those fucked-up mysterious letters that were sent by messenger to Queen Cordelia, but she's wept incessantly ever since she's received them, and reads the stupid bullshit over and over again, and then cries some more. You

Englishmen and your ladies are all psychotic, neurotic, moronic screwballs," the opinionated cavalier concluded and related. "At least that's my unsolicited determination. I mean, one-minute Queen Cordelia's all radiant sunshine, and the next she's freezing rain, as she alternates and vacillates between smiling and sobbing. The fuckin' fantasy-oriented, dumb-ass Bitch seems to be chronically fascinated with theatrically staging both comedy and tragedy drama in real life."

"Does she utter any sounds or words like 'Holy Shit!' or 'Ooh-ah, ooh-ah, ooh-ah, yes, yes, yesssss'!" the old pervert Kent curiously asked the French officer.

"She kept on yelling, 'Sisters, sisters, shame of immoral ladies, and 'Oh father, oh father!' So, all I could conclude from hearing her astonishing drivel was that Lady Cordelia was recalling having sex with her father, and also with her sisters at the same time. And now the royal broad feels both pleasure and guilt from those sensational memories that are deeply ingrained in her complex psyche," the presumptuous cavalier over-zealously hypothesized and remarked. "Lady Cordelia is one sick hussy. I'll definitely attest to *that* observation any time, any place!"

"Was the indecisive French King still here in Dover when Queen Cordelia read the letter?" the busybody Kent inquired. "If he was still here standing on this shore, his rival Burgundy would've had, please excuse me for using a popular cliché, he would've had a terrible French hemorrhage."

"That I can't verify," the gossip-mongering cavalier succinctly answered. "It's a verity that I can't verify."

"Did you know that old King Lear is supposed to be in town? Has he miraculously made it safely here?" Kent asked the Frenchman, without realizing that the subject of his inquiry was loosely seated stationary on a stolen horse right next to him. "Lear desperately wants to kick some ass as soon as he figures-out where his feet are, and who the hell the goddamned enemy is."

"I don't know if that horse-shit news is good or bad about your feeble-minded King arriving here," the French officer all-too-frankly articulated. "I understand that Lear couldn't even sink a solid-lead toy ship in his bathtub."

"Yes, King Lear's so plenty pissed-off that he gave Queen Cordelia's inheritance to her two dog-hearted, illegitimate sisters, Goneril and Regan," Kent told the Frenchman as Lear sat dozing and snoring atop his borrowed pilfered plow-horse. "Some influential Dover people believe that the King has lost all his sensibilities."

"You just got to feel sorry for the bad luck son-of-a-bitch!" the Frenchman admitted as the officer shook his head in dismay. "Your King seems to be sleeping while Cornwall and Albany's armies are amassing thousands of Britain's best yeomen to encounter us in combat. When's that stupid ineffective out-of-touch bastard King ever going to wake-up?" the cavalier critically said without knowing the identity of the renowned monarch sleeping next to him atop the purloined plow-horse.

"Who the hell knows?" Kent replied, shrugging his skinny shoulders. "But I want you to take us to your main camp, and then we can arrange to find and reunite this here aged, fatigued, slumbering fellow with your enchanting, prospective Queen Cordelia."

* * * * * * * * * * * *

Several hours later, resolute Cordelia entered her pastel-blue tent to confer with several underlings. "Quick, you French fanatics," Queen Cordelia imperatively ordered. "All of you wine guzzlers muster-up search parties that are not drunk and fanatically celebrating, and then go out and find my Old Man, King Lear."

"What the hell is happening?" a curious knight stepped-up and interrupted. "Is Your Liege under siege?"

"According to sketchy military reconnaissance reports, King Lear's somewhere in the vicinity, hiding-out with the Earl of Kent, and possibly also with the blinded fellow, the Earl of Gloucester, in one of the many weed-oriented flower fields around here," Cordelia explained. "Now go and search every *acre* and punch every local male peasant in the balls, and then don't forget to search those nearby lowlife *achers,* too! And Doctor," the prospective Queen instructed her chief surgeon, Dr. Morte. "Go along with the search party in case King Lear requires your specialized services. Now party on, dudes!"

A minute thereafter, a messenger entered Cordelia's tent and proclaimed, "The British soldiers are coming! The British are coming! And without any damned sticky semen saturating their battle uniforms!"

"I shall dedicate the French victory over the forces of Albany and Cornwall to my dear Father," Cordelia declared to her attending, apathetic French officers and knights. "We've expected this two-prong assault, and our armies are fully ready for combat, if they haven't already discovered some unsavory, bawdy inns, or some risqué bisexual brothels over in Dover. I strongly desire to be reunited with my failing father, either before he dies, or before the cowardly French soldiers most certainly get their asses kicked, and I don't particularly care which unreal event happens first. Now men, onward to victory!"

* * * * * * * * * * * *

A day later, Oswald rode his swift horse to Gloucester Castle and delivered a letter from Goneril intended for her new-found lover Edmund, which naturally (if discovered) would enrage Regan, who also was eager and ready to hop into the sack with the illegitimate disfigured creep with the enormous, throbbing, reproductive tool.

"Hi Harvey Lee, er, I mean Oswald," Regan greeted her sister's former paramour. "Are Albany's soldiers in place and ready to inflict injury and damage to the French invaders? I'm confident that soon everything else will be over at Dover!"

"Indeed Madam," Oswald confirmed, even though he never even learned how to baptize or distribute Holy Communion. "But I was so focused on delivering this missive that everything else, including that huge smear on your white-stained dress, is a big blur."

"Shit, Oswald!" Regan in distress exclaimed. "Now if blind Gloucester has the wherewithal to survive his most difficult journey to Dover, then the Old Fuck could have the capacity to inspire and incite rebellion against my sister and me, and our collective armies. It'll be bad enough of a challenge defeating the French, without the worry of insurrection among our own sex-starved soldiers. Why's it so much easier to make love than war?"

"Er, I momentarily forgot why I came to Gloucester," Harvey Lee Oswald admitted. "Now Duchess Regan. Why the fuck am I here?"

"Let me read that letter from Goneril you're holding in your hand!" Regan insisted to Oswald. 'I'll let this horny knave Oswald screw me, just so I can interfere into *their* affair. And also, even though Oswald has a big dick, I intend to get Edmund and his incredible pussy stuffer all to myself,' the always-scheming Duchess-widow wished.

"I don't think that it would be wise for you to read the letter," Oswald slowly and uneasily answered. "I do value my head and my gonads, you know!"

"Look, Asshole; I know you were screwing my sister Goneril like you both were two grunting wart-hogs in heat, and I also know that Edmund has cut into your action, and is now porking her right-through her double-mattress," Regan said straight-forward. "So, Harvey Lee, if you wisely share the contents of the letter from

Goneril, which I presume is intended for her lover-boy Edmund, I'll let you sample my eager beaver."

"One in the bush is worth two in the hand," Oswald shrieked a reversed aphorism in pure delight, as the former jerk-off anxiously handed-over the aforementioned love letter.

"And after we have delightful tantalizing sex," Regan told the easily-stimulated Harvey Lee Oswald, "and if you survive the ordeal, "I'll immediately dispatch you with a letter to Goneril, telling my sister that my husband Duke Cornwall is certifiably dead, and is about to be buried. And I want you to kill old blind Gloucester if you come across that dirty no-good double-crosser in your travails, er, I mean, in your travels."

* * * * * * * * * * * *

The blind Earl of Gloucester and Edgar had dismounted their "borrowed horses", and were presently climbing-up a hill that the Earl believed was a "White Cliff of Dover", from which he could leap in a spectacular suicide to be observed only by Edgar.

"Are we anywhere near the top of this steep, rugged hill yet?" Gloucester asked his disowned legitimate son. "Tell me a simple 'yes', and I'll most certainly be jumping for joy."

"Just think about how terribly arduous and precarious this steep ascension is, and you'll then realize what we're doing," Edgar twisted reality and told his father, since the climbers were not on the threshold of one of the high White Cliffs, but only walking-up a small hill. "This precipitous incline is terribly treacherous, almost as steep as a church steeple, and out of conscience, I feel inclined to tell you so! Don't you hear the inviting sea roaring, Father?"

"No; the only thing I hear is your stupid bullshit!" Gloucester adamantly disputed. "Lead-on, so that I may enact my fate."

"Okay, we've finally reached the most dangerous precipice," Edgar stated as he looked five-foot-down the ridge onto a flat plateau, and a subsequent safe landing area. "I see a fisherman down there on the beach casting his net. His head looks no bigger than a mouse's dick!"

"Well then," blind Gloucester replied. "Place me exactly where you're standing, so that I can successfully leap and plummet to my appointed death. And if I'm lucky, my fatal plunge will kill a French scout or two, along with myself! Now let go of my hand, you aggressive, shameless, faggot impersonator! But before I jump, here's another purse I'm carrying tucked-away, next to my sweaty balls," Gloucester entrusted to Edgar. "Take it, kind Friend. In it is a jewel. Its unremarkable value could get you laid, or blown, at least a hundred times in Dover's best, disreputable whorehouse! I prefer giving this gem to you, a cooperative Stranger," the mentally ill Gloucester said in a desperate, delusional moment, "rather than give it to either of my spiteful disobedient sons!"

"Thanks Old-Timer," Edgar mentioned to his blind father as the former favored son examined and admired the splendid jewel. "Now complete your intended suicide so that I can watch with amusement your final act on this lousy, intolerable Earth! And yes; it is wonderful Leap Year!"

"Oh Stranger; this despicable world I now renounce, because I hate everyone in it, except my true-blue son Edgar, whom I've recently egregiously abused," Gloucester lamented and wept. And then without any warning, the thoroughly-disoriented Earl of Gloucester jumped the full five-foot-descent, and next rapidly tumbled-down three body rolls onto the small plateau below, in an absurd, abbreviated, aborted suicide attempt.

A minute later, Gloucester regained his faculties and asked, "If I've fallen from the White Cliffs, then why am I still blind, and still fuckin' speaking and thinking? What kind of puny wick-dicked White Cliff was *that* anyway?"

"You must possess amazing wizard-like supernatural abilities!" Edgar shouted, feigning amazement from almost two meters above. "I just descended down a path to your location, and I'm astounded to observe that you're still alive and breathing, Old Man!" Gloucester's elder son creatively lied.

"I'm a dismal failure!" the Earl futilely bitched and moaned. "I couldn't even commit suicide, since I lack the necessary strength and intelligence. Yet I've somehow amazingly survived a fall that would've killed any ordinary man; blind or otherwise! I' must be part Divine! Yes, I must be part Divine!"

Then, just by sheer coincidence, King Lear arrived on the scene upon his borrowed horse, and soon dismounted and stepped onto that section of the vast plateau. "I am the King of Britain!" Lear announced to Gloucester and Edgar. "Did you hear me? I am the King of Britain!"

"What?" Gloucester exclaimed. "You are Lear; the tragic-oriented King of Britain? You're here on the White Cliffs of Dover reunited with your humble servant?"

"You must be a blind Old Codger if you can't recognize my identity in the flesh," Lear proudly answered.

"I know that magnificent voice," Gloucester marveled and determined. "I indeed recognize that fuckin', most-distinguished voice anywhere, I tell you!"

"My scumbag daughters Goneril and Regan have both maliciously deceived me," Lear reviewed and confided. "And now my fucked-up family is afflicted with adultery, tyranny, fraud, felony, suffering, machination, war, strife, rampant homosexuality, and other relative dangerous bullshit!" Lear grieved. "I mean to say that my cluttered mind has concluded that Gloucester's bastard son Edmund was kinder to his father than my aberrant, illegitimate daughters Goneril and Regan have been to me. And so, blind asshole, I've been rightfully punished for consistently having rampant sex with alluring whores!" Lear guiltily confessed. "Those two scurrilous Bitches have fucked-up my kingdom, and in the process, have ruined my elderly life. From the tits down, both of those savage, illegitimate whores are vicious, cruel, wicked, heinous, female Centaurs!"

"Oh, let me kiss your psoriasis-infected hand, Sire!" Gloucester shouted upon realizing his King's presence.

"Get the fuck away from me, you peculiar, pathetic, faggot, Old Shit Head!" Lear screamed. "There's entirely too much gay shit going on throughout all of Britain, without me being exposed to this depraved, queer advance of yours!"

"Does thou not know who the hell I am?" the blind Earl of Gloucester asked Lear. "I've kissed your smelly hand at least a thousand times before! You ought to learn to wipe your fat ass better, and stop eating so many damned green leafy vegetables!"

"I don't fuckin' recognize you from Methuselah!" Lear yelled at his noble, heartbroken subject. "Blind degenerate Fool; learn to see with your ears, and develop the nose of a hound dog. Then, truth will be more vivid and lucid! Shit! I'm beginning to sound like a goddamned erudite philosopher!"

"Could I assist you in any way?" the well-mannered Edgar asked the delusional King.

"Pull off my boots! My feet are still sloshing around in them!" Lear commanded to the befuddled Edgar. "If this old blind fellow gets-down on his knees, and thoroughly licks my toes, then I'll know that the Old Fuck is surely the Earl of Gloucester as he claims!"

Edgar did as his King instructed, and Gloucester got-down on his hands and knees, and ambitiously licked Lear's feet, just as he had performed hundreds of times in the past. The ruler and his nobleman rejoiced at being reunited.

An effeminate-sounding officer sent by Cordelia approached, discovered Lear, and next formally announced that the King was to be escorted to his daughter's tent. Distrustful Lear then believed that he was being arrested and taken prisoner by either Goneril or Regan, or perhaps by both "cat-fighting traitors".

Upon arriving at the French camp on the beach, the confounded Monarch demanded that a skilled surgeon attend to his many wounds, and that a nurse with healthy-looking breasts give him a complete bath, so that he could face either or both of his stealthy and villainous daughters with an immaculately clean appearance.

"You're without a doubt a royal Asshole, and I shall obey your whims that are cleverly disguised as commands," the gay officer stated. "For Your Majesty, I am the acclaimed Dr. Morte, and I don't think you want me operating on your ass, or on any other damned part of your old wrinkled-up, worn-out body! In my professional opinion, you'll make a really terrific cadaver!"

"Dr. Morte!" Lear hysterically screamed. "I know a little Latin, and I'm getting the hell out of here before I become a fuckin' autopsy!" the King shouted, as the crazy monarch garnered enough strength, and then frantically maneuvered away like a maniac seeking asylum.

"The King has been reduced to a mean-spirited, picayune wretch!" Dr. Morte snidely laughed to the now-petrified Edgar and the nearly-unconscious Earl of Gloucester. "Certainly, this most saucy, destitute fellow I just interviewed cannot be the eminent British King Lear as that fleeing old, frail geezer-impostor audaciously pretends!"

"How near is the French army?" Edgar asked Morte.

"Just a little further away than you could spit or piss against the wind," Dr. Morte cleverly answered, as the renowned mortician ambled in the direction of other officers searching for Lear to escort the unpredictable psycho back to Cordelia's camp.

* * * * * * * * * * *

After riding from Gloucester Castle, a very exhausted Harvey Lee Oswald arrived on the southern coast, and soon dismounted from his horse, and accosted Edgar and the Earl of Gloucester on the tiny plateau that was not far from the towering White Cliffs of Dover. The devious scoundrel stated that he must execute Gloucester with his sword to fulfill Regan's explicit command. Edgar advised Oswald to "chill-out" and abandon the scene, but the servant had *tunnel vision* when it came down to obeying Regan and murdering Gloucester, while also thinking about Regan and Goneril's sweet, delicious honey-wells.

"Leave the Old Coot alone!" Edgar warned and hollered at the very-focused Oswald. "If you don't leave us the hell alone, you're definitely cruising for a bruising, if not death itself! Do *you* Knave have a death wish?"

"Get out of my way you obstructive Dunghill!" Oswald stubbornly retorted. "Oh yes; I can almost taste desired power and smell *that* heavenly pussy from here!"

Edgar and Oswald then violently tussled and battled with swords, and the steward's lack of dueling skill was quite evident when in a mere ten second skirmish, the moronic rogue was run through-and-through, and then fell to the turf, mortally wounded, gradually bleeding to death during a final twelve gasping breaths.

"Bury my body and take my purse, even though it is regarded as feminine for a true macho man to carry one!" Oswald cried. "Give the letter you shall find on me to the magnificent Edmund, Future Earl of Gloucester. Seek him out, so that my death is not in vain. Shit! It's actually happening. I'm fuckin' dying!"

"*That* dying dirty, low-bred, son-of-a-bitch is almost as wicked as Edmund, Goneril, and Regan, all three evil fucks combined," blind Gloucester uttered to his victorious companion. "Dear Edgar; you might've just valiantly salvaged Lear's kingdom!"

"Sit-down in the mud, my weak and perplexed Father!" Edgar encouraged and gestured. "Rest your weary bones and your flimsy emaciated body." The son then read to his father Goneril's instructional letter, which urged Edmund to kill the Duke of Albany, and then marry the Duchess of Albany in order to keep the long-peckered ogre away from Regan's hungry snatch.

"Let's bury this knave before the voracious vultures descend!" Gloucester (who couldn't do shit because he was feeble, blind, incontinent, and virtually incapacitated) suggested to Edgar. "And poor King Lear has so much fucked-up activity going on in his lands that he'd be better-off selling coal, kerosene, and flammable peat in Hell. Our Ruler's plate is all-too-full!"

"Yes, my forgiven, contrite, penitent Father; after we, er, I mean I bury this vile underling named Oswald, I'll take you to visit a true friend, a loyal true friend," Edgar promised the weak-spirited Earl of Gloucester. "Yes, I now hear the drums beating in the distance. In fact, the enemy drums are not beating all by themselves. Soldiers are beating them," Edgar prattled. "Father, the French are now ready to pound the living crap out of your most repugnant native enemies and their troops; the doomed armies of Goneril and Regan! You're right, Father. King Lear needs a bigger plate!"

* * * * * * * * * * * *

Cordelia, the Earl of Kent, Dr. Morte and the cavalier French Gentleman were gathered in the Queen's pastel blue tent in the center of the invading army's Dover beach encampment. Cordelia's search patrol had successfully located and salvaged Lear, who was soundly sleeping and presently under the untrustworthy care of diabolical Dr. Morte. King Lear's youngest daughter and the indomitable Earl of Kent soon engaged in a meaningful dialogue.

"Oh, my dear Kent; how could I ever repay your devotion to my beloved Father?" Cordelia graciously praised the Earl. "You've been a true- blue Lord."

"A little couch dancing and strip-teasing would be satisfactory compensation, that is to say, after your forces triumph over your two illegitimate sisters' intoxicated armies," Kent joshed. "And if you masturbate while doing either couch-dancing or freelance stripping, then I would be most emotionally gratified."

"I do it for my husband, the French King, every night we're together, so when I perform for you Cunt, er, I mean Kent, I'll just pretend you're my horny kinky French spouse," Lear's disinherited daughter laughed.

Then, the notorious Parisian physician/surgeon/mortician entered the French Queen's pastel-blue tent.

"How is my fragile Father doing?" Cordelia asked Dr. Morte. "He hasn't evolved into his eternal sleep yet, has he?"

"He's as robust as your busty chest Madam," the dirty-old-man Doctor replied. "And I must say that your succulent-looking breasts are quite titillating, indeed! But perhaps I should awake the King before we have to attend his wake, which may result at any moment from lack of love, food, sustenance, and nutrition."

"Be especially careful when you awaken him," cautioned Cordelia. "He's quite a hypochondriac and liable to expire."

"I'll arouse him from his deep sleep by gently massaging his shrunken genitals," the insidious, lecherous, sex addict Dr. Morte predicted. "I don't want to be too *hard-on* your father, if you know what the hell I mean."

"You know your profession just like an accomplished prostitute knows hers," Cordelia smartly and directly returned. "But be sure to put fresh apparel on the King, so that he looks more like a King, and less like a fuckin' bag man."

The French Queen then accompanied Dr. Morte to *his* "Operating Tent". Cordelia shielded her eyes by cupping her hands to her face (just like a modest, meek, medieval woman would do regardless of social rank), while the orderly attendants (in a disorderly fashion) changed King Lear's tarnished, tawdry clothes, and also his dependable, disposable, smelly diaper.

"Oh Father!" Cordelia shrieked as Lear opened his eyes, wishing that he were dead and residing in Purgatory. "My sweet kiss will be like medicine on your lips!"

"I wish your sweet lips were medicine applied onto my teenage stiff pecker," the slowly-recuperating, incest-oriented Lear weakly replied. "But alas; my dick has been as limp as a crippled third leg these last two decadent decades."

"Sire, you've demonstrated an Olympian bravery quite rare to mortal soldiers," Kent falsely congratulated and praised Lear. "Men as courageous as you aren't born in Britain anymore, or for that matter, anywhere else in the dumb-fuck world. Lear, even though you're pretty fucked-up and senile yourself, you're still a great tribute to the human race!"

"Oh, my virtually unconscious Father, you've embarrassingly hovelled with swine, vermin, and evil scoundrels, all because you once wronged me, but I hereby fully forgive your misjudgment," Cordelia orally conveyed to the almost-comatose and incoherent Lear. "How are you feeling today, Your Majesty? Are you' feeling chipper? How's your general condition?"

"I feel like three-day-old shit!" Lear candidly confessed. "But honestly, my dear Cordelia; you ghostly apparition; you lost Angel of Death; you're indeed a celestial cherub possessing a blissful spirit that wonderfully transcends this baneful and condemned-to-Hell world!" the loony King uttered, thinking that he was dead. "Now kindly leave me the hell alone, Daughter, so that I may enjoy being deceased in peace, and get my immortal soul the fuck off this ass-backwards planet!"

"I was just concerned for your safety and welfare!" Cordelia sadly maintained. "I've always loved you for what you are!"

"Now, don't mock me, my heavenly Daughter!" Lear ranted and raved like a lunatic nutcase. "I just see shadows and images all over the goddamned place, and imagine they're all fucked-up people I once knew. Now, feed me adequate poison, my sweet obedient Cordelia; yes, prepare me an ample quantity of hemlock, so that I can die just like honorable Socrates had done in ancient Athens. Say; am I in France? I was never good in geography, or for that matter, in the art of the fundamentals of communication."

"You, Old Brave Dog; you're with the French Army in your own kingdom, just outside Rover, er, I meant to say 'Dover'," Kent rationally explained to his King.

"Bullshitting to an Old Fart like me is worse and more outrageous than performing excessive mental abuse," Lear plausibly answered the Earl as the monarch's errant, erratic mind gradually began escaping its captivity in dementia. "We're all stupid assholes at our own levels, whether we be kings, dukes, barons, lords, counts, squires, yeomen, jesters, chattel, knaves, or simply plain, old country bumpkin jerk-offs."

"Cordelia; trouble him no more with your plethora of trite interrogatives and declarations," wily Dr. Morte recommended. "He's living in a delusional near-death dream world; an in-progress fantasy, where nothing makes sense, just like our retarded daily reality seems inexplicable to us, most of the damned time."

"Could you stand and walk Your Majesty?" Cordelia asked her royal father. "We already know that you can ramble odd language from your mouth, and fart loudly out of your ass, just as well as anyone else in Britain."

"Forgive this Old Fool for his myriad transgressions, whoever you attending dumb Bastards and inquisitive, annoying Bitch happen to be!" Lear un-alertly and boisterously remarked. "Forgive and forget; that's precisely what I have to say to you dopey and anonymous Assholes! Forgive and forget, I command!"

A cavalier appeared at the tent's entrance, and quickly conveyed to Cordelia and Kent that the Duke of Cornwall had been slain by a common thug employee, and that the notorious bastard Edmund was leading the perverted Duke's knights and soldiers into major battle against the invading French Army.

"And what do you know about Edgar, the Earl of Gloucester's disenfranchised son?" Cordelia asked the informative cavalier.

"It's been reported, but not definitely verified, that Edgar and the Earl of Kent will be banished to Germany where they'll be perfectly content drinking potent beer, and eating a new tasty snack food the natives call pretzels."

"And what of the impending war if the two British armies unite to fight us?" the Queen asked the cavalier. "What are the odds of a French victory?"

"The war between Britain and France is bound to be brutal, and during this rocky period of uncertainty, expect much blood to be shed on both sides," the local-gazette-cavalier forecast without ever answering Cordelia's question.

"It's my menstrual time of the month, and I know exactly what you meant when you said much blood will be lost during this period," Cordelia irrelevantly pointed-out to the cavalier, while divulging her little secret to her very attentive audience (with the exception of the virtually unconscious Lear).

Meanwhile, Edmund and Regan had ridden horses to Dover, and were now standing in the center of the British camp, planning for the upcoming battle with the notoriously-coward French Army. Edmund was quite concerned and worried about losing the battle to "craven foreign encroachers", and the Earl of Gloucester's bastard son was also paranoid about getting slaughtered; and therefore, not being able to have sex with lusting royal bitches ever again. Out of character, the black-hearted bastard-son had an honest conversation with the Duchess of Cornwall.

"Have no fear dear Edmund," Regan sympathetically advised her new "very satisfying", deep penetration lover. "After our British knights and soldiers give the French invaders a severe and comprehensive thrashing, then *we'll* have more than enough time for our exquisite, amorous pursuits; but first, we'd have to take over that bastard Albany's lands and inherit his influential powers, and soon eliminate my bitchy sister Goneril. Then finally, true happiness will be ours," Regan expressed as the fascinated Duchess stared at Edmund's prodigious manhood coiled around like a snake inside his black tights. "By the way Edmund, how many times have you screwed Goneril?"

"Certainly, less times than I've vigorously pumped the poop out of you," Edmund deviously and evasively answered and lied. "You must admit Regan; variety is the spice of life, you know, and I just love my two main spice girls. Now then; let's get back to discussing the upcoming battle for the sake of love and war."

"Look over yonder!" Regan nervously prompted Edmund. "It's my witch bitch sister Goneril and Duke Albany entering the British camp, leading their knights and soldiers right this minute. I now think we have sufficient manpower to decisively trounce the French, and I'll avail myself of the opportunity to puncture my lily-white sister Cordelia's tiny tits once and for all," the insensitive, whoring Duchess of Cornwall expressed to Edmund. "And once the French are effectively dealt with and defeated, then we'll worry about eliminating Goneril and her notorious, playboy husband. I mean, why the hell do I have to be the only goddamned totally ice-hearted widow in my fucked-up family?"

In compliance with the demands of her huge ego, the newly arrived Duchess of Albany had her own contemplations. 'I would rather lose the battle than lose Edmund to my whoring bitch sister Regan, who is far from being a chaste nun,' Goneril evaluated, as the whore glanced ahead through her spyglass at Edmund's sausage curled round and round inside his very tight black leotards. 'And now that Regan's husband Cornwall's dead and buried and out of the picture, I'll have the inside track on landing Edmund and his wickedly hostile hose,' Goneril schemed. 'I must figure-out a way of swiftly eliminating my husband Albany in order for me to successfully compete with and eradicate my sleazy, slutty sister. But first, both she and I must play this sophisticated, politically correct, cooperation game, so that the fucked-up French can be thoroughly vanquished.'

"Hello Regan," Albany phlegmatically greeted his widowed sister-in-law. "I've gotten word that the fool Lear has made contact with Cordelia in the French camp, and that they're all sitting around a fire, roasting toasty marshmallows close to a nearby marsh. Has anyone here heard similar nonsensical reports?"

"Let's be frank, although we're both British and not Frenchmen. It doesn't freakin' matter about Cordelia and Lear," Goneril noted and added, while not extending the courtesy of even mentioning the deposed *King* as *her* castigated father. "We'll consolidate our British forces and beat the shit out of the cowardly French. Let's get serious about our joint enemy, and then we can decide how we'll attempt exterminating each other."

"Goneril; will you come with Edmund and me to my tent for a little stark-naked threesome?" Regan surprisingly asked her sister in a sidebar conversation. "I know we both have our monthly periods at the same time, so Edmund can enjoy our two tongues licking his huge throbbing manhood."

"Okay, Sis', that's a lot better than me smashing my crack open, bouncing up and down on that terribly long horseback ride all the way from Albany Castle here to Dover," Goneril assented.

Before the three sex addicts could leave the poorly constructed British tent, Edgar (without recognizing Edmund) came storming in, despite the fact that the weather was acceptably fine outside. Gloucester's older son quickly and solemnly addressed Albany, making an unusual request.

"Duke," Edgar began his preamble. "Open this informative letter before you fight the battle with the French. I assure you that the missive is not a trick forgery."

"Stay until I read the contents and then I'll decide whether to reward or kill you," Albany austerely stated to Edgar. "Right now, I'm leaning towards the latter. Either you or your half-brother has a bad reputation for forging phony documents! And incidentally, killing the messenger happens to be one of my favorite pastimes."

"No Sir!" Edgar replied and objected. "I'd rather just do my duty, deliver the missive, and then avoid all consequences, either positive or negative, but probably ninety-nine percent negative. I wanna' get the fuck out of here away from all you satanic crazies as soon as humanly possible!"

The sneaky bastard Edmund (wearing heavy armor and a helmet) then stepped forward and whispered into Duke Albany's ear that the French army was in sight, and reluctantly moving forward while all the lamebrain British soldiers were strangely walking backwards. But then, not-too-cerebral Edmund of Gloucester had to again open his big fat mouth.

"I urge you, Albany, to forget trivial written letters, and directly focus your attention and energy on the daunting task at hand! If we don't organize our combined manpower in a hurry, then you and I might be dick-less and ball-less in another few hours, and obviously to *you,* my close Friend, standing next to me," Edmund foolishly declared, "I apparently have much more reproductive meat to lose in such a catastrophe than you do. Now you know, Duke Albany, precisely how I feel."

"Okay; I'll muster my troops to catch-up with the French advance even if I don't exactly relish the novel idea," Albany loudly yelled back to Edmund, as the humiliated tiny-dicked Duke hastily departed the military strategy tent.

Edmund had time to ponder about his thriving love life for a moment. 'I love both Regan and Goneril, but each Bitch is intensely jealous of the other royal Whore. Oh Man, I'd love to see a vicious catfight materialize, and all over little old me, the guy with the incomparable lengthy stiff salami,' the delusional fiend imagined. 'My designs and villainy must be kept secret from Albany, or else I'll be administered a fuckin' instant sex change against my will. But if Albany ever extends mercy to Lear and to Cordelia,' Edmund fearfully speculated, 'then realistically, I might as well accept current reality, and with regret, perform the damned messy castration operation on myself.'

Act V

With the greedy Duke of Cornwall and the villainous Oswald both dead, the cast of characters has been narrowed. Cordelia's French Army was advancing towards the rank British ranks. Edgar did some surveillance near the White Cliffs of Dover, and reported to the blind Earl of Gloucester that the "disorganized French front line" had been getting its ass kicked, and that British dominance in the battle was quite evident. Gloucester panicked, crapped his pants twice, and then desiring to end it all, foolishly bolted and fled into an open field, idiotically seeking escape from cover and protection.

"Which one is Montgomery Cliff because that's the one I want to jump off of?" the paranoid, sightless Earl of Gloucester shouted. "Oh, I'm the type of guy that likes to roam around," Gloucester deliriously sang the catchy lyrics like a fanatical madman, "they call me the wanderer, the wanderer, I go around, around, around and, around ahhhhhhh!"

While Gloucester was plummeting off the White Cliffs of Dover (as he riskily played his own version of blind man's bluff), Edmund's minions had isolated and were capturing Cordelia and Lear, because the entire French Army had gone on strike during the battle-non-battle, and many of the troops, that would rather love than fight, were presently shacked-up in local British whorehouses.

"Officers, take these two derelict hostages away," Edmund (who had just returned from Cornwall) commanded several knights in rusty armor. "They're not to speak to anyone including each other."

"Can my father and I not see my sisters, Goneril and Regan?" Cordelia pleaded. "They'll want to give us an audience."

"Shut the fuck up, Traitor!" Edmund shouted into Cordelia's face. "Don't you understand plain English? You've been consorting with the fuckin' French enemy too long!"

"Let *us*, my all-too-rash faithful Daughter, learn to follow explicit directions and go directly to prison," Lear voiced his subjective opinion. "We'll sing like jailbirds in a cage. Some of history's greatest men have been incarcerated, Jesus Christ to name the most prominent One. We'll share old stories and anecdotes, and have a lot of bullshit to talk about. By the way, who the fuck are you again?" the demented old Lear asked Cordelia.

"Shut the fuck up, Old Fart!" Edmund shouted, and then spat into Lear's face. "You, old incontinent Fool, happen to be addressing the future King of England," the bastard son of the now-deceased Earl of Gloucester crudely ridiculed Lear. "Men, take these two assholes away before they drive me just as insane as they are!" Edmund instructed several celibate and gay guards that had been boycotting the local heterosexual, straight-sex brothels and bordellos.

After the two captives had been escorted away, Edmund hastily jotted-down a note and handed it to a Captain. "Here Man; take this paper, and follow the British assholes to prison. If you follow my instructions, then I'll make you the next Earl of Gloucester."

"I cannot pull an oxcart, even though I'm strong as an ox; nor can I eat raw oats as a horse does, because I have a bad food allergy," the imbecilic Captain weirdly explained. "Gee, that's been my only lofty goal in life!" the astonished Captain further exclaimed. "I get to temporarily be the Earl of Gloucester, by acting like a motley messenger. Life is good!"

The mentally-ill Captain speedily left Edmund's tent, and then Duke Albany, Goneril and Regan (accompanied by a number of fully equipped soldiers) entered to confer with Gloucester's bastard son. Naturally, a power struggle (between the upstart Edmund and the established Duke of Albany) was about to commence.

"Sir, you've served Britain well," Albany congratulated Edmund, as Goneril and Regan stared in admiration at Edmund's plump sausage coiled-around like a snake inside his black tights. "But now that we've soundly defeated the wimpy French Army, you must use your soldiers for security purposes only. What have you done with that retarded shit-head Lear? I understand that he's been captured and is under your jurisdiction."

"Both he and his traitorous daughter Cordelia I have sent to exclusive detention under heavy guard; all of those soldiers, each weighing over three-hundred-pounds," Edmund facetiously related to Albany. "A few brave articulations from my magical lips have drastically reduced the pair of royal idiots to mere commoners."

"Sir, in all due respect, I think you've indeed overstepped your limited authority," Albany chastised Edmund. "Your hour of fame and glory is indeed over. You, Edmund of Gloucester, are not my noble brother-in-law substitute as you pretend to be, but are merely a fucked-up, lowlife pawn in this fucked-up, upper echelon, royal-generated war. And regrettably," the Duke of Albany qualified, "you, Edmund, had accidentally been elevated to a General only, by *my* expressed permission and by *my* omnipotent will. The potent Duke giveth, and the potent Duke taketh away! Know your place, Knave!"

"Now brother-in-law, be more grateful for Edmund's highly-skilled services," Regan implored Albany. "I know I'm not only grateful for certain services rendered; I'm also quite gratified!" the

Duchess of Cornwall declared, as Regan again scrutinized Edmund's bulging reproductive equipment tightly stuffed inside his leotards.

"Ditto!" Goneril confirmed. "Edmund has done my sister and me, and oh yes, and the whole of Britain a great service!"

"Judging from your wide eyes, along with their pupils' possessive gazes, I suspect wife Goneril that you have the hots for this lowlife donkey-dicked sot Edmund!" Albany jealously yelled. "Woman, you'll soon lose your endowment just as surely as Edmund will lose his! And by your endowment, Wife, I mean first your sagging tits, and then your windfall inheritance!"

"You can't traduce our legal-regal rights!" Goneril adamantly balked. "Just because you have a wick-dick, Husband, doesn't mean that dear Edmund must suffer because he doesn't!"

"Guards, arrest this impostor Edmund for committing high treason!" Albany ordered. "In the future, Britain may have a big dick named Richard, but a big dick named Edmund is totally out of the question!"

"As the new Earl of Gloucester, I challenge you to a duel in that you've maliciously insulted my manhood," Edmund hollered-back at Albany as everyone including Edmund himself briefly stared-down at his enviable, coiled-up, sexual apparatus. "To the death Albany; I warrant and demand the privilege and honor of a duel, as a proud and valiant, recently-appointed nobleman."

"Let the trumpets sound and the strumpets open their legs!" Albany euphorically commanded. "Whether you know it or not Edmund, I can either appoint or disappoint military officers at my whim and fancy! It'll be my distinct pleasure to personally kill a treasonous menace to British civilization such as yourself," the now-berserk Duke Albany angrily berated his appointed opponent, as the antagonist demonstratively threw-down his pink, silk glove to make his challenge official.

Edmund, who was not wearing a glove, pulled one off of Goneril's hand and threw the white object upon the ground, indicating that he agreed with Albany's acceptance to duel. Then Goneril and Regan, not wanting to see Edmund get killed, rushed-out of the tent to demonstrate their opposition to the impending fight.

"I am but what *you* are; a dirty, rotten, filthy, worthless scumbag," Edmund boldly criticized the livid Duke. "And I've always aspired to be just as callous as you are, Albany."

And from the assembled guards present, out popped Edgar of Gloucester, disguised as an elite British soldier. After announcing his true identity, Edgar challenged Edmund to a duel, and the aspiring hero boldly insisted on being Albany's highly-competent substitute.

"I've been shunned and castigated by highbrow society all because of *you*, my bastard half-brother," Edgar defiantly accused his ambitious sibling for all present to hear and witness. "And *my* elderly, noble father has been blinded, and the admirable Earl of Gloucester is now dead, Edmund; all because of your blind greed and your grandiose aspirations. And my new buddy, the Earl of Kent, along with courageous King Lear, have both suffered excessive emotional hardship and excruciating physical pain, all because of asshole British politics influenced by *you* and your adulterous, bitch, whore, royal girlfriends," Edgar vociferously ranted at avaricious Edmund. "But indeed, much of this incredible tragedy has been generated by you; my fucked-up, mentally deranged, bastard half-brother."

Ten minutes later, (just as the duel was about to commence), a guard from the opposite side of the British camp entered the tent carrying a bloody knife, and the soldier informed everyone gathered that Lady Goneril had committed suicide, knowing that Duke Albany had found-out about her secret love affair with Edmund, and that Albany would certainly kill Edmund in a by-the-rules sword duel.

But before Goneril had stabbed herself in the throat, the greedy Duchess of Albany had poisoned *her* equally wicked sister Regan, so that neither of them would ever have to be unhappy living long mediocre lives, *not* being pleasurably screwed by the arrogant big-dicked, but-soon-to-be-deceased knave Edmund; who would certainly be maimed, castrated, and mutilated by the expert swordsman Albany. Next, the corpses of Goneril and Regan were brought into the tent as evidence of what shit happens when there is an ongoing royal rumble in progress.

"Cover their pallid faces!" Albany directed as the Earl of Kent belatedly entered the tent, finally accidentally by chance locating it. "My wife, a suicide, and my sister-in-law punished by poisoning! What moral justice! Now Edmund, thank God you won't be able to screw either of them, unless of course you're a sick macabre, morbid pervert, which I suspect you *have been* and are!"

"If I die in this duel, I predict that I'll screw both Goneril and Regan in the eternal afterlife, either every heavenly or hellish day!" embittered Edmund boastfully prognosticated. "That is, if there *is* any fuckin' afterlife!"

Edgar and Edmund then began dueling, and in thirty-seconds, the bastard half-brother had been mortally wounded, because the older legitimate nobleman happened to be better skilled and more highly trained in the art of sword combat. But in his dying moments, Edmund displayed some semblance of benevolence and penitence.

"Here in this writ tucked inside my pocket are instructions to hang Cordelia," Edmund gasped. "May the gods be steadfast in defending her innocence. I regret that this revelation follows her recent demise!" And with those last words, Edmund expired.

"Take this impostor's body outside to be immediately buried!" Albany barked to several subordinates. "Bury the insolent Bastard in the dunghill outside the camp!"

Then, noble King Lear, saddened, despondent, and weak, entered the tent carrying pure-hearted Cordelia in his arms. The ill-fated French Queen had been hung under secret orders given by her half-sister, the illegitimate Goneril. "She's gone forever!" the King uncontrollably wept. "My arduous life has become an accursed, goddamned, perpetual tragedy."

"Is this the essential meaning of life?" Kent philosophically asked those standing inside the royal tent. "Human existence is basically struggle, sacrifice, cruelty, war, jealousy, slavery, drudgery, murder, assassination, envy, greed, revenge, and last-but-not-least, an abundance of relentless bullshit trumping incessant horseshit, along with a plethora of ubiquitous chicken shit! I hope for history and for posterity's sake, that there's more to human life than that which I've just indicated."

"Who is this magnificent Mage that has illuminated my flagging spirit?" Lear pondered and asked. But then, stark reality impacted the sorrowful King's overtaxed, deluged mind. "Shit! Cordelia's body is getting heavier by the second, but consistent with my personal biography, I'll persevere in extending this horrible ordeal, just like I've done with everything else. Why the hell couldn't I have been born an immortal, omnipotent god, instead of being conceived as a fucked-up mortal royal pain in the ass."

Then, someone present in the gloomy tent finally recognized Kent's identity and acknowledged the aged noble. "My Liege! It is your loyal adviser and counselor, the Earl of Kent!" the victorious Edgar communicated to his lugubrious, haggard-looking King. "And please Your Majesty," Edgar of Gloucester elaborated. "Don't you dare ask me exactly how the hell this crazy, senile, itinerant, bizarre, mother-fucker ever got all the way here to Dover from many locations all over Southern Britain!"

"Yes, my treasured and beloved King. I've followed your every move all over Southern Britain, and have paid dearly for it, I can assuredly attest," the rejuvenated Earl of Kent's lips sincerely related from his patriotic heart. "But I must candidly confess that the entire, stellar adventure was well-worth the damned experience, and I'd gladly do the extraordinary exploit all over again, if I had the friggin' youth, strength and opportunity."

"You're welcome to remain as my distinguished attorney, advisor and court astrologer," Lear gratefully thanked and promised the Earl of Kent. "I find you, Kent, to be almost as wise as the renowned roving sage who possesses the venerable appellation Baron Folly! Now then, loyal friend, Kent; help me put Cordelia down before I get a triple hernia, and require a quadruple bypass!"

"I profess my loyalty to your reign, soon about to be terminated," Albany stated, paying tribute and homage to the failing King. "Hail Lear, King of Britain! May your prestigious, esteemed name go down in the anals, er, I mean in the annals of history!" the somewhat-disconsolate Duke respectfully wished and praised. "And I wholeheartedly mean *that* particular hope and reverence, that I've just sincerely expressed for the benefit of everyone's posterior, er excuse me Your Majesty, I meant to articulate 'for the benefit of everyone's posterity'!"

"Hail Lear! King of Britain!" everyone (still living) standing in the tent lauded and exclaimed. "Hail Lear! King of Britain!" everyone loudly reiterated, for the shouters had nothing better to do.

"I feel devastated, both in body and spirit! Please forgive me, Kent, for all of the pain and misery I've caused you!" King Lear uttered with trembling lips, as the beleaguered monarch finally came to his full senses. "Life on this fucked-up planet is indeed a cruel hoax; a cruel tragedy! I'll see you Kent in the next world, if there really is a fuckin' next world! I only hope that it will be better than this one."

And with those bittersweet words, the much-tortured King collapsed to the ground and died; a broken and bewildered old man.

Edgar and Albany remained active principals in English history, honorably and benevolently governing Britain with honor. And the kind-hearted pair, conclusively put the troubled land's many familial adversities buried deep in its medieval past.

"The Merry Wives of Windsor"

Act I

The setting for "The Merry Wives of Windsor" is England in the mid-sixteenth century. The loveable, intoxicated, fanatical scoundrel John Falstaff was again up to his usual antics and hi-jinks, causing trouble, ripping-off wealthy people, flirting with married women, and characteristically making a general nuisance of himself.

Jovial, corpulent John Falstaff, out to exhort women and extort their money, was up to his old shenanigans, playing havoc with the aristocratic higher echelon aristocrats and their attractive wives in and around Windsor Castle. An embarrassment to the Crown, Falstaff and his notorious hit-men were robbing honorable citizens left and right (with impunity), and were getting away with their flagrant skulduggery activities. But the legendary rogue was about to outsmart himself when "Big John" tried getting involved with Mistress Meg Page, and also her vivacious friend and constant companion, Mistress Alice Ford, who took a page out of Mistress Page's playbook.

Justice Shallow and his nephew, Abraham Slender, accompanied Parson Sir Hugh Evans to pay a special visit to the Page residence. Justice Shallow, Esquire, although not too deep intellectually, immensely disliked Sir John Falstaff, and vowed to his cowardly nephew to take the knight errant to England's highest court, if the mischievous rogue dared to attempt any further illicit activity involving *him*, according to the magistrate, "the soon-to-be dubbed knight".

"My principal aspiration, Nephew Slender, is to become the Chief Justice of the Country, and I'll not allow the iniquitous Sir John Falstaff to stand in my way!" Justice Shallow insisted as the three gentlemen approached the Page home. "In fact, I'll persecute the audacious bastard, er, excuse me Reverend Hugh; I'll prosecute the troublemaking scoundrel the first opportunity I get. Falstaff's excessive immorality is not above the law, no indeed!"

"Sir John is a slippery devil who religiously greases himself every morning, just to escape indictments and convictions," Slender insisted, further aggravating his already pissed-off uncle. "It would take you, Uncle Shallow, a full three centuries to apprehend and prosecute the evasive fiend while Sir John's been busy perpetually persecuting you. It would be far easier to find and dig-up that historical faggot Attila the Hun's body, that's mysteriously buried somewhere on the European plains, than to administer justice to one reprehensible John Falstaff, who used to be your friend!"

"I'll be willing to act as an arbitrator, or as a judicial mediator between you and Sir John Falstaff," Parson Sir Hugh affably joked to chagrined Justice Shallow. "I am of the Church, and will gladly broker a satisfactory compromise. But the essential problem here Justice Shallow is that you have grievances and complaints against Sir John, and the infamous knight doesn't seem to care one iota, nor give a crap about either you or your grievances. I'm sad to opine that you're just like water cascading right off of Sir John's back! And the knight exhibits no particular qualms about you, Justice Shallow, if I might add. John Falstaff persecutes you better than you can ever prosecute him!"

"Well, Sir Hugh. If I were a young man again, I would terminate that loudmouthed drunkard in a second with my sword!" Justice Shallow boasted, showing his inflated-but-damaged ego. "But let's be candid here! I know that my nephew Slender has his eyes focused on young Anne Page, you rambunctious horny toad, Nephew Abraham! And since many of the merry wives of Windsor have gay and bisexual husbands," Justice Shallow generalized and elucidated, "Sir John Falstaff's chances of having an affair with a heterosexual lady are greatly enhanced. But we have to keep the obese lover boy knight away from Anne Page, so as to keep my Nephew Slender in the running, so to speak."

"Is it *that* obvious?" skinny Abraham Slender asked his conniving uncle. "I try to conceal my feelings. That's why I specifically wear my shirt sleeves cut at the elbows in order to disguise my emotions."

"Well then," Parson Hugh laughed. "Young Anne Page, as you're well-aware, has a sizeable inheritance of seven-hundred-pounds coming her way, which incidentally is seven times as much as young Abraham Slender here weighs! Ha, ha, ha! Anyway, Justice Shallow; I can tell that you have your eyes transfixed both on Anne Page's inheritance, and also on her firm rock-hard breasts. Now then Justice," the Reverend Hugh continued his sage analysis. "Let's simply accept the very evident facts. You're far too old to be courting Anne Page, but you can control her money; that is, if you get your knuckleheaded nephew Abraham here a viable contestant in the wooing race for her affections. That more plausible marriage of your nephew to Anne ought to be your dedicated modus operandi; you wily, horny, Old Goat!"

"Yes, Reverend Hugh. That's very logical, for I would have a slim chance of winning her hand in any serious romantic competition!" skinny Abraham Slender stupidly stated. "As for myself, I would be perfectly happy with two-hundred-pounds. Then, I wouldn't look like I'm suffering from malnutrition or participating in a major famine."

"Well, Gentlemen, getting back to our original conversation, I hear that Sir John Falstaff is at the Page house right now," Reverend Hugh contributed. "Let's knock on the door and see what the Hades materializes. Remember your main objective, Justice Shallow. You want to get your incompetent, mentally-challenged, nephew Abraham here married to pretty Anne Page, so if you wish to accomplish your greedy goal, I suggest that you should discreetly diminish your ongoing quarrels with Sir John Falstaff."

Master Page answered the rap upon the wooden door, and opened the squeaky, swinging portal to welcome his "three distinguished guests" inside the well-decorated and luxuriously furnished home. Anne Page's father gratefully thanked Justice Shallow for the delicious venison that the family was about to enjoy for dinner.

"Beating around the bush is not a good practice, either in sex or in politics!" Justice Shallow bluntly remarked while shrugging his bony shoulders in disgust. "Master Page, I'd like to speak with Sir John Falstaff about an important matter, if you don't mind. I believe that the bastard, er, excuse me Reverend Hugh, I believe that the culprit has wronged me, and presently, I politely seek retribution."

Just as Justice Shallow was criticizing the notorious, affable knight, much to his dissatisfaction, Sir John Falstaff and his henchmen Bardolph, Nym, and Pistol nonchalantly entered the parlor room. The fearless, half-inebriated knight got right to the crux of the matter, thereby escalating Justice Shallow's worry.

"Justice Shallow; I hear you intend to register a complaint about me to the King and his illustrious Council of vain nincompoops!" Sir John assertively stated. "What the hell's your gripe? Has some heartless, inconsiderate hoodlum stolen your diapers and crib?"

"I accuse you and your unethical ruffians of beating the stuffing out of my good men, of killing one of my prized deer on my personal preserve, and then giving the meat to the Pages; and finally, I accuse you of vandalizing and trashing my sacred hunting lodge, so that's why I intend to lodge an official complaint with the Crown!" Justice Shallow asserted.

"But I never kissed, raped or even screwed your daughter!" Sir John haughtily replied and laughed. "In fact, Nimrod, I didn't even get my fat middle-finger wet! Did I boys?" Sir John added, much to the amusement of Bardolph, Nym and Pistol, and much to the mortification of Justice Shallow, Abraham Slender, and all-too-pompous Reverend Hugh.

"You're a damned disgrace to humanity!" Justice Shallow yelled at the tall and chunky Sir John. "Falstaff; you have no noticeable couth or integrity in your defective character! The Council shall learn all about your myriad, illicit activities, I promise you!"

"It's all a lot of trivial bullshit that you've cited, and the Council members will laugh their balls off listening to your hyperbole and exaggerated horse-crap!" Sir John articulated, casually dismissing the Justice's allegations, as Reverend Sir Hugh's face turned tomato red, and his eyes rolled-up, glancing at the ceiling. "Now Asshole Master Abraham Slender; do you have anything unmeritorious that *you* would like to say to me?"

"Yes; you and your three rowdy rogue accomplices roughed me up good when I tried defending my uncle's lodge against your trespassing, and your wanton ransacking, and then your thugs maliciously split my head open with your pummeling fists in the process!" young Abraham Slender accused Sir John. "You're not a knight! You're a damned unskilled butcher!"

"I see that there are three peacemakers who will negotiate a compromise before this dispute eventually gets to the King's Council," Reverend Sir Hugh diplomatically butted-in. "There's Master Page; there's the landlord of the Garter Belt and Pink Panty Inn, and then there's me. I trust that the three of us can come-up with an amicable and equitable settlement."

"Pistol, did you pick Master Abraham Slender's purse after you supposedly contributed to bashing his head in?" the thoroughly amused John Falstaff asked his nefarious confederate. "Tell the truth, now! Do you actually gain satisfaction and enjoy punching the feces out of effeminate jerk-offs?"

"No, Sir John!" Pistol said and snickered with a wink. "I'm not a goddamned thief or street pickpocket, and I'm not a nose-picker masquerading-around as the boogie-booger man, either! Thou are lying and maligning my good reputation, Abraham Slender, you feckless, scurrilous Scumbag!"

"I saw the whole thing and nothing happened!" Nym piped-in, adding to the general confusion. "The whole damned alleged occurrence at the aforementioned lodge can be categorized as a non-event. I know, because I was there trespassing."

"I think that Master Slender has drunk himself out of his five sentences (senses)!" Bardolph injected into the rather bizarre debate/discussion. "I mean, our eminent King hasn't had one goddamned *census* since he began his reign, and reportedly, the garrulous, hollow-headed, idiot Master Slender has five, ha, ha, ha!"

"If I ever get drunk again, it'll be me with good God-fearing men like Reverend Hugh and Master Page, and not with blasphemous sinners, lecherous knaves, and devil-worshippers, like you Bardolph, you Pistol, and you Nym!" weakling Abraham Slender yelled at his imagined adversaries, who incidentally were laughing their rectums off at his petulant behavior and his careless commentary.

"I don't deny that we deny everything!" Sir John interrupted and guffawed. "This rich entertainment is definitely worth a king's ransom! Ha, ha, ha! The stage should know such genuine comedy!"

The loud argument was quelled with the appearance of young Mistress Anne Page, carrying a tray of glasses filled with wine into the parlor. The attractive girl was accompanied by Mistress Meg Page, and *her* mother's constant friend, Mistress Alice Ford. Much to prudish Reverend Hugh's embarrassment, and jealous Justice Shallow's chagrin, Sir John unexpectedly gave Mistress Alice Ford a big smooch on the lips.

Master Page, sensing potential danger developing, wisely invited Sir John, Bardolph, Nym, Pistol and the women into the adjoining dining room to set the table for their delicious (stolen) venison meal, while Justice Shallow, Abraham Slender and Parson Sir Hugh remained in the parlor.

The droll fool Simple (Slender's obedient servant) entered the house to join his master for some benign camaraderie.

"Oh, hello Simple," Slender greeted. "If you weighed several thousand more pounds, you'd be a simple-ton, ha, ha, ha! Have you brought along your favorite *Book of Riddles?* You really need it, you preposterous Knave, to improve your ability to communicate."

"No, Master Slender. I believe I had lent the text to either Alice Shortcake or to Miss Strawberry Longcake!" Simple dumbly joked, feigning a formal aristocratic response. "Do you not recall?"

"Now Simple, you irascible Fool; listen carefully to the sage and erudite Justice Shallow's remarks, for my distinguished uncle is an accomplished Justice of the Peace, who can't even control the peace inside his own fuckin', er, excuse me Reverend Hugh; the peace inside his own darned personal hunting lodge!" Slender suggested.

"Let's cut to the chase, you old, sly fox Shallow, and we'll discuss the prospect of marriage," Reverend Hugh constructively suggested in order to readjust the rather ridiculous conversation back onto the proper track.

"Reverend Hugh, you wish to marry Justice Shallow?" Simple inanely asked and giggled. "Gay marriage is unheard of in these post-medieval times!"

"I'm hinting that perhaps Master Abraham Slender should court Mistress Anne Page, so that Justice Shallow can scrupulously govern over the gorgeous young lady's inheritance she'll be receiving from her deceased, generous grandfather!" the sly, conniving, coy Parson recommended.

"I sort of like her except for her pageboy haircut!" Slender seriously acknowledged and criticized. "But realistically, Mistress Anne's anticipated inheritance seems quite compatible with my future good fortune! I could really use the additional cash!"

"Get serious for a second you dysfunctional Ignoramus!" Justice Shallow admonished Slender. "Do you think, Nephew, that you can love Miss Anne? Do you have any notion of what the hell love is?"

"I'll do anything to please you, Uncle, even marrying a rich, good-looking, well-stacked doll with a weird-looking pageboy haircut!" Slender conceded and chortled. "And if things don't work-out, I'll experiment and marry the girl again, just to see what the hell went wrong the first damned time around."

Mistress Anne again entered the parlor from the dining room. "Gentlemen, the deer dinner has been prepared, and the venison is on the table, although Sir John Falstaff humorously claims that your goose is cooked, Justice Shallow," the young woman aptly quoted and commented. "What a remarkable sense of humor that man has!"

"Good! I'll say the Grace Prayer, because the scandalous rogues already sitting in the dining room really need all of the blessings they can accumulate!" Parson Hugh chuckled and shared.

"I'm not hungry, and I'll not indulge!" callow Slender maintained, winking incessantly (from a nervous twitch) at Mistress Anne. "Master Esquire Shallow here is a Justice of the Peace, but I fear that no peace can be established or accomplished between him and that insolent troublemaker, Sir John Falstaff!"

"How come you can't have dinner with us?" Anne innocently asked Abraham. "Is there something wrong with your stomach?"

"I don't know if I could sit-down and truly enjoy a good meal, because I bruised my leg yesterday climbing over a fence I was mending, and my thigh doesn't seem to be mending too well, either," Slender said to Anne Page, seeking emotional sympathy and consolation. "I think that the fence will mend itself sooner than my leg will. Why are your dogs barking so loudly? Are there bears or ferocious wolves prowling around in the area?"

"They must smell the blood from your lacerated thigh!" Anne Page jested to Abraham Slender. "But I'm afraid that your lame excuse about being lame is in truth a vain (vein) attempt at gaining my attention and also, my concern about your welfare! Now Gentlemen," the comely girl politely implored the men sitting in the adjoining parlor. "I invite you for the last time into the dining room to partake of Sir John's marvelous venison!"

"I think that young Slender would rather be attending an impromptu stag party!" Simple joked, much to the blushing Anne Page's delight. "The horny old fellow needs to grow antlers!"

"Come Gentlemen!" Master Page entreated as the man of the house stepped into the parlor. "Dinner is being served! Actually, we're all being served! The dinner can't serve anything! Ha, ha, ha."

"I must humbly decline your invitation!" Master Slender uttered, while cowardly chickening-out of his agreement to woo Mistress Anne. "I have to go to my uncle's hunting lodge and finish cleaning-up all the trash and scattered debris. Enjoy your venison while I'm straightening-out the mess that Sir John and his fiendish thugs have destructively created! Their massive demolition would be enough to have made Attila the Hun desire becoming a goddamned Vandal!"

* * * * * * * * * * *

The following day, the community matchmaker Parson Sir Hugh dispatched Abraham Slender's nutcase servant Simple on a simple errand to deliver a letter to Mistress Quickly, asking the busy-body Blue Boar Inn wench to intercede with the voluptuous Anne Page on Master Slender's behalf.

"You might find Mistress Quickly doing a quicky at wacko Frenchman Dr. Caius's house," Parson Sir Hugh told the near-retarded Simple. "Now, go quickly to Mistress Quickly, but don't disrupt her quicky."

"I'll do as you've admirably instructed!" Simple agreed, receiving the sealed envelope.

"Mistress Quickly and Mistress Anne Page are bosom friends," Parson Hugh clarified without intentionally referring to the women's busts. "I'm confident that Mistress Quickly will throw in a good word for young Abraham Slender at the appropriate moment. His bizarre uncle, Justice Shallow, used to be one of Mistress Quickly's best clients before the poor fellow went impotent!"

* * * * * * * * * * *

The following morning, the inimitable Sir John Falstaff was desperately tottering on the edge of bankruptcy, so the conniver abruptly fired Bardolph, who then immediately sought and obtained employment from the proprietor and host of the Garter Belt and Pink Panty Inn, where quite incidentally, Falstaff, Bardolph, Nym and Pistol often frequented.

"Yes, Sir John," the Garter Belt Panty Inn host said, as the inn's esteemed owner drew the renowned knight and his henchmen four brews from the tap. "I'll reluctantly absorb Bardolph's two pounds a week stipend. Your disreputable companion can tend bar, work the taps, take care of my almost-empty wine cellar, and pimp one of my prostitutes on the side. And since your man Bardolph really knows his shit, I'll even make him curator of the inn's cesspool!"

"Go on, Bardolph!" Sir John commanded his former employee and aide. "An old villain's cloak becomes a new bartender's jerkin, you jerk-skin jerk-off! Go learn the trade of tapster, so that you can tap dance on the bar counter just like Mistress Quickly does! Ha, ha, ha!"

"As long as I don't have to do nude couch or lap dances, I'll work here," Bardolph bitched. "But the second that drunken assholes begin stuffing bronze coins down my tights, I'm fuckin' out of here!"

After Bardolph obediently followed the inn host down the steps to inspect the dark, dank wine cellar, Sir John explained to Nym and Pistol that his former employee had been taken-off the payroll because "the unskilled filcher" had been eating and drinking more than he had been stealing for the company. "Do either of you two unscrupulous vultures know the Ford family?" Falstaff asked his thieving colleagues.

"I do!" Pistol acknowledged. "What do you wish to do? Mistress Alice Ford is a lousy cook, so there's no way she's going to help you increase your two-yard-wide waist! What a pathetic waste your fuckin' waist is! If you were a prized hog, John, you would've been slaughtered and butchered forty-years-ago, yes, you would've; you ultra-fat slab of bacon!"

"Now stop the insinuating insults!" Sir John sternly demanded. "Alice Ford is giving me the eye, and my keen senses perceive her deep longings for me to make mad, passionate love to her," Sir John lectured, as Nym and Pistol almost pissed themselves laughing. "Alice, I strongly suspect, quite obviously craves my attention and companionship. I can tell by the look in her bright blue eyes and by her batting eyelashes. And the local gossip says that Mistress Ford controls her rich husband's money, while the flamboyant Casanova carelessly cavorts around with a legion of expensive whores and hookers."

"Her husband is into pork bellies, and I see that Mistress Ford is, too!" Nym added for Pistol's entertainment before imbibing several mouthfuls of ale, and then choking and cackling some more. "Some of Master Ford's hookers looked like briny fishermen! Ha, ha, ha!"

"Okay you moronic Fuck-heads!" Sir John rankled at Pistol and Nym. "Here's a sort of love letter that I've prepared to be delivered to Mistress Ford, for whom I would ford the *Thames* for her precious affection and purse. And here's another similar letter I've penned for the expressed purpose of Mistress Meg Page to read. Both women keenly desire to initiate amorous relationships with me, because their husbands ignore and neglect their emotional needs while carousing all over Windsor with costly, sex-starved hussies. The two bitches need a caring gigolo, and that's precisely where I fill the bill. Then, I could exhort and extort a small fortune from the two gullible dames, afford to rehire Bardolph for the fourth time, and next, enthusiastically pursue my career of being a crazed knight dedicated to embarrassing the Crown!"

"The sun must be shining in dunghills all over England today!" Pistol applauded and laughed. "Either that or shining where the sun never shines; way up inside Sir John's enormous colon! Ha, ha, ha!"

"Yes, Sir John, your pipe dreams are leaking, and you have in my estimation less than a fat chance of landing either rich bitch!" Nym sarcastically cackled and mocked his employer. "What the fuck do you want Pistol and me to do, Sir John? Pretend to be Hermes and Mercury? Ha, ha, ha! Shit! They're basically the same gods!"

"Exactly, you dumb-ass Fool!" Falstaff confirmed. "But since you insincere, irresponsible Assholes refuse to cooperate with my caper, I'll have my page Robin wear his hood over his pimply face, and anonymously deliver the love letters to Mistress Alice Ford and to Mistress Meg Page. Now, if you'll excuse my farting and my parting, I'm going to get the fuck out of this fucked-up inn, and practice being an accomplished gigolo!"

After Sir John staggered-out of the very popular and well-patronized Garter Belt and Pink Panty Inn, Nym and Pistol agreed to collaborate on sabotaging Falstaff's anticipated love interests.

"I believe we've just been fired just like Bardolph was," Nym complained. "Sir John can't tolerate friendly buffoonery and jokes anymore! I'll be damned if I'm going to humble myself like Bardolph did and work in a goddamned whorehouse, and keep the cesspool empty, and the wine kegs full, and the beer taps loaded."

"Aye Nym! I think it's time for us to collaborate!" Pistol concurred. "I know the Page family pretty well and...."

"And I know the Ford folks pretty well," Nym volunteered his services to the mushrooming conspiracy alliance against Sir John. "We'll be like fucked-up Cupids, waking lovers up by shooting our arrows and darts up their asses instead of into their hearts!"

"Get your darts and your bow ready for that conceited, unrealistic fat-fuck beau, Sir John Falstaff!" Pistol told Nym. "Why is my name Pistol? I'm much more deadly with the bow and arrow than I am in fuckin' shooting a handgun! Ha, ha, ha! Let's drink to our new pact Nym! Ha, ha, ha!"

* * * * * * * * * * *

"John Rugby! You leather-headed-baller hailing all the way from Leatherhead!" Mistress Quickly yelled to an intoxicated Garter Belt and Pink Panty Inn employee. "Run to the cracked window and watch for one of my favorite upstairs clients, Dr. Caius, approaching the building. Your boss is a flamboyant Frenchman, and prefers oral sex to the standard boring penetration method preferred by most stupid-shit Englishmen."

"I'll do you a favor because you just did one for me," John Rugby agreed. "Well actually, you gave me two heads: one on my free bonus beer, and the other on my erect dingle; that's the one that goes on my ever-shrinking line of credit!"

Just then, the tiny-dicked Peter Simple entered the inn and sought-out Mistress Quickly to deliver the letter of recommendation for Abraham Slender, addressed to her from Parson Sir Hugh.

"You' say to me that your asinine name is Peter Simple, and that Master Slender is your truthful boss. I know Abraham. Isn't he the exceedingly tall jerk-off with the gargantuan, grizzled beard that looks like two beavers glued together at their asses?" Mistress Quickly asked.

"Yes, that describes the dumb-fuck exactly!" Simple verified. "Master Slender has more hair on his face than a giant gorilla has on its entire fuckin' body, including its balls!"

"Does your master sort of strut when he uses his long gait while entering his front gate?" Mistress Quickly asked. "I mean his strides are about two-yards-long, and I'm speaking about backyards long and not just six-feet in length. Your employer is a really tall bastard, your Master Slender, isn't he? I'll bet he houses quite a prodigious salami between his legs, judging by the length of his strides and by the size of his hands, jaw, and feet."

"That I would not know Mistress, because I'm basically a pink tunnel expert, and not a goddamned pecker-checker, or zealous fellatio administrator, or a certified dick-licking authority," Peter Simple smartly explained. "Sometimes, it's best to just have tunnel vision, and not get involved with venereal diseases!"

"I see!" Mistress Quickly courteously answered. "Well then, Peter Simple; tell your Master Slender that Mistress Anne Page might just love him tender," the inn's Madame awkwardly rhymed. "I promise to represent his love for her, since Parson Hugh Evans is one of my most frequent, secret clients over at the Blue Boar Inn, over in Eastcheap; and I'll see that this important letter gets to her."

"That would be absolutely terrific Mistress Quickly!" Peter Simple simply declared. "I'm a devout Christian and don't want to lose my virginity in such a bawdy and risqué dump such as this Garter Belt and Pink Panty establishment, so I'll be on my way now and spend some idle time over at the Blue Boar Bordello!"

No sooner had Peter Simple left the premises that John "Jack" Rugby came charging into the back dining room to alert Mistress Quickly that his demonic master, Dr. Caius, was about to enter the inn and cause a ruckus.

"Quick John!" Mistress Quickly ordered. "Hide inside this closet until *the maniac's* business here is finished. If your gruff master catches you hanging-out in this glorious establishment, your boss will have you hanging-out on a gallows' platform that he'll have specially constructed for you in his cemetery backyard!"

A minute later, a weird conversation ensued inside the popular town brothel. "I need my vitamin and sperm development sex tablets!" Dr. Caius yelled, referring to a placebo/aphrodisiac that Mistress Quickly kept stored for him in the nearby closet.

"Don't expend your vital energy walking over there!" Mistress Quickly said, while trying to protect the hiding John Rugby from being discovered by the emotionally-volatile doctor. "I'll retrieve several of the sex enhancement pills for you, Dr. Caius! I'll get the tablets with the strongest formula that will make your manhood grow to be two-inches-long."

After Mistress Quickly returned with the two phony aphrodisiac tablets, Dr. Caius popped them into his mouth, and washed them down with twelve ounces of cold ale. "Where the fuck is that disobedient, aberrant servant of mine, John Rugby?" the French physician bellowed. "I need to severely punish that recalcitrant, unfaithful knave!"

Fearing his master's wrath, the little rascal came out of hiding. "Here I am, Sir!" Rugby nervously piped-up, sneaking-up behind Dr. Caius, who then reactively spilled the remainder of his ale all over his freshly pressed formal suit.

"What the hell are you doing coming out of the fuckin' closet?" Dr. Caius admonished the freckle-faced scamp. "Is your same-sex partner in there, too? Are you one of those Homo Erectus fags?"

"Little John was just playing a small hide and seek game with an imaginary Friar Fuck!" Mistress Quickly spoke-up and giggled, to change the direction of the mercurial-tempered doctor's reprimand. "John's an honest, straight young man, who perhaps likes masturbating in dark enclosures when no one's around. Now, then Dr. Caius, would you care to accompany me to bed and shoot off your miniature cannon?"

"Not today, Mistress! I'm too fuckin' stressed-out to get a decent erection, let alone to expel a sticky ejection! I'll save my ejaculation for tomorrow when those delayed-action aphrodisiac tablets will kick-in. Now then, why was that nutjob Peter Simple just scooting-out of here? You'd better fuckin' tell me, or I'll take my business over to the Blue Boar Whore Inn lickety-split! And as you know Mistress Quickly, I'm perhaps your best customer at either place!"

"Well, Dr. Caius, that simpleton Peter Simple simply delivered a letter addressed to Mistress Anne Page, originating from his horny boss, Master Abraham Slender. I promised to give the missive to my friend Anne the next time I see her, which will probably be later on this afternoon!"

"What!" Dr. Caius exclaimed with his thundering voice rattling the row of pewter mugs lined-up above the inn's downstairs ale-serving bar. "Hand me a quill and some paper. I must author a letter of protest to Reverend Hugh Evans right this fuckin' minute!"

"And exactly what are you going to write in the letter?" Mistress Quickly respectfully asked. "Do you wish for the Parson to marry Master Slender and Mistress Anne Page?"

"You must be fuckin' insane, Woman!" the livid Dr. Caius boomed. "I happen to love Anne Page myself, and I'm deeply offended that *that* newsy, nosy matchmaker, craven Parson Hugh Evans has violated *our* longtime friendship. This letter is officially challenging Reverend Evans to a duel!"

"But Parson Evans is not a fighter; the reverend is a man of the cloth!" Mistress Quickly argued and pleaded. "He's a respected minister in the community!"

"Hugh Evans is a gossiping, interfering, cowardly imbecile that has performed his devious mischief for the last time!" Dr. Caius yelled. "He's a man of the cloth all right! And he'll be wearing a burial cloth over his chest and body sooner than fuckin' later! That fucked-up cutthroat is going to have his throat cut by me! I plan to administer a serious beating to the minister. Now Rugby, tarry not here, if you value your testicles! My dog loves to retrieve stones, especially the human glandular type!" the oddball Dr. Caius threatened Rugby. Deliver this letter to Parson Hugh right this minute, or else we'll be needing a coffin for two!"

"Yes Sir! Yes, Master Chaos, er, Dr. Caius; right away!" Rugby emoted as the lad grabbed the letter and dashed-out of the Garter Belt Panty Inn's front door, pissing his pants all the way to the street.

"Anne Page is my ideal woman, and I resent Parson Hugh Evans butting into my secret love affair while representing Abraham Slender's slim chance efforts!" Dr. Caius hollered, his voice echoing throughout the almost-empty inn. "The Reverend is interfering with my sacred happiness!"

"Aren't you overreacting a bit to a little commonplace love rivalry?" Mistress Quickly critically chided Dr. Caius. "Haven't you studied basic geometry? Love triangles are prevalent throughout England, Europe, and the whole goddamned world!"

"I'll kill that gutless, scheming minister if I also have to decapitate his head and his dick!" Dr. Caius loudly predicted. "The sanctimonious asshole son-of-a-bitch ought to know he's messing with the wrong adversary, and that eventually, his interfering meddling is going to get the parson either maimed or fuckin' killed. Anne Page is gorgeous enough to be worth fighting for!"

"But Parson Hugh Evans is not clairvoyant!" Mistress Quickly quickly exclaimed and insisted. "If he had known that you were interested in Mistress Anne, then certainly the Man of God wouldn't have acted on Abraham Slender's *behalf*"

"You mean on Slender's two *be-halves,* after I slice that lousy bastard in two, right after I mortally wound the none-of-his business, interfering agent, Reverend Hugh!" the incensed doctor maniacally screamed. Then the Doctor left the landmark inn in a pissed-off frame of mind, as Mistress Quickly shook her head in absolute disgust.

A half-hour later, Fenton, a gentleman of considerable domestic repute, approached Mistress Quickly on her way to the Page home to chat with her close friend. Fenton expressed his genuine love for the vivacious Anne Page to Mistress Quickly, and gave the inn hostess-matchmaker a gold coin to put in a good word for him.

'Holy souls in Heaven!' Mistress Quickly thought. 'An incredible love quadrangle exists between Dr. Caius, Master Abraham Slender, Master Fenton, and that knockout bitch, Anne Page! I don't think Anne cares one scintilla about any of the three arrogant shit-heads, but each of the three buffoons believes that I can influence Anne into favoring his romantic advances! But poor Reverend Hugh is going to get the brunt of this three-way-competition when the gentle pastor is not even a goddamned black-hearted suitor directly involved in the rivalry, but still will be challenged to a duel by envious Dr. Caius!'

Act II

Sir John Falstaff had never thoroughly theorized the matter, but Mistress Alice Ford and Mistress Meg Page had again met at the Page house, and discussed their love letters that the ladies had received from the "delusions of grandeur" errant knight. The dignified females were not-too-thrilled to know that Sir John was attempting to hustle both married women, and had the audacity to believe that he could pull the caper off.

"Look, we both know we're vain old bags and are flattered by Sir John Falstaff writing to us like we were innocent, love-searching seventeen-year-old virgins," Mistress Meg Page told Mistress Alice Ford. "Not only is our despicable suitor a fat, loudmouthed slob, but he's also a horrible poet with the writing and literary skills of a ten-year-old, mentally challenged, discipline-problem child."

"Sir John is to romantic poetry what King Herod was to the children of Bethlehem; an absolute butcher!" Mistress Alice Ford snootily replied. "The chubby asshole thinks he's still a handsome gallant knight looking for fair damsels either trapped or incarcerated inside ivory towers. Perhaps that phlegm-ish, Flemish drunkard should pursue his peculiar, fantasy adventures, and seriously fraternize with those insane, liberal, professors teaching over at the goddamned university! I suggest that we be as parsimonious in our mirth as Parson Sir Hugh when we're in the chunky knight's lackluster, un-illuminating company."

"Alice, let's get revenge on the brazen bastard!" Mistress Meg Page decided and declared. "I mean, from what I can discern, both letters were equally nauseous and horrendous. The presumptuous jerk has more fat around his girth than a sperm whale possesses blubber. Yet he writes in this zany letter that he lusts for my bust; that lascivious, corpulent, obnoxious bull elephant!" Mistress Page exclaimed with authentic rancor evident in her tone of voice. "But if the screwed-up in the head knight tells us he thinks he's a sailor, we'd better batten-down our hatches, because that probably means he wants to go below deck and check out our hulls!"

"What kind of ruse can we pull on this voracious social cannibal?" Mistress Alice Ford asked her best friend. "His ego needs deflating as well as his gigantic belly!"

"Here's exactly what we ought to do to fix his love-boat for good!" Mistress Meg Page imagined and stated. "Let's bait the narcissistic asshole, and lead the self-indulgent jerk-off on; making him think that the over-the-hill gigolo has a real shot at shacking-up with either or both of us. We'll send him into hock with our extravagant tastes, and make the artificial Don Juan so destitute that he'll have to pawn his horse to the gregarious Host over at the bawdy and tawdry Garter Belt and Pink Panty Inn."

"Well, my husband has such a jealous streak embedded in him that when it's activated, I fear for Sir John's life, should my spouse find-out about *his* audacious and unsolicited advances," Mistress Alice Ford divulged. "Now Meg; let's contrive an excellent plot that will make Sir John regret having these distortions of chivalrous grandeur in the twilight of his years, when the chubby geezer ought to be sitting in his room nostalgically and sentimentally pondering his inglorious past!"

Pistol and Nym had buttonholed Master Ford, and had clued the husband in about Sir John wishing to shack-up with *his* over-the-hill, post-menopause wife Alice. The recipient of the incredible news was not-too-pleased.

"I can't believe this bullshit you've just told me!" Master Ford related to Pistol and to Nym, as the three satisfied patrons departed Eastcheap's Blue Boar (and Whore) Inn. "I mean my wife Alice is now a sixty-year-old painted-faced, wrinkled-up, old hag who is sagging all over her chest, and also from her uninviting plump ass. Falstaff must be blinder than a bat, or have a bad case of glaucoma if the cock-sucker sees anything physically alluring in her! What a misguided idiot he must be! My wife's nipples touch her toes whenever the bitch bends over!"

"Sir John doesn't give a shit what a woman looks like, just so the imbecile could woo her high and low, pork her good, and then filch her money, which is really her husband's hard-earned sacrifices converted into gold coins," Pistol explained to the already-highly-irritated and volatile Master Ford. "In basic terms, Falstaff's like a bastard predator dog, out to screw every hot neighborhood bitch the bastard thinks is also in heat!"

"My wife hasn't been in heat her entire, fuckin', non-fucking life!" Ford strenuously balked. "At least she hasn't fuckin' ever been in heat with me! This entire scenario you're describing is a travesty!"

"Take heed of *our* warning!" Pistol told Ford as Nym nodded his head in agreement. "Do you see Sir John's massive waistline? Well, that's two-hundred-and-seventy-five-pounds of raunchy-smelling, accumulated, sperm backed-up all the way from his asshole to his belly! Yes Sir, Master Ford; that's exactly what the fuck you're looking at when you view his enlarged paunch! Now excuse me Gentlemen," Pistol said to Ford and Nym. "I must go over to the Garter Belt and Pink Panty's pantry to visit Bardolph and borrow some fresh money that he's gotten in the way of tips."

"Well, I'll try and catch that pernicious philanderer Sir John in the act," Master Ford confided to Nym after Pistol stepped across the street. "I'll not be hoodwinked by that playboy hood's winking!"

"Sir John has grievously wronged Bardolph, Pistol and me," Nym alleged to Ford, "and you're next on his hit list, because you're a rich target, and you have an available vulnerable wife, I believe, Alice is her name. That fat fuck Falstaff pretends to love your wife, and if the playboy succeeds, you'll pay dearly both in your marriage and in your' fuckin' highly treasured bank accounts, which will soon be dwindling-down to zero! Good day, Master Ford! I must now pay a visit to Reverend Bacchus in the back room over at the Garter Belt and Pink Panty's pantry to get caught-up on some past missed liquid libations. I might even eat a fur-burger with my ale."

'I'll definitely seek-out that swindler Falstaff, and catch him in the act trying to seduce Alice,' Master Ford strategically thought. 'And if I do discover that sperm whale in bed with my dumb fuck wife, I'll first cut his dick off, and then carve-up his two-hundred-and-seventy-five-pounds of sperm blubber that's been anchoring-down his corpulent waist and abdomen.'

Later that morning, Mistress Quickly had paid a visit to Mistress Meg Page's home to confidentially discuss the unprecedented love quadrangle with her daughter Anne involving Abraham Slender, Master Fenton, and Dr. Caius.

"Anne's in her room priming herself and admiring her features in her vanity mirror!" Mistress Meg Page expressed to her frequent visitor. "Mistress Quickly; Alice Ford and I would like to discuss some women's strategy with you a little later on. I promise, it won't take more than an hour of your valuable time."

"Okay, anything's better than working horizontally in a bed, or for that matter, toiling on my knees in one of the upstairs' rooms over at the Garter Belt," Mistress Quickly admitted. "Instead, I'll gladly sit on your comfortable sofa, politely drinking tea, munching on delicious pastries, and discussing the demise of one totally fucked-up male chauvinist pig, Sir John Falstaff."

* * * * * * * * * * * *

Master Page and Master Ford met outside the Blue Boar Inn over in nearby Eastcheap, and compared notes on information supplied by Nym and Pistol concerning John Falstaff's purported and intended romantic escapades with their "cheating Windsor wives".

"Do you think there's any truth in these abominable reports?" Ford asked Page. "How do we know that those ruthless scoundrels Nym and Pistol aren't envious of Falstaff's widespread reputation, and then the two derelicts invented an imaginative canard to trick us. Believe it or not, the public regards Falstaff to be a knight of high dignity, isn't he? Perhaps we're just too jittery and ejaculating prematurely over nothing but a trite triviality."

"True, my good Friend! Nym and Pistol are lowlife fiends that have recently been discarded from that scoundrel Sir John's employ!" Master Page objectively indicated to Master Ford. "Both jerk-off jackals are as fuckin' trustworthy as cobras on the prowl, and the pair are as honorable as those vile traitors Cassius and Casca that furtively plotted against and then assassinated Julius Caesar."

"I don't totally doubt my wife Alice's veracity," Master Ford skeptically remarked. "But I regret that I'll only be able to decapitate Sir John Falstaff once, if I catch him in bed with my spouse, who won't even give me head. And then, I don't care if I have to shamefully hang from the gallows for my sweet revenge! I'll cut-off Alice's flabby tits, too, if she's guilty of infidelity to *our* non-existent sex life! Hey, here comes the merry Host of the Garter and Panty Inn strolling our way with Justice Shallow. Maybe the gregarious Host can shed some illumination on these despicable rumors concerning *our* wives that are circulating all around Windsor."

"How would you two Gentlemen like to accompany Master Page, first to his house, and then to mine, in order to view some possible sins in action?" Master Ford said to Justice Shallow and the amiable

Host, while needing two reliable non-family witnesses to testify on his behalf at *his* imagined assassination trial.

"Sir, a more urgent matter must presently be resolved!" Justice Shallow answered Master Ford in an alarmed, heightened voice. "Dr. Caius has challenged Parson Sir Hugh to a duel to the death over a picayune matter too complicated to explain for a lack of time. The Garter Belt Inn Host here, and I, have sent each combatant to different dueling scenes, but there's always the possibility that the opponents might accidentally meet while each idiot is methodically searching for his foe. We law-abiding, responsible citizens must make certain that the Host's and my mis-directions given to Dr. Caius and to Reverend Sir Hugh have not been ignored and abandoned," Justice Shallow preached in place of the absent Parson Sir Hugh Evans, who might soon be slain.

"Now before we leave, is it true Master Ford that you have a certain grievance against one of my best patrons, the cavalier, inimitable, but often-rowdy Sir John Falstaff?" the Garter Belt and Pink Panty Inn Host asked the offended fellow.

"Yes!" Master Ford tersely responded. "Yes!" the man reiterated.

"Good then! You shall wear an appropriate disguise and use the alias name Brook!" the Host suggested to Master Ford. "Leave it to me. I'll organize all of the applicable details. But first we must keep that hothead fanatic Dr. Caius and his prospective victim Reverend Hugh Evans distant from each other before the Parson has to officiate over his own goddamned funeral Mass. As you can easily determine, it's a very urgent matter!"

"I rather like the code name Brook!" Ford indicated to the creative-minded Host. "It sounds kind of like a stream-of-consciousness term, emblematic of good literature."

"Let's immediately proceed and scour the town!" Justice Shallow impatiently interrupted the small-talk exchange. "I understand that the French doctor is awfully deft at handling both a saber and a sword. Reverend Hugh might just as well sign his own death certificate before the one-sided duel commences! The minister's frail life is definitely in jeopardy!"

'Master Page might trust his fuckin' wife, but I sure as hell don't trust Alice!' Master Ford concluded while not giving one second's thought to Reverend Hugh's life being in imminent danger. 'Oh well; I hope I don't talk too much jargon while wearing my disguise as Brook. But I don't fuckin' want to sound like a goddamned babbling brook, either!'

* * * * * * * * * * * *

"Look Pistol," Falstaff said to his former employee while the two rogues were loitering in front of the infamous Garter Belt and Pink Panty Inn. "I won't lend you a single or a married copper coin, simply because our business relationship is temporarily, if not permanently terminated, and that's as a result of a minor cash-flow problem I'm currently experiencing. And besides Pistol," Falstaff pontificated; "you want to be a big shot, don't you! You still owe me a gold crown for taking Miss Bridget Goodbody upstairs at the Sixty-Nine Tavern and Recreation Parlor over in Coventry. You're a wild baboon Pistol that wants to be an alpha gorilla, or to put it in more relevant contemporary terms, you're an empty pistol thinking that he's a goddamned loaded cannon!"

"Look here, Sir John, you blabbering, bungling, blundering, Fat Fuck. I know you've gotten some supplementary income lately from extorting money from the area Amalgamated Hooker and Prostitute Guild," Pistol asserted. "Can't you just share a little of the loot? I'm fuckin' starving, and I can't expect the fucked-up government to look out for my welfare, now, can I? Stop being so fuckin' frugal and share a bit of your bonanza!"

"Gratis shows no gratitude!" Falstaff weirdly and indecipherably answered. "Now Pistol, you uncouth, waste of humanity; go pick a few pockets; pilfer a few purses; or sell your ugly, smelly-assed body on the streets to rich blind women, you worthless piece of trash. Now if you'll excuse me, I have an appointment inside the prestigious Garter Belt to escape your incompatible company! Appointments generally are always better than disappointments, ya' know! Now leave me the fuck *alone* with your insistence on a loan!"

"Good morning, Sir John!" Mistress Quickly greeted her longtime client inside the Garter Belt and Pink Panty Inn. "I'm in a bit of a thither this morning, since I'm training a visiting prostitute from the Blue Boar, who just got fired from her job over there. So, Sir John; there's no time for a, pardon the expression, no time for the usual supreme-deluxe Quickly' quicky. What's your chauvinistic pleasure besides the usual straight sexual variety?"

"That's okay," Sir John responded in defense of his damaged ego. "Sex this early in the morning seems too tedious and monotonous after experiencing over two-thousand lustful, lusty whores in my legendary lifetime. But Pistol told me you had some germane information to share that hadn't originated in Germany. What's up?"

"I've gotten word concerning *you* in regard to the favors of Mistress Alice Ford," Mistress Quickly revealed in a soft tone of voice. "Are you at all familiar with the history of that sophisticated Lady? She's taken me into her confidence, you know!"

"Well, what about Mistress Ford? Did she drown fording the *Thames?*" Falstaff facetiously asked and joked.

"Well, Sir John; somehow you've gotten her so hot and bothered that she can't piss or shit straight," the Garter Belt and Pink Panty Inn visiting hooker had adroitly informed me of Mistress Ford's dilemma that the inexperienced prostitute had heard circulating through the Windsor grapevine. "That flirtatious letter you had sent Alice has won her affectionate heart, but more importantly, it's juiced-up her love tunnel something fierce. She's even asked me if she could have a secret rendezvous with you upstairs in my highly-specialized and well-equipped S and M Whip Room!"

"Are you sure you aren't shitting me?" Falstaff questioned his informant's credibility. "I wasn't expecting to hear any affirmative reaction to my dispatch for at least several more days!"

"Mistress Ford has thanked heaven a thousand times for your very timely letter," Mistress Quickly exaggerated at least ten to the third power. "And Alice has asked me to inform you that her vindictive husband will not be in the house between ten and eleven today. My distressed friend had related to me the following message last night: 'Instead of Sir John typically going before noon to the Dew Drop Inn, tell him 'Do drop in'!"

"Between ten and eleven you say?" Sir John asked for verification. "I'll have to listen carefully for the tower clock to bong like bongos ten times! I can't wait to hump and pump Alice!"

"Yes, Alice's husband will be out of the home for a scheduled business meeting, and as you might've already heard," Mistress Quickly whispered while feigning sincerity, "their love life no longer exists. It's rumored among the merry wives of Windsor that Master Ford has some sort of chronic sperm duct blockage! Because of his disability condition, Master Ford feels inferior and has a definite ego problem, and Alice's husband is extremely jealous of any man with or without a hard-on. Even the King smiling at *his* wife and saying an innocent 'Hello' makes Master Ford's erratic, possessive, temper travel right through the roof!"

"I promise I'll not let Alice down, and will pay her a visit at the prescribed time!" Sir John proudly stated as if he had achieved (with facility) something spectacular. "I'm glad that we didn't have a quicky this morning Mistress Quickly. Now, I don't have to build-up my sperm reserve to replenish my normally ample and enviable supply! Thanks for providing me with the valuable information about my next lover, Mistress Alice."

"I maintain that you'd better grow a second set of testicles, because Mistress Meg Page has a wet love canal waiting for you, too!" Mistress Quickly confided to the already-elated fat, over-the-hill knight. "Now unfortunately, Meg's husband is seldom out of the house, but Mistress Page also desires to have an extra-marital affair with you, come the first opportunity; perhaps even a threesome with Alice Ford involved. Now, I know Sir John that you've made love to as many as six women in a single day, so these two new ones shouldn't constitute any major challenge for you!"

"Thanks to my myriad charms, I've led a charmed sex life for sure!" Sir John boasted before blowing his huge nose upon his sleeve. "Now tell me; both women have confided in your excellent advice, but does Mistress Alice Ford know about Mistress Meg Page's amorous intentions regarding an adventurous, romantic affair with me, or vice-versa?"

"Neither woman knows about the other having the red hots for you, even though they're absolutely the best of friends," the wily Madame informant prevaricated. "Perhaps you can send your page Robin over to check-out the Page residence. Her husband is fond of Robin, and will not be suspicious of your inevitable affair with Meg upstairs while Robin might be distracting Master Page downstairs should the husband by chance show-up prematurely, which might then induce you, Sir John, to ejaculate prematurely! As you appreciate and know, in sex, timing is everything!"

"That's very clever strategy, indeed, and it's certainly worthy of implementation!" Sir John conceded. "And Robin, of course, will think that he's simply paying a social visit while the young fool is cleverly being used as a pawn on my game board to distract Old Man Page. Pretty slick plan you've conceived, I must confess."

"Yes; teenagers are so naïve and gullible, and so unaware of the adult wickedness that exists all around them!" Mistress Quickly philosophized and added. "Oh, to be young and innocent once more! It's too bad that youth is wasted on the young."

"Here's a purse of money to recompense for your good counsel!" Sit John said, handing several silver coins to his personal lady matchmaker. "I must commend you on your stellar arranging skills!"

After Mistress Quickly left the premises with her easily earned compensation, Bardolph approached Sir John (at a table) with a full sack of imported vintage wine. "Sir John; here's a little treat for you that's been paid for by a gentleman sitting over there named Brook (Master Ford in disguise). He wishes to speak with you and indulge in your wonderful company, and be exposed to your vast empirical knowledge about anything and everything."

"Invite the Gentleman over, Bardolph!" Sir John acknowledged and directed. "I'll be a good listener, downing several more sacks of savory wine before my next scheduled disappointment, er, I mean delightful appointment at ten. Shit! I'm getting an erection just thinking about two succulent Windsor beaver hides!"

Master Ford disguised as a visiting British merchant approached Sir John's table and introduced himself as "Brook; Mr. Donny Brook". Then Brook (Ford) continued his awkward preamble by saying, "God bless you, Sir. We were both sitting in this tawdry, bawdy inn without merry company, so I figured I'd share some fine wine with you and become acquainted with a new-found friend."

"Sit your ass down, and make yourself comfortable!" Sir John cordially stated before telling the newcomer to the inn *his* name. "Incidentally, thanks for the sack of expensive wine. What's on your mind besides a baldhead, Master Brook?"

"Hear me out, Sir John!" the masquerader said, feigning a modicum of sincerity. 'Here's a bag of money in exchange for your sage advice, for I've heard around Windsor-town that you're a gentleman and a scholar, and truly quite proficient in the practice of courtesy and wisdom."

"That's very generous of you!" Sir John gratefully acknowledged, as the destitute knight swiftly confiscated the money sack that had been placed upon the table. "What the hell do you wish to discuss that warrants my expertise? Confidentially, I happen to know plenty of shit about almost everything."

"I'm a man of many unique and eccentric follies, and I wish to share one of my peculiar fantasies with you," Brook (Ford) persuasively fibbed. "Now then, Sir John; there's a gentlewoman residing here in Windsor. I believe her name is Mistress Alice Ford. And I hear that her husband is a real jealous, mentally-unstable bastard, who positively goes berserk from time to time!"

"Yes, I'm vaguely acquainted with the two people you've just mentioned," Sir John concurred before imbibing another mouthful of delicious imported wine. "What about Mistress Alice Ford?"

"I've long desired meeting her, but being a timid man, I've been lacking the resolve or the courage to take the initiative," Brook (Ford) slyly lied. "I've purchased many expensive gifts to present to her, but then my will always chickens-out whenever I feel inspired to visit the dame, especially when her unpredictable husband is away from Windsor conducting business."

"And you've never spoken to her; never felt her tits, or never got your middle finger wet fondling around up inside her divine pussy?" Sir John asked.

"Never!" Brook replied, gritting his teeth while nearly telling the truth. "Never!" the masquerader angrily repeated.

"Your delightful mirth is nearly as large and as wide as my disgusting girth!" Sir John hardily laughed before ravenously guzzling-down some more tasty wine. "Now please be more definite and tell me your true purpose in consulting my sage opinion about Mistress Alice Ford."

"Since you, Sir John, are a reputable man of honest discourse and discreet intercourse, I wish that you woo Mistress Ford while representing my intense love for her," Brook suggested.

"Are you some kind of fucked-up voyeur?" Sir John rudely asked his tablemate. "Are you going to masturbate in a closet listening to Mistress Ford swooning her heart out over my amorous advances?"

"All I wish is for you to put in some good words for me and to introduce her to me, so that I don't have to take that difficult first step all by myself," Brook (Ford) convincingly insisted. "I assure you that the rest of the wooing will be exclusively up to me."

"I'll accept your good gesture and good will!" Sir John stated before gulping down some more delectable imported wine for breakfast. "I guarantee you, Mr. Donny Brook, that I can easily fulfill your fucked-up request as you've so far described it."

"How can this all be arranged?" Brook (Ford) anxiously inquired. "I know you're reputed to be a miracle worker, Sir John, but what can be done on such short notice?"

"As lady luck would have it, Master Donny Brook, I'm slated to meet Mistress Alice Ford at her residence between the hours of ten and eleven this very morning. Her jealous and rascally knave of a husband will be preoccupied with an urgent business transaction between those glorious hours," Falstaff elaborated to Brook. "You'll have your golden opportunity to accomplish your fucked-up love goal between ten and eleven. Just remember Master Brook', to the wise experienced man, love is merely pleasurable sex, and fuckin' nothing more! Ha, ha, ha! And I hope ya' get some sticky semen all over your right hand while pounding away in the closet! Ha, ha, ha!"

"I'm blessed to having made your incomparable acquaintance!" Brook (Ford) grossly exaggerated. "Do you know this asshole husband of hers, Master Ford?"

"I hardly know the feckless knave, but understand that he's a complete clueless, self-centered, jerk-off!" Sir John disclosed before consuming another mouthful of savory spirits. "He's a pretty rich and pathetic son-of-a-bitch bastard, though, and his wallet's going to keep me happy for at least the next several years as I employ my advanced gigolo methods on his gullible and vulnerable, easily-flattered wife."

"Aren't you afraid that your activities with the elegant Mistress Alice Ford might be discovered by her jealous husband?" Brook (Ford) asked. "He sounds like he's a desperate, savage individual."

"I'll kick his ass all the distance from Windsor to Kingdom-come if the degenerate asshole squawks one critical word about me to anyone around the town!" Sir John haughtily declared. "Now Master Brook, meet me outside the Ford house in a few hours, just before ten. Then you'll get to see a real Casanova in action!"

Sir John demonstrably finished-off the remaining ounces from the wine sack, slowly rose, belched, loudly farted seven consecutive times, and then excused himself. Next, the cocky fellow slowly staggered out of the Garter Belt and Pink Panty Inn. Brook (Ford) sat there seething and fuming, and contemplating his intensifying animosity, and also plotting his imaginative retribution for the inebriated obese knight.

'What a damned epicurean, hedonistic asshole that fat fuck Falstaff is!' Brook (Ford) concluded and reasoned. 'My wife is a false, unfaithful woman that can, in my judgment, no longer be trusted! My fabulous fortune is in jeopardy because of her infatuations with this ignoble, obese, asshole, Sir John Falstaff! Master Page trusts his faithful wife, but I can't mine! I'd rather trust a thief walking my horse than my idle wife alone at home, looking and longing for male companionship!' Brook (Ford) imagined. 'My only ambition is to now catch Sir John in the act with Alice, and then I'll get my supreme revenge on that no-good family-breaking bastard!'

* * * * * * * * * * *

The Frenchman Dr. Caius was angry that Reverend Sir Hugh had not showed-up for the scheduled duel that the Garter Inn Host had fraudulently arranged.

"John (Jack) Rugby, stop playing with your balls and tell me what fuckin' time it is!" Dr. Caius demanded to his subordinate.

"It's ten-minutes past the hour, and no detectable signs yet of the parsimonious Parson!" Rugby added, infuriating the doctor even more. "Maybe he's officiating at a burial, or at a Christening, or perhaps at a Bible-burning demonstration; or some other monolithic religious bullshit like that!"

"Damn it, Jack!" Dr. Caius yelled in frustration. "The preacher might as well be officiating at his own funeral if he dares show his ass in this grassy, weed-infested, vacant lot. There's one thing I detest more than fuckin' cowards, Jack, and that's fuckin' cowardly priests, ministers, and rabbis. Now then, pathetic Jack Rugby; take-up an imaginary sword and pretend to be dueling with me!" Dr. Caius ordered his obedient aide.

"Are you insane?" Rugby boisterously replied. "You're liable to kill me with either a real sword or an imaginary one! You're way more fucked-up than I ever thought you were! Thank God! Here comes the Garter Belt Host now to save my tender ass from brutal extermination! And there's Master Slender, Master Page, and Justice Shallow heading this way, too!"

"Bully good morning to you, bully, Doctor!" the Host cheerfully greeted. "Fine morning for a duel! Where's your adversary?"

"Why are you four assholes here?" Dr. Caius defensively asked. "Are you designated to be witnesses to the brief killing, so that I can be sued by the Parson's estate with all of my money going to his fucked-up gay congregation?"

"We simply came here to see the exciting fight!" the Host enthusiastically declared. "I'm sure you're unaware that Reverend Hugh became a Parson because he had killed over three-hundred opponents in duels throughout Ireland and Germany prior to moving here to Windsor. The expert swordsman then became a minister to erase the extreme guilt that Hugh Evans felt from executing three-hundred highly-trained opponents."

"Well then, if the cocky Reverend ever shows-up, he'll have the last thrilling match of his life!" Dr. Caius countered with a degree of new-found fear evident in his faltering tone of voice. "I'll only wait here for six-more-hours for the notorious coward to show his florid face, and not one second more," Caius lectured to his apathetic second, John Rugby.

"Your intrepid opponent is a sage fellow, my friend," Justice Shallow said to Dr. Caius. "Parson Sir Hugh is a curer of souls, and you're just a mere curer of bodies. Isn't that true Master Page?"

"As true as the gospels and the rest of the Holy Scriptures, too, including the insane Book of Revelations!" Master Page confirmed. "You should seek peace, esteemed Dr. Caius, as much as our eminent Justice of the Peace does!"

"If you should severely wound Parson Sir Hugh," Justice Shallow told volatile Dr. Caius; "then, Sir Sawbones Surgeon, I do believe that it's your absolute moral and legal responsibility to heal him, and if you should luckily kill him, either accidentally or deliberately, it's your liability to pay for his funeral expenses and to compensate for his financially stressed church's massive accumulated debts!"

"This is fuckin' blackmail; goddamned, unprecedented extortion!" Dr. Caius protested. "It's against all decency and chivalry!"

"Those abstract terms you've just cited, Doctor, are but obsolete anachronisms from the distant past!" Justice Shallow profoundly vociferated. "Now, I hereby urge you to abandon your preposterous quest for presumed retribution, and to return to the safety of your home before you kill Reverend Sir Hugh, and destroy your whole life by foolishly sacrificing your total wealth. Forget this valor bullshit that you're advocating, and seriously think precisely about the words 'practicality' and 'bankruptcy'!"

The Host took Justice Shallow, Master Page, and Slender aside for what Dr. Caius's young aide Jack described as "a rugby huddle".

"Now listen-up, Men," the local inn's Host confidentially stated. "Reverend Sir Hugh is hiding-out in the village of Frogmore, five miles from here, until this dueling bullshit is finally over. I'll escort the Doctor home, and you three degenerates are to journey to Frogmore and inform Reverend Sir Hugh that everything's been satisfactorily settled, and that the fucked-up minister's inferior life is no longer in immediate danger. And I understand that the natives have a terrific inn in Frogmore where the prostitutes dance naked on the tables, and allow the patrons to trim *their* fluffy bushes with tiny scissors!"

"That's all I need to hear!" Justice Shallow replied. "Let's go to Frogmore right this minute, men!" the deranged magistrate entreated Master Page and his nephew Abraham Slender. "I spent three wonderful years in the Kalahari, and I know just how the Bushmen trim their ladies' snatcheroos!"

"Say, wait a minute!" Dr, Caius imperatively shouted to Slender. "Aren't you the varmint that Parson Sir Hugh was representing to Mistress Anne Page, the glorious angelic woman of my dreams?"

"Hell no!" Slender denied. "I'm just a visiting academic expert on South African Bushmen and their wonderful, exotic, erotic habits, and nothing more!"

"Well then," the Host said to the indignant and combustible Dr. Caius. "Let's cut through a few vacant fields, and I'll take you to a house where your ultimate love Mistress Anne is visiting. Perhaps you can utilize your time a little more wisely, hustling your heart's desire, rather than spending your fabulous energy killing Reverend Sir Hugh, and then squandering your fortune and your life paying for your stupid reckless deed as reparation!"

"Very well, then!" Dr. Caius cooperatively agreed. "Come along Jack; at my heels!" the Doctor ordered the obedient, junior jerk-off Rugby "We're going to attend a scrum, and possibly an entire scrimmage, over at a house across yonder fields. I don't want you to hang-around with those other Gentlemen, and learn to your detriment all about the evils of becoming a bona fide, on the prowl, authentic British bush-man!"

Act III

Beautiful Anne Page was not at the house where the Host had thought she had been, so Dr. Caius became angry with his "blundering guide", and the weirdo surgeon, the Inn Host, and John (Jack) Rugby then trekked the five-mile distance from Windsor to the bustling village of Frogmore, where the enraged physician theorized Reverend Sir Hugh was hanging (hiding) out. Parson Evans and Simple were idly standing and waiting in a remote field outside Frogmore reviewing recent events.

"Look over yonder to the west!" Simple directed Parson Sir Hugh's erratic attention. "That's Justice Shallow, Master Page, and Abraham Slender walking this way."

Soon, the three trekkers spotted and approached Reverend Sir Hugh and Simple. "What are you doing? Waiting to get your ass and guts smeared all over this fallow field?" Justice Shallow shouted to the now-neurotic Parson. "Why wait for Judgment Day when it's cursing precursor is intently stalking you!"

"What the heck are you talking about?" the seldom-cursing Parson asked. "You make no sense at all, whether you're drunk or sober!"

"Below yonder ridge you can see the Host of the Garter Belt and Pink Panty Inn, accompanied by Dr. Caius and his servant Johnny Rugby, coming this way," Slender pointed-out to the now-trembling and lip quivering Preacher. "Now keep your weapon concealed, and we might be able to dicker some kind of agreement while your dick is still attached to your out-of-shape body."

"Disarm the combatants' weapons before the two fools dismember each other!" Justice Shallow ordered Master Page and

Abraham Slender. "This fight could only result in a one-man massacre."

"I want to attack and maim this cowardly priest, or whatever the hell he is!" Dr. Caius vehemently objected. "I want to paralyze the snoopy bastard so that the troublemaker suffers for the rest of his life! Then, there'll be one less rectum in the rectory tonight!"

"You've made both of us the laughingstock of Windsor and the general vicinity!" Parson Sir Hugh volleyed-back to his determined physician enemy. "My good reputation has been blemished Dr. Caius; all because of your stupid, capricious, queer sensitivities."

"Let's have peace on earth and goodwill towards all assholes like you two Morons!" the Host yelled, castigating both Dr. Caius and Parson Hugh Evans. "As they say in Spain, 'Paz hermanos'."

"Fuck you; fuck your promiscuous business partner Mistress Quickly, and fuck the fucked-up Garter Belt and Pink Panty Inn, too!" Dr. Caius bellowed to the Host as Reverend Sir Hugh repeatedly administered the Sign of the Cross while mumbling some rhythmical church phrases in Latin.

"Gentlemen; I had intentionally deceived both you Dr. Caius and you Parson Sir Hugh to avoid someone getting injured or mutilated in an unnecessary, brutal conflict, which obviously could lead to a cruel death, or perhaps even two," the Inn Host communicated. "I had deliberately sent you two phony gladiators to separate places to allow for a cooling-off period; whereby, we could come to an honorable termination of these possible lethal hostilities. Let's have peace on earth; and not wanton violence and murder!"

After giving his rhetorical presentation, the Host left everyone standing with their mouths agape, and then the inn proprietor began trekking back in the direction of Windsor. Soon Justice Shallow, Master Page, and Abraham Slender left the grassy field, walking behind the Host, who was completely unaware of and oblivious to their trailing presence.

"Well, Parson Sir Hugh. Now that those self-righteous assholes have confiscated our swords and daggers, what do you have to say for yourself, since you've made complete fools out of the both of us?" Dr. Caius indicted his designated foe as Simple and John Rugby listened to the beginning of a potentially huge quarrel.

"Everyone's a fool, but only honest ones like myself are brave enough to admit it!" Parson Sir Hugh answered, sounding a bit like a disciple of Socrates. "Since you now share my public mockery and disgrace, I suggest that we become friends and allies and have a common enemy. Such collaboration could be mutually beneficial!"

"Who might that asshole enemy be?" Dr. Caius demanded knowing. "The Bishop, the Cardinal, the Pope, the King?"

"That scurvy Host of the infamous Garter Belt and Pink Panty Inn!" Parson Sir Hugh cited. "That devious jerk deliberately tricked both of us by sending us to different locations."

"That's a really good decent idea Parson!" Dr. Caius concurred. "Now I'll treat you to an expensive dinner at a very special place I know over in downtown Frogmore."

"What is it?" Parson Sir Hugh asked. "Is it in a church hall?"

"I think it's called the Sixty-Nine Whorehouse Inn Bed and Breakfast, or something bizarre like that!" Dr. Caius prattled. "I've heard a lot of good gossip about it from my Windsor friends, Rudy, Jezebel, and Sam Delilah."

"I just love places with numerical names," Reverend Hugh acknowledged. "In my book Sixty-Nine, sounds just as good as any other darned arithmetical numbers that exist in the after*math* of potential violence."

* * * * * * * * * * * *

The meeting between Mistress Alice Ford and Sir John Falstaff was postponed until the following day at ten o'clock sharp, mainly because of other significant events in Frogmore that had attracted the attention and the imagination of many male Windsor residents. But the spiteful Brook (Master Ford) desired to organize as many witnesses as possible to convict Sir John of taking advantage of his chatty wife's suspected proclivity towards infidelity. Using the non-clever guise of providing wine and entertainment at a quarter past ten o'clock at his high-society house, Master Ford invited selected guests (witnesses) over to corroborate his intended allegations against the delusional, non-sensational Sir John Falstaff.

At 9:30 a.m. Robin (John Falstaff's page) came to the Page front door to escort Meg Page over to Alice Ford's place.

"Oh Husband; I just have to see my friend Alice!" Meg said to her disenchanted spouse. "We have so much Windsor fake gossip to get caught-up on! If our spouses both died, I think I would consider marrying Alice, since we're so close now! How frivolous and ridiculous my comment was!" Meg incessantly rambled-on to dubious Master Page. "Unfortunately, Husband; same sex marriages are forbidden everywhere, even in immoral places like Denmark, France, and the Vatican!"

'What the fuck's going on here? A threesome?' Master Page nervously speculated. 'I've always suspected my wife of extra-marital, kinky stuff, but now Meg is going to hop into the goddamned sack with Alice, and that fat, sloppy, obnoxious slob John Falstaff, the insufferable bonehead perhaps being under the covers with both hussies! This is a very sad day; yes, it most certainly is!'

"See you later, Dear!" Meg said to her doubting and jealous mate. "Have a wonderful day farting around town! Make sure that your excessive gas doesn't propel yourself all the way to Frogmore!"

"Yes, my Darling!" the irritated spouse with the newly developed irritable bowel syndrome answered with a forced smile. "I'll have a simply marvelous time farting around Windsor with the other old fart men! Tell Alice that I said 'hello'!"

According to Master Ford's shrewd plan, he and Master Page met Justice Shallow, Abraham Slender, Parson Sir Hugh, and Dr. Caius in front of the Garter Belt and Pink Panty Inn.

"All of you soon-to-be eyewitnesses, er, I mean male guests follow me over to my place!" Master Ford insisted. "I promise you some fine entertainment!"

"Sorry to cancel-out on you, Master Ford," Justice Shallow grunted and apologized. "But my nephew Abraham Slender and I must honor a late breakfast appointment with the buxom Mistress Anne Page. We had scheduled the important brunch several days ago, and when you changed your house party visit from yesterday to today, there was a difficult time conflict."

"Yes, I have designs of someday soon marrying Anne Page, and this 11:15 breakfast get-together is a good beginning to achieve that blessed end," Abraham Slender added.

"You have my encouragement!" Master Page, said to the grizzle-bearded Slender. "You'll make a fine son-in-law even, if you look like one of the apostles, either St. Peter or Judas, I think!"

"What the fuck's this shit about breakfast with Anne Page!" Dr. Caius objected, since the belligerent maniac too had tender feelings towards Mistress Anne. "Fuck your party Ford! I too am later going to the breakfast with the young Mistress Page!" Dr. Caius maintained, while unilaterally and daringly inviting himself to the brunch engagement.

"What do you think Master Page of Anne's other suitor, Master Fenton?" Justice Shallow suavely asked.

"He's a devil that used to hang-around with the rowdy Prince Henry and that fucked-up scoundrel Poins," Master Page disgustedly answered. "Hopefully and preferably, my impressionable daughter

Anne will marry either Abraham Slender or Dr. Caius. My wealth and fortune wait on my consent, and my consent is leaning in the direction of those two eligible wooers. That Fenton character is an absolute long shot."

"Please; someone come to my re-scheduled party!" Master Ford begged. "I'll have wine and cheese, and maybe even some rare novelty entertainment for you to view! Don't poop-out on me now, you poop-heads! I'm counting on your cooperation!"

Almost everyone abandoned the scene, leaving poor rejected Master Ford standing in front of the notorious Garter Belt and Pink Panty Inn all by his lonesome. 'Oh well; I guess I'll just have to catch that louse Sir John Falstaff porking Alice while eating-out Meg, or porking Meg and eating-out Alice all by my fuckin' self!' Master Ford lividly imagined, as a trace of smoke escaped out of his wiggling ears.

* * * * * * * * * * * *

Not only did Parson Sir Hugh Evans and Dr. Caius seek revenge on the peacemaking Host, but also Mistress Alice Ford and Mistress Meg Page wanted to get satisfactory retribution against the devil-may-care Sir John Falstaff. Ten o'clock was about to chime on the village square clock, as Robin preceded his egotistical master, Sir John Falstaff, to the Ford home. To Sir John, everything was going like clockwork.

Mistress Ford ordered her two burly servants Robert and John to take the giant clothesbasket filled with dirty rags, discarded towels and stinky underwear, and then place the huge object in the hallway next to the master bedroom door. "When I tell you," Mistress Ford gave Robert and John some last-minute instructions, "take this large basket and carry it down to the *Thames* riverbank and then dump its contents into the muddy river!" the woman specifically ordered the two brawny weightlifters.

"Everything's all set from my end!" Mistress Meg Page told Mistress Alice Ford. "Here comes that impish rascal Robin now to your front door to check and see if your husband's still at home. Both our spouses love the facetious imp! The cute little lad is inadvertently doing surveillance work for his disgustingly corpulent master, Sir John Falstaff."

"Hello Robin! What's new in Sherwood Forest?" Mistress Ford joked. "Have you pestered the Sheriff of Nottingham yet today?"

"I trust that Master Ford is not home to amuse me with some parlor games and tricks," Robin mentioned, alluding to Falstaff's expected visit. "That being the case, Sir John is going to enter your house via the back door. That's the same way he likes to give and receive sex, at least that's what the hell all the fellows over at the Belt and Garter tell me. Basically, Sir John likes entering exits, and the knight believes that a rear end is an entrance and not an exit!"

"Does Sir John know that I'm in the house visiting Mistress Ford?" Mistress Page asked.

"No, Mistress! He's unaware of that fact; I am sure!" Robin honestly replied. "That coincidence, I'm sure, will be a pleasant surprise to him."

"Good then! I'll hide myself in the spare bedroom with a view of the street, and see if any visitors arrive while Alice and Sir John are together," Meg Page said to Robin. "You might call that activity my 'window of opportunity', ha, ha, ha!"

"Okay Robin, go out back and tell your master that I'm home alone!" Mistress Ford commanded the naïve page. "And make sure you emphasize 'home alone', or else I'll have my ferocious pet bulldog bite your post-pubescent testicles off!"

After Robin left the house to meet Falstaff, Mistress Meg Page whispered something salient to Mistress Alice Ford. "This necessary moral lesson will teach Sir John to know the difference between elegant ladies and atrocious whores, and not to mistake one for the other," Mistress Page stated to Mistress Ford. "The clumsy oaf certainly lacks manners and manors, for the chivalrous, rich knight the fool falsely claims to be, and for the country estates the braggart doesn't have!"

Sir John entered the Ford house via the rear door, and immediately began professing his love for Alice. "Oh, my heavenly beauty! My life's ambition has been fulfilled at the very sight of you! I'm glad I've not died and gone to Heaven before this precious moment!"

"Oh, sweet Sir John, woo me some more!" Mistress Ford begged. "I need foreign male affection, very badly."

"Oh, perfect woman; if your screwball husband were dead, I would swear it before the King and his Council that I would marry you!" Falstaff bullshitted. "The courts of France and Spain know not such radiant female pulchritude as you wondrously possess! Your magnificent eyes sparkle like diamonds, Alice, and your rich, red lips look like bright shining rubies."

"I fear that you love Mistress Meg Page more than you love me," Alice Ford cleverly countered. "You do believe that she's prettier than I, don't you?"

"Oh, my sweet British wallflower! It's quite true that I find Mistress Page quite attractive, but her overall beauty pales when compared with your stunning, gorgeous, appearance," Sir John flattered and egregiously lied. "You must certainly be Venus in disguise! Yes, a contemporary Aphrodite."

"Okay, Sir John! Cut the happy horse-shit and get to the point!" Mistress Ford matter-of-factly said, surprising the cocky, fatuous, fat Falstaff. "Now hurry up! We only have an hour to do our amorous business! Kiss me, you big Lunk, er, I mean Hunk! Then, feel and caress my soft breasts; and then romantically carry me into the master bedroom! Thrill me, Sir John! Thrill me!"

Just as Sir John puckered-up his lips, Robin bolted into the hallway and loudly announced, "Mistress Ford! Mistress Page is at the door panting and sweating, and cursing like crazy! She says she needs to speak to you right now!"

"You'd better hide, Sir John!" Alice directed her obese suitor. "Mistress Page loves to tattle and expand short stories into tall tales! This is indeed a most delicate situation to handle and resolve without residual repercussions!"

Mistress Page came into the main section of the house and swiftly paced down the hallway ranting and raving. "Alice, what the hell have you done? You're publicly shamed! You're scorned! Your fine reputation is ruined forever! Damaged beyond repair!"

"What on Earth are you ever talking and ranting about?" Alice theatrically challenged.

"Your husband is only a block away, charging over here with the Windsor constables to search for a gentleman, more specifically, a very dangerous prowler that had been spotted hiding in your backyard and about to break into your house," Mistress Page (as planned) alerted her good friend. "Your husband is shouting in public that the intruder or interloper, or whatever the hell he is, happens to be inside this domicile at your improper consent and solicitation! The hostile mob is going to search every niche, nook and cranny to find the vile trespasser, or criminal rapist, or barbaric molester, or whatever the hell he is!"

"Good grief!" Alice screamed. "Meg, what should I do?"

"If the trespasser is in the house, get him the hell out of here as quickly as possible!" Meg Page hollered, feigning alarm. "Do this

405

successfully Alice, or else your good life and reputation among the Windsor gossipers is up in smoke! Think and act fast!"

"The gentleman I'm keeping can also be ruined by this atrocious scandal!" Mistress Ford dramatically yelled. "I would rather lose a thousand pounds solid gold than to have this prominent, innocent man trapped and detected inside this reputable house! I must avoid sensational village gossip at all cost!"

"Have your male companion hide inside the giant laundry basket among the foul-smelling greasy rags and wash towels!" Mistress Page loudly suggested so that Sir John could easily hear. "Then have your brawny servants Robert and John carry the buck basket and dump its contents into the *Thames* next to Datchet Mead," Meg then lowly whispered.

Hearing the wild clamor inside the house, along with the vengeful men vociferously shouting at the locked door, Sir John voluntarily climbed into the immense buck-basket and covered himself up with putrid-smelling rags and towels. Then Mistress Ford summoned her muscle-bound servants Robert and John to immediately lug the heavy basket away to the River Thames.

The two long-haired Samsons quickly tugged and dragged the immense basket to the back door, and then maneuvered it into the back-yard, placed a sturdy pole between the canvas metal loops, hoisted the buck-basket upon their sturdy shoulders, and slowly walked ahead, carrying their very heavy burden several blocks to the banks of the *Thames*.

The incensed, churchgoing, village men, defending the sacred institution of moral marriage, finally broke the front door down, burst into the house, and began searching every crack and crevice (except of course, Mistress Ford and Mistress Page's cracks and crevices) in an effort to discover condemning evidence of Alice's "undesirable paramour".

While the intensive search and manhunt were underway, Meg whispered to Alice, "I've got some more imaginative tricks up my petticoat to further stymie that fat slob rogue, John Falstaff!"

"Let's get Mistress Quickly to convince Sir John that our beaver cracks are steaming hot and wet for the immense pig to eagerly enjoy feasting upon our luscious, squiggly, bearded clams," Mistress Ford whispered back. "But just about now, Sir John is being tossed into the murky *Thames!* Ha, ha, ha! I can't control my bladder! This giggling is too intense! I'm going to piss myself! Ha, ha, ha!"

"This is a damned wild goose chase!" Dr. Caius yelled at Master Ford. "We can't find a cunt hair anywhere in the whole damned spotless place! Now I no longer feel like eating a delicious brunch!"

"Master Page and Parson Sir Hugh also hollered from different locations that no stranger was hiding anywhere in the Ford dwelling.

"You'd better apologize to your wife and buy her a piece of jewelry each day for the next six months!" the Parson bellowed into Master Ford's face. "Your false accusations and insinuations were completely unwarranted, and therefore, totally deleterious to your wife's superb character! You appear to be a phony accuser bearing false witness, Master Ford!"

"Pardon me, Gentlemen, for this embarrassing, unforeseen inconvenience!" Ford begged the community prosecutors for forgiveness. "We'll take a stroll through the park, and then I'll buy you all the most expensive meal, and the finest imported vintage wine on the inn's menu!"

"But what about our wives?" Master Page asked Master Ford.

"That's the only reason I left my morning business to come over to your place!"

"We'll take the leftovers home from the inn for them to munch on!" Ford nervously indicated. "Both those overweight bimbos need heavy-duty diets!"

After overhearing their husbands' conversation, the eavesdropping wives had their own private dialogue. "Now, where the hell is Sir John Falstaff when we need him the most?" Alice Ford whispered and intimated to the equally-shocked Meg Page. "Our husbands have become dirty-rotten, no-good, bastard, chauvinistic pigs! They're the ones that should've been dumped into the goddamned *Thames.*"

* * * * * * * * * * * *

Fenton, a fine young gentleman, showed-up at the Page home the following morning to woo Mistress Anne, but the young fellow got the impression that Master Page resented his presence, along with his presents. The well-matched young suitor and Anne were engaged in an intensive "evaluation of circumstances" conversation inside the Page's well-furnished parlor.

"I sense that your old man hates my guts, my brain, my eyes, my ass, and my testicles, too!" Master Fenton complained to the gorgeous gender-confused girl with the pageboy haircut. "He hates and distrusts any man besides himself!"

"Father's just angry because of all the nasty gossip circulating around Windsor about mother having an affair with that outrageous fat slob Sir John Falstaff," Anne attempted to clarify, giving Fenton more encouragement in his marriage pursuit. "In fact, Mother and Father are strongly considering moving the family to Frogmore, where there's supposed to be a higher morality practiced, along with a lower gossip level evident than that which exists here in Windsor."

"Dear Anne, I fear that your father worries that he'll have to contribute too much to your dowry, and he's also cognizant that I'm a mild-mannered gentleman of noble blood and heritage, but suspects that I'm an unemployed suitor out to unethically pilfer his accumulated wealth," Fenton explained. "Your dad accurately perceives me as a wild university student, solely engaged in extra-curricular activity, frequenting bawdy inns, and often visiting popular brothels. Truthfully Anne; I've never felt so woebegone in all my bad-luck life."

"Father's usually a straight-shooter, whether he's aiming his bow and arrow at one of Justice Shallow's deer, or taking a leak in the family outhouse," Anne answered. "In the final analysis, dad is always prudent and just."

"Well, darling Anne, I must honestly confess that at first I was very interested in you because of your father's great assets, but now, I'm more fascinated by your firm buttocks and solid breasts than I am by his accumulated fortune! I mean, you have assets, too. Feminine assets!" the lazy, indolent, penniless Fenton expressed. "Your love is far richer than your father's great fortune, both figuratively and literally speaking."

"Father's simply testing you to determine if you have the mettle when you awkwardly meddle to be his one and only son-in-law!" Anne meticulously confided to Fenton. "Father's not into either heavy mettle or heavy meddle, if you know what the hell I mean."

The pleasant-but-frank chat was rudely disrupted by a commotion at the front door. Mistress Quickly, Justice Shallow, and his stranger-than-weird nephew Abraham Slender, were arguing and making a racket (not a tennis one either). Slender was yelling that he was going to obtain a pipe to bend over Fenton's head. Mistress Quickly' quickly entered the parlor, and the Madame requested that Anne come to the front door and help mediate the dispute-in-progress.

"Master Abraham Slender would like a word with you!" Lady Quickly informed Anne. "It's quite urgent!"

"I wish it were only a one syllable word as you have stated!" Anne replied with a frown accentuating her facial features, clearly showing her preference in wooers. "But since Abraham Slender happens to be both my father and my mother's first choice in my marital suitors, I'll respectfully honor my parents' intentions. Oh, Mistress Quickly. What a world of vicious, ill-favored faults in which I must live and survive! Please excuse all of this extraordinary chaos Master Fenton, but I'm drowning in an overwhelming choice crisis!"

"Well, Mistress Anne," Mistress Quickly indicated. "Master Slender is legally employed and earns a handsome three-hundred-pounds a year. Unfortunately, you must make a difficult decision between love and money. Slender's money will still be there twenty-years from now, but I'm not so damned sure about Master Fenton's damned love lasting more than a decadent decade."

Anne stepped into the foyer in a rather confused state of mind, and met the impatiently waiting Slender and Shallow, who suddenly turned from hostile to cordial. Justice Shallow was the first to speak.

"Mistress Anne," the town magistrate prefaced. "My horny nephew here loves you with a passion, and seeks your hand, and also the rest of your body, in Holy Matrimony," the Justice announced. "In fact, Master Slender says he loves you as much as he does any woman in all of Gloucestershire, Frogmore, or Windsor, and the fine fellow promises to maintain your happiness like a decent, God-fearing gentleman should."

"Maintain me!" Anne squawked. "Your nephew makes me sound like I'm a goddamned house or a friggin' oxcart! Pray tell, of all the impudent gall! Master Slender wants to maintain me! Ha! Stop speaking for your intimidated nephew and let the asshole suitor account for himself! Doesn't your damned lame-brained nephew understand that I'm a liberated woman?"

"My uncle means that I'll keep you happy and sustained," formerly reticent Slender endeavored to clarify. "And if I should regrettably die before you do, Mistress Anne, you'll be guaranteed half my annual income, which is a tidy hundred-and-fifty-pounds a year. And if I suddenly croak, you'll be entitled to inherit my summer cottage over in Frogmore!"

"I'll leave you two enamored lovebirds alone for a minute to converse in private to resolve this momentary, minor lovers' quarrel!" Justice Shallow said, winking at his nephew.

"Master Slender!" Anne Page exclaimed in an effort to discourage the favored suitor's suit. "What is your will?"

"My will?" Slender nervously replied. "I haven't made my will out yet because, by the grace of God, I've in perfect health!"

"No, you bungling Ignoramus! I meant what are your intentions with me should we have to, by necessity and arrangement, get married?" Anne demanded. "Clarify your position on that matter."

"Now, Mistress Page; we'd have to consult with your generous father and with my stingy uncle to see exactly what should be done with you!" Slender stupidly answered the already-insulted young lady. "They're calling the shots here, you know! Your father is better equipped to render an explanation than I am! They're both Windsor bigwigs who can actually afford big wigs!"

Master and Meg Page then sauntered into the foyer via the hallway. Anne's parents were quite assertive and emotional.

"What's that lackadaisical lover boy Fenton doing lounging-around inside our house?" Master Page screamed at his sensitive daughter. "Learn to love and accept Master Abraham Slender here!" Then, Master Page turned his attention to the apprehensive Fenton, anxiously sitting and squirming on the parlor room sofa. "This is not a goddamned haunted house, so stop haunting it with your presence and your cheap presents! Don't you understand plain and simple Middle English, Master Fenton! My daughter's already taken, and she'll be properly maintained and sustained in the future, too!"

"Master Fenton," Meg Page interrupted, trying to establish a degree of civility and diplomacy to the squabble-in-progress. "Please find yourself a suitable mate over at the Garter Belt and Panty Inn; or at the Blue Boar Inn in Eastcheap, or at the Sixty-Nine Bread and Breakfast over in Frogmore!"

"Speak to Mistress Meg!" Mistress Quickly advised the totally flabbergasted Fenton. "Say something decisive like you want to get laid, but only with her!"

"Mistress Page, in spite of all the vehement protests, I must defend and again profess my love for your sweet, precious daughter Anne," Fenton courageously stated while decisively rising from the sofa. "I'll not surrender my suit so easily, as long as your darling daughter shows me interest. Doesn't Anne have any say in this important matter? After all, it is her damned life!"

"Mother, please don't force me to marry yonder ugly fool, Abraham Slender!" Anne neurotically begged. "Just his hideous appearance, let alone his peculiar meaner demeanor, scares the living shit out of me!"

"I seek you a better husband!" Meg Page agreed with her daughter, while referring to nixing Abraham Slender.

"Yes; I do believe that Dr. Caius is a suitable candidate!" Mistress Quickly butted-in (without turning her enormous ass), adding fodder to the general confusion.

"Shit, Mother! I feel like a piece of property rather than a gifted heiress!" Anne argued and cried. "I don't wish to lead the rest of my life feeling like a vegetable vegetating with that bearded pepper, this hairy onion!" Anne yelled and sobbed while pointing at a completely mortified and dumbfounded Abraham Slender.

"Master Fenton; my daughter is extremely upset, and I must counsel her in private," Meg Page maintained. "Please act like a gentleman and cease interfering in our family quarrel, er, I mean matter. We'll talk another time when things are more tranquil!"

Fenton was also emotionally disheveled by feeling rejected, but the unemployed, idealistic college student left the Page abode without further adding to the intense quibbling. Being the self-appointed community matchmaker, Mistress Quickly took the initiative to take full responsibility for the family crisis that had suddenly developed.

"This bullshit is all my doing!" Mistress Quickly readily admitted. "Mistress Meg; I urge you to not let your daughter marry this selfish fanatic Abraham Slender, or that irascible, moody, old fart nutjob, Dr. Caius! Favor Master Fenton, for the young man's a gentle human being, and the other two suitors are, beneath their suave veneers, covetous animals! In fact, to show his deep love and affection, Master Fenton has just handed me this cheap ring to give to Anne!"

"I resent being referred to as an animal!" Abraham Slender yelled, before exiting the comfortable home and violently slamming the front door.

"You're too goddamned lazy to be a beast of burden, you fucked-up donkey that's not-yet-grown into an adult jackass!" Mistress Quickly screamed out the window at the fleeing and frightened Abraham Slender, who was being swiftly pursued by the equally frightened Justice Shallow.

* * * * * * * * * * * *

Inside the Garter Belt and Pink Panty Inn, Sir John Falstaff was mentally reviewing his recent, unanticipated plunge into the muddy murky *Thames River*. The aged, fat knight figured he would drown his troubles in "deported wine", since the *Thames* had nearly drowned him right into the hereafter.

'I was maliciously treated like a barrel of butcher's offal, and then mercilessly dumped into the polluted river!' Falstaff lamented, feeling sorry for himself'. 'I have a kind of affinity for sinking in deep water, and my damned clothes weighed me down when the currents kept preventing me from floating over to the muddy bank. Besides being too wet for comfort, that damned filthy river was too friggin' cold, too! That freakin' water was a lot deeper than Justice Shallow's miniature mind, that's for goddamned sure!'

Bardolph approached Sir John's table with a cheap sack of wine and a relevant message. "Mistress Quickly wants to speak to you about the quicky you didn't receive over at the Ford house! Ha, ha, ha, Sir John!" Bardolph laughed and scoffed. "You've gone downhill rapidly ever since I left your employ! Ha, ha, ha, you fat fuck! It's a goddamned miracle that you were able to float to save your worthless mortal soul! Ha, ha, ha; you buoyant, flamboyant son-of-a-bitch! Ha, ha, ha!"

After surviving Bardolph's insulting derision, almost as effectively as Sir John had survived the *Thames* debacle, Mistress Quickly approached Falstaff's favorite table (and her worst) inside the dingy Garter Belt and Panty Inn.

"Sir John, I speak to you on behalf of Mistress Alice Ford, who deeply regrets the rude interruption of your special visit yesterday to her bed," Mistress Quickly began her monologue.

"I had enough of ford in the *Thames,* thank you, very much," Sir John haplessly punned. "I think I'm all forded-out, and can't afford any more fuckin' fording at the fuckin' Ford residence!"

"The unfortunate incident was not Alice Ford's fault," Mistress Quickly argued in her friend's defense. "She's sorry for being partially responsible for your near-death experience! Now, Alice yearns to see you again later this morning, after you finish your wine breakfast of course!"

"What does the wench want to do this time?" Sir John rankled. "Have me thrown off a ship inside a potato sack into the middle of the goddamned English Channel? I swim like a pregnant African elephant, ya' know!"

"Master Ford is going bird hunting this fine pheasant, er, I mean pleasant morning, and that'll give Alice a good chance to do some bird hunting in her bed, if you catch my drift," Mistress Quickly persuasively mentioned, giving Sir John an emphatic wink of her eye. "She'll once again be free between the hours of ten and eleven. This time, Mistress Ford promises to make your second visit much more fruitful, and much more memorable, than your first aborted rendezvous happened to be."

"Tell her I'm a sensitive, frail man who can't endure much more physical discomfort and potential violence!" the maverick Sir John told his mercenary confidante. "I promise you; I'll again visit her haunted house at the scheduled time. Not only am I a glutton for food and drink, but I've recently discovered that I'm also a fuckin' addicted glutton for punishment! I must be one of those fucked-up, misguided masochists ya' often hear about!"

No sooner had Mistress Quickly conveyed her essential message to Sir John that Master Brook (Ford in disguise) entered the Garter Belt and Pink Panty Inn and ambled over to Falstaff's familiar centrally-situated table.

"Now Master Brook, I'm sure you've heard the false vicious rumors eddying around Windsor about what had transpired between me and that maniac Ford's wife!" Sir John said. "That petulant asshole belongs in an insane asylum!"

"Please explain; what the hell happened there?" Brook (Ford) inquisitively asked. "I mean, Sir John, in Windsor as well as in Frogmore, rumor is often more true than actual fact!"

"Yes Sir, Brook. I was present at the Ford house paying a friendly social visit when her crazy, fucked-up husband arrived in a fit of unbridled jealousy," Sir John graphically explained. "After the Lady and I had kissed, and I had gently massaged her breasts, Sir John falsely bragged. "Ford and his rabble of village vigilantes wildly ransacked the house and went absolutely berserk, searching every damned place at least thrice."

"Well, Sir John. The gossip mill has it that you weren't found anywhere inside the home!" Brook (Ford) cunningly stated. "And that great escape only adds to your fantastic national reputation! How the hell did you manage to evade detection, anyway? Have you learned a few tricks from Merlin's magic book? Are you studying alchemy and perverted sex upstairs at this inn?"

"Well, Master Brook. Mistress Page came screaming into Mistress Ford's house yelling that Master Ford was coming with a posse of crazy assholes to brutally kick my fat butt," Sir John revealed before imbibing a mouthful of wine. "And then, I was instantly instructed to swiftly hide inside an immense buck-basket. Incidentally, both bitches strongly desire for me to pork them, you know! I just have to wish that I have enough sperm juice to accommodate both the hussies in a single day!"

"A buck-basket?" Brook (Ford) exclaimed and asked.

"Yes; and believe me when I tell you it smelled like shit underneath all of Master Ford's smelly, brown-stained underwear that almost made me suffocate to death from the putrid stench!" Sir John emphatically stressed to the already stressed-out Brook (Ford). "Then several muscle-bound freaks in the Ford's employ carried the mammoth buck-basket on a sturdy pole down to Datchet's Mead, and the transporters next dumped the dirty laundry along with my fat ass into the even dirtier *Thames!* What a gross humiliation to my dignity *that* ugly bullshit act was! Now after I've solemnly given you my true story with Mistress Alice Ford, are you still interested in being introduced to her?"

"Yes, I'm still desperate for you to break the ice for me," Brook (Ford) fibbed. "I've never before been hot and horny for a married bitch in all my days on this fucked-up planet as I am right now! I immensely need your indispensable services."

"Well Sir, her husband will be out of the house going bird-hunting I believe after ten this morning," Sir John honestly related to his disguised nemesis. "You can come to the Ford home and hide in the closet Master Brook, to frenetically masturbate your dick off if you'd like, while listening to me expertly and passionately wooing that promiscuous, kinky whore."

"No thanks for the moment!" the emotionally disheveled Brook (Ford) answered. "I need a rain check! Perhaps the next time!"

"If that's what you like Brook, anything you say!" Falstaff casually replied as he arose from his creaky, rickety wooden chair. "But remember, you owe me a sack of imported wine since I have to leave your illuminating company in such a rush! I'll have to work fast to pump a large load into good old Alice's steaming hot pink love tunnel; that is, before her fucked-up, paranoid husband comes home from his quail expedition! Bring a sack of gold coins in addition to the standard sack of wine, the next time you wish to obtain my sage advice about hitting on Mistress Ford! See you later, Senor Brook. Ha, ha, ha!"

After Sir John stepped-out of the virtually empty Garter Belt and Pink Panty Inn, the disguised, jaded husband mulled matters over in his troubled mind. 'I'm no fuckin' wild bull, but I'm horn-mad!' Brook (Ford) thought. 'I'll turn into a belligerent Minotaur if I have to! I'm going to castrate that fat fuck son-of-a-bitch if it's the last fuckin' thing I do!'

Act IV

Parson Sir Hugh Evans showed-up early at the Page home to tutor young William, Master Page and Meg's adopted, pre-pubescent son, reputed to have ugly mood swings and a classic case of post-medieval child manic-depression.

"Okay, Master William, hold your head high! No need for you to be crestfallen!" Parson Sir Hugh urged the often-uncooperative and defiant lad. "Adults are really your friends!"

"Come on, Billy! Get your senses and wits together!" Meg Page demanded. "Stop acting like a bratty, immature little snot-nose!"

"Now William," Parson Sir Hugh corrected, trying to harness his diminishing patience; "what's the number in the word 'nouns'?"

"In school we study numbers in arithmetic!" William remembered and argued. "Nouns' are what we study in English grammar! What kind of young, ignorant asshole do you think I am?"

"No William, 'numbers' also exist in English grammar!" Parson Sir Hugh corrected. "Number in English refers to singular for just one item or object. and plural refers to two or more things. Consequently, the word 'nouns' would be plural."

"I wish this was the after*math* of this stinking English lesson!" uncooperative William complained. "Your lousy paragraphs are worse than death sentences!"

"Would you like to now study the genitive case in Latin?" the tutor asked William.

"How can you get your genitals in a case?" the boy queried. "That ball-breaking trick would be rather painful, wouldn't it Parson?"

"Well, yes, I suppose it would be, now that you've mentioned it in *that* oddball context!" the minister impatiently-but-politely admitted and smiled. "Well, now William; let's get on with some splendid pronouns. Repeat after me the pronouns used in verb conjugation," Parson Sir Hugh lectured. "First we'll do the singular pronouns: I, you, me, he, she, it."

"You said a naughty phrase," William accused Parson Sir Hugh. "You definitely said, 'He shit'!"

"No, I didn't say any such thing!" Parson Sir Hugh objected with his face suddenly turning crimson. "I said the pronouns 'he, she, it'!"

"You've said it again! Naughty-naughty!" William insisted. "You explicitly said, 'He shit'."

"Perhaps we should explore verbs instead. Now William," Parson Evans proceeded with his unique grammar lesson. "We have two basic kinds of verbs in English: verbs of being, which are harder to learn and identify, and of course, we have action verbs! Now can you give me some fine examples of action verbs?"

"What about 'suck' and 'fuck'?" William vulgarly communicated. "They show plenty of action, don't they?"

"Er William; you've erred again. Perhaps I'll visit you again when we can have a more erudite and mature exchange of academic ideas," Parson Sir Hugh suggested. "If you were in class, I'm sure your schoolmaster would penalize you for making such insolent and inappropriate comments."

"If either Master Tarrington or Master Slender ever tried penalizing me up the ass, I'd cut his damned dick off with my rusty pocket knife!" William declared to the bewildered and besieged Parson, who was an English tutor before the British had bagpipe tooters, or even a century or so before fatso Henry the VIII was himself' an English Tudor.

* * * * * * * * * * * *

Sir John Falstaff was again visiting Mistress Alice Ford in her husband's absence (while her spouse engaged in quail shooting with his bow and arrow). The wary, corpulent knight briefly interrogated his rich female delight, desiring to begin their rocky romance with some small-talk.

"Are you sure your crazy, jealous husband isn't anywhere in the vicinity?" Sir John anxiously asked. "I don't feel like getting dumped again from a tremendous-sized buck-basket into the goddamned murky *Thames!* That's far worse than being dumped into a damned rat-infested dunghill!"

"Don't worry, Sir John!" Mistress Ford replied and assured. "Go into the master sleeping chamber, get yourself ready for some serious action, and then hop into my bed while I prepare myself properly."

When Sir John commenced following Mistress Ford's explicit directions, Alice and Meg were outside in the hall deliberately speaking loudly, so that Falstaff could easily overhear their very contrived conversation.

"Truly Alice," Mistress Page's voice boomed. "I'm glad you have nobody at home. Now we can talk plainly and candidly."

"Exactly what did you want to discuss?" Mistress Ford asked. "How the *Thames* is so dirty that fish are dying in it, or how terribly infected the river is because of all the filthy, disgusting, fecal matter that's daily dumped into the contaminated water?"

"No Alice! I'll make this little tale short and sweet!" Meg loudly promised. "Your loony husband is going berserk again, and barking all over Windsor worse than a rabid dog! I've never seen a man go on such a wild and furious tirade! Thank God that Sir John is not here again, or else, the mammoth sperm whale might not survive having his limbs and penis amputated!"

"But why is my husband so pissed-off?" Alice asked while holding back giggling. "He had his warm oatmeal, broccoli, and prune juice this morning."

"Your crazy husband has told my spouse that he's going to pretend that Sir John is a chubby quail, and shoot his ass with his bow and arrow, regardless of whether or not fat Sir John is flying in the air, or scooting and skittering around on the damned ground!" Meg described, feigning seriousness. "I'm happy to learn that Sir John is not here in this house, or for sure the poor excuse for a human being would soon be measured this evening for his funeral suit! My husband says he's never seen your spouse so hostile and so crazy."

"How close is my husband from the home?" Mistress Alice asked before she then bit her tongue to hold back laughter.

"He's at the end of the block and pacing this way with his bow and arrows, and possessing a menacing grimace, er, excuse me, a prodigious frown on his face," Meg reported.

"Oh shit, Meg! Sir John is here and presently hiding in the master bedroom!" Alice very audibly hollered in a pretend confession.

"You'll be shamed and mocked, and that sperm whale surely will be harpooned and murdered!" Meg promptly and im*promptu*-ly prompted. "Better to be shamed, Alice, than fuckin' murder! I recommend that you immediately get that annoying, fat fuck out of this house if you don't want to testify at a goddamned murder trial before Justice Shallow!"

"Should we again hide him in the buck-basket? I can get Robert and John right this instant!" Alice insisted in a harrowed and hurried-tone of voice. "Sir John can become a basket case again!"

Hearing the gist of the women's excited chatter, Sir John wildly thrust-open the master bedroom door. "I'll just dash out the front entrance and sprint right by your husband before he could ever have a chance to raise his bow!" Falstaff said to Alice Ford. "I'd rather get shot in my ass than in my balls!"

"But Sir John!" Mistress Meg Page argued. "Master Ford has three of his workmen with loaded pistols accompanying him over here. Your ass is going to be filled with quail shot before you can get the damned lead out!"

"Then, I'll escape through the chimney and gently roll off the roof into the side sticker bushes!" Sir John ludicrously vociferated. "I got to fuckin' get rolling sooner or later! Either that or be mercilessly shot inside the buck-basket with goddamned buckshot! Don't you have a kiln hole I could crawl into? I'll just pretend I'm an inflated snake or an oversized rabbit!"

"A scummy rat's more like it!" Mistress Alice Ford curtly corrected. "I have a great idea! I find that I think best under pressure! We'll disguise you in a woman's nightgown with a tall plumed hat, so that my husband will think you're a lady friend paying Meg and me a visit," Alice proposed. "My former obese maid had kept such a gown in the spare bedroom. Quick, Sir John! We have no time to waste! Into that spare room over there and put the huge gown and the large hat on your immense skull if you don't wish dying an inglorious and ignoble death! Mistress Page will gladly help you with your magnificent costume!"

When Sir John and Meg Page exited the hallway, Mistress Alice Ford reckoned and comprehended the true scenario. 'My near-sighted and far-sighted husband hated our insufferable, chunky maid, Lady Brentwood, and just fired her fat ass last week. When my jealous spouse sees Sir John wearing Lady Brentwood's dress and hat that she had given me as gifts last week to donate to charity, then we'll see precisely what the hell happens. My husband's eyesight is so bad that he couldn't hit a red barn with a bow and arrow standing only ten-feet-away!'

Just as Robert and John were again exiting the house with the loaded buck-basket, Master Ford briskly entered the front door accompanied by Master Page, Justice Shallow, Parson Sir Hugh, and the cantankerous Dr. Caius.

"Stop right there, Robert and John!" Ford commanded and demanded. "I was fooled once by that deceitful buck-basket trick, but I won't be hoodwinked again! Drop that container immediately, so that I can thoroughly inspect its dirty contents!"

"There's nothing but dirty clothes and smelly rags and your putrid brown-stained underwear in this buck basket!" Justice Shallow determined. "You should learn to wipe your ass better."

"You've gone stark-raving mad!" Dr. Caius yelled at Master Ford. "I wish I were a psychiatrist instead of a body doctor, so that then I could possibly diagnose and cure your major mental malady!"

"In the name of the Father, and of the Son, and of the Holy Spirit, Amen!" Parson Sir Hugh said, making the sign of the cross to chase away any evil demons lurking about inside and inhabiting Master Ford's unique body.

"Now cheating Woman!" Ford exclaimed to Alice. "Try telling and convincing me that you're a modest, honest, virtuous, faithful wife! I dare you!"

"Are you not ashamed that the buck-basket contains no man?" Alice Ford rebuked her distrustful husband. "Doesn't that fact reveal something pertinent about your suspicious, paranoid nature?"

"Empty the entire buck basket onto the floor so that I can make sure with my own two eyes!" Ford screamed, not placing full credence in Justice Shallow's initial inspection. "My need for vigilant jealousy is both reasonable and justified! I've never been so pissed-off in all my blessed life!"

"If there's a man inside that smelly, stinking basket, the poor soul has already suffocated and died a flea's death!" Mistress Ford again reproached her incensed marital partner. "Your uncouth behavior Husband is without a doubt entirely unwarranted!"

Robert and John flipped over the colossal buck-basket, but no man (let alone the chubby, gargantuan Sir John Falstaff) had been hiding inside; just regular laundry that required washing, scattered all over the wood-planked floor.

"I guess I was wrong about the buck-basket!" Ford apologized.

"The imaginary intruder exists nowhere else but in your diseased brain!" Master Page concluded and criticized his best friend.

"I'll not be your sport being ridiculed and laughed-at over an inn supper table tonight!" Ford bellowed to Page. "You're all trying to make an insane asylum case out of me! Search the entire house for that sleazy, fat, villainous culprit! Robert! John! Refill the buck-basket immediately and get that smelly, messy thing the hell out of my house right this instant!"

John Falstaff then exited the spare bedroom dressed as Lady Brentwood. But the perceptually impaired Master Ford believed that Sir John actually was the obese maid that *he* absolutely despised and had recently fired.

"What's this audacious bullshit all about Alice?" Ford screamed, showing his vibrating tonsils. "Get this goddamned witch out of my house! Get out of my house! Get out of my house!" Ford hollered as the infuriated fellow began ferociously punching, pounding, pummeling, and kicking the disguised Sir John, who unskillfully attempted protecting himself from absorbing the flurry of clenched-fisted blows.

"Husband, you should be ashamed of yourself maligning and nearly crippling this old helpless woman!" Alice Ford reprimanded her spouse. "Give her free passage out of *this* house immediately! Make a path, for I fear for her safety! Cease your hostilities Husband! You need temper-management lessons badly! Perhaps Reverend Sir Hugh could save you from yourself?"

"I'm a common minister of the gospel, and not an accomplished exorcist!" the Parson clarified. "Exorcisms are out of my area of expertise! But apparently, your out-of-control husband requires the services of more than one highly-skilled exorcist!"

"Hang that fat old hag witch!" Ford boomed as Sir John finally made his exit out of the house wearing Lady Brentwood's massive nightgown and grotesque plumed hat.

"You heinously beat-up Lady Brentwood, and now the abused dame might file assault and battery charges against you with the Constable!" Alice chastised her still-livid husband. "Fine Man you are; nearly beating a defenseless woman to death! If you try violently molesting me in a similar fashion, you'll pay with your bony ass in jail, that's for damned sure!" Mistress Ford boisterously yelled. "Never doubt my word again, if you value your shriveled-up, non-functional, numb- nuts!"

"Bless my balls, Parson Sir Hugh, while I still have them attached to my toro, er, I mean, to my torso!" Master Ford requested of the now totally-rattled and befuddled minister.

* * * * * * * * * * *

Some aristocratic Germans visiting England had desired hiring three of the Garter Belt Host's horses. Bardolph had alerted the inn's Host of the request, which would amount to an unexpected windfall profit for the almost-bankrupt bar and whorehouse proprietor.

"These German Lords are going to meet the Prince at the King's court tomorrow morning," Bardolph told the Host.

"Which Prince are they going to meet?" the Host asked. "Horse prints, or Prince Henry! Ha, ha, ha! Do these Germans speak English? If so, I'd like to confer with the barbarians."

"Yes, and they know all the damned curse words, too!" Bardolph answered his former boss. "I'll get the fucked-up assholes for you right away. The dumb shits were asking me if we had an Octoberfest in Windsor! Ha, ha, ha. Don't those stupid German tourist shits know that it's still summertime!"

"Well, Bardolph; these damned Germans have been staying in my favorite upstairs' rooms all week, and have interrupted and curtailed my prostitution business in the meantime," the Host bitched. "They'll pay plenty for their three horses; at least five days of sex worth anyway. Send those foreign, raucous, riotous bastards over here so that I can read them the goddamned riot act for acting like an insolent mob!"

* * * * * * * * * * * *

Alice Ford and Meg Page figured that it was time to level with their husbands about the tricks and stunts that the merry wives had been pulling on Sir John Falstaff to stifle and humiliate the notorious knight for his presumptuous audacity in actually believing that the two married women cared one speck about his amorous overtures. Master Ford, Master Page, their convivial wives, along with Parson Hugh Evans, were conscientiously discussing the humorous capers inside the Page living room.

"Why this is undoubtedly one of the best all-time pranks I've ever been associated with!" the Parson commended the two merry Windsor wives. "And you say that you both received the twin love letters within a quarter of an hour of one another? This presumptuous Sir John must think he's God's gift to women."

"Yes, Reverend, and the stupid asshole wrote the exact same sentences and paragraphs in each of the letters, word for word!" Alice Ford bitched. "So much for originality and integrity, the duplicating, duplicitous fat fool!"

"That heretic sinner deserves to be punished even more than he has been already!" the spiteful and now vengeful Master Ford proposed. "He's as despicable as a man could ever be!"

"Our wives are pretty creative when it comes-down to destroying a proud man's ego!" Master Page pitched-in. "Let's have our ladies organize another embarrassing caper to thoroughly con and scam Sir John! That corpulent gourd needs to be disgraced again! Let's have our own special little vendetta against that annoying, frivolous rogue, Sir John Falstaff!"

"We'll get him to come to the park at midnight," Meg Page plotted. "Now we have a specific setting, time, and place! But what about the hoodwinking aspect?"

"Well, it worked twice so let's try it a third time," Alice Ford opined. "Meg and I will be the bait to make the fat rat come to the cheese, with the ignoramus stumbling right into our ingenious trap!"

"I got a brilliant idea that'll make Sir John into an absolute clown, the absolute Windsor laughingstock!" Meg Page piped-up. "There's an old local legend about a predatory creature with horns named Herne the Hunter, who roams around Windsor Forest during midnight trying to hide from winter's approach. The beast surreptitiously stalks around and kills stray animals that wander into his path near a very feared magical oak tree."

"And we'll have Sir John come into the Forest wearing a Herne the Hunter outfit with a set of deer antlers on his head," Alice Ford said. "And then...."

"And then," Meg Page picked-up on the trend of thought, "we'll have little William, my daughter Anne, and a few neighborhood children dress-up as fairies and elves. They'll according to plan, leap-out at Sir John, you, and me and then....."

"And then you and I Meg will run away with all of the fairies and elves still dancing, and skipping, and running-around befuddled Sir John dressed as Herne the Hunter with the deer antlers on his head," Alice laughed. "The costumed children could even...."

"Have small sewing needles in their hands and tiny candles in their crowns, and the kids could pinch and puncture Sir John's blubber with their sharp needle points, and also burn his fingers, fat ass and his exposed legs with the lighted tapers removed from their crowns," Meg declared. "Oh, if this stunt works, it'll be so rich and jolly!"

"I'll teach the children their special dances and behaviors," Parson Sir Hugh eagerly volunteered. "And if you two Gentlemen care to donate financing for costumes and materials to the project, I'll even buy them some suitable masks to wear on that stellar evening."

"My daughter Anne will be the Queen of the Fairies that night, but only in fantasy, but not in gay and lesbian everyday reality!" Meg Page carefully differentiated.

"And we could use the fun-filled occasion to surprise our daughter Anne," Master Page injected. "When she's prancing around Sir John dressed as Queen of the Fairies, my favorite suitor Abraham Slander will sneak into the revelers from the forest shadows and steal-off with *my* unassuming daughter."

"And I'll masquerade as a certain Master Donny Brook and get a handle on what Sir John's honestly thinking and planning over at the pedestrian Garter Belt and Pink Panty Inn," Master Ford added. "I deliberately included the word 'Pink' because we'll all be tickled pink! Ha, ha, ha!"

"I like the cute prank idea because it's very honest, good-natured knavery that we're plotting!" Parson Sir Hugh evaluated and contributed. "No one gets hurt too badly; Sir John gets his just dose of humiliation for our amusement, and Anne gets hitched to the intended wooer Abraham Slender, just like both her kind-hearted parents' desire."

But Mistress Meg Page had designs of her own that did not parallel those of her husband. 'On second thought, Dr. Caius has much more money to offer Anne than does that foolish, pathetic excuse for a schoolmaster, Abraham Slender,' Meg thought. 'I'll go one step higher on the plotting ladder than my ridiculous husband has climbed upon, and have Dr. Caius on the Windsor Forest scene to steal Anne away before that perverted knave Abraham Slender dashes onto the rustic stage, and attempts snatching my precious daughter, and then absconding-away with her into the night, surreptitiously eloping off to Leatherhead to get married.'

* * * * * * * * * * * *

Strange things were also happening over at the disreputable Garter Belt and Pink Panty Inn. Abraham Slender's servant Simple entered the establishment to speak with the garrulous Host.

"Marry, Sir, even though I don't believe in gay nuptials," Simple simply began like a veteran simpleton speaking in Middle English. "Master Slender has dispatched me here to address the honorable Sir John Falstaff."

"His room is upstairs under a shingle marked 'The Prodigal'. Go and knock three-times, and the fat prick will answer the door," the Host tersely replied.

"But Sir," Simple persisted in his peculiar discourse. "I saw an old, obese, ugly woman enter Sir John's chamber, so I prefer that I speak with him down here rather than converse up there. I wouldn't wish to disturb the unpredictable knight, for he's exceedingly irrational and volatile when either fazed or aroused, so I understand."

"That old, fat, ugly woman is probably my old fat ugly wife servicing that obese, old, fat, ugly asshole right now!" the apathetic business-as-usual Host assumed and then revealed. "But I'll call Sir John now. just in case another old, fat, ugly bitch besides my promiscuous spouse is giving Sir John one of her trademark penis massages. Bully Sir John! Bully for Sir John!"

"What the hell's going on down there?" Falstaff shouted from the upstairs railing. "It sounds like the Apocalypse events have begun without me!"

"If that's not my lummox wife up there servicing you, then you're violating the goddamned house rules!" the distrustful-but-pragmatic Host yelled-up to Falstaff.

"There was an old, fat, ugly woman with a nightgown and a weird-looking bonnet up here, but I think she's squeezed her elephant ass through the window and is now gone!" Sir John unskillfully fibbed. "Maybe she's a damned spy from the Wild Boar Whore Inn across the street, or whatever the hell the name of that fleabag flophouse is now called!"

"Sir," Simple shouted-out with his hands forming a makeshift megaphone around his mouth. "Master Slender claims that a fellow associated with you named Nym has cheated the jerk out of a chain. Master Slender thinks that the old woman then cheated Nym out of the chain afterwards."

"The old, fat, ugly bitch that was up here told me that the very same man that had cheated your Master Slender out of the chain also had cheated her!" Falstaff lied to protect himself. "Now, who the hell am I to believe in this dangerous, fucked-up world?"

"Well then, Sir Knight. I have other more relevant things to speak to you about besides that old, fat, ugly bitch that had disturbed you this fine morning," Simple added.

"Stop wasting my valuable time with your preposterous, dunce-shit rhetoric!" Falstaff yelled-down and then yawned. "I need to catch-up on my beauty rest! Stop boring me with your fucked-up, trite, meaningless bullshit!"

"Well, Sir Knight," Simple apprehensively disclosed, "Master Slender has asked me to inquire of you whether you have some inside information that Mistress Anne Page desires his hand in marriage. Since you supposedly know all about all sorts of activities inside the Page house, my Master figured that...."

"Tell your cowardly Master that from what the hell I know, your boss has dibs, or in plain English, the inside track on Mistress Anne Page," Falstaff confirmed. "Now leave me the hell alone before I fart my ass right off of this precarious balcony, and fuckin' landing, squashing, and crushing you to death!"

"I'll deliver those most excellent tidings to Master Slender!" Simple hollered-up, and then excitedly and carelessly rushed out of the risqué establishment.

Suddenly, the tapster Bardolph came running into the main area of the Garter Belt from the back entrance. "Master Host; come quickly! Your plow-horses that you claim to be thoroughbreds have just been stolen. I was leading them into the barn when three sinister German Dr. Faustus-type thugs threw my ass into a drainage ditch, and then the felons took-off, riding the fresh animals in the direction of Eton, or east of Eton."

"They merely were borrowing the horses to meet the anonymous Duke and our synonymous Prince Henry at the King's palace," the Host calmly answered. "Those terrific Germans are honest men who have already paid me for the horse rentals. You probably antagonized them Bardolph, as is your gruff demeanor, so the passive gentlemen tossed your pathetic ass into the muddy ditch. At least, that's my sage interpretation of events! I hope you didn't get trench-mouth in the damned ditch!"

Then, Parson Sir Hugh, a rare (but believable) visitor to the Garter Belt stepped into the inn and divulged, "Host Master Quickly; three evil, cheating Germans that have stolen horses in Reading, in Maidenhead, and in Clitshit, are said to be in Windsor claiming that they must meet with Prince Henry and an imaginary British Duke," the trustworthy-but-gossipy minister reported. "Now be on the lookout for those ruthless, marauding thieves, because they'll steal your eyes out of their sockets, and the German pirates will sell them to a gullible, rich, blind man."

As soon as Parson Sir Hugh exited the infamous inn, Dr. Caius created more turmoil by rushing-in and saying to the befuddled Host, "There's been talk around Windsor Proper that you've been entertaining certain German barons here," the delusional physician said all out of breath. "There is no such proper Duke in all of Britain, and I think you've been fuckin' improperly duped!" Dr. Caius inadvertently rhymed. "Those Germans are uncivilized vermin!"

"Assist me Sir John!" the now-distraught Host loudly pleaded to his sometimes-chivalrous patron. "You're an honorable Knight! Help me apprehend and punish those detestable German villains! Of all the brazen audacity!"

"The whole world, but especially Britain, is full of mendacious cheats, and most recently I've had my share of being fuckin' cheated!" Falstaff yelled to the perplexed Host. "Please excuse me Master Proprietor, because I must fart in the middle of your dire horse theft emergency!"

Mistress Quickly' quickly entered the Garter Belt and Pink Panty Inn to voluntarily add to the chaos, and to help bait Sir John.

"Good Knight," the gossiping matchmaker hollered-up to Sir John, who was preoccupied belching and simultaneously loudly farting. "Mistress Alice Ford is all black and blue, and I suspect that her lunatic, jealous, dysfunctional husband has been beating the liver bile out of her. There's not a white spot visible anywhere on her exposed skin, including what once was her beautiful face!"

"She might be black and blue as you say, but yesterday, I was beaten into every fuckin' color of the rainbow, and then some, by that fucked-up husband of hers!" Sir John yelled-down and then loudly burped and farted to eliminate some congestive-digestive gas. "That insane jerk-off Ford mistook me for his former fat, ugly, old maid-maid, Lady Brentwood, whom the demented psychopath claims was a demonic fortuneteller and satanic tarot card reader, evilly disobeying the moral teachings represented in the *Holy Bible!*"

"Sir John; I insist that I immediately speak with you in your rented chamber," Mistress Quickly demanded. "There's matters of urgency that need to be addressed and discussed right now!"

"Okay, Mistress Quickly! Only if you promise me an exceptional quicky!" Sir John humorously stipulated.

* * * * * * * * * * * *

While Mistress Quickly and Sir John were talking and screwing-around up in his rented room, quixotic Master Fenton stepped into the Garter Belt and Pink Panty Inn.

"Master Fenton, my addled mind is in a quandary, so please don't talk to me!" the beleaguered Host stated while *his* business partner wife was having sex upstairs with Sir John. "My finest horses have been pilfered from right under my very nose!"

"I promise to give you a hundred-pounds more than you've unfortunately lost with your nearly dead missing horses!" Fenton said, promising the Host anticipated money that *he* expected to soon receive from Mistress Anne Page's dowry. "Mistress Anne loves me dearly, and we intend to get married. Here's a letter in my hand that outlines certain provisions that must be met, so that I can marry Anne and have instant access to a portion of her family fortune."

The letter written by the fair maiden stated that at midnight at Herne Oak in Windsor Forest, Anne Page will be dancing around the tree as "the Fairy Queen".

"My fuckin' horses have just been stolen, Fenton, and you're telling me that your sweetheart has turned gay, and will be dancing around Herne Oak as a horny, fucked-up Fairy Queen!" the totally aggravated inn Host screamed. "I think you're more fucked-up than Sir John Falstaff is, or ever was! Now what the fuck do you really want with me?"

"Now, here's my drastic dilemma!" Fenton said with a stern expression upon his visage. "I've learned that Master Page wants Master Slender, the fucked-up schoolmaster, to dash onto the forest scene and elope to Leatherhead with Anne to get married!"

"Why the fuck would Slender ever want to marry a lesbian who thinks she's a female fairy?" the Host incredulously asked Fenton. "I always suspected that *that* asshole Slender was gay too, with that high-pitched voice he has!"

"No, you don't understand!" the frustrated (sexually and otherwise) Fenton tried explaining. "Anne's mother desires for her to marry the temperamental Dr. Caius, while her father desires Anne marrying that insidious asshole Master Slender."

"Well then, who is Anne Page going to obey? Her father or her black and blue mother?" the bewildered and confused Host asked the handsome young wooer.

"Neither!" Fenton exclaimed. "She's going to marry me! Now Host, you know everyone in Windsor! I need for you to get me a vicar to perform a non-vicarious wedding ceremony uniting Anne Page and me in *Holy Matrimony* just after midnight!"

"Well, if you can wheedle a hundred-crowns out of Anne Page's dowry to compensate me for my stolen horses, and for my invaluable contacts, and for my indispensable social services," the Host insisted and agreed, "then Master Fenton, you're guaranteed an authentic, legitimate priest to conduct the ceremony. I'm basically a gambling man, and like betting on long shots!" the Inn's Host confidentially admitted. "And quite frankly, in my whole life's experience Master Fenton, you're the longest shot I'm ever fuckin' encountered!"

Act V

"Mistress Quickly, this is the third time that you say Alice Ford and Meg Page wish to engage in extramarital affairs with me," Sir John complained, as the wholly frustrated knight spoke to the accommodating woman on her knees assiduously administering fellatio to him. "Sometimes good lick, er, I mean good luck lies in odd numbers like three and thirteen!" Falstaff acknowledged just before achieving an excellent liposuction-type orgasm. "Ahhhh, yes!

I theorize that affairs with rich, married women could be quite messy and explosive."

"I'll provide you with the chain to strap your antlers on, you horny Old Man!" Mistress Quickly explained. "True, Sir John; it does seem quite odd-but-unique, that is to say, you meeting Alice and Meg at midnight in Windsor Forest near the fabled Herne Hunter's Oak. Just look at the great dual romances involved, and then everything else will seem trivial in comparison. Just think about abundant love and the luxury of money, and the entire frivolous adventure will make perfectly good sense to you. Those two well-to-do women really have the hots for you, I must say."

"You can now attend to your other duties!" Falstaff said to Mistress Quickly as the fat slob superficially scrubbed his genitals with a wet-but-soiled washcloth. "I'll bravely enter Windsor Forest tonight and hang-out there in the cold with my antlers on my head near the haunted Herne Oak, and see what the hell happens. But if nothing substantial materializes, then this'll be the last friggin' time I'm wasting my energy pursuing the two affluent Windsor bitches."

Sir John stepped downstairs and was met by Master Donny Brook (Ford). Naturally, Sir John had to vent his dislike for Master Ford and *his* jealous temper.

"That lousy knave Ford mauled, battered, and bashed my ass yesterday, awfully terrible," Sir John grieved to Brook (Ford). "That imbecilic son-of-a-bitch fuck-head was motivated by jealousy and by frenzy. The mangy bastard mercilessly beat the shit out of me, thinking that I was a certain cleaning woman, Lady Brentwood, whom he absolutely loathes and abhors like he does all other whores; the illogical, insane, maniacal prude. Anyway, Master Brook," Falstaff continued his warped and graphic elucidation. "I now resent and hate that mother-fucker more than I do any other dumb-fuck on this accursed Earth. I'll get even with that hostile bastard, Ford; I promise you Master Brook. And because I seek vengeance on that loony son-of-a-bitch, I'll safely deliver the black and blue Mistress Alice Ford into your hands, and needless to say, into your reliable custody!"

"I'm much obliged to you!" Brook stated with a wink. "Yes, Sir John; as you say, I'll really owe you!"

* * * * * * * * * * * *

Meanwhile, schoolmaster Abraham Slender (with the cooperation of Master Page and Justice Shallow) was preparing for his special participation in "the Herne Hunter saga", using the fiasco as a clever guise to elope with gorgeous Anne Page. The three conspirators reviewed their ruse under the Herne Oak in Windsor Forest.

"We'll hide here in the woods and have some gay talk until Anne and the fairies appear, and the kids, all dancing around Sir John!" Master Page said to Slender.

"I can't wait to steal off to Leatherhead with your well-endowed daughter!" Slender confided to Master Page about the travesty about to happen. "The suspense of waiting to elope to Eton with your endowment, er, I mean endowed Anne is what's really exciting me!"

"It's past ten now, and we have only two more hours until midnight!" Justice Shallow appropriately chimed-in. "Then Nephew; you can ring Anne's chimes after the two of you elope to Leatherhead and get officially hitched."

"Let's wait for the targeted horned-victim to show-up!" Master Page laughed. "I don't know who is hornier; Sir John dressed as Herne the Hunter, or Satan himself', Ha, ha, ha!"

* * * * * * * * * * * *

Shortly thereafter, Meg Page, Alice Ford, and sadistic Dr. Caius showed-up inside Windsor Forest to soon join-up with their fellow conspirators. The three new arrivals were going-over final preparations for deceiving Sir John Falstaff.

"Listen-up, Dr.!" Meg Page exclaimed to her chief, favored ally in performing the highly anticipated Herne Hunter Windsor Forest prank. "My daughter Anne will be dressed entirely in green. From my perspective, you're still in the race as far as marrying Anne is concerned, and that's what Alice and I are grooming you for!"

"Thanks for your support, and for your redundant instructions, which I've memorized thirty times already!" Dr. Caius politely answered. "Now I'll go to my designated battle station so that everybody leaves me the hell alone for a few minutes. Then, I'll be able to differentiate in complete solitude between my sore head and the hemorrhoids inhabiting my sore ass!"

"My erratic spouse is going to be pissed when he learns that Anne has eloped with sinister Dr. Caius, and not with that blundering imbecile Abraham Slender!" Meg Page feared and related to Alice Ford after Dr. Caius had quietly departed to meditate behind a tall tree. "My husband's emotions will quickly shift from amusing fun and games at humiliating Sir John, to dreadful anger upon learning of Anne's surprise marital fate! But that's a natural consequence of my spouse not trusting his devoted wife! Sort of a self-fulfilling prophecy, wouldn't you agree, Alice?"

"Where's Anne and Parson Sir Hugh right now?" Alice answered with a question of her own. "They should be here by now."

"They're hiding on the other side of Herne's Oak, and when the two spot you and me talking with Sir John," Meg explained, "that's when they'll light their crown candles, pick-up their sewing needles, swiftly encircle Sir John, and then proceed to attack and puncture his ass and testicles from all directions. His heavy head antlers will encumber the foolish lummox from adequately defending himself!"

"Sir John the dumb-fuck buck will be mocked and scorned right out of Windsor when everyone in town learns of this marvelous stunt!" Alice Ford commended her cunning accomplice. "Sir John will be both betrayed and amazed by our treacherous enterprise."

"Okay, the hour is near!" Meg whispered to Alice. "Let's proceed to the gigantic Herne Oak and lure our tantalized rat into its awaiting trap! This is better than comedy night at the opera house! Ha, ha, ha! I'm so happy that I think I have to shit!"

* * * * * * * * * * *

"Okay you fairies!" the suspected pedophile Parson Sir Hugh announced to Anne Page and the dozen faggot-dressed children. "Remember your assigned parts! And boys, remember your *parts* in your hair, too! Ha, ha, ha! Now don your vizards and follow me into the forest, and pretend that I'm a pie-eyed pied piper. And whatever you do, you daffy juvenile delinquents, don't deviate from the ten-times rehearsed script we had practiced; you little deviant deviates!"

* * * * * * * * * * *

'The Windsor clock in the town square has tolled twelve midnight, and I feel like I have a ton of bats in my belfry with this fucked-up set of heavy antlers strapped onto my head!' Sir John thought as the encumbered knight reluctantly entered the almost-dark forest under a full moon. 'Christ! Do I feel horny! Where's the fuckin' stag party? Ah yes! My cherished doe mates Alice and Meg have plenty of dough! Ha, ha, ha! If I fall into a huge dirty linen basket, I could then be a buck in a buck-basket! Ha, ha, ha! Shit! My brain is really fucked-up tonight!'

"Is that you, my dear deer, Sir John of Herne?" Alice Ford beckoned the beleaguered antler-headed figure, clumsily approaching and *stag*gering through the woods. "Over here Sir John! Over here!"

"Oh Alice! It's truly rutting season, and I so passionately long to mate with you!" Sir John's voice boomed as the encumbered fellow tenderly embraced his wealthy, fantasy woman.

"Darling, Sweetheart," Alice politely replied. "Meg Page is here too, so that we can soon have a pleasurable threesome going!"

"In forty-degree temperature?" Sir John loudly protested. "I'll freeze my ass, er, I mean my goddamned tail off!"

"Don't speak too loudly!" Alice Ford cautioned the irascible knight. "My jealous husband is a cockeyed hunter, and with you being dressed like a deer, Sir John, you might get a few unexpected arrows puncturing your fat ass!"

"Are you two Bitches, er, I mean you two beautiful ladies trying to scare me?" Sir John asked as the pair of women swiftly scampered-off into the darkness. "I never frighten too easily! In fact, I never frighten at all! Hey! What the fuck's going on?" Sir John shouted as the figure with huge antlers was suddenly surrounded by a pack of children disguised as curious pixies and fairies.

The little masked tricksters ambitiously danced and pranced around Sir John, and began pricking him everywhere (including his vulnerable prick) with the distributed sewing needles, and then the merry rascals proceeded burning his hands, feet, balls, and face with the small, lit tapers the diminutive revelers were carrying.

'Holy Shit!' the besieged knight remembered and reckoned. 'I've got to remain calm, despite the excruciating suffering, because anyone that speaks to or speaks with fairies shall die according to local, primitive superstitions, which I'm not about to fuckin' defy or challenge! Fuck!' Sir John realized in frustration. 'That little gay fairy just torched and scorched my dick! Ouch! Ouch! Yes; according to local folklore, if I dare move, I might be transformed into a four-hundred-pound mound of shit! How can I become a pile of shit if I'm getting the fuckin' shit knocked out of me now by these midget fairies! Ow! Ouch! Ow!'

Master Page then loudly sounded a hunter's horn, which signaled for all of the dancing fairies and pixies to instantly disperse into the dark woods. The antler-headed John Falstaff held his genitals gingerly from the great torture that had recently and savagely been administered. Then, Master Page, Master Ford, Alice Ford, and Meg Page mutually converged upon the very distressed and victimized "Herne Hunter/Knight".

"Okay, you jerk-off Knight in shining Amour," Master Page punned. "The moment of truth is at hand! This has been your well-deserved atonement for trying to hoodwink Master Ford and *our* wonderful soul-mates, the merry wives of Windsor."

"I feel more like a horse's ass than I do a wild buck in heat!" Sir John admitted, as the stunt's victim removed his antlers that had been dangling from the left side of his unkempt beard. "I suppose it's deer hunting season, and I'm the only damned buck in the whole fucked-up forest! I must confess; I've certainly earned this fuckin' scandalous disgrace! My pride and my dignity have been completely shattered, if not devastated!"

"You never stood a pistol shot into an empty barrel of air at wooing either myself or Meg Page," Alice Ford attested to the still very puzzled Sir John. "This time you've been out-schemed and out-manipulated royally, Sir John Falstaff!"

"I now wish that I was a misguided gay bastard, and was trying to hustle Master Ford and Master Page instead of their all-too-shrewd merry wives!" Falstaff regretted and guiltily uttered. "That more intelligent tact would've certainly been more damned productive, and truthfully, a lot less damned dangerous!"

"Sir John; kindly learn to faithfully serve God and your King, and forget all of your hedonistic tendencies and proclivities!" Parson Sir Hugh preached. "You still have sufficient time to repent before Judgment Day arrives!"

"I'll never distrust my wife again, especially if and when I'm told she's having an affair with a Fat Fuck like you!" Master Ford scoffed at the silly-looking and emotionally defeated Falstaff. "You, my Knight, looked much better Sir John when you were artistically disguised as Mistress Brentwood!"

"I promise not to pursue eating any more English muffins," Sir John said and pledged with a smile, "but that doesn't mean I can't enjoy munching on and licking any French croissants, or any hairy Spanish pink tacos!"

"Yes, Sir John, perhaps you should curtail all of your licentious, sinful habits like fornicating with loose women, drinking three sacks of wine a day, along with your constant flagrant swearing and perpetual swindling," the holier-than-thou asshole Parson Sir Hugh sanctimoniously stated.

"Well, Gentlemen!" Meg Page stated while also speaking for Alice Ford. "Now that we've thoroughly belittled, browbeaten, and tortured Sir John, much to our great delight, everyone here present, including our favorite muttonhead, Sir John, is invited over to my place for a delicious meal of roasted venison, compliments of the very generous Justice Shallow."

"Anyway, right now my daughter Anne is being married to Master Abraham Slender, Justice Shallow's extraordinary nephew," Master Page informed and chuckled. "This was indeed a most tremendous caper we've played on Sir John, on idealistic Master Fenton, and on pretentious Dr. Caius."

"That's what the hell you think, Husband!" Meg Page corrected. "*Our* daughter Anne is presently being married to the wealthy and distinguished Dr. Caius!"

Just then Master Slender and Justice Shallow came sprinting through the woods into the clearing, where everyone was standing below the historic (well, legendary) Herne Hunter Oak. The gossipers were curious about the cause for the pair's sudden alarm.

"What the hell's the matter, Master Slender?" Master Page curiously asked. "Is my horny daughter chasing you all around creation already?"

"I grabbed someone in a green dress as you had directed me to do, and when my partner and I got out of the forest and were heading towards Leatherhead, I soon discovered that my mate was a local choir boy dressed-up as a fairy, and the masquerading personage was not my darling Anne Page!" frustrated Slender lamented and balked. "What a goddamned bummer! Er, excuse me, Parson Sir Hugh for my poor vernacular! I really have to work on my goddamned nomenclature, especially when I'm fuckin' angry!"

Then, under the fine illumination of the full moon, the equally perturbed Dr. Caius came scampering through the forest (from the opposite direction on a narrow trail) and was frenetically dashing toward the legendary Herne Oak.

"I've been cheated! I've been cozened!" Dr. Caius vehemently protested. "In the dark, I had accidentally kidnapped a freckle-faced kid, and not the gorgeous Anne Page! The jerk-off garcon, or paisano, or whatever the hell he was, er, excuse me, Parson; anyway, the little creep was wearing a green gown and was all dressed-up like a fairy faggot holding a magic wand! I've been wickedly cheated, I tell you! Wickedly cheated!"

"I had changed at the last minute the color of Anne's dress from green to white," Mistress Quickly (who had just come onto the forest scene) informed the stunned gathering. "The entire fiasco was really my own doing!"

"Well then, who knew about the white dress?" Master Page asked in astonishment. "That's the man who would escape to Leatherhead with my daughter Anne."

"Master Fenton!" the Windsor/Eastcheap/Frogmore matchmaker Mistress Quickly quite quickly replied. "And here comes the newly married couple, right now!"

"Anne and I have been deeply in love and committed to each other for quite some time," Fenton disclosed to the shocked folks assembled (all that is, except Mistress Quickly and Mistress Meg Page). "Dear Anne refused to get married for money or for status! She simply desired getting married for love! And I knew for a fact that none of her other wooers loved her half as much as me, Master Fenton; bless my rewarded soul!"

"Well, I'll have to magically change from being a total jackass to being a gorilla's stepfather!" Sir John illogically exclaimed. "This fucked-up forest tale is more fucked-up than I'll ever be, that's for goddamned sure! Er, sorry about my aberrant choice of parlance, Parson Sir Hugh!"

"Welcome to the Page family!" Anne's father sincerely said to Fenton, while warmly shaking his hand, and then warmly embracing his knockout daughter.

"Let's go Master Donny Brook, er, I mean dear Husband, to the Page home for a most spectacular wedding feast," Alice Ford said to her spouse, as the often-drunken Sir John finally realized the wily Ford's dual identities.

"Yes!" Meg Page exclaimed and concurred. "Everyone's invited to the gala celebration! Even you, *our* illustrious and lovable over-the-hill playboy, Sir John Falstaff!"

"The Taming of the Shrew"

Introduction

Christopher Sly (a drunken mendicant who in actuality has little to do with this story) was being scolded by Hostess Hilda Gruntlube, and then was quickly kicked-out of the popular country alehouse.

"I'm not a 'lowlife rogue' as you've so maliciously labeled me," Sly insisted to no avail. "All I did was accidentally break two glasses of inferior quality and craftsmanship! That's why I refuse to pay for the ten beers I had drunk! You insulted me, you fat ugly Bitch in front of six of my friends, and a goddamned room full of strangers!"

"I'll call the sheriff and his constable if you don't get the hell out of here and never come back again!" the disgruntled Hilda Gruntlube yelled at Christopher Sly as the bum meandered-off, staggering and tottering. "You're more trouble than you're worth, and if ya' wanna' know the truth, I wouldn't waste my time showing-up before a legal court, and as an outcome, not get a pittance out of you! But on second thought, it might be worth it to see your ass sitting in stocks and bonds, with you being deservedly mocked in the village square!"

'Let the goddamned sheriff, the constables, and all the king's horses and all the king's men come and arrest me, for all the fuck I care!' Sly thought as the loser eased his back against a tree and slid his body down to the ground. 'Fuck 'em all! Fuck the whole goddamned world!' Then, the intoxicated fellow fell asleep, dreaming of a better life and a better wife.

Christopher Sly loudly snored his troubles away, subconsciously trying to build his self-esteem. Soon, a wealthy nobleman and his jovial servants on horseback passed by the inebriated Sly, and spotted the old alcoholic sitting there, prone on the ground; the riders wondering whether Sly was dead, or presumably soused.

"Perhaps today's lengthy hunt will be fruitful after all," the huntsman/aristocrat jested. "Is that worthless son-of-a-bitch still breathing?" the nobleman asked a dismounted attendant.

"He's fast asleep, Master!" the servant indicated after a cursory inspection of Sly. "The jerk-off has beer on his breath, but features a healthy pulse! And the lousy sleeping bastard is even occasionally farting, too!"

"Well, that's truly great!" the nobleman laughed. "Let's take this no-good shit-head home with us. I want to play a joke on him for my own enjoyment, because in this miserable day and age, a rolling stone gathers no moss; and therefore, I can't get no satisfaction. Someday those words might be famous, ha, ha, ha!"

"But this good-for-nothing dumb fuck smells like a stinking tavern barroom, and he's got putrid vomit caked all over his raggedy shirt and pants!" the kneeling servant mildly objected. "This pathetic asshole is a complete mess!"

"Clean him up at home; wash his mangy hair; trim his unkempt beard, and then dress him in my finest pajamas," the nobleman ordered. "Subject this poor excuse for a human being to beautiful music, and have sweet incense burning near his bed to provide a little atmosphere to help improve the atmosphere. This wretch might still someday be reformed and educated."

"Won't that crazy bullshit seem mighty peculiar to him when the hideous fuck eventually awakes?" a second servant on horseback asked the thoroughly-amused country baron. "Culture might seem odd to an uncivilized lowlife vulture like this wretch!"

"That's the whole idea of my social experiment, you stupid Shit!" the country gentleman scoffed at his not-too-brilliant underling. "We must convince this intoxicated dreg that he's someone important; a rich asshole with lots of servants and property. You and I both know that this hapless old fuck is Christopher Sly, the notorious village drunk, but we must convince him that he's a wealthy and powerful aristocrat, just to see how the hell the nincompoop reacts to his new status. Are you ready to initiate my little ploy for diversion's sake?"

"Yes!" the six delighted servants unanimously agreed. "Yes!" the newly appointed pranksters gleefully reiterated.

A traveling group of unemployed actors approached the scene on horseback, and the leader asked for directions to Italy.

"You're just outside of London, England and heading north toward Coventry!" the noblemen incredulously responded. "You're more disoriented than my Chinese cook and my Japanese geisha girl! You're definitely my kind of people!"

"Thank you, Sir!" the thespian leader politely answered. "Neither my troupe nor myself are very good at geography! We thought we were still in Coventry heading south toward London."

Suddenly, the huntsman/nobleman got an inspiration. "Kind Actors and Actresses; you've come at a most excellent time for me, and I guarantee a most propitious opportunity for you!" the nobleman exclaimed. "I could use your wonderful, eclectic services to perform a play for a sick elderly friend of mine. Could you talented folks accommodate my wishes?"

"Well, in that we could use a good meal and some additional money to travel on to famous Venice to seek employment there," the lead actor declared. "Sure; we'd be very interested in obtaining a small side job. Do you desire for the play to have nudity, sex, S and M, or weird gay characters?"

"No, just a common ordinary straight play will do!" the nobleman laughed while stroking his beard. "My chief steward shall escort your traveling company to my mansion, and assist you in any props or necessary items your production might require. You wouldn't mind performing your show in my giant master bedroom?"

"No Sir!" the head actor laughed. "We'll do it in your smallest outhouse if you'd like!"

"Fine! Here are several gold coins as an advance payment! A dozen more will follow upon completion of your ludicrous performance!" the nobleman generously stated. "You may eat and sleep tonight in my luxurious manor house, and tomorrow evening, perform your marvelous play. That'll allow you sufficient time to rehearse your key parts in my barn, but I'm warning you, gypsy troubadours; don't do anything un-stable! Ha, ha, ha!"

"Terrific! Excellent!" the head actor dramatically exclaimed. "This coincidental encounter, kind Sir, is indeed a very fortuitous opportunity for us!"

Later that afternoon, Christopher Sly awoke in the nobleman's enormous, comfortable bed, all clean and sober, and surrounded by accommodating servants who volunteered to shave, dress, and provide wine to the now-astonished and bewildered derelict.

"Where the fuck' am I?" Sly inquired. "I've never swallowed-down fancy wine in my entire life! Does it taste delicious like ale? And I wear the same fuckin' clothes each and every day! In real life, I'm a goddamned vagabond and tinker wannabe', and now, I must be fuckin' dreaming this most wonderful fantasy! I'm fucked-up Christopher Sly, a total failure!"

"Master, please don't degrade your abundant dignity!" a servant diplomatically suggested while feigning genuine sincerity. "You're exceedingly tired, and I believe that your thinking is a little skewed. Why do you say you're poor, when in fact, you're one of the richest men in this part of the world?"

"Yes, what you say must be fuckin' true!" the sly Sly uttered with a degree of uncertainty. "But ask the fat, ugly wench Hilda Gruntlube over at the Wincot Alehouse who the hell I am! I owe the bitch at least a dozen silver coins for my accumulated debts, or else I'm banned forever from the unsophisticated premises!"

"Master, I assure you that you're certainly worth many thousands of coins, and gold ones at that," a giggling servant insisted. "You have the finest hunting hounds in the entire area; the most fabulous horses; the most loyal servants, and the most beautiful Mistress who is deeply saddened because you're temporarily ill."

Christopher Sly stuck his hand into a pan of steaming hot water and almost scalded his skin off. "Holy fuckin' shit!" Sly boisterously screamed. "I'm not dreaming or fuckin' hallucinating after all! This is fuckin' reality, and not a goddamned illusion! But since I'm convinced that I'm now some sort of influential high-ranking person, bring my' lady here and fetch me a large container of beer. I need to get laid badly, and to someone else besides my ugly toothless wife."

"Oh Master!" the smiling and then snickering nobleman said to Christopher Sly. "Your formerly befuddled mind is once again healthy, my Lord, and we're all so happy about the transformation. How foolish of you to dream that you were a destitute peddler! What a screwball nightmare that terrible frustration must've been!"

The following evening, one of the actresses entered the bedroom, pretending to be Christopher Sly's devoted wife. The attractive, well-dressed lady informed Sly that his doctor demanded that the recovering fellow view a play production to fully regain his emotional stability. "The laughter will do you good!" the voluptuous woman recommended and encouraged. "The fun and entertainment will completely cure you of your brief affliction."

"Good idea, my beautiful Wife; even if I don't know your goddamned name!" Sly answered. "I'll consent to seeing this play! But for my information, what in the hell is its title?"

Another actor associated with the traveling band entered with a whip, and a barred wooden box containing a nearly blind rodent resembling a mole. Sly curiously peered into the barred cage at the strange-looking mammal with the long, pointed snout.

"What the fuck is that?" Sly incredulously asked the fellow holding the cage and the whip. "Is the name of your weird play 'How to Box a Furry Rodent'?"

The main actor carefully placed the cage on the floor and began hostilely lashing the whip at the frightened, beady-eyed creature scrambling about inside. "No Master! The play that you're about to witness is appropriately titled 'The Taming of the Shrew!' Ha, ha, ha! And your phony wife is an actress in this play, so she won't be able to sit by your damned side watching it, while holding either your unproductive hand, or your reproductive gland! Ha, ha, ha!"

Act I

"The Taming of the Shrew" opens with Lucentio (a wealthy heir from Florence) accompanied by his elder servant Tranio, arriving in Padua where the lucky, rich teenager desired attending the renowned university to delay the onslaught of adulthood and responsibility. Lucentio had chosen the *University of Padua* because, in the mid-1500s, the city was a major center of Renaissance art, culture, knowledge, and theater.

"I'll tell you, Master," aged and wise Tranio said to Lucentio upon entering Padua. "Forget about all this intellectual bullshit relating to art and culture, and focus your energies and attention upon sex, partying, loose women, and food and drink. The biological aspects of life are where pleasure lies!"

"Is that why you always have indigestion and require frequent enemas?" Lucentio indulgently laughed. "Just remember, Tranio! Money talks, and bullshit walks! That's the only reason I'm listening to your ignorant, verbal horse-shit, simply because I'm a gentleman, and I must practice courtesy and extend it to even a lowlife Piss-head such as yourself!"

"Yes, young Lucentio. Your father Vincentio is a great merchant doing business out of Florence and Pisa, and the rich tycoon even has a lien on the *Leaning Tower* there, ha, ha, ha!" Tranio imaginatively quipped. "And unlike the famous leaning edifice, your affluent old man desires that you yourself mature into a tower of strength. Doesn't your pappy Vincentio realize that it's impossible to make chicken salad out of chicken shit? Fuck Aristotle, Ovid, and Homer! I'm telling you Lucentio that those dead assholes will only distract you from getting your rocks off!"

"I need to develop my academic skills in rhetoric, theater, logic, mathematics, history, metaphysics, and science, and I'll never receive those specialized trainings from you, Tranio," Lucentio maintained. "Indeed, I can learn much from the ancient Greek stoics. And if you knew so fuckin' much, dear Tranio, you wouldn't be my damned servant wiping my ass when you aren't kissing it; you dumb hedonistic Fuck!"

Lucentio and Tranio forgot about debating when the new arrivals encountered on the street a mild dispute going-on between two garrulous men and an old codger. The visiting pair stopped their conversation to eavesdrop on the argument-in-progress. The intense discussion involved two suitors, Gremio and Hortensio, debating an old fellow Baptista about having the opportunity to court the ancient fossil's younger blonde-haired daughter, Bianca. But inflexible-minded Baptista insisted that the suitors' intentions should be denied until the parent could successfully marry-off his older, dark-haired daughter Katherina, who had a terrible and shameful reputation for being a bitchy shrew.

"Now Gremio and Hortensio," Baptista persisted and wrangled. "Listen to me. If either of you two obdurate Fools wishes to court my older daughter Katherina, then you're certainly welcome to do so. But if you try and woo Bianca, like I've already told you two Clods, you'll both have to wait until Katherina is wed. Is that perfectly clear?" the old geezer stated with Katherina and Bianca standing directly behind him.

"You meant to say that we should be carting nasty-tempered Katherina instead of courting her," Gremio balked. "Your older daughter is an untamed, vile, bossy bitch, who is only compatible with the goddamned Devil! She belongs in a cage on the back of a circus cart!"

"Father, you've reached a stalemate with these two potential stale mates for Bianca," Katherina chimed-in. "Gremio and Hortensio are both men with long noses that look like hoses, and the assholes probably possess short hoses that look-like noses. Why in the world would my younger sister ever want any part of these two arrogant, old fuck Assholes?"

"Unless you learn manners, no educated man will ever show even the mildest interest in you," Gremio replied, attempting to chastise Katherina. "You're the Bitch of bitches, no fuckin' doubt about it!"

"Keep talking like that, you fucked-up, wrinkle-skinned, ancient Bastard, and I'll improve your face's appearance by scratching and lacerating the ugly thing all up! My fingernails are lethal weapons!" Katherina answered back to the aged Gremio. "And then, I'll beat your head into pulp by repetitiously slamming a three-legged stool against it, you three-legged freak of nature!"

"My Katherina is rebellious because she thinks that I've always favored Bianca," Baptista apologized to Gremio. "But her belief is a suspicion that's not strongly founded in truth. If Katherina were more civilized and cultured," her father insisted, "she could get anything that she wants! But she's truculent and obstinate in her fucked-up ways, and refuses to ever concede, negotiate, and compromise!"

"She must drink vinegar for breakfast every morning!" Hortensio theorized and stated. "A goddamned venomous viper has a prettier tongue than she has! Katherina is stark-raving mad, and must've annually experienced a skein of three-hundred and sixty-five-day-long goddamned bloody periods to prove it! That's why she's always fuckin' ragging on men!"

"Master," Tranio softly said to Lucentio. "Aren't you fuckin' glad that you're who you are, and not this troubled old man Baptista? The Old Fart probably wishes he was John the Baptist, and having his head cut off to escape this cruel and miserable world!"

"I think I'd rather screw a dozen tigresses than to try and pump that ornery-but-beautiful, black-haired, absolutely gorgeous, super-wench Katherina!" Lucentio related to his astute servant. "Let's listen to more of this fascinating bullshit argument! Tranio, I believe I can get a better education on the streets of Padua than I can obtain inside the damned academic university, that's for damned sure!"

"Now Bianca, get inside the house so that your ears don't have to hear any more of this escalating altercation!" Baptista instructed his younger, sweet daughter. "Go inside now and avoid participation in this unnerving confrontation!"

"Sister, the next time Father gives you a dumb-shit command, stick your thumbs into his eyes, and then roughly and fiercely rotate them as I'm used to doing," Katherina told Bianca. "And if you have to gouge his eyes out to establish your dominance, then by all means, do it as your first priority! Stop being his goddamned puppet and stick-up for yourself for a change! Learn to assert yourself, Bianca! And that'll be one goddamned less lock on your chastity belt, which should be removed and lost, or forever destroyed in the first place!"

"Your older daughter ought to be locked-up in a zoo cage if not in a jail cell," Gremio recommended to the beleaguered Baptista. "Hortensio and I are only interested in courting pristine Bianca!"

Before Bianca honored her father's intentions and entered the family home, the comely young lady announced to Gremio and Hortensio, "I must go and study my books so that I can be eligible to qualify for entrance into the university. I can learn more from astute, benign teachers than I can from constant street quarreling and bickering."

"Gremio and Hortensio, if either of you two know of a suitable tutor for my dear Bianca, let me know, for being a chauvinistic old fellow, I believe that only males should attend the university!" Baptista requested of the two unsuitable suitors. "Now Katherina; you may stay here with Gremio and with Hortensio, for one of the local shits might be stupid enough to propose marriage to you!" Then, the aggrieved father entered the house to confer with his favored daughter, blonde-haired Bianca.

"I need a goddamned special appointment to talk with Father, yet the asshole constantly flourishes Bianca with gifts and favors," Katherina protested to her two greedy male companions, who both pretended being deaf and mute to her grievance. "I might as well go inside the house too, rather than be bored-to-death standing outside here with you two prune-faced, simpleton Fuck-heads!"

After Katherina re-entered her father's home, Gremio and Hortensio reviewed the very difficult situation, and decided that they should be friendly competitors for Bianca's hand in marriage, since neither of them had a prayer's chance in hell of desiring to be triumphant in *his* pursuit of Katherina.

"Let's be happy rivals for Bianca's hand, which as you know, my friend Gremio, is unattainable under the present circumstances," Hortensio suggested. "In the interim, we can be decent chums, can commiserate with each other, and can merrily go to taverns, inns, and raucous whorehouses together!"

"Perhaps the first one who finds a qualified tutor for Bianca will have an advantage in the competition," Gremio declared to his now-amiable opponent. "Either that, or whoever finds a husband for the implacable Katherina would enjoy an even bigger advantage."

"A goddamned eternity in Hell would be more desirable than a life here on Earth with that saucy, vitriolic bitch!" Hortensio aptly returned. "I'd rather be dick-less than to have to try and pork that mouthy wench! Or Gremio, being crucified would seem like a plausible and feasible alternative! And no fuckin' dowry in the world would be worth such an excruciation; not to mention the goddamned daily anguish and verbal abuse that would befall Katherina's humiliated, crestfallen husband! Married to Katrina would mean no more hard-ons for the rest of your miserable life."

"True Hortensio!" Gremio agreed with his pompous rival. "There's little sweetness in a rotten apple, and Katherina's cunt must taste like raw sewage! Could you imagine that wench administering a blowjob? She'd bite your damned dingle-off whole, chew the son-of-a-bitch up, and then spit it out like inferior sausage, just for spite! I believe that the competitor who sprints faster in this race shall earn the hand of Bianca. How do you feel about our peculiar arrangement by necessity?"

"It's a tall task finding Katherina a husband!" Hortensio concurred. "It's best that we focus our ambitions on obtaining a skilled tutor for chaste and pure Bianca. The first already stated objective involving the courtship of Katherina would be a frivolous pursuit, bordering on absolute madness! I mean, dear Gremio,"

Hortensio emphasized, "you could never fuck Katherina on your honeymoon night because the bitch will have already either cut or bitten your dick and your nuts off! Let's get the hell out of here before we're both violently castrated. I'm sure you'll amply agree, my friend Gremio, that Katherina is definitely not desirable for either wedding or bedding!"

When Gremio and Hortensio eventually ambled around the corner, Lucentio and his loyal, elderly aide Tranio thoroughly evaluated what their eyes had just witnessed, along with what their pricked ears had just heard.

"Those two knuckleheaded suitors made the wise decision!" Tranio verbally related to Lucentio. "That Katherina is a vicious wildcat who has the disposition of a rebellious, insane female gorilla. That's one female ape I wouldn't want to fuckin' monkey around with! I wouldn't consider screwing that Medusa-type monster if she had the last remaining wet pussy on the face of the Earth!"

"Ah Tranio, I must confess that I've experienced love at first sight!" Lucentio confided to his cynical, veteran servant. "That luscious blonde-haired broad Bianca is absolutely a knockout! I'll be dreaming all day and all night about that charming and vivacious chick with the golden beaver."

"Master, you're just momentarily and stupidly infatuated over blonde beaver; firm tits, and nice ass! Puppy love, that's all it is!" Tranio counseled his employer. "Learn to think with your head, and not with your penis, and I assure you, you'll avoid major problems in your future life! Remember Master, your brain is in your head, and not inside your throbbing cock!"

"True Tranio," Lucentio conceded. "But emotion often transcends reason and dominates my thinking. In fact, it's presently reigning supreme in my pea brain. Bianca's sweet innocent face makes me desire to prematurely pop a load, and then instantly come all over her good-looking features!" the rich kid visitor to Padua maintained.

"Look, Master Asshole; remember why the fuck you came here to this fucked-up city!" Tranio reminded his youthful master, administering a reality check to his vernal and callow boss. "You could've easily whored around in Florence, and I'm not talking about your old girlfriend, either! But now we come here to Padua, and you instantly fall in love with the first bitch you see without even saying a fuckin' word to her!"

"Tranio! I just got a magnificent brainstorm!" Lucentio merrily declared. "I'll volunteer my services to become Bianca's tutor, and woo her in the process. I could get either that old joker Gremio or that cad Hortensio to introduce me to her, and to recommend my professional services. The fuck-heads both said they'd like to win old man Baptista's favor by getting the services of a competent house instructor for the curmudgeon's younger daughter."

"You stupid Asshole!" Tranio challenged. "You're here in Padua to learn cultural shit, and now you're acting like an academic know-it-all wanting to tutor that fair-skinned, blonde-haired doll! Ya' want to know something. I'll bet that Old Baptista must've whored around in his younger days, because Katherina is dark-skinned with dark hair, and her sister Bianca is white-skinned with blonde hair. I suspect that there's fucked-up genetics prevalent in *his* family!"

"Enough of your foolish conjecture and prattling!" Lucentio lectured Tranio. "Now here's my terrific plan. We'll switch places, you and me; and then you'll pretend to be my scholarly master, and I'll impersonate you, even though I've never learned how to be an asshole subordinate! One word of erudite advice, Tranio. Just don't keep pulling rank on me, you rank Moron!"

"What the fuck would your old man Vincentio think about *this* incredible, materializing bullshit?" Tranio curiously asked. "He'll certainly regret ever sending you to magnificent Padua if he ever found-out about this oddball caper you're considering."

"Father is closed-minded, and would think exactly as you've described it. He would perceive and interpret my plan as impractical bullshit that violates the social-order!" Lucentio acknowledged. "Now let's duck into this alleyway and change clothes. And when my young servant Biondello soon arrives in Padua, I'll tell him to regard you as his master and me as his equal. What do you think of that amazing shit, Tranio?"

"I think that your loony lark is merely asking for foolish trouble, and that's why the fuck I like and hereby endorse it!" Tranio enthusiastically answered. "Your father instructed me to obey you when here in Padua; and thus, although I'm no fuckin' Arabian genie of the lamp, I must admit that your outrageous schemes are my commands, as long as my death is not immediately imminent. I can't wait to become a fucked-up wealthy aristocrat! I suppose that as soon as we change and exchange our clothes, my name will be Lucentio, and you'll be my slave, Tranio."

"That is correct, my observant servant!" Lucentio verified. "I always wanted to know what the life of a knavish vassal was like, and now here's my fuckin' chance. Look there! That impish rogue Biondello is approaching us now!"

"Master, why are you wearing Tranio's clothes and why is your servant wearing yours?" Biondello curiously asked. "Are you two idiots practicing some new form of homosexuality that I'm unaware of? I've heard of cross-dressing and gay transvestites, but this exhibition is completely ridiculous!"

"This is no fuckin' time to jest, Biondello," Tranio (Lucentio) admonished the page. "For your information, I've recently killed a man and must change my identity in a hurry! I must alter my appearance by necessity, and you must go along with this imaginative ruse; otherwise, I'll feel obligated to alter the appearance of your already fucked-up freckled face! Do you now fuckin' understand my predicament, asshole valet?"

"Er, yes Master Lucentio, er, I mean Master Tranio!" Biondello stammered. "But I can't imagine this loser, gambler, and notorious womanizer Tranio, ever being rich and powerful! Just the thought of that nonsensical notion boggles my impressionable mind!"

"Look Biondello! Forget all about this murder canard you just heard!" Tranio (Lucentio) rankled. "Your fucked-up Master is now an avid protagonist, and not a goddamned antagonist! Now then, Bordello, er, I mean Biondello; your unscrupulous and fanciful Master has the hots for a young blonde-haired chick named Bianca, and we must use these disguises to trick her old man Baptista into allowing me Lucentio, er, I mean me Tranio, to tutor *his* lovely daughter!"

* * * * * * * * * * * *

A friend of Hortensio's named Petruchio (from Verona) showed-up in Padua with his servant Grumio (not to be confused with Gremio, the elderly pantalooner trying to woo Bianca). Hortensio confidentially told Petruchio about the incredulous situation involving sisters Katherina and Bianca. Petruchio, an ambitious fortune hunter and practicing gigolo, was soon inclined to woo Katherina, so that Hortensio would have the inside track to become Bianca's chief suitor.

"Ah Grumio, it's great to get out of Verona and visit my old buddy Hortensio," Petruchio said to his servant as the pair finally reached his friend's pad in Padua. "Knock on the door, and let's see how tough your knuckles are, and how long it takes them to bleed!"

"Okay Master, but don't knock me while I'm knocking on this door!" Grumio complained. "You're the only man I know who has his bloodless period every damned day of the month, you quarrelsome, demented Lord, you!"

"Never mind saying those flippant comments, Asshole!" the petulant Petruchio commanded. "There's a bell near the gate! Pull the clapper, or else I'll ring your bell good by wringing your ears off your Neanderthal skull with my strong hands!"

Hortensio answered the bell, and immediately recognized his old chum from Verona, along with *his* zany servant. The resident cordially invited the two fatigued travelers to step inside and enjoy his warm hospitality.

"Ah, welcome to Padua, Petruchio," Horetensio greeted. "And you too Grumio, which sounds a little too much like Gremio."

"Yes Hortensio; I've had to punch Grumio in the head at least a dozen times between Verona and Padua, so that's why the idiot looks like a goddamned knucklehead," Petruchio laughed. "If only stubborn Grumio wouldn't be so difficult, and learn to follow simple, basic directions! But as you can plainly see, I can't knock any damned sense into the ignoramus's skull!"

"Knock it off, Master!" Grumio bitched. "My head is hurting so badly from all of your knocking and punching, that I think I hear something called 'rap music' inside!"

"Go find the pantry Grumio, and help yourself to the cookie jar," Hortensio suggested. "But be sure not to put your face and cranium inside the narrow glass opening, or else your head might be jarred again! Ha, ha, ha!"

After Grumio left to explore and inspect Hortensio's pantry and snack supply, the amiable host and Petruchio struck-up a friendly dialogue. The host Hortensio asked his visitor why he had journeyed all the way to Padua from Verona.

"I wasn't having too much luck finding and hitting on a rich bitch back in Verona, so I figured I'd come here to Padua and get a hot lead from you," Petruchio informed an amused but suddenly inspired Hortensio. "Nowadays, it's far easier to get laid or smacked in the face by an unappreciative, wealthy hussy than it is to marry her. Now then, my father Antonio has recently died and left me a sizeable fortune, but being the greedy bastard that I am, I want more wealth in the form of a substantial dowry," Petruchio explained. "I'm in quest of an eligible and desirable rich woman here in Padua. Do you have any available recommendations?"

"A shrewd fellow like you deserves the challenge of courting a savage shrew!" Hortensio cleverly phrased to Petruchio. "Now, I know a particular rich bitch, but I dare not wish her upon you or anyone else! She might bite your dick off while you think you're getting some good head from her, the first time she goes south with her mouth! I hope that my introductory description will discourage you from meeting the incompatible Bitch!"

"If the shrew is wealthy, that's my only real criterion," Petruchio indicated. "I can tame any shrew by killing her with kindness. Tell me more about this rich strumpet you've been describing. I'm becoming very interested; almost intrigued."

"Well, this Katherina that I know is quite beautiful and wealthy, but she has the temper of a fierce ocean tempest," Hortensio very deliberately related. "Her father Baptista is a fine gentleman who cannot control her vehement and intolerable outbursts. Personally Petruchio, I wouldn't wed Katherina for a full dozen-and-a-half, active-and-profitable gold mines."

"I like romantic challenges," Petruchio bragged as fat Grumio returned to the living room from the pantry, eating his seventeenth spicy cookie. "Now please tell me more about this fellow Baptista and his uncontrollable daughter Katherina."

"Minola Baptista is a pleasant and polite fellow, but his older daughter Katherina is quite obnoxious, abominable, and quite frankly, very dangerous," Hortensio conveyed to his fascinated guest. "And this mercurial-tempered shrew Katherina has a scolding tongue that's worse than scalding water. I'm warning you, Petruchio, that sex with Katherina is analogous to putting your dick and your testicles into a lethal bear trap!"

"Although I don't yet know this most-interesting toxic wench Katherina, believe it or not Hortensio, her father Minola Baptista and my father Antonio were at one time good friends," Petruchio recollected and verbally shared. "Could you accompany me to Baptista's home so that I could be properly and formally introduced to this villainous feline you've depicted, this Katherina Baptista?"

"If this Katherina knew my Master as well as I do," Grumio interrupted, "then the contemptuous wench would not say a word for the rest of her life if the two deserving-each-other imbeciles were to marry. Signior Petruchio is an avid animal trainer, and my stern master can easily convert this atrocious shrew Katherina into a cagey woman," eavesdropping Grumio stated to Hortensio without *his* opinion ever being requested. "My Master Petruchio will make this ferocious cat into a tamed kitten so that his intriguing male dominance could get to her pussy without fearing having his dick amputated during fellatio."

"Well now, Petruchio," Hortensio excitedly stated while pretending to ignore Grumio's irrelevant remarks. "Dark-haired Katherina is the older sister of Bianca, the blonde-haired doll that I wish to court and marry. However, there's another suitor involved in this fascinating scenario, and his name is Gremio, a loony elderly town pantalooner. But old Baptista has stipulated that first Katherina must be married-off before I could compete for the lovely Bianca's hand in marriage, so that's where you, my cherished friend, fit into this complex love equation. Petruchio, you couldn't have fuckin' visited me at a more favorable, or should I say, 'more opportune time'!"

"This arrangement sounds pretty reckless and fucked-up to me!" Grumio rudely assessed and shared his unwanted and unsolicited opinion. "I might viciously get simultaneously killed by two crazy people instead of just by one!"

"Okay Petruchio," Hortensio remarked while again ignoring Grumio's inane evaluation and commentary. "Here's the essence to my ingenious plan. I'll dress-up as a sophisticated music instructor disguised to tutor Bianca. We'll show-up at Baptista's house using the guise of the old fellow being an acquaintance of your dead old man, Antonio. I'll get to tutor the blonde-haired Bianca, and you'll get to meet and flirt with the dark-haired Katherina. Gee, I wonder if Bianca's pussy is blonde, or dark haired?"

Not wanting to hear any more "disgusting scheming bullshit" between Hortensio and Petruchio, Grumio stepped outside and soon met-up with Lucentio (Tranio) and his servant Tranio (Lucentio). "Hello," Grumio greeted the itinerant pair. "Are you looking for another servant?" the dumb-ass clown innocently asked. "My Master has gone bonkers, and I need a change of venue before he goes stark-raving ballistic."

"Er no; my friend and I are just reviewing some lecture notes in literature that I'm practicing to recite later on. I'm about to audition to tutor a beautiful woman, and I need to make a good impression upon her father," Tranio (Lucentio is now dressed and disguised as the tutor Cambio) informed the somewhat-impressed Grumio.

"You two assholes seem to be more fucked-up than the two I had just left inside that wonderfully-constructed house over there," Grumio all-too-honestly stated. "One thing's for damned sure. There're more assholes in Padua than there are toilet seats in this fucked-up town's outhouses."

Just then Hortensio and Petruchio exited the house, and soon met-up with Grumio, the idealistic Cambio (Lucentio is disguise) and a new arrival Gremio, the ancient-looking city pantalooner. The men initiated an impromptu chat, and soon discovered that they were all heading to Signior Baptista's nearby residence.

"Ah Petruchio, this old fellow Gremio is my chief rival for Bianca's perfumed hand," Hortensio cordially explained. "We've mutually decided on a friendly competition. And my friend Gremio," Hortensio continued his discourse, "Petruchio here is also a highly skilled music teacher auditioning to professionally instruct Bianca in that special art," Hortensio lied.

"Ah yes, Hortensio; glad to see you again. And hello Petruchio," Gremio, the elderly-but-suave pantalooner, acknowledged. "What a remarkable coincidence this is indeed! Now here is Cambio (Lucentio) who is a highly skilled literature teacher I have brought along to teach Bianca poetry and the like. The blonde-haired cherub of our dreams will be a university student by next semester, no doubt about it! She'll learn classical music from Petruchio, and literature from Cambio!"

"This is absolute bullshit!" Grumio said as everyone paid little attention to the servant's annoying, exaggerated peeving. "I would've stayed in Hortensio's pantry longer if there were more cookies inside the damned glass jar."

"Well then," Hortensio said to old and withered Gremio. "We can now peacefully continue our friendly rivalry for Bianca's hand in marriage. This very ambitious fellow Petruchio, who is pretending to be an eminent music teacher for Bianca, wishes to court and marry Katherina, and that leaves the field open for you and me to pursue Bianca's sought-after affections," Hortensio reviewed for the almost senile Gremio. "And your clean-shaven poetry and literature tutor, young Cambio here (Lucentio) can also instruct her in another important university subject."

"If you were smart, Signior Cambio," Grumio said to Lucentio, "you'd refrain from your poetic refrains. It would be most wise for you to go back to your studies, rather than to enter into any kind of complicated arrangement with these crazy, conniving, unscrupulous mental cases! I have a concealed knife if you'd like to attempt committing suicide!"

Old Gremio ignored the servant Grumio's grumbling and mumbling to Cambio (Lucentio), and then asked Petruchio a pertinent question. "Sir; are you aware of Katherina's many faults? She's a brawler, a man-hater, and a shrew of the worst magnitude!"

"Just the type of belligerent woman that I positively adore, admire, and find absolutely fascinating," Petruchio boasted and

449

related. "I do have an advanced diploma in animal training, you know, and I specialize in subduing wild felines like panthers, tigers, leopards, cheetahs, prostitutes, and lionesses."

"This newly discussed information sounds quite great and most fair!" Gremio the loony pantalooner expressed to his fellow strategists. "Petruchio woos Katherina, while surreptitiously tutoring Bianca in music; you Hortensio and I vie for Bianca's hand in marriage, and Cambio here (Lucentio) teaches Bianca literature and poetry. I'll therefore wholeheartedly go along with Petruchio's suit for Katherina's hand and dowry. What is your heritage Petruchio?" Gremio inquired. "You must be a rich fellow to be able to sufficiently bankroll the courting of the volatile Katherina?"

"My deceased father was the famous Antonio of Verona, an extremely wealthy whore and harlot slave trader and bordello owner," Petruchio accurately divulged to his new colleagues. "I inherited quite a considerable fortune, and plan to add to it with Katherina's substantial dowry from this old, liberal, poor disciplinarian fellow, Minola Baptista. I can't wait to get started on this romantic enterprise," Petruchio enthusiastically declared. "I just simply love bawdy, argumentative, and unruly women! And if this Katherina is a dominatrix with a whip and chains, I'll soon love the hostile bitch even more!"

"You're a brave and daring man, Petruchio!" Gremio generously complimented. "I'll cooperate with your suit, and with your aggressive pursuit of Katherina! Better fuckin' you, than me! You've got more fuckin' audacity than I could ever dream of possessing!"

"Look Assholes, er, I mean distinguished Gentlemen," Petruchio crudely replied and then corrected himself. "I've heard and experienced severe hurricanes beat against cliffs that I've been marooned on, and I've heard cannon balls whizzing by my ears on the battlefield. A goddamned shrew's mouth cannot frighten me unless it has spiked barbs like a cudgel's attached to it, and she's then sticking her lethal dagger-tongue into my vulnerable ear!"

* * * * * * * * * * * *

Lucentio (Tranio), accompanied by Biondello, met-up with Cambio (Lucentio/Tranio) at Baptista's front door, and was formally introduced to Hortensio, to Gremio, and to Petruchio. The stage was now set for the courting of both Katherina and Bianca.

"Sir," Hortensio said to Lucentio (Tranio). "Are you a suitor to either of Baptista's daughters, black-haired Katherina, or blonde-haired Bianca?"

"Are not the streets as free for me as they are for you?" Lucentio (Tranio) smartly answered. "Is not the air ours to share and enjoy? Cannot I enjoy viewing the parks and the splendid buildings of Padua the same as you do?"

"Well then, evasive Stranger," Hortensio said to Lucentio (Tranio), "I must inform you that you're at a distinct disadvantage. This gentleman Gremio and myself are the principal suitors to the blonde-haired Bianca. This fellow Petruchio to my right is a suitor for the hand of perilous Katherina. And this fellow Cambio here (Lucentio) is an accomplished tutor of literature for Bianca's academic advancement. And now. Sir; your coincidental presence obviously complicates this expanding conflict even more!"

"Well then," Lucentio (Tranio) explained. "I'm a rival suitor not to be trifled with, or dismissed too easily, even though Master Gremio, I understand, is a sort of suitor by trade. My name is Lucentio, son of Vincentio of Florence and Pisa, and I'm here in Padua to also court the beautiful Bianca. Let's now enter the house and drink some sweet and mellow wine together as three friendly rivals. Don't look so shocked, Gentlemen!" the newly-announced fucked-up suitor said to Hortensio and Gremio. "I'm a lot richer than both of you two dumb mother-fuckers put together!"

'Nice going, my faithful servant Tranio!' Cambio (Lucentio) the prospective literature and grammar tutor appreciatively thought. 'Your fantastic bravado was very illuminating, just like *my* real name that you're impersonating is!'

"Okay," Hortensio reluctantly agreed. "But I suggest one further modification to *our* alliance. Petruchio, forget your tutoring assignment. I'll be Bianca's music instructor, Licio."

"Fine with me," Petruchio assented. "I don't particularly care what new names you blustery Assholes assume; just as long as I remain myself" Petruchio of Verona, courting this irascible and unbearable Padua shrew Katherina Baptista! I can't wait to meet and tame the contemptible Bitch!"

Act II

When Petruchio, Lucentio (Cambio/Tranio), Gremio, Hortensio and Tranio (Lucentio) entered Minola Baptista's splendid mansion,

Petruchio surprised the old geezer by announcing to Baptista that he was a suitor for Katherina's hand. Then, the haughty Petruchio introduced the nearly-blind Baptista to Hortensio as talented Licio, the music teacher to instruct Bianca, and possibly Katherina, also; and then Gremio, the garrulous pantalooner, presented Cambio (Lucentio/Tranio) as Bianca's "well-versed and articulate literature professor". Finally, Tranio introduced himself as Lucentio, the son of wealthy Vincentio of Pisa and Florence as being another friendly rival seeking the hand of sweet and innocent Bianca. All of those aforementioned formalities were happening in the parlor, while in another room, Bianca was begging volatile Katherina to untie and free *her* hands.

"Good Sister; please un-tether my bonds!" Bianca urged Katherina. "I promise to respect your age, and even involuntarily perform cunnilingus on you if you should again order me! Please untie me now! My wrists are starting to bleed!"

"Tell me which of your suitors you prefer, and I'll untie you!" Katherina yelled at Bianca. "Tell me or you'll remain my personal hostage, and who the hell knows what a crazy girl like myself might decide to do with you!"

"Sister, to this very day I still haven't found that special face that lights my fire!" Bianca honestly cried and begged. "Shit! I better not die a virgin, or I'll definitely commit suicide if you don't first kill me before I make-up my mind!"

"Thou art lying, Bianca!" Katherina shouted. "I believe that you love that fucked-up fellow Hortensio the most! Yes, it's that lousy creep Hortensio, isn't it?"

"I would prefer that Hortensio were to woo *you!*" Bianca screamed to Katherina. "The covetous merchant is much more your type, and I'm not talking about newspaper or poster print either!"

"Then, you must favor old mediocre Gremio the pantalooner to get inside your pants and under your petty petticoat!" Katherina yelled. "Gremio is not a comedian who will keep you in stitches. You'd be better off marrying a human-sized worm!"

"That's not true, Kate! Untie my hands so that I can go and study my lessons!" Bianca pleaded. "Unlike you, I want a college education to improve myself."

"You really want me to untie your hands so that you can go masturbate your button!" Katherina bellowed. "Go rub your silly squiggly clit off your tiny crotch, for all the hell I care! Ha, ha, ha!"

Baptista excused himself and left his guests' company to step to another part of his mansion to referee in the disagreement between his two opposite-minded daughters. The new arrivals slowly entered the adjoining room to eavesdrop on the very vocal family argument.

"Katherina, why are you so insolent to my authority and so abusive to your kind younger sister?" Baptista yelled to his bellicose older daughter. "You possess a shameful, devilish spirit, and feel that you must persist in exhibiting it when we have honorable guests in *our* house! Please show some basic decency and discretion, will you?"

"Father, your precious younger daughter must have suitors and a husband, while I'm neglected and ignored like a discarded, weatherworn, old shoe," Katherina hollered at her nearly-blind parent in her own defense. "Don't you dare talk to me and make excuses when I'm in such a turbulent mood! I'm liable to fuckin' strangle you out of sheer anger, and out of my rising need for revenge! Now leave me the fuck alone, or I'll tie you up just like I've done to Bianca!"

"I'm totally embarrassed by my daughter's delirious semantics!" Baptista turned and apologized to his guests standing in the hallway. "Katherina is a combination typhoon and maelstrom!"

"God save you from your bitch of a daughter!" old Gremio said to his upset neighbor, Baptista. "She's both crazy personified and crazy amplified! I do believe that Katherina needs an exorcism performed on her by a bishop, or perhaps even by a full-fledged cardinal, or most favorably, by the Pope himself in Rome!"

"Signior Baptista," Petruchio impulsively interrupted. "As you already know, I'm an opportunistic gentleman from Verona, seeking your daughter Katherina's hand in marriage. I've heard plenty about her beauty, and her wit, and her wonderful sociability, and also her humility; not to mention her abundant modesty."

"Are you daft, Man?" Baptista incredulously answered. "My daughter Katherina will butcher you up, and gladly sell your meat to the corner marketplace. She's worse than any devil or demon residing in Hell, and would make diabolical Satan desire to amend his errant ways and ascend into Heaven. You must be talking about my Bianca, and not about that horror mental asylum case study, Katherina!"

"On the contrary," the jolly Petruchio replied with a less-than-genuine broad grin. "Now, here is a terrific music tutor Licio (Hortensio) I've brought along to teach Bianca and Katherina in the cultural aspects of both Orpheus and Apollo's favorite pastime."

"And may I present good Cambio (young Lucentio)," Tranio acting as Lucentio said to Baptista. "This young man is an extraordinary scholar in literature and pornography. If you recall from my short introduction in the other room, I'm Lucentio (Tranio), son of Vincentio of Pisa and Florence. I've traveled all the way from Pisa via Florence to Padua to also woo your blonde-haired beauty, the virtuous and incomparable Bianca."

"Your father is a mighty fellow in Pisa, laundering his prostitute trading money into a chain of pizza parlors and other clever front businesses," Baptista remembered and stated. "You, Lucentio (speaking to Tranio) are very welcome in my house by virtue of your father's most excellent reputation."

"Licio and Cambio," Baptista said to Hortensio and to Lucentio respectively. "Take your equipment and your academic books and start tutoring my daughters immediately. Katherina especially needs all of the education and all of the culture that her ferocious feline mind can absorb! And Cambio," Baptista continued his exposition, "I believe that you're an expert on languages. Those Latin verb conjugations have always been Greek to me! Ha, ha, ha! To tell you the truth, I don't give a flying shit what Caesar did to the Gauls, or what the hell the primitive Gauls had the gall to do to that Roman rascal Caesar!"

A servant was summoned and instructed to lead Licio (Hortensio) and Cambio (Lucentio/Tranio) to their respective newly-appointed responsibilities, industriously tutoring Baptista's two daughters. Biondello followed his master Cambio (Lucentio) into a side suite of rooms, carrying the necessary literature and poetry books.

"Now then, Gentlemen," Baptista said to Petruchio, to Gremio and to Lucentio (Tranio). "Let's take a brief stroll into my apple orchard, and then into my olive grove, to discuss our new relationships. Then, we'll enjoy dinner together once I feel I know all three of you jackasses better."

"Signior Baptista," Petruchio nervously interrupted. "I have many important duties and obligations awaiting me back in Verona. Forgive my haste, but I must immediately have permission to woo Katherina; otherwise, I'll be neglecting my myriad responsibilities, for I'm indispensable to my family's businesses and affairs. Does my sincere request have your approval? What sort of dowry does my suit of your bad-mouthing daughter entail?"

"Well now, Petruchio, you blunt Fellow, and may I add that I admire that particular characteristic in you," Baptista uttered and qualified. "You'll be entitled to half of my properties, estates and deeds, and to twenty-thousand gold crowns, which incidentally have never been worn by any fucked-up kings or dukes. And, oh yes, noble Petruchio; you have my consent to woo Katherina, but I wish you lots of luck in your asinine endeavor!"

"And if I marry Katherina and die before her, she'll be entitled to all of my inherited land and wealth," Petruchio proudly and confidently answered. 'Little does this old geezer Baptista know that I've virtually gambled my father's entire fortune away on wine, women, song, gay whorehouses, and card playing, and that my inheritance will be at best minuscule.'

"How do you intend to win my daughter Katherina's love when there is no love for anyone but herself in her empty heart?" Baptista asked Petruchio. "I think that my question represents a tall order on your part, and I truly believe that you're biting-off more than you can either chew or swallow!"

"It'll be like two raging fires converging," Petruchio said in a simile to Baptista, "but in *our* conflagration relationship, my inferno will be far too powerful for Katherina's small blaze, and my potent flames will soon envelop and consume her. Then, she'll be a part of me, and be all mine to boot. I promise you; I won't be intimidated by her ruthless temper, and I know just how to domesticate your wench, er, I mean your precious, older daughter."

Suddenly, Licio (Hortensio) came dashing from the mansion into the orchard, loudly screaming and holding his bleeding head. Baptista wondered what sort of disaster had happened to his daughters' newly appointed music tutor.

"How come you look so pale, Licio? Did Katherina clobber you with a pail?" the nearly-blind patriarch questioned the music tutor, whom *he* never recognized as the devious pretender Hortensio.

"Your wild and furious daughter Katherina did a musical score on my goddamned head!" Licio (Hortensio) moaned and groaned. "That unsavory bitch should've been a soldier, or an ancient Roman gladiator, or perhaps a self-defense instructor beating the shit out of uncivilized barbarians. I had handed her a lute, and then she broke the instrument over my skull," Licio (Hortensio) grieved. "I don't think that Katherina would make a good orchestra musician, even if she has memorized all of the notes, and all of the music in the whole fuckin' world!"

"Tell us the specific details of your conflict with my daughter," Baptista asked the disheveled tutor.

"At first, I was about to get-out my guitar to accompany her horrendous lute playing," Licio (Hortensio) lamented, "but I'm glad that I never had a chance to begin the lesson; otherwise, I'm quite sure that *that* ornery female wildcat Katerina would've gotten my dick and my balls caught inside the guitar strings, and then the object would've been twisted around and rotated, until my genitals would've been snapped-off from my abdomen! It's far more painful thinking about that grotesque possibility of me being abused by a G-string, than have me worrying about having my head brutally split open by a lute, and about me bleeding profusely all over your goddamned polished floor, and upon your expensive Oriental carpet; not to mention shedding my precious blood inside your impeccable apple orchard."

"Shit Baptista! I now love your abrasive-tongued older daughter ten times more after hearing Hortensio's, er, excuse me, Licio's graphic testimony," Petruchio bragged. "I really long to have an extensive chat with the vociferous wench, er, I meant to say, with that beautiful brunette girl!"

"You must be more fucked-up than I had originally thought you to be!" Baptista abruptly criticized. "Petruchio; I have no skills in standard psychiatry or any other pseudo-social-science, but I know of a very competent physician who may be of practical service to you, even though the doctor exclusively deals with the theoretical facets of mental health!"

"No thank you, Signior Baptista!" Petruchio promptly replied. "I don't think that your psychiatrist friend could cure Katherina's mental maladies, but I do believe that my superb psychological methodologies can work a miracle! Unlike Licio, I'll soon possess Katerina's G-string!"

"Okay, Licio, your scalp cuts were only superficial, and your head has stopped bleeding," almost-blind Baptista observed and commented. "Go now to Bianca's room and replace her in-progress literature lesson with some fundamental music instruction. I'm sure you'll find Bianca much more cooperative and receptive than you had found Katherina to be," Baptista optimistically predicted. "The worst that could happen is that her pet squirrel crunches your nuts while you're employing your marvelous tutoring!"

"I again entreat you Signior Baptista!" Petruchio stubbornly implored. "Please allow me to converse with Katherina. I know how to handle such a belligerent shrew, and I refuse to be henpecked by her. If the wench, er, I mean your older daughter scolds me, I'll tell her she sings like a fabulous meadowlark, and not like a lackluster mockingbird. If the bitch, er, I mean your older daughter grimaces or frowns, I'll describe the sullen expression on her countenance as being radiant as roses during a morning, downy snow," Petruchio boasted. "And if your big titted, er, excuse me Signior Baptista, if your firm-breasted, well-endowed daughter Katherina refuses to accept my spectacular wooing, then I'll continue repeating our wedding date to her in very polite vernacular, as if she had actually acceded to the aforementioned calendar appointment."

"God save you, my fine young Man!" Minola Baptista marveled and remarked. "Lesser men than you have been dominated, insulted, and mortified by similar woman to my irrepressible Katherina. You have my blessing to proceed!"

A servant was then directed to escort Petruchio to Katherina's study room. "Good luck, Sir!" the neurotic servant said. "My uncle is the local undertaker, and he'll be glad to take care of and dispose of your Earthly remains!"

"Hello Kate!" Petruchio began his wily-minded taming of the nasty-tempered shrew. "Kate is your name, isn't it?"

"You dumb chauvinistic Asshole! My damned name is Katherina, and I friggin' hate its enunciation!" Baptista's older daughter snottily answered. "Call me by my despised right name, or else you'll suffer the fuckin' consequences."

"Ah bonny Kate, that's what your true name is, both here and in Emerald Ireland," Petruchio continued his suave narration, much to his listener's *ire* and indignation. "And I'll bet that there's no more adorable and lovable Kate in all of Christendom. Your inimitable beauty is quite breathtaking to say the least! I'm indeed humbled by its overwhelming radiance, and hardly have the wherewithal to ask for your hand in marriage," Petruchio praised, utilizing plenty of hyperbole. "Come now, Kate, and sit on my lap, and perform some sexy naked lap dancing, if couch dancing, or sofa striptease is not your particular forte!"

"You no-good, mealy-mouthed Bastard!" Katherina scolded at her visitor, and then nastily slapped Petruchio across his face. "I'll put welts all over your hairy Italian body!"

"Ha, ha, ha!" Petruchio loudly laughed, the force nearly shaking the walls. "Hit me once more Kate, but this second time, much harder! But if you assault me again, I promise to loosen a few front teeth in your mouth with a savage strike of my own! I used to wrestle snorting bulls, python snakes, and hungry crocodiles from time to time in my younger days when I had worked in a traveling circus, and I still retain the various skills! Ha, ha, ha!"

Kate tried smacking Petruchio again, but was unsuccessful in her malicious attempt. "Let go of my hand!" the shrew squawked. "You're certainly no country gentleman! You're probably a notorious molester; perhaps even an evil combination of a pedophile abductor and a boorish womanizer!"

"Not at all, my thrilling Kate!" Petruchio gently responded while maintaining a tight grip on Katherina's clenched right fist. "I find you to be attractive, genteel, docile, sweet, fair, and quite wonderful! Now, I finally realize that I've been specifically born just for the stellar purpose of taming your harsh temper. Kate, we were made for each other! Don't be shy and trying to feel secure while acting jaded!" Petruchio encouraged. "Now stop behaving so crabby, because I absolutely love crabs, and always kiss them before boiling the crustaceans in steaming hot water! You're exactly like the archer virgin goddess Diana; and conversely, I'm very much like the very skilled Cupid, him having the more accurate bow and arrow than his goddess counterpart, Artemis. Now forget all of your latent inhibitions and overt aggressions, venomous shrew, and I now wholeheartedly implore you to wildly kiss me, Kate!"

"Fuck you, you heinous Brute!" Katerina yelled at the eccentric, aggressive man, as Baptista's older daughter was finally able to wrench her right arm away from Petruchio's strong grasp. "Fuck you and all the other fuck-heads in your fucked-up family!" the shrew screamed as she bolted-out of the room like a lightning flash.

Meanwhile, Baptista, Gremio and Lucentio (Tranio) re-entered the mansion from their meaningless trek through the blood-laden apple orchard and olive grove. The group soon encountered Katherina being chased through the house by Petruchio. Baptista was both stunned and shocked at what his eyes were witnessing when Katherina suddenly stopped dead in her tracks.

"Now, Signior Petruchio, I see that when you had said you were interested in the pursuit of Katherina's hand, you had actually meant in pursuit of her entire body!" Baptista mused and uttered. "This astounding phenomenon which my poor-vision-eyes have beheld has to be an all-time historic first!"

"I had told you Signior Baptista that I had little time to waste here in Padua searching-for and finding the most sensational, available wildcat woman in your fair city," Petruchio rationalized and declared. "That's why the hell I was chasing Kate all over your magnificent home, and why all of your frightened, scaredy-cat servants have quickly evacuated the property. Kate now knows that I won't merely accept the word 'no' for an answer."

"Now, Katherina, why do you look so much down-in-the-dumps when we live so far away from the Padua refuse, trash. and garbage center?" the widower Baptista asked his older offspring. "What has caused your disconsolate disposition?"

"How can you possibly call me your daughter when you wish me wed to this paranoid, maniac lunatic?" Katherina protested to Baptista. "I'd rather enter a nunnery, have a sex/gender operation, and then transfer to a strict-discipline monastery than to spend one unfortunate evening with this affectionate, jerk-off suitor! He's a barbarian of the worst ilk!"

"Kate is as modest as a white dove, and only shows anger to conceal her tender and vulnerable inner core," Petruchio eloquently bullshitted and philosophized. "She's just trying to protest her pent-up chastity, her flagging patience, and her wonderful virginity."

"You're totally full of shit!" Kate yelled into Petruchio's face. "In fact, you're doubly full of shit!"

"You see Signior Baptista, Kate really loves me below this brutal and callous external façade she's projecting," Petruchio insisted. "I mean, the hussy couldn't stop kissing me in the privacy of her bedroom, but she now feels motivated to show contempt for me while in public; she's being afraid to openly express her deep-rooted love and affection for me," the suitor from Verona hypothesized and stated. "Those that have labeled my dear Kate a hostile shrew are sadly mistaken, for when we're alone, Kate smothers my neck and face with sensational smooches, and I have at least three hickies to prove it. I've never encountered such an affectionate doll before!"

"You're a fuckin' boldfaced, bullshitting, total liar!" Katherina screamed at Petruchio. "You're a fibbing Asshole; yes, an Asshole of the greatest magnitude!"

"Come now, Kate," Petruchio sedately urged, much to Baptista's amazement. "I'll take you to Venice and buy you the most exquisite wedding gown from my dear friend, the city's most exclusive merchant. And Minola Baptista, Sir; you can prepare a splendid wedding feast second to none, and invite hundreds of noteworthy guests! I propose that Kate and I get married next Sunday."

"You have my blessing, dear Petruchio!" the joyous Baptista consented, being quite glad to get rid of the contemptuous and reprehensible Katherina safely from his house. "And I surely hope that you're man enough, Petruchio, as you've so admirably claimed, to pump and screw all of the evil demons out of dangerous Katherina's crotchola on your wedding night!"

"Well now, I must soon attend to social business, and purchase myself some exquisite wedding clothes," Petruchio announced to the assembled group. "And I want *our* wedding ceremony to be the first time that Kate kisses me in public!"

"This is all total bullshit!" Katherina hollered. "That wily bastard is a lying son-of-a-bitch! His sugary, facetious, frivolous bullshit is non-acceptable to my dubious ears!"

* * * * * * * * * * * *

After Petruchio departed the urban mansion of urbane Minola Baptista in an ecstatic and spirited frame of mind, Katherina retired to her private room to contemplate and to sulk about the inexplicable madness that had recently transpired. The time interval left Gremio the loony pantalooner, Lucentio (Tranio), and Baptista alone to discuss the current situation regarding Bianca.

"Baptista, Sir; I've never seen anything quite like that spectacular male angst exhibition in all my days surviving on this despicable planet!" Gremio asserted. "I wouldn't want to be Petruchio for all of the tea in China, and for all of the expensive China in your dining room cabinet."

"This is indeed a match made in Hell because it certainly was never consecrated in Heaven," Minola Baptista claimed, shaking his head in full bewilderment. "Don't be surprised if Lucifer himself shows-up in priestly garb to publicly officiate at the impending church wedding ceremony."

"Well, Signior Baptista," Gremio said, intentionally changing the subject. "In regard to Bianca, she's now free to marry also, and please remember; I'm your benign neighbor and claim first dibs. If you recollect, I had seen her first as a child, and later was the first to mention my benevolent intentions to you."

"But Signior Baptista, I'm Lucentio, son of the wealthy merchant and prostitute importer and exporter Vincentio of Pisa and of Florence," Tranio boldly orated with his right hand held over his heart. "And I also love the dear, fair-skinned Bianca more than words can express, and more than thoughts could guess. Even though I'm a rich fellow, I can love your daughter as much, if not more, than this graybeard loony pantalooner standing next to me!"

"Now then, I'm pleased to announce that whoever can render a greater reverse dowry to me for Bianca, then that jerk-off, er, I meant to say, *that Gentleman,* shall win her hand in Holy Matrimony," Baptista revealed, while creatively inverting the tables on a standard-type Italian nuptial arrangement. "Now, who pray tell is the highest bidder in my presence? You Gremio, or you Lucentio?"

"Well, Signior Baptista," Gremio awkwardly stuttered. "I have my comfortable house situated right next to yours, and I have gold and ivory chests loaded with fine-woven imported linen. And I own a large farm out in the Tuscany countryside, having a hundred milk-producing cows, and also several dozen well-conditioned oxen; not to mention a multitude of crowded chicken coops and smelly pigpens. And if I die a day after my wedding to the fair Bianca, all of those stellar possessions will naturally become yours and hers."

"And what can you offer Bianca and me?" the coy Baptista asked Lucentio (Tranio), who owned absolutely nothing except the clothes on his Master's back. "Would your proposition exceed that which the generous Gremio has put on the table?"

"My offer can beat the pants off of that pantalooner," Lucentio (Tranio) stated and fibbed, without any distinct authority or license to do so. "Bianca will get at least four well-furnished opulent mansions located in both Florence and Pisa, and she'll receive a wonderful income of two-thousand gold crowns a year, which is mere regular petty interest on my ancillary stock and bond investments. And to top that incredible incentive," Lucentio (Tranio) paused his lying prattle, "she'll own controlling interest in six of the finest merchant ships sailing the *Adriatic* and the *Mediterranean*. My father has argosies sailing all over the damned world! Bianca will undoubtedly be the richest woman in all of Padua, not to mention the wealthiest damned dame in all of Northern Italy."

"See here, Gremio; can you top Lucentio's (Tranio's) lucrative offer?" Baptista asked.

"But what if you Baptista should happen to die before this young whippersnapper Lucentio does?" Gremio challenged. "What then? You'll receive nothing!"

"It's possible that an accident could happen to me, and Baptista could outlive my Verona ass!" Lucentio (Tranio) effectively argued.

"These are all quite valid points to weigh!" Signior Baptista readily acknowledged. "The promises must be thoroughly evaluated."

Then finally, the old pantalooner Gremio realized that his accumulated fortune was no match to Lucentio's litany. "No, my good neighbor, I cannot compete with this gregarious stud's braggadocio," Gremio replied in a melancholy tone of voice. "I must hereby surrender my marriage suit to this brazen, haughty, wealthy fellow, Lucentio of Verona."

"Then, that settles it!" Baptista determined and declared. "However, there's one caveat that must be resolved. Lucentio, once I get confirmation from your father Vincentio endorsing your extravagant marriage proposal suit, then voluptuous Bianca will be all yours; tits, ass, cunt, pubic hair, clit, ovaries, vulva, and all! In my senile mind, it is for all purposes finished!" Minola Baptista articulated with great relief. "Katherina will be wed to Petruchio next Sunday, and Lucentio (Tranio) will be married to Bianca the following Sunday! I figure that from Lucentio's generous offer, that my personal wealth will soon be at least quadrupled."

The pantalooner Gremio stepped to the door and vented his frustration at being outbid and outdone by the younger Lucentio (Tranio). "Lucentio, I figure that your father Vincentio must be more of a fool at heart than he is a mastermind at business. An ordinary old Italian fox would not be so kind to subsidize a naïve son, and for *him* to squander a fortune on a doomed marriage."

'Holy shitcakes!' Lucentio (Tranio) thought. 'What the fuck have I said without any power to do so? I only intended to do my Master Lucentio (now Cambio/Tranio) well! This precarious dilemma I'm now in is really fucked-up! It's actually more a debacle than a dilemma! I must now creatively find a suitable substitute, a worthy replacement for the nobleman/merchant Vincentio, and have *him* act and pretend being Lucentio's fabulously wealthy old man. Who the hell is available to play such a convincing part and completely deceive the nearly-blind Baptista? Let me fuckin' fully think this terrible puzzle out! Holy Christ! I feel like I'm about to shit my pants at least twice!'

Act III

With the pantalooner old Gremio dropping-out of the intense competition for Bianca's hand in marriage, this left Hortensio (Licio the music tutor), and Lucentio (Tranio), along with Cambio (Lucentio) left in the rivalry. However, Lucentio (Tranio) had given Minola Baptista great promises that the rich Vincentio of Pisa and Florence might be unwilling to fulfill. The rivalry between Hortensio (Licio) and Cambio (Lucentio) heated-up inside Baptista's mansion, when the elder music suitor discovered that the junior literature suitor was also interested in actively courting and wooing blonde-haired Bianca.

"Hey, you mediocre violin player. I'll not play second fiddle to you!" Licio (Hortensio) scoffed at Cambio (Lucentio) as the latter was patiently instructing Bianca. "Now, this blonde-haired lady's literature lesson time has expired, and I'm the one that should be teaching her a music lesson, and not you. I think that you, Young Man, might have sinister, amorous intentions on your mind, other than engaging in seemingly innocent poetry and literature! Thou has the makings of a villain; a surreptitious villain at that!"

"Have you forgotten Licio the novel entertainment that Katherina had inflicted upon your hard head with the lute?" Cambio (Lucentio) lucidly reminded the already-aggravated Hortensio. "Stop acting like you're a pissed-off woman; cease behaving and whining like a petty, frigid, and tense whore!"

"Look, you beardless young Bastard," the livid Licio (Hortensio) lividly wrangled. "Go through fuckin' puberty; get some hair under your armpits and around your dingle, and then I'll find time to argue with you. You're now cutting-in on my music time with Bianca!"

"Listen here, you preposterous, fraudulent, pitiful Ass," Cambio (Lucentio) audaciously responded. "You haven't the slightest idea of how music had originated, or how it was ordained. Poetry and philosophy are much more worthy and difficult subjects to analyze than simple music scales, notes, and chords!"

"I don't have to listen to this ridiculous bullshit from a mush-mouthed teenaged Punk like you!" Licio (Hortensio) bristled and gesticulated. "Show some basic courtesy to the situation and to our individual time constraints, you quarrelsome, juvenile delinquent!"

"Look Gentlemen!" Bianca intervened. "I'm not limited to any time frames with either of you two arrogant, egotistical, pedagogues. I'll decide what I wish to learn, and when I wish to master it! Now Signior Cambio, you handsome devil, you; please interpret for me this particular line here from the *Iliad*."

While Licio (Hortensio) was preoccupied pouting and tuning his musical instrument, Cambio (Lucentio) whispered several scrambled, rambling verses to Bianca. "The passage reads Bianca: 'Hic ibat Simonis', I am Lucentio'; hic est', son of the wealthy Vincentio of Pisa and Florence. 'Sigeia tellus'; I'm disguised as a literature and poetry tutor to win and receive your much-cherished love. 'Hic steterat'. My servant Tranio is impersonating me, but in fact, and in deed, 'Priami regia celsa senis salsa'; I'm the true one and only Lucentio, only pretending to be naïve and penniless Cambio performing this perfunctory service in quest of food money'."

"Madam Bianca, my instrument is now tuned and ready to play!" Licio (Hortensio) angrily announced. "I suggest you abandon your literature venue with this young creep, right now! He's beginning to make a nightmare nuisance out of himself."

"Don't *fret* Signior Licio!" Bianca courteously responded as the blonde beauty pointed to his guitar. "Oh, the treble seems to be a little off key! Perhaps more adjustment is necessary!"

"Spit in the hole and adjust the tuning again!" Cambio (Lucentio) directed Hortensio. "And if you see your reflection, it'll be the spitting-image of yourself!"

"You dirty, rude, young Bastard!" Licio (Hortensio) yelled at Cambio (Lucentio). "I know exactly what kind of hole you're thinking about spitting into!"

"Now, Signior Cambio," Bianca pleaded to Lucentio as the frustrated Hortensio again attempted tuning his musical instrument. "Let me see if I can interpret and construe the next difficult passage on my own. 'Hic ibat Simonis'; I know you not. 'Hic est Sigeia tellus'; I trust you not. 'Hic steterat Priami'; take heed, he hears us not, and is unaware of our amorous flirting. 'Regia celsa senis salsa sauce'; presume not and despair not, for truly, all is not lost!"

"Madam Bianca; I believe that my instrument is now fully in tune!" Licio (Hortensio) indicated. "Please listen carefully to my adroit strumming!"

"Lady Bianca doesn't give a shit about *your* instrument, your dangling limp tool, or about your boring strumming!" Cambio (Lucentio) intrepidly stated while alluding to another (more biological) apparatus altogether. "Quite frankly, dumb-ass, your bass sounds a little base!"

'This son-of-a-bitch handsome knave Cambio is endeavoring to court *my love* from right under my long snout!' Licio (Hortensio) finally realized. 'I'll not insult my dignity and compete for Bianca's affections with a fiendish, lowlife, penniless tutor strongly wanting to be a destitute school teacher!'

"In time, I shall believe, but now, I'm subject to suspicion and distrust," Bianca softly confided to the somewhat-disappointed but not discouraged Cambio (Lucentio). "I now think that it's time for me to practice my music with Master Licio, who at the moment seems to be a bit dejected."

"Madam, before you learn to play this instrument, you must watch my fingering!" Licio (Hortensio) advised.

"You must watch-out for his wet fingering!" Cambio (Lucentio) criticized his principal rival. "I meant to say, my dear Bianca, that Licio's finger is wet from spitting into his guitar hole, and wiggling the wet appendage around inside!"

"Now please ignore that punk scalawag and pay attention to my pithy instructions," Licio (Hortensio) directed the easily-distracted Bianca. "Concentrate on your treble, and not on that fellow's trouble! Now my Dear, to comprehensively study my next objective, let's focus on the gamut."

"I'm tired of the gamut," Bianca complained. "And I'm tired of the gamut of your poor teaching methods! Let's start playing some old-fashioned popular music, and stop with all of these silly scales; you pedantic Imbecile!"

Before additional verbal conflict could occur between Cambio (Lucentio) and Licio (Hortensio), a messenger entered the room. and the pesky adolescent informed Bianca that Minola Baptista desired for her to help clean-up the house in preparation for Katherina's wedding on Sunday.

"Farewell, sweet Masters," Bianca said to the dumbfounded Cambio and Licio. "I must attend to my household duties. Unlike my sister, I heed and obey my senile father's commands."

'I don't trust this Cambio jerk-off!' Licio (Hortensio) imagined. 'This post-pubescent punk-prick is indeed in love with Bianca. I can tell by looking at the throbbing bulge in his tights. I'll gladly abandon my suit for Bianca rather than compete with an asshole, lowly school tutor for her warm soft hand; the no-good disrespectful, cocky son-of-a-bitch!'

* * * * * * * * * * * *

On the Sunday wedding day, Minola Baptista stood worried in front of his Padua mansion, wondering why his prospective son-in-law Petruchio was late arriving at the residence on what should have been the most important day of *his* life.

"Signior Lucentio (Tranio)," Baptista neurotically beckoned. "You don't suppose that Petruchio has chickened-out and gotten cold feet? It'll be quite embarrassing to me if Katherina is left standing in the church without the victim, er, I mean groom ever showing-up! On second thought, perhaps Petruchio is smarter than I had given him credit for being," Baptista remarked. "Master Lucentio (Tranio), what's your take on this un-glorious shame I think I'm presently experiencing? You seem to be a man of some academic intelligence. Please share your opinion."

"I say that you should exhibit trusting fortitude, and wait and give Petruchio the doubt of the benefit, er, I mean the benefit of the doubt," Lucentio (Tranio) counseled. "Maybe there's a feasible explanation for Petruchio being dilatory. I mean, Signior Baptista, if this day were his funeral, we could then accurately refer to Petruchio as the *late* husband of Katherina."

"I'm the one who should be fuckin' shamed, besides my social-conscious status-oriented father!" Katherina angrily blurted-out. "I'm forced to give my hand in marriage to a man who's almost a stranger without having any definitive say in the matter. I resent being fuckin' treated like property," Katherina objected. "A damned slave has more rights and privileges than I currently do! It serves you right for being embarrassed Father, for impetuously arranging such a hasty wedding! In all honestly, you deserve the humiliation that being a completely fucked-up fool absolutely warrants!"

"Have patience please!" Lucentio (Tranio) cautiously advised the old man and his petulant daughter. "Petruchio's a good fellow and wouldn't neglect his sacred commitment. I don't think that you're being deliberately stood-up by him, Katherina, or being deceitfully tricked by him, Signior Baptista!"

"What the fuck do you know about anything, you stupid dumb-dick Asshole?" Katherina wildly screamed and cried at Lucentio (Tranio). "You fuckin' have the low mentality of a common house servant!" the unhappy bride yelled as Minola's older daughter briskly stepped into the house and energetically slammed the front door behind her.

Suddenly, Biondello scampered-down the street to the Padua mansion, quite obviously all excited and out of breath. "Master Lucentio," the boy correctly said to Tranio. "Petruchio is on his way. But he's wearing an old jerkin; a pair of tattered pants; a dirty pair of boots; an old rusted sword; archaic armor on his chest, and his shaggy-mane horse looks like its blind in one eye, and ready to collapse on the ground and die."

"Is his preposterous servant Grumio accompanying him?" Baptista incredulously asked.

"Yes Sir!" Biondello exclaimed. "The lackey looks like he just climbed-out of a very full cesspool."

"Perhaps this is some sort of peculiar jest?" Lucentio (Tranio) suggested. "I gotta' admit; I really like Petruchio's bizarre style! He does have a flair for the dramatic!"

"I don't really give a medieval shit how Petruchio looks!" Minola Baptista excitedly declared. "I'm just fuckin' glad that he's come back to Padua, and that I can dump vulgar Katherina on him! The wedding can now take place!"

Petruchio and his impish servant Grumio rode-up to Baptista's mansion on decrepit-looking plow-horses; both men were all soiled and unkempt. Baptista stood there with his mouth agape as the father of the bride-to-be witnessed the gross violation of social wedding etiquette and big-event haberdashery decorum.

"Where is Kate, my lovely bride?" Petruchio inquired. "Signior Baptista, why do you look so flabbergasted?" the flamboyant groom asked. "Have you just seen a comet or a meteor cross the sky? Are you in the process of dying by any chance?"

"Well, Petruchio, as you know, this is *your* wedding day, and your abnormal, late appearance is most remarkable to say the least," Baptista all-too-politely replied. "You are indeed an eyesore, even though neither of my pupils is hurting! I must admit that your weird behavior is a departure from the ordinary."

"And what was so important that you had been detained from arriving here on time?" Lucentio (Tranio) asked and interrogated Petruchio. "Were you hit by an asteroid or by an errant shooting star when you found-out that Signoir Minola Baptista was Biblical Moses resurrected?"

"Suffice it to say that Grumio and I had to fight-off a dozen determined bandits that had savagely accosted us on the trail to Padua!" Petruchio fibbed. "And it took quite some time for us to finally get the unruly robbers arrested and to the jail. Incidentally, where the hell is Kate? It's almost time for the ceremony!"

"Petruchio, don't let Katherina see you wearing those pathetic rags!" Lucentio (Tranio) seriously urged. "Go into my mansion's guest room and put on another set of more satisfactory clothes. You do look like a lazy vagabond with not a penny to your name! You, Sir, appear to be a gutter wretch!"

"I'll go and visit Katherina right now and plant a lengthy kiss upon her lips, er, the ones on her mouth!" Petruchio said as the rogue slowly dismounted from his lethargic-looking plow-horse. "She'll be instantly buoyed by my zesty effervescence!"

"Does that mean you've changed your mind about marrying my incorrigible daughter?" Baptista feared and asked. "I really can't blame you if that's the case."

"Look here, my future father-in-law; your beautiful daughter is marrying me and not my goddamned clothes," Petruchio emphatically lectured. "And it's downright foolish for me to be out here chit-chatting with you when I should be inside repeatedly kissing my magnificent Kate! Doesn't *that* bullshit stand to reason?"

Petruchio and Grumio entered Baptista's home as Katherina's father and Lucentio (Tranio) shook their heads in total disbelief. Lucentio (Tranio) volunteered to go inside and try and convince Petruchio to wear more appropriate apparel for his scheduled wedding, and agreeing Baptista told the impostor to abruptly enter the mansion and try to persuade Petruchio to don more suitable garments that were "better matched and tailored" to the occasion. "On second thought," Baptista stated to Lucentio (Tranio), "I'll see if I can talk some sense into Petruchio myself."

'I have to find a man to imitate being Vincentio of Pisa, my father, er, I mean Lucentio's father,' Lucentio (Tranio) pondered. 'I gotta' figure-out how I can get Lucentio married to Bianca a week from now, and somehow satisfy all of the expenses and properties I had promised that old fart Baptista!'

* * * * * * * * * * * *

At the crowded church, the bride and groom stood before the priest, who was peering at the groom's unsavory appearance. And when the cleric asked Petruchio if he was prepared to take *his* sacred wedding vows, the unpredictable groom grabbed the *Holy Bible*, wrenched it from the dumbfounded priest's hands, and then repeatedly clobbered the friar over the head with the revered black book yelling, "Aye, gogs wouns (Yes, God's wounds!)" Then, the highly-agitated Petruchio violently flipped the priest onto the church's tile floor, and after the stunned wedding official stood-up with a shocked expression upon his face, the cowardly priest dashed from the altar and fled out of the edifice via a side door.

Katherina was trembling at the altar in response to the manner in which the groom Petruchio had treated the solemn, pious priest. Then, after placing a cheap copper wedding band on Katherina's finger, Petruchio drank all of the wine from the priest's chalice, and next carried his astonished bride down the aisle as everyone standing in the pews stood gawking and gaping at the unprecedented spectacle. It was indeed the most outrageous and craziest wedding ever to take place in the normally-somnolent city of Padua. But soon, the entire assembled congregation stood in unison and applauded the impromptu/improvised rite that the attendees had just witnessed without any church priest officiating.

At the wedding feast (being conducted at Minola Baptista's mansion), Petruchio had a surprise announcement that was not taken too receptively by anyone in attendance at the massive reception. The unpredictable groom stood upon a chair, and after gaining everyone's attention, the self-appointed husband made a rather startling pronouncement.

"I'm sorry to inform everyone that my bride and I must go in haste and participate in an important mission," Petruchio loudly stated, much to the mortification of Signior Baptista and the many invited banquet guests. "So, therefore, asinine Folks, we won't be dining with any of you Assholes this afternoon, or for that matter, any time soon! Arrivederci!"

"What the hell's this shit all about?" Minola Baptista challenged Petruchio. "First of all, you show-up at the church looking like an indigent rag-picker; then you beat the shit out of the reverent priest at the sacred altar; next you sacrilegiously guzzled-down the sacred wine from the holy chalice, and now you arrogantly tell us you're too busy to dine with family and guests at your own wedding reception!" the old man balked. "What the fuck gives here? Do you have a penchant for causing scandals? Are you a fuckin' space alien?"

"Look, my easily perturbed father-in-law. I have important business to attend to at *our* destination, and my wife must accompany me right now!" Petruchio insisted as the groom again deliberately traduced wedding protocol and social expectation. "Now, all of you invited and uninvited Folks can kindly enjoy meeting my uncle and my other fucked-up relatives in attendance! But right now, I have other issues of paramount importance to contend with, that incidentally, happen to eclipse your trivial wedding banquet!"

"I've never been so blatantly insulted and disgraced in all my life!" Minola Baptista yelled at the all-too-nonchalant Petruchio. "You're a shameful, repulsive, abomination! You're an uncouth, disgusting, ingrate that's completely infatuated and enamored with himself, and I'm absolutely ashamed to call you' my son-in-law!"

"Thanks for the generous compliments!" Petruchio facetiously answered with a broad smile upon his countenance. "Truthfully, I had no idea that my performance today had been so meritorious, and would be held in such high esteem!"

"Stay Husband, if you really love me!" Katherina entreated. "My father's wishes must be honored, for his prestige and his reputation are on the line!"

"Bullshit!" Petruchio sternly and adamantly replied. "Let's get the fuck out of this dump, Kate! I won't come back to this fucked-up shanty until after the oats have eaten my horses; or until the pig shit in my farm pens starts flying around! You're leaving Padua right this instant, and going with me to my exclusive country pad."

"This is absolutely an odious ignominy, me being publicly disparaged and humiliated like this!" Signoir Baptista protested to no avail. "I must defend my honor! I refuse to see my daughter treated in such a bellicose manner!"

"I refuse to go away with you'!" Katherina balked to Petruchio. "You cannot make me do anything against my volition! I won't leave this goddamned house until I'm fuckin' good and ready! Do you hear me, Husband?"

"On guard!" Baptista shouted to Petruchio as *he* and his relatives drew their swords from their scabbards. "On guard because I can't catch you off-guard, you wily Bastard!"

Petruchio and Grumio drew their swords and assumed defensive fighting stances. Then, in an instant, the intrepid hero Petruchio latched onto Katherina, hoisted the shrieking bride up upon his left shoulder, and then dashed-out of the opulent mansion, followed close behind by his loyal subordinate and servant, Grumio.

Act IV

At Petruchio's farmhouse outside of Verona, Grumio divulged to another servant Curtis what had transpired between their Master and Katherina on the horseback ride from Padua. The two underlings were discussing the extraordinary adventures while warming themselves next to a fireplace.

"Oh man, Curtis; did our Master and his mistress have some wild experiences on our bumpy expedition from Padua to here," Grumio began his recollection. "It was pretty incredible bullshit, indeed. I just gotta' tell you the remarkable juicy gossip, which of course happens to be all fuckin' true!"

"Why should I believe you, a dwarf with only a three-inch-long erection that looks like a wriggling larva? Ha, ha, ha!" Curtis belittled his short, under-endowed peer. "What I want to know is did Master Petruchio screw the shrew along the journey? That's what the fuck I wanna' know!"

"At least I've got a dick that gets erect, you impotent Dolt!" Grumio volleyed back. "Maybe I'll cut your limp dick off, roast the sucker over the fire, and have a small breakfast sausage to eat! Ha, ha, ha Curtis! Now then; do you want to hear the whole fuckin' story, or don't you?"

"Come on you swindling Scoundrel, get on with your lame tale, for I'm presently bored with your conversation; and also with your fucked-up company," Curtis smartly retorted. "The table's already all set for today's dinner, and there's little fuckin' left to do right now except listen to your monotonous bull-crap. Shit, Grumio. I really wish that I was sleeping!"

"First of all, Curtis; I had selected an ornery horse for Lady Katherina to ride. Of course, only after Master Petruchio had told me to have such a mount ready for the tempestuous Bitch during the great wedding reception escape," Grumio revealed.

"And was the mercurial-tempered bitch capable of controlling the restless steed?" Curtis asked.

"Well then, Curtis; and this is pretty damned amusing," Grumio laughed and then belched, almost regurgitating. "Lady Katherina's horse stumbled while we were fording a small swamp, and the animal flipped over. The screaming wench tumbled from her colt, which was more like a goddamned bronco, and next the hussy inelegantly plummeted into soft black mud."

"What did Master Petruchio do?" Curtis laughed and then loudly involuntarily farted a long blast for thirty-seconds.

"He faked lashing me with his whip, and the witch Bitch was fooled, and she actually thought the disciplinary action was for real!" Grumio disclosed. "Katerina then started begging our master to cease his fake physical reprimanding, and the shrew sat there in the shallow stagnant water sulking, all covered with black mud on her face; on her hands; and the bride was still wearing her fancy, no-longer-white, wedding dress. All the while, the wench was shouting to our Master, who was pretending to still be berserk. 'Don't hit him'! It wasn't Grumio's fault!' Ha, ha, ha! And then, our illustrious Master hollered at the top of his lungs, 'I'll beat the shit out of an elephant's turd if I fuckin' want to! Ha, ha, ha'!"

"Well, you've really made my day!" Curtis guffawed. "But if Petruchio beat the crap out of you, how come you're still full of shit? Regardless Grumio; did anything else of humor, or of consequence, happen on the trip home? Ha, ha, ha! Excuse my excessive farting, but I'm doing my digestive system good by clearing-out all of this noxious, offensive-smelling gas! Ha, ha, ha!"

"Consider this, Curtis, you idiotic gaseous, sewer-like Asshole. Lady Katherina's horse had broken its bridle, and our spare horse had galloped-away during the amusing swamp incident," Grumio related to his thoroughly entertained peer. "And Master Petruchio made the begrimed, filthy Wench walk behind him and me, with us sitting together on horseback the last four-miles home, as if his bride were a captive slave; or hostage, or some other bullshit prisoner; or weirdo like that. Master told the crying Katherina, 'You're a genuine sight to behold, but not a sight to be held! Ha, ha, ha!"

"The bridal bride's horse had just lost its bridle!" Grumio humorously added. "Ha, ha, ha! I think I just shit-out my large intestine, Curtis; ha, ha, ha!"

"And I perceptively observed that when you finally arrived here to the farm house," Curtis said, still giggling and gesturing, and farting, "Petruchio paid little attention to Lady Katherina's incessant bitching, but instead, ordered Philip, Joseph, Nicholas, Nathaniel and Gregory to take care of his precious horses, as if the steeds were his more favored wives, ha, ha, ha! Our enviable Master was even screaming-out the names of imaginary servants that I've never heard of to attend to his disobedient steeds! Ha, ha, ha! It was both surreal and melodramatic! Ha, ha, ha!"

"I guess the horses were still unstable, Grumio; ha, ha, ha!"

"And then Curtis, as your limited and narrow mind can recollect," Grumio proceeded with the events of the night before, "our cunning Master acted like a possessed tyrant, running all around the house, and chastising all of the servants, both real and imaginary, for not having everything in order, while completely ignoring his wife's protests and grievances. It was truly fuckin' rich to watch and hear!"

"Anything else to report?" Curtis asked.

"Yes, my friend; and then the sage Master Petruchio complained to the cook about the tough mutton our employer was eating, while not heeding a word that his pissed-off wife was blabbering," Curtis laughed before expelling a quantity of intestinal gas originating from his esophagus. "And when Lady Kate told him that the food was delicious, our Boss grabbed it off her plate and threw her sumptuous mutton at the cook, who had to duck-down! It was quite a phenomenon to witness and hear! I really was impressed at how our Master was systematically dismantling Lady Kate's inner wall; brick by fuckin' brick! Ha, ha, ha! It was psychological warfare at its fuckin' best!"

"Keep going!" Curtis laughed.

"And when Lady Kate asked about supper alternatives. because the volatile banshee was exhausted from her arduous ordeal traveling from Padua to here," Grumio chuckled, "Master Petruchio said that he wasn't hungry, and that the couple would eat tomorrow evening instead, because according to his peculiar, unorthodox, atheistic, religious faith, the recent groom preferred fasting *after* marriage. Ha, ha, ha!"

"And all throughout the night, Lady Kate was loudly bitching about not eating and about not sleeping, and Master kept killing her with kindness; and then, praising everyone in the house except her," Curtis recalled and shared. "Master Petruchio believed that he could make her control her fierce temper by pretending to accidentally knock Lady Kate out of bed three times while complaining about a hard pillow and an uncomfortable mattress, and about inferior blankets, in addition to grimy, smelly sheets! It was absolutely household comedy at its finest! Ha, ha, ha! And then when Lady Kate was finally exasperated…."

"Master Petruchio expeditiously disassembled the bed, claiming that the frame had been poorly constructed, and the newlyweds had to then sleep upon the floor!" Grumio laughed as he too lost control of his bowels and started egregiously farting, matching Curtis, fart for fart. "Our Master has suddenly become a bigger shrew than Lady Katherina is, and to my knowledge, Curtis," Grumio chortled, "our superior is still a fuckin' male, because I saw him taking a lengthy piss into the stench-laden dung-pile last night, while standing behind the barn! Ha, ha, ha!"

"And then, in the middle of the night, when Lady Katherina finally dozed-off from exhaustion upon the floor," Curtis continued the review of the bizarre series of events, "Master dressed himself in his hunting clothes and brought his bloodhounds into the bedroom, and their relentless barking and ferocious fangs scared the living shit out of Lady Kate; not to mention our Boss's frantic tooting of his hunting horn! Ha, ha, ha! Poor Kate now believes that her husband is absolutely insane, way beyond being simply crazy! Petruchio had deftly conducted a major imaginary foxhunt inside his own bedroom, but instead of pursuing a fox, our Master's pretend hounds had found pussy odor; Katherina's pussy, Grumio," Curtis coughed and laughed with long snot strands hanging out of his nostrils. "I think my goddamned appendix is about to burst-open and spill my guts all over the fuckin' floor! Ha, ha, ha!"

"That's exactly how Master Petruchio has trained his falcons and his sleuths, and the genius is now using the same successful techniques on Lady Kate!" Grumio realized and declared towards the end of the servants' jocularity.

"What the hell outrageous methods are they?" Curtis laughed.

"Starvation and sleep-deprivation!" Grumio cackled before nearly choking to death. "Don't be surprised if Lady Kate starts flying around the house like a bird of prey, or sniffing the corners and the floor like a tamed on-the-prowl ferocious bloodhound! Ha, ha, ha! Master Petruchio really knows how the fuck to treat and tame predators, both animal and human, ha, ha, ha!"

* * * * * * * * * * * *

Back at Minola Baptista's Padua mansion, Lucentio (Tranio) and Licio (Hortensio) were discussing how Bianca seemed to be favoring Cambio (Lucentio/Tranio). Naturally, the authentic Tranio tried persuading Licio (Hortensio) to drop his futile courtship suit, for (after a reality check) *he* was contemplating doing the exact same thing for his master, Lucentio (Cambio).

"Signior Licio (Hortensio)," Lucentio (Tranio) said while the two men were standing inside the parlor. "Haven't you noticed that Bianca is falling in love with that irascible rascal Cambio? They're always making silly goo-goo eyes at each other, and cooing, too."

"Signior; since we're now almost friends, I'll tell you my inclination on the subject," Licio (Hortensio) replied. "If you drop your suit for Bianca's hand, I'm of the persuasion to do likewise. I mean, why the hell should I sacrifice my hard-earned fortune for a little young blonde pussy in a queer inverted dowry situation invented by Baptista; when in fact, a rich old Venetian whore with wonderful flabby, flaccid tits wants to marry me? Do you get where I'm coming from?"

Before Licio (Hortensio) and Lucentio (Tranio) could shake hands to solidify their prospective deal, Cambio (the real Lucentio) and Bianca stepped into the mansion's parlor.

"Now Mistress Bianca," Cambio (Lucentio) lectured. "We've been assiduously studying the topic, or should I say the abstraction known as love, and it's now time to bridge the gap between theory and practice. Wouldn't you agree with my premise?"

"Do you wish to teach me love in practice as well as in theory?" Bianca coyly responded. "Oh no! Our conversation has been overheard by my other two rather impetuous suitors; Signiors Licio and Lucentio."

"Bianca; Signior Lucentio (Tranio) here and I have both noticed that you seem to have the hots for Signior Cambio," Licio (Hortensio) rather bluntly articulated. "Are our sage observations, along with our mutual suspicions about your marriage intentions, correct?"

"Yes, Master Licio. Cambio has won my heart and the rest of my desirable anatomy, too!" Bianca admitted. "We're both hornier than a couple of warty toads!"

"Well then; I must confess to you Lady Bianca that my name is not Licio, and I'm not a goddamned lowlife music tutor either! In disguise, I'm Hortensio, a *former* suitor of yours."

"And I too withdraw my suit and my ambitious pursuit of your many charms," Lucentio (Tranio) disclosed. "I realize that your affections are now all directed to your sex education teacher, er, I mean to say, to your most excellent literature and poetry pedagogue, Master Cambio."

"Thank you for surrendering your oaths, you big oafs!" Cambio (Lucentio) verbally reacted. "I never did quit my quest of the lovely Bianca, because quite candidly, I've had a wicked hard-on that wouldn't quit ever since I arrived here in Padua! I mean, I haven't pissed in over four days."

* * * * * * * * * * * *

Biondello approached Cambio (Lucentio) and Lucentio (Tranio) inside Minola Baptista's side garden. The young messenger was quite euphoric about an important matter.

"Master Cambio (Lucentio)," Biondello said all out of breath. "A distinguished-looking gentleman who is a carbon-copy of your old man Vincentio is presently walking up the street. I think you ought to buttonhole and talk to him."

"Yes; good work Biondello!" Cambio (Lucentio) commended. "We'll hire the old geezer, dress him up in expensive threads, and tell him exactly what the hell to say on cue. Then, I'll be able to marry Lady Bianca next Sunday, even if the marriage is conducted under false pretenses, but who really gives a shit?"

"Indeed, and I hope that the priest who had been brutally mauled by Petruchio has recovered from his multiple injuries sustained in the violent church assault," Lucentio (Tranio) added. "Petruchio literally threw the book at the molested friar, the *Holy Book!* Ha, ha, ha! Let's stop this elderly duplicate fellow now, and make him a proposition the impostor can't refuse! Ha, ha, ha!"

"Where are you heading old-timer?" Cambio (Lucentio) asked the lackadaisical ambler. "Could you use a little extra spending cash?"

"Why yes I could!" the old codger graciously exclaimed. "I'm from Mantua, and I'm on my way to Rome to view the *Colosseum;* and then I'm off to Tripoli to gaze at the majestic shores."

"Well now, you're lucky to be alive!" Lucentio (Tranio) told the old wanderer. "The fucked-up jealous Dukes of Mantua and Padua are quarreling over shipping rights and access to Venice. Citizens from both cities have been warned in bills posted almost-everywhere that their lives might be in jeopardy should people from Padua visit Mantua, and vice-versa. Old Man," Lucentio (Tranio) emphasized and coyly whispered, "we might've just saved your delicate ass from being pulverized!"

"Thank you, kind Gentlemen!" the very old curmudgeon gratefully acknowledged before loudly farting four distinct, different-sounding toots. "I was unaware of the grave political problem to which you've just diplomatically alluded. I'm deeply indebted to you!"

"Have you ever been to Pisa?" Cambio (Lucentio) asked the wrinkled-skinned old coot. "It's quite a delightful city. Even the crazed astronomer Galileo is enchanted with its high leaning tower."

"Yes, many times!" the senior citizen remembered and answered. "I have many relatives in Pisa in the pizza business, and they're all rolling in the dough when they aren't rolling the dough!"

"Well then, do you know an old nobleman mogul by the name of Vincentio?" Cambio (Lucentio) proceeded with his rather skillful, ongoing interrogation.

"Why no; but I've heard much about him!" the old chap revealed. "I understand that he's a very prosperous merchant of tremendous, and perhaps incomparable wealth!"

"Well, Sir, I'm Vincentio's only son and heir, and I'm asking you to do me a mighty big favor," Cambio (Lucentio) told the old fogey. "I want you to pretend being my wealthy pop, Signoir Vincentio? Are you game Old Man?"

"I like folly as much as the next idiot does!" the old, good-natured wanderer stated. "And when I was a young man, when Julius Caesar was still alive, I had studied being an actor. The rest of the bullshit you desire to be implemented ought to come easy to me! And I'm not stymied by minor snafus, or by major snags. Explain what the hell I need to know, and my acting ability will *stage* it. To tell you the truth, Young Fellow. I crave excitement and trickery. At my fuckin' age, I don't give a shit whether I fuckin' live or fuckin' die!"

* * * * * * * * * * * *

Petruchio's austere disciplinary measures of sleep deprivation and food fasting were paying-off with Katherina showing signs of being domesticated as if she were a wild animal being trained and coming under human control. Even Grumio was instructed to not provide the Lady of the House with any kitchen victuals to eat.

"Grumio, I'm feeling dizzy and believe that I'm starving from malnutrition," Katherina complained to the inane servant the following morning. "Don't you have any decent food in the pantry, or meager crumbs or morsels hidden in the cupboard?"

"The only thing I have is some rotten tripe that's guaranteed to give you food poisoning and diarrhea," Grumio related, his words consistent with the instructions that his master had given him. "And it's a lot fuckin' better to die from starvation than from having your entire digestive system become unraveled from terrible stomach cramps. I'm no goddamned woman, Lady Katherina, but I imagine the pain I'm describing is a thousand times worse than your monthly period cramps!"

But a half hour later, Petruchio entered the dining room and made an announcement to Katherina that thoroughly surprised his new wife, and that instantaneously stimulated her good side.

"Kate, look here! I've brought you some delicious meat with a tasty sauce that I've personally prepared for your hungry palate," Petruchio enthusiastically announced. "Now all you have to do is say the brief phrase 'Thank you!', and then you may have it. Otherwise, I'll throw the tasty meat to my famished bloodhounds, and you can watch them devour the delicious food, and I'll never share my meat with you again, either at the supper table or in bed."

"Thank you!" Kate politely and humbly replied. "Thank you so much, my dear Husband," the partially-tamed shrew said, prior to consuming the steak as if she was a starving canine.

"And now, Kate," Petruchio continued with his exceptional training methods. "I've taken the liberty of procuring for you this most fabulous dress to wear to Bianca's wedding this coming Sunday. Isn't it absolutely stunning?"

"Oh yes! I can't wait to try it on!" Katherina joyously exclaimed. "Let me try on the fancy hat, too. I want to see myself in the mirror wearing it."

"Sorry Kate! On second thought, this lousy hat looks like a goddamned cereal bowl!" Petruchio exaggerated. "I must rip it up, for you'd look incredibly unfashionable wearing this embarrassing, fucked-up monstrosity!"

"But it's the latest vogue!" Katherina bitched. "Gentlewomen of culture and sophistication wear *this* contemporary style!"

"When I'm convinced that you've become 'gentle' as in the word gentlewomen," the husband lucidly maintained, "then I'll allow you to wear a similar type of hat." And then crafty Petruchio disappointed his distressed wife again. "I'm examining this dress I had purchased in Venice for you, and it's terribly flawed here at the seam. Its overall appearance looks a lot like an oxcart, and the grotesque sleeves look like doorways. I can't allow you to wear this ugly thing to Bianca's wedding!" Petruchio insisted. "Remind me to beat the shit out of that churlish tailor back in Venice who had sewn it. The incompetent asshole is probably a damned close relative of that snobbish obnoxious priest I had beaten the shit out of last Sunday in Padua!"

"But I see nothing wrong with the magnificent dress!" Katherina protested. "Please let me have it! It's positively beautiful!"

"No, Kate! You must learn to be un-pretentious and un-ostentatious, just like I am!" Petruchio slyly indicated. "You'll go to the wedding looking like a pauper, just like I'm going! And if you behave yourself, I'll even teach you how to beat the shit out of the attending priest, just like I had done during our nuptial ceremony. Remember Kate, our purses and our bank account must be proud, and our appearances must always be shabby and humble! Otherwise, Kate, you'll be spoiled just like the smelly tripe that not even my carnivorous hounds will dare eat."

"But when are we leaving for my sister's wedding?" the worried wife queried. "I'm already looking forward to returning to Padua!"

"We'll leave this afternoon and get there by dinner," Petruchio estimated and stated. "That ought to give us sufficient time to make the short journey."

"That's goddamned impossible!" Katherina balked. "Do you think I'm stupid? I know geography, Husband. We'll definitely miss supper, and won't get to Padua until midnight! That's fuckin' rude and discourteous!"

"Look, my sweet, Kate. Whatever I say and do, you automatically take an opposite course as is your nature," Petruchio politely and shrewdly argued. "If you keep bothering me with your petty objections, and with your disturbing contradictions, then we won't be attending Bianca's wedding at all. Now do you still desire going to the church function or not?"

"Er, yes!" the confused Katherina answered.

"Well then, Wife; if you want me to kiss your hand, you must first learn how to kiss my ass!" Petruchio figuratively declared, as the experienced chauvinist gently kissed Katherina's hand, much to her heightening chagrin.

* * * * * * * * * * *

Meanwhile, back in Padua (outside Minola Baptista's mansion), Lucentio (Tranio) was giving the old hired, itinerant wanderer/actor some last-minute instructions. Biondello was attentively listening to the comprehensive briefing.

"Now that you have your fantastic, expensive costume on, you can pretend that you're Vincentio of Pisa and Florence, Cambio's, er, I meant to say Lucentio's rich father. Yes, *Old Man;* you look exactly like Lucentio's old man, ha, ha, ha!"

"But Signior; twenty years ago, when I was staying at a lodge called the Pegasus back in Genoa, I had cheated this honest man Minola Baptista out of a thousand ducats playing cards. But since then, I've joined 'Gamblers' Anonymous', and have reformed my errant betting habits," the aged impersonator recalled and replied.

"Whatever the fuck you do, don't mention the nouns Genoa, Pegasus, or gambling during our creative ruse," Lucentio (Tranio) advised the old pretender. "Just focus on being wealthy Vincentio of Pisa and Florence and being Cambio', er, I mean, Lucentio's father, and nothing else. You're lucky that Baptista didn't lodge a complaint to the local constables before you managed to leave the infamous Pegasus Lodge."

"Now Biondello," Lucentio (Tranio) said to the rascally, obsessive-compulsive youth. "Have you delivered the message to Baptista that we had discussed and reviewed last night?"

"Affirmative; I told him that Lord Vincentio was in Venice and that he'd be showing-up here in Padua sometime this morning!" Biondello proudly stated. "And here he is; standing right next to us! What a marvelous canard this is! A theatrical play couldn't have more dumb bullshit in it!"

"Good then! Let's go inside and introduce this wonderful fake Vincentio to Signoir Minola Baptista!" Lucentio (Tranio) directed. "Jesus Christ! I hope that Baptista doesn't want to sprinkle Holy Water on this impostor Vincentio's forehead, just like his ancestor John the Baptist used to do at the River Jordan! Ha, ha, ha!"

* * * * * * * * * * * *

"Signior Baptista," Lucentio (Tranio) announced to the confused and nearly-blind old man. "Here's my famous father, Vincentio of Pisa and Florence. He's traveled here to Padua to attend my wedding to Bianca tomorrow. But first, my father wishes to consummate the dowry agreement with you that I had promised to broker."

"Yes," the false Vincentio spoke-up and agreed. "I've come to Padua to settle-up some outstanding debts that my idealistic son has accumulated in the form of promises. But when a young man is in love, money oftentimes is of little consideration or consequence? Wouldn't you agree Signior Baptista?"

"Er, why yes?" the impressed Minola Baptista concurred. "That is really quite true!"

"Now then, kind Sir. Do you have the papers for us to sign to officially give the imminent marriage our blessings?" the false Vincentio asked Baptista.

"Yes; I'll have the city clerk dispatch them here immediately," Baptista nervously answered. "Indeed, I've smartly proposed a reverse dowry, since your son loves my daughter Bianca so much. And once the legal papers are signatured, my consent will be forthcoming! We'll sign the papers at the town hall, because I have too many servants with large ears and larger mouths that might report the big news too prematurely. Are you amenable to my simple suggestion, Signior Vincentio?"

"Why certainly!" the former, unemployed actor acceded. "Whatever you say, Signior Baptista! You're calling the shots; even though neither of us is holding a glass with any whiskey in it!"

"I suggest that we dispatch Bianca's tutor Cambio (Lucentio) to alert the town clerk of our coming!" Lucentio (Tranio) submitted his input to the conversation. "That might expedite the signing of the marriage contract between our two famous families."

"Excellent point!" Baptista exclaimed. "Cambio (Lucentio) is a trustworthy young fellow who'll execute *that* easy errand without any difficulty."

* * * * * * * * * * * *

No sooner had Cambio (Lucentio) been sent on his vital messenger mission to the city clerk's office, that Biondello caught-up with him to deliver a very important communication.

"Here's the plan!" Biondello said and rapidly panted. "Tranio (Lucentio) will be keeping old Baptista occupied, bullshitting trivia with your impostor father; that oddball actor who, after our little scam, plans walking from here to Tripoli right through the blue *Mediterranean*. You must take Bianca to the old priest who is still recovering from the beating that Petruchio had administered. The church official agreed to secretly marry you and her at St. Luke's Church, because the apprehensive priest is afraid of getting beaten-up again when marrying Bianca in a public ceremony; especially since I've informed him that Petruchio might be attending the Church Mass as the Best Man."

"But why all the rush?" Cambio (Lucentio) asked Biondello.

"Because at any time, our tricky plan might be discovered," Biondello quoted Tranio. "Then, you'll lose Bianca if Signoir Baptista feels that he's been flagrantly deceived. She'll have to then marry either Gremio, the loony pantalooner, or Hortensio, who still fuckin' thinks he's Licio; not to mention that nutcase Tranio, who doesn't have a dirty penny to his name."

"I see!" Cambio (Lucentio) realized and concurred. "Bianca must get to the old priest, so that *we* can tie the knot before old Baptista gets wind of the fact that he's been royally hoodwinked."

* * * * * * * * * * * *

Petruchio and Katherina were riding on horseback on a dusty road leading to Padua. Again, the husband was very critical of his wife's reluctance to cooperate, but then, the clever spouse would deftly switch into his suave and gentle mood whenever Katherina became defiant and bitchy.

"For Christ's sake Kate! Hurry-up and stop dallying!" Petruchio loudly yelled. "At this rate, we'll never reach your father's house before the goddamned wedding. I wonder if the same old fart priest is going to officiate as the craven *one* that had tried marrying us? Look how brightly the moon is shining!"

"Husband! Are you visually impaired?" Katherina questioned her swift-minded mate. "It's broad daylight, and that's the sun up there shining brightly, and not the goddamned moon! You must be perceptually handicapped!"

"Look Wife; if you can't tell the difference between the sun and the moon, then you must either be mentally retarded or mentally insane, whichever!" Petruchio insisted and equivocated. "I know it's the goddamned moon that's shining because it greatly resembles your fat mooning ass!"

"Then how do you know it's not Jupiter, Venus, or Mars, since it's nighttime according to your erroneous misperception, and there're other objects in the dark sky, including all the twinkling stars?" Katherina reasoned and replied.

"The object in the sky is whatever the hell I call it!" Petruchio politely insisted. "And if I say it's the fuckin' moon, then you must go along with my infallible determination, or go without food, drink, clothing, shelter, or sleep. Is that fuckin' clear?"

"Yes, my demanding Husband; that is fuckin' clear!" Katherina assented. "You know everything, and I know absolutely nothing, but

I must be willing to learn everything from you! I wish I lived in a future age where possibly a law exists forbidding spousal abuse!"

"And if you persist in annoying me with your trite driveling, we'll immediately go back to the Verona farmhouse and begin our arduous journey to Padua all over again; is that fuckin' clear Kate?" the husband hollered from atop his horse.

"Positively, my omniscient Husband!" Katherina deeply sighed. "And if you want to call that bright object up in the sky a candle, or a dildo on fire, then it must most certainly be either a fuckin' candle or a burning dildo!"

"Now you're finally beginning to see the fuckin' light!" Petruchio chuckled as the gentleman on horseback momentarily glanced-up at the sun, which he still identified as the moon. "Now, let's get moving or else I won't have the opportunity to beat the crap out of that old fucked-up priest again! Say Kate; maybe he'll be willing to complete *our* wedding ceremony this time?"

"I doubt it very much!" Katherina quickly answered. "He'll probably never open a damned *Bible* again for the rest of his mortal existence on this totally-lunatic planet!"

* * * * * * * * * * *

Petruchio and Katherina caught-up to, and were about to pass, an elderly gentleman on horseback, heading in the direction of Padua. After learning that the old fellow was also traveling in their direction, Petruchio invited the elderly coot to ride along.

"I'm Vincentio of Pisa and Florence," the impressively well-dressed gent amiably introduced himself. "I'm going to Padua to pay a surprise visit to my son Lucentio, who is enrolling as a student in the splendid university there. The school has a fine reputation for its classical studies," the famous merchant opined and communicated. "One must be exposed to theoretical academics before a person can adjust to the mundane practicalities of business, at least, that's always been my personal philosophy."

"Well, this is indeed quite a remarkable coincidence!" Petruchio laughed. "We're truly related. I've heard that your son is getting married tomorrow morning to my wife's sister, Bianca. Don't tell me you know nothing of this wedding?"

"Er, yes I do!" the real Vincentio fibbed, trying to conceal his sudden shock and embarrassment.

"Yes Vincentio; the fair blonde-haired Lady Bianca Baptista comes with a most excellent dowry that'll make you proud of your son Lucentio's choice for a bride!" Petruchio assumed and articulated. "And besides *that* interesting item, as a terrific bonus, Lady Bianca is very beautiful, too! I'm sure you'll be extremely happy with your lucky son's superb selection."

"I always knew that my Lucentio was very intelligent!" Vincentio smiled and laughed. "It must be my paternal genetics admirably kicking-in, ha, ha, ha!"

'If a man desires to be happy for the rest of his life,' Petruchio conjectured, smiled, and then rhymed, 'the fellow should never make a pretty woman his wife. But conversely, an ugly wench that can be a superior cook, in my humble estimation, Signoir Vincentio, is indeed the best kind of wife to have!'

Act V

Being unaware of the secret plot of Cambio (Lucentio) and Bianca to furtively get married, and also being totally unaware of Lucentio's (Tranio's) reverse-dowry promises to the shrewd Minola Baptista, Petruchio, and Katherina led Vincentio to *his* son's (Lucentio's) modest Padua residence. Upon arriving, venerable Vincentio insisted that Petruchio come inside and enjoy a drink with him after *their* long journey into the city, just before Katherina was instructed (by her husband) to patiently wait outside on horseback.

While Grumio was diligently knocking on the door for *his* master, the false Vincentio took a glimpse from the window and yelled outside to the disruptive servant, "Who the hell are you down there knocking down the gate? You must have brass knuckles; you brass-balled-Knucklehead!"

"Is Signior Lucentio home?" the real Vincentio inquired to his likeness standing in the window. "I need to make contact with my idealistic-but-irresponsible son. It's the weekend, so I figure he's not studying at the university!"

"Please tell Lucentio that his father Vincentio is outside and wishes to see him!" Grumio yelled-up to the window from behind the front gate. "It's an urgent matter that requires immediate remedy!"

"What the hell are you talking about?" the impostor Vincentio shouted-down from the partially-opened window. "I'm Lucentio's rich father, and I don't savor ordinary people impersonating me!"

"Enough of the stupid bullshit!" the all-too-frank Petruchio hollered-up. "Get your ass down here right this second, and let us inside, or else Asshole, there's going to be big trouble brewing without a neighborhood distillery in sight!"

Biondello showed-up outside the small apartment house, and the real Vincentio immediately recognized his minor employee who was indeed still a minor. 'Oh no!' the lad thought. 'Now this dramatic bullshit is really going to upset the goddamned applecart!'

"Biondello, don't pretend that you don't know who the hell I am!" Vincentio demanded from his low-echelon servant. "Where's my itinerant son Lucentio? Speak the truth, or lose your service to me and to my benevolent son! Have you forgotten me already, after less than a month, you impudent, unappreciative little Rogue?"

"Sir; how could I forget you when my eyes never saw you before in my whole damned life!" Biondello neurotically prevaricated. "Your ridiculous comment is wholly illogical!"

"Forget losing your paltry job!" the real Vincentio nastily rankled. "Perhaps I can talk to the local gallows' warden and see what appropriate punishment can be arranged for you, you disloyal, traitorous, punk Scamp!"

"Signior; how could you be Lord Vincentio of Pisa and Florence when that is he staring out the window?" Biondello argued, pointing up. "It's either he standing up there, or it's your twin brother that you don't even know about!"

"Take that you little, egotistical Punk!" Vincentio shouted as the visiting entrepreneur fiercely slapped Biondello ten-times across the face. "I'll get the goddamned truth out of you, as long as my frail hands don't fall off my flimsy wrists!"

"Help! Help! I'm being assaulted by an incensed, wealthy madman!" Biondello screamed as the page sprinted down the street, seeking immediate shelter from being mutilated. "I've been wickedly molested by a raving lunatic! Help! Help!"

Petruchio and his reformed wife were now standing beside the real Vincentio, and the husband evaluated the raucous scenario. "Perhaps we ought to just watch whatever materializes rather than open our mouths and complicate matters ever worse than they already are!" Petruchio advised the now-shocked Katherina, whose bloodshot eyes presently perceived dual Vincentios.

Then, the fake Vincentio exited the house and confronted the real Vincentio outside. "What the hell were you doing beating on my innocent servant like that!" the old codger absurdly admonished his totally appalled, authentic duplicate. "I ought to call the constable and have you arrested on the spot, even though there's no spot evident on this dirty street for you to be standing on! You're probably a goddamned active pedophile, besides being a fake Vincentio in disguise! Go to the goddamned church and molest several innocent, unsuspecting Castrati choir boys!"

"Of all the astounding, unwarranted audacity!" Vincentio yelled back at the belligerent impostor. "You pretentious Villain! I've come all the way from Pisa via Florence to visit my wonderful son Lucentio, and this is the kind of fucked-up reception I get?"

As the wild argument escalated, Lucentio (Tranio) showed-up at the modest apartment house, seeking-out the real Lucentio, who was busy at the church being secretly married to Bianca.

"Who the hell are *you* dressed in my son's expensive clothes?" Vincentio demanded of the newly-arrived Tranio. "What kind of fucked-up masquerade party is this utter fiasco that is now being conducted in broad daylight? Whatever fuckin' happened to civility and sanity? I hereby accuse *you* of murdering my naïve son, and pretending to be him in the flesh, with your ulterior motive being to extort money from honorable decent citizens in my good name!" Vincentio yelled to his servant Tranio, whom he did not recognize in *his* son's stellar apparel.

"This man is Lucentio," the false Vincentio attested. "He's going to marry Minola Baptista's daughter, Bianca, later today! We're all invited to the ceremony; that is, if the intimidated priest ever shows-up to conduct it!"

"What the fuck are you lying about?" the real Vincentio rankled. "This moronic jerk-off is Tranio, whom I now recognize with his hat off and his bald head showing. This idiot has been my son's servant for fifteen-years now, at my generous expense, and apparently, at my great aggravation too, mind you!"

"Perhaps we should locate and notify the Constable to resolve this harsh dispute!" Petruchio lowly whispered to Katherina. "This whole fucked-up scene is getting completely out of hand!"

Just as the two aged Vincentios were about to come to blows, Biondello returned with scratches all over his face and forehead, and the beleaguered youth was accompanied by the real Lucentio, along with his new bride, Bianca.

'Oh shit!' Tranio thought. 'Now we're really being discovered, foiled, and ruined! I knew I should've entered a monastery and became a gay monk, or perhaps a gayer abbot!'

But the real Vincentio was rather thrilled to discover that his doted-on son Lucentio was still alive, and had not been criminally disposed of by Tranio, who had been furtively impersonating him and boldly wearing *his* clothes.

"Pardon me, Father, for all of my juvenile, grievous offenses I've committed," Lucentio said, kneeling-down on one knee in front of Vincentio. "But I'm deeply in love with this beautiful doll here, Bianca, and we just got married at the rectory, and if you stick around Father, you'll get to see the bandaged-up priest publicly marry us again at noon."

Finally, sizing-up the extraordinary situation, the wise, real Vincentio intelligently recommended that everyone go to Minola Baptista's mansion to discuss and negotiate the terms of contract between the two dignified families. Everyone was amenable to that provision, including the false Vincentio, who was happy to receive his handsome stipend from Lucentio (along with some sumptuous food), and who was thrilled at learning that he could forever keep his new expensive haberdashery.

Petruchio and Katherina stayed behind, still recovering from the hilarious spectacle the couple had just witnessed. Their romance was finally beginning to germinate, almost a week after their rather strange, un-rehearsed, wedding ceremony.

"Kate, once you learn obedience, self-control, submission, and decent fellatio, then I'll finally gladly screw your ass right through the goddamned mattress!" Petruchio sincerely promised. "Now kiss me, Kate!"

"Right out here in the middle of the street?" the wife answered with her mouth agape. "I do have my inhibitions, you know!"

"Why not?" Petruchio returned. "Even though we're in fuckin' Italy, doesn't mean that we can't French kiss! Love often arrives better late than never!"

"Oh, my sweet Husband! I love you with all of my heart!" the overwhelmed spouse cried and sobbed, and then demonstratively French kissed Petruchio.

'Now that my Wife evidently has been sufficiently tamed,' Petruchio reasoned, as the sagacious gentleman indulged in the prolonged passionate kiss, 'I can finally vigorously screw the shrew until my one and only dick falls off.'

* * * * * * * * * * *

Later that afternoon, three newly married couples and their families cheerfully gathered at Minola Baptista's mansion for a joint wedding feast. The blithe newlyweds were Petruchio and Katherina, Lucentio and Bianca, and Hortensio and his rich (formerly widowed) wife Priscilla of Venice (with the wonderful flabby, floppy, flaccid, tits). In a corner of the extensive banquet dining room, the inimitable Petruchio was being subjected to some merciless taunts and some heavy teasing about being married to "a notorious shrew".

"Hortensio; I understand that you're scared of your obstinate widow!" Petruchio jested. "Perhaps you should take a few lessons from me in the art of wife training! Over the past week, I've become quite an authority on the matter."

"At least my Priscilla is not as much of a shrew as your stubborn wife Katherina is!" Hortensio laughed, with young Lucentio listening in at the head table. "Katherina is enough to make a man not only contemplate suicide, but actually following through and doing it!"

"Well now, how would you two chauvinistic Gentlemen like to engage in a little friendly wager to see who has the most obedient and dependable wife?" Petruchio proposed to Hortensio and to Lucentio. "Now tell me, who is willing to put his fuckin' money where his mouth is?"

"What the hell did you have in mind?" Hortensio curiously asked. "Do you want to see which ornery bitch gives the best blowjob, and then whoever pops a load first, wins the bet? Ha, ha, ha! No; that sort of insane contest would never do, because then it's two conditions instead of one!"

"No; you ignominious, ignoramus Asshole!" Petruchio haughtily replied to Hortensio. "Now Gentlemen; I genuinely suggest that we wager a meager hundred crowns each. Here's the damned lowdown, so listen carefully. We'll each at the same time send a servant to fetch a wife, and then whichever woman returns first to this room, well, that bettor wins the prize money. What the hell do you say about my fascinating proposition, Hortensio? What about you participating in my challenge, Lucentio?"

Both grooms hesitantly agreed with Petruchio's strange-and-irregular terms, and the three available servants were swiftly dispatched at the same time to retrieve the three wives. The three bettors impatiently waited to see exactly what would happen.

"Lucentio's immature servant Biondello quickly returned, and the youth reluctantly reported that Bianca was too busy chatting with her bridesmaids and with Priscilla's Maid of Honor to immediately come to her husband.

"Who the fuck did you marry?" Petruchio aggressively chided the embarrassed Lucentio, whose head was now crestfallen. "Did you wed the Queen of England, or did you marry the Queen of Clubs? Certainly not the Queen of Hearts, Ha, ha, ha!"

And then Hortensio's numbskull servant anxiously returned with bad news for the quickly-disappointed husband. "Sir; Lady Priscilla is seriously involved in combing her hair and putting on her heavy-duty makeup, and your new wife insists that you must go and see her at your earliest convenience!"

"Your new wife must think that her brown shit doesn't stink, or that her perfumed piss isn't yellow!" Petruchio verbally battered Hortensio. "If you were smart, my Friend, you would eagerly run away to either Africa or to Borneo! Have you ever heard of a distant remote uncomfortable place called Siberia? Ha, ha, ha!"

And then Katherina passed through the portal and appeared in that cozy corner of the room, and the elegant lady courteously and respectfully announced, "Husband, what is your wish? Why have you summoned me?"

"Katherina, go in haste and fetch Bianca and Priscilla, and have the vain bitches immediately come into the dining room to enjoy a toast to *our* health, happiness, and prosperity, in that particular order!" Petruchio loudly requested. "And thanks to your steadfast promptness my dear, Wife, I'm now two-hundred-crowns richer! Ha, ha, ha!"

"Well, Petruchio, you're smarter than I ever gave you credit or cash for!" Hortensio indulgently laughed while patting his idol on the back. "I see that I have plenty of relevant bullshit in regard to wife training to learn from you! Ha, ha, ha! You know more about women than I know about flabby tits!"

"A woman's heart and tongue should be as soft and smooth as her breasts!" Petruchio lectured to his captive listeners. "I think I'll open an academy for henpecked husbands!"

Katherina returned five-minutes later with Bianca and Priscilla, who were both unaware of any wager being placed on *their* loyalty and punctuality. The other two females seemed quite upset at being solicited on such short notice, if one could judge by the peeved expressions on their faces.

"What foolish duty warrants my immediate attention and presence?" Priscilla scolded Hortensio. "I'm already finding you to be quite imperious and intolerable, this second time around! I was in an upstairs bedroom trying to get my breasts to stay inside my new formal dress, and then you had to interrupt me with this utterly stupid roll call shit!"

"And Husband," Bianca said to Lucentio. "I hope that you don't make a habit of ordering me to be in a specific place at a designated time on demand! I have important shopping and visiting to do the next several months all over Italy! And besides; I need to have a hundred-crown-allowance each and every week for spending on various luxuries! I don't think that *that's* too tall of an order to handle, now do you?"

"Kiss me, Kate!" Petruchio commanded. And when Kate willingly and lovingly obeyed her husband's benign direction, all four bystanders looked upon the amazing event with their mouths wide open in pure admiration and envy. Finally, Hortensio and Lucentio realized that Master Petruchio was indeed the supreme expert at taming a shrew.

* * * * * * * * * * * *

Christopher Sly wildly applauded and whooped to show his appreciation of the dramatic presentation of the improvised play "The Taming of the Shrew". No sooner had the appreciative bum ceased his clapping that the nobleman (whose country house Sly had been staying at while the vagrant was learning to be a high-brow aristocrat) rained on the gleeful, disillusioned man's parade.

"Pay attention, you lazy slacker Christopher Sly; I have some bad news for you. Your little charade is over, and it's back to shirking daily responsibility for you! It's time for you to get back into your raggedy clothes, and get the hell out of here!"

"But Sir; I thought I was an eminent and esteemed nobleman just like you!" Sly awkwardly objected. "I can't go back to being an aimless, roving vagabond after I've seen how the spoiled upper crust lives! That's inhumane treatment you're subjecting me to! I can only conclude from *this* negative experience that the upper crust consists of a bunch of crumbs held together by dough!"

"Well, Christopher Sly," the humored nobleman answered with a broad smile on his face. "I also have some *good* news to report. These actors need a person playing a drunkard in their next play, and you fit the bill perfectly. Thanks to your wondrous adventure experienced in my manor home, you now have employment in a traveling group of thespians. Congratulations!"

"Thank you, Sir!" Sly humbly exclaimed. "But to tell you the truth, much the same, I'd rather be a gainfully-unemployed, fucked-up nobleman like you are!"

"Now Mr. Sly; I'm sure you'll fit the part just fine!" the traveling company's head actor confidently chimed-in. "We're traveling troubadours, unemployed most of the time, too, and may I add Sir Christopher, that when we do earn some money," the chief thespian chuckled, "well, then, we get ripped to the gills just like you do, and as a result, we have a gay old time sleeping against termite-infested tree trunks!"

"Romeo and Juliet"

Act I

In the year 1450 A.D., (almost a half century before Columbus discovered America), two feuding families living in Verona, Italy absolutely detested each other. These were the famous Montagues and the legendary Capulets, and even the servants that were loyal to the pair of constantly disputing clans were always hankering for an imbroglio, or for an out-and-out altercation. Animosity abounded around every corner wherever Montagues coincidentally encountered Capulets. Sampson and Gregory were pedestrian servants working in the Capulet household, who also shared their employers' disdain for the rival Montagues.

"Here comes several Montagues ostentatiously prancing down the street!" Sampson observed and informed Gregory. "I'll stab one of them in the ass with my pen-knife, and then run away like the true coward that I am! I wish I wasn't so bald-headed and had long hair!" Sampson told his peer. "Then, I would be able to kick any Montague's ass, including that snot-nosed 'romeo', Romeo!"

"Sampson, you're just a dumb fucked-up servant, and not a strong long-haired Old Testament Biblical character, so that might be a rather lamebrain idea you've just concocted; you pathetic, miserable, cocky Bastard!" insecure Gregory strenuously disagreed. "Those crazy Montagues are nothing to trifle with! They're all highly-skilled swordsmen that'll carve us up like we're pigs' meat and chopped-liver! There's a big difference between feeling like chopped liver and actually being chopped liver!"

Sampson foolishly confronted his imagined Montague enemies in the center of the street. "Look you Shit-heads! The Capulets are better masters of pugilism than the fucked-up Montagues are! That's why I'm not fuckin' working for you asinine Assholes!"

"What the fuck did you say, you' no-good, lowlife, lying Bastard?" Benvolio Montague yelled into Sampson's fat face! "I'll cut both sides of your dumpy ass off so that you won't get any more half-assed ideas like the one you've just expressed! Be prepared to defend yourself; you insulting, obnoxious Knave!"

"I understand that the Montague damsels give good maiden head! Is that fuckin' right?" Sampson further instigated and agitated. "Did you just screw and then munch-on one of your maiden's maidenhead? I say this language mockingly, because your fuckin' breath smells like a store full of rotten sea bass!"

As Benvolio drew his sword to fight and castrate both Sampson and Gregory, the notorious dueler Tybalt (Lady and Lord Capulet's nephew) alertly noticed the fracas developing, and voluntarily entered the fray. Soon, Tybalt was standing in front of Sampson and Gregory, and facing the audacious Benvolio.

"Okay, you Montague scumbag," Tybalt shouted at the now-apprehensive Benvolio. "Since you've already-drawn your sword, I challenge you to a duel! Soon, craven Benvolio, you'll be diced into mince-meat! When I fuckin' get done this small episode with you, you'll wish that you were chopped-liver, and you'll need a damned tiny cheese-box for a coffin!"

"I was only trying to keep the peace!" Benvolio hollered back at Tybalt. "But if I find it necessary, I'll defend myself and my honor against you; you despicable Rodent; I'll fight you regardless of your infamous reputation for being a wanton killer!"

But then, ordinary citizens of Verona, tired of the perpetual feuding between the two proud, antagonistic families, turned into instant street vigilantes and came running from all directions to punish the participants in the heated argument. The disorganized enforcers were all brandishing and wielding swords, knives, and clubs, and shouting, "Down with the Montagues! Down with the Capulets! Down with fucked-up feuding!" and "Let's beat the shit out of those belligerent, quarrelsome Assholes!"

When all of the escalating ruckus reached a culmination, old Lord Capulet and Lord Montague exited their respective mansions to evaluate the source of the pandemonium.

"Give me my sword!" Old Capulet ordered his wife. "You know, the one above the mantel that's shaped like a fish!"

"Here, fuckin' fight with this, you Old Fart!" Lady Capulet screamed at her handicapped, stubborn husband as the family matriarch offered her arthritic husband a crutch. "Your goddamned bow legs are as limp as your penis has been for the last thirty-years! I think ya' have a bad rickety case of rickets!"

"Come on, you senile Old Fuck!" Lord Montague challenged Old Capulet from across the street. "I challenge you to come on out here, and then you won't act so cool with only half a culo to shit out of after I get done with you!"

But then, thankfully, Prince Escalus and his guards came onto the scene and interrupted the brawl before the neighborhood could escalate into a major killing zone. When everything quieted down,

Prince Escalus criticized the escalating series of disputes between the hostile Montagues and the bellicose Capulets.

"This ongoing bullshit has got to stop!" the Prince of Verona admonished and remonstrated the pissed-off participants. "You' boisterous jerk-offs are disturbing the peace! I'm sick and tired of warning you feuding Assholes for the third time now, in just two weeks! From this moment on, I hereby decree that anyone caught fighting in the streets without the proper city permit will be publicly executed without having a fair and decent trial! Is that edict fuckin' clear?"

After being officially reprimanded and publicly threatened, the neighborhood residents returned to their various preoccupations and employments, and the royal procession reorganized, slowly moving in the direction of the City Prince's opulent palace.

"Benvolio, have you seen my son Romeo anywhere?" Lady Montague asked the brazen young swordsman, whom the ever-dangerous Tybalt had almost decapitated. "I'm really happy that the boy had avoided the clamorous and almost deadly feuding incident! That's what I love about my docile son! He's basically a pacifist who doesn't use his fists. Romeo's a lover and not a fighter."

"I saw him walking over a bridge this morning, and Romeo told me he desired to be alone," Benvolio reported to Lady Montague. "I think the kid was headed towards the woods to either work his stick, or to take a healthy shit! I believe that Romeo's tired of receiving inadequate blowjobs from ugly wenches, and has decided to lose his virginity and finally get laid with a cheap prostitute for the first time!" Benvolio rather discourteously and imprudently joked to Lady Montague. "I hope he wasn't too hard on his hard-on, and I trust that Romeo hasn't chaffed-up his tool as of yet!"

"Curb your tongue you rascal, Benvolio, or else, you'll find it lying at the curb or in the street gutter, you totally indiscreet Fool!" Lord Montague threatened the callow youth, simply to appease Lady Montague's fierce temper, and to assuage her mounting chagrin. "Perhaps the confused idiot is looking for love and not kinky sex? I'd call our son Romeo a horny son-of-a-bitch if my fearsome dyke wife wasn't standing here right next to me!"

After Lady Montague vigorously kicked her feeble, demented husband three times in the testicles, Benvolio spotted Romeo further down the street, and dashed over to the dashing young man, who was only casually strolling along. Benvolio wanted to tell Romeo about the tremendous melee that had been disrupted by Prince Escalus's benign intervention.

"Hey, favorite horny Cousin! How's it hanging?" Benvolio greeted Romeo. "Is your dingle really dangling?"

"Let's go to an inn and get a bite to eat," Romeo suggested. "I can't seem to satisfy my sexual desire, so I'll have to settle for quenching my thirst and gratifying my empty stomach's appetite! Benvolio, I think I really need to find that one special girl to love and to screw. Do you know what the hell I mean?"

"Romeo, why buy a cow and get married when you could get your milk free every day, and not have to pay for it," Benvolio laughed and kidded. "Your problem is that you're too fuckin' selective. Yes, you need less discriminating taste! Just screw any kinky bitch that comes down the road, and stop looking for that one special female; or else, you'll never get laid until you change your fucked-up sex philosophy. Now then, Cousin; let's go sample some sumptuous food and some delicious drink. I'll bet I get ripped before you even begin to get grogged."

As the young cousins sauntered down the street, Romeo revealed more about the cause of his melancholy. "Benvolio, we've been close pals ever since we were mere toddlers in diapers with smelly shit-stained asses. I must divulge to you a personal secret. I love this gorgeous knockout doll named Rosaline, but she seldom if ever looks in my direction; and in fact, the raunchy bitch gives the impression of totally ignoring me," the young idealist maintained. "My mind is in a quandary. What the fuck should I do?"

"I'm telling you Romeo; don't fuckin' waste your time on hustling some unreachable, pristine, virgin chick! Go for the ugly hens that have been roosterized more than once!" Benvolio lectured. "Then, you'll be just like me, and getting to look and strut-around like a proud capon with my cape-on! Ha, ha, ha! You got to master the four F's Romeo: find them, feel them, fuck them, and forget them! It's all just as fuckin' plain and simple as that! Try screwing your first woman with both of you having masks on!" Benvolio suggested and jested. "That usually takes the fuckin' guilt out of it when you don't know who the fuck you're fucking, or what the fuck the bitch looks like!"

"Maybe you're right after all!" Romeo acknowledged. "Four F's in adult life sounds plenty better than four F's on my grammar school report card! Anyway, good Friend, enough of your irritating bravado and your frivolous sexual innuendo, my illustrious companion Benvolio. Say Cousin," Romeo observed and remarked. "Here's the friggin' neighborhood tavern! I hear that they've got some terrific prostitutes humping and pumping in those upstairs bedrooms! After we eat and drink a-plenty, let's get it on; that is, if we have any damned money left in our shallow pockets for adult, female entertainment!"

* * * * * * * * * * * *

A week later, Old Capulet was visited by Count Paris, who incidentally never had traveled to France. The Count was interested in courting and marrying Capulet's pretty daughter, Juliet.

The wily rich aristocrat Paris had once expressed his greedy intentions (of committing statutory rape on a young girl, rather than on an already-naked statue) to his dying father, who had guaranteed the lustful County Paris of inheriting his massive estate.

"If my daughter's willing, she has my utmost permission, and I'm sure she'll be willing after I twist her arms if she becomes too contrary and obstinate," Old Capulet told the avaricious, churlish Count. "But tonight, I'm having a gala masquerade party and feast at my residence, and you're invited to attend. Who the hell knows Count? You might find a hussy there more intriguing and enchanting than my Juliet!"

"It's springtime Lord Capulet, and as you know, come April, a man's fancy turns to love. Now getting back to the subject at hand, I'll be there at your big happening, Lord Capulet," Count Paris boringly indicated in a monotonous tone of voice. "But how will I know which women are beautiful, and which ones are hideous-looking if they'll all be wearing masks?"

"Count Paris, I suggest that you buy a calendar. It's now late July, and not early April, as you've just rather erroneously presumed and stated!" the sometimes-cognizant Capulet patriarch courteously corrected his covetous sex-addict guest. "And after the masquerade party concludes, everyone will have to take their masks off to eat, and then you'll be able to check-out all the available chicks in attendance!" Capulet logically explained. "I mean, Count Paris; my daughter Juliet is only fourteen-years-old, and you might just be robbing the cradle, you ornery rich devil, you." Then Capulet reconsidered something that his experienced mind deemed rather salient to consider. 'Sometimes, I think that the more money someone has, the more stupid he becomes!' Juliet's father mused and surmised. 'This wealthy cad Count Paris is an excellent example of exactly what the hell I mean!'

That afternoon, Old Capulet gave an illiterate servant a list of important names, and instructed the not-too-erudite individual to go and inform all those invitees whose names appeared on the scroll to attend the planned festive masquerade party. The bewildered servant was scrutinizing the list out in the street, but since the fool hadn't learned how to read, he was completely stymied by his basic assignment. It was at that precise moment that Romeo and Benvolio staggered out of the local tavern, and the overwhelmed Capulet servant anxiously approached the two Montagues with a befuddled look upon his face.

"Pardon me distinguished-looking Gentlemen, but could you assist me in identifying the names scribbled on this paper?" the servant requested. "The names are written in a crabbed script, and since I'm not a crustacean, I can't interpret them."

'Ah,' Romeo thought as the whimsical dreamer silently read the names. 'Lady Rosaline's name is indeed itemized.' Then, Romeo orally read the names, which the servant then attempted to memorize in their exact order. The Capulet employee was so grateful for Romeo's assistance that he surprised the Montague with a generous offer.

"If you two eligible Gentlemen are heterosexual bachelors and not crazy-minded gay Montagues, you're both invited to the big shindig tonight at Lord Capulet's place!" the servant suggested, not realizing whom he had been addressing. "The party begins at seven p.m. sharp, and be sure to bring and wear masks along with proper attire."

"Thank you!" Romeo politely replied. "If my friend and I aren't doing anything special this evening, we might just drop-in. It's always better to conveniently drop-in and party than it is to drop-off and die, you know."

"So, Romeo, I saw your eyes light-up and a super bulge appear in your tights when you were reading the list!" Benvolio jested. "Who knows? Maybe some other dolls will be there who are prettier than this Rosaline babe you're always chattering about! And if you're exceptionally lucky, you might even get to score with old Lady Capulet! Ha, ha, ha! Please remember Romeo," Benvolio specified, tongue-in-cheek. "There's more than one fish in the ocean, and more than one prostitute in the whorehouse!"

"I'll go to the masquerade party, even if it's at the gaudy Capulet dump!" Romeo related to Benvolio. "I love to take risks. However, we must be cautious so that we're not discovered. Smoking will be hazardous to our health if the Capulets set us on fire! But Benvolio; I imagine that we'll be like daring crusaders spying inside the Muslims' camp!"

"That's why I fuckin' enjoy your company!" Benvolio praised his favorite cousin. "You're the most idealistic, fucked-up, jerk-off in the entire Montague family of fucked-up jerk-offs! I strongly suspect that the Lady Rosaline is simply an imaginary person; a mere figment of your fertile daydreaming."

"Believe it or not Benvolio," Romeo steadfastly insisted, "I like masquerade parties better than I like warring political parties, or inter-family feuds! I wanna' live to be at least a hundred."

* * * * * * * * * * * *

While Romeo and Benvolio were cutting each other up, Lady Capulet had the family nurse summon Juliet to her study for a brief conference. The mother asked her knockout daughter how she felt about the prospect of getting married, specifically getting hitched to the rich pompous, notorious playboy, Count Paris.

"You were born in July, and that's where the hell we got the stellar name Juliet!" Lady Capulet informed her pristine daughter. "And besides considering *that* totally irrelevant, immaterial nonsense, your full name made a really cute easy-to-remember rhyme: Juliet Capulet! And let me tell you something else a little more pertinent, Juliet. When you were an infant, you were such a ravenous weaner that you almost sucked my damned tits off! I mean my nipples still hurt and ache almost fourteen fuckin' years later."

"Marriage Mother!" Juliet answered with an exclamation. "I haven't really thought about it! I mean I haven't even gotten my first damned period yet! Couldn't I just get laid a few times to see how the hell I like it? When my maidenhead gets broken, I'll just pretend I'm having my first damned period!"

"Well, Juliet, County Paris has asked for your hand in marriage," Lady Capulet diplomatically explained. "Actually, he wants to marry all of you!"

"How the hell can one rich idiot be an entire County?" Juliet marveled and questioned. "That really seems to be a tad absurd and out of the ordinary; calling anyone a County."

"Think it over, my beloved Daughter," Lady Capulet advised. "He's a rich son-of-a-bitch, and can afford anything your little heart, or your virgin crotch desires. Money can compensate for a lot of ancillary faults."

"After I meet this Count Paris, I'll let you know how I like him," Juliet promised. "I only hope that Count Paris doesn't get plastered and barf all over my tits."

A stodgy, stuffy, dumb-waiter having a prodigious frown upon his countenance rapped at the doorway and interrupted the females' private conversation announcing, "The guests are beginning to arrive downstairs, and we don't have enough guest rooms to accommodate them." The anxious mother and her naïve daughter decided to continue their intimate dialogue later that evening.

"Excuse me Juliet for not catering to your needs, but I must supervise the caterers catering to our masquerade guests' culinary preferences!" Lady Capulet austerely declared. "Call me dilatory!"

"Why the hell should I call you Dilatory when you're my goddamned Mother, Lady Capulet!" Juliet futilely answered.

* * * * * * * * * * *

Wearing imaginative costumes and expensive masks, Romeo and Benvolio anonymously crashed Lord Capulet's private "invited guests only" masquerade party. And to add to the trauma of the drama, Romeo had brought-along another close friend, Mercutio for moral support. But at the gala event, the Montague encroacher was getting acid indigestion, but not from ingestion.

"What the hell's wrong with you, Romeo?" Mercutio asked his pal from behind his five-pound mask. "You're holding your stomach as if you're constipated and have to take a royal shit! Do you have excess gas trapped in your all-too-sensitive intestines? I'll jump on your back and help you expel the excess gas out of your ungrateful ass, and then you'll propel straight across the party room!"

"I had a terrible nightmare last night without a female horse anywhere in sight," Romeo awkwardly tried explaining. "I dreamt that something horrible was going to happen involving a duel between an anonymous Montague and a Capulet. And sometimes, dreams have dual meanings; even when they don't involve duels! Do you now comprehend my apprehension, Mercutio?"

"Well Romeo; don't worry about a thing, let alone worrying about all things!" Mercutio advised his good chum. "After you gorge yourself with a variety of foods, you'll have more gas that you can fart-out when Benvolio and I simultaneously jump up and down on your skinny back. And don't expect that Cupid's dart will make you fart any better, either!" Mercutio described and chuckled. "Here Romeo! Sample some of this tartar sauce on a cracker! I've never tasted any tartar sauce tarter than this tartar sauce! I think it was invented by the Teutonic knights, who as you know, used two different tonics to tame their long wild hair at night!"

"Yes, Romeo!" Benvolio indulgently laughed. "Look for women with blisters on their lips, because those bitches give the best blowjobs most frequently! That's how the whores get those wonderful blisters because the harlots suck at a blistering pace! Ha, ha, ha! And Romeo," Benvolio added. "I'm referring to the lips on their mouths, and not to their entrancing love tunnel entrances! Ha, ha, ha!"

At the festive party, Old Lord Capulet (who had arthritis all over his body, except in his penis) welcomed all his aristocratic guests and told the crowd to "Eat, drink, and be merry, without being excessively gay or blatantly homosexual in public!" Then, the orchestra musicians started playing their waltz selections, and the masked guests began mingling and interacting. Romeo noticed a female (Juliet) standing across the banquet room, and the trespassing Montague casually asked the same dumb illiterate servant that had approached him with the guest list in the street her name.

"That's Juliet Capulet!" the mask-less servant answered. "The County Paris has the hots for her snatcheroo, and I'm not talking about jalapeno peppers either!"

'She's got an hourglass figure!' Romeo reckoned. 'I hope she's not filled with sand!' Then, Romeo asked the dunce-like servant, "Are you sure her name's not Sandy?"

"No, Asshole! How many times do I have to tell you!" the feisty servant bristled. "Her fuckin' name's Juliet Capulet!"

'Oh my God! Her skin is like soft winter snow! I hope she's not too flakey! I feel love swelling in my lonely *heart,* and it feels really swell, even though I need to eliminate a quantity of intestinal gas,' Romeo inadvertently rhymed and punned. 'The best-laid plan of mice and men is getting laid, and nothing more! Ah! Sweet forbidden fruit! All of the other males at this party look like gay fruitcakes, but I can't resist the temptation of porking that curvaceous bitch Juliet, over and over again!' Romeo fantasized.

But then, the ever-vigilant Tybalt suspected that Romeo was a Montague by observing the adolescent's juvenile behavior, and by overhearing *his* shrill high-pitched, staccato voice. "Uncle Capulet," Tybalt said with a degree of urgency in his enunciation. "I must get my sword. That young jerk-off standing over there with a huge bulge in his tights is definitely a Montague. I believe his name is Romeo! Obviously, the brazen fuck had the balls to crash your posh party, and he's even wearing a military-style safety helmet on his head!"

"Show admirable restraint, Tybalt!" Old Lord Capulet cautioned. "Just pretend young Romeo is wearing a seat belt in addition to his military crash helmet! This Romeo punk has a decent reputation around Verona as a virtuous and well-mannered youth, and he's well-liked among all the city women, too!" crazy Capulet confidentially disclosed to the uninterested Tybalt. "I don't want trouble transpiring under my roof tonight, you impetuous Retard; even if Romeo's public name is Rufus Tard. Now go have some punch before you punch Romeo, and unnecessarily start a wild, fuckin' fracas!"

"I still don't like this bullshit of a Montague audaciously and disrespectfully coming into this enemy house and acting like he owns the whole damned place!" Tybalt adamantly squawked. "And who the hell knows how many other unwelcome intruders are also interloping into our private territory? You should stick your right eye inside the back of my friar's costume, Lord Capulet, because I think you've been fuckin' hoodwinked!"

But while Tybalt and Old Capulet were quibbling, Romeo stepped over to Juliet and romantically asked, "May I take your hand?"

"No, Creep! It's attached to my wrist, and I need it to pick-up things, and to wipe my delicate ass with, too!" Juliet balked.

"No, Doll! I meant to say, would you care to dance with me!" Romeo clarified. "I know that you need your hand to perform other commonplace, mundane functions! That's a given."

"Why not? Saints kiss by clasping hands!" Juliet answered in an appropriate metaphor. "And look! The saints come marching-in!"

"If hands could kiss as you've so poetically alluded," Romeo cleverly enunciated, "then my lips do the same! Pucker up, baby, while I smooch you into ecstasy!"

The couple immediately fell in love, but their instant romance was interrupted when Juliet's obnoxious nurse ambled over. "Madam; your concerned mother wishes to converse with you. She's been watching your amorous activities, and is curious to know who the hell you're talking to. I mean, *this* bullshit conversation is like a goddamned soap opera in progress."

When Juliet finally departed to answer to her domineering mother, Romeo realized something pertinent. 'Shit! This is the Capulet house, and that fantastically attractive girl's name is Juliet Capulet! There's little reason to that rhyme that can effectively explain how love can ascend above and dominate both logic and reality! I'm in really deep-shit now; and that high crap is more powerful and lethal than quicksand ever was!'

"Romeo, let's get the fuck out of here before some major catastrophe happens!" Benvolio urgently urged. "I feel danger closing in on us! Even Mercutio is scared shitless, if the foul odor, emanating from his grimy leotards, is any indication. Let's hightail it out the front door before we three are discovered and get our asses kicked right into our intestines, with the impacts leaving a trail of our entrails all over the fuckin' floor! Let's get the fuck outa' here!"

"You're right on target, Benvolio!" Romeo promptly agreed. "I don't need my precious colon turning into a semicolon!"

On the way out the door, old Lord Capulet intercepted the three disguised trespassers and amiably addressed them. "Why are you Gentlemen leaving so early? Are you not party animals?"

"We must return to our separate homes to empty our sick wives' bedpans, and to place sanitary napkins on our dining room tables!" Romeo told the somewhat-confused and already-senile Lord Capulet. "But we're glad that we came to the fiasco, even though none of us came! Great party! Have a good one!"

Then, old Capulet realized that it was past his bedtime hour, so the family patriarch unexpectedly broke-up the masquerade party before the guests could take off their masks, or before any food was ever eaten from the massive banquet tables. The disgruntled, pissed-off visitors all exited, wondering if there was a better party going on over at the Montague mansion across the street.

Act II

When all of the unhappy, mumbling and grumbling guests were prematurely leaving the aborted masquerade/feast extravaganza, the Capulet's wary and inquisitive nurse had a few words to share with Mistress Juliet.

"That masked young man you were kissing was not the County Paris," the Nurse softly indicated. "His name is Romeo, and the fuckhead is the son of Lord Montague, your father's bitter enema, er, I meant to say your father's bitter enemy. I thought I'd especially clue you in on that situation, because all your life, Juliet, you've been basically clueless."

"My only true love originates from my family's extreme enmity for its historical enemy!" Juliet sobbed and regretted, employing convoluted language. "Why couldn't I have been born on another fuckin' continent? Why must I have to be a restless mistress in distress in this dress?"

"And to add exasperation and exacerbation to aggravation, dear Juliet, when your mother and father, along with the rest of the mercurial Capulets, find-out *that* handsome young stud's true identity," the wary and gossipy Nurse predicted, "that's when the shit will really start sizzling in the hot frying pan!"

Several hours later, Romeo (the gander) just had to get another gander of his fair goose, Juliet. 'If only I could goose her once and screw her twice!' the newly-inspired suitor thought. 'My heart is now my dick, and my dick is now my throbbing heart! I must see voluptuous Juliet one more time. I'll scale the orchard wall, and then climb-up to her balcony. This all-too-twisted love shit really has me fuckin' climbing the walls!'

That cloudy, dark evening, after Romeo had clambered-up and had disappeared over the garden/orchard wall, his nutcase friends Benvolio and Mercutio were searching for his missing ass, and for the rest of Romeo, too.

"Call him, Mercutio!" Benvolio urged. "That dumb-shit Romeo is around here somewhere!"

"Why should I call Romeo Mercutio, when his fuckin' name's Romeo, and *I'm* fuckin' Mercutio!" Mercutio exclaimed to Benvolio. "Stop incessantly breaking my vulnerable balls! It's either *that* scenario, or it's the fact that sometimes you just don't make any fuckin' sense at all! But Romeo is outa' sight, and I suspect that the romantic fool has been blinded by Cupid's dart, and has vanished into oblivion, because he thinks that Juliet Capulet is outa' sight!"

"You're a hundred-percent correct in your assessment, Mercutio!" Benvolio concurred. "I believe that Romeo is motivated by craving to stick his penis inside his Venus, and I'll bet he's crazily climbed-over this orchard wall to get to her sweet snatcheroo. I mean, let's go to the inn and drink some suds in our fancy duds," Benvolio recommended. "We can't find someone who doesn't wish to be found. When Romeo realizes that the many liquids that he normally drinks can be put to better use by pissing beer and ale rather than shooting semen, then he'll rejoin us, and thoroughly-appreciate our stellar and illuminating company. I can't believe that our gullible friend Romeo has forgotten all about his imaginary Rosaline, and now has the hots for sexy Juliet Capulet!" Benvolio theorized and declared. "I mean, if both families didn't live on the east side of Verona, then this scenario would be a classic west side story!"

But then, while climbing-up a side rose-bush-trellis, amorous Romeo took a glance-up and recognized an almost mesmerized Juliet, staring-out at the shining stars from her bedroom window. 'What a wondrous beauty!' the young stud thought. 'Her bright light beaming from her radiant being is like the marvelous sunshine pushing-away the darkness of night. I hope I don't get a bad case of astrology-madness, getting too close to my shining star.'

But Juliet, almost in a self-induced love trance, was speaking from her balcony, enticing an imaginary Romeo to ascend higher, and for his pulsating-dick to ascend higher, too. Suddenly, the suitor got several painful rose thorns (that had penetrated his leotards) embedded in his scrotum, all happening in his awkward but highly focused ascent. 'Shit! My already aching balls are now being mutilated into tiny meatballs!' the love-struck fellow regretted. 'How am I ever going to screw lovely Juliet if my balls are bleeding and experiencing excruciating, dual agonies during painful sex?'

"Oh Romeo, Romeo, wherefore art thou Romeo? You're a cherished, divine angel of the highest magnitude! If only you were anyone but a diabolical Montague," Juliet sadly lamented and sighed. "But alas, you're too proud of your family name! And alas again, I'll have to change my last name to yours, just so that we could be together in marital bliss; whether our incorporation has been sanctioned and blessed by our stubborn fathers, or not! What a complicated pity this entire stinking love shit is! Alas; I regret being a victimized Capulet lass!"

The eavesdropping Romeo (now standing near the roof's eaves) spoke-up and startled the daydreaming fair maiden. "I'll hold you Juliet, and then hold you to your vow; and I'm not talking about the letters a, e, i, o, or u, even though *I owe you'* my love!" the mesmerized lover stammered. "Oh Juliet! You sleep with soap in your hole! I'll kiss your snatch and pee into the night! Oh, pardon my clumsy diction!" the young man stuttered, as Romeo finally clambered-over the wrought-iron railing onto the girl's private balcony. "You sleep with hope in your soul! I'll snatch a kiss, and flee into the night! That's what the hell I had meant to say originally, Juliet, despite the fact that my initial expression was quite original!"

"If your love is true, I'll send my nurse and my illiterate servant to you tomorrow morning at nine, and if you respond favorably, I'll make plans to marry you, even if we must secretly elope," Juliet promised her new-found wooer. "But we can't talk too loudly, or for too long, dear Romeo; otherwise, my nosy, horny nurse might come-out here and try to nurse you on her big, succulent breasts!"

"I pledge that I'll show my allegiance by telling your illiterate servant, and your large tits' nurse, that I truly love you!" Romeo euphorically answered as his head and lips drew nearer to Juliet's face and mouth. "Juliet, we *can't elope,* even if we were melons!"

But then Juliet's watchdog nurse began calling her name, and so Romeo had to quickly descend from the balcony without either obtaining a kiss, or getting a cheap-thrill feel; and consequently, in his perilous descent, the sex-starved bachelor received more thorns stuck through his tights, and others lodged inside his delicate scrotum sac. And then, after suffering that particular combined hurting, the stupid lummox tumbled-down the vertical rose trellis, and finally landed inside a small, filthy, mud puddle.

"Good night, my Love!" Juliet giggled and softly whispered-down as the fair maiden blew Romeo a kiss from the balcony, with her silhouette outlined upon a sheer curtain that was illuminated by bedroom candles in the pale, summer moonlight.

'Shit!' Romeo thought and peeved when the young Montague rose to his feet, and then quite gingerly climbed-back over the orchard/garden wall, and next unexpectedly tumbled onto the cobblestone street. 'First thing tomorrow morning, I must go and see the good Friar Lawrence, and tell him what the hell has happened. He'll be able to give me some professional advice and assistance. The priest is an acknowledged expert on the subjects of marriage; of heterosexual and of homosexual love affairs; of gay marriage; of sodomy, and also, Friar Lawrence is an acclaimed authority on pedophilia. I'm becoming just like the sun! Both it and my sensitive aching dick are rising in the east just like yeast!' Romeo mused. 'Ah, yes; waste no time to arise fair sun, and assassinate the jealous and spiteful moon that haunts my spirit! Soon, I shall feel like mighty Jupiter, either penetrating your Venus, or your anus, oh beautiful Juliet! A rose by any other fucked-up name would still be a goddamned rose!' Romeo sobbed as the entranced lover pulled several new thorns out of his throbbing scrotum sac. 'Oh God; how I lust for her bust! Sometimes love really sucks! Parting is such sweet sorrow!' Romeo finally considered as the suffering romantic removed the last two thorns from his abused scrotum.

* * * * * * * * * * *

"Good morning, Father'!" Romeo greeted the reclusive Friar Lawrence. "Good morning is always better than bad mourning!"

"You're right about *that* salutation when you call me Father!" Friar Lawrence replied. "I've fathered many illegitimate children all over Verona and vicinity. Now tell me, young Romeo; why are you up so early? If you want to make a confession, I suggest that you go to the police! Ha, ha, ha! And Romeo, I notice that your leotards are all ripped around your posterior! You should learn to fart more politely and less intensely! Ha, ha, ha!"

"I'm in love Father, even though we're both in Verona," Romeo awkwardly explained. "And I can't get the image of this fantastic girl out of my mind!"

"Oh, now; I fully understand your modus operandi, young Romeo! So, you're again fantasizing about having that imaginary girl Rosaline swirling-around inside your fanciful mind, so that you can jerk-off more effectively!" the hermit friar jested. "But such normal mental pornography and its accompanying masturbation constitutes only a venial sin, and not a more serious mortal one! Are you sure you don't need me to give you absolution?"

"Father Lawrence, (who was not from Arabia), this incredible Woman I'm describing is not a figment of my wild imagination, or some sort of mental manifestation; or a random bizarre illusion as you have implied!" Romeo maintained in a decisive tone of voice. "I've wonderfully fallen in love with a loco local doll named Juliet Capulet. Chide me not, kind Friar! As you well know, *our* families have been feuding for over a damned century now, and I've contritely and not tritely approached you in good faith. I want you to marry us; preferably secretly in order to avoid a big family feud; perhaps the biggest one since feudalism went out of style among middle-aged men back in the Middle Ages."

"My morning was going pretty damned smoothly until you arrived and broke my most excellent fantasy bubble!" Friar Lawrence snapped back. "But this feuding bullshit between the Montagues and the Capulets must cease. If I could arrange a workable truce using *your* marriage as a peace vehicle, I will have engineered something very special that will both merit and warrant Prince Escalus's Noble Peace Prize. The prospect of receiving *that* great recognition is worth the potential danger associated with attempting the rather perfidious exploit! And if my *idea* works, and I earn Prince Escalus's coveted Noble Peace Prize, I pledge to you Romeo that I'll rename this antiquated, ruinous, born-again Christian, Verona church 'The Immaculate Conception'. Your unanticipated visit, dear Romeo, has really made my day, and I must congratulate you for being a very precocious and intrepid young man!" Friar Lawrence commended. "Now, if you'll just stay for a few more minutes, and listen to the introduction of my upcoming sermon on the subject of 'Sodomy'; er, excuse me Romeo; as I was saying; my upcoming sermon on Sodom and Gomorrah."

* * * * * * * * * * *

The following morning, Benvolio (the unemployed rich-kid) and the un-gainfully unemployed Mercutio were sauntering around the city streets looking for their love-struck friend, Romeo Montague, who hadn't come home the night before according to the "local gazette" Mercutio.

"I spoke with old man Montague early this morning, and Romeo was out all night," Mercutio told Benvolio. "I hope he's not out for the count; Count Paris that is, ha, ha, ha!"

"Well, listen to this extraordinary bullshit!" Benvolio answered with a degree of detectable disconsolation in his faltering voice. "Lord Montague told me that Tybalt is pissed-off that Romeo had crashed the masquerade party at the Capulet mansion, and that the enraged bully-villain had a nasty letter loaded with invectives sent to the Montague mansion."

"Great God in Heaven!" Benvolio exclaimed. "Tybalt's gone postal I'll bet, sending that letter! He wants to challenge Romeo to a duel!"

"You're right on the money!" Mercutio concluded and replied. "And Romeo is the type of gullible asshole that will stupidly fight Tybalt, even though young Montague doesn't even know how to hold his penis when taking a piss, let alone how to fight to the death with a sword. Our friend would have a better chance of winning a damned swordfight with Tybalt if the Capulet was a damned paraplegic!" Mercutio argued. "You asked me, friend Benvolio, where that devil Romeo is? Well, he'll soon be with the other demons in Hell, or with the angels in Heaven once that vindictive and formidable tyrant Tybalt gets through with him."

"Romeo will have been smitten twice!" Benvolio deduced and added. "Once by Cupid's arrow, and the second time by Tybalt's sword. The second execution will definitely be more lethal than the first, which as you know, is a very slow marital death that could last for possibly six or seven very ugly decades. Romeo was much better off having his fantasy affair with the imaginary Lady Rosaline. At least one of Rosaline's hostile, pretentious relatives would only kill him in a bizarre illusion, and not in reality! Holy shit! Thank the Lord, Mercutio! Here comes that fanciful wanderlust Romeo, now pacing this way in all his sartorial splendor!"

"First of all, I want to *apologize* to you two Nimrods about not going inn-hopping with you guys, even though my name's Romeo and not Apollo!" the love-struck youth stated. "Putting it succinctly, my mind was in love, and my body was in Verona. But I feel that both my brain and my anatomy are now mutually in a quagmire, and also, in a quandary. What the hell's the latest scuttlebutt around town? Is Juliet pregnant?"

"No Romeo; but you gave us the slip last night, but it wasn't one that belonged to Juliet Capulet!" Mercutio added (because he was once an Accounting Major at the local university). "It's chilly this morning, so you ought to be wearing Juliet's petty coat, ha, ha, ha! But nevertheless, my salubrious, salacious Friend, it's good seeing you still alive. However, in regard to area gossip, which incidentally involves losing your ass and also your nuts," Mercutio proceeded to elaborate, "there's something important we must tell you; so just hold your horses, you rambunctious Italian stallion!"

Mercutio and Benvolio were about to reveal to Romeo that Tybalt was out to malevolently slay him (although mercurial Mercutio's humor usually slayed Romeo), but *their* purpose was preempted when Juliet's gossipy Nurse interrupted their inane conversation.

"Which one of you dawdling dimwits is Romeo?" the Nurse arrogantly began. "I'm alluding to the Romeo that's been roaming all over Verona; yes, the asshole who also wants to roam all over Juliet's pristine body. I'd like to speak privately with him, whoever the Montague dunce may be."

Romeo guiltily identified himself, and Mercutio and Benvolio politely stepped aside to have an aside. "Mercutio and I are going to lunch at your father's house to report that you're safe and sound," Benvolio yelled to Romeo; "despite the fact that you're not trapped inside a safe and dumped into the nearest sound or bay. We'll catch you later alligator; that is, if you're still falling in love, ha, ha, ha!"

"What's the story?" Romeo asked the Nurse. "Confidentially I'm more into plays than I am into stories."

"Unfortunately, and much to my dismay, Mistress Juliet says that she loves you," the wily Nurse reluctantly revealed. "I told her that you were indeed a saucy fellow out to make the rest of your life gravy, but my Mistress did not believe my good advice. She'll see you again, preferably alive rather than dead."

"Please tell sweet Juliet that I'll marry her at Friar Lawrence's ramshackle church, that'll soon be renamed the Immaculate Conception. Tell her to be there at two this afternoon," the prospective groom articulated. "I know I can trust you with our great secret. I'm generally a good judge of character."

"Lady Capulet and I have tried to persuade Juliet that the Count Paris would be an excellent choice for a husband, but your devoted girlfriend stubbornly ignores our wise counsel," the Nurse divulged. "The dumb little Bitch won't listen to reason, and wants to marry you. So, don't try putting the make on me, Buster, for if you pucker-up, I'll surely give you a stiff slug right in the kisser. I collect and eat wall-climbing snails as a hobby, you know!"

"Tell Juliet that I love her dearly," Romeo said to the garrulous Nurse. "And I'm glad that she sent you, and not that illiterate servant Peter with the gargantuan peter."

"Come my son, Peter!" the Nurse directed her illegitimate offspring. "This stupid-assed jerk-off doesn't know that incest is best! He doesn't have a fuckin' clue!"

* * * * * * * * * * *

The itinerant and easily-distracted, gossipy Nurse had been gone for three hours, and Juliet impatiently waited in the garden/orchard for her return. 'Where can she be? Her errand should've only taken half-an-hour?' Juliet worried. 'It's a good thing she's not a prostitute working on a per-trick hourly basis! If that were the case, my Nurse would be a destitute prostitute! Shit! The city clock just struck nine! I hope my servant remembered her assignment and is not presently playing with Peter's peter!'

The on-a-mission Nurse finally returned, and desired talking about the Capulet aborted masquerade party flop; about quilting bees; about women's underwear haberdashery, and also about fox hunting expeditions, but Juliet persistently demanded to learn of Romeo's reaction to *her* sincere message of love.

"Nurse, whatever the hell your real name is, send Peter away to stay at the gate!" Juliet insisted on having her conversation private. "Maybe after your recalcitrant son kicks the bucket, the idiotic sex maniac can help his namesake St. Peter guard the resplendent Pearly Gates of Heaven."

"The young dowry-seeking asshole, Romeo, says he'll meet you at two in the afternoon at Friar Lawrence's tenement residence that *he* calls a rectory!" the Nurse hesitantly disclosed. "Go there, and the stupid-assed, award-seeking priest will marry you two noodle-heads! Are my explicit directions clear in your fucked-up mind?"

"After Romeo and I are wed," Juliet ecstatically expressed, "you, he, and I can nurse-down several bottles of imported wine!"

* * * * * * * * * * *

Romeo was pacing and waiting for Juliet to arrive at Friar Lawrence's place as scheduled. "I wish Friar that I had worked in a restaurant in my early teens, for then, I would be better suited for waiting on Juliet," Romeo crazily remarked to fill a distinct void in the conversation. But soon afterwards, Juliet arrived and brightened up Romeo's life in a jiffy (while Romeo's gross mind was engrossed thinking about giving Juliet's love tunnel a premium jiffy lube).

"Oh Romeo, words can't express how much I love you, even though we've known each other for less than a day!" Juliet earnestly emoted. "I left my vanity in front of my dressing mirror, and then enthusiastically rushed over here to this dilapidated church! My damp crotch is accumulating much juicy dew, as I wish to soon deluge you with my genuine love fluid!"

"Oh, beautiful Juliet; I can't wait to explode my warm juices into your luscious pink love cave!" Romeo unromantically answered. "I tend to have more semen than the average seaman. Honestly, it's embarrassing having to stand here erect with an erection in these torn and tattered retarded leotards! The pain is hard on my hard-on!"

"Okay, it sounds like you two are really ready to engage in Holy Matrimony, even though you aren't even engaged!" Friar Lawrence intimated to the intimate couple. "I'll marry you two lovebirds at once, because it's not common practice or tradition to marry people twice! It's always better to have tradition than extradition; that's precisely what the hell I always say!" the nutcase friar joked. "But from what I see and hear, the Church's teachings have been successfully confirmed, even though I'm about to perform the *Sacrament of Matrimony:* and literally speaking, according to your powerful sex drives, the ancient, sagacious maxim that states: 'Two shall be made one!' Now, my dear young couple, that rather gnostic religious quote makes perfectly good sense!"

Act III

That same early hot summer afternoon, Benvolio insisted to Mercutio that the two Montague comrades should go home and seek sanctuary from the perilous streets that seemed to be teeming with antagonistic Capulets. But Mercutio chided the temporarily paranoid Benvolio, because Romeo's stubborn cousin had the reputation for being an instigator, picking on the smallest of excuses to initiate an altercation with a suspected enemy.

"I don't know," Mercutio emphasized to Benvolio. "I might not know jack, but Romeo has become like a jack who's the jackal of all jackasses wanting to friggin' jack-off all the time."

"I hear that *that* beast of the Capulet boys, Tybalt, wants to fight for the right to party, without any Montagues invited or attending," Benvolio insisted. "That bullshit is basic out-and-out, Italian-style, discrimination! But getting back to your last statement, Mercutio, Romeo better be like Jack be nimble, Jack be quick, or else his tender ass is going to be burnt jumping over a goddamned blazing candlestick! Oh fiddlesticks! Oh shit!" Benvolio nervously yelled. "I should've heeded your sage advice! Here comes that bastard Tybalt now, along with several of his bully henchmen."

"Where the fuck's that coward Romeo?" Tybalt began his tirade. "I would like a word with one of you two degenerate Imbeciles!"

"One word will suffice, and that word is 'Asshole'!" the quick-tongued Benvolio haughtily countered the livid antagonist. "If you're trying to provoke trouble, Tybalt, you don't have to look further than the length of your long, ugly, hose nose! Now, just because this is a public *square,* that Verona fact doesn't fuckin' mean that you have to moronically act like one!"

"The public can look and gawk all they want!" Mercutio glibly added to the developing and escalating tumult. "And all they'll plainly see is you Tybalt, a public nuisance, creating more unnecessary, bothersome havoc! But if you wish to go somewhere else to settle your presumed grievance, we'll gladly go with you into a side alley! Otherwise, Benvolio and I will stand right here and hold our ground!"

"Gaze upon me, you effeminate gay Montagues! You two freaks look like minstrels having their menstruals!" the sharp-tongued Tybalt verbally returned (using nouns, pronouns, an adjective and a functioning preposition, too). "Who wants to take me on?"

But just as Mercutio was about to challenge Tybalt to a duel, the devious nemesis spotted Romeo nonchalantly strolling up the street in *his* direction. "Oh, wonderful day! Here comes the idiot that I fuckin' want to punish, walking right into my trap!" the felonious fiend Tybalt exclaimed. "Young Asshole; you've insulted the Capulet name by rudely crashing the family's private masquerade party!" Tybalt directly accused his selected foe. "Defend yourself rogue Romeo on this major traffic artery, if you have any Montague honor flowing in your blood veins!"

"I now honor the Capulet name as much as I do the appellation Montague!" Romeo intelligently answered. But before the young man could specifically explain to Tybalt that Juliet and he had just decided to secretly get married, Mercutio, thinking that Romeo was too smitten with love to courageously duel with Tybalt, accepted the scoundrel's challenge as his good friend's worthy substitute. "Humility is a virtue, but honor is a virtue of greater value! I'll cut off your ears, Tybalt, and then have them sewn onto your tiny testicles!" Mercutio yelled in an utterance of exaggerated bravado.

The two duelers squared-off, much to Romeo's consternation and horror. The worried young man urged his cousin Benvolio to help him stop the fight before someone, namely Mercutio, became seriously injured or killed.

"Tybalt! Mercutio! Prince Escalus has expressly forbidden all brawling and feuding with swords anywhere in Verona!" Romeo futilely shouted. "Cut this crazy bullshit out, immediately. Words are always better than swerds, er, I mean swords!"

Just as Romeo lunged-forward to stand between his noble cousin and Tybalt, the agile Capulet swordsman ducked-down and reached in under Romeo's extended arm, and mortally wounded the momentarily distracted Mercutio. The valiant friend of the proud Montague family held his side, and soon collapsed to the street, anguishing in his swift demise.

"Romeo, a pox on the houses of Montague and Capulet!" Mercutio coughed and gasped. "May a terrible plague afflict both despicable families!" the stabbing victim cursed. "I'm fuckin' dying! The gash in my chest is severely gushing! I fear that the damned gap is grave enough to put me into my early grave!"

"I only tried stopping the fight to announce to you and Tybalt that Juliet and I have seen Friar Lawrence, and that we're now, all supposed to be friends and allies!" Romeo cried. "But now all of that good faith his evaporated into thin air!"

"Let's get Mercutio into a house, otherwise, he'll die out here on the street like a rabid distempered dog!" Benvolio told Romeo as Tybalt and his henchmen had already bolted-away from the tragic scene, and the fleeing Capulets were then hastening down the cobblestone street. All the while, Romeo was on a guilt trip, feeling personally responsible for Mercutio's dire situation. But after Mercutio stopped breathing, Benvolio orally committed himself to avenging his favorite friend's cruel death.

"I'm going to slay that mother-fucker Tybalt, if it's the last thing I do!" Benvolio pledged to the emotionally-addled Romeo. "Soon, the evil Capulet killer, too, will be pushing-up daisies in the goddamned local cemetery!"

But then, the dastardly Tybalt (like a true culprit) returned to the scene of the crime to view the result of his terrible malice. Romeo shouted a bold ultimatum to the Capulet instigator.

"Mercutio's spirit seeks company in the hereafter!" Romeo yelled at the pugnacious Capulet. "You cheated when you thrust your blade under my arm and caught the brave Mercutio defenseless and by surprise. One of us is going to join his ghost, and it ain't fuckin' going to be me! Tybalt, be ready to meet your Maker!"

Romeo, who had spent the last five-years shadow-fencing with a wooden sword in the Montague's dark and dismal wine cellar, drew his shiny new birthday-present weapon, and within ten-seconds of ferocious parrying, *he* had amazingly stabbed Tybalt in the chest, instantly incapacitating the vile knave.

Seeing that Tybalt had been killed, Benvolio yelled at Romeo to evacuate the area before either incensed citizens exited their houses (to beat the two to death with clubs, sticks, and knives), or Prince Escalus arrived on the scene to take Romeo into custody, and pronounce an execution date for the gallows. The two Montagues scurried-away from the death setting as people (fifteenth century versions of ambulance chasers) flocked to the crime scene.

"What the hell happened here?" Prince Escalus incredulously asked. "Who is responsible for this carnage?"

A bystander reported for all to hear, "Tybalt had murdered Mercutio, and then Romeo sought revenge and had efficiently disposed of Tybalt. Then the Montague murderer cut out of here!"

"That honest crime spectator got the whole spectacle right!" another eyewitness assertively verified. "He must be a fuckin' optometrist with superior vision!"

And then, Lady Capulet rendered her subjective opinion of what had transpired. "Romeo and Benvolio were definitely the instigators of all this violence!" the matriarch indicted. "And their erroneous observations and conclusions are quite biased and prejudiced! That irascible loudmouth bastard standing there is a friend of the Montagues, so Prince Escalus, pay no heed to his fallacious testimony! Romeo had to cheat to slay Tybalt! There's no way that he could've defeated the highly-skilled Tybalt in a fair fight! That's why the hell that incorrigible, cowardly punk Romeo ran-away like the true gutless scumbag that he is! I beg your indulgence, kind Prince! I sue for justice!"

But then old Lord Montague approached the Verona Prince and felt a moral obligation to defend his son's character. "If Tybalt had dispensed of Mercutio, as has been accurately reported, then Romeo was quite justified in defying the established law by killing Tybalt! The Bible explicitly states, Prince Escalus, 'An eye for a tooth, and a testicle for an epididymis, or some crazy absurd jargon like that!"

But after hearing all the opinions and versions rendered, the sage Prince Escalus ruled, "Since Tybalt had started this disgraceful tragedy by killing Mercutio, and since Romeo committed the second murder by getting rid of that malicious troublemaker Tybalt to avenge Mercutio's death, and based on my previous pronouncement regarding feuding and the like, I hereby rule that Romeo is not to be sentenced to death, but is to be ostracized from Verona. Banishment and exile from Verona are Romeo's deserved punishments for killing Tybalt. Raw violence should not ever escalate in my city," Prince Escalus emphasized.

* * * * * * * * * * * * *

Juliet was unaware of what had happened to Tybalt and to Mercutio. The gullible fourteen-year-old girl was preoccupied plucking the petals off of a daisy and monotonously reciting, "He loves me; he screws me not. He loves me; he screws me not!" Then, Juliet became more pensive and reflective as the girl gazed-upon her appearance in the garden's reflection pond. 'Tonight, Romeo will climb my wrought iron balcony, and we'll legally hop into the sack to see what our intense lovemaking will have wrought. I can't wait to have my lousy cherry busted, and possibly soon enjoy my initial coming-of-age first period! Sometimes, doing stupid things ass-backwards is more exciting and thrilling than following standard tradition!' Then, the enthralled girl merrily sang, "When the moon hits your eye, like a big tomato and cheese pie, that's amore!" Juliet whimsically amused herself. "When the anchovies make you drool, just like pasta-fagioli, that's amore!"

But the girl's mental concentration, along with her sweet reverie, were abruptly interrupted with the appearance and the voice of the seemingly ubiquitous family Nurse. "Your cousin Tybalt is dead, and he had been killed by your precious lover, Romeo, in a villainous sneak attack," the shallow-minded Nurse revealed, relying heavily on hearsay. "Prince Escalus has rightfully banned your lover from the city, so I'm going to dispose of this climbing rope that *he* had planned to use to scale-up to your bedroom, and do some foreplay, followed by some highly focused cherry-picking. But that neurotic Dope's not going to do the rope-a-dope this evening; that's for damned sure! Your evil significant-other has maliciously taken the letter 't' from the good word 'trust'!"

Juliet was grief-stricken, and she began whimpering and then crying. "Despite the evidence that Romeo has brought shame to *our* name, if I cannot have my beloved Romeo, then I would prefer to die!" the saddened girl pouted and wept. "Life is not worth living without the comfort of love!"

"No, you foolish, rueful Child!" the bossy Nurse disagreed. "Don't kill yourself out of self-pity! I know where Romeo is hiding, and I can arrange a secret rendezvous. I'll see to it that he meets you tonight before he flees the city. But since I'm in your employ, I must tell you the unvarnished truth as I know it to be. Your lover-boy Romeo is hiding-out with a criminal named Fernando in Friar Lawrence's underground cave hideaway beneath the priest's dilapidated church."

"Oh, my faithful Nurse; I entrust you with this ring!" Juliet pleaded, because the wench was too lazy and too spoiled to deliver it herself. "Take it to Romeo as a token of my love and affection. I wish for him to be wearing it when he eventually feels compelled to leave Verona forever!"

* * * * * * * * * * *

While Juliet was giving the ring instructions to her trusty Nurse, Father Lawrence was informing Romeo of all the pertinent events that had recently been evolving in Verona. All during the informative revelation, Romeo was languishing in grief.

"You're pretty damned lucky!" the sanctimonious Friar solemnly said to his temporary ward. "Prince Escalus is only banning you from Verona for killing Tybalt, and not ordering the usual death sentence. This measure certainly represents a very lenient punishment. But don't despair Romeo. Perhaps in the future, merciful Escalus might change his ever-vacillating mind. I mean, stop acting like its damned doomsday, or something really ugly or morbid like that," Friar Lawrence suggested. "You're only being banished to Mantua, and not to Hell, or even to friggin' Purgatory. Oh well, you young Colt; there goes my damned Noble Peace Prize award, tossed right out the friggin' window!"

"I'd rather die than be sent-away to live as a reckless recluse in Mantua," Romeo peeved. "How can I ever live without Juliet, the inspirational love of my life?"

Now, if Romeo or Friar Lawrence had an ounce of brains, the bride and the groom, already quietly married by the hermit priest during Juliet's visit to the remote church's rectory, would have easily ventured to a honeymoon destination outside Verona. And also, (as a result of ineffective decision making), the two dim-wits (Romeo and Father Lawrence) could have still stolen Juliet away *that* evening, and Romeo and Juliet could have lived peacefully in an isolated, rustic cottage somewhere in the hinterlands. Or, Juliet and Romeo could have just told their families the truth about their clandestine wedding, and hung-around Verona to see if their parents would give them any propitious financial support. But instead, Romeo allowed the unorthodox and cowardly Father Lawrence to contrive several crazy plans that were certain to backfire.

"Someone is rapping on my door!" the nervous Friar said to himself, momentarily forgetting that young Montague was standing nearby. "Quick Romeo! Dash into my study and pretend that you're being studious for once in your lackluster life!"

Juliet's gabby and incompetent Nurse had showed-up at Friar Lawrence's humble dwelling to deliver the aforementioned ring, and to relate to Romeo that Juliet wished for her renegade husband to risk a hernia or castration a second time by ascending the flimsy rose trellis up to her bedroom's balcony; the purpose of the visit being to comfort the young bride's sadness over the dual deaths of Mercutio and Tybalt.

"Go and see your fourteen-year-old wife," Friar Lawrence suggested and urged. "Then, you could leave Verona before daybreak, trek to Mantua, and seek asylum there in a monk-operated sanatorium. I'll give you a letter of introduction, and I'll keep in touch with you Romeo, using your servant Balthasar as a vital courier. Now then, get the hell out of here, and don't bother my ass until you irrationally decide to freakin' get married again in a more legitimate venue; namely in *my* church, instead of my rectum, er, I mean my rectory!"

Meanwhile, at the expansive Capulet mansion, the Lord and plastered Count Paris (who both knew nothing about Juliet's secret wedding) were conferring about arranging a marriage (and spectacular wedding reception) between Capulet's fourteen-year-old progeny and the straightlaced, drunken, aristocrat playboy.

"I'm here to woo and not to woe!" the totally soused Count divulged and then hiccupped. "I often say 'woe be' gone Lord Capulet, just to disperse my woebegone moods! Ha, ha, ha!"

"I predict that Juliet will forget all about Tybalt's death, if I demand that she marry a rich lush such as yourself," Lord Capulet told the burping and belching Count. "Then, Juliet will once again be happy, and I can get the little troublesome Bitch out of my house. Count France, er, I mean Count Paris; I grant you permission to marry my Daughter Juliet, this coming Thursday, three days from now, which oh yes, let me see, would logically make today Monday on my porno' calendar."

But while the serious consultation between Lord Capulet and the intoxicated Count Paris was occurring downstairs, Romeo was flirting with his teen wife on the black wrought iron upstairs' balcony. And if Juliet was just smart enough, or had the backbone to leave the security of her all-too-familiar and her all-too-comfortable home environment, many problems (and the rest of the plot to this famous play) could have been satisfactorily avoided.

"Must you go so soon, my handsome Husband?" Juliet sadly asked. "Haven't we gotten beyond the damned necking and making-out stage of our relationship? Isn't it penetration time?"

"The robins are beginning to chirp, and the bees are starting to buzz, and quite frankly Juliet, that's all the hell I know about the birds and the bees," Romeo blushed and confided. "And if I dare stay here in your father's mansion after dawn, something amazing just dawned on me! I'll probably be executed if I've neglected to leave Verona as the omnipotent Prince Escalus has decreed. But fair Juliet, I would surely stay in your opulent home, and get apprehended and die for you, if that's what the hell you desire!"

"No, my precious Romeo! Depart the premises immediately!" Juliet emotionally answered. "I wish I were a male, for then, I'd have the balls to leave with you!"

"Juliet!" the obnoxious Nurse called from the hallway. "It's time for your cookie and milk snack break! And then, Mistress, Lady Capulet desires to discuss some significant, recent, current events with you downstairs!"

"Oh, kiss me, Romeo, and you can later think about munching on my cookie while I'm munching on mine that was baked in my mother's kitchen!" Juliet insisted. "I suppose that's the way the cookie's gotta' crumble! And I promise to vigilantly wait every day for your hot and steamy love letters."

After Romeo hazarded a double hernia by again awkwardly descending the un-sturdy rose-flower trellis, the all-too-curious Nurse entered with the serving tray of cookies and milk, and then hastily exited the bedroom. Next, Lady Capulet stepped-in, noticed Juliet crying her retinas out, and the matriarch thought that her daughter was mourning Tybalt's death.

"I have some superb news from the suburbs to cheer you up!" the mother informed her sorrowed and distraught teenager. "Your magnanimous Father and I have arranged your marriage to the wealthy Count Paris, whom you should outlive by fifty-years, because the rich fool has got only about one-tenth of a functioning liver. This means, Juliet, that your avaricious Father and I won't have to provide a dowry. And Lord Capulet and I can greedily keep all of our money in our lucrative interest-bearing stock management account, and also in our profitable bond portfolio."

"Oh no, Mother! I can't marry that scurrilous, drunken, son-of-a-bitch!" Juliet panicked and exclaimed. "Count Paris is the biggest asshole in his entire suburban county!"

"I know the great turmoil your emotions are experiencing!" Lady Capulet tried empathizing with her sometimes-insolent child. "That callous and ruthless no-good bastard Romeo Montague has terminated your dear cousin Tybalt, and that particular calamity has gotten your sensitive heartstrings all unraveled."

But then, Lord Capulet stepped into the bedroom to read the riot act to his rebellious, acne-faced, teenage daughter. "Juliet, read my lips!" the fully-aggravated Father sternly warned. "Either marry Count Paris on Thursday at St. Peter's Church, or I'll kick you the hell out of this fine house and onto the street, where you can beg like a leper and live sucking-on greasy offal gotten from garbage bins. Thank goodness Prince Escalus hasn't created, or legislated, any child abuse laws yet! Now either you marry the horny, kinky, drunken, fucked-up Count Paris on Thursday, or get ready to pack your bags; and don't let the door collide with your skinny ass on the way out! Or, if I prefer," Lord Capulet austerely indicated, "I'll violently shove your ass off the upstairs balcony, and then you'll really be grounded, if not permanently paralyzed."

Naturally, Lord and Lady Capulet believed that the parents were acting in their daughter's best interest, because just the year before, immature and impulsive Juliet had threatened to find a husband in an Oriental mail order "Spouse and Gay Men's Catalog". But when the defiant girl refused to listen to her parents' repetitious horse crap, the ruling Capulets angrily left her room, cursing up a storm of unmentionable expletives. A half-hour later, Juliet had an instruction to give to her trouble-making, personal servant.

"Nurse, you must escort me to see Friar Lawrence for some self-improvement advice," the confused girl told her inquisitive aide. "My parents are quite upset and hostile towards me right now, and I so badly want to be screwed by my husband Romeo, and not by that cavalier asshole, the ever-intoxicated, and I assume limp-dicked, Count Paris."

"Forget about Romeo!" the Nurse imperatively shouted. "Don't be stupid! Have it made for the rest of your life by marrying the affluent Count Paris! You will be able to live a life of luxury in Florence, in Venice, or at Lake Como."

"Get the hell out of my bedroom, or I'll puncture both of your sagging tits with my long-sharp sewing needles!" Juliet menacingly threatened her all-too-newsy Nurse.

Act IV

Count Paris was counting on Juliet marrying him, so the infamous playboy paid an impromptu visit to Friar Lawrence to hastily make *his* nuptial arrangements, which in reality, was more optimistic than visiting the priest to make his funeral arrangements. Now, if Father Lawrence were an intelligent, honest man, the cleric would have simply informed the impetuous Count that Juliet had already been married (by him) to Romeo, and then no further conflict should have transpired in this incredible domino-effect death story. "You want to get married in three days," Father Lawrence quipped. "But usually Count Paris, the full ceremony only takes about an hour."

"Unfortunately, Venus doesn't smile in a grieving house, although both you and I fully know that houses don't grieve, but the people in them do. Now then Father," the intoxicated visitor slurred and elaborated, "Lord and Lady Capulet are exhilarated and want to obviously accelerate the wedding event happening," Count Paris declared, ascribing and transferring the blame for the reason for haste in the preparations to Juliet's parents. "And I figure that in three days, I'll have sufficient time to sober-up, and possibly after re-evaluating the circumstances, rescind my decision to participate."

Friar Lawrence was about to give his sacred blessing to the Count Paris marriage, but then Juliet came into the priest's study (without having the courtesy of knocking on the front door to the ramshackle rectory/cave), and the Capulet girl was astonished to see Count Paris kibitzing with the formerly trusted marriage official.

"Oh, my goodness," the cranky Paris uttered and then burped. "It's my future Wife who has come in the flesh to shrive her litany of venial sins. I must confess that I myself haven't done a shrive since I had been a loyal sergeant in Prince Escalus's army seven-years-ago. Are you ready to wed me, dear Juliet? Speak your heart's true intent!"

"Whatever will be, will be! The future's not ours to see!" Juliet queerly and peculiarly replied. "Stranger things have happened in this screwed-up world, I'm quite sure of *that* oddball concept, you rich, drunken Dud!"

"Now then, call me a frustrated thespian, but I must candidly tell you Juliet that I have an affinity for enacting and staging the dramatic," Friar Lawrence boasted. "Now Count Paris, please go into my study and count the number of living and dead cockroaches that abound in every crack, crevice, cranny, and niche residing in there. I'll rejoin you in around half-an-hour in case your limbs, your head, and your dingle all decay and fall off in the meantime."

"Why have you come, my Dear?" Father Lawrence asked the emotionally unstable girl. "Have you finally killed your nosy, newsy Nurse? I find that woman rather irritating!"

"No Father; I'm not here for an examination of conscience or to confess any accumulated sins, but I felt that I must see you alone for a private consultation!" Juliet reviewed and articulated. "Please help me Friar Lawrence, or else, I might succumb to the strong suicidal urges that my vulnerable weak will is presently experiencing and struggling with."

"Okay, Young Lady," the priest reluctantly assented. "Don't commit suicide. Let's make it look like you *have* committed suicide! Now, I precisely know what's bothering your spirit Juliet, and I have the perfect imperfect solution," Friar Lawrence (an uncertified and unlicensed amateur alchemist) peculiarly explained. "I've concocted a secret formula in this vile vial. Drink the *solution* and your whole body will go into a fantastic, catatonic, coma-like state, giving the extraordinary appearance that you're dead. You'll have no detectable pulse or any evidence of vital signs like breathing and heartbeat working. Every asshole in Verona will be tricked by *our* in-genius clever ruse!"

"But Friar, if I'm supposedly dead, then how the hell am I to be reunited with my banished husband, Romeo?" Juliet wondered and queried. "What's this vile vial shit all about? I require an explanation right this minute!"

"Now Juliet, I happen to love whimsical nursery rhymes and fractured fairy tales, despite the fact that I'm celibate and not gay like many of my religious, homosexual peers," Friar Lawrence maintained. "You'll be placed in your family's enormous tomb, and then I'll write a letter to Romeo over in Mantua, and soon thereafter, young Montague will trek on over here to Verona to wake you up with a gentle kiss, just like you were a beautiful Sleeping Beauty! Who says that plagiarism is out of style?" the crazy, lunatic priest asked his female client. "This insidious, womb-to-tomb bullshit is what makes religion plausible and attractive to the general population! And then, my dear Juliet; we wily priests capitalize on people's hopes and fears, and offer them a distinct choice between Heaven and Hell! It's basically all that simple, you gullible Simpleton!"

"Where will Romeo and I live if I'm still alive after I'm supposedly dead?" the completely puzzled and baffled Juliet asked her demented adviser.

"You'll both be living over in Mantua," Friar Lawrence calmly explained. "Don't worry! I'll arrange everything with some of my many contacts!"

"But Father, wouldn't it be a hell of a lot easier for me just to go to Mantua right now and live with my exiled husband rather than try and enact all of this ludicrous bullshit about drinking the mystical formula, and then pretending to be dead, while I'm giving the appearance of being dead?" Juliet objectively challenged. "This entire deceitful enterprise that you've presented seems quite preposterous in both scope and sequence!"

"The world is pretty fucked-up, Juliet, and that's why the people living on this planet must think and do imaginative fucked-up things just for diversity's sake. And besides, I always enjoyed dabbling in creating new and unusual apothecary prescriptions!" the incompetent and misguided priest revealed. "Now then, take this special unproven experimental batch of chemicals home and drink the vial, er, I mean, swallow-down the special fluid inside the vial, and let's see what the hell happens. That off-the-beaten-path activity ought to be a lot easier to swallow than your impending marriage to that perverted alcoholic Count Paris, who is loudly belching and farting in the adjacent room! But let's put first things first, Juliet," the delusional priest elucidated. "You must consent to marrying Paris; I mean the damned Count, and not the damned city."

Juliet returned home to the Capulet mansion and considered the weird prospect of her awakening from her extended slumber inside the family's burial vault, which was situated right next to the Capulet's pole vault. 'What kind of priest would ever consider marrying a fourteen-year-old girl twice within a week? Oh well, life really sucks, but I fear that death does nothing, not even sucking!

This liquid shit in this vial better not be poison! I hope the hell I'm not crossing that fearful eternal bridge, and permanently joining Tybalt and Mercutio's ghosts flitting-around in the afterworld,' Juliet pensively evaluated.

And then, the upset girl irresponsibly followed Friar Lawrence's easy directions and chugged-down the mysterious liquid from the vile vial, and in a matter of two suspenseful minutes, the girl-bride collapsed onto the bedroom floor. The following morning, Juliet's busybody. disoriented Nurse discovered the teen's un-busy body, which was motionless upon her room's Oriental rug.

"Oh, lamentable day! Oh, detestable day! Juliet's deader than a deadbolt lock!" the Nurse screamed, drawing the attention of everyone else in the mansion. Naturally, Lord and Lady Capulet were shocked and stunned at discovering the apparently horrible fate that had descended on their precious, unworldly daughter. The chill of winter frost had evidently taken the bloom off of the elder Capulet's treasured sweet, teen flower.

"Our Daughter is now going to St. Peter's Church as a pale corpse and not as a blushing bride!" Lady Capulet cried and moaned. "The church bell's tolling will be macabre instead of cheerful! This is an unbearable tribulation that I'm suffering, that *we're* suffering! That pirate Angel of Death has wickedly stolen and absconded with my dear Daughter's angelic spirit!"

"And to think that I've hired twenty cooks and thirty butlers and maids to accommodate the wedding feast's five-hundred invited guests," Lord Capulet lamented. "Nurse; tell Peter to fire Paul and the other nineteen hired chefs and thirty domestics. I'm not going to rob Peter to pay Paul, that's for goddamned sure!" the parsimonious Lord Capulet exclaimed. "Peter has run out of money, and parasite Paul has run out of credit!"

Within an hour, the conniving all-too-pious Friar Lawrence and the bewildered-but-rich Count Paris were told of the sobering news of Juliet's terrible death, and the disappointed groom finally showed some genuine emotion in the form of sober meditation.

Act V

Romeo was hanging-out in Mantua (which was better than hanging in the Verona gallows), waiting for news of relevant developments occurring back in his native city. But one day, young

Montague's servant Balthasar arrived and encountered the ostracized young man wandering-around the city's notorious red-light district.

"Romeo, I have some bad tidings to report!" Balthasar reluctantly said. "Your wife is dead from an unknown cause, and Juliet's body's been placed in Lord Capulet's mausoleum. At least she's being laid to rest above ground, and not being interred inside the insect-infested Earth. Your Juliet's been laid to rest in the marble monument right next to the Capulet's backyard pole vault!"

"That bad news really sucks!" Romeo told Balthasar. "We'll leave for Verona tonight, and quite frankly, I don't give a short shit if I get caught and hung or not. Have you any other news from Friar Lawrence?"

"No Master; I didn't know that I was supposed to obtain any info' from him!" the servant nervously answered. "That oddball priest doesn't know what the fuck he's talking about, anyway! Like most priests and bishops, Friar Lawrence makes more fuckin' sense when he says absolutely nothing at all!"

"I can't live without Juliet's love and support!" the disconsolate young griever confessed to Balthasar, who was not certified like Father Lawrence was to hear confessions and give absolution. "The next time I become disconsolate, I vow that I'll break into Juliet's tomb, drink-down some potent poison, and dejectedly take my own meaningless life! I feel as hollow as an empty cavern!"

"What is your plan?" the servant asked.

"Now my faithful Balthasar," Romeo said after inquiring about his chemical acquisition, "here's a crown to buy me some quality ink and paper. And oh yes, you pathetic Imbecile. I'll also need a quill pen with which to write. And then, you can keep the remaining change as a tip to spend as you wish."

"While Balthasar was preoccupied purchasing the paper and quill pen, Romeo was visiting a disreputable Mantua chemist. "This potent poison is sufficient to kill twenty normal or abnormal men!" the don't-give-a-shit, fully-dishonest apothecary told Romeo. "It's guaranteed to instantly damage and destroy every major organ in the body within thirty-seconds. In fact, Sir," the unethical businessman continued his descriptive sales pitch, "it's one of my most popular products; especially among pissed-off men that wish to conveniently dispose of their bothersome wives, or their interfering mothers-in-laws. It's also a favorite among vengeful, scorned, jaded women that want to get even with their cheating husbands."

"Good! I'll purchase a jar of that lethal shit!" Romeo eagerly stated to the disingenuous, warty-faced merchant behind the grimy counter. "The sooner I get the fuck off the face of this disgusting. fucked-up Earth. the better off I'll be! I despise the world and all of its convoluted laws, and all of its contemptible fucked-up customs. Now, here's forty-ducats Old Man to pay for the transaction, you wretched gnarled-up. pathetic Knave! And believe it or not, you unethical, back-alley, Apothecary Mixologist, this payment in gold coins I'm giving you is greater poison than the lethal chemicals that I'm illegally procuring from your illicit, black market, underground economy shop!"

"That's what the fuck you think, Junior Montague!" the very contemptible chemist/merchant replied. "I recognize you from police posters tacked to poles and trees all over the fuckin' city."

Back in Verona, Friar Lawrence had written a letter to Romeo. A procrastinator/friend, Friar John, had been delegated to deliver the missive to Romeo in Mantua. But when Friar John visited Father Lawrence at St. Peter's Church, the designated courier had a bad luck *sob* (son-of-a-bitch!) story to relate.

"The house of prosecution, er, I mean the prostitution dormitory in which I was staying, had an epidemic of communicable venereal diseases among its scurrilous occupants. And the Verona Prince ordered the entire place to be quarantined," Franciscan Father John declared to his disappointed religious friend. "No one was allowed in or out of the home for a full week, and everyone inside was suffering and scratching from mysterious, sex-related infections, all far worse than any gonorrhea or syphilis I've ever had or seen. Consequently, Father Lawrence, I was unable to deliver the letter that you had entrusted me with. I suppose that *that's* the inherent risk people take when they start screwing around, especially with the city police doing undercover work under the covers! What a fuckin' scandal this incredible story's going to be once it becomes public gossip!"

"Get me some carpenter's tools in a hurry!" Friar Lawrence ordered Father John. "We'll definitely need hammers, crowbars, and chisels, you cheap, covetous, incompetent chiseler. Next time, stay at a fine hotel and not at a dirt-cheap brothel. But for now, Father John," Friar Lawrence remarked, getting back on subject. "Juliet Capulet is scheduled to wake-up in three hours, and Romeo won't be there at the mausoleum because the youthful husband never read the letter that I had penned, that you never delivered. I knew I should've trusted Prince Escalus's postal service rather than stupidly giving the vital missive to an irresponsible Boob like you!"

"Have sympathy for me, Friar Lawrence!" Friar John pleaded. "I've got more crabs around my genitals than there are lobsters in the whole Verona fish market! I'm just itching, Father, to get the fuck out of my own skin!"

* * * * * * * * * * * *

Count Paris had sobered-up enough to visit the Capulet mausoleum and pay his last respects to Juliet, when his servant (holding a lantern) alerted him' that visitors (who were Romeo and Balthasar arriving from Mantua) were approaching on horseback. 'I'll hide in the bushes and avoid detection! It might be several of Prince Escalus's tax collectors spying on me!' Paris suspiciously thought. 'Those pestering bastards are present everywhere! Those arrogant, nasty, pricks think that I owe them a damned living!'

Romeo and Balthasar furtively entered the area where the Capulet mausoleum was situated. "Now hand me that bouquet of delicate flowers, and take this very important letter to my completely delirious Father, Lord Montague. The dispatched communication will explain precisely what I plan to do next, and why the hell I'm doing it!" Romeo instructed Balthasar outside the Capulet huge, white marble monument. "Right now, I'd like to be alone with dear Juliet, so get your fat ass the fuck out of here before you permanently wind-up inside this morbid structure, too."

While Romeo was using tools left outside the mausoleum by Father Lawrence and by Friar John (because the listless priests were too lazy to expend energy and open the sealed tomb themselves), Count Paris stepped from the shadows and suddenly surprised the preoccupied, melancholy Romeo.

"You're the belligerent asshole Montague that killed Tybalt, a former valued acquaintance of mine!" Paris curtly accused the innocent-minded youth. "And now Juliet has died because of the colossal sadness and sorrow that your diabolical actions have generated. I won't allow you to do anything else to hurt the noble Capulet family. Now, I insist that you leave Juliet's tomb alone, or else you'll surely die!"

"I don't take orders from you, or from anybody associated with the self-righteous Capulets!" Romeo snapped back, deliberately dropping his hammer and crowbar, and then reaching for his sword. "Your loose-tongue gabbing might result in a chest stabbing!"

"According to Prince Escalus's imperial decree, you're never supposed to return to Verona again!" Count Paris recollected and stated. "That means that I'm going to have to arrest your ass, haul you off to jail, and let the constables and the gallows' executioner deal with you, you condemned Villain!"

Romeo would not submit to being apprehended or arrested without a fight, so the two opponents squared-off and began intense dueling. Within a minute of very savage combat, Paris was mortally wounded and laid bleeding to death on the soggy turf.

Several minutes later, Romeo remembered the Count's true identity. 'This dead scoundrel was a relative of my deceased friend Mercutio, his distant cousin, I believe!' Romeo sadly reflected. 'And now I've killed in fair fights two men, Tybalt Capulet and this feckless Count, and I'm also implicated in Mercutio's unfortunate murder. Forget Mantua!' the saddened young man grieved. 'At this rate. I'll be exiled either to Jupiter or to the planet Saturn. I'll place Paris's body inside the tomb near Juliet's corpse. Then, I'll drink-down the powerful, lethal poison the Apothecary in Mantua had concocted, and soon, I'll join my wife, Mercutio, and Mercutio's cousin somewhere in infinity.'

And after gently depositing Paris's body on a vacant slab inside the Capulet mausoleum, Romeo leaned-over and kissed Juliet upon her pallid lips. 'I'll eternally rest here between the bodies of your playboy paramour, County Paris, and you, dear Juliet!' Romeo sobbed. The disenchanted lover then quickly drank-down the Apothecary's toxic poison, and soon keeled over, lying beside his wife's motionless figure.

A few moments thereafter, Friar Lawrence and Balthasar entered the tampered-with tomb, just as Juliet was awakening from her drugged slumber. The girl was shocked beyond belief upon discovering that both Romeo and Count Paris were lying dead inside her family tomb.

"We must get the hell out of this macabre sepulcher at once!" the craven Father Lawrence commanded revived Juliet, while holding a flickering torch in his quivering right hand. "Let's claim ignorance, and let the Verona authorities then sort-out all of the gory, gruesome details. I'll link you up with a colony of nuns, Juliet, and you can spend the rest of your years praying and meditating inside a peaceful convent! Please, my dear Young Lady, I must repeat; let's get the hell out of this all-too-sordid place!"

But still-groggy Juliet had become immobile, with her body becoming virtually paralyzed in enduring her overwhelming grief. And so true to form, cowardly Friar Lawrence, and scared shit-less Balthasar, hastily fled the scene like two spooked jackrabbits.

Juliet gazed upon handsome (but dead) Romeo's pale face, slowly removed his dagger from her husband's belt-sheath, and then after tenderly kissing Romeo's lips, the Capulet heiress methodically shoved and plunged the knife deep into her heart. At that moment, three corpses lay inside the seemingly-accursed Capulet tomb.

Paris's alarmed servant had summoned several of Prince Escalus's guards to the bad-luck Capulet mausoleum, and several other soldiers had simultaneously apprehended Friar Lawrence and the scared shit-less Balthasar, who both had been frantically scampering away from the doomed tomb. The series of unfortunate tragedies represented a major blessing in disguise.

Soon, Prince Escalus and the beleaguered Lord and Lady Capulet arrived at the family mausoleum. Friar Lawrence felt guilty and responsible for several of the deaths that had resulted from his poor advice, and from the priest's indiscreet, impractical judgment.

"I had secretly married Romeo and Juliet several days ago without the knowledge of the Montagues or the Capulets," the penitent cleric ironically confessed. "My sincere intention was to try and spare Juliet of a second unwanted marriage to Count Paris, so I concocted a special formula to make her sleep, while all along, the girl appeared to be dead with hardly a noticeable pulse, along with very slight breathing," Friar Lawrence sorrowfully divulged to Prince Escalus. "Now on the basis of what I've observed, since I theorize that Romeo had killed Count Paris in a duel, and then *him* believing that Juliet was already-dead in the mausoleum, I speculate that the emotionally affected Montague lad drank some of his own poison, the remainder of which has been found in his flask. Finally, Prince Escalus," the remorseful priest concluded and shared, "upon awakening, Juliet, seeing both her husband and Paris lying dead, then stabbed herself with Romeo's dagger. I apologize Prince for the domino-effect death mess that I've created! Perhaps I'm a reprehensible, pernicious, villain after all. Dispense with me however you deem necessary. My reputation in Verona isn't worth shit anymore!"

"I forgive you, Father, and hereby exonerate you from all allegations of wrongdoing," Prince Escalus mercifully declared for all present to hear. "Although you fucked-up big time with your lousy advice, and with your foolish mystery formula, you still had honorable intentions throughout your enterprises, even though you had implemented them in a foolish manner. But sometimes, the best of intentions, on occasion, ultimately result in producing disastrous consequences, as we've all recently found-out."

"I had only desired to have Romeo and Juliet live happily together in Mantua," Friar Lawrence disclosed and wept. "And now, just look at all the accumulated evil my actions have wrought! If only I possessed the courage to kill myself, too!"

Balthasar then presented to Prince Escalus the letter that Romeo had authored back in Mantua that had been addressed to Lord Montague. The lengthy missive's content verified Friar Lawrence's oral testimony. "Your statements of remorse have been graphically validated, and you're now officially vindicated!" Escalus said to the still-saddened Friar. "The next time you get any bright ideas, present them to me first for my approval!"

Then, the emotionally-drained Prince gave a most compelling speech. "The noble Capulets have lost Juliet and Tybalt, and the proud Montagues have lost Romeo. And Mercutio and Count Paris have also died in this horrendous series of tragedies," Prince Escalus emphasized. "The entire city has tremendously suffered as a result of needless feuding between the two competing families. Let this tragic and woeful sequence of events serve as a catharsis for everyone in Verona; an epiphany, and also a sober reminder for each and every one of us," Prince Escalus stressed. "I strongly suggest that both you, the Montagues, and you, the Capulets, discard your personal differences, and genuinely shake hands to guarantee the safe future of Verona. Do it now, my good-hearted Citizens, or otherwise, I'll feel motivated to leave this fine city and work for my lunatic cousin, a crazy, depraved, black-market Apothecary doing a fabulous cash business over in Mantua."

About the Author

Jay Dubya is author John Wiessner's pen name. John is a retired New Jersey public school teacher, having diligently taught the subject for thirty-four years. John lives in Hammonton, New Jersey.

Counting *Poe: Pelted, Pounded, Pummeled and Pulverized*, John has written and published sixty-two total books. *Pieces of Eight, Pieces of Eight, Part II, Pieces of Eight, Part III* and *Pieces of Eight, Part IV* all contain short stories and novellas that feature science fiction and paranormal plots and themes. *Nine New Novellas, Nine New Novellas, Part II, Nine New Novellas, Part III, Nine New Novellas, Part IV, One Baker's Dozen, Two Baker's Dozen, Snake Eyes and Boxcars* and *Snake Eyes and Boxcars, Part II* are short story collections all written in the spirit of the *Pieces of Eight* series.

Other Jay Dubya adult-oriented fiction are the works *Black Leather and Blue Denim, A '50s Novel*, and its exciting sequel, *The Great Teen Fruit War, A 1960' Novel*. *Frat Brats, A '60s Novel* completes the action/adventure trilogy. Jay Dubya also has produced two irreverent Biblical satires, *The Wholly Book of Genesis* and *The Wholly Book of Exodus*. A third satire *Ron Coyote, Man of La Mangia* is a parody on Miguel Cervantes' classic novel, *Don Quixote* published in 1605. *Thirteen Sick Tasteless Classics, TSTC, Part II, TSTC, Part III* and *TSTC, Part IV* are satirical works that each corrupt thirteen classic stories from American and British literature and from Greek mythology. *Fractured Frazzled Folk Fables and Fairy Farces* and *FFFF & FF, Part II* satirize and corrupt famous children's literature stories. *Mauled Maimed Mangled Mutilated Mythology* is another popular adult-oriented satirical/parody work that pokes fun at twenty-one famous classical myths. *O. Henry: Obscenely and Outrageously Obliterated* is another satirical adult rewrite. Finally, *Shakespeare: Slammed, Smeared, Savaged and Slaughtered* and *Shakespeare: S, S, S and S. Part II* poke fun at the famous works of the great playwright.

The author has also penned a young adult fantasy trilogy: *Pot of Gold, Enchanta* and *Space Bugs, Earth Invasion*. *The Eighteen Story Gingerbread House* is a collection of eighteen new children's stories. And last but not least, two non-fiction works are *So Ya' Wanna' Be A Teacher* and *Random Articles and Manuscripts*.

Jay Dubya really likes '50s music and he also listens to songs by the Beatles, *ELO*, the Carpenters, the Beach Boys, Fleetwood Mac, the Eagles', the Rolling Stones, John Mellencamp and John Fogerty.

Author Biography

Born in Hammonton, NJ in 1942, John Wiessner had attended St. Joseph School up to and including Grade 5. After his family moved from Hammonton to Levittown, Pa in 1954, John attended St. Mark School in Bristol, Pa. for Grade 6, St. Michael the Archangel School in Levittown for Grades 7 and 8 and then Immaculate Conception School, Levittown, Pa. for Grade 9. Bishop Egan High School, Levittown Pa was John's educational base for Grades 10 and 11, and later in 1960, the aspiring author graduated from Edgewood Regional High, Tansboro, NJ. John then next attended Glassboro State College, where he was an announcer for the school's baseball games and also read the nightly news and sports over WGLS, GSC's radio station.

John Wiessner had been primarily an English teacher in the Hammonton Public School System for 34 years, specializing in the instruction of middle school language arts. Mr. Wiessner was quite active in the Hammonton Education Association, serving in the capacities of Vice-President, building representative and finally, teachers' head negotiator for 7 years. During his lengthy teaching career, John had been nominated into "Who's Who Among American Teachers" three times. He also was quite active giving professional workshops at schools around South Jersey on the subjects of creative writing and the use of movie videos to motivate students to organize their classroom theme compositions.

John Wiessner was very active in community service, being a past President of the Hammonton Lions Club, where he also functioned for many years as the club's Tail-Twister, Vice-President and Liontamer. John had been named Hammonton Lion of the Year in 1979 and in 2009, received the prestigious Melvin Jones Fellow Award, the highest honor a Lion can receive.

John also was a successful businessman, starting with being a Philadelphia Bulletin newspaper delivery boy for two years in the late 1950s in Levittown, Pennsylvania. After his family moved back to New Jersey in 1959, John worked at his grandparents and his parents' farm markets, Square Deal Farm (now Ron's Gardens in Hammonton) and Pete's Farm Market in Elm, respectively. He later managed his wife's parents' farm market, White Horse Farms in Elm for three summers.

Also, in a business capacity, for 16 summers starting in 1967, John Wiessner had co-owned Dealers Choice Amusement Arcade on the Ocean City, Maryland boardwalk and also co-owned the New Horizon Tee-Shirt Store for eight summers (1973-'81) on the Rehoboth Beach, Delaware boardwalk. In addition, "Jay Dubya" was a co-owner of Wheel and Deal Amusement Arcade, Missouri Avenue and Boardwalk, Atlantic City. And then, for 18 summers beginning in 1986, John had been the Field Manager in charge of farm crew-leaders for Atlantic Blueberry Company (the world's largest cultivated blueberry farm), both the Weymouth and Mays Landing, New Jersey Divisions.

After retiring from teaching in 1999, writing under the pen name Jay Dubya (his initials), John Wiessner became the author of 62 books in the genre Action/Adventure Novels, Sci-Fi/Paranormal Story Collections, Adult Satire, Young Adult Fantasy Novels and Non-Fiction Books. His books exist in hardcover, in paperback and in popular Kindle and Nook e-book formats.

In January of 2022, John Wiessner (Jay Dubya) was nominated into Marquis Who's Who in America, and in April of that same year, was one of nine distinguished Who's Who in America members honored with Lifetime Achievement Awards, all nine sharing an article of recognition appearing in the Wall Street Journal.

Google: Jay Dubya books